The Biography of an Institution

The Civil Service Commission of Canada, 1908–1967

J. E. HODGETTS

WILLIAM McCLOSKEY

REGINALD WHITAKER

V. SEYMOUR WILSON

The Institute of Public Administration of Canada
L'Institut d'Administration publique du Canada

McGill–Queen's University Press
Montreal and London 1972

©Public Service Commission of Canada 1972
International Standard Book Number 0-7735-0140-1 (Cloth)
International Standard Book Number 0-7735-0159-2 (Paper)
Library of Congress Catalog Card Number 72-87185
Legal Deposit 4th quarter 1972

Design by Anthony Crouch
Printed in Canada by T. H. Best Printing Company Limited

To the Memory of

Abraham Martin Willms

1921—1968

Contents

Part Two

Preface

THIS IS THE STORY OF AN ACT, the people who created and changed it, the organization vested with responsibility for administering it, and the evolution of procedures designed to implement the objectives adumbrated in the Act. The statute around which individuals and institutions rallied over a period of fifty years to play out their roles and responsibilities is the Civil Service Act of 1918. Although the Civil Service Commission, as the agency vested with primary responsibility for the administration of the Act, appears as the central institutional actor in the story, the cast of supporting (and opposing) characters is almost as numerous as that featured in a Hollywood epic. Close to half a million Canadians have been under the jurisdiction of the Act at one time or another, its terms governing their mode of entry, their career patterns in classification, pay scales, and promotion, as well as many other conditions of service. Senior departmental officials had to work through the Commission, which carried an unusually extended mandate to initiate or approve their decisions affecting departmental personnel. Organized staff associations had to orient their structure to the classification system and gear themselves to the full range of personnel practices, ranging from efficiency rating forms to promotion appeals and grievance, which were Commission inspired. The other key managerial agency of government, the Treasury Board, came to share with the Commission certain ambiguously defined authority which brought the two agencies into conflict as often as collaboration.

The Civil Service Act and the Commission not only occupied the front centre of the stage for the government as employer, they also occupied one of the most politically sensitive and exposed positions as ostensible guardians of the public service against the pressures from an entrenched system of patronage. The ideal of the merit principle, advanced by civil service reformers with a fervour exceeded only by the vagueness with which it was defined, provided the raison d'être for the Act and the Commission. That the role of guardian of public virtue, as expressed through Commission priorities and procedures, was not necessarily compatible with the role of central personnel manager for the civil service will become apparent as the story unfolds.

Critical reassessment of one's past is said to be the first step in self-knowledge and self-adaptation. Few individuals, unless prodded by their psychiatrists, undertake this venture. Institutions are amenable to the process but just as prone as individuals to keep the results of searching self-scrutiny to themselves. This retrospective analysis of sixty years' experience with administering both the Civil Service Act of 1908 and 1918 is, therefore, the result of an unprecedented decision by an institution to open its past to scrutiny, and to have this record appraised in the light of contemporary developments. This enterprise was made possible only because its prime subject, the Public Service Commission, generously provided funds and courageously made records available to us. The courtesies and facilities extended by the Commission are hereby warmly acknowledged, with special thanks to the Chairman, John Carson, to Mrs. Mary Johnston and her library staff, to Mrs. A. McCuaig, Supervisor of Stenographic Services, to R. F. (Bob) Smith for his unfailing attention to our administrative needs, and to a host of public servants and officials who submitted to interviews and offered critical appraisal of the manuscript at various stages (most of whom are listed in the Bibliography). We are also indebted to the Literary Executors for granting us access to the Mackenzie King Papers and to the Honourable J. W. Pickersgill for similar access to the St. Laurent Papers. Thanks are also due to Dr. W. I. Smith, the Dominion Archivist, and his staff for their invaluable assistance during our stay at the Public Archives of Canada. To the unsung heroines of the typewriter, Maureen Harrington, Pamela MacDonald, Mrs. Agnes Lessard, Sandra Casey, and Mrs. Marjorie Miscampbell, our special thanks for meticulous typing of successive drafts.

This work is the result of a genuine team effort in which we collectively accept responsibility for selection of facts, emphasis, and interpretation. We wish to stress that, if failings there be, none are attributable to the exercise of any veto power on the part of the sponsoring body. In this context, we would add that the Institute of Public Administration, under whose auspices this volume appears and for which it granted a publication subsidy, is also totally dissociated from any endorsation of the views expressed.

We have divided the book into two sections: part 1 concentrates, for the most part, on the history of the organization starting from the passage of the 1908 Civil Service Act and culminating in the introduction of the 1967 legislation which fundamentally reshaped the old Civil Service Commission. Part 2 endeavours to deal in some detail with selected topics of interest which tended to crop up during the research on the book: leadership within the CSC, management development, the merit principle and its application, etc. *These topics are by no means exhaustive*: time and the available data precluded any treatment of other topics equally important in staffing policy.

Our notes are placed at the back of each chapter to facilitate easier reading for our general audience. The documentation of our text is rather heavy, hence our decision not to clutter up the flow of our story on each page with detailed notes. We hope that this decision will not be too much of an inconvenience to those wishing to check carefully our sources while reading the text. Readers will also see that in our notes the title of an article is usually given with no other information. This should be no cause for dismay; simply turn to the Select Bibliography at the back of the book and all information on the article will be found.

During the last four years we have pleasantly collaborated in a creative enterprise which has proved intellectually stimulating for all of us. As a fitting memory of this experience, we have decided to let alphabetical sequence determine the order of our names on the title page. We wish to emphasize, however, that this sequence should *not* be interpreted as reflecting, or as not reflecting, our relative contributions to this work.

Finally, we respectfully dedicate this volume to the late Professor A. M. Willms, who died shortly after he had accepted the Commission's invitation to direct this project.

Part One

Chapter One
To Break a Habit: An Organization Is Born

*Institutions, as many have said, are tools
for "building civilization," but they do not,
like most tools, lie wholly outside and
apart from the individuals who use them.
They are, on the contrary, our own habits
which, entering into our vital organization,
exert upon other phases of our personalities an effect, which we cannot safely
ignore. Institutions are not merely our
instruments; they are part of ourselves.*

Floyd H. Allport, *Institutional Behavior*

THE AIM OF THIS BOOK is to describe and explain the genesis, evolution, and adaptation of a well-entrenched organization, the Civil Service Commission of Canada. The framework for inquiry and explanatory analysis we have employed rests on a theory of bureaucratic development which emphasizes the importance of the external environment to an organization, even as internal goals of self-preservation and prestige are held to influence the inner dynamics of institutional adjustments. Other descriptive-analytical models are available, but, in our view, they are less helpful in achieving a comprehensive picture of the vicissitudes of an evolving organism within a changing, though uniquely Canadian, environment.[1]

Since the end of World War II, an increasing number of social scientists have turned their attention to the study of human organizations, and have developed numerous analytical perspectives vital for an understanding of organizational activity. One of these perspectives has been the conception of the organization as a living, social institution.[2] From this point of view, although organizations are social units deliberately constructed and reconstructed to seek specific goals, they possess a life of their own. From the very beginnings of an organization, many internal problems may arise, resulting from the needs for an ideological raison d'être, for a homogeneous

3

outlook on the surrounding environment, and, particularly in periods of organizational crises, for creative leadership. At the same time, organizations are adaptive social structures, taking cues, hostile or otherwise, from their environment, and learning to adapt to changing political or wider social circumstances.

In the process of developing and implementing their most important function, namely, the legal goals defined in their organizing statutes, these units during their life cycles develop vested interests which force them to focus on the goals of self-preservation and prestige. It must be emphasized that the latter goals should not be stressed as the preeminent pursuits of all organizations. However, in the conduct of their day-to-day responsibilities, organizations must of necessity be concerned with the positions they take on important issues, and for the sake of their own preservation, be prepared to defend the logical inferences of these positions.

Prestige is primarily concerned with the organization's relative position in the social hierarchy of formal structures committed to the same goals. Several factors are of importance here. If the goals assigned to the organization are generally assessed to be important, the organization will have a correspondingly high status. Similarly, an exclusive, rather than a shared, responsibility for a particular objective considerably enhances the organization's status. Under these circumstances it could logically be expected that an organization possessing some scope for choice would choose options which would increase its prestige. Another factor in assessing prestige is the important ongoing role that creative leadership plays in all organizations. As we shall see, this factor has been of considerable importance in the growth and respectability accorded to the Civil Service Commission of Canada.

In studying organizational life cycles, four different ways have been identified in which these formal structures come into being.[3] Organizations have on many occasions been created through the "routinization of charisma"; namely, the gathering of a group of men around a dynamic and unique personality for the specific purpose of propagating certain aims. Sooner or later, as the leader passes from the scene, this grouping of men transforms itself into a routinized organization in order to perpetuate his ideas. A good Canadian example of this type of routinization is the formation and perpetuation of the Social Credit movement in Alberta.[4] Formal structures may also be deliberately created by groups in society or by political decision-makers in order to fulfil certain aims. The use of existing organizations may have been ruled out for a variety of reasons. Illustrative of this type was the role played by the late Clarence Decatur Howe, a cabinet minister in both the King and St. Laurent administrations, in the creation of crown corporations.[5] A new organization can be created as an offshoot of an already established agency or department, primarily because the activity in which it is engaged has become increasingly important, thus meriting separate facilities. The creation of the Canadian International Development Agency, formerly the External Aid Office attached to the Department of External Affairs, serves as an example of this in Canadian government. Finally, an organization can be formed as a result of the "entrepreneurship" of a particular group of people, who, in promoting a specific policy, were successful in obtaining significant support in establishing an organization devoted to the propagation of their objectives. The role of the Consumer Association of Canada, and its relationships with politicians and senior civil servants in Ottawa, is a good illustration of this type of organization.[6]

These four modes of organization have three basic characteristics in common. During the initial stages of organizational life, they are usually influenced either by strong advocates with a purpose to fulfil, or by zealots with missionary fervour; they usually undergo a period of steady growth; and, in order to survive as organizations, they must seek sources of external support. These three characteristics are, of course, interrelated, for they are all underscored by one basic purpose: the need for organizational survival and success. Anthony Downs suggests that "officials in almost every new bureaucracy place a high priority on creating conditions that will ensure the bureau's survival."[7] Yet this characteristic is endemic to organizations at all stages of their life cycles, for, as Downs suggests, "few bureaus ever achieve such perfect autonomy that they are immune from threats to their survival."[8] Downs has indicated two main reasons why organizational personnel are interested in the survival of their organization. First, zealots in the organization usually feel strongly that the goals they pursue have a high priority, and failing adequate organizational performance, these goals will most likely be cast aside as unimportant. Second, organizational members value the survival of the bureau in terms of their individual self-interest.

For these reasons, an organization will be vitally interested in avoiding serious conflict with interest groups or other organizations that have the power to alter its status. Evading this type of conflict considerably enhances the chances of survival and success for the organization. Survival and success are also related to another organizational goal: the creation of relative autonomy. As Peter Clark and James Wilson have indicated:

The proliferation of associations and the division of labour in society has meant that there is almost no way for an organization to preserve itself by simply seeking ends for which there are no other advocates. Thus, the maintenance of organizational autonomy is a critical problem. By autonomy we refer to the extent to which an organization possesses a distinctive area of competence, a clearly demarcated clientele or membership, and undisputed jurisdiction over a function, service, goal, issue, or cause. Organizations seek to make their environment stable and certain and to remove threats to their identities. Autonomy gives an organization a reasonably stable claim to resources and thus places it in a more favourable position from which to compete for those resources. Resources include issues and causes as well as money, time, effort, and names.[9]

Autonomy can reduce organizational conflict by allowing the organization greater scope for independent action, but it may increase it by making responsibility for failure more difficult to circumvent. Furthermore, autonomy can foster greater security by increasing the organization's ability to deal with situations of conflict when these occur.

In essence, organizations are thus viewed as continually asserting their rights to self-preservation. Whether a specific organization has the ability to tide over the numerous vicissitudes of its life depends on a number of factors: its ability, first of all, to withstand adverse pressures from its environment; its style of leadership at crucial periods of its history; the necessity to maintain or to change its goals when it becomes expedient to do so; its ability to effect coalitions when these are to its advantage; and its success in maintaining organizational integrity throughout this period of coalitions and shifting alliances.

Phillip Selznick further amplifies this mode of analysis by making the important distinction between an organization and an institution. Drawing on the pertinent work of Chester Barnard, Selznick defines the term "organization" as "a certain bareness, a lean, no-nonsense system of consciously co-ordinated activities. It refers to an *expendable tool,* a rational instrument engineered to do a job." There is a deliberate concentration on technique as the organization goes through a period of rapid growth in both its size and the relative significance of its functions. This growth, however, only occurs in response to external environmental conditions favourable to the expansion of the organization's functions. Institutionalization of an organization, however, is a "process," an ability "to *infuse with value* beyond the technical requirements of the task at hand." He continues: "It is something that happens to an organization over time, reflecting the organization's own distinctive history, the people who have been in it, the groups it embodies and the vested interests they have created, and the way it has adapted to its environment."[10]

The process of changing from an organization into an institution permits the observer to detect a number of interesting aspects of organizational behaviour.[11] For example, faced by a number of constraints, the existence and aggressiveness of other organizations, or the degrees of freedom allowed under the legislation for which the organization is responsible, the bureaucratic hierarchy will choose a "best point" at which the organization could safely operate. Furthermore, because prestige and self-preservation are interdependent factors, many of the bureau's strategic decisions involve a trade-off between them.

In planning its course of action, the organization has a number of choices. Within certain limits it can decide on the goals for which it will be held responsible, as well as the strategies it will maintain in order to perform the selected functions. It can decide to encourage or discourage the sharing of responsibility for an objective with other organizations. In addition, since prestige involves judgement by the public, the organization will attempt to influence the manner in which the public views it through its publications, its public relations performance, and the various other contacts it fosters through interest groups and other intermediaries. These elements, which reflect the inner dynamics and tension within an organization, suffuse the history of the federal Civil Service Commission, and we shall have frequent occasion to document these themes in the ensuing chapters.

It should be clear that the inner dynamics of bureaucratic evolution are profoundly responsive to the external environment of the organization. J. E. Hodgetts has argued: "An examination of the administrative mechanism is not particularly rewarding unless the policies which that mechanism is designed to implement are also described. And these policies, in turn, are understandable only in terms of the broader social, political, and economic environment to which they are a response."[12] The concept of organizational environment embodies two meanings: the social aspects of the environment which help to shape attitudes and perspectives of the human actors within the organization at a particular period in time; and the physical aspects, that is, the structural changes taking place in the organizational environment to reflect changing attitudes and perspectives. We shall endeavour to deal with both the physical and social aspects of the environment. Specifically, the physical aspects refer to such features as the creation of statutory provisions to crystallize new attitudes adopted, and the structural changes within the milieu which prepare the organization to handle its new role proficiently and expeditiously. In short, this approach emphasizes the fact that the organization is conceived as an "instrument," that is, as a rationally conceived means to the realization of expressly announced goals. Chapters 3, 13, 14, and 15 are centred around this environmental perspective.

The social aspects of the environment emphasize changes in organizational patterns which are considered the results of unplanned, cumulative responses to certain "threats" to the equilibrium of the organizational system. Responses to problems are seen as being importantly shaped by shared values which are deeply internalized in the society in which the organization exists. Therefore our discussion of the merit principle (chapter 18), and the importance of management theories which seek to concretize the concept of efficiency in government (chapter 4), emphasize this link between the more normative considerations of the society and the efforts to grapple with and solve a problem of some magnitude within the organization's milieu. Similarly, the enduring theme of the Civil Service Commission's independence and responsibility only to Parliament has been largely shaped by efforts to rid the bureaucratic system of the "venal practices of patronage." It was the mounting pressure from the environment to break the habit of patronage that generated the impulse to create the Civil Service Commission. For sixty years (1908–67) it was to wrestle, sometimes single-handedly and often against indifference or outright hostility, with the task of organizational survival, goal protection, and functional response to changing political and managerial needs in the field of personnel administration.

Since the initial and continuing key to civil service reform was the desire to eliminate patronage, a brief description of its relevant manifestations is in order. With the perspective that hindsight enables the investigator to obtain, we conclude that the elimination of patronage was not the exclusive key to reform its advocates believed it to be; it was a necessary, but not sufficient, condition for the development of an efficient civil service. But what is important is that at this time the elimination of patronage was seen as the *sole* condition, and the strength of this conviction brought an organization into being whose statutory goals were explicitly wedded to this belief. From Confederation to the passage of the new Civil Service Act in 1918, no less than six major inquiries into the federal bureaucracy dealt at length with the "patronage evil."[13] During this same period, Hansard, the newspapers, and the popular periodicals were replete with charges concerning the practice of patronage in the civil service. The evidence is overwhelming that the major environmental motive of civil service reform in Canada was the elimination of patronage. It is therefore somewhat curious that the practice of patronage has never been the subject of sustained analysis on the part of Canadian social scientists and historians. An exploratory inquiry into the practice of patronage during the first fifty years of our national history is clearly in order if only as an indication of the need for a more detailed and systematic assessment of the subject.

This caveat is strongly emphasized. The initial analysis and the empirical evidence on patronage practices presented here suggest some qualifications which the conventional wisdom needs to consider in its treatment of the subject. However no claims are made for its definitiveness; although suggestive, the analysis remains exploratory at the present time.

VARIANTS IN THE PRACTICE OF BUREAUCRATIC PATRONAGE

The word "patronage" has been used to cover a variety of alleged malpractices in government, and our interest lies only in those aspects of patronage that affected staffing in the bureaucracy. Insofar as it affected staffing it was not a homogeneous practice; certain variants may be identified. The most common was *political nomination*, in which persons were appointed to positions in the civil service on the basis of party credentials. This mode of appointment is well illustrated by this newspaper item of 1906: "There was a meeting of the Liberal Association on Thursday, with a full attendance of delegates. The object of the meeting was to nominate a successor to the position of customs officer in (Havelock) made vacant by the death of the late A. Fiddes. There were only two nominations, Alex Waddel and J. W. Curran, the other candidates withdrawing. A ballot resulted in J. W. Curran receiving thirty-six votes and A. Waddel seventeen. Mr. Curran therefore received the nomination. He is well suited for the position, and his being chosen gives general satisfaction."[14] There were certain distinct characteristics about this variant. First, it took place at the local constituency level, with local party members, as well as the Member of Parliament, participating in the allocation of positions. Because there were always fewer positions than applicants, various methods of elections were devised.[15] Second, most of the appointments were to vacant posts of a menial nature in the Outside Service,[16] such as post office clerks, letter carriers, labourers, and construction workers. Most of these positions were seasonal in nature, with a high turnover rate to be expected under normal circumstances.

It is extremely difficult to reconstruct the precise extent of political nomination to such positions throughout the country. No reliable statistics were compiled, not only because statistics were not generally kept at this time, but also because any such figures could be used by political opponents. Both the advocates and adversaries of political nomination played a nebulous numbers game in describing the extent of the practice. Adversaries always stressed the "large number" of persons turned out of office to make way for new political appointments with a change in government. The system's advocates, on the other hand, emphasized that it applied mainly to the positions which became vacant under normal circumstances.

Lacking any objective information, debates on the subject usually degenerated to the level of partisan invective.

An exception to this general picture was the attempt by Professor R. MacGregor Dawson to produce statistics on political nomination during the war years, from 1915 to 1917.[17] Dawson claimed that the Government took advantage of the wartime emergency to swell the ranks of the civil service with some 23,000 political nominations. More reliable statistics, however, indicate that the service in fact increased by only 16,700.[18] Dawson's figures seem to have included members of the RCMP and the militia —groups excluded from the definition of civil servant in the 1918 Civil Service Act. He also failed to distinguish between regular civil servants and casual workers. More seriously yet, he failed to recognize the large turnover necessitated by the war. Not only were regular civil servants leaving to join the armed forces, but an expanded service was also necessary to meet the special demands of the war effort. Normal examination procedures had to be suspended for the sake of expediency. To attribute these special selection methods entirely to the Government's appetite for patronage is stretching the point altogether too far.

In addition to political appointments in the lower ranks of the civil service, political nomination has always existed, and continues to exist, at the level of appointments by the Governor in Council, where political considerations are part of the input in making final selections.[19] Interestingly enough, civil service reformers rarely criticized this variant; instead they reserved their moral condemnation for lower rank appointments. This implicit class bias of reformers did not go unnoticed. Dr. W. L. Grant, head of the Civil Service Reform League, was criticized in precisely these terms by the editor of the *Kingston Whig-Standard* in 1929:

> One of the strongest reasons why I am in favour of the patronage system is because of the unfairness of the present method. If there is a vacancy for a position as a letter carrier, or a Customs House clerk, the applicants are supposed to deal wholly and solely with the Civil Service Commission. As a matter of fact they usually pull every wire possible, and interview any and everybody whom they think may have some slight influence at Ottawa. Theoretically, however, they deal wholly and solely with the Civil Service Commission and theoretically too, the Commission lets nothing else influence it in making the appointment, than the qualifications of the applicants as presented to them by the candidates themselves. But, if a senatorship is vacant or a judgeship, do the applicants have to pass any examination? Not at all. Usually these juicy political plums fall to the ones who have the most influence politically. Peculiarly we never hear much criticism of these appointments,

and yet usually they are straight examples of patronage for they always go to friends of the party in power. The same thing happens when we require an ambassador to Tokio [*sic*] or Washington. These are nice positions—positions of honour and distinction—and they quite rightly go to political friends. I have never had it satisfactorily explained to me just why, when one advocates that the ordinary party worker should receive some reward for his labour, without the interference of a Civil Service Commission, there should be a lot of ridiculous talk about "pork barrels" and "feeding at public troughs," but when some active political lawyer receives a judgeship there should be editorial commendation. There seems to be a tendency to build up in this country what I once referred to as a $5,000 aristocracy. If a political worker is appointed to a position to which is attached a yearly salary of $5,000 or over, he is a great public servant, but if some hard ward worker gets a $2,000 job, he is feeding at the public trough.[20]

Dr. Grant replied that "patronage does not work out there too badly," and that those filling higher positions have maintained a "high standing of ability and integrity." Such was not, however, the case in the lower echelons:

After all, the great difficulty is the motives and the men. I can imagine the patronage system working quite well in the Kingdom of Heaven. If you take the Calvinistic doctrine of grace, for instance, it really is a doctrine of hand-outs (laughter), and I can imagine the patronage system working well in such a place. My contention is that it does not work so well in twentieth century Canada, which is a fine country, but not the Kingdom of Heaven.[21]

In other words, the higher one ascends in the bureaucratic hierarchy, the closer one attains to godliness. By 1935 a more consistent civil service reform program was being advanced by the CCF intellectuals in the League for Social Reconstruction. The League's Research Committee viewed *all* political nominations as "evil" and "pernicious," and advocated the establishment of the position of Commissioner of Appointments to ensure that selection of the senior ranks "would be kept as clear as possible of political entanglements."[22]

Political nomination could also apply to positions to be filled from within the ranks of civil service personnel. Here the facts are even more difficult to ascertain. While civil service reformers and the Civil Service Commission did maintain that most deputy ministers, owing their own positions to political nomination, engaged in widespread "bureaucratic patronage," these charges were publicly denied by all the deputy ministers, both before a special committee of the House of Commons and in a signed memorandum addressed to the Prime Minister.[23] The truth appears to be somewhere in between, as evidenced by the manner in which Sir George Murray treated the problem during his investigation of the civil service in 1912. After listening to the arguments from both sides, Sir George concluded that the interference of the CSC in matters of promotion was undesirable, but admitted that the sole reliance on deputy heads to promote on the basis of merit was not without dangers. Nevertheless, he recommended that departmental promotions be the prerogative of the deputy heads, and requested the repeal of the provision requiring a certificate from the CSC before promotions were official.

Another variant of political patronage is the concept of "to the victor belong the spoils," a practice allegedly Jacksonian in origin, under which a wholesale rotation of civil service personnel occurs whenever a new administration achieves power. Lord Bryce described the essential features of the system: "That a place in the Public Service is held at the absolute pleasure of the appointing authority, that it is invariably bestowed from party motives on a party man, as a reward for party services (whether of the appointee or of someone who pushes him); that no man expects to hold it any longer than his party holds power, and that this gives him the strongest personal reasons for fighting in the party ranks."[24] Lord Bryce's third feature, that no man expected to keep his post any longer than his party held power, has fallen under serious questioning by political sociologists analysing American historical data.[25] On the available evidence, Dawson appears to be even less justified in referring to the years from 1867 to the 1920s as the period of the spoils system in Canada.

Following the defeat of the Conservative Government in the 1873 election, Sir John A. Macdonald, just before leaving office, made a number of appointments to the civil service.[26] It is difficult to believe that Macdonald would have taken the trouble to appoint party supporters if he knew that they would be automatically dismissed by the incoming Government of Alexander Mackenzie. One may surmise that the appointees therefore expected permanent tenure. A Member of Parliament from Cape Breton claimed that many of these were dismissed by the new Government, but when pressed for substantiation, he named only one individual, while suggesting that there were "other minor appointments" which he would not name.[27]

The same element of uncertainty emerges once more in the election year of 1878. Dawson maintains that the "return of the Macdonald administration in 1878 led to so many dismissals from the Service that the situation was felt to be intolerable."[28] No evidence was advanced in justification of this assertion. While charges and countercharges crossed the House of Commons, no overall figures were quoted, and the facts were generally obscured by partisan political infighting.[29]

In the ten months following the election of 1896, Dawson claims that 473 employees were dismissed by the incoming Laurier Government, 196 of whom were dismissed for reasons of "offensive political partisanship."[30] If we can assume that the entire federal civil service for this period numbered about 10,000 employees,[31] then 196 political dismissals represents a turnover of less than 2 percent—scarcely a system of wholesale rotation with a change in government. In 1897 the Governor-General, Lord Aberdeen, confirmed this view in a letter to Prime Minister Laurier: "I am well aware from what has been mentioned by yourself and other ministers that the dismissals actually carried out form only a very small proportion of those which the Government have been asked, nay urged, to effect . . . I know that an attitude of resistance to such pressure has been maintained by members of the Government and moreover a purpose, largely carried into practice, of declining to sanction dismissals except where really sufficient cause for such has been made out."[32]

Dawson saw the return of the Conservatives in 1911 as one of the darkest pages in the history of the spoils system in Canada. According to the *Canadian Annual Review*, "In less than four months 236 postmasters were dismissed from office, and in three years [that is, between 1911 and 1914] almost 11,000 employees had resigned or had been removed. The reason for which the majority were turned out was the old one of political partisanship and little time was wasted in inquiries or investigations."[33] As part of the evidence to support this statement, Dawson cites 363 separate questions asked in the House of Commons by Opposition members concerning dismissals. While most of the answers to these questions were not published in the Sessional Papers, a close check of the published answers indicates that many of the alleged dismissals were based on rumours circulating in local districts; in some cases, the "dismissed" officers had been removed from particular positions and placed in different postings. While there were undoubtedly dismissals for political purposes, the mere citing of questions did not constitute *ipso facto* evidence of dismissals. Another factor not taken into account by the critics of patronage was that a very considerable number of the 11,000 (if indeed, that figure is correct) resigned their positions voluntarily to join the armed forces at the outbreak of World War I—the first few months of which would be included within the three-year period following the accession to power of the Conservatives in 1911. An exact figure on civil service enlistments in this period is not available, but during the year 1915 there were at least 4,730 civil servants who joined the armed forces.[34] It is not an unjustifiable assumption that voluntary recruitment must have run as high or higher in the enthusiasm at the beginnings of the war, and this casts a heavy shadow on the credibility of the figure of 11,000 political dismissals.

THE FUNCTIONS OF PATRONAGE

The closest approach to a theoretical framework for assessing patronage as a political activity has been offered by Robert K. Merton utilizing "structural functionalism" as an analytical tool.[35] Merton has in effect attempted to explain the "functions" of patronage at a given point of time in American political development, and also as part of the transformation of the political structure over time. This approach has raised a series of questions. Why political patronage? What are the various levels and forms of this authority? Under what conditions has it been possible for reform of a patronage system to be successful?

In answering the first question, the moralistic approach is limited in its explanatory power. The ready answer given by the moral reformers was that man's greed inevitably led to the fostering and encouragement of this pernicious practice. On the other hand, the patronage system can be viewed as a procedure which, at a particular historical stage, may fulfil certain "functions" some of which might not be fulfilled in the absence of patronage. While we may abstain from judgements as to the ultimate historical justification of the patronage system—thus avoiding the difficult task of proving that no other possible system could have accomplished the same ends—it remains useful to examine patronage within a "functional" rather than a moral perspective, and to seriously consider the various arguments put forward on its behalf.

The most common argument is that patronage was necessary for the building of a party system, which was in turn necessary for the building of a national political system.[36] O. D. Skelton discussed the financial difficulties of political parties, and while deploring the practice of patronage, recognized that some rewards had to be offered to political workers if the party system was to be maintained.[37] Another argument rested on a notion of administrative responsibility, which could only be maintained, it was asserted, if the people's elected representatives had full control of the bureaucracy. This in turn was only possible if the government could freely place its own appointments within the administrative system. In this view, the minister, being responsible for the effectiveness of his department, would ensure that the most capable persons would be placed in the leading posts.[38] The argument against a powerful Civil Service Commission or other such independent body was that it could not get to know prospective candidates in the various constituencies as well as M.P.'s could.[39] There was also, on the part of M.P.'s, a considerable fear of "bureaucratic patronage": the creation of a civil service family compact.[40]

How was the partisanship of civil servants manifested? One form reported in the United States has been *macing*, that is, a systematic assessment made on the salaries of appointees by the party in power. The evidence for such a practice in Canada is scanty. The *Report of the Committee on Election Expenses* claims that it took place in Canada, but offers no evidence.[41] In the 1930s the League for Social Reconstruction maintained that the practice was widespread in many cities throughout the nation.[42] The only evidence which could be located to indicate that this aspect was considered during the drafting of civil service reforms is contained in a terse paragraph of the 1918 Civil Service Act prohibiting civil servants from contributing to the coffers of any political party.[43] This strict prohibition was again reiterated in the 1961 Act,[44] but by 1967 there was a dramatic change in attitude when the new Public Service Employment Act not only recognized as legitimate the desire of civil servants to contribute to the party of their choice, but also gave them permission to be candidates in any political elections.[45] Generally, however, the emphasis in Canadian legislation from 1908 onwards appears to be concerned with maintaining the impartiality of civil servants rather than protecting them from any widespread macing procedures.[46]

In the past the influence of the politician on the public servant has been one side of the coin; the other side was the activity and influence of the public servant in politics. The two were interdependent: as long as the public servant participated in politics he would look to his patron or party for reward; and when his party was unsuccessful the opponents would "punish" him and reward their own partisans with public office. We have already looked at the latter and have made some tentative conclusions as to its practice. What then can be said about the political activity of civil servants in Canada?

A perusal of early Canadian newspapers indicates that there were many charges about civil servants' political activities, but very little proof. For example, the *Mail and Empire* in 1874 accused cabinet ministers of having instructed their subordinates to vote for the Government.[47] It must be remembered that in this period voting was by public declaration, there was no secret ballot, and consequently a vote meant an open avowal for party and candidate. In 1877 the secret ballot was adopted, and henceforth the right of public servants to the vote was seldom disputed.

The public servants' involvement in election campaigns, however, became more and more of an issue. If two or three civil servants were exposed in their "nefarious activities," the newspapers were usually scandalized and tended to inflate the matter out of proportion.[48] The evidence is again impressionistic, but the following exchange between a deputy minister and a questioner during the hearings of the Royal Commission into the Civil Service of 1891–92 gives quite a different view:

I sometimes get a man whom it is difficult to employ profitably owing to his frequent application for leave of absence on the plea that a minister or a member wants him to go away.

Q. What do you mean by the member wanting him to go away?
A. *I have been told by a clerk that he was wanted in his county on political matters.*
Q. Does this happen frequently?
A. *No, it happens at times.*
Q. At election times?
A. *Yes, but this applies to temporary clerks only.*[49]

As with the evidence for the "spoils" assertion, the indications are that the activity was sporadic and that those who engaged actively in the campaign were a minority and usually on the margins of the civil service—the temporary clerks, labourers, postmasters, and letter carriers.

PATRONAGE AND INEFFICIENCY

The major appeal of those who were crusading for the elimination of patronage was that as long as the foregoing practices continued, the civil service could never become efficient. It was the simple equation of patronage with inefficiency—laying all the ills of bureaucratic structures at the door of the "patronage evil"—that proved the clinching argument.[50] Apparently it never occurred to the reformers that in principle, as well as in practice, one could have an inefficient public service with or without patronage.[51] It is significant that Professor L. D. White maintains that from 1789 to 1829 the American federal civil service, although practising recruitment of staff by patronage, achieved more economical and possibly higher standards of administrative efficiency than the British civil service. These studies have led Professor S. E. Finer to question the linkage between inefficiency and the patronage system.[52]

Concurrent with the patronage system in Canada were some serious inefficiencies in administration. There is a question of what was cause and what was effect, but so long as archaic administrative forms existed, the best personnel in the world could not have operated the system very much more efficiently than the incumbents. Within some key departments at Confederation there were problems of lack of central control and internal coordination.[53] During that period, the question of administrative responsibility was a central practical issue in public administration because of the pre-Confederation rapid turnover of political heads of departments, and the reluctance of many administrative heads of semiautonomous agencies to be dictated to by ministers whose political tenure was, to say the least, rather tenuous.

In 1867, the new civil service relied heavily on the administrative structure of the United Provinces, with virtually no recruitment of personnel from the Maritimes.[54] Federal business in the "remote" Maritimes was handled by a few officials in Ottawa, who were aided in their work by a small number of civil servants recruited from the old provincial service. This, of course, raises some questions as to how knowledgeable this group of bureaucrats was about local problems in the Maritimes.[55] When decentralization of services was recognized, it was implemented without any systematic planning. Decentralization in any administrative structure requires not only key trained and trusted individuals to command strategic posts within the decentralized system, but also inspections and expert central audit to ensure efficiency and discourage corruption. As Professor Hodgetts has shown, the pre-Confederation public service was forced to decentralize at a time when these measures were nonexistent.

Often, there were no clearly defined or settled policies to be administered; staff members in the regions were invariably of inferior calibre; and, partly because of very low wages, they were susceptible to corruption. The central safeguards, which were all the more necessary under such circumstances, were of the more rudimentary or cumbersome type. The situation called for first-class bookkeeping practices, intelligent, independent departmental auditors, and full-time inspectors. Instead, departmental books were consistently in arrears, and often not very intelligible; departmental financial controls were poor; and inspection was normally regarded as a subordinate part-time activity of overworked headquarters' staff. Yet, "the amount of paper work was prodigious, apparently on the assumption that the extent of headquarters' control was proportionate to the number of reports and accounts submitted by the local agents."[56]

The extent of this problem could be discerned by the Report of the Royal Commission of 1868–70, which investigated conditions within the civil service. The Report concentrated on the problems of internal administration, the central concern of a bureaucracy put together on very short notice. Explaining the discrepancies existing in record-keeping, the Commission illustrated its point by outlining the procedure followed in the Department of the Secretary of State:

In the Ordinance Lands Branch, the agent generally only reports the answer which should be given; although it appears that he sometimes drafts it. These reports and drafts are copied by press in his office and the letter is written, and copied by hand into the letter book in the Secretary's office. In the Indian Branch, the Deputy Superintendent always writes the letter, and it is copied by hand in his office. It is then sent to the Secretary's office to be signed, and is again copied by hand . . . the copying a letter thrice over by hand, into two books kept at opposite sides of the same passage, is a most unnecessary multiplication of labour.[57]

In 1912, Sir George Murray echoed similar criticisms of the bureaucratic structure he was asked to investigate. In a report which was notably clear of criticisms pertaining to political patronage, he pointed to administrative inefficiencies: the duplication of work, the lack of decentralization, the nonexistent organizational procedures for Privy Council meetings and record-keeping; and the absence of delegation of responsibilities to departmental personnel other than the deputy head.[58] When all these other factors are taken into consideration, it appears reasonable to assert that the simple connections made between patronage and inefficiency have been inadequate to explain the administrative problems of the bureaucracy.

There is one aspect of the patronage-inefficiency equation that bears further examination. Critics were most often at pains to point out that many able and hard-working civil servants were conscientiously fulfilling their duties, but were placed in an inferior position vis-à-vis an echelon of party appointees relying on political influence rather than on their own merits. This was a pointed charge. Obviously the existence of such a situation was not only detrimental to efficiency in itself, but was also conducive to poor staff morale. However, the relevance of this criticism is lessened when it is recalled that patronage was strongest among the lower and more marginal posts.

It is of more than passing interest that in the United States, the moralistic identification of patronage with inefficiency, along with the parallel idea that the abolition of patronage would, *ipso facto*, mean the abolition of inefficiency, reached its evangelical peak in the late nineteenth century. By the early twentieth century, however, there was a general move toward an understanding that efficiency was a problem *in itself*, not necessarily linked to patronage.[59] In Canada, concern remained fixed primarily on patronage as the root of all administrative ills for many decades after the tide of moralism had begun to ebb in the United States. It is doubly curious that this should have been so, when the evidence clearly indicates that the incidence of patronage in Canada never approached the levels that it reached in the United States.

Nevertheless, the public embarrassment and other difficulties attendant on dispensing patronage seem to be the recurring theme which made the practice a burden to most politicians, particularly the executive. By the turn of the century, politicians on both sides of the House indicated that they were being influenced by public opinion calling for some measure of civil service reform in Canada.[60] The Liberal Government of Sir Wilfrid Laurier appointed a royal commission on May 9, 1907, to investigate the internal workings of the federal civil service. By August of that same year the Conservative party, under the leadership of Robert Borden, significantly added to its party's platform, as a major policy plank, the need to eradicate patronage in the civil service of Canada. This was the first time in Canadian history that a party elevated civil service reform to the front rank of its policy pronouncements.

One much publicized instance of bureaucratic corruption occurring in this same period must have given impetus to the reformers. The parliamentary sessions of 1906 and 1907 were rocked by scandals within the Government. The Opposition had charged that all was not well in the Department of Marine and Fisheries, and a subsequent investigation by Mr. Justice Cassels into these allegations led to the suspension of three civil servants and the resignation of the deputy minister.[61] Shortly thereafter the Government decided to adopt one of the major recommendations of the 1907–8 Royal Commission. On June 17, 1908, Bill No. 189, the Civil Service Amendment Act, 1908, was given first reading in the House of Commons, its major feature being the creation of a Civil Service Commission.

NOTES

1. For example, one could utilize the framework of rational choice as enumerated in the numerous Annual Reports of the Civil Service Commission. Another is the descriptive framework provided by R. H. Dowdell in "The Elements of Personnel Management in the Civil Service of Canada." While being extremely helpful in understanding the structural framework within which personnel management is conducted, Dowdell's framework does not provide reasons for the CSC's or Treasury Board's behaviour in personnel management decisions.

2. Amitai Etzioni, *Modern Organizations*; Phillip Selznick, *TVA and the Grass Roots*. This analysis uses interchangeably the words "bureau," "organization," and "formal structure."

3. This summary owes an intellectual debt to Anthony Downs, *Inside Bureaucracy*, p. 5.

4. C. B. Macpherson, *Democracy in Alberta: Social Credit and the Party System*.

5. C. A. Ashley and R. G. H. Smails, *Canadian Crown Corporations*.

6. Helen J. Dawson, "The Consumers' Association of Canada," see particularly pp. 105–11. Another example of this is the case study done by the same author on the Canadian Federation of Agriculture, *Canadian Public Administration* 3 (June, 1960), pp. 134–49.

7. Downs, *Inside Bureaucracy*, p. 8.

8. Ibid., p. 9.

9. Peter B. Clark and James Q. Wilson, "Incentive Systems: A Theory of Organizations," p. 158.

10. Phillip Selznick, *Leadership in Administration*, pp. 5 and 16–17. (Emphasis added.)

11. This statement is not meant to infer that the behavioural traits enumerated here are confined to this critical period of the organization's life. Rather, this process of change is best observable at that time because the organization is consciously changing its outlook within a time span easily handled by the observer.

12. J. E. Hodgetts, *Pioneer Public Service: An Administrative History of the United Canadas, 1841–1867*, p. viii.

13. These include the Royal Commissions of 1868–70, 1880–81, 1891–92, 1907–8, 1911–12, as well as Judge Cassels' inquiry into the Department of Marine and Fisheries of 1907.

14. The *Huntingdon Gleaner*, cited in the *Canadian Magazine* found in the Borden Papers, Public Archives of Canada (PAC), vol. 305, 179054–55. All further references to the Borden Papers are to those in the PAC.

15. For a description of the workings of this system, see Sir Robert Borden, "Problem of an Efficient Civil Service," Canadian Historical Association, *Report of the Annual Meeting*, 1931 (reprint).

16. That is, outside the national capital.

17. R. MacGregor Dawson, *The Civil Service of Canada*, pp. 88–89.

18. Dominion Bureau of Statistics (DBS), Finance Statistics Branch, *Statement of Civil Service Personnel and Salaries in the Month of January, 1912–1924* (Ottawa: King's Printer, 1925), table A, p. 9.

19. See remarks of the Honourable Judy LaMarsh, former Secretary of State, in House of Commons (H.C.), *Debates*, March 15, 1968, pp. 7683–85. (All further references to *Debates* are to those of the House of Commons.) For an analytical discussion of the factors involved in such selections, see Reinhard Bendix, "Bureaucracy and the Problem of Power," pp. 194–209.

20. Canadian Civil Service Research Conference, *Proceedings of the Sixth Annual Convention*, 1929, p. 50.

21. Ibid., p. 54.

22. Research Committee of the League for Social Reconstruction, *Social Planning for Canada* (Toronto: Thomas Nelson and Sons, 1935), p. 278.

23. H.C., Special Committee Appointed to Inquire into the Operation of

Chapter 12, 8–9 George V, An Act Respecting the Civil Service of Canada, 1923, *Proceedings and Evidence*; Report of the Committee of Deputy Ministers on Civil Service Matters, December, 1922, King Papers, PAC, *Memoranda and Notes*, vol. 61, C48184–92. All further references to the King Papers are to those in the PAC.

24. Quoted in Dawson, *Civil Service of Canada*, p. 25.

25. The first known criticism of the historical validity of the spoils system was Erik Eriksson's article "The Federal Civil Service under President Jackson," pp. 517–40. Based on statistical data, Eriksson's argument was that Jackson did not inaugurate a "spoils system," and that few civil servants in fact lost their jobs under his administration. More recently, the sociological research of Seymour Martin Lipset and Sidney Aronson has substantiated Eriksson's original hypothesis. See Aronson's "Status and Kinship in the Higher Civil Service: The Administrations of John Adams, Thomas Jefferson and Andrew Jackson" (Ph.D. thesis, Columbia University, 1961); and Lipset, *The First New Nation*. In the British public service, tradition and precedent gave the occupant of a position a strong claim to that position even when patronage was at its worst. E. N. Gladden, *Civil Service or Bureaucracy?* p. 48.

26. Macdonald himself admitted to 101 appointments. *Debates*, February 22, 1877, p. 205. George Casey, a strong antipatronage reformer, claimed 147. *Debates*, March 15, 1875, p. 711. Five years later an Ottawa newspaper asserted that 659 late appointments had been made. *Ottawa Free Press*, September 26 and October 4, 1878.

27. *Debates*, May 18, 1874, pp. 105–6.

28. Dawson, *Civil Service of Canada*, p. 42.

29. *Debates*, March 19, 1879, pp. 551ff.

30. Dawson, *Civil Service of Canada*, p. 72.

31. This is an estimate only. The DBS had no record of the total number of public servants by year until 1912. The *Montreal Journal of Commerce* of July 18, 1914, gave the total number of officials in the Inside Service for the year 1896 as 4,109. Other statistics available up to the year 1918 show that, on an average, the Outside Service had one and a half times as many employees as the Inside Service. On this basis we can arrive at an estimate of 10,000 for the entire service.

32. Aberdeen to Laurier, May 16, 1897, Laurier Papers, PAC.

33. Dawson, *Civil Service of Canada*, p. 82.

34. Memorandum (undated), Borden Papers, vol. 198, 110664–65.

35. R. K. Merton, *Social Theory and Social Structure*, pp. 71–81. Merton argues that in the structural context of the American city in the late nineteenth and early twentieth centuries, power was diffuse and fragmented. In response to this situation there emerged the party "boss" who could deal with all the elements in a fluid environment, from the street corner to the Governor of the State. Merton enumerates four major "latent functions" which were performed by the party machine: a welfare service for the immigrants and the poor, given in return for votes; a protection service for small business, in return for party funds; an avenue of social mobility for the immigrants; and a stabilizing mechanism of control over criminal activities, through the setting of standards and the defining of limits. Merton argues further that where civic reform movements unseated the bosses, these functions were not performed with consequent social problems.

36. Frank H. Underhill, "The Development of National Political Parties in Canada," in Underhill, *In Search of Canadian Liberalism*; E. Scott Reid, "The Rise of National Parties in Canada," in Hugh Thorburn, ed., *Party Politics in Canada*.

37. "We must frankly recognize that the political party is a necessary part of our governmental machinery, and recognize too, that it cannot be maintained on air. . . . The method adopted in the past has been to reward the party workers by Civil Service jobs, or by cash from a fund contributed in part by men who honestly favour Conservative vs. Liberal principles. . . . In England they sell titles, not contracts to fill the campaign treasury . . . a party member must contribute to his party chest just as a Church member contributes for the spread of his faith." (O. D. Skelton, "Our Foes at Home," pp. 101–5)

38. *Debates*, June 30, 1908, p. 11665. Academic support for this viewpoint can be found in Max Weber's work on bureaucracy. See A. Diamant, "The Bureaucratic Model: Max Weber, Rejected, Rediscovered, Reformed," in F. Heady and S. L. Stokes, eds., *Papers in Comparative Public Administration*, pp. 59–96.

39. *Debates*, May 10, 1918, pp. 1725ff; April 12, 1918, pp. 707ff.

40. *Debates*, May 10, 1918, p. 1739. Some members demanded that lists be produced showing the number of relatives each public servant had in the bureaucracy.

41. *Report of the Committee on Election Expenses* (Ottawa: Queen's Printer, 1966), pp. 87–88.

42. League for Social Reconstruction, *Social Planning for Canada*, p. 274.

43. 8–9 George V (1918), c. 12, s. 32.

44. 9–10 Elizabeth II (1961), c. 57, s. 61(1).

45. 14–15–16 Elizabeth II (1967), c. 71, s. 32.

46. It is also significant to note that the evidence we have on macing indicates that, to the extent it did take place, it was found in the menial contracting jobs in the local constituencies.

47. *Mail and Empire*, May 20, 1874.

48. In November, 1876, the *Canadian Monthly* asserted: "The price of a commission in the government service is the free exercise of a glib tongue, deftness in canvassing, unscrupulousness in everything. Serve the party day and night, secure us an electoral triumph by fair means or foul, and you shall be quartered for life on the public treasury."

49. *Report of the Royal Commissioners Appointed to Enquire into Certain Matters Relating to the Civil Service of Canada*, 1892, p. 132. (Emphasis added.)

50. A typical example is the remark made by the Secretary of the Civil Service Commission in 1929: "The best method of judging any system is by its results. The results of patronage were inefficiency, extravagance, disorganization, and injustice; the Merit System, on the other hand, has brought about business methods, efficiency, economy and democracy in the Service." (Civil Service Research Conference, *Proceedings of the Sixth Annual Convention*, 1929, p. 62)

51. The "sure cure" remedy for inefficiency came to be known as the "good people syndrome" in the United States. One commentator describes the orientation: "[Early civil service reformers] were so understandably perturbed about 'spoils' and so eloquent in portraying the effects of its eradication that their

solution—recruitment by competitive examinations—came to be regarded as a panacea. [They encouraged] the belief that all we need to do is to 'get good people' . . . [if] the efficiency of the organization is impaired, we simply need more 'good people.' [This orientation] stymies needed action, excuses inactivity, and gives a false sense of security born of faith in a sure-cure remedy." ("The Distorted Spirit of '83," *Personnel Administration* 5 [November, 1942], p. 2) It must be conceded that poor systems can be improved by good people, and that good systems mean very little if run by poor people. However poor systems will continue to be poor if drastic administrative overhauls are not instituted to rectify deficiencies. In the absence of this overhaul good people could only marginally improve the system; indeed, most of them would undoubtedly quit in disgust and frustration.

52. L. D. White, *The Federalists*; idem, *The Jeffersonians*. The criterion for White's assertion is not entirely clear, and Professor S. E. Finer utilizes it without being explicit as to the comparative evidence. However, having said this, it in no way diminishes Finer's original contention that the argument linking patronage and inefficiency is open to some serious questioning. See Finer, "Patronage and the Public Service," pp. 329–60.

53. At Confederation there were administrative problems in the Departments of Crown Lands of Public Works, of the Interior, and of Marine and Fisheries. See Hodgetts, *Pioneer Public Service*.

54. The Blue Book reveals that of the 263 employees of the federal civil service located at headquarters at Confederation, at least 220 had been previous employees of the provinces of Canada. Hodgetts, *Pioneer Public Service*, pp. 274–79.

55. Professor Hodgetts records that at the time of the setting up of the new departments, some Maritime Members of Parliament expressed dissatisfaction as to the lack of Maritime representation in the bureaucracy. Ibid., p. 275.

56. Ibid., p. 277.

57. *First Report of the Civil Service Commission*, 1869, p. 17.

58. The reforms advocated by Murray will be discussed in chapter 2. For his report, see *Report on the Organization of the Public Service of Canada*, by Sir George Murray.

59. Paul Van Riper, *History of the United States Civil Service*, pp. 225–26; Dwight Waldo, *The Administrative State: A Study of the Political Theory of American Public Administration*, pp. 28–29.

60. *Debates*, May 26, 1908, pp. 9132–33.

61. *Debates*, April 1, 1908, pp. 6003–5.

Chapter Two

The Early Civil Service
Commission, 1908–1917

A central aspect of the fate of being Canadian is that our very existing has at all times been bound up with the interplay of various world empires. One can better understand what it is to be Canadian if one understands that interplay.

George Grant, *Technology and Empire: Perspectives on North America*

THE CIVIL SERVICE COMMISSION, although "created" in 1908, had certain antecedents which directly shaped the manner in which it conceived its task. The most important of these was the extent to which the British experiences in civil service reform directly affected the somewhat groping experiment being attempted in Canada between 1868 and 1908. British reform influence was at first slight, but it grew in importance within two decades after Confederation. For example, the influence of the British reforms was more apparent than real in the 1868–70 Canadian Royal Commission Report on the civil service, in the sense that although passing references were made to the Northcote-Trevelyan recommendations, no concerted effort was launched to copy any of these reforms when the Royal Commission made its recommendations to the new Federal Government.[1] The 1880–81 Royal Commission on the Canadian federal civil service was much more forthright however: "We do not assert that the English system is in every particular suitable to the wants of the Dominion; but with such modifications as we will presently submit, we believe the adoption of its essential principles would be an effectual remedy for all the important defects of our system."[2]

This slow development of learning from the British experience is in itself understandable, for even the British did not immediately introduce the rather novel recommendations which Sir Charles Trevelyan and Sir Stafford Northcote made to the British House of Commons in 1853. In

England, although a Civil Service Commission was created in 1855 to take care of recruitment procedures to the bureaucracy, it was not until 1870 that the Gladstone Ministry issued an Order in Council which introduced the concept of competitive examinations to fill vacancies in the civil service. Eleven years later the influence of this reform was demonstrated in Canada when the Federal Government accepted the recommendation of the 1880–81 Royal Commission that a board of civil service examiners be created to examine would-be recruits to the service on their academic knowledge. Even the format of the Canadian examination system was essentially the same as in Great Britain: a preliminary test to prevent those unfitted for the civil service from competing, to be followed by a selecting examination. By 1891, the Royal Commission into the workings of the civil service appointed by Sir John Abbott's Conservative Government recommended, both in its final Report and in the draft civil service bill appended to that Report, the formation of a federal Civil Service Commission to conduct recruitment to the service on the basis of merit.

When the 1907–8 Royal Commission on the civil service advocated the creation of a Civil Service Commission, it was therefore an echo of earlier calls for reform. The 1877 Select Committee of the House of Commons appointed to "inquire into the present condition of the Civil Service" had recommended that an independent Civil Service Commission be created to appoint, promote, and manage civil service personnel.[3] Under the Civil Service Amendment Act, 1908, the Board of Civil Service Examiners was replaced by a Civil Service Commission composed of two members having the rank of deputy minister, who held office during good behaviour and could be removed only by the Governor-General on an address from the Senate and the House of Commons. While the CSC was a "new" creation, in the sense that there was never a central personnel agency for the federal public service before this time, some of the organizational machinery and personnel of the old Board of Civil Service Examiners were co-opted into the new organization. A significant personnel transfer from the Board was Mr. William Foran, who, from 1896 to 1908, served as the secretary for the Board of Civil Service Examiners, and who, in his capacity as secretary to the CSC, was destined to exert a profound personal influence over the fortunes of the central personnel agency until his retirement in 1939.[4]

The CSC was authorized to set open competitive examinations for entrance into the Inside Civil Service, and to test and pass, upon the qualifications of candidates, "for promotion in the Service, and to issue certificates with respect thereto."[5] According to the Act, applicants had to be British subjects and between the ages of eighteen and thirty-five.[6] In section 10(1) the CSC was authorized to investigate, on its own initiative, and to:

26

report upon the operation of the Civil Service Act or of this Act, and upon the violation of any of the provisions of the Civil Service Act or this Act or of any regulation made either of the said Acts, and upon the request of the head of a department with the approval of the Governor in Council, to investigate and report upon the organization of the department, the conduct and efficiency of its officers, clerks and other employees, and any other matter relative to the department; and in connection with, and for the purpose of, any such investigation the Governor in Council may invest the commission with all or any of the powers vested in a commissioner appointed under Part II of the Inquiries Act.[7]

As a response to the Courtney Commission's observations on the growing complexity of the Inside Civil Service, the old organizational format of personnel consisting of minister, deputy minister, principal and chief clerks, and other minor clerical help was changed, and a reform which was essentially British in origin was adopted. Provisions were made, for the first time, to recognize the growing complexity of the civil service by dividing personnel into three broad divisions, each with a corresponding salary scale. Section 5(2), (3), and (4) provided for the following classification:

The First Division shall be divided into:
Subdivision A, consisting of officers having the rank of deputy heads but not being deputy heads administering departments, assistant deputy ministers, and the principal technical and administrative and executive officers;
Subdivision B, consisting of the lesser technical and administrative and executive officers, including the chief clerks now holding office and not eligible for subdivision A.
The Second Division shall consist of certain other clerks, having technical, administrative, executive, or other duties which are of the same character as, but of less importance and responsibility than those of the first division. This division shall be divided into subdivisions A and B.
The Third Division shall consist of the other clerks in the Service whose duties are copying and routine work, under direct supervision, of less importance than that of the second division. This division shall be divided into subdivisions A and B.

Further salient provisions of the Act were the grading of examinations according to the positions to be filled (section 13), the substitution of qualifying tests for examinations for technical positions (section 21), and the implementation of a probationary period of six months before permanent appointment (section 20). The Act provided stiff penalties for partisan political activity or attempts by civil servants to influence members of the CSC:

> No person shall, directly or indirectly, solicit or endeavour to influence a member of the Commission with respect to the appointment of any person to the service, or with respect to the promotion of, or an increase of salary to, any officer, clerk, or employee in the service.
>
> Any person who, directly or indirectly, solicits or endeavours to influence a member of the Commission in favour of his appointment, promotion or increase of salary, shall be deemed to be unworthy of such appointment, promotion or increase, and it shall not be accorded him; and if he is employed in the Civil Service, he shall be liable to immediate dismissal.
>
> No officer, clerk or employee in the Civil Service shall be debarred from voting at any Dominion or Provincial election if under the laws governing the said election he has the right to vote; but no such officer, clerk or employee shall engage in partisan work in connection with any such election.

Finally, the legislation provided that the Secretary of State was to be charged with the administration of the Act, and was further authorized to lay before Parliament, within fifteen days after the commencement of each session, a report of the CSC's activities during the preceding year.[8]

THE EARLY YEARS, 1908–1912

In the late summer of 1908 the two Commissioners provided for by the Civil Service Act of that year were appointed: Adam Shortt of Kingston, Ontario, and Michel G. LaRochelle of Montreal.[9] Little is known of Lt.-Col. Michel LaRochelle. He was born in 1867, studied law in the office of Sir Wilfred Laurier, and was secretary to Laurier from 1887 to 1889. He ran in the Quebec provincial election of 1900 as a Liberal and was defeated. In 1907 he refused the nomination for the federal riding of Richelieu. His acceptance of the Civil Service Commissioner's position in 1908 leads one to surmise that he no longer wished to be engaged in the rough and tumble world of politics, and was prepared to serve the country in an administrative capacity.[10]

The second Commissioner had a much more illustrious background. Adam Shortt was a distinguished academic, professor of political studies at Queen's University from 1892 to 1908, a Fellow of the Royal Society of Canada (1906), a past president of the Canadian Political Science Association, and twice first vice-president of the American Political Science Association.[11] In 1907, Dr. Shortt, through his earlier interests and scholarly work on the problems of taxation in Canada, became involved in the implementation of the Industrial Disputes Investigation Act, which was made into law that same year by the Dominion Parliament. The legislation, commonly called the Lemieux Act after its parliamentary sponsor, the Minister of Labour, the Honourable Rudolphe Lemieux, was the creation of William Lyon Mackenzie King, then Deputy Minister of Labour. The Act was considered unique in the world's labour legislation in that it sought to ensure compulsory investigation of labour disputes by the Government without resorting to binding awards. The intention, as Dr. Mackintosh of Queen's University indicates, "was that careful investigation would resolve many difficulties and that a public report would so focus public opinion that compromise and settlement would prevail over the strike and the lockout." Dr. Mackintosh continues: "Shortt's success under the Lemieux Act was astounding. Aside from the pervasive and enduring influence of an ardent teacher, it is his greatest single achievement. The bald facts are, I think, very impressive. From April 20, 1907, to May 12, 1908, he was chairman of eleven boards under the IDI Act. The disputes affected 15,000 workers. In every case there was agreement not only among the three members of the Board, but by employers and employees alike."[12]

There is no doubt that this success in conciliation enhanced his prestige in government circles, leading, in turn, to his eventual appointment as Civil Service Commissioner.[13] Shortt's acceptance and appointment was fortunate for the CSC. He possessed two of the basic qualities needed for leadership for the organization if it was to survive its initial threshold period: he was well known to the Canadian public and was a strong advocate of civil service reform. His interest in civil service reform was not altogether new, for he was already a leading exponent of moulding the civil service after the British model.[14] During the first year of the central personnel agency's life, however, the importance of its work was to be overshadowed, so far as the Government was concerned, by events of more significant political import than civil service reform. The ten-year period between 1908 and 1918 was virtually dominated by events taking place in Europe which directly affected conditions in Canada. These included the naval crisis, a storm which had been long brewing and which finally erupted in 1911; the outbreak of World War I, with all its consequent agony at home concerning Canada's role in the conflict; and, finally, the formation of the Union Government in 1917. These were all important events which, at first, overshadowed the impetus for further significant reforms in the federal civil service.

Adam Shortt, during his period of tenure as Civil Service Commissioner, fostered a considerable amount of public interest in, and support for, the CSC's role in personnel administration. The Shortt Papers are replete with constant demands for his services as an after-dinner speaker at banquets of reform groups, the Canadian Club in the urban areas throughout Ontario and the West, and various boards of trade. Popular demands for his services even came from such faraway cities as Washington, Boston, New York, and Chicago. The tremendous grass-roots support which he engendered for the work of the CSC was to stand it in good stead in later years.

Notwithstanding the Government's preoccupation with other matters in 1911, the extent of Dr. Shortt's influence can be gauged by the new Government's willingness to accept the advice he tendered to Sir Robert Borden concerning certain aspects of administrative reform. Shortly after assuming the office of Prime Minister, Borden, it appears, requested a memorandum from Dr. Shortt and one D. Malcolm, seeking their advice on improvements for civil service administration.[15] The memorandum was forthright in its criticisms of existing administrative machinery, and argued for the adoption of many of the reforms advocated by the Northcote-Trevelyan Report of 1853. Foremost among the criticisms was the deplorable lack of Treasury control: "In Britain alone do we find a system which is at once sufficiently effective and entirely suited to our system of government, as framed on the British model. The British system of 'Treasury Control' is worthy of most serious consideration in view of the present and prospective needs of the Canadian Executive Government."[16] The Canadian Treasury Board, Shortt argued, was analogous to its British counterpart in name only, it being a committee of Council, with no staff and machinery to expedite effective control functions. He pointed to the increasing influx of technical personnel into the civil service and advocated a special category for this group of civil servants, as was the practice in the British civil service.[17] He argued for better treatment of civil servants with regard to their superannuation, and he visualized the CSC solely as an effective recruiting organization, as was the case in Britain, the other functions of personnel being left to the departments and the proposed chief control agency, the Department of Finance.

His most important recommendation was to urge the Government to appoint a senior British officer to carry out a thorough investigation of the federal civil service. This, it will be recalled, was one of the specific duties assigned to the CSC under the Civil Service Amendment Act, 1908. "Reform is so much needed in so many directions that the Government cannot deal with the matter piecemeal. We would suggest that, before they take any important step, they should have had before them a full report from an impartial Commission appointed to consider the whole question. The

Commission should comprise as one of its members the ablest and most experienced official of the British Treasury whom that office can be persuaded to lend for that purpose. The assistance of such an official will be of the utmost value."[18]

In a letter to Earl Grey, the recently retired Governor-General of Canada, Shortt jubilantly noted that the new Government was very favourable to changes needed in civil service administration. The Commissioner indicated that the success of his advice to the new Government was due, for the most part, to Earl Grey's counsel to him as to the proper timing for such suggestions to the new administration.[19] To expedite the task of administrative reform, there was a need for the "employment of an official from the British Treasury. In the selection of the proper man, upon which so much will depend, I trust we shall be able to avail ourselves of the advice and assistance of Your Lordship."[20]

The Borden Papers indicate that the Commissioner's advice was accepted by the Prime Minister. Through the efforts of Sir George Perley, later to become Canadian High Commissioner in London, Borden was able to obtain the services of Sir George Murray, a former permanent Secretary of the Treasury in England.[21] Sir George spent a short period of three months in Canada, during which time he gathered information for a brief, but nevertheless perceptive, analysis of the problems affecting the Canadian civil service. His Report called for the inclusion of all recruitment procedures under the jurisdiction of the CSC; a clearer delineation of the First, Second, and Third Divisions; the creation of a special division for technical personnel; the lowering of the age limits for admission to the civil service; a noncontributory pension scheme with compulsory retirement; and a decrease in the number of temporary clerks employed by the Government.[22] Murray saw the necessity for relieving the Cabinet of much of the administrative detail with which it was burdened, and for decentralizing the work load so as to give ministers and deputy ministers an adequate share of the tasks of administration. The abolition of the Treasury Board was advocated, for it was felt that this institution was an administrative anachronism. The Treasury Board's supposed powers over estimates and appropriations were to be transferred to the Department of Finance.

The Murray Report was not implemented. True, there were some institutional changes made as a result of these recommendations, but the bulk of the criticisms and advice for reform was not heeded or acted upon by the Government.[23] Several reasons suggest themselves for the Government's inaction in this regard. Of first consideration is the nature of the inquiry. In a passing critique of the Report some twenty years later, Sir Robert Borden expressed the opinion that the recommendations were "elaborate and far-reaching but went considerably beyond the scope of the proposed inquiry," and that it was "such a wholesale and far-reaching programme that it would have been out of the question to have carried it out in full."[24] The Report was indeed broad in scope, and it was perhaps politically inexpedient for the Government to act upon it in its entirety; but these criticisms do appear rather weak in view of the fact that the Government's terms of reference were quite broad in the first place. Murray was commissioned during his brief Canadian sojourn of ninety days to report on:

1. The methods employed in the transaction of public business.
2. The control of appropriations and expenditure.
3. The administrative methods and operations of the chief spending Departments, including:

   (a) the manner in which appointments to the public service are made.

   (b) the manner in which promotions within it are made.

   (c) the manner in which retirements are effected.

   (d) the classification of the staff and the distribution of duties in each Department and the duplication of the same or similar work in two or more Departments.

   (e) the distribution of the work between the several Departments or authorities.

4. Generally the manner in which the public business of the Dominion is administered.[25]

Moreover, despite the fact that the CSC had recommended a supporting staff for such an investigative study, no such personnel were placed at Murray's disposal. The result was that there were no detailed blueprints as to how some of the reforms could be implemented. The limitations on the Commissioner's time, the extremely broad nature of the terms of reference, and the reluctance of the Government to supply supporting staff for this one-man effort preclude any serious criticisms of Sir George's effort.

Regarding Murray's recommendation for the abolition of Treasury Board, Borden felt that it was somewhat superficial in that the Commissioner had failed to understand the historical reasons behind the creation of the institution in a Canadian context.[26] This criticism would have been a cogent one if the Treasury Board was indeed fulfilling its statutory functions, but as a cabinet subcommittee substantiated in 1920, all statutory functions of the Board had been inoperative for years.[27]

Another reason given for the failure of implementation was that "there was strong opposition, in various quarters, to doing away with the Commission's powers over promotions, to a non-contributory system of pensions, and to the stricter distinction between the First, Second, and Third Divisions."[28] From the CSC's correspondence to the Prime Minister, it was clear that this organization, responsible for staffing functions, had no such qualms about the Report.

In retrospect, it appears that if the Murray reforms, or any other reforms for that matter, were adopted in Canada at this period of crisis, it would have been fortuitous. The foreboding clouds of an impending war, followed in a few months by its actual outbreak, were to keep the Government preoccupied with the situation from 1914 onwards. As Borden stated: "In Canada, as in Great Britain, the imperative purpose of the Government was to throw the full power of each nation into the conflict, for upon its issue hung the future of the British Commonwealth. Thus a meticulous adherence to Civil Service enactments and regulations was not the main purpose of the administration in either country."[29] This may be taken perhaps as one good reason why the Murray reforms were never seriously entertained by the Government.

PERSONNEL ADMINISTRATION, 1908–1917

The Civil Service Act of 1882 had organized the federal bureaucracy into a five-tier form: at the apex, the deputy minister, and, in descending order of importance, chief clerks, then first-, second-, and third-class clerks. From this tier system, a theoretical departmental hierarchy was adopted to achieve a balanced ratio of clerical help: one chief clerk, two first-class clerks, four second-class clerks, and eight third-class clerks. In actual practice, however, the bottom of this system was congested with third-class clerical appointments, and the upper echelons of the bureaucracy were maintained as intended. Career development and rapid advancement on the basis of one's merit were millennial concepts. As one commentator asserted: "Nothing short of the chief clerks being stricken by paralysis every three or four years could create any hope for the scores who were submerged in the lower classes. As a matter of fact there are in the public service at Ottawa a very large number of capable men who are being held down to small salaries and subordinate rank."[30]

The Civil Service Act of 1908 sought to alleviate this problem by providing for further subdivisions of the old classifications. What was roughly comparable to the administrative class in the British civil service (First Division) was divided into Subdivisions A and B. Both Second and Third Divisions were also subdivided. But although there were more classified positions to be filled, the Government's action in mechanically utilizing the old salary scale to effect this new classification only aggravated, rather than mitigated, the central problem, namely, the poor salary scales for civil servants.

This defective administrative arrangement only served to compound existing difficulties in personnel administration. To offset this central defect in the legislation, the various departments, exercising what Professor Norman Ward has called "the sturdy tradition of departmental autonomy,"[31] promoted staff members solely on the basis of the increased cost of living, rather than on meritorious service or on the nature of the duties to be performed. The result was that no uniform principles of organization were enforced. In 1912 Sir George Murray pointed to this central defect: "Men will be found in one Department with high salaries doing work which is performed by a much lower class in others; and the numbers of the various classes have been increased from time to time to meet the supposed claims of individuals without any special reference to the nature of the duties to be performed. It would be easy to quote numerous cases in which an officer has been allowed to proceed from one class to another without any change of work whatever, merely because it was desired to improve his position."[32] The CSC repeatedly pointed to the same condition, Commissioner Shortt complaining to the Prime Minister that "the culmination . . . [of this state of affairs] must be to make of the Civil Service an army of generals."[33]

Between 1908 and 1913 the CSC's internal statistics reveal that an average of four hundred and ten positions were yearly classified as temporary, to be filled, for a six-months' duration, by the departments.[34] Although acknowledging that part of this staffing "problem" was caused by the difficulty which the CSC was encountering in recruiting qualified permanent male clerks at the salaries offered, the CSC drew attention to the fact that these temporary positions did allow a certain amount of patronage to continue. As Commissioner Shortt intimated to the Prime Minister: "Members of Parliament on both sides of the House have assured me that the worries of local patronage afford the chief drawback to the position of Member of Parliament. They all agree, however, that until patronage is legally taken out of their hands, they cannot escape it, inasmuch as to do so would have the effect of transferring a too numerous section of voters to the camp of their opponents. Where, however, the patronage is removed altogether, neither party gains or suffers and the better Members of Parliament are most relieved."[35] Other staffing problems were the need for a statutory age limit for retirement, some provisions for superannuation benefits for civil servants, and the necessity for a classification system for the rapidly growing ranks of scientific personnel in the employ of the Government.[36]

These proposed reforms all suffered the same fate as the Murray Report of 1912, and for essentially the same reasons. The CSC remained solely a recruiting agency with a clerical staff of about twenty-four persons.[37] For the Government, personnel administration remained a non-priority item, but the CSC's inability to take the initiative in these areas was also due in part to another difficulty: a leadership crisis which had existed since the creation of the organization and which was further aggravated during the Conservative administration of Borden.

PERIOD OF INSTABILITY, 1912–1917: CRISIS IN LEADERSHIP

Between 1908 and 1911, it appears that the smooth functioning of the Civil Service Commission was hampered by personality clashes between Commissioners LaRochelle and Shortt. Evidence from the Shortt Papers indicates that Dr. Shortt envisaged his role as one senior to his counterpart and expected no misunderstanding on this point. As Shortt informed Borden in 1911, apparently this did not turn out to be so:

The only other concrete matter which it is necessary to deal with in this memorandum is the composition of the Civil Service Commission itself. It was rather an unusual experiment to provide for a Civil Service Commission of two members with equal authority, yet without any provision for possible differences of opinion between them. The Commissioners are required to deal with many matters of detail in the administration of the Act, and with hundreds of appointments and promotions involving special phases of qualification. Yet not one of these matters can be effectively dealt with unless there is a complete coincidence of judgement as between the Commissioners. A difference of judgement involves the paralysis of appointments or promotions without any provision for solving the difficulty. To understand the nature of the situation one need only consider how long the work of the Government could be carried out if there were two Ministers or two Deputy Ministers for each department, and if each pair had to agree at once on the general policy and the special action to be taken in the case of every matter coming before them, or in the alternative to get nothing done. That under existing conditions the work of the Civil Service Commission has not been paralysed long before this is doubtless a legitimate matter for surprise. There are, however, a number of cases in which the inevitable has happened, and much inconvenience has been occasioned to at least three departments on account of differences in judgement as between the Commissioners as to the proper method of making certain appointments. The official interpretation of the Justice Department, and the concurrence of the Ministers and Deputies in the departments affected, have not availed to settle the matters in dispute, indeed all that is necessary on the part of a Commissioner, to paralyse the functions of the Commission is simply to do nothing and say nothing. The difficulties connected with the suspended appointments now pass over as a legacy to the new Government.

Needless to say no such situation as that involved in the Civil Service Commission exists anywhere else in Canada or in any other service of which we have record. In Britain, it is true, there are two Commissioners of the Civil Service, but one of them is Chief Commissioner and has the right to decide matters in which there is a difference of opinion. Obviously the Canadian Act should be amended in one of three directions. (a) By providing for one Commissioner, (b) If there must be two Commissioners, one should be Chief Commissioner with a deciding vote, the other having the right to record his dissent and the reasons for it, (c) By providing for three Commissioners, one to be chairman with any special powers deemed necessary; otherwise the majority voice should decide, and the minority should have the right to record dissent. Some change is indispensable if the Commission is to discharge its functions properly.[38]

The Government concurred in this analysis of the problems of the CSC, and in 1912, through an amendment to the Civil Service Act, opted for the third recommendation by providing for a chairman and two other Commissioners, the former considered to be the senior member of the group and official spokesman to Parliament and to the public.[39] Shortt, however, appeared to have favoured the one-man commission, for on the two occasions when he was responsible for drafting provincial civil service legislation, he was successful in making recommendations to this effect.[40]

The relations between the Conservative Government of Borden and the illustrious Dr. Shortt remain historical conjecture on our part. The evidence accumulated, however, indicates that when Borden achieved office in 1911, he had a very high regard for the past accomplishments of this academic. By 1912, however, the Government had its reservations about Dr. Shortt, and he was not accorded the newly created position of chairman of the CSC. Indeed five years were to pass before Shortt was to resign from the CSC, clearing the way for the appointment of a chairman. The Government followed a deliberate policy of leaving the reform on the statute books, thus signifying, at least to Dr. Shortt, its displeasure with his performance. Indeed, no other option was open to the Government: the removal of the popular advocate of reform from his *de facto* position as chairman would have been politically damaging to say the least.

As a "moral entrepreneur" concerned with the elimination of patronage from the bureaucracy, Shortt had succeeded in institutionalizing the crusade calling for reform in government. His campaign, and the support it received, operated with an absolute ethic: patronage was evil without any qualification, and effective measures had to be enforced to eradicate the practice.[41] Giving full support to this view were the majority of the nation's newspaper editorials, popular luncheon clubs, reform movements in both Canada and the United States, and a phalanx of academic colleagues of the Civil Service Commissioner.

As discussed in chapter 1, this "moralism" of the reformers undoubtedly led them to establish overly simple objectives and blinded them to other ramifications having a significant bearing on the achievement of administrative efficiency. However, there is much to be said for the view that in a large-scale organization, important changes, particularly along the lines we are now discussing, are very hard to accomplish unless pressed by a leadership touched with some "fire in the belly." The fervour of the moral entrepreneur cannot therefore be outrightly dismissed as misguided.

Furthermore, Shortt's campaign in Canada had strong humanitarian overtones. He was genuinely concerned with the plight of the lower clerical workers of the civil service whose positions were most susceptible to patronage abuses. Sociologist Howard Becker's description of this posture of the moral entrepreneur is analogous to Shortt's outlook:

> The crusader is not only interested in seeing to it that other people do what he thinks right. He believes that if they do what is right it will be good for them. Or he may feel that his reform will prevent certain kinds of exploitation of one person by another. Prohibitionists felt that they were not simply forcing their morals on others, but attempting to provide the conditions for a better way of life for people prevented by drink from realizing a truly good life. Abolitionists were not simply trying to prevent slave owners from doing the wrong thing; they were trying to help slaves to achieve a better life.[42]

From this quarter of the civil service Shortt also received full support for his moral campaigns. As chapter 8 will indicate, the majority of the staff associations, although in perpetual conflict with each other on many civil service matters, have generally been united in their support of the CSC's activities to eradicate patronage practices in civil service appointments. Confronted then with this tremendous groundswell of support for the CSC, the Government would have found it politically inexpedient to remove the Civil Service Commissioner from his position. The ordeal alone of having to face the public debate in the House of Commons was enough

37

to ensure political prudence on the part of the Government. Prime Minister Borden therefore continued to mark time by leaving the clarification of Shortt's status in a state of limbo:

> *Mr. Marcil:* As to the personnel of the Commission, if I remember rightly, a statute was passed about two years ago authorizing the appointment of a third member of the Commission. That statute, however, seems to be a dead letter. In answer to a question put by me last year, the Government replied that there was no chairman of the Commission; that both Commissioners were on an equal footing. I think both members of the Commission are hard-working men, and that they have had a more strenuous time than they expected when they were appointed. Does the Prime Minister intend to complete this Commission, or is the statute to remain a dead letter?

> *Sir Robert Borden:* I think I was asked that same question both last session and the session before, and I give the same answer now that I gave then, namely, that we thought it was desirable to make some amendments to the Civil Service Act, that other matters in regard to it were under consideration, and that, pending those amendments, we thought it unnecessary to make the additional appointment. My honourable friend is quite correct in his appreciation of the status of the two Commissioners.[43]

Perhap's Borden's negative image of Shortt was greatly buttressed by an unfortunate incident in 1915. In a public address quoted in the Ottawa newspapers, Dr. Shortt implied that the Government had been blatantly engaged in patronage to the tune of some ten thousand appointments. This accusation pointed to one cabinet minister, the Honourable Robert Rogers, Minister of Public Works, who was indeed quite well known for his political indiscretions.[44] Shortt, however, took his statistical information from a newspaper report without checking the accuracy of the claim. As a result, he was forced to retract his assertions privately to the Prime Minister, admitting quite frankly his error of judgement. But the damage was already done, and he was forcefully attacked in the House of Commons by members of the Government, while being defended by the Liberal Opposition. The Dominion Archivist, Dr. Doughty, summed up Shortt's predicament:

> I know that it was common opinion after the attack in the House by the Honourable Mr. Rogers that Shortt could not very well remain for any length of time in his position, and soon after that occurrence, an effort

was made to create the Board [of Historical Publications]. But when it was finally accomplished, it was thought that the Government had found a satisfactory way of relieving Shortt from his unfortunate position.[45]

Adam Shortt's naiveté was his idealism. He assiduously strove to develop in Canada the British model of public administration at a time when the political climate was not receptive to such changes. A well-known student of his, Liberal Senator Andrew Haydon, was later to assess his performance in the following terms:

> He talked of the Indian service as an ideal, and of the eagerness with which Oxford and Cambridge men, for example, felt honoured in competing under the British system of civil service examinations. He visualized the days when many of our young Canadians, in the laudable anxiety to serve the state, would seek employment by becoming part of the permanent governing body of the country, for such is the civil service since parties and administrators come and go. He should have known that in Canada at least this was quite impossible. But he had by nature a certain Scottish stubbornness that never knew defeat, and with characteristic courage he set out to administer an almost impossible piece of legislation.[46]

Borden, however, found that Shortt, while being "a man of conspicuous ability," was not "altogether suited, either by his previous academic experience or by his temperament, for the duties of Civil Service Commissioner."[47] Shortt's temperament, it appears, consistently demanded adherence to civil service legislation enacted in 1908. The Government, however, considered civil service legislation to be of minor importance compared to the overriding need to bring the war effort to a successful conclusion. Thus, civil service legislation was frequently violated in pursuit of this major objective.[48] If only Borden's side of the story is considered, the image which thus emerges is that of an uncompromising Commissioner refusing to be influenced by the exigencies of war, and wishing to carry out the letter of the law. The evidence accumulated for this study, however, gives a somewhat different view of Adam Shortt. Although an idealist, he was, as Senator Haydon intimated, a realist in his understanding that "the faults and follies of mankind" could only be mitigated slowly over a period of time.[49] Indeed, a year after his resignation from the Civil Service Commission, Shortt complained rather bitterly that the central personnel agency had become much more stringent in expediting the letter of the law than it had under his leadership.[50] Shortt, according to Borden, had very little administrative talent,[51] but the prestige he brought to the job of Civil Service Commissioner certainly helped the organization to weather the first few years of its existence. By 1917, then having outlived his political usefulness, Dr. Shortt was only too relieved to leave the position of Civil Service Commissioner and accept the more congenial position of chairman of the Board of Historical Publications at the National Archives of Canada. He frankly admitted in his private correspondence that he had urged the Government to expedite the creation of the Board even before the 1915 incident, and that his resignation from the CSC and transfer to the Board was a mutually acceptable agreement between the Government and himself.

Upon Shortt's resignation in October, 1917, the Government moved quickly to provide the CSC with the full roster of commissioners provided for under the 1912 amendment. Commissioner LaRochelle continued to serve in his position. Two new Commissioners were appointed: the Honourable W. J. Roche, as the first official chairman of the CSC, and Mr. Clarence Jameson, the Conservative M.P. from Digby, Nova Scotia. Little is known of Jameson prior to his appointment other than the fact that he was first elected to the House of Commons in 1908 and re-elected in 1911. He had not particularly distinguished himself as an ardent civil service reformer in the House, but neither had he demonstrated an antipathy to the cause. Roche, a medical doctor, was first elected to the House of Commons in the general election of 1896 and became the Conservative Whip for the West in 1901. He was appointed Secretary of State in Borden's administration in 1911, and the following year he relinquished this post to become the Minister of the Interior and Superintendent-General of Indian Affairs, the position he held until his appointment as chairman in 1917. Roche, although not a particularly outspoken advocate of reform, brought to the CSC considerable administrative abilities garnered from his ministerial duties. One correspondent of Prime Minister Bennett who had worked under Roche in the Interior Department described him as certainly no "world beater," but as "a sincere, conscientious and painstaking administrator" who, seven years before the classification of the Outside Service, had designed an adequate classification scheme for part of his department.[52]

Between 1908 and 1917 the CSC remained largely an *organization*, mechanically performing the task of recruitment for virtually autonomous departments. Efforts initiated by the CSC's hierarchy to further remodel the civil service after the British practices in public administration largely failed for two main reasons: a leadership crisis developed in the CSC hampering the organization's capacity; and the timing for such reforms was not as yet politically propitious. *Institutionalization* of the organization had, however, begun. In the public eye the CSC increased its favourable image by legitimizing the moral crusade so ably conducted by the illustrious Dr. Shortt. This was a period when moral reformism was concerned more with ends than with means. The Shortt tenure must therefore be viewed more as a period of consolidation for the CSC rather than a period of successful enforcement of the civil service legislation to eradicate patronage practices. Within one year after the resignation of Dr. Shortt, wider political events were to set the stage for the most fundamental changes so far experienced by the Canadian federal administrative structure.

NOTES

1. In advocating reforms for the making of new appointments, the Commission did indicate a passing knowledge of the new British reforms: "It is to be hoped, however, that the improvement in that respect, which has taken place in England, may be found worthy of adoption here." (*Second Report of the Civil Service Commission*, 1869, p. 32)

2. *First Report of the Civil Service Commission*, 1881, p. 20.

3. H. C., Select Committee Appointed to Inquire into the Present Condition of the Civil Service, 1877, *Report*, p. 5.

4. Foran's influence within the Civil Service Commission will be dealt with in succeeding chapters. For a brief résumé of his career in the public service, see the commentary on the occasion of his retirement in *Civil Service Review* 12 (March, 1939), p. 28.

5. 7–8 Edward VII (1908), c. 15, s. 10(1). The Canadian federal bureaucracy was divided into two services up to 1918: the Inside and the Outside. The Inside Service was comprised of those positions in and around the federal capital. The Outside Service consisted of federal employment in the various provinces or areas outside Ottawa under federal jurisdiction.

6. Ibid., s. 14.

7. Ibid., s. 10(1).

8. Ibid., ss. 42, 43, and 44.

9. Privy Council (P.C.) 1992 (September 4, 1908).

10. His relations with both the Liberal and Conservative governments appeared to be cordial, except for one instance in 1919 to which he alluded in a letter to Borden upon the latter's retirement from the Prime Ministership in 1920: "Quant à la delicatesse de vos procédés à mon égard, je vous prie de croire que j'en conserverai un bien fidèle souvenir. Je n'oublierai jamais la sympathie que vous m'avez toujours montrée. Le Maintien de mon status officiel

en 1919, alors qu'il était en péril, en fut l'une des dernières preuves." (LaRochelle to Borden, July 14, 1920, Borden Papers, vol. 16, 4124–25)

11. This information was obtained by a systematic search of the Shortt Papers, at present in the possession of the Douglas Library at Queen's University, Kingston, Ontario. All further references to the Shortt Papers are to these.

12. W. A. Mackintosh, "Adam Shortt, 1859–1931," pp. 170 and 171.

13. The extent of his popularity can perhaps be gauged from one of the many letters he received throughout 1907 and 1908 from federal cabinet ministers. One example comes from part of a letter which the Minister of Agriculture wrote to him on March 16, 1908: "Let me assure you that my colleagues in the Government appreciate no less than myself the value of the services you have rendered during the year; often, I am aware, at great personal inconvenience and to the disturbance of your leisure and of your normal duties and engagements. I believe I may add that the public also fully recognizes its indebtedness to you in respect to this same matter." (Lemieux to Shortt, March 16, 1908, Shortt Papers)

14. Before his appointment as Commissioner, Shortt was one of the luminaries in the Civil Service Reform League of Canada. See Borden Papers, vol. 305, 179054–55.

15. "Memorandum on Improvements Required in the Dominion Civil Service," prepared by A. Shortt and D. Malcolm, n.d., Borden Papers, vol. 229, 128577–93.

16. Ibid., 128581.

17. He wrote, "The classification and salaries for technical positions, though not the selection of persons to fill them, are features of departmental arrangement which in Britain are subject to Treasury Control." (Ibid., 128588)

18. "Memorandum on Improvements," 128591.

19. Shortt to Grey, January 22, 1912, Grey of Howick Papers, PAC, vol. 25, 006326.

20. Ibid., 006327.

21. Perley to Borden, February 5, 1912, Borden Papers, vol. 229, 128344–47.

22. *Report on the Organization of the Public Service of Canada*, by Sir George Murray. Hereafter cited as the Murray Report.

23. A change was effected whereby cabinet meetings were less encumbered with the minutiae of departmental administration, and attempts were made to rationalize the system of keeping accounts by first appointing experts to investigate the system and then establishing a method conceived to effect more adequate controls on public expenditures. See P.C. 2402 (September 24, 1913) and P.C. 2403 (October 8, 1913).

24. "Memorandum Respecting Professor Dawson's Work on the Civil Service of Canada," prepared by Borden, n.d., Borden Papers, vol. 265, 148851–52.

25. See Murray Report, p. 3.

26. Sir Robert Borden, "Problem of an Efficient Civil Service," Canadian Historical Association, *Report of the Annual Meeting*, 1931 (reprint), p. 15.

27. "Memorandum Regarding the Treasury Board," Treasury Board Records, PAC.

28. Borden, "Problem of an Efficient Civil Service," p. 15.

29. Ibid., p. 16.

30. J. L. Payne, "The Civil Servant," pp. 508–9.

31. Norman Ward, *The Public Purse: A Study in Canadian Democracy*, p. 235.

32. Murray Report, p. 21.

33. "Confidential Memorandum for the Prime Minister on the Report of Sir George Murray with Reference to the Organization of the Public Service of Canada," prepared by Shortt, August 30, 1913, Borden Papers, vol. 229, 128564.

34. Ibid., 128547–48.

35. Ibid., 128552.

36. The Royal Commission of 1907–8 gave the first official recognition to the growing importance of scientific personnel in the civil service. *Report of the Commissioners*, 1908, p. 19.

37. Interview.

38. "Memorandum on Improvements," 128589–91.

39. 2 George V (1912), c. 10.

40. See J. Castell Hopkins, *Canadian Annual Review of Public Affairs, 1917* (Toronto: Canadian Annual Review Ltd., 1918), p. 824, and ibid., 1918, p. 675. See also John Campbell to Shortt, December 9, 1916, and Shortt to G. A. Warburton, January 4, 1918, Shortt Papers.

41. Shortt himself, as indicated a little later on, was not rigidly moralistic on these matters. He however gave leadership to a movement which embodied all the moralistic rhetoric of the early twentieth-century reformers.

42. Howard S. Becker, *Outsiders: Studies in the Sociology of Deviance*, p. 148.

43. *Debates*, February 9, 1916, pp. 665–66.

44. *Debates*, February 25, 1915, p. 471.

45. Arthur G. Doughty to Borden, July 30, 1931, Borden Papers, vol. 282, 158419.

46. Andrew Haydon, "Adam Shortt," p. 619.

47. Memorandum prepared by Borden, n.d., Borden Papers, vol. 282, 158428–29.

48. Borden, "Problem of an Efficient Civil Service," p. 16.

49. Haydon, "Adam Shortt," pp. 612–13.

50. Shortt to Foran, March, 1918, Shortt Papers.

51. Interview.

52. E. H. Finlayson to R. B. Bennett, December 1, 1932, Bennett Papers, PAC, no. 137, 91950–51. All further references to the Bennett Papers are to those in the PAC.

Chapter Three

The Reforms of 1918

I am informed that the Secretary of the Civil Service Commission, when he was called into conference by Mr. Maclean, took exception to the wide scope of our proposal; but he was informed that it was our purpose to go to the utmost limit with a view to the elimination of patronage in every possible aspect.

Sir Robert Borden, *Canadian Historical Association Report*, 1931

THE HISTORY of events surrounding the Borden Government's decision to form a Union Government and to call a general election has been the subject of much historical discussion and need not be reiterated here.[1] What is important for our purposes, however, is that in the Government's statement of policy to the country two significant issues were stressed. Along with the commitment to increase Canada's contribution to the war in Europe, the other major issue was the Government's full intention to proceed with sweeping civil service reform. The leading journals and newspaper editorials in English Canada had linked the issue of civil service reform to the necessity of expediting the war effort, for without reformed government it remained questionable how an "efficient and ungodly" German juggernaut could be successfully brought to its knees. The editor of the *Westminster Hall Magazine and the Farthest West Review* best epitomized this line of thinking when he hurled thunderbolts of fire on the heads of "corrupt politicians": "After fair opportunities of forming a judgment, I am forced with sorrow to the bitter and humiliating conclusion that the political life of Canada is the most sordid of the World's English-speaking communities. In at least two of our provinces we have proved unworthy of representative institutions and are helpless in the hands of corrupt autocracies, and if the terrible ordeal through which we are passing does

45

not lead us to penitence and prayer for a rebirth of the national conscience and a sense of sanctity of the institutions under which we live, we are not worthy of a place beside our august mother in the most holy cause she has ever espoused."[2]

Immediately after the elections in the fall of 1917, the Government announced its intention to initiate reform measures, the Civil Service Commission having already been directed "to make a report to the Prime Minister as to the necessary steps for that purpose." One month later another communique added: "It is believed that a Government derived from both political parties and strengthened by special representation of agriculture and organized labour, can act with greater freedom and independence than a Government which held office under old conditions."[3] Two committees of the Privy Council were immediately created by the Government after the election. The War Committee had as its vice-chairman the Honourable Newton Rowell, a leading Liberal from Ontario, while the other committee, given responsibilities more directly affecting domestic affairs and the development of natural resources, was chaired by the Honourable A. K. Maclean of Nova Scotia. "Efficiency in government" was the keynote during the winter of 1917, and Borden, Maclean, Rowell, and Sir George Foster were preeminently the key cabinet ministers concerned with the pursuit of this goal.

Foster's interest in the elimination of patronage was for many years tied to his major concern of establishing organizational efficiency in the civil service, so that a strong and efficient government could effectively advance the interests of Canadian business abroad. Early in 1911, following the Laurier Government's decision to introduce reciprocity with the United States, a group of prominent Toronto businessmen, many of them associated with the Canadian Northern Railway project and all of them formerly Liberal supporters, formed a committee known as the Toronto Eighteen, to oppose the Laurier Government and to effect a bargain with the then Opposition leader, Robert Borden. The Manifesto of the Toronto Eighteen was published in the *Mail and Empire* of February 20, 1911, and called for a continuation of the policies of Canadian economic nationalism which the Macdonald Government and, up until 1911, the Laurier Government, had followed. Obviously fearful of the effects of free trade on the railway business in Canada, the committee was also keenly interested in gaining foreign markets for Canadian products other than in the United States. In order to build up a prosperous export trade, the members believed that a stronger and more efficient government and civil service were essential, especially a Department of Trade and Commerce that could act to open up markets abroad.

On March 1, 1911, Z. A. Lash, Q.C., a railway promoter and leader of the Toronto Eighteen, Lloyd Harris, M.P., and J. S. Willison, formerly editor of the *Globe* and by then a Tory sympathizer, met with the Honourable Clifford Sifton in his Ottawa office and agreed to lay seven demands before Borden in order to determine whether the Toronto Eighteen would abandon the Liberals and throw their support to the Conservatives. Among the demands were these three:

(1) That the future Government, while giving proper representation to Quebec and to the Roman Catholic element, should not be subservient to Roman Catholic influences in public policy *or in the administration of patronage.*

(4) That Mr. Borden should pledge himself *to place the outside civil service under control of the Civil Service Commission.*

(5) That Mr. Borden should agree *to reorganize the Department of Trade and Commerce,* place the Department in charge of a strong Minister without *undue regard to party considerations,* and establish a commercial consular service in foreign countries in order to protect Canadian interests and extend Canadian trade.[4]

Foster was obviously the type of "strong" Trade and Commerce Minister the Toronto Eighteen desired. His later roles as the Minister of Trade and Commerce exactly during the period when Canada began establishing commercial consular services in foreign lands, as chairman of the Griffenhagen inquiry on governmental efficiency, and as a strong champion of these efficiency experts in the face of considerable opposition to their work, substantiate his connections with the civil service reform movement.[5]

It has been exceedingly difficult to obtain a composite picture of the role that the Honourable A. K. Maclean played in the reform measures implemented by the Borden Government. However, from the scattered newspaper reports of his performance in the House of Commons, Maclean had over the years built up a favourable image as an "honest" politician. For example, the *Globe* on February 18, 1916, reported in its front page Maclean's role in the budget debate in the House of Commons: "Mr. Maclean suddenly lifted the debate to its highest plane. Tracing certain of his trenchant criticism of Government unjustifiable expenditure to the inevitable curse of party patronage, the Halifax man threw aside the mantle of a mere political advocate, and made a stirring and statesmanlike appeal to both sides of the House 'to introduce business and conscience' into their dealings with the estimates." Other known facts about him are that he was a close friend and confidant of a leading reformer, the Honourable Newton Rowell, and that he was charged with the duty of preparing and presenting to Parliament the Civil Service Act of 1918.

Newton Rowell had a more formidable public image. In his private correspondence as well, he appears as a politician imbued with a strong sense of the moral justification of his mission in politics.[6] His controversial actions of 1917 in joining the Union Government were agonizing for him, but he had felt rather strongly that his duty to Canada demanded his full support of the war effort. In such circumstances, party loyalty was of secondary importance. In a letter to a personal friend, the Honourable H. C. Brewster, Premier of British Columbia, he confided:

> If a national government, then, is in the public interests, it must include representative Conservatives as well as representative Liberals. . . . One of my hopes of a union or national government would be that it would have courage to eliminate party patronage, and give us a new start. It is the curse of both parties. It has bedevilled the war situation so far. I see no hope that it would not, in some measure at least, bedevil the war situation under the Liberals if they formed a Liberal government . . . nothing would contribute more to the future welfare of Canada than the elimination of party patronage and graft. We should, out of the sacrifices of this war, develop a spirit that would put an end, so far as it is humanly possible to put an end to that kind of thing.[7]

Upon taking office, the new Union Government moved to expedite its election promises. The decision was quickly arrived at to clean the Augean stables of the civil service by strengthening the CSC, the only agency existing at the time with the capabilities to perform the mission. The CSC found itself faced with a task of gigantic proportions, and as the opening quotation of this chapter indicates, some strong reservations among the organization's senior staff were expressed as to its capabilities in performing its new duties. Commissioner Jameson graphically relates the difficulties in his testimony before the 1923 Special Committee on the Civil Service:

> At that time the staff of the Civil Service Commission consisted of twelve persons, and on the 3rd of February, 1918, the entire public service was handed over to us en bloc. It was a tremendous piece of work, to endeavour to administer it. History tells us that about 5,000 years ago, Pharaoh of Egypt bade the chosen people that they were to make bricks without straw. If it may not be considered irreligious, I think the task entrusted to them was little more difficult than that which was imposed upon the Commission in the handling of the public service of Canada, with an untrained staff of twelve. I think the only comparable thing would be the administering of patronage by a Union Government.[8]

The first official indication of the Government's intentions was the Order in Council, P.C. 358 of February 13, 1918, which brought the appointments in the Outside Service under the CSC's jurisdiction, and considerably increased the central personnel agency's powers vis-à-vis the Inside Service. An earlier unpublished Order in Council, however, which had formed the basis of P.C. 358, contained an interesting reference (deleted in the published version) to the CSC's role in proposing new legislation:

> The Prime Minister further observes that shortly before the announcement of policy [i.e., the elimination of patronage and patronage lists proposed by Borden before the election in 1917] . . . he had communicated with the Civil Service Commission and asked that a report should be prepared outlining the steps and measures which in the judgment of the Commission would be necessary for the purpose of carrying into effect the policy set forth. . . .
>
> The Prime Minister further observes that in the opinion of the Civil Service Commission it will be necessary for the purpose of fully carrying into effect the proposal for Civil Service Reform above mentioned to enact further legislation and they are of the opinion that a new Civil Service Act should be prepared and submitted to Parliament at the next Session if possible. *They further report that they are prepared to recommend suitable legislation for the purpose indicated and the Prime Minister recommends that they be authorized to proceed with the preparation of such legislation* in order that it may be submitted to Your Excellency in Council. . . .
>
> The members of the Commission, however, are of opinion that pending the enactment of new legislation alluded to it is both feasible and desirable that certain regulations should be enacted under the provisions of the War Measures Act, 1914, and in pursuance of any other powers vested in Your Excellency in Council and they have submitted to the Prime Minister the regulations hereinafter set forth which are now presented for the consideration of Your Excellency in Council.[9]

The use of the War Measures Act, albeit temporarily, to effect civil service reform was indeed drastic medicine to administer. This fact again serves to illustrate the temper of the times. The regulations included in the Order in Council provided a preview of the reforms intended for the civil service: the departments were prevented from recommending to the Governor in Council technical personnel for appointment, a right which they had enjoyed under the 1908 Civil Service Act. All temporary employment was curtailed, and the CSC was made the sole agency to certify all personnel in the civil service.

The Civil Service Act of 1918 can hardly be called an original document. All indications point to the fact that it was hastily conceived. Indeed, in keeping with the reaction to patronage practices, the emphasis was overwhelmingly on control mechanisms. It must be remembered that the passage of the Act was impelled by the immediate pressure of reformers imbued with the moralistic vision of a civil service cleansed of patronage and thereby automatically rendered efficient for the conduct of the business of a nation at war. It was, as W. L. Grant said, "a great piece of political righteousness for which Sir Robert Borden deserves the highest praise."[10] The timing of this act of moral rehabilitation had to be linked with a coalition government, which many viewed as the only instrument capable of overriding partisan considerations. The sense of the uniqueness of the opportunity this provided gave strength to the reformer's broom which swept in a wide and ruthless arc, to leave the newly reconstituted CSC in full legal command of personnel administration throughout the entire civil service.

THE CIVIL SERVICE ACT, 1918–1919

This urgency to apply remedial surgery to a much maligned bureaucracy can be detected from the composition of the Act. Of its fifty-three clauses, nineteen were copied from the Revised Statutes 1906, chapter 16; nine from the 1908 Civil Service Amendment Act; three from the Civil Service Amendment Act of 1910; one each from the Civil Service Amendment Acts of 1912 and 1917; and four were mixtures of previous legislation. Professor Caiden claims that of the remaining sixteen clauses, seven combined old legislation and new provisions, and six were rearrangements of previous legislation.[11] Many of these provisions were obviously conceived as temporary, for in the following year the Act was revamped, leaving only twenty-five clauses untouched.

The Civil Service Act of 1918 (amended 1919) extended the principle of appointment by competitive examination to the civil service and charged the Civil Service Commission with the responsibility to organize and classify the entire civil service.[12] More specifically, the Act was divided into four main sections. Part I was devoted to describing the nature of the CSC's hierarchy (number of Commissioners, their status and salaries), the duties allotted to it, and the penalties which the CSC should prescribe for such offences as fraud and impersonations in competitive examinations. Part II dealt with more general concerns: rational organization of the civil service, probations, leave of absence, dismissals and resignations, hours of attendance, and political partisanship. Part III described the manner in which examinations were to be conducted and how their results were to be enforced. Part IV was concerned primarily with in-house problems: classification, appointments, promotions, transfers, and compensation.

Clearly, the most important function given to the CSC was the administering of civil service appointments by competitive examinations. Both sections 43 and 44 made it clear that the Act contemplated much more than the mere elimination of unfit candidates, as was the case under the old Board of Civil Service Examiners and in the 1908 legislation. The Act prescribed open competition for all positions, and the compiling of a fixed list of eligibles from which appointments would be made to the civil service in order of standing.

Appointments were all probationary for a six-month period, during which time the deputy head could decide to reject or approve the appointment, or extend the probationary period of the appointee for another six months (section 13). The CSC was given full powers to regulate promotions (section 45), temporary appointments (section 51), sick leave (section 26), and transfers (section 46). The power of dismissal remained the sole prerogative of the Governor-General in Council (section 28[1]). In any case of separation from the service following the decision to abolish a redundant position, provision was made in the Act for the pension of the employee so separated, the latter also being eligible under the Civil Service Act for preferential consideration for reappointment to the service in positions which he was qualified to fill (section 29[3]). The CSC was also given full responsibility to, "from time to time, as may be necessary, recommend rates of compensation for any new classes that may be established hereunder, and may propose changes in the rates of compensation for existing classes."[13]

Great emphasis was placed in the Act on reorganization. The CSC was literally given a carte blanche mandate, subject only to the control of the Governor in Council, to reorganize the civil service:

> The Commission, as soon as may be practicable after the passing of this Act, shall, after consulting with the several deputy heads, the heads of branches and other chief officers, prepare plans for the organization of the Inside Service and the Outside Service of each department and of each branch or portion of the civil service, such organization as far as possible to follow the same general principles in all branches of the civil service. As soon as the plan of organization is completed for either the Inside or Outside Service or any branch or portion of the civil service, such plan or organization shall be submitted for the approval of the Governor in Council.
>
> If, *after such approval*, the deputy head or the Commission is of the

opinion that any such plan of organization might with advantage be in any way changed, the Commission shall in a similar manner prepare a report upon such proposed change, and shall submit the same for the approval of the Governor in Council. No change shall be made in the organization of any department until it has been so reported upon by the said Commission.[14]

This section of the Act reveals particularly the tight controls imposed on the civil service. The Act provided no real opportunity for the deputy head to play an important part in the reorganization of his department. According to the legislation, the CSC could bypass the deputy in its reorganization work, and only after the approval of the Governor in Council could the deputy minister submit his objections to the proposed reorganization. This procedure was fraught with potential dangers for the CSC as the following chapter will indicate in detail. The Government, however, was explicit in its intentions: patronage in recruitment had to be eradicated, and this could only be assured through the strengthening of the CSC and the institution of the merit principle in civil service appointments. Interestingly enough, a careful perusal of the Civil Service Act fails to disclose a precise definition of the merit principle. What the legislation contained instead was a statutory description of the mechanics of the merit *system*, with the *principle* taken for granted.

Section 38 of Part III came closer than any other part of the Act to hinting at the underlying philosophy:

> The examinations held by the Commission to establish lists of persons eligible for appointment may be written or oral or in the form of a demonstration of skill or any combination of these and shall be of a character fairly to test and determine the relative fitness and ability of candidates actually to perform the duties of the class to which they seek to be appointed. Any investigation of training and experience and any test of technical knowledge, manual skill, or physical fitness that in the judgment of the Commission serves to this end may be employed.[15]

This section would seem to indicate that the merit principle was employer-centred; that is, merit was viewed as the potential "fitness" of candidates for the "duties of the class to which they seek to be appointed." The Act required the CSC to organize the newly combined Inside and Outside Services "upon general principles applicable to all departments and branches." The CSC itself understood that it was required to "classify the several offices and positions in the various departments and branches of the service, both Inside and Outside, clearly defining the duties of each and the salaries adequate thereto; and to place each officer, clerk, and employee in a proper place under such plan of classification."[16] Section 52 of the Act prescribed that the Outside Service should be classified according to "schedules containing lists of the positions and the duties and salaries attached thereto," and section 42 specified that the Inside Service should be classified according to a set salary schedule of ten grades. This focus was clearly coordinated with the philosophy of scientific management embodied in the new classification system. Duties, rather than persons, were to be classified, and personnel were to be hired as component parts of the existing machinery.

The negative definition of merit—freedom from considerations of political patronage—was also touched on in the legislation. Section 32 prescribed that, under threat of dismissal, no civil servant "shall engage in partisan work in connection with any such election, or contribute, receive, or in any way deal with any money for any party funds." Having thus indirectly advanced both a positive and negative definition of the merit principle, the law went on quickly to enumerate exceptions, exemptions, and limitations to the same principle. Indeed, far more space was devoted to what the principle would *not* cover than to the elucidation of what it would cover.

The same section, section 38, which laid down the basis of determining "fitness," also contained this significant sentence:

> Examinations shall be open to all persons who may be lawfully appointed to any position within the class for which the examination is held, with such limitations as may be specified in the regulations of the Commission as to age, sex, health, habits, residence, moral character and other qualifications that are in the judgment of the Commission requisite to the performance of the duties of such positions.

The specification of sex was clearly of great significance for the application of merit, but given the circumstances of the time, no further legal elaboration was deemed necessary. No dissent seems to have been voiced, nor was there any discussion of the question.

Rather more pressing at this time was the question of age as a standard of hiring. In 1919, a new section (section 41[2]) stipulated:

> The Commission, with the approval of the Governor in Council, may by regulations prescribe the several limits of age within which persons shall be eligible for appointment to positions in the civil service.

Residence requirements were also spelled out in section 41(1):

> No person shall, without the authority of the Governor in Council, be admitted to any examination unless he is a natural born or naturalized

British subject, and also has been a resident of Canada for at least three years.

No further legislative elaboration was proffered for the stipulations about health, habits, moral character, and other qualifications found in section 38.

Special preferences were built into the legislation. These fall into three major categories: veterans, local residents, and those who already held government jobs. Section 39(1)(a) provided that

> in all examinations for entrance into the Civil Service persons who have been in active service overseas on the military or naval forces of His Majesty or of any of the allies of His Majesty during the present war; who have left such service with an honourable record or who have been honourably discharged, or when any persons who have served as aforesaid have died owing to service overseas the widows of such persons, and who in either case obtain sufficient marks to pass such examinations, shall, irrespective of the marks they have obtained, be placed in the order of merit on the list of successful candidates above all other candidates.

Moreover, even some of the provisions limiting other candidates could be waived in the case of veterans. Section 39(1)(b) stated:

> The provisions of any Statute or regulation prescribing an age limit and physical requirements with respect to any appointment in the civil service shall not apply to any such persons (i.e. veteran) if the Commission certifies that he is of such an age and in such a satisfactory physical condition that he is then able to perform the duties of his office and will probably be able to continue to do so for a reasonable period after his appointment.

Section 43(3) provided that local people should receive local jobs:

> Except as to appointments to positions in the headquarters of the several departments and other positions of the civil service of Ottawa, the appointments to any local positions in any province, shall, so far as practicable, be made from *bona fide* residents of such locality.

Preference was also to be given to existing employees. Section 45(1) provided that "vacancies shall be filled, as far as is consistent with the best interests of the civil service, by promotion." Section 45(2) specified:

> Promotion shall be made for merit by the Commission upon such examination as the Commission may by regulation prescribe. The Commission may by such regulation restrict the competition at such exami-

nations to Employees or to Employees of a certain class or classes of a specified seniority, and may prescribe what marks may be obtained by such employees for efficiency and seniority. Such marks shall not, however, exceed one-half of the total marks that can be obtained at the examination.

Moreover, the age requirements for positions were to be waived for existing employees. According to section 41 (3),

any person holding a permanent appointment in the civil service may enter for any open competition or examination if such person when first appointed was not older than the maximum age prescribed for the position for which the examination is being held and if successful thereat may be appointed irrespective of his age.

Section 32 (2) extended a preference to former civil servants:

The list of eligibles for each class of positions in the civil service shall be made up first of names of persons who have previously held permanent positions in such class and who were laid off in good standing under the provisions of this Act, and then names of persons who have been examined by the Commission and found qualified.

Another broad area of limitations was in regard to positions exempted from the Act. Deputy ministers and private secretaries to a minister of the Crown or "other members of the Government," along with royal commissioners or members of boards, were exempted. Section 38A, however, went much further:

The provisions of this Act shall not apply to positions in connection with the Government railways or any railway owned or controlled by His Majesty, or to any position on any Ship of His Majesty until Parliament otherwise enacts; and in any case where the Commission decides that it is not practicable to apply this Act to any position or positions, the Commission, with the approval of the Governor in Council, may make such regulations as are deemed advisable, prescribing how such position or positions are to be dealt with.

Nor were competitive examinations necessary in all cases, even for those positions remaining under the jurisdiction of the Act. In the event of a vacancy, section 43 (1) provided that the CSC, "if necessary to prevent any serious interference with the public business, but not otherwise, may fill the position at once by making a temporary appointment."

On the question of bilingualism, the legislation of 1918–19 was somewhat restrained. Only one section, section 40, even mentioned language, and it merely prescribed that notice of every examination be printed in both English and French and that "every examination under this Act shall be held in the English and French language, at the option of the candidate." The existence of two languages was nowhere else so much as mentioned. Language skills were clearly not viewed as part of an individual's "merits."[17]

THE CSC's CONCEPTION OF ITS TASK

It is interesting to speculate on the degree to which the Civil Service Commission was responsible for the form and content of the Act which it was called upon to implement and administer. The reference made to the unpublished Order in Council which formed the basis of P.C. 358 (see p. 49) indicated that the newly constituted CSC was advising the Prime Minister as to the appropriate legislation required. There are therefore indications to suggest that the CSC seized this opportunity to mould the Civil Service Act into the form it desired. The Act, for example, delegated a wide variety of personnel functions to the Commission, other than those of appointment and promotion. A perusal of the CSC's Annual Report for 1917–18 suggests in no uncertain terms that the major thrust for the inclusion of these other functions in the Act came from the CSC itself.

The intention of the Report was to explain the meaning of the 1918 legislation to Parliament and to the public, but the CSC's emphasis reveals a great deal. The principle of the Act, the CSC argued, was the promotion of "efficiency and economy in the non-political Civil Service." To attain this, the legislation provided for the establishment and administration of the "merit system," a term to which the CSC gave a much wider definition than it has come to mean in the present day. The merit system, according to the Report, consisted of two distinct parts: the first is concerned with the selection and appointment of individuals to the civil service "without regard to their politics, religion or influence"; the second is concerned with "applying the methods of scientific employment to maintain the efficiency of these selected employees after they enter the service."[18] In contrast to the emphasis placed by Borden on the elimination of patronage, the CSC directed its attention as much, if not more, to the second part of the merit system.

Although emphasizing that the selection process was its "primary and most important function,"[19] it is evident from the Report that the CSC felt that the most challenging and exciting portion of its work would result from its duties which called for the application of "scientific employment" methods. It obviously felt that the recruitment function was a rather routine task requiring little direction once the proper type of competitive examination was chosen.[20] The Act was fairly specific in defining the CSC's role in the selection process, and therefore there was no need to strongly assert its authority in this field. In fact, the Examination Branch is not once mentioned in the whole Report. By contrast, a great deal of attention is lavished upon the other functions of the CSC, particularly those dealing with classification and organizational work. The optimism and enthusiasm with which the CSC greeted these functions, as well as the readiness with which the central agency was able to demonstrate that they constituted a vital component of the merit system, suggests that the whole philosophy regarding the merit system had not only been well thought out long before the 1917–18 Report, but had exerted a strong influence on the form of the legislation recently passed by Parliament.

The CSC was formed with three main divisions: the Organization, Examination, and Assignment Branches. The stress which the Report placed upon the Organization Branch, however, makes it clear that it was considered the most important among the three divisions. The ambit of the Organization Branch was to include the administration of all "those functions having to do with the investigation of departmental organization; the design of revised plans of organization; the classifying of positions in existence at the time of taking effect of the law, classifying of new positions created from time to time; and the investigation of all matters pertaining to organization and classification and their interpretations."[21] The "first and biggest task" to fall to the Organization Branch was the classification of the service. Because classification required a huge investment of specialized talent for a relatively short period of time, the CSC felt it impractical to delegate total responsibility in this area to the Organization Branch. As the following chapter will relate, the central personnel agency acquired the services of a firm of classification experts, the Arthur Young Company of Chicago, to proceed with the classification of the service under the auspices of the Organization Branch.

The CSC considered the main body of the initial classification work as a transitory phenomenon which, once completed, would require only periodic readjustment. The primary field of concern for the Organization Branch lay in the area which the central personnel agency termed reorganizational work. To this task the CSC attached three distinct functions: administration of the classification, organization studies and reports, and special investigations.

The first of these pertained to the adjustment of the classification scheme: the classification of new positions and reclassification of old ones as the situation warranted, as well as the setting of salary schedules and departmental establishments. The CSC considered this a relatively routine task and observed that "a greater value" lay in the second of these roles, "that of serving the departments in assisting them to perform, without waste, the highest quality of service to the public." This function, as the forerunner of the modern practice of "Organization and Methods," was intended by the CSC to engage the problem of inefficiency in combat. The Civil Service Commission was to make an attack upon two sides: first on defective organizational structure, and second on inefficient and uneconomical procedure and methods.[22] It was in anticipation of exercising this authority that the central personnel agency displayed real enthusiasm for the task at hand, and genuine optimism for the rewards to be won:

> It is the purpose of the Commission to make surveys and prepare reports which will be comprehensive and constructive, and, with the co-operation of the departments, will give effect to measures for the correction of recognized faults in the services. This work is the function of the Organization Branch which is constituted as the investigating arm of the commission. Its effective use opens a field for possible economics which cannot be estimated. Opportunities for promoting improved and increased service to the public are equally great.[23]

The Report pointed out that the CSC did not exercise its reorganizational powers in a vacuum, but required the goodwill of the departments to smooth the way. However, in the absence of such cooperation, the CSC had full recourse to its authority granted under the Inquiries Act:

> The Act implies that the use of the instrument shall be made with the co-operation and for the benefit of the departments, and at the same time arming the commission with inquisitional power when the situation may demand.[24]

In addition, the legislation gave the CSC the authority to conduct investigation of "special matters arising in the public service," either *on their own initiative* or on that of the Governor in Council.[25] The CSC also expressed its readiness to make effective use of these powers in order that real financial benefits might accrue to the service:

> In recent years the people have evidenced growing interest in the administration of the public service. They are demanding more and better service. Now, as never before, the greatest economy is necessitated by the financial burdens resulting from the war. A considerable responsibility for the attainment of these ends rests upon the Civil Service Commission. It is preparing to meet that responsibility in large part by the liberal and considered use of its investigational power, and is planning the work of its Organization Branch that it may be an effective partici-

pant in the accomplishment of a high degree of economy and merit in the public service.[26]

The CSC Report for 1917–18 is a revealing document, for it did much more than explain the elements of the Civil Service Act to the public and to Parliament. The Report reveals that the CSC viewed the Civil Service Act of 1918 as providing it with the tools to approach the problem of efficiency and economy in a very thorough and systematic manner. This attitude is somewhat remarkable, viewed in the context of the atmosphere in which the Act was passed. Although Parliament expressed grave concern over efficiency and economy in the civil service, the debates over the clauses of the 1918 legislation reveal a predominant interest in those sections which would eradicate political appointments, while those clauses dealing with the Commission's organization and classification work drew relatively scant attention.[27] Clearly the initiative for including those functions relating to "scientific employment" methods in the Act came from the CSC itself.

Granted this, it is instructive to note that the whole concept of the merit system put forth in the 1917–18 Report obviously bears a strong resemblance to the ideas of the scientific management school of thought. The Commissioners' two-sided definition of the merit system, for example, closely parallels that offered by E. O. Griffenhagen for the "employment problem" of the Civil Service of Canada. Griffenhagen was the acknowledged North-American expert on scientific management, and was at that time employed by the Arthur Young Company to set up the Canadian classification scheme. He pointed out that "the problem is to man the organization (after its form and requirements have been described), from among all available candidates, with those persons best qualified for the respective positions, and to provide for their adequate compensation and just treatment, for the advancement of the most efficient, and for the removal of the inefficient."[28] The very term "scientific employment" moreover suggests a strong influence from scientific management thought. These ideas appear to have been brought to bear upon the CSC primarily through its powerful Secretary, William Foran. Two of the Commissioners had only recently emerged from the political arena, and it is natural to expect that they would be primarily concerned with combatting patronage than with introducing scientific employment. The development of the Commission in the next few years, in fact, shows this to be the case. The third Commissioner, M. G. LaRochelle, never really indicated a great deal of interest in this area. Foran, on the other hand, had served with the CSC since its inception in 1908, and had been connected with the cause of civil reform from an early date. In 1915 he was elected vice-president of the Civil Service Assembly of the United States and Canada, and in the following year became its president. The Assembly during those years served as a medium for the spread of ideas of civil service reform and scientific management, with which Foran undoubtedly came into contact.[29] In fact, no less a person than Griffenhagen stated that Foran, in his capacity of president of the Assembly, became "thoroughly conversant with the best modern practice in Civil Service administration," and was the person in the Commission primarily responsible for the initiation of the classification project by the Arthur Young Company.[30] With the arrival of two new Commissioners in 1917 it was natural that Foran would play a part in the negotiations between the Government and the CSC over the Civil Service Bill in the following year.

Ironically, at the climax of a decade of agitation for reform of the civil service, when politicians of all partisan persuasions, as well as academics and press observers, seemed agreed on the appropriateness of the British civil service model for Canadian emulation, the 1918–19 legislation leaned much more heavily on the administrative culture of its southern neighbour. As the first Report of the new CSC made clear, the "first and biggest task" was the classification of the service according to the precepts laid down in the Report. These precepts were accepted in the preparation of the new legisation and more particularly in the first few years of its administration by the CSC. Founded on scientific management originating in the United States, these precepts became the decisive influences on Canadian ideas and practices, just at their most formative stage. Thus the moral fervour behind civil service reform was reinforced by the "rational" and "objective" respectability claimed for the scientific management ideas imported from across the border. The unusual partnership was doomed to be muted when the recommendations of the experts were washed away in the early twenties by a rising tide of anti-Americanism.

1. For Borden's personal account, see R. L. Borden, *Memoirs of Sir Robert Borden*, vol. 2.

2. *Westminster Hall Magazine and the Farthest West Review* 7 (April, 1915), p. 23.

3. Sir Robert Borden, "Problem of an Efficient Civil Service," Canadian Historical Association, *Report of the Annual Meeting*, 1931 (reprint), p. 17.

4. J. S. Willison Papers, PAC, vol. 105, 38488–92. (Emphasis added.)

5. See chapter 4 for a full discussion of these events.

6. Historian Blair Neatby supplies us with some insight into the personality of Rowell, and the enemies he made by joining the Union Government. King wanted to appoint Rowell to a cabinet post by 1926, but he met considerable opposition in his efforts: "The Customs Department needed to be reformed and Rowell would ensure a rigidly honest administration. King was soon reminded, however, that Rowell had managed to alienate most of the elements of the Liberal Party in Ontario during his career: Laurier Liberals, French Canadians, and Irish Catholics while he was in the Union Government, the 'wets' by his temperance campaigns, and the 'continuing Presbyterians' by his part in the United Church Movement." (H. Blair Neatby, *William Lyon Mackenzie King: The Lonely Heights* [Toronto: University of Toronto Press, 1963], p. 173)

7. Rowell to H. C. Brewster, September 7, 1917, Rowell Papers, PAC, vol. 3, 1890. See also Rowell to Maclean, May 18, 1917, ibid., 1699–1702.

8. H.C., Special Committee Appointed to Inquire into the Operation of Chapter 12, 8–9 George V, An Act Respecting the Civil Service of Canada, 1923, *Proceedings and Evidence*, pp. 894–95.

9. Unpublished P.C. 273 (January 31, 1918). (Emphasis added.) The final official draft was dated February 13, 1918. See Borden Papers, vol. 82, 44603–6.

10. W. L. Grant, "The Civil Service of Canada," p. 434.

11. Gerald E. Caiden, "The Federal Civil Service of Canada," p. 29.

12. 8–9 George V (1918), c. 12, was amended by 10 George V (1919), c. 10.

13. It is of interest to note that no mention was made of Treasury Board in the 1918 Act. The legislation specified that "such proposed rates of compensation shall only become operative upon their approval by the Governor in Council, and, where any increased expenditure will result therefrom, when Parliament has provided the money required for such increased expenditure." (Ibid., s. 45B[1])

14. Ibid., s. 9(1) and (2).

15. 8–9 George V (1918), c. 12, s. 38.

16. Civil Service Commission of Canada (CSC), *Annual Report*, 1917–18, p. 20.

17. The theme of language as it pertains to the merit principle will be discussed in chapter 18.

18. CSC, *Annual Report*, 1917–18, p. 16.

19. Ibid., p. 17.

20. Ibid., pp. 27–28.

21. Ibid., p. 22.

22. Ibid., pp. 25–26.

23. Ibid., p. 27.

24. Ibid., p. 24.

25. 8–9 George V (1918), c. 12, s. 4(1b), 4(1g), 4(3), 4(4).

26. CSC, *Annual Report*, 1917–18, p. 27.

27. *Debates*, April 12, 1918, pp. 694–723; May 10, 1918, pp. 1721–66; May 11, 1918, pp. 1768–1826.

28. Arthur Young and Company, *Report of Transmission to Accompany the Classification of the Civil Service of Canada*, p. 36.

29. The Assembly was closely allied in the United States with the National Civil Service Reform League and the National Municipal League. Griffenhagen and other leaders in the field of scientific management often addressed the Assembly. Fred Telford for years served as secretary of the Bureau of Public Personnel Administration, an offshoot of the Assembly. See Charles P. Messick, "Civil Service: Then and Now"; J. J. Donovan, "The Civil Service Assembly: 1906–1956"; and "Officers of the Civil Service Assembly of the United States and Canada, 1906–1956," in *Public Personnel Review* 17 (October, 1956), pp. 308–11, 312–19, and 320–31.

30. Young, *Report of Transmission*, p. 72.

Chapter Four

Classification, Reorganization, and Reaction, 1918–1921

Some day a Gibbon or a Macaulay will write the history of the classification of the Civil Service of Canada. In ponderous sentences he will reveal the errors, the mistakes, and even the crimes committed in the name of efficiency. It will be an amazing revelation.

The Civilian 13 (June, 1920)

THE PASSAGE of the 1918 Civil Service Act and the launching of the Civil Service Commission on its long career in government personnel management came at a time when critical changes were taking place in theories of organizational methods. *Scientific management* and the *classification movement*, both American in origin, were decisive influences on Canadian ideas just at that point when they were at their most formative state. Scientific management was a general term applied loosely to the first wave of management theory to arise in America in the late nineteenth century. The most prominent figure associated with scientific management was Frederick W. Taylor, the engineer who first devised the technique of time-study. However, there were other theorists associated with various schools, who were also part of the scientific management movement. What most scientific management theorists held in common was the view that work could be studied in terms of its component parts or motions, and that the most efficient method of work was that method which involved the minimum necessary motions in the shortest possible time while accomplishing the given task. Since work was considered a mechanistic process, it was believed that the application of the scientific method of analysis would ultimately yield the "one best way" of accomplishing every possible task. This would in turn make possible a "scientific" method of determining wages—ideally a piece-rate system which would allocate to each worker the precise market value of his productivity, that is, his efficiency in approaching the "one best way" model in his own work.[1]

In the early decades of the twentieth century, a number of historical factors came together to make scientific management a popular concept, not only in industry but in government as well. The general demand for the end of political patronage in government was coupled with a desire for more efficient administration, which could only be possible if all civil service positions were to be classified by function. An attempt to analyse the *component elements* of jobs was inspired by the example of scientific management in studying the component elements of work; once these elements were analysed, examinations could be devised to determine which candidates were best qualified to fill specific positions—the central concern of the merit system of selection. At the same time the development of new methods of uniform cost accounting necessitated a uniform job terminology, which would also allow for more efficient financial control of the bureaucracy by the legislature. The common philosophical thread running through all these developments was an emphasis on work as an abstract phenomenon, analytically separated from the worker. To the practitioners of civil service classification this meant that what was to be classified was always the *job*, never the person.

THE CLASSIFICATION OF 1919

That the Canadian civil service was ripe for drastic changes in organization and structure by the end of World War I was apparent to almost all observers at the time. The dramatic legislative innovations enacted by the Union Government in 1918 were themselves only the signal for a wave of practical changes which were to follow. It was one matter to proclaim the new era of merit in the public service; it was another matter to devise the machinery which would effect the desired results.

The new legislation was not the only factor compelling change. The war had caused great organizational strains within the administration by sheer weight of numbers. In 1913 the Government had employed a total of 22,621 persons; by 1919 the number had almost doubled to 41,825.[2] "War branches" had been able to offer higher wages than civilian branches, thus disrupting whatever salary uniformity had previously existed. The examination system had been ignored or circumvented because of the emergency situation. With the war's end, however, such conditions were hardly in keeping with the new merit system.[3]

The Civil Service Commission believed that sections 42 and 52 which classified both the Inside and Outside Services respectively were inconsistent, and suggested that the existence of two separate types of classification within one service would lead to intolerable administrative problems.[4] It also believed that the method prescribed for the Outside Service, that of "duties, responsibilities and authority," was "accepted as the only logical and workable basis of classification," while the method prescribed for the Inside Service was a purely "arbitrary" grading made on the basis of the present salaries of incumbents. The CSC therefore decided to reclassify all positions on the basis of duties, and to recommend "such legislation as would be necessary to apply the resulting classification to the entire service."[5]

The CSC immediately recognized its own inadequacy for the immense task ahead in classifying the public service and decided to bolster its newly formed Organization Branch with a team of outside consultants. "After a thorough canvass of the professional field, the Commission found that the firm of Arthur Young and Company was engaged in this highly specialized line of work and was well able to furnish experts of the kinds and numbers needed." With these words the CSC explained its choice of consultants, adding that the firm, established for twenty-five years, had an experienced staff of civil service specialists, and had been employed by the American, British, and French governments.[6] In 1923, Commissioner Jameson elaborated further on the events surrounding the hiring of Arthur Young and Company: "They were recommended to us by a Mr. Cather-wood, who was associated with the United States Civil Service Reform Association. We asked them to come to Ottawa and discuss matters with us, and a representative of their firm came to Ottawa and discussed the subject and we engaged them."[7] In answer to a question in the House of Commons in 1920, the CSC went so far as to assert that before making its decision it had "ascertained that this firm had the only staff on the continent employed in this special work."[8]

There can be no doubt at least that the CSC was engaging consultants who were in the vanguard of the classification movement. At least two of the consultants involved in the Canadian work, E. O. Griffenhagen and Fred Telford, were generally acknowledged as leaders in the development of classification analysis. Indeed, Griffenhagen is spoken of as the pioneer in this field.[9] Once the decision had been made to adopt an American-style duties classification, the CSC could not have done better than to go to Griffenhagen and his associates.

After the firm had been hired and the course ahead charted, the detailed work of classification began. Since such a task had never been undertaken before, it is worth indicating just what was specifically involved in classifying a large bureaucratic structure. In 1924 Telford, drawing on a decade or more of practical experience, described the main stages of the process: first, the selection, authority, and technical staff of the classifying agency must be determined, with special emphasis laid on the question of authority; then all the relevant facts must be collected with regard to all existing jobs, with the primary focus on the opinions of the workers themselves, rather than on those of their supervisors; finally, classes must be determined into which all jobs with common duties are tentatively allocated and class specifications developed. At this point the classification agency is ready to present its preliminary plan for the consideration of the civil service, the politicians, and other interested parties. In view of what happened in Canada in 1919, it is especially interesting to note that Telford made outside criticism an integral part of the entire process, and even suggested public hearings to provide the necessary feedback in response to the first tentative proposals. When all reasonable adjustments have been made, the classification plan can then be formally adopted; since an organization is a changing structure, some formal method of accommodating future adjustments is also necessary. The classification plan itself is normally a series of job descriptions, with specification of duties and qualifications, exact lines of promotion, and usually a salary schedule.[10]

In the Canadian case, questionnaires were sent to all employees to determine their duties, and these were verified by their superior officers. This procedure appears to have horrified Dawson, who stated: "Cards were sent to all civil servants asking for information about their positions, and rashly adding that if there were not sufficient room on the card to describe their duties another sheet might be attached. Many availed themselves of this unexpected opportunity for showing their value to the nation."[11] This did not seem to have bothered the classifiers to any appreciable extent, although it may have caused a certain amount of resentment on the part of the superior officers who were expected to verify the information. The entire process comprises sixteen distinct steps: with fifty thousand persons being classified, this involved some eight hundred thousand separate actions.[12]

REACTION TO THE CLASSIFICATION

After a gestation period of about nine months, the new classification plan was delivered to Parliament in June of 1919.[13] The infant was a cause not of rejoicing, however, but of shock, bewilderment, and disgust. As a somewhat embarrassed parent, the Civil Service Commission pleaded: "The proposed classification, when submitted in concrete form, was a scheme 'so new and strange' that not Parliament, the country, nor the Service itself could comprehend or fully appreciate all that it stood for . . . its very scope and completeness complicated the situation and confused the judgment. The entire proposition was so novel to the people of this Dominion that Parliament hesitated to commit itself to an approval, while the Service was in doubt as to how it would work out in practical application."[14] The object of this confusion was a volume of 678 pages, listing about seventeen hundred separate classes. Class titles along with definitions were provided, as well as sample duties. A statement of minimum requirements was included, dealing with education, experience, technical knowledge, and special aptitudes. Lines of promotion were enunciated, showing the next highest as well as the next lowest position, and a salary schedule was appended to each class.

That the classification represented a radical innovation cannot be disputed. For once Canada was not simply copying a long-established and time-tested practice. Although the concept of the classification had been developed in the United States, Canada was in a sense pioneering in the practical application of the system, by subjecting such a large bureaucratic system as the Canadian civil service to a plan which in the United States had only been applied to state and municipal jurisdictions. Indeed, when the American federal government later adopted a classification plan—on the advice of E. O. Griffenhagen—the Canadian plan was used as a model.[15] The classification of 1919 could be seen as a large-scale experiment. The experimental approach, of course, involves both trial and error. In view of the complexity of the task—and without the benefit of modern data-processing methods—it seems altogether remarkable that the consultants were able to complete the initial classification in the limited time available. Moreover, they themselves viewed the initial classification as a set of proposals open to correction.

Tolerance was not, however, a characteristic of the critics. "The instant the *Classification* was published," Dawson related with not a little contempt, "the whole service was in uproar. Appeals poured in by the thousand." With obvious relish, Dawson repeated some of the contemporary references to the *Classification*: " 'the joke book,' 'the yellow book,' 'the best book of short stories in the English language.' "[16]

Meetings were held with deputy ministers where detailed questions of application were examined. Some conflict developed, and the evidence seems to indicate that the Commission overrode many objections: "In no one of these departments does the Deputy Minister approve the classification of every position. The Commission does not feel that this is proof of inaccurate classification; indeed it feels that if it were to agree with the wishes of every department it would not be fulfilling its duty as expressed in the law, namely, that of providing for a uniform standard classification as between departments."[17] Four years later, a number of deputy heads testifying before a parliamentary committee expressed a high degree of discontent over the system, citing its complexity, its apparent inelasticity, and most important, its failure to set up a viable promotional system.

These officials also felt that their views reflected a similar dissatisfaction among their subordinates. Some went so far as to suggest the complete abolition of the system altogether and a return to the pre-1919 system of a handful of loose, general classes.[18]

The opposition of the civil servants themselves, although somewhat muted at first, rose in vehemence as the effects of the classification became clearer. The major source of opposition was on the matter of salaries, and there can be no doubt that in this matter the Arthur Young firm made a serious, perhaps disastrous, miscalculation. They had assumed that the great wartime inflation would prove to be a temporary aberration, to be counteracted by a quick return to prewar price levels. They therefore calculated all salary schedules on a prewar cost-of-living index and proposed a system of temporary bonuses to help bridge the transition.[19] As it turned out, there was no transition: prices continued to rise, and civil servants were left with grossly inadequate salaries and a clumsy, insecure, and haphazard system of ad hoc bonuses to make up the difference. Of course this error was essentially one of economic forecasting and did not ultimately impeach the value of the classification itself, which was analytically separate from any specific salary schedule. It was, nevertheless, an error which did much to sour the attitudes of the civil servants who suffered its ill effects.

The complexity of the classification was a common complaint—and one which was to echo down through the years—yet the net result of the complaints was, as we shall see, to increase the complexity of the system rather than to simplify it. When critics spoke of "complexity," they were perhaps groping their way uncertainly toward a very real problem inherent in the system, that of promotion. As Dawson justly pointed out:

> All positions are deemed to call for special talents, and each is filled through an examination of its own designed to test these special qualifications. But therein lies its basic weakness. Some civil servants . . . should unquestionably be chosen because of the special knowledge or skill which they happen to possess at the moment of their candidature; but for others . . . the knowledge of their duties which they might have at entrance is comparatively unimportant. The really vital question is their inherent ability and what they will be capable of doing after they have been trained by years of experience in the department. . . .
>
> The entire scheme is avowedly built about the idea of a continual flow of promotions from the bottom to the top. Entrance to the service is supposed to take place through the lower positions, and the ambitious young employee will go from there, step by step, to the uppermost rung of the ladder. Unfortunately, the splendid simplicity of the plan breaks

down in practice. . . . An employee entering with the common school education which the *Schedule* demands for certain of the lower posts finds that if he is to reach his goal he must acquire in odd moments, a university education with perhaps graduate work in certain subjects. The rosy future held out by one part of the *Schedule* thus disappears completely when confronted with the practical demands of another part, and the classification which is so elaborately exact breaks down on one of its fundamental principles.[20]

The paradox was that in turning for advice to the United States, famed for its progressive business methods and traditions of liberal enterprise, Canada received a plan for a civil service structure of much hierarchical complexity, with much built-in rigidity, within which upward mobility might prove very difficult.

On the other hand, Professor Dawson's alternative—the British tradition of the administrative generalist—raises some equally grave doubts. It has been recently suggested that the British system is more of an isolated accident of history than a viable model for other nations, and that countries such as Canada, being from the start concerned essentially with the development of economic resources, have always placed a premium on technical specialists.[21] To an extent, then, Canada's course was already predetermined by her history and her economic needs. And as we have already suggested, the Canadian Government and the Civil Service Commission had by 1918 already accepted much of the contemporary American ideology of business efficiency. In this context, the administrative generalist was something of a nonstarter.

The organized civil service became increasingly vocal in its opposition. Although the Arthur Young Company had echoed a major demand of the Civil Service Federation of Canada (CSF) when it suggested the creation of employee advisory councils,[22] salary complaints and misgivings about promotion possibilities led to a high degree of antipathy to the plan, which was also reiterated by the Civil Service Association of Ottawa (CSAO). The original complaints centred around specific grievances, but after the experience of the Griffenhagen reorganization of the civil service (which we shall deal with later), a new reason was found for hostility to the classification: anti-American nationalist feeling. "The American experts," said the CSF in retrospect, "left the classification of the Canadian civil service in an inconglomerate mass, inconsistent, inaccurate and unworkable"; the Federation spoke approvingly of the "capacity of Canadians to put their own house in order with their own brains and experience better than by the employment of foreign experts, however highly paid."[23] It was thus with a certain amount of exasperation that the CSC must have viewed the behaviour of the CSF and CSAO, as described by Commissioner Roche to Prime Minister Meighen in 1921:

> The antipathy of the civil servants to American experts is of a somewhat recent date. No such objection was offered when the Arthur Young Company was originally employed, in fact they were welcomed by the civil servants generally, as they realized there was no firm in Canada with trained experts in this particular line. It was only after the salaries did not meet their expectations that this firm and its employees became so unpopular. A curious commentary, however, of the antagonism of the Civil Service Association and Federation to the employment of aliens is their own action, when in 1919, in order to get expert advice upon the Arthur Young's classification, a deputation was sent to Chicago . . . to interview a certain Mr. Jacobs, who was at the head of another such firm . . . and whom they brought to Ottawa to advise them as to what improvements, alterations, etc. could be made in the classification as prepared by the Arthur Young Company.[24]

So much for the purity of patriotic zeal.

One of the more spectacular by-products of the Arthur Young classification was the formation of the Professional Institute of the Civil Service of Canada, which was founded as a means of combatting the threat which professionals saw in the new classification.[25] Their main complaints seemed to have centred around inadequate salaries and inconsistencies in the application of the classification to professionals among the various departments. At their second annual meeting in 1921, a committee, which had been set up a year earlier to prepare a memorandum "deprecating" the employment of American experts, recommended that all "scientific professional positions" be made into a single class, with six salary grades.[26] The Professional Institute clearly felt that the classification was too complex. In view of the fact that much of the hostility was articulated in terms of anti-Americanism, it is interesting to note that its proposed scheme for reclassification of professionals was modelled very closely along the lines of the classification adopted by the U.S. Civil Service Commission for application to technical positions—and that the Institute used its source as a major selling point for the plan.[27]

The Associated Federal Employees of Ottawa (AFEO), affiliated with the Trades and Labour Congress of Canada, also severely criticized the classification, but went further than other civil service organizations in suggesting that "the only possible method of financing a satisfactory classification is through the Joint or Whitley Councils." This same organization put great emphasis on establishing a less complicated system as well as raising strong complaints against the pay scales.[28]

72

THE BOARD OF HEARING

The anger of the civil servants did not stop with the American consultants, but began to spill over onto the Civil Service Commission which had hired them. This situation produced something of a crisis among the Commissioners.

The Commissioners were in fact divided over the issue. Chairman Roche believed the classification scheme to be beneficial to the service and useful to the CSC.[29] Commissioner Jameson, on the other hand, was opposed to the classification from the beginning.[30] Roche later reported to Meighen that "it is a well known fact that . . . strained relations, to put it mildly, existed between my two colleagues on the Commission and the employees of the Arthur Young Company."[31] Within a few weeks of the publication of the classification in June, 1919, Jameson was put in charge of revising the plan. He immediately set up a Board of Hearing and Recommendation "in order to bring this [revision], so far as possible, into line with the views of the Service."[32] Such a revision was in fact an integral part of the classification process, but in the controversial atmosphere of the time, and with Jameson—a known opponent of the whole scheme—being placed in charge, the revision could well be interpreted as an attempt by the CSC to restore its favourable image in the eyes of the civil service associations by dissociating itself from the classification.

This inference becomes even stronger on a close inspection of the Board of Hearing. Jameson created the Board with himself as chairman presiding over four other members. Of these, two represented the departments and were nominated by the deputy ministers. The other two represented the civil servants and were nominated by the Civil Service Federation, the national association of a variety of civil service organizations. The CSF was chosen because, as Jameson wrote, it represented "most of the organized Service" and afforded "the one direct channel known to me, through which to obtain the necessary expression of appeals."[33] The official purpose of the Board was "to afford a convenient means of hearing objections to the Classification" and to make the revised form reflect "so far as may be [possible], the viewpoint both of the Departments and the Service."[34] The Board dealt with matters referred to it from the CSC and reported its recommendations back to the CSC for approval.

At first the Board heard mainly departmental appeals. Three months after the original publication of the classification, a revised edition was presented to Parliament,[35] and formed the basis for the major amendments to the Civil Service Act passed in the fall of 1919.[36] In view of the prevalent criticism of the classification as being absurdly long and overly complex, it is instructive to note that the three months of heated criticism between the preliminary and final classifications produced about a hundred more pages and some two hundred additional classes.

The revision did not, however, halt criticism. The work of revision went on, both through the offices of the CSC and through the continued functioning of the Board of Hearing. The attitudes which found expression on the Board, particularly those emanating from the two CSF representatives, suggest that the Board served more as a forum to soothe the outraged feelings of the civil servants and to regain their confidence in the CSC than as a serious attempt to improve the classification system. The atmosphere in which the Board sat was one of open hostility to the Arthur Young Company. One of the CSF representatives later testified that "the Board of Hearing had a battle royal with the Arthur Young Company before we were able to lay unholy hands on the classification that they had prepared."[37] The other CSF representatives went further:

> The Arthur Young Company naturally objected to the board of hearing, when the board took that classification and abolished many of the positions in the Post Office service alone, cutting that down wholesale, and in the Custom service also, and changed the classifications around quite a bit, and making it more pleasant and workable. At the same time, it afforded an opportunity for groups of civil servants to come before the board and make their complaint. *It relieved the Commission, and it relieved the Government*, and in that way I think established very mutual good will, in the days of stress, of 1918–1919–1920.[38]

The CSC eventually bowed to pressure and decided to hear personal, as well as departmental, appeals, and machinery was set up with the Board of Hearing to handle the extra work.[39] Again it seemed that the motive was as much to relieve the CSC from criticism as it was to do justice to the classification. Roche was not at all impressed by the validity of most of these complaints, but Jameson now seemed to be ascendant.[40] The CSC, in fact, openly asserted that the whole procedure was as much for its own benefit as it was for that of the civil servants:

> They [the employees] realize that the question of the co-operation of employees in the management of their own affairs is on trial and are approaching the problem with an open mind free of any prejudice. It is too early to predict what the result of these personal appeals will be, but if the procedure followed does nothing more than convince civil servants that the Commission desires to play no favourites but to handle all matters in a fair, just, and equitable manner, it will have justified itself.[41]

74

Under Jameson's guidance the CSC's efforts to convince civil servants of its interest in their welfare and to gain their confidence appear to have succeeded. The main result of the establishment of the Board of Hearing was to draw the organized civil servants closer to the CSC. Both the majority of civil servants and the deputy ministers looked upon the Board of Hearing as a friend in the struggle against an unacceptable classification system.[42] So far as its practical impact on the classification itself, the main result seems to have been to *increase* the much criticized complexity. By the time the Board concluded its hearings, it had caused the abolition of 158 classes, but had at the same time created 587 new classes.[43] Despite the inflated claims of the CSF members of the Board of Hearing that the Board had placed a "bungled" classification on a "sound working basis,"[44] the classification system was to remain for some fifty years on the same basic foundation laid by the Arthur Young Company in 1919. The revisions no doubt cleared up inconsistencies—as indeed the experts themselves expected—but they also added appreciably to the size and complexity of the system. What the avalanche of criticism certainly did accomplish, however, was to make the CSC wary of innovative behaviour. Not for many years would it again dare to carry out under its auspices such a radical undertaking. This attitude was further consolidated by the events immediately following the classification.

GRIFFENHAGEN AND ASSOCIATES: CANADA'S FIRST GLASSCO

The 1918 Act had required the Civil Service Commission to organize the service, with "such organization as far as possible to follow the same general principles in all branches of the civil service," and then to classify the service on the basis of this organization.[45] The CSC, however, had decided to proceed in the reverse order. One of the reasons given for this reversal was the lack of information upon which reorganization could be based; it was hoped that the classification would yield more information.[46] An additional factor was the insistent demand of the staff associations for pay revisions; it was thus believed that the classification was a more pressing priority.[47] Although it was not acting in strict accordance with the Act, the CSC maintained that it had merely reversed the steps involved and that it intended to use the information collected in the classification as the basis for future organizational work and efficiency studies to be carried out by the Organization Branch in the departments.[48]

Although the decision to give priority to classification effectively delayed the commencement of reorganizational work in the departments, the Commission did reaffirm its intended role in this area through its participation in two projects which, it was hoped, would provide a model for reorganizational work in the future. In the summer of 1918 the CSC engaged the Arthur Young consultants to report upon the Commission's office organization and procedure. Three months later the firm produced a report establishing a model organizational framework, as well as outlining the duties and responsibilities of each position within this framework. The report affirmed the necessary connection between good organization and efficiency and expressed the belief that the early adoption of the plan by the CSC would "exhibit to the Government a complete plan of organization applied to its own business as the first step towards carrying out its statutory function of preparing plans of organization for all government departments."[49] The Commissioners appear to have basically accepted the plan as laid down in the report, and proceeded to organize the CSC along the lines suggested.

The second reorganizational study conducted under the auspices of the CSC at this time was an investigation into the operation of the Printing Bureau. The CSC again called in the Arthur Young consultants.[50] The latter concerned themselves with the introduction of "up-to-date business principles and practices" in the Bureau, and comprehensive recommendations were made, the acceptance of which saved the Government about $740,000 and brought about a reduction in Bureau staff of 400 employees (36 percent of the total). Although there was some criticism of these results, the general impression of outside observers was highly favourable.[51] The CSC was elated with the results: they were "a credit to the Dominion Government and a testimony to the abolition of patronage, the establishment of the merit system, and efficient government ownership and operation."[52] The Commission apparently looked forward to more such campaigns against inefficiency: "The times require the most drastic retrenchment and the country demands it. The Civil Service Commission has set this as an essential objective, and if Parliament will permit the carrying out of the reorganization of the Public Service strictly along the lines already laid down and now being put into operation, millions will be saved to the people and the Service itself will be benefited."[53]

The consultants themselves—now constituted separately as Griffenhagen and Associates[54]—informed A. K. Maclean that in their short stay in Ottawa they had not found it possible to close their eyes to "shortcomings in organization, to instances of duplication and of conflict, to examples of unnecessary work, of wasted effort, of extravagant practices, or of group and individual inefficiencies." Griffenhagen made a plea for the progressive nature of a businesslike approach to government: "The widespread demand for greater economy and more businesslike methods of government has affected municipalities to a remarkable degree. Many cities have definitely accepted the idea that the administration of the local government should and can be managed in an efficient manner, and that public waste is as serious a matter of concern to every citizen as that of a private company is to the stockholder."[55]

The Government evidently agreed and was prepared to continue such efficiency studies. Yet despite the high enthusiasm of the CSC in 1918–19 for waging war against inefficiency, by 1920 the CSC made it clear that the struggle would have to be carried on without its help. The decisive influence in draining the CSC of its earlier zeal would seem to be the violent opposition aroused by the classification. The sudden realization that the innovation and reform, to which it had been so enthusiastically looking forward, would also create a hostile and difficult environment within which to operate seems to have struck the CSC with an almost traumatic force. The ringing words of 1917–19 on its future role in reorganization of the service contrast curiously with its behaviour in May of 1920 when the Government decided to retain the services of Griffenhagen and Associates to reorganize the remaining government departments. By the terms of the Civil Service Act, the CSC should at least have retained authority over the work. Instead the Commissioners declined to be involved, citing the "peak load of work we had at this time."[56] Yet despite the fact that the CSC, through the Board of Hearing, attempted to publicly dissociate itself from the Arthur Young classification, when the Government sought the CSC's private opinion of the consultants, the response was quick and emphatic: the CSC had "no hesitation in commending in the strongest possible way the work of Arthur Young and Company in connection with the organization of the Department of Public Printing."[57]

The cabinet meeting of May 28, 1920, indicated that uppermost in most of the ministers' minds was the problem of curtailing the burgeoning costs of government operations. Impressed by the Griffenhagen work in the Printing Bureau, the Cabinet concluded that "many millions of dollars can be saved in the Government operations by an application of up-to-date scientific principles of organization and operation."[58] On May 31, Griffenhagen and Associates were officially employed to begin the task of reorganizing the departments. They were to report directly to the Council Subcommittee on Reorganization and Efficiency of which Sir George Foster was chairman.[59]

Although nowhere expressly stated, it is clear that the original understanding between Griffenhagen Associates and the Government was for a thorough study, encompassing all aspects of reorganization, not only within the departments but also within the various agencies, boards, and councils as well.[60] In the preliminary stages of the study the consultants limited their work to exploratory investigations. General studies attempted to determine the size and nature of departments as well as their powers and duties. They were astonished to find that the Canadian Government apparently knew very little about its own administrative structure.[61] After a general picture began to form, studies were launched into the financial and accounting control methods of the Department of Finance, as well as into the matters of staff records and payroll systems. The Council Sub-committee also earmarked the Post Office and the Customs and Inland Revenue Departments as requiring special reorganization; the consultants began specific inquiries in these departments.

Fears of widespread disarray in departmental organization were confirmed at the outset of the investigaton. A lack of concern for the orderly development of functions had over the years resulted in a proliferation and duplication of activities which could better be rationalized on a functional, rather than on a departmental, basis. For example, large-scale lithographic work was being conducted not only by the Department of Printing and Stationery, but by at least four other major departments as well.[62] Another example was the highly decentralized Department of Agriculture, where many units were engaged in similar activity and were often quite unaware that others in the same department were doing the same work.[63] Lack of organization went so deep, the consultants felt, that a "sweeping reorganization" of all departments "might be found to be justifiable."[64]

The investigators even found cause to criticize the physical accommodation of government departments. The "gothic style of architecture" favoured for government buildings in Ottawa was found to result in offices which were "small and poorly ventilated and in some cases poorly lighted." Thousands of feet of space were thus wasted, and typing pools to expedite secretarial work were difficult to create.[65] But worse than this was the scattered geographical locations of departments, which were often spread about the city in haphazard fashion, leading to extensive costs for communication between the units.[66]

Turning their attention to the auditing functions of the federal administration, the consultants found that "the essential element of an audit is lacking where there is no standard imposed by the auditor as to how the necessity for and legality of the claim against the government is to be proved."[67] They broke down the Auditor-General's duties into six categories: prescription of uniform accounting practices; certification of parliamentary authority for payments of public moneys; certification of parliamentary authority for all expenditures; examination of appropriation accounts; checking of all vouchers and other essential financial documents; and examination of the government accounts. Of these duties only the last three were being effectively implemented, since a pre-audit was all but impossible owing to the practice of issuing letters of credit to departments.[68] Payroll procedures also came in for criticism.[69]

These initial discoveries gave further impetus to the massive investigation of governmental operations. For some seventeen months a staff of approximately twenty people were employed on a full-time basis by the Council Subcommittee. The results were as varied as they were prolific. The consultants submitted about seventy-four reports covering all aspects of government for the consideration and approval of the Subcommittee.[70] The work of the consultants can be divided into four general categories. First was a plan to incorporate the twenty-five departments and over fifty boards and commissions into a compact arrangement of eleven major departments.[71] Second was a series of reports dealing with the general accounting and finance problems of the Government, with heavy emphasis on the development of an adequate system of expenditure control, and a pre-audit system.[72] Third was the attention paid to systematizing the routine clerical work common to all government departments.[73] In the fourth category was perhaps the most important aspect of the consultants' work: the reorganization of the Departments of Customs and Revenue and the Post Office. Recommendations for these two reorganizations were contained in fifty-nine reports and numerous memoranda.[74] The consultants estimated that in these two departments more than $3,000,000 could be saved if their "economy and efficiency" recommendations were implemented.[75]

Despite the gargantuan efforts of this "first Glassco," the practical results were surprisingly few. Although it is now difficult to assess accurately how many of the task force recommendations were actually approved and ultimately implemented, the dominant impression remains that the majority of the proposals never advanced past the discussion stage.[76] E. O. Griffenhagen himself later confided in a letter to Mackenzie King's private secretary in 1922: "There were many valuable ideas developed on such matters as general organization, inter-departmental relationships, and particularly budget making, appropriations, financial control, and accounting procedure. It has been a great disappointment to me that these ideas were not utilized and made effective and that the undertaking was allowed to grow cold and lose much of its value."[77] Following King's electoral victory over Meighen in 1921, Griffenhagen and Associates attempted persistently for over a year to interest the new Prime Minister in continuing the work of the Subcommittee, but without success.[78] By the time the Liberals came into power, the American consultants as well as the entire reorganization of the service had become distinct political liabilities, which the cautious Mr. King wished to keep at arm's length. The task force had, within little more than a year, been caught up in a whirlwind of political events not of its own making, but which nevertheless ensured its failure.

Ultimately the Council Subcommittee went the way of so many royal commissions, special committees, and task forces in Canadian history: it pinpointed a problem, devised a solution, and then promptly expired, leaving the original situation unchanged. Several specific reasons may be advanced for the apparent failure of the Griffenhagen undertaking. From the very beginning, the Subcommittee had to face the problem of the exact nature of the audience to which it was to address itself. Was it to be the bureaucracy itself, the federal Cabinet, Parliament, or the Canadian public? The Griffenhagen consultants, who would appear to have believed implicitly in the complete separation of politics from administration, did not concern themselves with any questions beyond the abstract ones of administrative efficiency. Faced with serious, even disastrous, misunderstanding of the nature of their work on the part of civil servants, Parliament, and the press, the consultants chose to rely—in vain, as it turned out—on the Government to issue a public statement to clarify the situation.[79] They seemed to have had no feeling for the acute political sensitivity of their work. Nor did they have any sense of human relations in their dealings with the people they were organizing, or even of the need to communicate the meaning of what they were doing—a failure which cost them dearly in public support.[80] And it does not seem that they learned from their public relations fiascos: in trying to persuade the King Government to continue the reorganization work, Griffenhagen boasted that during their short stay in Ottawa, "our efforts were given exclusively to persistent work in inducing department officers, *by every means we could bring to bear*, to put into actual effect the improvements that had been outlined."[81]

In the public service at large there was violently hostile reaction to these methods. The use of such alarming innovations as time and motion studies,[82] and the suspicion that the introduction of more efficient automated methods would endanger the jobs of many employees, led to acute morale problems. It was claimed that civil servants were "resorting in many cases to the most underhand methods of currying favor with the so-called experts, and with deputy ministers and branch heads, so that they will be kept on in their present positions."[83] Evidence further indicates that as the Griffenhagen inquiry increasingly became a political issue, considerable opposition was aroused in Cabinet to the Subcommittee's activities, as indicated by the Postmaster-General's request to Foster that the Griffenhagen work be directed to "some other Department, where their work could be useful."[84] Faced with a politically explosive situation, the Government did not come down strongly on either side, but simply let matters drift.

The staff associations, on the other hand, were only too eager to offer various solutions to the problem. The CSF argued that since the CSC had statutory authority over reorganization, the contract with Griffenhagen and Associates was *ultra vires*.[85] The Associated Federal Employees of Ottawa went much further: reorganization, it maintained, was a matter for joint consultation between government and employees.[86] Meighen had no intention of entertaining such demands, and engaged in angry exchanges with the associations.[87] The efficiency work soon became lost in the cross-fire.

Whatever legitimate complaints employees may have had of the time and motion study analysis of their work, and however little they may have liked being organized along the mechanistic lines of scientific management theory, their complaints were unfortunately articulated most often in the form of irrational anti-Americanism and general zenophobia. For example the CSAO and CSF breathlessly informed Meighen in 1921 that "alien efficiency engineers have assumed control of Canadian Government offices. . . . Officials feel a daily humiliation in being subjected to the supervision, which is nothing less than espionage, of foreigners. Men and women cannot be expected to go to their work with zeal when they realize that their movements are watched and noted by an alien body of mercenaries."[88] All this at a time when there was a grand total of eight such "mercenaries" in the entire service.[89] The issue gave Parliament an opportunity to fulminate against "trading and trucking with the Yankees,"[90] and when anti-Americanism wore thin, it was duly noted that Mr. Griffenhagen and an employee named Wolf bore "names reminiscent of his Majesty's late enemies"[91]—thus linking the firm with the recent atrocities of Kaiser Wilhelm. They were accused of such nefarious acts as causing the removal from offices of "patriotic pictures, such as that of General Foch and the British bulldog."[92] Soon Griffenhagen rose to leading rank in the politician's demonology, and even began to take on the status of a Gothic monster ("the claws of the Griffenhagen"),[93] whose horrendous exploits grew ever more blood chilling: "The government had to get Arthur Young and Company and Griffenhagen from a foreign country, and send them sword in hand into these different departments to kill, slay, destroy, and kick out those people for whom the ministers had no use."[94]

By way of contrast, Sir George Foster's private judgement was that Griffenhagen and Associates "have done a good work hampered as they were by passive and active opposition. . . . It is a thankless task to attempt any reorganization in the Civil Service. Everyone professes desire for efficiency and economy. As soon as one begins to work for it everyone opposes and criticizes."[95] In February of 1921 the Subcommittee commended the valuable work done by the consultants and gave them the required two months' notice, while making the very dubious assertion that "a sufficient basis has been laid upon which the further reorganization of the Governmental Departments may be carried out by trained officers of the different Departments working in connection with the Civil Service Commission."[96]

It was the latter point which was the weakest link in the whole process. The Government's approach to reorganization at this time had been to visualize the civil service as a simple mechanism in need of an overhaul, rather than as a political system, comprising power centres which inevitably collide when a change in relationships is introduced. Innovations, however logical and businesslike, can only be consolidated over time, through persistent and exhaustive efforts to secure adjustment and compromise. "I can call spirits from the vasty deep," thundered the boastful Glendower. To which Hotspur nicely replied, "Why, so can I, or so can any man; but will they come when you do call for them?"[97] The Subcommittee called, and thought that was sufficient. Only the CSC at this time could have ensured the continuity of the reforms and prevented the unnecessary disruptions. Unfortunately the classification had all but swamped the Commission's small and inexperienced staff. Moreover, the strong hostility roused by the Griffenhagen investigation marked out for the CSC an area of activity which it would tend to avoid for many years. The realization of just how insecure the CSC's position was in political reality, despite the sweeping statutory powers of the 1918–19 legislation, shifted its focus rapidly from reformism to a desire to maintain a sympathetic environment. Despite its first flush of enthusiasm for enforcing efficiency on the service, the CSC quickly realized that to disturb bureaucratic inertia is the surest means of creating hostility.

The prodigious amount of work accomplished by the Griffenhagen Associates within so short a space of time was ample testimony that as efficiency engineers they indeed practised what they preached. It is thus ironic that an efficiency study of such magnitude proved to be, at least in part, a waste of public resources, although a number of valuable piecemeal reforms did result.[98] Neither the consultants nor the Subcommittee had the means or the authority to carry through to a successful conclusion their overall schemes for administrative reconstruction.

The immediate aftermath of the 1918–19 legislation was perhaps the most critical period in the history both of the CSC and of personnel administration in the public service. The sweeping legislative provisions provided a wide field of possibilities for the CSC as a personnel control agency, a field which at first it seemed ready to occupy. The period of flux from 1918 to 1921 instead saw the CSC's legions first waver and then fall back in confusion as they became aware of the power and hostility of the opposition. The classification and reorganization battles were decisive struggles; even though the CSC did not take to the field in charge of reorganization, it watched, and learned, from the defeat of the "foreign mercenaries" who were employed for this purpose.

NOTES

1. For a general treatment of the scientific management movement, see Samuel Haber, *Efficiency and Uplift: Scientific Management in the Progressive Era.*

2. DBS, Finance Statistics Branch, *Statement of Civil Service Personnel and Salaries, 1912–1924* (Ottawa: King's Printer, 1925), p. 9.

3. CSC, *Annual Report*, 1917–18, p. 20. In the United States the war appears to have had a strong impact on the development of personnel theories. The expansion of the bureaucracy and of the armed forces resulted in a new appreciation of personnel as a specific area of interest for management. As a result, new standardized personnel specifications and means of testing for the required skills were developed. See Cyril C. Ling, *The Management of Personnel Relations: History and Origins*, pp. 322–37.

4. See chapter 3 for a description of these two sections of the Act.

5. CSC, *Annual Report*, 1917–18, p. 21.

6. Roche, LaRochelle, Jameson to M. Burrell, Secretary of State, in Arthur Young and Company, *Report of Transmission to Accompany the Classification of the Civil Service of Canada*, p. v.

7. H.C., Special Committee Appointed to Inquire into the Operation of Chapter 12, 8–9 George V, An Act Respecting the Civil Service of Canada, 1923, *Proceedings and Evidence*, p. 896.

8. It went on to state that "this same staff has just been chosen, after a thorough-going investigation as the only one qualified to classify and standardize the service of the city of Philadelphia." (Parliament, unpublished Sessional Paper no. 139, April 28, 1920) (All further references to the Sessional Papers are to those of the Parliament of Canada.) The firm of Arthur Young was formed originally as a public accountancy firm in 1895. The principal partners were apparently all British born. Except for an office in London, most of the firm's operations were in the United States, centred in Chicago, but with other offices in New York, Pittsburgh, Milwaukee, Kansas City, and Los Angeles. By 1919, it employed some four hundred persons in all. The Industrial Engineering Department, under Griffenhagen, was organized in 1911, and was involved in the pioneering classification work in the Chicago area. By the time of the Canadian classification, it had already acted as consultant in classifying various private firms, including such giants as the Pullman Company, Commonwealth Edison, and the First National Bank of New York, as well as a number of governmental jurisdictions such as the states of Maryland, Illinois,

and South Carolina, and the cities of Philadelphia and Baltimore. Concurrently with the Canadian work, the Griffenhagen section of the Arthur Young Company served at the head of the directing staff for the U.S. Congressional Joint Commission examining the organization of departments and duties of individual positions in the federal service within the District of Columbia (approximately one hundred thousand employees). See the memorandum prepared by a Mr. Bailey, August 23, 1921, and sent by C. H. Payne (private secretary to Sir George Foster) to Meighen, August 26, 1921, Meighen Papers, PAC, vol. 38, 19724–32. (All further references to the Meighen Papers are to those in the PAC.) See also unpublished Sessional Paper no. 78A, October 29, 1919.

9. See Charles W. Lytle, *Job Evaluation Methods*, p. 102; E. Lanham, *Job Evaluation*, pp. 6–7; Ling, *Management of Personnel Relations*, p. 286. Griffenhagen was in charge of the efficiency division of the Chicago Civil Service Commission, 1910–11; supervised the installation of duties classifications in Cook County and the State of Illinois, 1911–12; and held leading posts in various civil service boards and organizations. See *Public Personnel Studies* 2 (September, 1924), p. 184. Van Riper refers to Griffenhagen as "instrumental in the development of the new position-classification system." (*History of the United States Civil Service*, p. 220)

10. Fred Telford, "Methods of Developing and Administering Classification and Compensation Plans in the Public Service," *The Annals* (1924), pp. 254–61.

11. R. MacGregor Dawson, *The Civil Service of Canada*, p. 95.

12. 1923 Committee, testimony of Commissioner Jameson, pp. 900–901.

13. Arthur Young and Company, *The Classification of the Civil Service of Canada*, June, 1919.

14. CSC, *Annual Report*, 1918–19, pp. 9–10.

15. United States Congress, Joint Commission of Reclassification and Salaries, *Report Submitting the Classification of Positions and the Schedules of Compensation for the Respective Classes in the Washington Service*, 1920, pp. 15–16 and 149.

16. Dawson, *The Civil Service of Canada*, p. 95.

17. Unpublished Sessional Paper no. 139, April 28, 1920. See also 1923 Committee, p. 898.

18. See testimony of the deputy heads, 1923 Committee.

19. Young, *Report of Transmission*, pp. 24–27.

20. R. MacGregor Dawson, "The Canadian Civil Service," pp. 293–94.

21. V. Subramaniam, "The Relative Status of Specialists and Generalists: An Attempt at a Comparative Historical Explanation." Hodgetts has also pointed out that in pre-Confederation Canada the most important government departments were those dealing with natural resources and economic development, and possessing technical staffs. J. E. Hodgetts, *Pioneer Public Service: An Administrative History of the United Canadas, 1841–1867*, p. 41.

22. Young, *Report of Transmission*, pp. 60–62.

23. 1923 Committee, pp. 222 and 224.

24. Roche to Meighen, August 26, 1921, Meighen Papers, vol. 19, 10716. This curious incident demonstrates the extent to which both the defenders and the antagonists of the 1919 classification were operating within the American framework of management thought. J. L. Jacobs and Company—the firm presumably referred to by Roche—was as much a part of the American classifi-

cation movement as Arthur Young and Company. See William E. Mosher and J. Donald Kingsley, *Public Personnel Administration*, p. 360.

25. Professional Institute of the Civil Service of Canada, *Silver Jubilee History, 1920–1945* (Ottawa, 1945), pp. 10, 59–60; Saul J. Frankel, *Staff Relations in the Civil Service: The Canadian Experience*, p. 23.

26. *Institute Bulletin* (Journal of the Professional Institute of the Public Service of Canada), March 5, 1922. This proposal was put before both the CSC and the Cabinet, and was also brought to the attention of the 1923 Parliamentary Committee. See 1923 Committee, testimony of J. M. Swaine, pp. 280–83.

27. 1923 Committee, p. 281.

28. F. W. Patterson (President, AFEO) to Meighen, March 2, 1921, Meighen Papers, vol. 18, 10475–79; Patterson to Meighen, January 21, 1921, ibid., 10448–54; 1923 Committee, testimony of Patterson, pp. 289–90. It might also be pointed out that the voices of the organized service were not quite unanimous in opposition. The President of the Dominion of Canada Public Works Federation testified in 1923 that the Young classification was excellent insofar as it described positions of which he had professional knowledge, and that its only deficiency was its incomplete application: "It is too efficient to suit the service." (1923 Committee, testimony of T. A. Matheson, pp. 505–9) It might also be pointed out that most members of this association were engineers; the industrial engineers of the Arthur Young Company were probably well qualified to classify such positions.

29. H.C., Special Committee on Bill No. 122, An Act to Amend the Civil Service Act, 1918 [1921], *Proceedings and Evidence*, testimony of Roche, pp. 127–31.

30. 1923 Committee, testimony of Jameson, pp. 896–97.

31. Roche to Meighen, August 26, 1921, Meighen Papers, vol. 19, 10716. The Civil Service Association of Ottawa and the Civil Service Federation of Canada wrote to Meighen complaining that the CSC had informed them that the services of the Arthur Young Company had been "most unsatisfactory." Meighen questioned Roche on this point, and Roche replied that while he himself had never suggested such a view, it was no doubt true that one of the other Commissioners had done so. See also Meighen to J. C. O'Connor and T. R. L. MacInnes, September 10, 1921, Meighen Papers, vol. 19, 10736–40.

32. CSC, *Annual Report*, 1918–19, p. 11.

33. Jameson to O'Connor, July 31, 1919, cited in ibid.

34. Ibid., p. 12.

35. Arthur Young and Company, *Revised Classification of the Civil Service of Canada*, September, 1919.

36. 10 George V, c. 10.

37. 1921 Committee, testimony of O'Connor, p. 378.

38. 1923 Committee, testimony of D. L. McKeand, pp. 227–28. (Emphasis added.)

39. An appeal went first to a preliminary committee of three persons representing the employee, the department, and the Organization Branch of the CSC. If the decision was unanimous, it was referred directly to the CSC; if not, to the Board of Hearing.

40. In 1921 Roche wrote to Meighen that "individual notices were sent out to the entire Service of Canada, practically inviting any person who was not

satisfied with his or her classification to appeal before a certain date, which resulted in hundreds of appeals being filed which were of a trivial nature and many of which would not have been lodged at all had it not been for those notices." (Roche to Meighen, August 26, 1921, Meighen Papers, vol. 19, 10715) The 1918–19 Annual Report of the CSC had stated quite clearly that in the Commissioners' judgement the bulk of the protests were from a small minority, "viewing it from the selfish angle of personal application," and that the goal of a service "organized on a sound business basis . . . economically administered" had to be maintained. "That everyone concerned will be fully satisfied with the final settlement is perhaps too much to hope for. Half a century of unscientific methods under a system founded on no definite principle, a happy-go-lucky, hit-or-miss affair, in which political exigencies controlled and merit was a very secondary consideration, could not but develop many startling anomalies and finally evolve a badly balanced and lopsided structure. But the incompetent employee appointed as a reward for political services would be the last to recognize this feature of the case; consequently, there are bound to be many dissatisfied with their rating under the new classification." (CSC, *Annual Report*, 1918–19, pp. 10–11)

41. CSC, *Annual Report*, 1920, p. 7.

42. See testimony of R. R. Farrow (Deputy Minister of Customs), 1921 Committee, pp. 220–22; and testimony of D. L. McKeand, George A. Mountain (President of the Professional Institute), J. A. Elrick (General Secretary of the Amalgamated Civil Servants), P. T. Coolican (Acting Superintendent of the Post Office), G. J. Desbarats (Deputy Head, Department of Defence), 1923 Committee, pp. 226–32, 264, 412, 715, 718. See also *Civil Service News* (organ of the CSF and CSAO), October 21, 1920, p. 8, and January 17, 1921, pp. 3–4.

43. 1923 Committee, testimony of C. V. Putman (chief of the CSC Organization Branch), p. 72. There is some confusion surrounding the precise number of revisions, cancellations, and additions to the original classification. The Board of Hearing reported that by 1920 the Organization Branch of the CSC had created 100 new classes, deleted 67 old ones, and revised 304. In the same period the Board itself had revised 64 classes. Report of the Board of Hearing to Hon. N. W. Rowell respecting the recommendation of the Board and postal service classification, Meighen Papers, vol. 18, 10417. The copy of the revised classification, held by Commissioner Jameson, contains a CSC memorandum signed by Jameson, dated September 14, 1921, indicating that since the issue of the classification, the total number of classes added was 531; 123 had been abolished; and there had been 512 revisions in salary and 213 revisions in definitions, etc., for a total of 1,379 changes. The discrepancy between the Jameson memorandum and the Putman testimony can be explained by a time difference of a few months. (Although it has not been possible to fix a precise date to the termination of the Board of Hearing, it would appear to have concluded in 1922.) In any event, the trend toward more classes, rather than fewer, is evident from all the figures.

44. CSF to Mackenzie King, July 28, 1922, King Papers, Correspondence, Primary Series, vol. 71, 60963–64.

45. 8–9 George V (1918), c. 12, s. 9.

46. 1923 Committee, testimony of Jameson, p. 896.

47. Wartime inflation had seriously depressed the purchasing power of civil

service salaries. Commissioner Jameson later testified: "The organized Civil Service was tremendously strong, and it raised the slogan, 'Equal pay for equal work.' They wanted classification on the basis of duties and qualifications, and they did urge the Commission. Perhaps we yielded where we should not have yielded, but it was a troublesome time. There were strikes threatened. It was a trying time for the departments and the Commission . . . I thought it would not be necessary, but finally the service prevailed upon the Commission to give them classification based on duties and qualifications, claiming that it was the only way that they could get equal pay for equal work." (1923 Committee, pp. 896–97)

48. CSC, *Annual Report*, 1917–18, p. 23.

49. Arthur Young and Company, "Civil Service Commission of Canada: Report on Office Organization and Procedure containing Proposed Manual of Rules," November 30, 1918 (typescript), p. 5.

50. The task had been handed to the CSC by the Government in March of 1918 prior to the passage of the 1918 Act, on the basis that the upcoming legislation would grant the CSC authority "to generally consider questions related to the efficiency of the service." (P.C. 562, March 15, 1918) A board of inquiry appointed by the CSC recommended that outside experts be secured to continue the investigation; the outside experts were, of course, the Arthur Young consultants.

51. A. L. Lewis, of Southam Press, who had headed the 1918 Commission investigating conditions in the Bureau, which had originally called for reorganization, made a supplementary report on conditions following the Arthur Young study, in these euphoric tones: "We are amazed! What was probably as inefficient and unhappy an organization as could very well be found anywhere has been changed into one, we do not hesitate to say, as efficient on the average as any in Canada. . . . We believe it has been very satisfactorily demonstrated that a Government institution can be favourably compared with a high class and purely commercial one." (Sessional Paper no. 91, March 17, 1921) The report was delivered to the Government at the beginning of 1921.

52. CSC, *Annual Report*, 1918–19, p. 17.

53. Ibid., p. 24.

54. On January 1, 1920, the Industrial Engineering Department of Arthur Young and Company was separately established under the name Griffenhagen and Associates and incorporated under dominion law. This firm was later employed by the City of Montreal and the Bank of Montreal for organizational and classification work; also undertaken was a budgetary study for the province of Quebec, and consultancy services for Massey-Harris Ltd. and Canadian Cereal and Flour Mills, Ltd. See memorandum prepared by W. G. Bailey, a partner of Griffenhagen, August 23, 1921, and sent by C. H. Payne (private secretary to Sir George Foster) to Prime Minister Meighen, August 26, 1921, Meighen Papers, vol. 38, 10724–32. The change in name did not involve any major change in personnel.

55. Griffenhagen and Associates, "Report: Opportunities for Effecting Economics and Bettering Service in the Dominion Government Administration," April 28, 1920, part 1, p. 8, Borden Papers, vol. 265, 148990.

56. 1921 Committee, testimony of W. J. Roche, pp. 130–31. Roche stated that he had advised the Cabinet that, "instead of these organizers reporting to our commission, and through our commission, and placing the responsibility

on us they make a recommendation to the Governor in Council, they should report direct." In a private communication to Meighen the same year, Roche was more frank, citing the "strained relations" between the consultants and Commissioners Jameson and LaRochelle: "No doubt it was because of the constant irritation that I pointed out was going on, that the Government decided to have the work of re-organization carried on under the supervision of a Sub-Committee of the Cabinet." (Roche to Meighen, August 26, 1921, Meighen Papers, vol. 19, 10716)

57. Sessional Paper no. 216, June 21, 1920.

58. Ibid.

59. P.C. 1238 (May 31, 1920). See also Memorandum, June 11, 1920, Foster Papers, PAC, vol. 27, File 5094. All further references to the Foster Papers are to those in the PAC.

60. The task force understood that one of its primary duties was to submit a blueprint for the general organization of the administrative departments of the Government of Canada, which it did in Report no. 16. In their initial report to A. K. Maclean, the consultants had commented critically on all aspects of internal organization which they believed were hampering the achievement of "business-like methods" in the departments. "Opportunities for Effecting Economics," part 1, pp. 1–9.

61. As Griffenhagen and Associates commented: "There was nowhere to be found a comprehensive picture of the administrative structure. Instead of a careful plan for each related activity of the work, the enquirer sometimes found an almost complete lack of information as to the activities of some of the divisions of the larger departments. It was not uncommon during the preparation of the charts to be informed by higher officials, who should have been better posted, that certain divisions shown as part of the organization of their departments did not exist." ("Organization," ibid., part 2, pp. 12–13)

62. Ibid., p. 11.

63. Duplication of research activities in the Department of Agriculture was responsible for a considerable waste of public funds from "overmanning, high clerical, stenographic, and messenger expense, purchase of unnecessary equipment, high travelling costs, employment of an unnecessary number of administrative chiefs, and general loss through failure to plan for each class of work as a unit." (Ibid., pp. 15–16)

64. Ibid., p. 11.

65. "Building Space and Office Layout," ibid., part 3, pp. 19–20.

66. The case of the Department of the Interior was cited: branches were located in thirteen separate buildings, and employees of one branch were sometimes located in the offices of another branch. "These widely scattered offices make this a very difficult organization to handle efficiently; to give a general idea of the result of such housing, the department has five automobiles engaged in carrying files from one branch to the other. One of these, during the year 1918, covered 11,000 miles. A large volume of correspondence originates in the Langevin Block and is forwarded from there to another building for the purpose of securing the signature of the Secretary, after which it is sent to still another building for mailing." (Ibid., pp. 21–22)

67. Ibid., p. 26.

68. Ibid., p. 27.

69. They noted the "vicious" practice of paying permanent employees in the

middle of the month for the entire month's services. Ibid., p. 29.

70. Griffenhagen to King, January 5, 1922, King Papers, Corr., Prim. Ser., vol. 74, 62778.

71. See chart, "Present Organization: Proposed Organization," December, 1920, King Papers, *Memoranda and Notes*, vol. 61, C48132.

72. These recommendations mirrored the then popular practice in the United States of providing a firm accounting base for the routine conduct of business by instituting a control, object-of-expenditure budgetary system. See United States Presidential Commission on Economy and Efficiency, *The Need for a National Budget* (Washington: United States Government Printing Office, 1912), pp. 210–13. Griffenhagen and Associates recommended a "revision of the audit procedure to provide a systematic current audit of all claims by representatives of the Auditor General, such audit to be before payment except where it is deemed advisable to provide an immediate independent audit by some other authority." (Council Subcommittee on Reorganization and Efficiency [Directing Staff], Report no. 37, October 14, 1921, p. 12, King Papers, *Memoranda and Notes*, vol. 61, C48057–89)

73. This category included recommendations concerning the payment of employees, uniform procedures on staff records, the standardization of official forms and office equipment, and the replacing of précis clerks by the introduction of an "efficient filing method" for all the departments. Ibid., pp. 14–15 (C48073–74).

74. W. G. Bailey to F. A. McGregor (secretary to King), March 30, 1922, containing proposed letter to members of the Cabinet on reorganization, King Papers, Corr., Prim. Ser., vol. 69, 59018–24.

75. Ibid.

76. Of well over a hundred reports and memoranda presented to the Subcommittee, marginal reforms embodied in five reports obtained the approval of the Privy Council. See P.C. 296 (February 7, 1921).

77. Griffenhagen to McGregor, November 7, 1922, King Papers, Corr., Prim. Ser., vol. 74, 62786.

78. At least twenty letters were exchanged between Messrs Griffenhagen and Bailey and King's office, between January 5, 1922, and November 25, 1922, King Papers, Corr., Prim. Ser., vols. 69 and 74.

79. Griffenhagen to Foster, June 14, 1920, Foster Papers, vol. 27, File 5139.

80. In all fairness to the consultants, it must be noted that the development of the human relations school of management lay in the immediate future. But the simple failure of communication was obviously a cause for inefficiency in what was purported to be an efficiency study, a point for which the following case, if it may be believed, furnishes some evidence: "One very important officer of the Department, who has been in it for a number of years . . . has had his entire staff taken away from him, has had his own office moved to another building and has sat there for two to three weeks without work, without staff, and without instructions. We are advised that when he inquired from his Deputy Minister, or his Assistant Deputy, they knew absolutely nothing about these experts' plans, that he was as much in the dark in the whole matter as the most junior clerk in his Department." (Patterson, President of the Associated Federal Employees of Ottawa, to Meighen, March 22, 1921, Meighen Papers, vol. 18, 10537)

81. Griffenhagen to King, January 4, 1922, King Papers, Corr., Prim. Ser., vol. 74, 62778–80.

82. The associations claimed that officials were being demoralized "by the knowledge that an alien investigator is peering at them through a partly opened door." (T. R. L. MacInnes, President, CSAO, C. F. Spence, First Vice-President, CSAO, and J. C. O'Connor, President, CSF, to Meighen, August 16, 1921, Meighen Papers, vol. 19, 10722)

83. Patterson to Meighen, September 16, 1921, Meighen Papers, vol. 19, 10747.

84. P. E. Blondin to Meighen, February 16, 1921, ibid., 10667–68.

85. O'Connor to Borden, June 17, 1920, ibid., 10592.

86. At the 1920 annual convention of the Trades and Labour Congress of Canada, the AFEO successfully sponsored a resolution favouring the adoption of national and departmental councils along the Whitley Council approach in the British civil service. Patterson to Meighen, September 16, 1921, ibid., 10747.

87. For example see Meighen to MacInnes, et al., September 10, 1921, ibid., 10736–40.

88. MacInnes, Spence, and O'Connor to Meighen, August 16, 1921, ibid., 10720.

89. Memorandum from G. D. Robertson to Buskard, October 7, 1921, ibid., 10751–52.

90. *Debates*, May 28, 1919, p. 2912.

91. MacInnes, Spence, and O'Connor to Meighen, August 16, 1921, Meighen Papers, vol. 19, 10722.

92. Ibid.

93. *Debates*, March 18, 1921, p. 1111.

94. *Debates*, March 11, 1921, p. 833.

95. Foster Diary, January 31 and February 2, 1921, Foster Papers, vol. 2.

96. Report of the Chairman of the Subcommittee on Efficiency and Reorganization, February 2, 1921, cited in P.C. 296 (February 7, 1921).

97. Shakespeare, *Henry IV*, part 1.

98. The cost to the Canadian government of the services of Arthur Young and Company and Griffenhagen and Associates cannot be reconstructed exactly, but the minimum cost can be computed as $75,235 for the original classification (including $47,491 paid directly to the Arthur Young consultants), $67,683 for application of the classification, and $150,000 to Griffenhagen and Associates for reorganizational work. This gives a total of close to $300,000, and it is clear that other, hidden costs were involved. All in all, the estimate of $350,000 sometimes suggested in Parliament may not have been far off the actual amount—by no means an inconsiderable sum at that time. (Sessional Papers no. 78B, October 29, 1919, and 98A, April 29, 1920)

Chapter Five
The Twenties: From Lion to Lamb

Those he commands move only in command
Nothing in love; now does he feel his title
Hang loose about him, like a giant's robe
Upon a dwarfish thief.

Shakespeare, *Macbeth*

IN THEIR FIRST two years of operation under the new Act of 1918 the Civil Service Commissioners had attempted to implement their conception of the merit system in the federal civil service. Although circumstances had forced them to modify the exact mode of implementation as outlined in the Act, generally the Commissioners had followed the precepts which they had enunciated in their 1917–18 Annual Report. The immediate concentration of the Civil Service Commission upon classification and reorganization problems in these years reflected the emphasis which the Commissioners had placed upon these aspects of the organization's various functions.

Within the organization this emphasis was reflected in the relative status of its two main branches. In contrast to the great stress placed upon the Organization Branch in the first Annual Report, the Examination Branch, as we saw earlier, had been virtually ignored,[1] and this inattention continued throughout 1918 and 1919. At the beginning of December, 1918, by which time the Commissioners had been in office for over a year and the Organization Branch heavily involved in the classification project for several months, the Examination Branch was criticized by the Arthur Young Company's report on the CSC's office organization and procedure for having "a wholly inadequate force to meet the examination program that the Commission must sooner or later adopt if it is to carry out its primary function of recruiting the civil service with appointees who have been tested and found qualified."[2] By June of the following year, the Commissioners had done little to rectify the situation, and the Report of Transmission contained the following recommendation: "That the Commission add to its premanent staff under a thoroughly qualified chief with broad knowledge of modern examination methods and with a high degree of organizing ability, a sufficient number of examiners to conduct with the aid of special examiners appointed from time to time, the tests necessary to maintain at all times the required eligible lists."[3] The CSC, however, continued to focus its attention on other matters, and the staff of the Examination Branch remained inadequate to handle the demands placed upon it. As a result, for the first two years the CSC found it necessary to allow some departments, subject to its approval, to make their own appointments.[4]

But the CSC's attempts to implement its initial economy- and efficiency-minded version of the merit system had not met with a great deal of success. Moreover, at the same time that it had suffered a drastic setback on the classification and reorganization issues, the CSC increasingly became a target for criticism from Parliament and the departments. The 1918 Act had not been a universally popular measure among all politicians by any means, and some of them seized upon every opportunity to strike out at the CSC. Such an opportunity presented itself in 1919 when it was publicly revealed that an employee of the Ottawa Post Office Department had secured CSC examinations prior to their use and had sold one of them to a fellow worker, a prospective candidate for an examination the following day. The substance of the attacks made in the House of Commons at this time, and reiterated in newspapers across the country, was that the Commissioners, aided by Foran, had consciously endeavoured to conceal the true facts of the case in order to prevent an investigation in which they would be implicated.[5] Although it was evident that nothing of the sort had occurred, and that the two men had illegally intercepted the examinations in the mail, the adverse publicity could do nothing but tarnish the image of the CSC.

In addition to this external criticism, the CSC was also beginning to encounter criticism within the civil service from the deputy ministers. To some extent many of them resented the wide expanse of power in personnel management granted to the CSC which they might otherwise have wielded. Moreover, the problems which the CSC had encountered in establishing its examination and appointment procedure and the tardiness of the system once in operation exposed it to the charge that it hampered rather than helped the public service.[6]

These criticisms began to convince the CSC that the defenders of patronage had been far from defeated in 1918 and were still seeking to reclaim their lost territory. The threat to its existence became even more of a concrete possibility in 1921 when Bill No. 122 was introduced into the House of Commons. The Spinney Bill, as it was popularly called after its sponsor, proposed to remove a large number of positions from the CSC's jurisdiction. The bill was subsequently referred to a parliamentary committee with Spinney as its chairman, and the CSC was publicly forced to defend its exclusive responsibility to make appointments to these positions. In the following year, the opposition and criticism of the deputy ministers had also grown to such an extent that King was forced to appoint a committee of ten of their number to study the problems facing the civil service. They produced a report which seriously attacked the CSC's competence and challenged the area of its jurisdiction.[7]

By the early 1920s the CSC was thus in serious difficulty. Not only had it failed to fulfil the promise made in 1918 of effecting massive changes in efficiency and economy through improved classification and organization, but its competence to make appointments and promotions in the wide area of its jurisdiction was being openly challenged from various directions. In the face of these threats, the CSC was forced to focus its attention on the preservation of its very existence. The pursuit of this goal, in effect, resulted in a new orientation toward its role in creating an alternative to the patronage system. To much of the country, the whole issue of the 1918 Act had been the victory over the evils of patronage, and by predicating its own existence in terms of maintaining this victory, the CSC was assured of a strong base of popular support. In short, the principle of efficiency and economy, which had so infused the 1917–18 Report of the CSC and had served to guide its first administrative ventures, became completely overshadowed and dominated by the struggle against the evils of patronage through the establishment of a system of competitive examinations. But to change horses in midstream is always a difficult manoeuver. In this case the endeavour succeeded, but only because the CSC was continually prepared to compromise its authority and jurisdiction by eschewing areas and issues of potential conflict with the departments and the Government.

The re-evaluation of its position had actively begun by 1920. During this and following years the CSC began to focus its attention, both in operation and in theory, on the creation of a competitive system of examinations for appointment and promotion as a viable alternative to the patronage system. This interest was reflected on an operational level by a sudden flourish of activity in the previously ignored Examination Branch. As the Commissioners explained in their 1920 Annual Report, "the necessity for an adequate staff of experienced and well qualified examiners is becoming ever more apparent as it is realized that the success of the merit system is vitally dependent on the work of the Examination Branch."[8] During this one year, the staff of the Branch more than doubled, and the expansion continued throughout the 1920s, so that by the end of the decade it had eleven full-time examiners, almost twice the number of professional staff in the Organization Branch.[9] The Examination Branch, moreover, quickly regained control over the appointments which it had been forced to let the departments make in the 1918–20 period. Whereas the CSC had ratified more than ten thousand appointments made by the departments in 1919, by 1921 the Examination Branch conducted competitive examinations for all positions under CSC jurisdiction.[10]

The attempt to create an operational system of competitive examinations for entrance into and promotion in the civil service was matched on another level by the attempts of the CSC to direct attention, both publicly and privately, away from its other functions—the functions it had so extolled in 1918—toward the work it was doing here. Ignoring the vital part the CSC had played in framing the Act, Roche complained to the Spinney Committee of 1921 that classification and its related work was composed of only "subsidiary duties" which had been "dumped" and "imposed" upon the CSC, and which had unfortunately prevented it from devoting more time to the heart of its duties, the filling of positions in an impartial and objective manner.[11] In a revealing letter to the Prime Minister in 1923, Commissioner LaRochelle drew an even more explicit picture of the CSC's role:

> The Commission has no powers to exercise, but mere functions to discharge.
>
> Its chief duty, according to section 4 of the Act, is to hold competitive examinations in connection with appointments or promotions. Its other functions are merely of an accessory or transient character.
>
> It is so true that if the holding of examinations was to be taken away from the hands of the Commission, it would have no reason whatever to exist. It may therefore be said that it is above all, as in other countries, an examining body.
>
> With regard to the reorganization contemplated by section 9 of the Act—which is a passing operation, an administrative incident, a mere readjustment—it has to be done under the direction of the Ministers and Deputy Ministers. The part of the Commission in that specific operation is nothing but that of an aid or helper.
>
> The same thing may be said about eventual changes in the establishments of the departments.[12]

By 1924 this orientation had become even stronger. "The great fundamental principle of the [1918] Act," Roche told a public meeting in that year, was "the abolition of patronage and the substitution of the merit system of open competition." Forgetting the broad interpretation the CSC had given to the meaning of the merit system in 1918, LaRochelle told the same meeting that the merit system consisted of "nothing else than the selection and promotion of qualified and meritorious public officers, through competitive examinations held at the request of ministerial authorities."[13] Even in the depth of the Depression when the country was once again calling for efficiency and economy, Roche was still maintaining that "the keystone of the Civil Service Act is the principle of appointment by competitive examination."[14]

But the CSC needed to do more than merely direct public attention and its own energies toward its examination program. In order to rebuild the popular base of support which it had enjoyed in 1918, it was necessary to emphasize the fact that the patronage issue was by no means dead and that some dissatisfied politicians posed a continual threat to the existence of the merit system. The CSC was helped considerably in this by the frequent attacks upon it in the House of Commons throughout the 1920s. These attacks actually worked to its advantage by engendering the fear of a possible return to the patronage system. By playing upon that fear, which it undoubtedly and in all sincerity believed to be a valid possibility, and by picturing itself as the bulwark against it, the CSC easily rallied a continuing base of support to which it could appeal whenever it felt itself endangered. In 1924, the Citizens' Research Institute of Canada, a group centred in Toronto and concerned with various public issues, established a branch to deal with civil service affairs. At its yearly meetings the Civil Service Research Conference, as it was called, primarily concerned itself with detailing how the merit system of competitive examinations could successfully defeat the old patronage evil.[15] The CSC itself played no small part in advocating the creation of this group and in garnering support from it by continually warning of the tenuous existence of the merit system. "We cannot expect to change the moral tone or the political evils of a generation at once," Roche told the first annual convention of the Conference, and he warmly applauded the formation of this group to help maintain a vigilant eye on the politicians.[16] In the discussion following Roche's remarks, the chief executive officer of the CSC, Secretary William Foran, made a similar plea:

> I do not believe the time will ever come in Canada when you will have a Government who will want to interfere with the main provisions of the Civil Service law, but we must have a strong public opinion behind the Government, and that is the reason why we look with a great deal of favour upon the establishment of this Civil Service branch of your Institute.
>
> We feel that if there is any danger of the law being interfered with in any material respect, if you gentlemen would rouse public opinion it

97

would cause a Government to hesitate before proceeding with a measure of that kind, and in that way you can be of great service to your country. . . .

I hope you will keep this one fact in mind, that if at any time you want any information from the Commission which would enable you to prepare . . . a pamphlet or booklet on any feature of the merit system, that you will not hesitate to apply to the Commission for that information.[17]

What is evident above all else from the CSC's public standpoint, and what is precisely most difficult to understand from a contemporary vantage point, is the euphoric sense of moral reformation which it saw itself as representing. The struggle against patronage had clearly become a moral crusade identified with the forces of decency, civic-mindedness, and efficiency. It is perhaps not completely accidental that the movement against patronage was contemporaneous with the peak of the long struggle against liquor. The two movements bear a strong ideological resemblance in the moral fervour of their campaigns and in the widely alleged dangers contained in the object of their attention.[18] The temptation of patronage, like the temptation of the "demon rum," could at times be positively overwhelming, even for the strong and morally upright. As Foran said to the Civil Service Research Conference in 1925:

When a man gets into public office, he does not care very much about a theory. When you are not interested in politics a theory strikes one as being the correct thing. It is the correct thing. But when you get into public office you find it is very inconvenient, and I have known a great many men who were very strong reformers, but after they got into public life became very lukewarm in regard to reforms of the public service. . . . You know it is a very nice thing when in office to be able to oblige your friends. It is natural and human and I do not say that we would not all do it if we could, but *the thing is to put it beyond our reach. Every man who wants a good Civil Service law should protect himself against himself*, because he feels if he has the giving of the office he wants to give it to his friends, and if there is a law which prevents him from doing that he can always seek its protection.[19]

It was exactly this protection of oneself against the baser drives and urges of one's own nature which the CSC claimed as the great benefit of the merit system of competitive examinations. As Roche explained in 1924:

There is no teaching of history and no process of reasoning that will not unfailingly lead us to the conclusion that the element of favouritism and spoils politics can be excluded from the Public Service only by the establishment and maintenance of competitive tests to which every qualified person has free access and which secure to the best merit properly demonstrated the best title to appointment. The competitive principle . . . is the very soul of Civil Service Reform. . . . To understand [the merit system] is the first if not the only argument needed to make a supporter. To bring its just principles and its practical methods distinctly before the intelligent classes is therefore a patriotic and paramount duty.[20]

The endeavour to reduce the problem of administering the merit system to a question of morality struck a strong and responsive chord within the country. The Commissioners as well as Foran were invited to make public speeches to various organizations, and many newspaper editors were usually more than willing to print letters and articles from the CSC explaining its position. In addition, numerous articles of this sort appeared in newspapers across the country during the 1920s which, as an official of one civil service association told the 1923 Committee, bore "all the ear-marks of having been prompted by the Commission or some of the employees." By means of such "newspaper propaganda," the official continued, the CSC tried to make its own existence synonymous with the preservation of the merit system.[21] In this purpose the CSC largely succeeded. In 1928 W. L. Grant introduced Newton MacTavish, one of the Commissioners appointed on the resignation of Jameson and LaRochelle, to a group interested in civil service administration with these words: "There is a deeper truth in the saying of John Bright [that] 'There is no permanent greatness for a nation except that it be based upon morality,' and Dr. Newton MacTavish, as one of the three Civil Service Commissioners of Canada, is one of the three chief guardians of the morality of our national administration."[22]

By taking the matter to the country to gain a base of support, the CSC succeeded in institutionalizing this aspect of its functions. No government by 1930 would have had the temerity to suggest the abolition of the CSC and a return to the patronage system. This in itself was a significant and commendable achievement. Yet in light of the danger which the CSC continually pictured as lurking just around the corner, it is interesting to consider whether any government would have wished for this solution, even if it would not have had to face a large public outcry. Although individual backbenchers continually called for a return to patronage throughout the 1920s, the Government always maintained a strict neutrality on the matter. Meighen had been too closely connected with Borden to have risked any such move. Similarly, it is evident from King's papers that he never gave serious thought to such a plan. King received countless pleas from Liberals during the course of the 1920s, calling for him to restore the old system and claiming that the CSC was filling the civil service with Conservative supporters. He generally took the tack of agreeing that a terrible situation prevailed, but maintained that his hands were unfortunately tied by the 1918 Act of Parliament.[23] He was obviously greatly relieved that the CSC had lifted the burden from the Government and on this ground alone never considered any move against it. When pressure became too great to resist in 1923, King simply did what Meighen had done in 1921—he created a parliamentary committee to study the problem.

Despite King's own feelings on the subject, attacks continued to emanate from the backbenchers of the House. However, from a contemporary perspective, it is evident that with the hostile attitude toward patronage running deep across the country, these criticisms actually aided the institutionalization of the CSC by inflating the threat to its existence out of proportion. Even during the 1930s, whenever the CSC felt itself threatened or endangered, it had only to appeal to the moral basis for its existence in order to gain widespread public support. Unfortunately, the success of this appeal in these years conditioned the organization to rely upon it long after the morality issue was not of primary concern for the merit system. In the late 1940s and in the 1950s the need was not for a system which protected a man against himself, but for a positive instrument of personnel policy. Yet it was essentially on this basis that the CSC remained oriented until the reassessment of the Heeney years.

The CSC and Departmental Reorganization

One of the concomitant features of the Civil Service Commission's endeavour to switch its main emphasis to the establishment of a merit system of competitive examination was its adamant refusal to become involved in departmental reorganization work. This refusal, in fact, was the obverse side of its attempt to institutionalize itself as an examining body. The same pervading sense of weakness which had led it to turn toward this aspect of its duties also led it to avoid conflict which would only make it more prone to criticism. The Griffenhagen experience served as a dramatic warning of the severe opposition of the civil servants and the departments to further enterprises of this sort. Under these circumstances the CSC exhibited an evident lack of initiative in reorganization work.

The 1918 Act, however, had laid upon the CSC the responsibility for such work,[24] and it could not openly disclaim interest in this area, particularly in light of the previous enthusiasm which it expressed for this

100

type of endeavour in its 1917–18 Annual Report. Consequently, whenever questioned on the subject, the Commissioners and CSC officials would strongly reaffirm the CSC's interest, but would quickly follow this by emphasizing the practical difficulties in exercising its responsibilities. They had actually used this approach as early as 1920 in refusing to follow the terms of the Act by having Griffenhagen's reorganization work carried out under its auspices.[25] But they continued to use this same excuse throughout the twenties, maintaining that classification and reclassification consumed too much time to make a start on reorganization work. Before the parliamentary committee of 1923, Commissioner Jameson listed this reason for delaying the commencement of the general departmental reorganization provided for in the Act. He also added that the bulk of reclassification had been completed at that time, and expressed eagerness to get on with the task of reorganization.[26] Yet almost a decade later Secretary Foran repeated the same refrain to the Lawson Committee of 1932: "Our reorganization has not proceeded very far because of the preliminary work we have had to do in connection with the reclassification of the service, but now we are ready to go on with the surveys in the departments."[27]

More to the point with regard to the delay was the opposition of the departments. Jameson told the 1923 Committee that the cooperation of the deputy heads was an "absolute necessity," for if the CSC tried to impose itself on the departments, its employees would be put in the position of "unwelcome guests" which would utterly frustrate their work.[28] The Annual Reports of the CSC picked up Jameson's argument and reiterated it over and over again. The Report for 1925 is fairly indicative of the approach taken:

> The Civil Service Commission has consistently urged a strong program of general reorganizations for the Civil Service of Canada. The efforts of some departments and their branches to establish themselves as self contained units, have resulted in a multiplication of highly paid supervisory positions with a full complement of specialists and duplication of expensive equipment. . . . It is submitted that if the Commission were to receive the necessary measure of support, not only could large economies be effected but the general condition of the service would be improved.[29]

The only way the CSC felt it could be assured of this cooperation was if the Government armed it with an order in council as it had during the investigation of the Printing Bureau.[30] The CSC, however, failed to persuade the parliamentary investigation of 1923 of this necessity, and the Committee reported that the CSC already possessed the requisite authority required under the Inquiries Act and urged it to get on with the job.[31]

Following the report of this Committee, the CSC approached the Government to solicit its views with regard to what action the CSC should take. Foran subsequently had an interview with the Prime Minister on the topic, and it was decided to proceed with the reorganization work. Under whose direction this was to be conducted is just not clear, but in anticipation of this the CSC was to conduct a preliminary survey of the civil service. The Commissioners, however, even balked at this prospect, unless they could be assured of the Prime Minister's official and written support. As Foran told King's secretary:

> If the Government is going to undertake any work in connection with the reorganization of the Public Service, it is important that they should have before them a comprehensive report of conditions as they really exist. It is this report that the Prime Minister is anxious that we should prepare, but you will understand that, unless they have specific instructions from him to go to work upon it, the Commissioners would not care to undertake the task.[32]

It appears that the authorization demanded was never forthcoming from the Prime Minister's Office.

In the following year the CSC appeared before the Senate Committee investigating the efficiency of the civil service and submitted a memorandum on reorganization of government departments or branches.[33] The study did not deal with the reorganization of any specific department, but made twenty-two tentative suggestions where economy might be effected, primarily by grouping common services between and within departments. Interestingly, these suggestions appear to have been drawn from the unimplemented recommendations of the Griffenhagen inquiry. The Committee reaffirmed that "the proper body to undertake the work of reorganization is the Civil Service Commission. Its powers, under the Act of 1918, give it the necessary legal authority, and the intent of the Act was, *inter alia*, that the Commission should proceed with the organization of the Civil Service." The Committee also lent a somewhat more sympathetic ear to the tale of the CSC's difficulties and saw fit to recommend:

> That an Order-in-Council be passed instructing the Civil Service Commission to proceed with the reorganization of those departments of the public service which have not been reorganized within recent years, and enjoining deputy heads to render the Commission the fullest cooperation and assistance. This order should further require the Commission to report to the Governor in Council and to Parliament in all instances where their work is hampered or delayed by lack of cooperation upon the part of Deputy Ministers or their chief officials.[34]

In its 1924 Annual Report the CSC printed the recommendations of the 1923 Committee concerning reorganization work beside those of the 1924 Committee.[35] Accompanied with only a few explanatory remarks, this ostensibly stood in mute testimony to the ultimate triumph of the validity of the CSC's argument for an order in council.

The Government ignored the recommendation of the 1924 Committee and, as a result, the CSC's plans got no further. The Organization Branch proceeded with a limited amount of reorganizational work in the following years, but such work was always done on the invitation of the departments. Several witnesses before the Lawson Committee in 1932 insisted that the CSC had not shown any initiative in the area at all unless called in, a point confirmed by C. V. Putman, the head of the Organization Branch.[36] The departments for their part considered the staff of the Organization Branch incompetent,[37] and initiated a great many projects themselves without reference to the CSC, except for the final approval.

In contrast to its success in establishing its role as the guardian of the merit system, the CSC had, by the 1930s, failed to gain wide acceptance for its competence to perform a significant part in the direct promotion of economy and efficiency in the civil service through the creation of better organizational structures. It may very well be that departmental opposition to reorganization work by the CSC was formidable enough to give the CSC cause for hesitation in executing its duties. There is also the unanswered question of why the Government never passed the order in council demanded by the CSC.[38] Yet the fact still remains that by the terms of the Act the CSC had the necessary authority to impose itself upon the departments, but refused to proceed without the added official support of the Government. It might be argued that this was the only reasonable course to pursue since the Act had obviously overlooked the crucial role and interest of departmental management in this area. Be that as it may, the CSC hesitated, not out of a commendable respect for departmental responsibilities, but out of a sense of weakness: it continually expressed the willingness to proceed once the necessary support which it felt it required was obtained. Thus, the CSC's refusal to take the initiative in reorganization work helped it over the difficult trials of the twenties by reducing institutional conflict, but it weakened the organization for the future. When the depression years called for a renewed emphasis on economy and efficiency, the CSC showed itself incapable of rising to meet the situation.

THE PROBLEM OF INDEPENDENCE

The sense of vulnerability which had inspired the Civil Service Commission to seek public acclamation for its right to make appointments and promotions in the civil service and had made it shrink from strongly asserting its role in departmental reorganization was the result of the peculiar circumstances in which the CSC found itself in the early 1920s. But it is important to realize that the CSC's weak position in these years was compounded by the fact that the Commissioners were themselves not in a strong position to assert the organization's independence from the outside forces which would encroach upon its territory. This situation had originally developed more from an unclear understanding of the dynamics of power relationships than from any deliberate policy. But as the CSC began to encounter bureaucratic opposition, it was to the distinct advantage of entrenched interests to maintain this state of affairs.

In the parliamentary debates over the Civil Service Act of 1918, the independence of the CSC from governmental control was a subject which received very little treatment. While the politicians dutifully acknowledged the need for an independent commission, they gave little consideration to the exact means by which the independence would be guaranteed. Because they conceived of the question of independence primarily, if not solely, in political terms, the problem became greatly simplified for them. The major necessity was to guard against the use of overt political influence upon the Commissioners. To secure their freedom from political or personal pressure, the Government proposed to place them on the same level as other semi-independent bodies. In this regard the Railway Commission apparently served as a model in framing the legislation.[39] All Commissioners appointed after 1918 were to serve for a ten-year term contingent upon good behaviour, and were to be retired at sixty-five years of age. They were responsible to Parliament and were removable only by the Governor-General on address to the Senate and the House of Commons. The stature accruing to their positions was that of a deputy minister, and their salaries, payable out of the Consolidated Revenue Fund, were independent of political control.

These provisions had been changed somewhat from the 1908 Act. In the debates over this legislation, Robert Borden had successfully argued that the best way to insure the freedom of the Commissioners was to give them the stature of judges and make their appointment for life contingent upon good behaviour.[40] The first two Commissioners, Shortt and La-Rochelle, were appointed under these conditions, as were Roche and Jameson in 1917. Borden's frosty relationship with Shortt may have given him second thoughts on the matter of tenure, however, for after 1918 all future Commissioners were limited to the ten-year term.

Despite the assurances of the Government, both in 1908 and 1918, neither piece of legislation made sufficient provision to guard the Commissioners' independence. In fact, they were never fully placed at the level of either judges or railway commissioners. Although the men appointed in 1908 and in 1917 possessed the life tenure accorded judges, they did not have their generous retirement provisions. This meant that, after growing old in the service of the state, these men would be thrown upon the mercy of the government in power to grant them a gratuity or retirement allowance. For men who were expected to maintain a strict detachment from the politics and influence of the party in power, the lack of such a provision was a drastic oversight. This same reprehensible feature was transferred to the 1918 Act, and the problem was further compounded by the ten-year tenure. Future Commissioners, although supposedly possessing the same stature as deputy ministers, did not even have their security of tenure to offset the lack of a retirement allowance. In fairness to the Government it should be pointed out that in 1918 no superannuation scheme existed for Canadian civil servants. The feeling may have been that to grant the Commissioners such arrangements, even though they were not civil servants as defined in the Act, would have represented preferential treatment. In a sense this may have been true; the railway commissioners, to whom they were compared in 1918, had no retirement provisions. But to counterbalance this fact, as well as that of their similarly short tenure, the railway commissioners had been granted much more attractive salaries than those enjoyed by most deputy ministers, including the Civil Service Commissioners. The chairman of the Railway Commission, to compare cases, received $12,500 to Roche's $6,000, while the assistant railway commissioner received $9,000 to the $5,000 received by Jameson and LaRochelle. The obvious disadvantages under which the Civil Service Commissioners laboured had unfortunate results when at least three of the first nine Commissioners appointed had need to resort to the humiliation of petitioning the Government for some kind of financial aid on retirement.[41] Such a situation severely weakened the independent status of the Commissioners. Men who were more dependent upon the good graces of the party in power, rather than on Parliament as a whole, were not in a strong position to assert the CSC's authority whenever it came into conflict with the Government.[42]

THE SPINNEY COMMITTEE AND THE EXEMPTION ISSUE, 1921–1922

The consequences of the Commissioners' relatively weak position soon became evident in the issue over exemptions to the Civil Service Act in 1921 and 1922. The 1918 Act had extended the Civil Service Commission's control over the entire service, but had provided that when the CSC felt it was not "practicable" to apply the Act to any position, it could, with the approval of the Governor in Council, make regulations stipulating how

105

such positions were to be filled. Initially the CSC seemed content with the reaches of its power; the 1917–18 Annual Report, in fact, sharply reprimanded the Board of Pension Commissioners for resisting CSC control over appointments to that body.[43] Within the next few years, however, the situation altered dramatically. The almost total concentration of the CSC on the time-consuming problems of classification and reclassification work had created great delays and difficulties in securing staff for some of the rapidly expanding postwar agencies. The CSC now felt, as Roche later put it, that "so drastic a measure at one step, such as taken in taking in the whole service was too big an undertaking,"[44] and in the fall of 1919 it recommended the exemption of the temporary employees of the Department of the Soldiers' Civil Re-establishment.[45] The employees of the Soldiers' Settlement Board followed in February, 1920, under the authority of an order in council sponsored by the CSC.[46] Officially the guiding principle in determining these exemptions, to keep them within the terms of the Act, was the CSC's inability to prescribe competitive examinations for the positions concerned, although Roche later admitted that the constant irritation between the CSC and the bodies concerned was as much to the point in helping to decide these cases.[47] By 1920, however, the CSC had begun to shift its emphasis toward its examining function, and consequently it was probably not anxious to exclude any more positions. At any rate, regardless of the real reason behind the earlier exemptions, the CSC refused to make any more, maintaining that it now had the resources to apply competitive examinations to all positions.[48]

In 1921, parliamentary accusations that the civil service had not become any more efficient after 1918, despite the existence of the CSC, induced E. K. Spinney to introduce a bill into the House of Commons which threatened to add to the exemptions by removing all manual labourers, a large number of postmasters, and all professional, scientific, and technical officers from under the Civil Service Act. Roche and Foran subsequently appeared before the Committee formed to consider the bill and were forced to defend the competence of the CSC to retain its jurisdiction in these cases. Although they successfully convinced the Committee of the disastrous consequences of such a measure, they had to give ground on the criteria upon which the CSC had made exemptions. Most of the members of the Committee were firmly of the opinion that those classes should be exempted which invariably caused hampering delays to fill—even when it was possible to fill them through competitive examinations. Both Roche and Foran acquiesced in the Committee's opinion and now expressed willingness to exempt positions under this condition.[49] The Committee decided to leave it to the CSC to decide what classes to exempt, but secured an amendment to the Act which clarified the relevant section to allow for exemptions on these grounds.[50]

Following the committee hearings and the amendment, the CSC hastened to study the matter, and in early 1922 sponsored several orders in council removing various positions, primarily those of manual labourers, from the jurisdiction of the Act. But in May of that year, it ran head-on into the new Liberal Government of Mackenzie King. The problem revolved around a proposed order in council which would have exempted 144 classes involving 12,804 positions. Under its authority to draw up regulations for the exempted positions, the CSC had always scrupulously endeavoured to protect the merit principle by specifying that selection for them was to be made "without reference to personal or political considerations and strictly on the merit principle."[51] When it included this provision in the order submitted in 1922, however, the Government returned the recommendation, refusing to pass it on the grounds that the accompanying regulations were "too cumbersome and unnecessary." The meaning of the Government's refusal was manifestly clear: it was an open demand that the CSC withdraw the clause regarding nonpolitical selection. The issue immediately produced a crisis among the Commissioners similar to that which had taken place three years earlier over the question of the CSC's answer to the criticism of the civil servants to the classification scheme. At that time Jameson and LaRochelle had concluded that the best policy was to forge a compromise and, as a result, the Board of Hearing was created. Roche, who did not hold the same views as his colleagues toward the results of the classification, had not fully agreed as to the proper response to the civil servants. Consequently he had tended to remain aloof from the Board and from the open criticism of the Arthur Young Company in which Jameson and LaRochelle indulged.

In 1922 the Commissioners split along the same lines. To Roche the issue at stake in the Government's refusal was a serious one. It was a question of safeguarding "the principle underlying the Act, to see that these positions were not filled through patronage."[52] He refused to amend the recommendation. Jameson and LaRochelle, on the other hand, bowed to the pressure of the Government and withdrew the contentious clause. When they submitted the order with only their two signatures, it received immediate approval. In the face of an intransigent Government and accommodating colleagues, Roche eventually capitulated and signed exemption orders without the clause in question. The Commissioners as a whole apparently drew a lesson from the affair, as thereafter they usually adopted a much more cautious and timid manner whenever dealing with the Government. For example, before submitting a recommendation to the Privy Council on freezing salary levels in 1924, the Commissioners canvassed the Prime Minister for the possible reaction of the Government because, "the Commission would not wish . . . to embarrass the Government by making such a recommendation, and would not submit it therefore, if Council was not likely to consider it favourably."[53]

THE COMMISSION'S FADING PRESTIGE

The Civil Service Commission's inability to resist pressure from the Government was certainly not enhanced by subsequent developments during the twenties. The 1918 Act had handed the CSC a tremendous range of duties and powers, the implications of which were only dimly understood at that time. When it came to transforming its statutory powers into action, it was inevitable that at times the CSC's interests might conflict with those of the Government as had happened in 1922 in the exemption issue. The conflict in this instance had been relatively minor, but it suggested the possibility that other more significant conflicts loomed over the horizon. In such a situation it is not at all surprising that no government would wish to strengthen the authority and independence of the CSC. On the contrary, the Government exhibited a general distrust of a CSC which would be independent and powerful enough not only to resist the pressures for patronage, but to decide other policy which might at times conflict with the Government's wishes.

This attitude was made evident by the Government's obvious disinterest in strengthening the position of the CSC. Actually, the Government seems to have pursued precisely the opposite course by consciously allowing the prestige of the CSC to decline in the years following 1922. In 1924 it raised the salaries of the deputy ministers, but failed to touch those of the Commissioners, even though they supposedly enjoyed the same rank. The salaries granted the Commissioners in 1918, while far below those of the railway commissioners, had compared favourably with those of other deputy ministers. In 1919 the Union Government had amended the Act to increase the salary of the chairman to $7,000 and of the other two Commissioners to $6,000 to match the increases received by the deputy ministers. However, when the salaries of the deputy ministers were increased once again in 1924 to $8,000, the Commissioners received no corresponding revision. They realized the effect this would have upon their stature and complained to King: "The Civil Service Commissioners claim that according to law and well established precedents, they are clearly entitled to such salary. Any discrimination against them would be a violation of law and precedents. . . . To place the Civil Service Commissioners in a lower grade than that of the Deputy Ministers would seriously impair their status and prejudicially affect the transaction of business daily carried on between the Commission and the various departments of the public service of Canada."[54] The Government turned a deaf ear to these pleas, and in the following years allowed the salaries of the Commissioners to fall even further below those of the deputy ministers. The Beatty Royal Commission (1929–30) in turn suggested that the Government raise the salaries of the Civil Service Commissioners, but to no avail.[55] Yet, not only was the Government content to let the Commissioners' salaries fall below those of persons occupying the same rank, but the Prime Minister announced in 1929 that Roche did not even possess the rank of deputy minister: "The head of the Civil Service Commission has not the position of a deputy minister corresponding to the permanent head of a government department. He is an officer who is appointed for a term of years under statute."[56] King later admitted his error with regard to Roche's tenure, but he did not alter—publicly at least—his opinion concerning the chairman's status.

At the same time that the CSC's prestige within the civil service was being weakened, its public image was seriously compromised by a scandal from within the organization itself. In 1926 Jameson and LaRochelle became implicated in the corrupt dealings which had been revealed in the customs administration. According to the evidence, these two Commissioners had on different occasions received several cases of liquor seized at the port of Montreal from a customs officer employed there. Over the protests of Roche, they had subsequently approved of a salary increase for the officer in question on the recommendation of the department. When the parliamentary committee established to investigate the shady dealings in the department uncovered the receipts for the liquor sent to the two Commissioners, it demanded explanations from them. The denouement of the whole affair was swift, as a friend of former Commissioner Shortt related:

> The speed with which the heads of Jameson and LaRochelle fell into the basket rivals the guillotine in its earliest days. On Wednesday they appeared before the Committee and acknowledged having received some cases of liquor from a rascal who was managing Custom's affairs as Bureau's [the Minister of Customs and Excise] factotum, and that they two as Commissioners had endorsed the recommendation of the Department that this fellow should have a $600 increase in salary; on Thursday there was a howl from the newspapers for their removal; on Friday morning their resignations were offered at the suggestion of the Prime Minister and promptly accepted. On Saturday morning as I was coming to the office I saw LaRochelle approaching. He wore heavy coloured spectacles. He tried to pass me without recognition but I com-

pelled an acknowledgement of my salutation. Poor fellow! He has been an awful fool, though I do not believe anything worse.[57]

On the resignation of Jameson and LaRochelle, King's office was inundated with demands that the Government appoint "two good party men" to replace the disgraced Commissioners.[58] This presented a considerable problem to King. If he appointed two men with a blatant partisan spirit, he would open the Government to the charge that he was attempting to transform the CSC into a patronage dispensing organization for the Liberal party. Similarly, to appoint two men on a strict nonpartisan basis would run the risk of alienating party supporters. The only real solution was to appoint relatively unknown party sympathizers, whose selection would not attract widespread public displeasure, but who would hopefully have enough political awareness not to embarrass the Government by taking it upon themselves to publicly assert the CSC's interests whenever they were impinged upon by the Government. Neither of the two men chosen, in fact, seems to have had any special qualifications for the position other than sympathy for the Liberal party. Newton MacTavish had been the editor of the *Canadian Magazine* for twenty years and was a personal friend of King. Although he had academic pretensions, they seem to have been disparaged by some members of the academic community.[59] The other appointee, J. E. Tremblay, had existed on the fringe of politics for several years as the private secretary to various Liberal ministers of justice.[60]

Unfortunately for the CSC, neither MacTavish nor Tremblay possessed sufficient ability or capacity to check the declining prestige of the organization, which, during their tenure, fell to the lowest point in its history. The two Commissioners whom they replaced had on at least two occasions —once following the uproar in the civil service after the publication of the classification scheme, and the other in the exemption issue—thought it best for the future of the CSC to compromise with the strong forces which exerted pressure upon it. MacTavish and Tremblay now carried this attitude one step further by attempting to satisfy practically everyone who had an interest in the administration of the civil service. Prior to 1926 the CSC had resisted political pressure from both Liberals and Conservatives. Members of Parliament were often in the habit of endorsing local candidates for positions, especially those of postmasters, but until 1926 the CSC had assiduously endeavoured to avoid giving these candidates any edge in the competition. Now, however, this changed perceptibly. In appointments involving postmasters, the local postal supervisor had a hand in drawing up the order of merit from which the CSC made the appointment. Roche began to suspect these lists and on one occasion openly condemned one of them. "This is one of a number of instances where the order of merit appears difficult to explain except by the fact that the MP for the constituency has recommended the applicant who has been placed first."[61] In most cases MacTavish and Tremblay acquiesced in the merit lists of these supervisors over Roche's objections, even though the lists had obviously been influenced by politicians from both major parties. In addition, the 1932 Committee investigating the CSC found cases suggesting that MacTavish and Tremblay at times appointed men with Liberal sympathies over their better-qualified opponents.[62]

Not only did these two Commissioners open the CSC to the operation of political patronage, but during their period of office the departments enjoyed unparalleled influence. MacTavish told the 1932 Committee that the "genius" of the Civil Service Act was that "the department must be suited" in appointments.[63] MacTavish and Tremblay followed this policy indiscriminately, often going outside the regular order of merit in order to appoint the department's choice of candidates.[64] They also regularly delayed appointments for inordinate lengths of time on the request of the deputy head of a department. These delays provided the department with the opportunity to temporarily install its own choice of applicants, allowing them valuable experience on the job, a factor which often influenced the outcome of the competition.[65]

Roche consistently opposed these practices, but he was unable to prevent them. When one Member of Parliament, J. A. Clark, inquired as to the reason for a delayed appointment, MacTavish and Tremblay informed him that it had been CSC practice since 1918 to delay a competition on the request of a deputy head, "although several times the Chairman had refused approval to such suspension when the reasons given by the department were not, in his opinion, sufficient."[66] This answer failed to satisfy Roche, who personally wrote an explanation to Clark:

> In order to give you a fuller understanding of the situation I would point out that, on March 18, 1926, prior to the appointment of my present colleagues . . . I placed on file a note to the following effect: "that when the Commission is requested to suspend action some good reason should be assigned, because the Commission is frequently blamed for the delay." This note was approved by my then colleague, Col. LaRochelle.
>
> On a number of occasions since the appointment of my present colleagues, I have refused to suspend action at the request of the department when no reason whatever was assigned for the delay, in accordance with the ruling of the Commission of March 18, 1926, but my colleagues on each occasion complied with the request.[67]

111

Roche's aggravated relations with the other two Commissioners had actually begun only shortly after they had assumed office. Within several months of their arrival at the CSC, MacTavish and Tremblay had, without Roche's knowledge, commissioned a study of the CSC's organization and procedure.[68] The supposed purpose of the study was to remedy the delays in CSC's procedure concerning which the two Commissioners claimed they had received numerous complaints. When Roche discovered the existence of the project, he vehemently protested that the two men chosen to conduct it had been appointed without the knowledge of even the heads of the branches in which they worked. The study nevertheless proceeded, and when completed, it almost tore the CSC apart. The Kemmis-Simmins Report, as it was called after its two authors, suggested a reorganization of the CSC, in which the officers of the Examination Branch and the Organization Branch would report respectively to either Tremblay or MacTavish. Roche was thus left in some vague coordinating position, while the heads of the two main branches would be left without jobs. Although the authors of the Report appear to have been genuinely concerned with improving the procedure and organization of the CSC, the manner in which the study was conducted and the suggested realignment gave the impression that MacTavish and Tremblay were attempting to organizationally isolate the chairman. This assumption is rather dubious, however, since neither Commissioner appears to have been aware of what precisely Kemmis and Simmins would recommend until the Report was completed. The Report was never implemented; it nevertheless had a decidedly harmful effect upon the morale within the CSC and poisoned the relations between Roche and the other two Commissioners. The CSC's image and prestige was also dealt another shattering blow when Roche complained of the matter to one M.P., who related the complaint to the Prime Minister. MacTavish and Tremblay subsequently rushed to tell their side of the story to several members of the Cabinet. King refused to become involved, but the strained relations within the CSC became a matter of general knowledge.

It would be unfair to MacTavish and Tremblay to fail to point out that these two Commissioners only further weakened what was already a weak organization. While it could rely upon strong public support to ensure its continued existence, this fact did little to help the CSC become a truly effective organization. Its poor position within the bureaucracy generally led it to search for a consensus for the exercise of its duties and to avoid any involvement in institutional conflict which would only serve to weaken this consensus. The CSC, for example, openly acquiesced in flagrant abuses of the practice of temporary employment by the departments. It ritually renewed temporary certificates on the request of the department for years on end, so that some persons remained in temporary positions for nine or ten years, despite the fact that the 1918 Act had attempted to put an end to this situation. When questioned on the probity of such a practice by the 1932 Committee, the Secretary of the CSC, William Foran, admitted that it had never attempted to stop the abuse because, "we try to get along with the departments as harmoniously as we possibly can."[69] Yet even when it did attempt to stop an open abuse, the CSC's inferior position often doomed the effort to failure. By the close of the 1920s the Government was making widespread exemptions to the Civil Service Act through statute, much to the consternation of the CSC. The CSC as a whole now felt, as Roche had done in 1922, that appointments made without regard to merit had the unfortunate tendency to undermine not only the principle of the Act, but its own authority as well. Although it complained of this in the Annual Reports, it was powerless to stop the drift in this direction.[70]

The Burdens of Leadership

The inability of the Civil Service Commission to assert its authority in these areas underscored its progressive loss of bureaucratic power and prestige throughout the twenties. But while in practice its freedom of action was limited and compromised in a great many ways, it found the legal fiction of its official independence increasingly difficult to bear. Like Macbeth, it found its title to hang loose upon it, "like a giant's robe upon a dwarfish thief." Attacked in Parliament, the CSC, unlike the departments, had no medium through which to present its views and argue its case before the Government and the M.P.'s. To overcome its embarrassing position at not having a minister to represent its interests, the CSC tried a variety of schemes. Although it officially reported to Parliament through the Secretary of State, the CSC in practice rarely subjected itself to this formality when contacting the Government. Instead, the Commissioners, as well as Foran, wrote the Prime Minister directly to seek advice and present their opinions. In addition, the CSC attempted to secure a voice to represent it in Parliament. During the days of the Union Government, A. K. Maclean had defended the CSC, but with the electoral defeat of the Conservative government, the practice was terminated. Throughout the remainder of the 1920s, Roche continually tried to resurrect this procedure. At a meeting with King in 1922, he suggested that a member of the Cabinet be delegated to take a special interest in civil service matters.[71] Although he moved slowly, for a time King seemed willing to meet the request. In 1925 the Prime Minister designated J. A. Robb, the Minister of Immigration, to act on the CSC's behalf, but before he could assume his new duties, Robb was reappointed finance minister.[72] The matter was then dropped until Roche again brought it forward during the hearings before the parliamentary committee of 1932. At this time, while Chairman Roche argued for a voice in Parliament, Secretary Foran suggested that the Government should establish a permanent parliamentary committee on the civil service through which the CSC could publicly offer a defence of itself.[73] Bland and Foran made the same suggestion before the 1938 Committee, but nothing ever became of the matter.[74]

The endeavours of Roche and Foran in this regard suggest an attempt to ease the burdens of leadership. This was matched by the fact that while the Government never really got beyond defining the independence of the CSC in terms other than freedom from political interference in appointments and promotions, neither did the CSC. To openly define the ambit of its powers could bring the CSC into conflict with other interests; to avoid this, the Commissioners, along with Foran, studiously refrained from making dogmatic pronouncements on policy. They were content, rather, to let these questions be decided in the day-to-day give and take of the bureaucratic power struggle. To rationalize their failure to offer strong and dynamic leadership to the organization, the Commissioners explained that they were mere dispassionate administrators and not policy-makers; they had no responsibility to define the role of the CSC—that was the task of Parliament. In a refrain which was to be repeated in the following years, Roche told the Spinney Committee of 1921:

We are trying to enforce the Act which you members have put in the Statute Book, but the difficulty is that you members have placed a certain Act, and a drastic Act it is, a very advanced Act—but it is in there by legislation, and the members of parliament, while most of them are very, very reasonable, some of them blame the Commission for enforcing their [i.e. the M.P.'s] own Act; that is unfair, insofar as the commission is concerned. We are living up to the provisions of the Act, and, if you desire to change the Act, do so, and we will then just as dutifully carry out whatever provisions the Act may provide.[75]

The tendency to picture themselves as detached administrators, who had the vast duties of the act "dumped" or "imposed" upon them in 1918, was essentially a disingenuous position, as it failed to take into account the important and vital role which they had played in drawing up the terms of the Act in 1917–18. It allowed them, nonetheless, to excuse themselves from adopting a positive leadership stance in the broad area of personnel administration.

114

In startling contrast to its position in 1918, and indeed to that of 1920, the CSC, by the close of the twenties, did not occupy a particularly advantageous or prestigious position within the Canadian federal bureaucracy. Time and time again during these years it had been forced to compromise its freedom of action for the sake of its continued existence or as the price for poor leadership. In many respects the CSC had entered the twenties like a lion, but had gone out like a lamb. Although its existence was no longer a matter of speculation by 1930, it could operate only within limits which were greatly circumscribed from what they had been in 1920. One should, perhaps, not be too surprised at this, given the extent of the legislation passed in 1918. The Civil Service Act was in a sense radical legislation designed to cope with a serious problem. It had obviously raised a host of conceptual problems that had not been thought through properly or even identified. It also imposed upon the CSC—partly through the CSC's own fault—responsibilities which the organization was ill equipped to handle. During the twenties, nevertheless, patronage was largely eliminated, some of the previously prevailing chaos disappeared, an orderly classification of positions was installed, and a superannuation system was established.[76] Placed into context against the historical background and the contemporary political backdrop, these were no mean achievements. It is not really too surprising, then, to find the efforts which the CSC expended in the process had seriously weakened the organization over the long run.

NOTES

1. CSC, *Annual Report*, 1917–18, pp. 9–33. The same fate extended to the Assignment Branch, in many respects merely an extension of the Examination Branch, and was concerned with the administration of the eligible lists and the certification of candidates.
2. Arthur Young and Company, "Civil Service Commission of Canada: Report on Office Organization and Procedure containing Proposed Manual of Rules," November 30, 1918 (typescript), p. 3.
3. Arthur Young and Company, *Report of Transmission to Accompany the Classification of the Civil Service of Canada*, p. 44.
4. Between September 1, 1918, and December 31, 1919, a total of 25,414 persons were appointed to the civil service, of which only 14,536 had been examined by the CSC. The remaining 10,878 persons were appointed by the

departments. CSC, *Annual Report*, 1918–19, p. 23.

5. *Debates*, March 3, 1919, pp. 160–66. See also CSC, *Annual Report*, 1918–19, pp. 19–20.

6. These facts became quite evident in the testimony of various deputy heads before the Spinney Committee of 1921. H.C., Special Committee on Bill No. 122, An Act to Amend the Civil Service Act, 1918 [1921], *Proceedings and Evidence*, testimony of E. L. Newcombe, W. W. Cory, A. Johnston, D. C. Scott, C. Camsell, pp. 9–24, 27–46, 55–76, 189, 191–205. Several other deputy ministers testifying before the Committee at this time did, however, emphatically support the CSC, although they criticized it for the delays in its procedure.

7. Report of the Committee of Deputy Ministers on Civil Service Matters, December, 1922, King Papers, *Memoranda and Notes*, vol. 61, C48184–92.

8. CSC, *Annual Report*, 1920, p. 13.

9. H.C., Select Special Committee on Civil Service and Civil Service Act, 1932, *Proceedings and Evidence*, p. 13.

10. CSC, *Annual Report*, 1919, p. 23; 1921, p. viii.

11. 1921 Committee, p. 51.

12. Memorandum enclosed in a letter from LaRochelle to King, February 5, 1923, King Papers, Corr., Prim. Ser., vol. 89, 75501.

13. Civil Service Research Conference, *Proceedings of the First Annual Convention*, 1924, pp. 104, 123. Hereafter cited as CSRC (1924).

14. 1932 Committee, p. 4.

15. See the proceedings of the CSRC for the period 1924–28. The files of the CSC contained documents entitled "Civil Service Papers" published in Toronto, September 30, 1925, probably by this group. These papers show an overriding concern with the patronage question.

16. CSRC (1924), p. 105.

17. Ibid., p. 111.

18. It is interesting in this regard that the Honourable Newton Rowell was in the forefront of these movements.

19. CSRC, *Proceedings of the Second Annual Convention*, 1925, pp. 138–39. (Emphasis added.)

20. CSRC (1924), p. 104.

21. H.C., Special Committee Appointed to Inquire into the Operation of Chapter 12, 8–9 George V, An Act Respecting the Civil Service of Canada, 1923, *Proceedings and Evidence*, testimony of H. C. House (President of the Associated Federal Employees of Ottawa), pp. 54–55, 285–88.

22. Canadian Tax Conference, *Proceedings*, October 12, 1928 (Toronto: The Citizens' Research Institute of Canada, 1928), p. 68. The Tax Conference, like the Civil Service Research Conference, was an outgrowth of the Citizens' Institute.

23. A letter which King wrote to a Liberal sympathizer in reply to a complaint concerning "a noted dissatisfaction about the civil service" is fairly typical in this regard: "I wish it could be possible to amend, in some way, matters with respect to the Civil Service. Unfortunately, it is only too true that, as respects most appointments, whilst we are a Government in office, we are not a Government in power. Parliament has given the Civil Service Commission far-reaching authority, and has placed its jurisdiction beyond our control, save by amendment of the Civil Service Act. This, I fear, could not be satisfactorily

effected with our representation in Parliament as it is at present." (King to S. J. Johannesson, December 30, 1922, King Papers, Corr., Prim. Ser., vol. 75, 63617–18)

24. 8–9 George V (1918), c. 12, s. 9(1).

25. 1921 Committee, p. 130.

26. 1923 Committee, pp. 937–38.

27. 1932 Committee, p. 100.

28. 1923 Committee, pp. 927–28, 936–38, 943–44. At one point Jameson even suggested that the CSC had no responsibility for reorganization work at all, "not unless we would be asked to undertake it." He later qualified his remark to read that "no attempt to reorganize a department would in my judgment be successful unless you have the cooperation of the officers from the deputy minister down." (P. 937)

29. CSC, *Annual Report*, 1925, p. ix. See also the Reports for the years 1926–32.

30. 1921 Committee, testimony of Roche, p. 127; 1923 Committee, testimony of Jameson, p. 938; 1932 Committee, testimony of C. V. Putman (chief of the CSC's Organization Branch), pp. 175–76.

31. 1923 Committee, *Report*, pp. xii, xiv.

32. Foran to F. A. McGregor, September 17, 1923, King Papers, Corr., Prim. Ser., vol. 86, 72968.

33. Senate, Special Committee on the Civil Service, 1924, *Report*, appendix no. 2, pp. 14–29.

34. Ibid., pp. 7 and 9 respectively.

35. CSC, *Annual Report*, 1924, pp. viii–ix.

36. 1932 Committee, p. 182.

37. Ibid., testimony of G. J. Desbarats and Dr. A. Beauchesne, pp. 362–65, 466.

38. One member of the Lawson Committee suggested that some deputy ministers, unwilling to countenance CSC interference into what they considered to be strictly matters of internal concern, had perhaps used their influence with the ministers to prevent an order in council from passing through the Cabinet. Ibid., p. 176.

39. *Debates*, May 11, 1918, p. 1801. Both A. K. Maclean and Borden made this point.

40. *Debates*, June 25, 1908, pp. 11339–41.

41. Jameson and LaRochelle both resigned from the CSC in 1926. Jameson died shortly after, but LaRochelle wrote several unsuccessful letters to Bennett over a period of years during the Depression pleading for a pension. LaRochelle to Bennett, July 9, 1931; May 4, 1932; April 26, 1933; Bennett Papers, no. 137, 91851–52, 91855–57, 91858. In 1932 an amendment to the Act provided for superannuation arrangements for Commissioners who were civil servants prior to their appointment. But as there were none in this category at the time, it did little to remedy the situation, and Newton MacTavish subsequently petitioned the Government for aid. MacTavish to Bennett, September 4, 1932, and May 5, 1933, Bennett Papers, no. 137, 91867–68 and 91875–77.

42. Walter Turnbull, King's former private secretary, maintains that the short tenure of the Commissioners with nothing to offset it, contributed in a large part to their weakness. Interview.

43. CSC, *Annual Report*, 1917–18, appendices A and B, pp. 37–42.

44. 1921 Committee, p. 364.

45. This was done by statute. 10 George V (1919), c. 29.

46. Although the CSC excluded other positions at this time, they were not too numerous and mostly of a minor nature only. These two bodies were the only large ones exempted.

47. 1921 Committee, pp. 52–53, 139–40.

48. In its Report, the Spinney Committee, summarizing the testimony, noted that when the CSC was asked why certain classes "had not been removed in the same manner and to the same extent as were the position(s) in the Soldiers' Settlement Board and the Department of Soldiers' Civil Re-establishment, the Commission replied, first, that the cases were not parallel and that the Commission was not prepared to admit that their continued intervention was impractical. On the other hand, they were quite sure that it was practicable for them to function with respect to all classes." (1921 Committee, *Report*, p. 414) See also the testimony of Roche, 1921 Committee, pp. 139–40.

49. Roche's capitulation on this point does not appear to be entirely academic or legalistic. The impression one gets from reading his testimony before the Spinney Committee is that he felt the CSC should and could administer examinations to all classes under its jurisdiction quite effectively. The Committee, in fact, had a difficult time convincing him of the need for further exemptions, and it was only as a result of its pressure that he cautiously came around to this position. Foran, on the other hand, seemed to have been more willing to rid the CSC of classes which were difficult to fill and which only brought it criticism. He told the Committee that all countries in the world had exemption lists, and the only reason that the one in Canada was not longer was because classification work had monopolized the CSC's time. It is difficult to judge whether Foran was completely candid or whether his enthusiasm came primarily as a result of the pressure exerted by the Committee. 1921 Committee, pp. 351, 360.

50. Before 1921 the Act allowed the CSC to prescribe how classes were to be dealt with to which it was "not practicable," in the CSC's opinion, to apply the Act. The 1921 amendment changed the wording to read that when the CSC felt it was "not practicable nor in the public interest" to apply the Act, it could exempt the positions in question. The change gave the CSC wider grounds on which to make exemptions. 11–12 George V (1921), c. 22, s. 1.

51. Information on this dispute is drawn from 1923 Committee, pp. 947–54, 963–69.

52. Ibid., p. 950.

53. Memorandum from F. A. McGregor to King, November 12, 1924, King Papers, *Memoranda and Notes*, vol. 61, C48326–27. This particular memorandum to King resulted from a telephone call from Roche to McGregor.

54. "Memorandum . . . Concerning the Salary of the Civil Service Commissioners of Canada," Roche, LaRochelle, Jameson to King, February, 1924, ibid., C48216–17.

55. The Beatty Commission recommended that the salary of the chairman be raised to $9,000 and the other two Commissioners to $7,500. It also suggested that the provisions of the Superannuation Act apply to them and that they be eligible for pension at whatever age they retire. Royal Commission on

Technical and Professional Services, 1929–30, *Report*, p. 28.

56. *Debates*, May 20, 1929, p. 2666.

57. William Smith to Adam Shortt, May 4, 1926, Shortt Papers. See also H.C., Special Committee Investigating the Administration of the Department of Customs and Excise, 1926, *Proceedings and Evidence*, testimony of Jameson and LaRochelle, pp. 1493–1511, 1531–53. Both Jameson and LaRochelle denied that having received the liquor in any way influenced their decision to grant the officer a promotion.

58. One letter King received from the head of the Ontario Federal Liberal party offers a good example of the feeling of party workers at this time: "I most sincerely hope and trust that nothing on earth will be allowed to prevent the immediate filling with two good party men, the vacancies in the Civil Service Commission. If ever a God given chance was thrown at a party by the enemy this is it. No one can ever know how many seats the action of the Commission has cost us during the last four years, but we all know it is a matter of thousands of votes and has deprived us of the work of hundreds of our former best workers who have seen all positions going to Tories." (A.C. Hardy to King, April 30, 1926, King Papers, Corr., Prim. Ser., vol. 132, 112211)

59. By 1931 W. L. Grant had apparently lost his conviction that MacTavish was "one of the chief guardians of the morality of our national administration." In one of a series of three articles in the *Montreal Gazette* in which he attacked the CSC for failing to cope with the need for efficiency and economy, he referred to MacTavish as the "unsuccessful editor of a struggling magazine."

60. Grant also had several unkind words for Tremblay, calling him "the somewhat shopworn private secretary of the Minister of Justice." (Ibid.)

61. Cited in 1932 Committee, p. 738.

62. Ibid., pp. 491–96, 532–39, 541–42, 735–38, 745–50.

63. Ibid., p. 35.

64. Ibid., pp. 491–96, 532–39, 715–65.

65. See, for example, the cases of the St. Arsène post office and the Sutton post office. Ibid., pp. 531–39 and 715–34, respectively.

66. Ibid., pp. 723–24.

67. Ibid., pp. 724–25.

68. This whole issue and its significance are discussed at greater length in chapter 15.

69. 1932 Committee, p. 92.

70. CSC, *Annual Report*, 1930, pp. x–xi; 1931, pp. xx–xxi; 1932, pp. xvi–xvii.

71. See memorandum, July 8, 1922, King Papers, *Memoranda and Notes*, vol. 61, C48161.

72. 1932 Committee, testimony of Roche, p. 17.

73. Ibid., pp. 17, 94–95.

74. H.C., Special Committee on the Operation of the Civil Service Act, 1938, *Proceedings and Evidence*, pp. 246, 526.

75. 1921 Committee, testimony of Roche, pp. 103–4. See also pp. 98–99 and 1923 Committee, testimony of Jameson, pp. 839, 909.

76. See chapter 8 for a full discussion of the superannuation system.

Chapter Six

The Commission as an Arbitration Board: The Salary Issue, 1924–1929

*The Civil Service Commission as an
arbitration board is a farce.*

The Organizer 3 (March, 1926)

ONE FACTOR PLAYED no small part in augmenting the general impotence which characterized the organization by 1930. In the protracted struggle over salary schedules in the years 1924–29, the one occasion on which it risked open conflict with the Government, the Civil Service Commission, for reasons of its own making, came out largely discredited.

When the Arthur Young Company had prepared its original classification scheme for the service, it had based the accompanying salary schedules on conditions as they had existed prior to the war on the theory that these conditions would reappear at the cessation of hostilities. The Government adopted the plan but, owing to the continued increase in the cost of living during the postwar years, found it necessary to supplement the salaries with bonuses each year. This method of rectifying the depressed state of salaries, however, proved fundamentally unsatisfactory. The specific amount of each bonus was predicated on an individual's classification, his present salary level, and his status as head of a household.[1] Because it was founded on the basis of the individual and not the job, the bonus destroyed the principle of "equal pay for equal work," the guiding rule of job classification.

In 1924, a subcommittee of Cabinet dealing with the hours of work and holidays in the civil service expanded its terms of reference to include a consideration of remuneration as a whole, mostly as a result of salary demands from the civil service staff associations. The postal associations, in particular, were vociferous in demanding a salary revision and, to give their demands urgency, were threatening strike action. When the subcommittee made its report, it recommended that the CSC undertake a revision of the salary schedules with a view to eliminating the bonus system.[2] The new schedules, it suggested, should take into account the bonus presently received, the hours of work, holidays, and the superan-

121

nuation plan instituted that year. It also recommended that the revision should be accomplished in conjunction with the deputy heads and the Board of Audit and, as well, that the CSC should allow the staff associations to present their views.[3] Finally, it suggested that the revision begin by considering the salaries of the postal employees and customs officers. The Government looked favourably upon the report and in March directed the CSC by Order in Council to proceed with an immediate salary revision of the entire service,[4] referring it to the report of the subcommittee as a basis for action.

The Act, however, had been somewhat imprecise in defining the CSC's exact role and powers in setting salaries. It had stated that the CSC was to recommend rates of compensation for new classes and was to propose changes in the rates of existing classes, such proposals to become operative upon approval by the Governor in Council. The Government's role in all this was not specifically clear. The Act had been similarly unclear in failing to specify where the initiative should come in commencing a salary revision and in its total lack of guidelines on which to base such a revision.

The Government had partially solved these problems in 1924 by taking the original initiative to begin the revision and by setting the guidelines for the revision through its Order in Council and through its referral of the CSC to the subcommittee report. More importantly, the Government seemed to interpret the Act to mean that the CSC could function as an arbitration board of sorts, attempting to arrive at a settlement between the deputy heads representing the Government, on the one hand, and the civil service associations representing the employees, on the other. Although this interpretation may not have been too clear at first, subsequent events made it quite evident.

The CSC was not entirely clear about the Government's wishes, and on April 4, several days after the Order in Council was issued, Jameson, at the head of a group of deputy heads, met with King and several cabinet ministers to seek further guidelines. It was perhaps characteristic of Jameson that he should want to insure that the CSC would do nothing to displease the Government, but on this occasion he was more accommodating than King wished him to be. Following the meeting he printed and circulated a report of the interview in the form of questions by the delegation of deputy heads and answers by the Government.[5] Although most of the questions and answers were rather innocuous and contained no more information than found in the Order in Council, there were two questions which Jameson might understandably have wished the Government to assume the burden of answering. The first of these was whether the revision might actually scale down the total compensation (salary plus bonus) in some cases. The Government responded that considering the other benefits of government employment which the CSC was to take into account in the revision, this might indeed be the situation in some instances. The second was that one group of postal workers had interpreted the directive concerning consultation with the staff associations as meaning that they were to be granted representation on a revising board or service council. In reply, King made it clear that "it is the desire of the Government that the Service should be afforded an opportunity of making their representations to the Civil Service Commission, but not that any boards should be established."

Several days later, King became rather disturbed when he received Jameson's printed record of the meeting. King had meant the meeting to establish only the broad outlines of policy, and did not want the impression to go abroad that the Government was attempting to influence the concrete terms of the revision. As he informed Jameson:

> I thought I had made it clear at the time of the Conference that the Government did not wish it to be considered that they were expressing any views with respect to the course the Commission should take in the revision of salaries, beyond such as were indicated in the Order in Council and the report of the Sub-Committee. . . . [The] Conference was not to be regarded as in any sense definitive of the duties of the Commission or the lines within which it was to be expected to proceed; rather it was to be considered wholly informal in character. . . .
>
> [In] a word, the Government will expect the Commission to deal with the question of salary revision in accordance with its own interpretation of the terms of the Order in Council and the Report of the Sub-Committee in reference thereto.[6]

King's letter to Jameson indicated that the Government would allow the CSC complete freedom to arrive at its salary recommendations within the broad terms of reference set by the Government. But it was fast becoming apparent that these terms of reference were to include the strong suggestion by the Government that the CSC should endeavour to arrive at some settlement between the postal employees and the Government. King had in part clarified this point at the conference with Jameson and the deputy heads when he informed them of the Government's view of how the CSC should conduct itself in relation to the staff associations. Several days following this conference, King further clarified the Government's position on the matter. The Order in Council and report of the subcommittee had stipulated that the revision was to be accomplished in conjunction with the deputy heads and the Board of Audit. The CSC had subsequently established a committee composed of these two groups to act as a sounding board for the various proposals. The Board of Audit, however, felt that it should play a larger role in the revision than that of consultant and soon refused to participate. When the CSC brought the matter to King's attention on April 9, he replied that the CSC alone was to undertake the revision. The Board of Audit and deputy heads were not to participate directly in the revision, but were to be merely "consulted" by the CSC.[7] In other words, the departments and Board of Audit were to be in precisely the same relation to the CSC as were the staff associations.

The Government's intention in this regard became all the more clear within a few more days. In accordance with the Order in Council, the CSC had first proceeded to consider the salaries of the postal employees and had heard representations from both the associations and the Post Office Department. Meanwhile the situation was approaching critical proportions with the postal associations continuing to threaten strike action if their demands were not met. The Government, however, did not feel it could meet their demands. In the hope of getting the associations to temper their publicly proposed rates, the subcommittee, which had originally suggested the revision, directed the Minister of Labour to approach the CSC with the request that it reveal the Department's proposals to the postal associations. At the very least, this suggests that the Government was of the opinion that the associations and the Department were the only bodies with interests to consider in this particular revision and that the CSC might hopefully reconcile these two camps. The CSC acquiesced in the Minister's request and on April 15 held another meeting at which time the postal associations strongly protested against the adoption of the Department's proposals. The CSC then proceeded to draw up its recommendations.

When the CSC finally submitted the first of its recommendations to the Governor in Council on April 30, the Government was stunned.[8] Maintaining that its recommendations were based on a survey of comparable rates in industry throughout Canada, the CSC completely ignored the Government's intention that it attempt to arrive at a reconciliation between the Department and the associations, and proposed rates which were substantially lower than either those which the employees had demanded or those which the Post Office Department had been willing to offer. It had, in fact, accepted the guideline outlined in the meeting of April 4 with Jameson, which suggested that total compensation might in some instances be reduced, and had applied it to the whole of the postal service: indeed, the proposals, if accepted, would have cost less in total than the present salaries plus the bonus received in 1923–24.[9] Furthermore, the CSC had gone completely outside the terms of reference of the

Order in Council and the report of the subcommittee to establish its own criteria upon which to base the revision. It had declined to alter the minimum rates of the entrance class, as suggested by both the employees and the Department, on the grounds that adequate supply prevailed at the present rates: "It has not been difficult to secure properly qualified postal employees at the minimum salaries presently offered and, for the most part, the Commission's eligible lists . . . contain the names of large numbers of qualified candidates for positions in the postal service in practically every center in Canada."[10]

This situation posed a serious dilemma for the Government. The postal associations had not been satisfied with the Post Office Department's proposals, and the fact that the CSC's salary recommendations were even lower than these could only serve to aggravate an already explosive situation. The Government was naturally eager to avoid any strike action and as a result returned the CSC's submission the day after receiving it. It requested the CSC to reopen the whole question and indicated that Charles Stewart, the Acting Postmaster-General, the officials of the Department, and the postal associations all wished for a further opportunity to make representations on the matter.[11]

The Government's desire was painfully obvious: it earnestly wanted the CSC to arrange a settlement between the associations and the Department. But on May 8 the CSC made it just as obvious that it adamantly refused to act in the capacity of mediator when it returned its original proposals without change to the Government.[12] The CSC had once again heard representations from the associations and the Department, but these had failed to impress it. In the CSC's memorandum of May 8, it defended instead its original position by presenting arguments against the proposals of the other two parties and arguments in favour of its own.[13] The most remarkable statement of the memorandum, moreover, revealed the grounds on which the CSC had refused to act as a mediator in the issue:

> The Civil Service Commissioners further respectfully represent that in recommending to His Excellency the Governor General in Council any changes in the rates of compensation of employees and classes of employees in the Public Service, as from time to time required, they have endeavoured to discharge impartially the duty which they owe to the employees; to the various departments of the Public Service, *and last but by no means least, to the taxpayers of Canada, whose rights and interests the Commissioners deem it no insignificant part of their duty to protect against undue exactions in this behalf.* That the drastic changes in basic rates requested by the Postal Employees as well as

the substantial increase in basic rates proposed by the Department would in their application to the classification of the Public Service as a whole involve a very large annual increase in the expenditure therefor.[14]

Thus, representing the taxpayers, the CSC introduced a surprising new third party, in defence of whose interests it felt justified in refusing to accede to the Government's desire to alter its original proposals.

This placed the Government in a rather preposterous position. Probably for the very first time, the Canadian Government was willing to increase the salaries of a segment of its employees, but was blocked by a body of Parliament's creation which claimed to represent the taxpayers, a group which the Government had always thought it represented. Clearly it was a state of affairs which could not be allowed to stand for long. For the moment, however, the Government attempted only to exert pressure upon the CSC. On May 12, it sent to the Board of Audit the CSC's recommendations and asked for the Board's proposals. The Board eagerly seized upon the opportunity to go through the revision process in which it had earlier refused to participate. After hearing representations from the associations and the Department, the Board presented its proposals on May 28. These amounted to a compromise between those of the CSC and those of the Department.[15]

Once it received the Board's recommendations, the Government invited the Commissioners to attend a meeting of the Privy Council on May 31. Obviously frustrated by the CSC's intransigent position, King, in preparation for the meeting, endeavoured to clarify its exact rights and powers in the whole matter. On May 30, his secretary inquired from the Justice Department whether either the Commissioners or the Governor in Council had the power to set salary rates. The Deputy Minister of Justice replied that the Governor in Council could only approve or reject the CSC's recommendations; he could not amend them.[16] There is no indication of what transpired in the Privy Council meeting, but two days later, on June 2, the Government sent the Board of Audit's report to the CSC with the request that it study the proposals and submit a final recommendation. On June 7, the CSC once again replied that it refused to amend its original proposals. This final report criticized various points in the Board's memorandum and closed by reiterating the CSC's duty to the taxpayers of Canada.[17] With this second failure on the part of the Government to induce it to suggest higher rates, the Cabinet relented and on June 9 approved the CSC's salary proposals for the Outside Service of the Post Office Department.[18] In the fall, the CSC made additional recommendations on the customs service which met with much less resistance and were passed by the Government on October 17.[19] By May of the following year (1925) the CSC completed its proposals for the remainder of the service and on May 6 an Order in Council put these into effect.[20]

The CSC had won the first round. But the Government was not so easily defeated. The CSC's recommendations had caused the Government a great deal of difficulty when the postal associations called a short-lived strike in 1924 to protest the new salary rates. To ease the situation the Government promised to appoint a subcommittee of Council to hear objections of the postal employees to the new rates once the revision was completed for the entire service.[21] In addition, it promised, in June, 1924, to pay sufficient bonuses to ensure that no employee would have his total pay reduced in any manner under the CSC's adopted schedules.[22] This last decision placed the salary situation back where it had been prior to the revision; the Government, in effect perpetuated in June a bonus system that it had set out to terminate only a few months earlier.

Following the completion of the salary revision in May, 1925, the Government, as it had promised, formed a subcommittee under the chairmanship of the Postmaster-General to hear complaints against the revision. It met with the postal associations on June 4 and later received representations from the Civil Service Association of Ottawa. The chief complaint concerned, of course, the modesty of the CSC's salary schedules, as well as the fact that the perpetuation of the bonus for some classes destroyed the principle of "equal pay for equal work." As a result of these meetings, and on the recommendation of the subcommittee, the Government directed the CSC in September, 1925, to proceed with an *upward* revision of the salaries in the postal service. The Government also stated that owing to the interrelationship of the salary schedules, the representations of the CSAO should be considered so that "a comprehensive decision that will apply to the entire Civil Service may be reached at the earliest possible date."[23] The CSC's terms of reference were patently clear: it was to provide a revision of salaries that was to confine itself somewhere between the limits set by the proposals of the various departments and the demands of the associations.[24]

The CSC once again proceeded with the revision and submitted its new proposals for the entire service in April, 1926. Although the precise terms of the recommendations are not clear, the CSC may once again have ventured outside its terms of reference, for the Government objected that the upward revision had not been large enough, particularly in the postal service, and again returned the proposals to the CSC for further consideration. However, the unstable political situation created by the constitutional crisis of 1926 delayed the CSC's reconsideration of the matter; the whole question became an election issue in Ottawa when

King promised that if returned to power he would use "what influence I can to see that the salaries are revised in accordance with the instructions given in the Order in Council, and in a manner which will take account of the position of the Service and the cost of living in our city at the present time."[25]

In the spring of 1927, the CSC submitted its new salary revision to the Governor in Council. Once again, in a fashion that was becoming almost ritualistic, the Government refused to ratify the proposals. On this occasion, though, the reason for the refusal was somewhat different. The associations had argued fairly unanimously for a flat increase of $300 for all classes. The CSC's proposed rates, on the other hand, had attempted to integrate the bonus system into the salaries, and had recommended $60 increases for the lower grades, $120 increases for the intermediate salary ranges, and $180 increases for the senior salary grades.[26] The Government, meanwhile, had referred the question to the subcommittee of Cabinet which produced its own proposals. The subcommittee had felt it best to meet the associations' adamant demand for a flat increase, but had scaled the amount down from the $300 demanded to $120, with an increase of only $60 for those who had received $120 or more in the revision of 1924–25. When the Government returned the CSC's proposals, it also sent along those of the subcommittee and asked for a reconsideration of the whole matter. The CSC, for the first time, acquiesced in the Government's demands and concurred with the subcommittee's recommendations. It subsequently recommended to the Government that the rates proposed by the subcommittee be adopted. The Government, of course, immediately accepted these recommendations.[27]

There are several possible reasons why the Government was able to induce the CSC to accept its wishes in 1927, but had failed to accomplish this two years previously. For one thing, the customs scandal of 1926 which rocked the Government had also penetrated the CSC, leading to the forced resignations of Jameson and LaRochelle. The implication of the Commissioners in the affair greatly discredited the CSC in the eyes of many people and served to weaken its resistance to pressure from the Government. Moreover, by the time of the CSC's capitulation, MacTavish and Tremblay, who later showed themselves unwilling to withstand pressure from any quarter, had already served on the CSC for several months.

Second, and probably more to the point, the CSC, and Roche in particular, had become convinced of the utter uselessness of any further resistance to the Government. Roche later told King that he personally had been opposed to any more increases in the service, "but in accordance with specific instructions contained in P.C. 1644 (September 14, 1925) to provide an *upward* revision of salaries, I became a consenting party to the recent increase of $120."[28] But Roche's conversion did not come lightly. Before he would consent to the revision, he succeeded in obtaining the Government's agreement to an arrangement which would allow the CSC to continue to pose as the protector of the public's purse. The widespread dissatisfaction with the salary revision had resulted in many deputy ministers approaching the CSC to argue for upward reclassification on behalf of individual employees. The great number of these individual appeals had presented a problem to the CSC, and in 1924 it had urged the Government to defer them until the entire revision was completed.[29] Now, in 1927, as the price for capitulating to the Government's wishes, Roche attempted to end all further salary increases by way of individual reclassifications. As he ominously warned King, "The situation is becoming rather serious, and if some effective means are not soon taken to check those requests from the Departments . . . within a few years a reaction will set in and public opinion will condemn both the Government and the Commission, and perhaps the Government more than the Commission, because of the increasing payroll of the Service."[30] The Government subsequently agreed to Roche's terms and tried to put an end to the salary appeals.[31]

THE PROFESSIONAL AND TECHNICAL CLASSES

Roche was aided in his endeavours at this time by the fact that some members of the Cabinet had come to share his economizing attitude. Although the subcommittee of 1927 had agreed with employees' objections to anything but a flat increase, the amount of the increase was a great deal smaller than the associations had demanded. The subcommittee, in addition, had accepted the rationale of the Civil Service Commission for maintaining salaries at their present levels in the entrance classes, and the revision had allowed for no increase in the junior clerical grades. But there was also another reason for agreeing with the parsimonious attitude of the CSC. In dealing with the question of salaries, the subcommittee had come to realize that a crisis situation was fast developing in the professional and scientific classes. While the two major revisions had bettered the position of the whole service in relation to the country, the salaries of these two groups were steadily dropping in relation to their counterparts in industry. A great many scientists, professionals, and technical personnel were forsaking the civil service for more lucrative positions elsewhere. The subcommittee felt this to be a distressing situation and recommended that the CSC proceed at once to consider the salaries of the professional, scientific, and translator classes. The Government concurred and forwarded the request to the CSC in March, 1927.

The recognition of this problem won a degree of support for the CSC's earlier economy-minded attitude. When it continued to refuse to accede to the entreaties of the Postmaster-General to raise the wage level in the postal service, the CSC came under strong criticism in the House.[32] However, on this occasion Finance Minister Robb rose to its defence, using the CSC's own argument that the market supply of labour should determine salaries:

> In the particular service which the honourable gentlemen have been discussing there is a surplus of applications for the positions, notwithstanding the salaries paid. The people who accept those positions know before they enter the service what the salary is going to be; they know what the minimum and the maximum are; they know of the pensions provided for their families. In this particular service there is a long waiting list all the time, but in the technical classes the experience has been that men are being drawn away from the service. Industry is offering them more than the government offers.[33]

Whatever opportunity this support offered the CSC to redeem its earlier failure was soon lost when it submitted its report on professional and scientific salaries in May, 1928.[34] The CSC had once again taken a very broad interpretation of its terms of reference, but on this occasion erred on the side of liberality rather than parsimony. It had used university graduation or its equivalent standing as the basis for distinguishing between the professional and scientific classes and those of the remainder of the service. It also included in this group all persons with a maximum salary range above $4,000 on the theory that they would possibly have professional and scientific personnel working under their direction. The salary increases it recommended for these classes ranged from $240 to $420. The effect of the CSC's report was thus to include in the professional and scientific category men in senior executive and administrative positions.[35] The salary increases would have applied to 2,080 positions and would have cost the Government a total of $750,000 annually.

The presentation of this report raised serious doubts and questions in the minds of some people in the Cabinet as to the competence of the CSC in handling salary matters. Perhaps the salaries of senior administrative and executive personnel did need to be rectified, but the Government had not requested the CSC to investigate these. There is even the suggestion that the Government was willing to grant a larger increase to those persons occupying purely scientific or professional positions than the CSC had recommended. The report had come at the end of a session, and during the recess the Government decided, in view of its objections to it, to remove the question from the hands of the CSC entirely. Accordingly, it created the Royal Commission on Technical and Professional Services under the direction of E. W. Beatty, the President of the CPR, to investigate the remuneration of technical and professional personnel, as well as all officers occupying the rank of deputy minister. When questioned in the House on the matter in the following session, King laid the responsibility for the creation of the Royal Commission directly on the doorstep of the CSC:

> Unfortunately the Civil Service Commission gave an answer that I do not think my hon. friend [Mr. Garland, Bow River] would approve of. Certainly the government did not approve of it. We think that the suggestion of the Civil Service Commission was most inadequate. We felt that the professional and technical men were entitled to much better recognition than the Civil Service Commission was prepared to grant them, and for that reason we appointed a royal commission to look further into the matter.[36]

King also added that he fully expected the Beatty Commission to recommend higher salaries than those submitted by the CSC.

When the Beatty Commission reported in February, 1930, the country had already entered the throes of the Depression; consequently its recommendations were never adopted. The Commission had run into the same problem encountered by the CSC in defining professional and scientific personnel, but had evolved a more acceptable solution. It had, like the CSC, used university graduation as the basis for making a distinction, but had supplemented this with the provision that scientific or professional positions should demand the continued application of technical, scientific, or professional knowledge already acquired by special studies before entrance to the civil service. It also attempted to simplify the numerous classes and grades of a scientific or professional character into two divisions containing a total of seven grades. The cost of the proposed salary increases was estimated to be the same as that contained in the CSC's report, but because of the more restricted definition this amount would be spread among fewer officers.[37]

Despite the failure of the Beatty Commission to produce any discernible effect, its very appointment signalled a defeat of sorts for the CSC. After 1929 it never regained any real ability or power to play a positive and independent role in the establishment of salaries in the civil service. During the 1930s and 1940s the real power in this regard lay with Treasury Board; former CSC employees have recalled that the CSC generally proposed rates that it knew beforehand (as the result of prior informal discussion) Treasury Board would accept. After the CSC's failure in the twenties, this was the only arrangement that would work.

In retrospect it is evident that the factors which combined to cause the CSC to forfeit its positive role in the area of pay determination were intimately connected with those which led to its failure to undertake departmental reorganizations. During the twenties the CSC had endeavoured to switch its primary emphasis away from its role in effecting economy and efficiency in the civil service toward its role in establishing a merit system of appointment and promotion. Its original orientation, though overshadowed, was never altogether lost, however, and the CSC continued to claim that it had a vital role to play in saving money for the country. This explains why the CSC exhibited such an interest in departmental reorganization, even though it never did get around to initiating such work. Similarly, it helps to explain the CSC's insistence that it represented the taxpayers in salary negotiations. Yet it is equally evident that the CSC's attempt to play a vital role in effecting economy and efficiency was simply not based upon a realistic appraisal of its environment. The CSC was incapable, for example, of conducting the departmental reorganizations specified in the Act because of its weak position in the bureaucracy. By the same token, the only way the CSC could have maintained some measure of independence in the salary matter would have been for it to act as an intermediary, aiming at an acceptable balance between the departments and the employees. The Government, in fact, earnestly wanted the CSC to function in this capacity. But by attempting to establish itself as the representative of a third interest (the taxpaying public) in the employer-employee relationship, the CSC found itself in a wilderness with no real base of solid or popular support to which it could appeal. With the rise of the Treasury Board in the 1930s, the CSC's argument fell flat, leaving it for years with a role of nominal power only in the area of pay determination.

The salary issue, thus, is significant in that it served to further weaken the CSC's position in the bureaucracy. Because of its untenable position in the salary negotiations, and as a result of its unsophisticated and unacceptable report on scientific and professional salaries, the Government came to further disregard and disparage the work of the CSC. Not only was this demonstrated by King's statement of 1929, but also by the Government's continual refusal throughout the 1930s to remedy the CSC's weak position. The CSC, by assuming the independent posture it had, became an embarrassment to the Government rather than the neutral body to whom the Government had hoped to turn, at worst, as a convenient scapegoat for unpleasant decisions concerning salaries, or, at best, as an authority on matters of classification and pay problems.

1. At first the CSC recommended the amount of the yearly bonus to the Government, but in 1923, for no readily apparent reason, the Department of Finance took over the bonus recommendation.

2. Memorandum of the subcommittee of Council on hours of work and holidays to the Governor-General in Council, March, 1924, King Papers, *Memoranda and Notes*, vol. 62, C48696–98. See also a similar memorandum, March 26, 1924, C48418–19.

3. The Board of Audit was established by the Government in 1923 to inquire into and report on the system of audit and to make recommendations to effectively control this system. It also was to undertake studies suggested by the Minister of Finance.

4. P.C. 530 (March 29, 1924).

5. "Minutes of Conference of the Sub-Committee of Deputy Ministers (Messrs Bell, Gaboury, Hunter, Jameson) with the Right Honourable W. L. Mackenzie King . . . and Members of the Cabinet," April 4, 1924, King Papers, *Memoranda and Notes*, vol. 62, C48422–24.

6. King to Jameson, April 12, 1924, ibid., C48427–28.

7. Foran to King, April 9, 1924, and King to Foran, April 12, 1924, King Papers, *Memoranda and Notes*, vol. 62, C48425 and C48429–30. The CSC also requested that King change the terms of the Order in Council at this time, excluding the Board of Audit from any part in the revision process. See also G. Beaupré (Secretary to the Board of Audit) to Foran, April 4, 1924, ibid., C48426 and Roche, Jameson, LaRochelle to the Governor-General in Council, June 7, 1924, ibid., vol. 61, C48316.

8. Roche, Jameson, LaRochelle to the Governor-General in Council, April 30, 1924, King Papers, Corr., Prim. Ser., vol. 100, 84700–701. For a more detailed analysis of the CSC's proposals, see memorandum from the Commissioners to the Governor in Council, May 8, 1924, King Papers, *Memoranda and Notes*, vol. 61, C48295–97.

9. The proposals of the Post Office Department would have cost the Government $13,487,000 and those of the employees $15,055,000. The recommendations of the CSC, by contrast, would have amounted to $12,956,000. The present salaries plus the 1923–24 bonus would have cost $13,134,000.

10. The maximum rates proposed for each class were likewise proportionally lower than either those of the Department or the employees.

11. E. J. Lemaire (Clerk of the Privy Council) to Foran, May 1, 1924, King Papers, *Memoranda and Notes*, vol. 62, C48433.

12. Memorandum from the Commissioners to the Governor-General in Council, May 8, 1924, ibid., vol. 61, C48287–304.

13. In defence of its proposals the CSC twice reiterated the claim concerning the availability of labour at the present minimum rates. It also argued that its proposals cost the Government the least of the three different proposals put forward and warned that, because of the interdependence of the classification system, an increase of salaries in one sector would unavoidably necessitate an increase in others.

14. Memorandum, May 8, 1924, King Papers, *Memoranda and Notes*, vol. 61, C48293–94. (Emphasis added.)

15. Board of Audit (G. Gauthier, J. C. Saunders, G. W. Edwards, W. G. Thomson) to the Acting Minister of Finance, May 28, 1924, King Papers, Corr., Prim. Ser., vol. 100, 84957–68. In the estimation of the Board, the demands of the associations were fatuously inflated and so it chose to ignore

these altogether. While it agreed with the CSC that the present minimum rates for the entrance classes were adequate to attract qualified personnel, it disagreed with specific features of both the CSC's and the Department's proposals. Consequently its recommendations sought to strike a mean between these two.

16. F. A. McGregor to E. L. Newcombe (Deputy Minister of Justice), May 30, 1924, and memorandum of Newcombe, May 31, 1924, King Papers, *Memoranda and Notes*, vol. 62, C48430 and C48440.

17. Roche, Jameson, LaRochelle to the Governor-General in Council, June 7, 1924, ibid., vol. 61, C48312–19.

18. P.C. 962 (June 9, 1924).

19. P.C. 10–1818 (October 17, 1924).

20. P.C. 712 (May 6, 1925).

21. "Memorandum re Revision of Civil Service Salaries," (unsigned), May 13, 1925, King Papers, *Memoranda and Notes*, vol. 62, C48642. The memorandum was prepared by King's staff to reacquaint the Prime Minister with the facts of the revision. See also C. Murphy to Dominion Postal Clerks' Association et al., May 7, 1925, King Papers, Corr., Prim. Ser., vol. 121, 102939–44. In his letter Murphy mentions and quotes from an earlier letter in 1924 from Charles Stewart, then the Acting Postmaster-General, to the various postal associations. In this letter, Stewart had promised the formation of the sub-committee.

22. P.C. 1099 (June 27, 1924).

23. P.C. 1644 (September 14, 1925).

24. It appears to have been a well-known fact that the Government wished the CSC to act as an intermediary. The CSC's past performance had failed to satisfy the Amalgamated Civil Servants of Canada, and it maintained that "the Civil Service Commission as an arbitration board is a farce," because no arbitration board would recommend salaries lower than what the employer had offered. *The Organizer* 3 (March, 1926), pp. 3–4.

25. Cited in "Memorandum of the Civil Service Association of Ottawa on the Subject of Salary Revision," December 1, 1926, King Papers, *Memoranda and Notes*, vol. 62, C48657.

26. "Memorandum [on] . . . the Treatment of Civil Service Salaries since 1918," prepared by the CSC Organization Branch for the Beatty Commission (n.d.), files of the Royal Commission on Technical and Professional Services, PAC, vol. 19.

27. P.C. 627 (April 2, 1927).

28. Roche to King, September 20, 1927, King Papers, Corr., Prim. Ser., vol. 148, 125590.

29. Roche to King, August 13, 1924, ibid., vol. 100, 84710–11.

30. Roche to King, September 20, 1927, ibid., vol. 148, 125591.

31. The Government had incorporated Roche's terms into the Order in Council of April 2, but as a result of Roche's later complaints in September that individual appeals were still being submitted, King attempted to bring the matter to the attention of the deputy ministers. King to Roche, September 21, 1927, ibid., vol. 148, 125593 and King to J. A. Robb, September 21, 1927, ibid., vol. 147, 125459–60.

32. *Debates*, May 2, 1929, pp. 2172–97. Part of a letter from the CSC to the Postmaster-General refusing to raise the salaries in the postal service was

read in the House on April 16, 1929. The CSC refused on the grounds that an increase here would upset the relativity within the remainder of the schedules. *Debates*, April 19, 1929, p. 1740.

33. *Debates*, May 2, 1929, p. 2182.

34. Roche, MacTavish, and Tremblay to the Governor-General in Council, May 21, 1928, files of the Royal Commission on Technical and Professional Services, vol. 24.

35. A confidential memorandum on the CSC's recommendations in the Beatty Commission files makes this point. It indicates that the result of the CSC's approach was "to include persons in positions not essentially of a professional or scientific character, for instance, archivists, librarians, publicity men, editors, translators, statisticians, inspectors, officers of the Civil Service Commission, trade commissioners, secretaries, carilloneur, etc. . . . To sum up, the proposal embraces not only purely professional and scientific classes but a considerable portion of the senior executive and administrative staff. In effect, the Commission says that employees in all these classes are underpaid." ("Memorandum re Re-classification of Professional Services," ibid.)

36. *Debates*, June 14, 1929, p. 3767.

37. Royal Commission on Technical and Professional Services, 1929–30, *Report*, pp. 12–13, 16, 24–27, 30. The Commission recognized that its definition did not by any means solve the problem of determining scientific, professional, or technical personnel, and that in the final resort the designation would often be arbitrary.

Chapter Seven

The Thirties: Depression, Austerity, and the Rise of the Treasury Board

And all the time Winnie-the-Pooh had
been trying to get the honey-jar off his
head. The more he shook it, the more
tightly it stuck. "Bother!" he said, inside
the jar, and "Oh, help!" and mostly, "Ow!"
And he tried bumping it against things, but
as he couldn't see what he was bumping it
against, it didn't help him; and he tried to
climb out of the trap, but as he could see
nothing but jar, and not much of that, he
couldn't find his way. So at last he lifted up
his head, jar and all, and made a loud,
roaring noise of Sadness and Despair.

A. A. Milne, *Winnie-the-Pooh*

IN THE 1920s, events in Canadian civil service personnel administration followed a course in many ways determined by factors which were internal in their nature. Developments, it might be said, followed an inner logic; the external environment did not intervene in an obtrusive fashion. The shrinkage of the Civil Service Commission's jurisdiction had been played out on a small stage where the other actors were the Government, Parliament, the departments, and the staff associations. Then in late 1929 came the great stock market crash. The dawn of the 1930s revealed a landscape which had been transformed. As the CSC faltered amid its strange new surroundings, another organization, Treasury Board, found in the arid ground of the Depression a soil in which it could grow and flourish. Personnel administration in the 1930s was dominated by two interrelated developments: the imposition of a general policy of harsh austerity and the rise of Treasury Board from a position of relative insignificance to the status of the chief government control agency.

THE EVOLUTION OF TREASURY BOARD

Before any adequate discussion of the events of the 1930s is possible, it is necessary first to examine the history of Treasury Board before the transformation of the Depression. Described as a "transplant of [a] tradition,"[1] the Canadian Treasury Board was modelled on the British Treasury Board which was something of a mythical body, being neither now nor then a functioning entity, as such, and which has not met as a body in over a hundred years. However, with the usual perspicacity of admiring colonials, Canadians set up in 1867 a board which was to act as an administrative unit with regular meetings, on the assumption that this was the correct "British way" of doing things. Apart from its somewhat doubtful origins, the Board's status as both a committee of cabinet ministers and a bureaucratic agency—in fact until recently an administrative division of the Department of Finance, with its own separate staff of civil servants—has further contributed to its peculiar lack of definition.

Until the Civil Service Act of 1918 the Board was "intimately concerned with appointments to the public service, and with the compensation of its members."[2] Because of its status as a committee of cabinet ministers, the Board was apparently an agency for the administration of the patronage system. In sharp distinction to its modern role as watchdog over the public treasury, the Board does not, on the available evidence, seem to have been at all concerned with economy in government. This role was more congenial to the office of the Auditor-General, and even to certain elements on the Commons Public Accounts Committee.[3] From 1896 to 1905 a Liberal Treasury Board continually overruled a zealous Auditor-General.[4] The Board could thus be viewed at this time as a rubber stamp for cabinet spending decisions. It should, however, be pointed out that the evidence is very sparse indeed, and that any conclusions lie mainly in the realm of speculation.

It does seem clear that while the Board held, from its beginnings, extensive statutory powers, there seems to be little support in the historical record for those commentators or writers who have started from the Board's post-World War II ascendancy and then read such ascendancy backwards into the more remote past. Investigating the Canadian civil service in 1912, Sir George Murray recommended that the Board be abolished, since it appeared to him to serve no discernible purpose.[5] When the Griffenhagen consultants to the Council Subcommittee on Efficiency and Reorganization reported on the workings of Treasury Board in the early 1920s, they noted that "the law specifies numerous specific duties many of which are not important in connection with the work now done," and went on to list a number of statutory responsibilities which were "inoperative"—although it should be noted that included among the "principal tasks actually done" were three areas of personnel administration: superannuation, resignation, and dismissals.[6] Contemporaries seemed more impressed by what the Board did not do than by what it did do.[7] Even World War I did not raise any clamour for a strong centralized control agency for public expenditure.[8]

As popular revulsion mounted against the "patronage evil," and as demands for a merit system increased apace, it became clear that the Board, as a none-too-lively agency directly under the political thumb of the Government, was an unlikely body with which to entrust the preservation of a merit system of personnel administration—if, indeed, many of the reformers had even heard of the Board, since even some senior bureaucrats were unaware of its existence. The 1918 legislation was quite explicit in its award of almost exclusive powers to the CSC. Appointments, selections, examinations, residence requirements, age limits, veterans preference, tenure, promotions, transfers, and classification were all the direct responsibility of the CSC. In line with Treasury Board's basic raison d'être as a control over expenditure, it was, however, stipulated that proposed salary rates could be enacted only with the Board's approval, although the initiative still lay with the CSC. Retirements were to be recommended by the Board.[9]

As previous chapters have made clear, the wide jurisdiction granted the CSC in law was for various reasons eroded severely in the period from 1919 through the 1920s. Yet Treasury Board does not appear to have actively re-entered the personnel picture, except for the revision of the Board's supervision of a large number of positions in the Outside Service exempted from the Civil Service Act in 1922.[10] During the 1920s the pace of Board activity seems indeed to have slackened. In 1918 the Board held sixty-six meetings; by the mid-1920s, a month or more might elapse between meetings, and the retirement of an employee might take two to three months to complete.[11] Certainly a perusal of Treasury Board minutes from the 1920s gives the impression of neither an active nor an influential agency at work: most of the matters dealt with were routine and few had any connection whatever with personnel matters.[12] White quotes the Acting Secretary of the Board in 1929 as admitting that in this era the Board was "relatively quiet, meeting infrequently, and deciding very little."[13] White seems wholly justified in concluding that the Board was "simply an agency which supported and in effect put the government *imprimatur* on anything dealing with establishments and organization."[14] As if in confirmation of this point, the Beatty Commission reported early in 1930 on problems of technical and professional personnel in the federal service without once mentioning Treasury Board.[15]

The coming of the Great Depression suddenly altered this entire situation. To understand why this should have happened, it is necessary to recall the economic philosophy of the times. It is now a tenet of academic orthodoxy among economists that the way to combat a depression is to expand government spending. But five years before Lord Keynes' *General Theory of Employment, Interest and Money* was to appear, along with the revolution in economic thinking which was to follow in its wake, the Conservative party under Prime Minister Bennett suddenly found itself in 1930 in charge of a shattered economy with no better idea of what to do than to fall back on the old verities of austerity and a balanced budget. That this should have been the policy response to the Great Depression is scarcely surprising: the Liberals were fully in agreement and the western protest groups had developed no coherent alternative. The restoration of business confidence was the main theme, and the most extreme austerity on the part of the Government was believed to be the key to such a restoration. Even the academic economists of the day fully backed such views. The Bennett Government accordingly gave highest priority to reducing the cost of Government and balancing the federal budget.[16]

But a policy of stringent austerity no less than a policy of governmental intervention in the economy requires, to be effective, an efficient and flexible bureaucratic apparatus with some capacity to plan intelligently. Much to Bennett's horror, it appeared that the economic and social chaos in the country at large was hardly any worse than the administrative chaos which had reigned in the federal bureaucracy for years insofar as financial control was concerned. Each department had a different accounting system, and the department heads had letters of credit in chartered banks, and often exceeded parliamentary grants.[17]

One of Mr. Bennett's first priorities upon assuming office was to determine the precise financial position of the Government. This proved to be a difficult task. The Department of Finance took six months to answer a request for information on the current state of government finances, and even then could not fully determine the Government's obligations.[18] The direct results of this situation were the creation of the office of the Comptroller of the Treasury and considerable reorganization of the entire machinery of financial administration in the Consolidated Revenue and Audit Act amendments of 1931.[19]

These developments indicate the thrust of the Bennett Government's reforms of the bureaucratic structure. White suggests that prior to the 1930s: "The weakness in the Canadian system was that neither the Treasury Board nor the Cabinet, both of whom were responsible to the House of Commons, took its responsibility in financial accounting seriously. Distribution of government money on a regional basis exceeded the responsibility of proper accounting to parliament."[20]

The terrible exigencies of the Depression put a severe clamp upon easygoing regional pork-barrelling. Further intensifying this trend were what one writer has called Mr. Bennett's "innate tendencies toward centralization," as well as the influence of those around Bennett who strongly urged centralization as an administrative principle.[21] The creation of the Comptroller of the Treasury was one aspect of this tendency. Another aspect of importance was that the removal of most accounting functions from the departments into a centralized agency left behind a great many personnel and pay records, the maintenance of which formed the nucleus of the first departmental personnel administration groups. Until this time, departments had so little authority that personnel matters were looked after, not by specialized officers, but by senior management officials. The beginnings of the departmental personnel function may be thus traced to the establishment of the comptroller's office.[22] This office was not however an isolated development, but rather one segment of a policy of centralized financial control. Of equal or of perhaps even greater importance was the revitalization of Treasury Board. In fact MacLean suggests that in the development of the comptroller's operations, "the major environmental factor was the rise of the Treasury Board to a position of dominance."[23]

The extension of Treasury Board control over departmental expenditures is a complex development, most of which is not strictly relevant to the present account.[24] But in the area of personnel policy, the Board collided with the CSC's actual or potential power under the 1918–19 legislation. To understand this clash it is first necessary to realize that the unemployment and deflation which were endemic to the 1930s had drastically curtailed government revenue. Since the Bennett regime favoured balanced budgets as a means of restoring business confidence, it was necessary not only to freeze expenditures but to actually cut back on them. But since relief and welfare costs were soaring, the Government inevitably looked to its own bureaucratic structure and sought to actively reduce the administrative costs of its own programs. Even here it faced severe limits. As the Prime Minister rather self-consciously explained: "In this period of depression—I hope I am not misunderstood—our civil service is overmanned, but the moment you start to reduce it you then find that you are facing relief for a great number of people that the taxpayers must pay for."[25] What could be done, however, was to cut the salaries of existing employees; freeze the existing establishments in departments; cut down promotions and salary increases; tighten up all the various personnel arrangements which involved the expenditure of public money; and ram through organizational reforms to achieve a higher level of efficiency and cut down waste in the expedition of public business.

Based on its previous record, Treasury Board might have seemed an unlikely tool for such purposes, but Bennett recognized that the Board was an inflatable dragon whose size and prestige depended entirely upon the amount of life breathed into it by the Prime Minister and his Minister of Finance. Bennett, as both Prime Minister and Finance Minister, was able to turn it into a very formidable dragon indeed. One civil servant who worked closely with Bennett recalled that the Prime Minister thought the Board could serve a useful function: "He rode the economy horse hard and ordered the secretary of the Treasury Board to cut all expenditures. Bennett took a personal hand in this as Minister of Finance and he conscientiously attended all Board meetings. There were so many influences to increase both expenditure and the size of the civil service that the Board had to act as a counter influence and it started issuing letters of refusal as well as Treasury Board minutes as authorities."[26]

Bennett was also able to place in the key role of assistant secretary— that is, as the permanent Finance Department official in charge of the Board's administrative staff—a man who very closely mirrored the Prime Minister's own enthusiasm for economy and austerity. W. C. Ronson was an exceedingly capable and hard-working official who seems to have more than fulfilled Mr. Bennett's expectations. One retired official told White that both Bennett and Rhodes, who succeeded Bennett as Finance Minister, wanted Ronson to intervene actively in civil service affairs: "Their instructions to Ronson were 'cut down.' " Another senior official maintained that "under Ronson the Board was usually negatively assertive in one sentence which said 'No.' " Ronson himself, many years after he left the Treasury Board, said that he had conceived of his role as "being sure nothing was put over Treasury."[27]

THE CSC IN THE BENNETT YEARS

The Civil Service Commission was looked upon with far less favour by the Bennett Government. On one level, partisanship may have been a factor. When the new Government came into office in 1930, it saw a CSC composed of a Conservative Chairman who was continually overruled by two Liberal Commissioners. In depression conditions, the demands for party patronage were even more fierce than usual, and the CSC stood in the way of those who wished to reward the party's friends in their hour of need.[28] In all fairness, however, it may be assumed that in the dozen years following the 1918 Civil Service Act, the importance of patronage to the party leadership had no doubt waned. More important in the CSC's decline was the public discrediting of its leadership and the irrelevance of its merit principle ideology to the conditions of the 1930s.

In early 1931 the third major scandal in the CSC's history broke in the press. An employee of the Examination Branch in Montreal, along with some civil servants from other departments, was convicted of accepting sums of money to fix examination results. A second examination scandal—there had been an earlier such scandal only twelve years before— was damaging enough to the credibility of the CSC's role as the upholder of morality in government recruitment, but the scandal eventually drew in the name of Commissioner Tremblay, who had exposed the matter in the first place. It was alleged in various quarters that Tremblay had "framed" the employee in question; while the employee seems to have been quite justly convicted, a sufficient amount of scandalous information about Tremblay's private conduct was circulated to create a generally unsavoury image of the CSC, an image which was in part responsible for the establishment in 1932 of a parliamentary inquiry into the CSC's operations.[29]

The Lawson Committee of 1932 probed deeply and disturbingly into the internal affairs of the CSC. Affairs such as the Kemmis-Simmins fiasco and the attendant adverse publicity in connection with Commissioners MacTavish and Tremblay did little to enhance the public image of the CSC.[30] The Committee finally recommended that, "being of opinion that the position of commissioner . . . calls for very special qualifications, because of the wide powers conferred on such commissioner," Tremblay and MacTavish be removed from office. Chairman Roche, they recommended, should also be retired, but in his case because of advanced age (he was seventy-three).[31] The 1918 Act had specifically stipulated that Commissioners were removable only by the Governor-General on joint address to the Senate and House of Commons, but the Government, indicating its disregard of the Commission's "independent" status, simply passed an amendment to the Act in 1932 which provided that "notwithstanding any provision of the said Act, the members of the Civil Service Commission now in office shall be retired from office by order of the Governor in Council on such date as he shall determine."[32] The following year the Government retired both MacTavish and Tremblay, but let Roche linger on until 1935 to spare him any suggestion that he had been linked with the misdeeds of his two colleagues.[33]

The Government did not, however, draw the obvious lessons from the case of the disgraced Commissioners. To replace Tremblay, the Government chose Adrien Potvin, editor and chief translator of the French Senate debates, apparently on political grounds. As soon as the position of French Commissioner had fallen vacant in 1933, the Prime Minister in effect turned over the power of nomination to his Quebec ministers.[34] The ministers could not agree on a candidate, and various political manoeuvres led to a stalemate. Potvin, the candidate of one faction,[35] seems to have been put forward mainly because of his party loyalty;[36] he had been an unsuccessful candidate in Quebec prior to the war. After a year had elapsed without an appointment having been made, the Prime Minister was still doubtful, referring to Potvin as "not sufficiently industrious to make him a suitable appointee."[37] Bennett's doubts may have been fed by Potvin's curious behaviour when he first applied for the job in 1932. Evidently believing that Bennett was dissatisfied with the CSC, he wrote a memorandum to the Prime Minister pledging that if he was appointed he would vote to abolish the CSC and all its branches. He also pledged himself to carry out "any other instructions that your government may issue, officially or otherwise."[38] Finally, however, Bennett was so flooded with demands for Potvin from French Canadians both inside and outside Parliament that he swallowed his doubts and on October 7, 1933, appointed Potvin as Commissioner.[39] Much more openly political was the appointment of J. H. Stitt in 1935. Stitt was a Conservative M.P. from Manitoba who had carried his seat by a tiny majority in 1930 and was apparently certain to lose in the next election.

Bennett's other appointment was of a different order, however. The naming of Charles H. Bland to the CSC in 1933 and his appointment as chairman in 1935 were not only free from any suspicion of political partisanship, but were well received from all sides. After the dismal record of four successive Commissioners from the outside being disgraced in office, the appointment of a man who had come up through the ranks was welcomed. Bland had entered the CSC in 1909 and, except for a brief period during the war, had spent his entire career in the CSC, where he had risen from the rank of examiner to that of chief of the Examination Branch and assistant secretary of the Commission. Yet if other appointments gave the impression of an organization which was mainly a green pasture for old party war-horses, Bland's appointment was indicative of the faltering independence of the CSC in another, more subtle, fashion. As a career civil servant, Bland was not a strong figure who would face down the politicians. Unlike Roche and Foran, his style was to stay out of the limelight and to avoid open conflict at all costs. He believed in compromise as the essence of success in administration, and thought flexibility to be a cardinal virtue. It was necessary always, he told his staff, to give up "the little things, in order to protect the big things," and to learn how to "horse trade."[40] He had demonstrated his skill along these lines even before he became Commissioner, when in a successful attempt to relieve the CSC from a continuation of the pressure to which it had been subjected over the MacTavish-Tremblay affair, he managed to engineer a deal with the members of the Lawson Committee. Bland arranged to release a large number of postmasterships from CSC control; formerly all post offices grossing more than $400 yearly were under the CSC, but this limit was raised to $3,000 per year under a 1932 amendment passed on the recommendation of the CSC. It has been suggested that this deal earned Bland his appointment the following year.[41] However, it is equally evident that Bland had genuinely impressed the Committee by the breadth of his knowledge and degree of competence, an impression which caused the Committee to single him out in its report for his "ability . . . integrity . . . [and] comprehensive grasp of the principles underlying the merit system and the Civil Service Act."[42] In one sense, Bland's accession to leadership of the CSC could be seen as a strengthening of the CSC as an organization, but in another sense it indicated a less independent policy. In yet another sense, it perhaps weakened the CSC vis-à-vis the Government in the peculiar circumstances of the 1930s, for Bland, a graduate of the Examination Branch, appeared to view the CSC's role as being almost exclusively tied to the administration and preservation of the merit system of selection. The Government, on the other hand, had gone on to other concerns.

The CSC's old merit ideology was suddenly irrelevant to the pressing problems of the 1930s. The problem was no longer how to get people *into* the public service, but how to get them *out*, and how to make the existing employees more efficient and less costly to the Government. In the moral fervour which accompanied the passage of the 1918 legislation, the CSC had been given authority in areas far beyond the recruitment-promotion core of the merit system, but these other areas were seen as ancillary to the essentially *moral* foundation of the CSC's authority. In the 1930s, however, civil service problems were redefined in more strictly economic terms. It followed from this that those functions which the CSC considered most important in terms of its own organizational ideology were no longer considered important in the wider bureaucratic and political environment, while those functions which the CSC considered ancillary had consequently become the most pressing concerns of the time, and in terms with which the CSC was ill prepared to deal, that is to say, in monetary rather than moral terms.

In no area had the CSC's failure to act been more spectacular than in the matter of reorganization. Early in 1931, Prime Minister Bennett rather bluntly gave the CSC the opportunity to, in effect, "shape up" to the new requirements. Writing to Chairman Roche, Mr. Bennett remarked straightforwardly that he wanted to know the reasons for the rapid growth of the civil service each year: "There is nothing in the business of the country to warrant it, and I can only conclude from the most careful consideration that I have been able to give to the matter that the selection of those alleged to be qualified to fill vacancies, has resulted in too many cases of unfit persons being placed in positions of importance. Several instances of this kind have been brought to my attention." In an even blunter postscript, the Prime Minister suggested that "the casual perusal of the numbers now in the Civil Service as compared with the number when the Commission was created will, I think, give any man cause for thought."[43] Roche replied with a memorandum placing the blame for staff increases on the departments which, he stated, initiated all actions in establishing new positions, as well as on the minister concerned, who had to sign any request going before Treasury Board. Roche also pointed out that new positions were created by Order in Council without reference to the CSC.[44] Finally, Roche suggested that considerable savings could be effected by a regrouping of the functions of a number of departments, as well as by the implementation of the Béique Senate Committee recommendations concerning reorganization, but specified that the CSC was still awaiting special instructions along these lines from the Government.[45] Considering that the CSC itself had authored the Béique recommendations referred to, that this had occurred in 1924, and that the CSC had been definitely given the power under the 1918 Act to carry out reorganizational work in the departments, its reply to Bennett constituted a somewhat perplexing performance. It might thus have seemed another ominous portent when the Prime Minister sent a further letter to the CSC asking simply how many employees were on the CSC's payroll and what the cost of maintaining the CSC was to the Government.[46]

Throughout 1931 the CSC made reports on changes in organization. Most of its recommendations were rejected outright by Treasury Board, which suggested forcefully that they were not money-saving recommendations at all, but rather the reverse.[47] The CSC itself replied that it knew how to achieve many economies, but that special authority was needed since previous recommendations had in some cases been ignored by the departments. At the same time the CSC sent a lengthy memorandum to the Secretary of State requesting a specific order in council to enable it to proceed with reorganizational work. The Secretary of State replied that the CSC already had the necessary powers conferred upon it by the Act.[48]

The ambiguity and evasiveness of the CSC's position on its responsibility for reorganizational work was brought into the public spotlight in hearings held by the Lawson Committee inquiring into the civil service in 1932. Committee members, informed by the press of the existence of Treasury Board,[49] began speculating whether such a body might not be better suited to carry out organizational studies. No witnesses were called from the Board, but some officials were asked to comment on the possible transfer of the Organization Branch to the Board. C. V. Putman, chief of the Organization Branch, admitted that at the CSC's current rate of progress, it would take at least 200 years to reorganize the entire service. He added nevertheless that he could not see "any great advantage to be gained by putting it under Treasury Board, *if we could proceed with a vigorous policy of reorganization.*"[50] William Foran's testimony on this point was very curious. He admitted that such a transfer "might be given consideration," but that the present system got better results since the CSC alone possessed an expert staff. He then admitted that the Organization Branch was doing nothing tangible, but added that it would be glad to undertake such work if requested. When asked if it did not already have the power to initiate such work, Foran replied that the Commissioners were "hesitant" and "wary" in the face of possible departmental resistance. When one M.P. suggested that a way out of this dilemma might be for the CSC to make its Organization Branch staff available to the Treasury Board when needed, Foran retorted that the CSC was "the personnel department of the public service and should deal with all matters affecting personnel"; he also denied that Treasury Board had any more authority than the CSC in this regard.[51] It was quite evident that Foran had impaled himself on the horns of a logical dilemma. He was saying in effect that the CSC was the only body which could take charge of reorganization because it was solely within the CSC's authority; yet at the same time he was arguing that the reason the CSC had not in fact undertaken such work was that it did not possess sufficient authority. C. H. Bland, then chief of the Examination Branch, was no more helpful in clarifying this confused situation. While he agreed that CSC recommendations to Treasury Board "could" be accompanied by all the background information collected by the Organization Branch so that the Board might be allowed to make an independent evaluation, he doubted that "Treasury Board can be expected to investigate in detail, or to particularize with the smaller things," although he did admit that the Board "does expect and rightly expects to control the larger questions of expenditure." Bland thus made a somewhat hazy distinction between major reorganizations which the Board might oversee, and the presumably "minor" reorganizations which the CSC might undertake.[52]

The deputy ministers made no attempt to hide their disdain for the incompetence of the Organization Branch, and initiated a great many projects themselves, without reference to the CSC, except for formal approval.[53] Even when requested by the departments, the Organization Branch had appeared unable to provide any reorganizational services.[54] After weighing the evidence, the Lawson Committee censured the Organization Branch:

Your Committee recommends to the Civil Service Commission that ways and means be sought to bring about greater cooperation between the Organization Branch of the Civil Service Commission and departmental officials with a view to obtaining necessary reorganization and equalized classification. In the opinion of your Committee very little has been accomplished by this branch of the Commission which, if strengthened in personnel, would perform a very necessary and useful function in promoting efficiency and economy.[55]

The fact that the order in council requested by the CSC was never granted indicates a want of confidence on the part of the Government and the deputy ministers in the CSC's ability to undertake such work.

The CSC, through its tireless advocacy of the merit principle as its sole ideological justification, had effectively painted itself into a corner. Yet the fact remained that the CSC, with a total staff of 173 at the beginning of 1931, had the potential resources with which to undertake reorganizational work, while Treasury Board, which as late as 1939 had a permanent staff of only 8 persons,[56] was limited in the amount of work it could undertake on a continuing basis. Perhaps because of lingering fears expressed by some members of the Lawson Committee over possible political interference in the civil service if a committee of Cabinet were to control organization, the Committee did not recommend the transfer of the Organization Branch to Treasury Board.

In any event, Treasury Board did not want the Branch under its jurisdiction. As one of Ronson's close colleagues recalled, the Board resisted the idea of assuming responsibility for organizational work: "Ronson did not want it; his main concern was the estimates."[57] Ronson had a low opinion of the abilities of the Organization Branch, but he was also firmly against Treasury Board taking on additional staff, for his Calvinistic attitude toward spending was strictly applied to his own organization. A former Board official recalled: "We had a saying around the Board: 'keep your own skirts clean.' "[58] Viewing the Board as an example of economy in government, Ronson presided over a "tremendously overworked" staff.[59] It would thus seem that Treasury Board was not in fact as viable an alternative to the CSC as might have appeared on the surface.

In the year following the Lawson Committee Report, the CSC was given another chance to produce. Prime Minister Bennett appears to have thought he had found an ally on the CSC in the person of Charles Bland. Working personally through Bland, Bennett undertook to ask Chairman Roche for a series of recommendations for economies in administration. Bennett had apparently considered placing Treasury Board in charge of requesting and considering such recommendations, but accepted Bland's advice against such a course.[60] Bland himself authored a memorandum listing a series of specific efficiency measures which would, he claimed, save the Government one million dollars annually. There was also, he suggested, "the wider question of reorganization of departments which would involve the setting up of an interdepartmental committee."[61] Bennett then requested Chairman Roche to set up such a committee, under the direction of Bland.[62] Five months later, Roche forwarded to the Prime Minister a progress report concerning action taken on Bland's specific suggestions (some successes, some failures).[63] Bennett thanked him for the "very very substantial economies in the operations of the public service." But he was quick to add: "On the other hand, there are those who still complain that we have not accomplished anything like we should have in that regard."[64] As to the fate of the interdepartmental committee and the "wider question of reorganization," there appears to be no further word in the historical record. It is doubtful that its results could have been very spectacular.

In any event, the fact remained that very serious questions had been raised concerning the efficacy of the CSC's holding responsibility for a task so intimately connected with the concerns of the executive power and so important to the public purse—questions that had not been answered in any effective manner by the CSC. In 1935, Ronson, in a Treasury Board memorandum, aptly summed up the case against the CSC in the following terms: given the diffusion of administrative and personnel authority in the federal service, some centralized supervision is desirable. There is no internal incentive toward economy without such supervision. The CSC can however never be expected to operate effectively in this regard for it covers only half the service, and, more importantly, it cannot exercise the necessary authority, for how could civil servants be given the "power to overrule not only the highest Government officials, but also the Government itself, in the matter of numbers of staff required to carry out Government policies?" Ronson concluded that "what seems to be required is an authority offering stout resistance to increases in staff, ever alert for chances to reduce, with all decisions issued by the Government." He therefore recommended the transfer of responsibility for organization from the CSC to Treasury Board, which as a committee of leading cabinet ministers, could exercise the required authority.[65] A few years later, Watson Sellar reiterated the case against the CSC by emphasizing that it held "power without . . . responsibility":

When the Legislature provides that appointments be by tests of qualification and this implemented by an instrumentality of Parliament, no one can take exception; but when the Legislature trenches on the field

149

of the executive government by providing that a body which is not responsible to the executive have the power to organize the machinery for working departments, I think an unwise policy is brought into play. The Executive is responsible for the working of the public service, and should be free to organize as it sees fit.[66]

Organizational work was only one point of conflict between the CSC and the Government in the early 1930s. The Prime Minister ordered that the salaries of all government employees be reduced by 10 percent and frozen. This desperate austerity measure, which affected more civil servants than any other, had a strong impact on their attitude toward the Conservative Government. Another of the blows struck in Mr. Bennett's war against waste in the bureaucracy was an Order in Council of June 14, 1932, which in effect constituted one of the major foundations for Treasury Board's new role in personnel policy known as the staff control regulations.[67] This Order abolished all permanent positions then vacant, curtailed promotions, and set up procedures designed to cut down on the number of temporary employees and to stop, wherever possible, the appointment of additional staff. Salaries could no longer be raised except by promotion, but promotions were, in effect, ruled out except when the deputy head and the minister stated in writing that if a vacant position was not filled "the public interest would suffer." As Ronson testified years later, the Treasury Board was concerned over the CSC's practice of granting increases through reclassifications of duties. "This," Ronson noted dryly, "put a stop to that." He went on: "The whole idea was to obtain economies wherever possible . . . by austere methods; but that is the only way you can get them in the Civil Service."[68] In retrospect, this Order in Council represented a most decisive break with the 1918 Act. Clearly the CSC's responsibility for personnel management was being radically reduced. Yet this change in direction appears to have passed unremarked by outside observers. One month after the Order was passed, a meeting of the Lawson Committee was disrupted when an M.P. read an excerpt from an Ottawa newspaper to the effect that Treasury Board now had more power than the CSC in staffing. The committee members knew nothing of the Order and consternation set in. One member even inquired as to what the Treasury Board was![69]

On July 18, 1932, a Treasury Board minute amplified the staff control regulations by providing for a twice yearly review of staff requirements to determine whether such requirements were justified or whether further reductions might not be made.[70] The following year an Order in Council (apparently on Treasury Board advice) provided for the compulsory retirement of civil servants at age sixty-five, except in exceptional circumstances.[71] Such cases not covered by superannuation would receive a gratuity up to a maximum of six months' salary. Ronson later claimed that 425 civil servants were thus retired and their positions abolished at an annual saving of $827,500.[72] As might be expected in a situation in which so many heads were rolling, a good deal of chaos and confusion developed in the departments. At the end of September the Board itself recognized the ill effects by permitting the CSC to fill vacancies in permanent positions on a temporary basis without the immediate authority of the Board, provided that such action was necessary for efficient administration.[73]

Once the full effects of the staff control regulations were felt, the CSC set up a barrage of complaints. The CSC Annual Report for 1933 is a catalogue of grievances against Treasury Board. It asserted that the service was still "labouring" under the staff control restrictions, and that the CSC had to arrange transfers to meet the needs of departments which the Board had flatly turned down. New appointments to permanent positions were being given only on a temporary six-month basis: "The Commission," the Report commented with understatement, "is not entirely in agreement with the Treasury Board on the value of this practice as an economic measure"; it cited both administrative problems and the destructive nature of such a system on the concept of a career service.[74] The following year the CSC enlarged on the latter point, with regard to the Treasury Board practice of allowing "acting promotions" without salary increases. This was an "eminently unsatisfactory condition of affairs," declared the CSC. "The small economies which are rendered possible by the procedure in vogue in no way compensate for the dissatisfaction and unrest which the policy has caused throughout the Service."[75]

These points raised by the CSC are particularly interesting, since it seems that to a certain extent at least the CSC represented a more employee-centred philosophy of personnel management than the Treasury Board, with more thought given to the implications of policy changes for morale and career development in the service. Another example was the long struggle waged between the two agencies over leave regulations. Treasury Board actions which drastically cut down leave privileges for long-term employees were opposed by the CSC on the grounds that "a leave system based upon length of service, which recognizes the right of an old employee to special consideration . . . tends to earn for the Government at little cost a name for generosity; to provide a comfortable feeling of security among all its employees; and to let each one know where he stands and what can be applied for in case of necessity without any feeling of being dependent upon special grace or favour or made the object of a plea for charity."[76] Treasury Board, on the other hand, never betrayed the slightest concern with employee morale or good human relations. Instead

151

of people, the Board seemed to see only salaries and expenses and to assume that efficiency simply meant cutting costs. Whether cost-cutting alone would increase productivity appears not to have troubled it, for it was almost exclusively concerned with the input side and apparently assumed that the output side would take care of itself.

Unfortunately all the attempts of the CSC to remedy this state of affairs ended in vain. In May of 1933, Secretary Foran addressed a letter to the Board concerning the staff control regulations. Citing the 1918 Act, Foran stated that the CSC had both the responsibility and facilities which the Board lacked, and asked if the CSC might therefore carry out the new regulations without special reference to Treasury Board. It was to no avail. The Board replied that the regulations were to be "strictly" adhered to.[77] There would be no retreat from the Board's new authority.

In the last days of the Bennett Government, some liberalization of the staff control regulations took place. On July 16, 1935, restrictions on permanent appointments and promotions were cancelled.[78] A month later annual salary increases were restored, but while the CSC had recommended increases to all those who had been promoted to higher grades during the period of the staff control regulations, Treasury Board caused this recommendation to be deleted from the Order in Council, and replaced by a provision which limited such increases to those who had rendered "meritorious service" and had increased their usefulness.[79] A further Order in Council two months later appears to have been put forward to mollify the CSC on this point, but since it did not extend to the employees who had been given *acting* promotions—the group which was the CSC's real concern—it in fact did little to heal the wounds.[80]

THE RETURN OF THE LIBERALS IN 1935

The defeat of the Conservative Government in October, 1935, and the return to office of the Liberals under Mackenzie King did nothing to alter the basic direction set by Mr. Bennett in the early thirties. W. C. Ronson on Treasury Board and Watson Sellar in the office of the Comptroller of the Treasury continued to place their considerable influence on the side of austerity and executive control of personnel matters. Once again the acute political vulnerability of Commissioners selected by the Prime Minister became evident. Although Chairman Bland was a career public servant genuinely above partisan suspicions, his two fellow Commissioners were acknowledged political appointments. While the Treasury Board changed its cabinet makeup automatically with the change in government, the Liberal regime faced a Civil Service Commission which appeared to the new ministers to be a Conservative enclave in the very heart of the bureaucracy. The point is not whether such a view was justifiable—in fact it appears to have been a very dubious assumption—but rather that the Government believed it to be true. Moreover, the merit principle in appointments was not really at issue; what was far more important was personnel policy and administration within the federal service, with all the fiscal and economic ramifications of these problems. It was highly unlikely that a new government coming into office after five years in opposition would grant to a Commission—whose membership was appointed by a former government—a controlling voice in the government's own personnel policy.

Early in the life of the new King Government, Treasury Board counterattacks began against the small gains the CSC had made in the dying days of the Bennett regime. In April of 1936 the Order in Council of the previous year, which had cancelled the restrictions on permanent appointments, came under Treasury fire. A new Order in Council, emanating originally from the Treasury Board, provided that the "proportion of permanent employees to the existing basic fixed establishment (normal staff requirements) of any unit of the Public Service shall not at any time exceed 80%, subject to such regulations as the Treasury Board may prescribe." In a phrase most revealing of the Board's managerial philosophy, the Order stated that the cancellation of restrictions on permanent appointments "has resulted in permanent appointments being made without regard to maintenance of a margin of temporary employees to provide for fluctuations in volume of work, greater flexibility of staff and *increased incentive to new appointees*."[81] This latter phrase reveals a management philosophy not unlike the statement attributed to an American capitalist in the 1920s: the greatest spur to efficiency on the part of workers is a long line of unemployed outside the factory gate. It is thus hardly surprising that the Treasury Board appeared to civil servants as representing the Government in its incarnation as "boss" and "exploiter."

In the late thirties, the overt signs of conflict between the CSC and the Board became less apparent. This development has led some to suggest that the conflict itself had begun to disappear, but such a view is difficult to substantiate. The same issues remained between the two agencies, and many of the same personalities continued in office. Treasury Board had unmistakably established its supremacy over personnel questions to the extent that they were money matters. But this was by no means the end of the affair. Almost *all* personnel questions could be viewed as money matters, one way or another, and yet the CSC's statutory authority in the personnel field had not been formally altered. Despite the telling criticisms levelled against its performance, the Organization Branch had not been transferred to Treasury Board. The CSC was perhaps coming to terms with its new role as an investigating agent for Treasury Board, but it would be an exaggeration to assume that this meant an inward reconciliation with the new power relations. If the CSC modified its public stance on interagency rivalries, this could be traced as much to the style of a chairman who was a career public servant as it could to any shift in the CSC's basic ideology and interests. It would, however, be a mistake to argue that the CSC saw the permanent staff of the Treasury Board as its major enemy. Although in the war years which were to follow, the arbitrary exercise of control by the Board's staff was to become painfully apparent to the CSC, in the thirties, the Treasury Board was seen more as a direct instrument of the Cabinet, imposing restrictions which were administered more or less automatically by the staff of the Board, but which had the objective effect of squeezing the CSC out of the picture. In retrospect we can now see that, quite apart from official government policy, the CSC was also facing a *bureaucratic* agency which was confidently feeling its way to a position of control over personnel questions, under the forceful leadership of a public servant, W. C. Ronson, who possessed a very coherent ideology which he wished to impose wherever possible on the conduct of government operations. The CSC stood in the way; therefore, the CSC fell under strong attack.

In all the key areas of conflict, the decisions had gone to Treasury Board. On only one ground did the CSC hold an advantage: numbers. The CSC had managed to retain its relatively large staff, while throughout the thirties, the Board maintained a staff of under ten persons. It was thus necessary for the Board to employ the CSC in an instrumental manner to provide much of the information upon which Board decisions could be based. But that it was Treasury Board which held the better hand can scarcely be doubted. After Bennett's revitalization of the Board, it would be a foolish government indeed which failed to make use of such a direct and practical channel for controlling costs. Certainly Charles Dunning, the new Liberal Finance Minister, was not one to let such an opportunity slip by. In 1938 Dunning began a detailed procedure for tying the estimates to specific departmental needs. This approach, White suggests, "involved increases in the staff of the Board, and eventually economic policy planning to analyse and develop priorities. The change also reflected the increasing importance of the Minister of Finance as chairman of the Board. Both Dunning and Bennett as Ministers of Finance were quick to recognize that in closely controlling the expenditures of the government the chairman of the Board could assume a critical position in the general policy plans of the government of the day."[82] Although this refers to matters not within our immediate range of interest, it does illustrate the impetus that the Board was building up as a control agency. Not only had the austerity policy of the thirties shorn the CSC of most of its positive work as a recruitment and selection agency, but its activities in other areas were falling increasingly under the supervisory control of the Board. As the depression decade drew to a close, it must have been obvious to most observers that the Treasury Board's star was waxing, while that of the CSC—slowly perhaps, and complainingly, but nonetheless surely—was waning.

And yet the Board's success story was not unclouded. The awkward fact remained that it had been quite unable to cut expenditures by a significant amount. In the fiscal year 1932–33, federal expenditures had risen to over $500,000,000. When the desperate measure of slashing civil service salaries by 10 percent was effected the following year, the rate of increase subsided somewhat, but after 1933–34, expenditures began climbing once again.[83] The attempt to balance the government budget during a depression is somewhat equivalent to ordering back the incoming tide—and in the light of Keynesian countercyclical theories, even less sensible. Of course this was not fully understood then, and the Board cannot justly be criticized on this count. But as a consequence, it took on something of the mean and petty fanaticism of a housekeeper doomed forever to chase dirt from an irredeemably dirty household. Despite mounting expenditures in the late thirties, MacLean notes: "Treasury Board had become accustomed to reviewing estimates and supervising expenditures and continued to exercise and expand its control. The Board was so active in these fields that it gained an unsavory reputation in the public service for arbitrarily refusing departmental requests in the interests of its view of good administration. Immediately before and during the war, the Treasury Board exercised what seems to have been too much control."[84]

In August of 1939 the quota restrictions imposed in 1936 were cancelled, and replaced by the provision that permanent appointment could be awarded after one year's temporary employment regardless of the proportion of permanent appointments already on staff in a department.[85] This move seemed to indicate something of a victory for the CSC, but less than a month later, Canada entered World War II and it became, as they say, a whole new ball game.

THE POULIOT COMMITTEE

If the depression years were a dark period for the CSC, the organization's fortunes must have seemed to have reached their nadir in 1938 when a special parliamentary committee was constituted to "enquire into the operation of the Civil Service Act,"[86] under the chairmanship of Jean-François Pouliot—a man once described privately by a member of Prime Minister King's staff as the "clown prince of Parliament." Dawson commented in 1939: "The Committee's first claim to notice must rest on the bizarre character of its proceedings, which have probably never been duplicated in Canadian history. For this the Chairman must shoulder the chief responsibility, for many members repeatedly protested against his eccentric behaviour and the way in which the investigation was being conducted."[87] In four months of hearings, which filled 1,555 pages of testimony, the Pouliot Committee relentlessly harried the CSC in an unsuccessful attempt to uncover the kind of scandals and evidence of incompetence which the Lawson Committee had revealed six years earlier. All of this took place amid a circus-like atmosphere similar to that of American congressional witch-hunts. When the members, and especially the Chairman, were not hurling insults and accusations at CSC officials, they turned their belligerence on each other, and committee meetings often erupted into chaotic quarrelling among the members.[88] The CSC was subjected to constant indignities, such as receiving, at 10:30 A.M., a demand from Chairman Pouliot to provide the Committee with the complete personnel files on every civil servant on a certain page in the government telephone directory—by 11:00 A.M.!

The major target of the Pouliot Committee was the Secretary of the CSC, William Foran. As previous chapters have indicated, Foran was for many years one of the most powerful and influential figures within the Commission. But Foran was more than an *eminence grise* exerting control behind the scenes. To the public and the politicians, he symbolized the CSC. It was Foran's signature that went on all posters advertising examinations, on letters to M.P.'s informing them that a candidate for whom they had written a letter of recommendation had failed to secure the appointment, and on letters to the unsuccessful applicants themselves.[89] In short, Foran was probably more widely known than the Commissioners themselves to the general public, and not always under the best circumstances. Because of his position Foran was often the scapegoat for attacks on the CSC itself. In the examination scandals of 1919 and 1931 unsuccessful attempts were made to link Foran's name with the misdemeanours of others. The Lawson Committee of 1932 recommended that Foran be stripped of most of his power within the CSC.[90] The Pouliot Committee went to inordinate lengths, without any real proof, to give the impression that Foran had secured civil service positions for his relatives.[91] Pouliot himself, engaging in that colourful rhetoric which was one of his more memorable qualities, called Foran the "bully of the Civil Service Commission" who was a "combination of Buffalo Bill and the late Bull Montana of the silent movies . . . the great boss of the Civil Service Commission." He also suggested that the CSC publish Foran's picture on the front page of its annual report.[92]

156

It is somewhat ironic that Pouliot should have termed Foran a "bully," for it was exactly that type of behaviour for which Pouliot himself was most famous. In one instance, Pouliot's own bullying of Foran became a public issue. When Foran attempted to read a statement defending himself in the face of Pouliot's accusations, Pouliot declared him out of order, and stated that his side of the story was of "no interest" and that he, Pouliot, would "not stand for any criticism."[93] The *Ottawa Journal* sprang to the defence of "simple justice and ordinary sportsmanship toward an old member of the public service" and warned that "democracy is not so entrenched in this country that it can afford too many of the spectacles that this particular Committee has provided."[94] Despite Pouliot's lack of repentence, it was clear that he had gone too far.[95] When the Committee met again in 1939, Mr. Pouliot was no longer chairman. Foran retired from the CSC in 1939, having already exceeded the normal retirement age, with an honourable record of over fifty years' service, despite the continual attempts of the politicians to smear his name.

The inquisitions of 1938 were among the sorest trials the CSC ever had to bear. Unlike the Lawson Committee hearings of 1932, no real scandals were ever uncovered. Indeed the somewhat degrading atmosphere probably enhanced, rather than diminished, the image of the CSC. Not for two decades, until 1959, was the CSC ever to be brought before a parliamentary inquiry again, and on this occasion the atmosphere was far more friendly. This contrasts sharply with the two decades between 1919 and 1939 when no less than seven House of Commons committees—not to speak of Senate committees—were launched to investigate the civil service in general.

It was not only Pouliot's excesses which caused Parliament to grow wary of civil service investigations; the leadership of Chairman Bland also did much to carry the CSC safely through the stormy seas. After the scandalous and incompetent behaviour of four earlier Commissioners, Bland's obvious integrity and ability gave the organization a new credibility in the eyes of the Parliament, the Government, and the public. Moreover, Bland's skill at rolling with any punch gave new meaning to the old maxim that a "soft answer turneth away wrath."

The 1930s was simply not a period for bold innovations. The leadership of Charles Bland was well fitted to the circumstances of the era. Wise enough to see the way the winds were blowing, but cautious enough not to overreact, Bland guided the CSC in a manner not unlike the way Prime Minister Mackenzie King guided the country. The internal and external shocks of the early 1930s had left the CSC adrift. The assessment of Michael Oakeshott on politics could, perhaps, be applied to the leadership of Bland: "In political activity, then, men sail a boundless and bottomless sea; there is neither harbour for shelter nor floor for anchorage, neither starting-place nor appointed destination. The enterprise is to keep afloat on an even keel; the sea is both friend and enemy; and the seamanship consists in using the resources of a traditional manner of behaviour in order to make a friend of every hostile occasion."[96] Bland was certainly not an heroic innovator, but he did keep the ship on an even keel. Perhaps no more could have been expected from any man in such a position in those troubled times.

NOTES

1. Such transplants, the same writer suggests, usually turn out to be "pale pernicious reflections of the original body." (E. M. Gruetzer, "The Role of the Treasury Board," November 15, 1961, p. 1, files of the Royal Commission on Government Organization, PAC, vol. 1)

2. C. J. Mackenzie, "The Treasury Board," speech delivered to the Junior Administrative Officers' Course, CSC, December 7, 1947 (mimeograph), p. 10.

3. On this latter point, Norman Ward states that "one could argue with considerable force that for several decades after Confederation the Public Accounts Committee was not merely a device whereby the Parliamentary Opposition sought to scourge the Government, but also an institution through which those middle-class English Canadians who had stern Victorian views about morality in public life, and the necessity for keeping all governmental expenditures to a minimum, sought to impose their views on more happy-go-lucky compatriots with other backgrounds." (*The Public Purse: A Study in Canadian Democracy*, p. 92)

4. Ibid., pp. 102–21. The Auditor-General, J. L. McDougall, was overruled seventy-six times by Treasury Board. On only seven occasions did he sustain his points over Board protests, and all these depended on legal rulings by the Justice Department.

5. *Report on the Organization of the Public Service of Canada*, by Sir George Murray, p. 9. For a fuller discussion of the Murray Report, see chapter 2.

6. "Memorandum Regarding the Treasury Board," n.d., Treasury Board Records.

7. In 1912, Rodolph Boudreau, Clerk of the Privy Council, noted in a memorandum that an Order in Council of October 5, 1896, had provided that questions of appointment, employment, promotion, salary, etc., be referred to

the Treasury Board before being dealt with by Council. Boudreau suggested that "as a matter of practice reference to the Treasury Board usually involves some delay as its meetings are not held so frequently as those of the Privy Council and there is no great saving of labour . . . as reports to the Governor in Council from the Board are usually read at length in Council." (Memorandum by Boudreau, January 30, 1912, Borden Papers, vol. 322, 192086–87)

8. Walter L. White states that the war was not however "a time when the Treasury Board could exercise any real executive authority," and quotes a member of the Finance Department (later to become a secretary of the Board) to the effect that during the war period, "he never heard of the Treasury Board." ("The Treasury Board in Canada," p. 80)

9. Retirement was one personnel matter with which the Board had traditionally dealt. Following the 1918 Act, however, the CSC appears to have abandoned this responsibility. Contrary to the recommendation of the Justice Minister, appeals on retirement decisions were being settled *before* the Board was even advised of such cases. For example, on December 6, 1920, the CSC's recommendations for retirements in the Secretary of State Department were sent directly to Council without Treasury Board intervention. With the return of a Liberal government in 1921, however, all reports had to be recommended by Treasury Board before their submission to Council. R. M. Coulter (Deputy Postmaster-General) to E. L. Newcombe (Deputy Minister of Justice), March 30, 1922, Treasury Board Records.

10. P.C. 1053 in June, 1922, exempted a large number of classes. P.C. 154 of February 7, 1925, authorized the Board to report upon all matters emanating from the CSC or from any department concerning personnel. The more specific references were to the creation, abolition, and reclassification of positions, resignations or dismissals, compensation, approval of temporary establishments and appointments, with regard to positions exempt from the Civil Service Act. Despite its somewhat broad terms, this Order was simply a follow-up to P.C. 1053. Mackenzie comments that "while this order afforded to the Treasury Board the opportunity of effecting more uniformity of treatment in relation to the sections of the Public Service falling outside the ambit of the Civil Service Act . . . the more active participation of the Board in staff cost control may be dated from 1932." (Mackenzie, "The Treasury Board," p. 10) The impression remains that Treasury Board delegated most detailed personnel work on the "prevailing rates" employees to the departments concerned.

11. "Memorandum Regarding the Treasury Board," Treasury Board Records; White, "The Treasury Board in Canada," p. 91; Coulter to Newcombe, March 30, 1922, Treasury Board Records.

12. See Treasury Board Minutes, PAC, 1920–30.

13. White, "The Treasury Board in Canada," p. 90.

14. Ibid., p. 116.

15. Royal Commission on Technical and Professional Services, 1929–30, *Report.*

16. Irving Brecher, *Monetary and Fiscal Thought and Policy in Canada, 1919–1939*; A. E. Safarian, *The Canadian Economy in the Great Depression*; *Report of the Royal Commission on Dominion-Provincial Relations* (Ottawa: King's Printer, 1941), vol. 1. Speaking in 1934, Leonard White noted that "during the three years which have just expired, there has been a very strong reaction against government and government expenditures. This reaction has

159

been somewhat violent." ("Effective Personnel Administration in the Federal Government," Civil Service Assembly of the United States and Canada, *Proceedings of the Twenty-Sixth Annual Meeting* [Chicago, October 4–6, 1934], p. 114)

17. In the years 1920 to 1930 departments spent over $8,500,000 in excess of what Parliament had authorized—a considerable sum in those days. R. D. MacLean, "An Examination of the Role of the Comptroller of the Treasury," p. 48. This situation was not only a natural result of the letters of credit system but also serves to point out the failure of the Treasury Board in the 1920s to exercise the control functions which were theoretically vested in it.

18. The Department formed a committee, headed by Watson Sellar and made up of four other officials, including W. C. Ronson, to provide Bennett with the required information. Ibid., p. 47.

19. Mr. Bennett himself explained the changes two years later: "When we came into power it was impossible to ascertain what the commitments of Canada were, and so legislation provides no right to claim anything due Crown (*sic*) by contract or otherwise unless the contract itself is registered with the Controller of Finance (*sic*) and since that Act . . . we have had a more orderly control of our financial operations and we have been able to tell you with precision at any moment just what our position is." (Quoted in J. R. H. Wilbur, ed., *The Bennett New Deal: Fraud or Portent?* pp. 29–30)

20. White, "The Treasury Board in Canada," p. 139.

21. MacLean, "Examination of the Role of Comptroller," p. 52. The influence of one Harold Daly, variously described as a Conservative "back-room boy" and as a party hanger-on, seems to have been of some importance. MacLean refers to Daly as a "centralizer 'par excellence.'"

22. Interview.

23. MacLean, "Examination of the Role of Comptroller," p. 57.

24. See Walter L. White and J. C. Strick, *Policy, Politics and the Treasury Board in Canadian Government.*

25. Quoted in Wilbur, *The Bennett New Deal*, p. 29.

26. Quoted in White, "The Treasury Board in Canada," pp. 111–12. White also refers to "colourful stories" related to him "of how Prime Minister Bennett used arbitrary methods in Treasury Board meetings to force his sometimes unorthodox views on unwilling ministers during the harsh years of depression." (Pp. 110–11, fn.)

27. Ibid., pp. 121, 123, 121.

28. The Bennett Papers in the PAC are filled with pleas for government jobs during the years 1930 to 1935.

29. Bennett to Roche, January 22, 1931, Bennett Papers, no. 130, 87196; Roche to Bennett, January 23, 1931, ibid., 87199–201; Bennett to Roche, January 23, 1931, ibid., 87202; Memorandum from the Commissioners to the Secretary of State, February 24, 1932, ibid., 87602–10.

30. See chapters 5 and 15.

31. H.C., Select Special Committee on Civil Service and Civil Service Act, 1932, *Report*, pp. ix–x.

32. 22–23 George V (1932), c. 40, s. 13(1).

33. E. H. Finlayson to Bennett, December 1, 1932, and Bennett to Finlayson, December 3, 1932, Bennett Papers, no. 137, 91950–52.

34. Bennett to J. A. LeFebvre, May 31, 1933, ibid., 91921; Bennett to D.

Lecompte, September 23, 1933, ibid., no. 136, 91624; A. E. Millar (secretary to Bennett) to P. G. Davies, ibid., 91619.

35. According to one of Bennett's correspondents, Potvin was promoted by Mr. Arthur Beauchesne, Clerk of the House of Commons: "The apparent stalemate in the appointment of the Civil Service Commissioner from Quebec has no other cause than a little *bargaining* engineered by Mr. Beauchesne, in favour of Mr. Potvin. . . . It is evident that Mr. Beauchesne is wandering a little far outside his official duties." (LeFebvre to Bennett, May 27, 1933, ibid., no. 137, 91920)

36. Onésime Gagnon to Bennett, September 21, 1932, and P. E. Blondin to Bennett, April 7, 1933, ibid., 91905 and 91844.

37. Bennett to Gagnon, May 5, 1933, ibid., 91915.

38. "Memorandum re the Civil Service," Potvin to Bennett, August 27, 1932, ibid., no. 130, 87685–89; see also no. 137, 91890.

39. P.C. 2106 (October 7, 1933).

40. Interview.

41. Interview.

42. 1932 Committee, *Report*, p. x.

43. Bennett to Roche, February 14, 1931, Bennett Papers, no 130, 87221.

44. The CSC had in fact recommended that the civil service regulations be amended so as to place all initiative for staff increases with the CSC. This advice was never followed.

45. Roche to Bennett, February 23, 1931, Bennett Papers, no. 130, 87294; "Memorandum Prepared for the Honourable Prime Minister Relative to Increase in Personnel of the Public Service," ibid., 87223–28; Report to the Governor in Council from the Commissioners, June 21, 1930, ibid., 87242–44.

46. Bennett to Roche, February 17, 1931, Bennett Papers, no. 130, 87226.

47. On December 5, 1931, the Board declared its opinion that, "at this time increases in the cost of personnel in the public service are not in the public interest, whether such increases are effected by the creation of new positions, reclassifications, or promotions." (Quoted in CSC, *Annual Report*, 1931, p. xii)

48. 1932 Committee, testimony of C. V. Putman, p. 175.

49. Ibid., pp. 113–15. The Committee's ignorance concerning the Treasury Board reflects not only the Board's previous insignificance but also the extent to which the executive branch under Mr. Bennett was proceeding without reference to the legislature. From the reminiscences of people associated with the Bennett Government, it may even be doubted that many cabinet ministers were kept informed of the new developments.

50. Ibid., pp. 181, 545–46. (Emphasis added.)

51. 1932 Committee, pp. 96–101.

52. Ibid., pp. 859–61.

53. Ibid., testimonies of G. J. Desbarats and Dr. A. Beauchesne, pp. 362–65, 466.

54. The following case from the Department of National Defence is instructive. In the words of the Deputy Minister: "The department drew up the plan to reorganize and went to the Commission with it. The Commission sent Mr. Boutin down at first and we asked him if he would put forward an organization scheme. He could not. I did not expect he could. Nevertheless I told him, 'The Commission is charged with reorganization. Will you come in and

reorganize this branch? We want it reorganized.' He said, 'What do you want done?' I said, 'I want the Commission to do something.' We did not get anywhere with that; so I said, 'Here is our proposed organization.' He took that ... and after a little over a year the Commission agreed with our recommendation." (Ibid., testimony of Desbarats, pp. 366–67)

55. 1932 Committee, *Report*, p. viii.

56. Mackenzie, "The Treasury Board," p. 14.

57. Interview.

58. Interview.

59. Interview. This same official recalls having to work long hours at the Board on Christmas day.

60. Bland stated, "I leave it to your judgment as to whether or not a Treasury Board Minute would be preferable [to a direct request from the Prime Minister]—personally I think not; also whether or not the recommendations should be sent to Treasury Board or to the Prime Minister—I think the latter course would be preferable." (Bland to Merriam, private secretary to Bennett, April 8, 1933, Bennett Papers, no. 872, 542639)

61. Memorandum from Finlayson to Bennett, May 30, 1933, ibid., 542656.

62. Bennett to Roche, June 1, 1933, ibid., 542671. Bennett suggested to Roche that "it would be quite impossible for you to undertake this work but may I hope that you will give every possible assistance to Mr. Bland, whose work you can greatly help by counsel and advice."

63. Roche to Bennett, October 27, 1933, Bennett Papers, no. 130, 87715–23.

64. Bennett to Roche, February 6, 1934, ibid., 87724.

65. "Supervision of Public Service Organization," internal Treasury Board memorandum prepared by Ronson, 1935, Treasury Board Records.

66. "Memorandum to the Minister of Finance on Civil Service Legislation," from Watson Sellar, March 5, 1938, in "Reasons for Suggesting Changes to the Present Civil Service Act," prepared by Sellar, 1938 (mimeograph), p. 1.

67. P.C. 44/1367 (June 14, 1932).

68. Royal Commission on Administrative Classifications in the Public Service, 1946, "Proceedings," 1, pp. 59–60.

69. 1932 Committee, pp. 113–15.

70. Treasury Board Minute, T. 146585½B., July 18, 1932, Treasury Board minutes.

71. P.C. 1561 (July 31, 1933).

72. Royal Commission on Administrative Classifications, 1946, "Proceedings," 1, p. 64.

73. H.C., Special Committee on the Operation of the Civil Service Act, 1938, *Proceedings and Evidence*, appendix no. 4, p. 496.

74. CSC, *Annual Report*, 1933, pp. 12ff.

75. CSC, *Annual Report*, 1934, p. 13.

76. CSC, *Annual Report*, 1933, p. 13.

77. CSC, *Annual Report*, 1934, p. 15.

78. P.C. 1/2035 (July 16, 1935).

79. P.C. 8/2387 (August 12, 1935).

80. P.C. 11/3161 (October 4, 1935). See also CSC, *Annual Report*, 1935, p. 14. Curiously enough, the CSC also blamed the Treasury Board for delegating it too much work: "With the changes made by the Treasury Board in the

Staff Control Regulations, it has . . . been necessary to investigate a great number of departmental requests for increases in staff, changes in classification, promotions, and reorganizations of methods and establishments. The strain placed upon the senior staff of the Commission has thus been heavy, and it is only through the courtesy and co-operation of other departments, which have loaned employees whenever possible, that the Commission has been able to carry on." (Ibid., p. 5)

81. P.C. 84/978 (April 22, 1936). (Emphasis added.)

82. White, "The Treasury Board in Canada," pp. 112–13.

83. MacLean, "Examination of the Role of Comptroller," p. 58.

84. Ibid. A concrete example may be seen in the provision of desk telephones. Instead of viewing the introduction of telephones as a progressive step forward in the development of an effective communications network, the Board viewed them as a generally unjustifiable luxury, and gave individual consideration to each application. Ronson candidly admitted that whether or not one received a desk telephone depended upon whom one "knew." Royal Commission on Administrative Classifications, 1946, "Proceedings," 1, p. 54.

85. P.C. 2259 (August 11, 1939).

86. 1938 Committee, p. iii.

87. R. MacGregor Dawson, "The Select Committee on the Civil Service, 1938," p. 180.

88. The flavour of such quarrels may be judged from remarks made by Pouliot to one of his colleagues, remarks later struck from the official record: "You are only a trouble maker. You understand nothing. You are dumb. You think you are a superman but you are only a pest in this committee . . . I cannot stand your actions any more." Quoted by Dawson, ibid., p. 181. One member complained to the Prime Minister that conditions in the Committee were "becoming increasingly intolerable," because of the Chairman's "dictatorial" and "offensive" manner, and stated that on one occasion he and another M.P. had to leave the hearings if "they were not to have some violent conflicts with the Chairman." If Pouliot was not put under "control," mass resignations from the Committee were threatened. Confidential memorandum for the Prime Minister, April 7, 1938, King Papers, *Memoranda and Notes*, vol. 155, C111496.

89. This was Foran's own explanation of his unpopularity. 1938 Committee, p. 648. See also the comments of Mr. Spence, M.P., who agreed with this assessment, ibid., p. 947.

90. 1932 Committee, *Report*, p. viii.

91. 1938 Committee, pp. 151–59; 426–46; 510–22.

92. Ibid., p. 647. H.C., Special Committee on the Operation of the Civil Service Act, 1939, *Proceedings and Evidence*, p. 194.

93. 1938 Committee, pp. 648–49.

94. *Ottawa Journal*, May 28, 1938, edit., quoted in Dawson, "The Select Committee on the Civil Service, 1938," pp. 181–82.

95. Pouliot wrote to King that the reason the *Ottawa Journal* defended Foran was because its editor "plays golf occasionally with Mr. Foran." (Pouliot to King, November 14, 1938, King Papers, Corr., Prim. Ser., vol. 257, 218900–901)

96. Michael Oakeshott, *Rationalism in Politics and Other Essays*, p. 127.

Chapter Eight

The Long Road to the
Bargaining Table, 1918–1938

The value of discussions for the staff associations with department heads, Civil Service Commissioners and Cabinet Ministers, has been dependent on the attitude these authorities have taken toward their visitors. Where the attitude has been positive, the discussions have some usefulness. The authorities have frequently decided to take action favourable or partly favourable to the requests of staff organizations. Such decisions have, however, been unilaterally made. . . . Where the decisions have been negative there has seldom been any attempt to deal with the arguments put forward by staff organizations, however carefully and painstakingly these may have been prepared. Representatives of staff organizations in such circumstances have nothing to console themselves with, except memories of interesting visits with eminent personages.

John Mainwaring, "Some Reflections on the Problem of Collective Bargaining by Federal Civil Servants," paper delivered to the Canadian Political Science Association, Ottawa Branch, February, 1957

AS THE THREE PREVIOUS chapters have shown, during the period of the twenties and thirties the Civil Service Commission faced a relatively hostile bureaucratic environment. There was, however, one interest group within the bureaucracy upon which the CSC could rely for strong support on nearly all occasions: the organized civil service. Unfortunately, the staff associations were also the weakest of the interest groups with which the CSC had to deal. Only a portion of the service was at all organized at this time, and the associations which did exist had no direct institutional relationship with their employer. Contact was maintained by means of memoranda delivered through the mail or by infrequent interviews with members of the Government. The associations themselves did not help their weak position by their hopelessly bitter internecine struggles and rivalries. They proved helpful to the CSC, nevertheless, by offering their continual and vociferous support through the worst of its trials.

Staff Associations in the Twenties

The establishment of a strengthened Civil Service Commission in 1918 had strongly commended itself to the associations by assuring them that in the future the advancement of civil servants would be on the basis of merit rather than personal influence. Although the classification of 1919 had strained relationships for a time, the creation of the Board of Hearing and its subsequent work convinced the associations of the CSC's goodwill toward their needs. Once the majority of their objections to the classification were swept away by the Board, the associations positively extolled the virtues of the new merit system. The *Civil Service News*, the joint organ of the Civil Service Association of Ottawa (CSAO) and the Civil Service Federation (CSF), told its readers in 1927 that most civil servants were paid what was due their position, and that if anyone had complaints the solution lay completely in his own hands, for merit was always rewarded: "It is within the power of each and every civil servant of Canada to so perform the duties assigned them (even though they may at present be lowly) with such zeal and regard for efficiency that their very efficiency will produce the result most desired by them—a promotion to higher duties which they can perform with equal energy."[1] This warm support for the system which the CSC administered was further augmented by the CSC's strong and successful advocacy of a superannuation system. The establishment in 1924 of such a system, in many respects far in advance of anything found in the private sector since it provided for equal payments from both employer and employee, was greeted with delight by the civil servants.

It is certainly not surprising, then, that as the CSC began to encounter an increasing amount of criticism from various quarters, the associations identified their own interests all the more closely with those of the CSC. It was simply a case, as the *Civil Service News* said, that the problems which faced both sides necessitated cooperation: "It is the view of the *Civil Service News* that the Service and the Commission must work together if our problems are to be satisfactorily settled, as neither body is likely to make much headway except by co-operation."[2] During the twenties the associations, with one exception, relentlessly pursued this policy, carrying it at times to extreme lengths by assiduously avoiding criticisms of the CSC, justified or not, which would only hand ammunition to those they called the "patronage mongers" in Parliament.

The spirit of partnership on the part of the associations and the CSC was thrown into relief by one civil service association, the Associated Federal Employees of Ottawa (AFEO),[3] who set itself up as the implacable and vociferous foe of the CSC. The AFEO was formed in 1920 from discontented elements in the other associations, primarily the CSAO. By far the most radical, militant, and articulate group, the AFEO was from its inception the only staff association to oppose simultaneously the classification, the Board of Hearing, and the CSC.[4] In the estimation of the AFEO, the first administrative ventures of the CSC had been drastic failures. The initial mistake had actually been made by the Government in 1917 with the appointment to the CSC of three men who had very little knowledge of civil service affairs. This situation had spawned the "second fundamental error," the hiring of "foreign classifiers" to wreck havoc upon the Canadian civil service. The AFEO publicly pilloried the CSC's efforts to remedy the disastrous results of the classification through the Board of Hearing as "nothing more than attempts to patch up a classification which, even as revised, still remains full of inconsistencies." The third great error in administering the service consisted in the reorganization work of the Griffenhagen concern which, to the AFEO, should logically have preceded classification, as prescribed in the 1918 Act, instead of following it. In the eyes of the AFEO these mistakes had exhibited the complete inadequacy of the CSC "to grapple with the problems of Civil Service Administration," and it called for the Government to put an end to the confusion by placing the Civil Service Commission "in charge of the work for which they were originally intended [i.e., making nonpolitical appointments and promotions], instead of allowing them to take to themselves practically the whole control of the Civil Service, through which very frequently indeed they hamper its activities, owing to ridiculous and unnecessary regulations."[5]

The initial point of departure between the AFEO and the other associations seems to have been the attitude adopted toward the creation of a Whitley Council scheme of employer-employee relations. At approximately the same time that the CSC had established the Board of Hearing in Canada, the British government had set up its system of Whitley

Councils to adjudicate disputes and problems in its civil service. The Canadian staff associations quickly became envious of this development, and from 1919 until the Depression their journals and meetings inevitably raised the issue of the desirability of such a system in Canada. The proposal went under various names—National Civil Service Council seems to have been the most popular—but the end in view was always the same in each case: a greater voice in the management of the affairs which urgently concerned their welfare and working conditions.

The difficulty between the AFEO and the other associations revolved around the fact that the CSC's role in establishing salary schedules and determining working conditions was seen to conflict with any system involving full-fledged councils in the true Whitley sense. The AFEO recognized and publicly welcomed this fact. As H. C. House, the President of the AFEO, told the 1923 Committee, "a council introduced leaving the Commission exactly those powers which it now has would be so feeble that it would be almost useless."[6] It was willing to allow the CSC to retain most of its authority in appointments and promotions, but maintained that all its other functions should come under the purview of the civil service council. The CSC, in fact, would become a mere appendage and servant to the council: "In a word their function would be to act as adviser and assistant to promote the smooth functioning of the joint council scheme in so far as it affects the personnel of the federal service."[7] Besides this, the AFEO also attempted to undermine the popular identification of the CSC with the merit principle. Before the 1923 Committee, House charged that the CSC consciously issued releases to newspapers to create the indelible impression on the public's mind that the preservation of the merit system rested solely upon the continued existence of the CSC. House suggested that this was far from being the case, and that a merit system could exist without the CSC.[8]

Apart from the existence of the CSC, the AFEO recognized that government inertia, and perhaps policy, also blocked the establishment of councils, and it attempted to apply direct pressure upon the Cabinet to remedy this situation. The AFEO was affiliated with the Trades and Labour Congress—the only civil service staff association to be labour affiliated until the 1950s—and through this body it managed to enlist the support of labour for its cause. Each year the Congress regularly passed a resolution pledging support for the idea of joint councils in the civil service, and the AFEO quickly brought these to the attention of the Government.[9] To supplement this pressure, the AFEO also managed to induce various labour unions across the country to write letters to the Government in 1920, complaining of its refusal to accede to the demands of the civil servants for the creation of councils. Meighen's Government, however, reacted quite unfavourably to this pressure, and the Prime Minister, through his secretary, wrote an angry letter of warning to the President of the AFEO: "Activity of this kind on the part of your organization is clearly a species of political interference and is not regarded as a conduct consistent with the proper discharge of the duties of the members of your organization to the country. I am therefore asked to advise you that should there be a continuance of this procedure on the part of your Officers the Government will have to consider at once what steps it should take in the public interest."[10] There is no indication whether or not the labour unions desisted from applying such pressure on the Government, but the officers of the AFEO did continue to send numerous complaints and memoranda on the matter of councils to the Government.

In contrast to the AFEO, the majority of other associations placed less emphasis upon the creation of a Whitley-type council than upon the preservation of the CSC with its existing powers. For one thing, the type of council advocated by the AFEO, while similar to the Whitley Council scheme, smacked of trade unionism and of the type of demands for workers' councils made in the private sector. Along with much of the country, they displayed a distinct aversion to such radical demands and resented any comparison with the general labour movement. Second, and more important, all the benefits they had secured in the last few years—the eradication of patronage, a "scientific" classification system, and a generous superannuation plan—had come as the result of the intervention of the CSC. Thus, to them the protection of the CSC was the single most pressing concern of the moment. In this regard they looked upon the AFEO's public criticisms as acts of sheer madness; they only served as encouragement for the mounting number of voices calling for a return to the patronage system. The AFEO's attacks upon the CSC and Board of Hearing had in fact met with a somewhat responsive audience in certain segments of the population, and various newspapers and politicians picked up and reiterated these charges. This had produced a situation in which the CSF and CSAO discerned that "hidebound politicians and party hacks are now conspiring a great moral wrong against the public service and the people of this country."[11] In an effort to remedy the unfortunate effects of the AFEO's criticisms, the CSF and CSAO jointly sent a letter to newspapers across the country emphasizing the cooperative attitude adopted by the majority of civil servants toward the CSC and the Board of Hearing.[12]

The associations' concern with protecting the CSC was significantly reflected in their own proposals and plans for a civil service council. Here they adamantly refused to consider any type of scheme which could not coexist alongside the CSC. At first this attitude arose more from a general ignorance on their part of what the Whitley Council system entailed. To them the whole thing was quite simple: the Board of Hearing had proved such a brilliant success in normalizing staff relations that it constituted conclusive proof that the council system could work in Canada.[13] The earliest suggestions for a council, in fact, simply involved an extension of the Board's authority into other areas, but which would be accomplished in complete cooperation with the CSC.[14] When the CSC's unwillingness to consider any further expansion of the Board's powers defeated this plan, they began to advocate a more traditional, national civil service council system, but a system that in essence was considerably less than a true Whitley system, since it left room for the continued existence of the CSC with its present powers and functions. For example, in testimony before the 1923 Committee, the Amalgamated Civil Servants of Canada (ACSC), a group centred primarily in the West and consisting largely of postal employees, recommended the creation of an elaborate system of councils on different levels. These councils were to be primarily *advisory* in nature and would deal only with the "general principles" governing working conditions, recruitment, hours of work, promotions, discipline, tenure, remuneration, and superannuation.[15]

With time the other associations came to approximate this position. The various associations appearing before the 1928 Committee on Industrial and International Relations, which considered the question of civil service councils, remained divided as to what specific questions the councils would deal with, but argued almost unanimously that the system should function in an advisory capacity, deal with matters of a general nature only, and not transgress any existing statutory enactment.[16] As the Civil Service Federation gladly noted: "While disagreeing among themselves as to details, different bodies showed practical unanimity as to principle. They proved that in no sense did they desire to uproot existing institutions."[17]

By this time the fate of the AFEO served to confirm the associations in their chosen path. For despite its intense efforts, the AFEO's endeavour to secure a Whitley-type council had ended in disaster for the organization. Although it had had a membership of over fourteen hundred in 1923,[18] within a few years it had disappeared. There is, unfortunately, little evidence indicating reasons for its demise. Most likely the AFEO's fate was linked to its decision to reject the CSC and to embrace wholeheartedly a council system. In taking this course, the AFEO had to rely solely upon its ability to bring pressure upon the Government to meet its demands. But it miscalculated both its power to mobilize effective pressure against the Government and the Government's resistance to such "radical" proposals. In any event, whatever the full reason for the AFEO's disappearance, the lesson it provided would certainly not fail to impress itself upon the other associations. Their chosen course of reconciling the desire for a council system with the existence of the CSC, while perhaps less courageous in some respects than that of the AFEO, was certainly much more realistic, given the temper of times.

ATTITUDE OF THE CSC

The insistence of the majority of associations upon the preservation of the Civil Service Commission and its powers is made all the more interesting when it is placed into context against the attitudes exhibited within the CSC toward the associations. These viewpoints, it is important to realize, are understandable only in terms of the differing conceptions among the leadership of the CSC concerning the role which the organization should adopt toward its environment. In 1919, in the classification dispute, and again in 1921, in the exemption issue, the compromise policy of Jameson and LaRochelle had won the day. In both these cases, as well as in the protracted salary issue, Roche had unsuccessfully sought to maintain the CSC's independence from the forces in its environment which would impinge upon its freedom of action. Yet what he had failed to accomplish in these cases, Roche later succeeded in doing in the CSC's relationship with the staff associations.

The differing attitudes among the Commissioners toward the staff associations were clearly exhibited before the 1923 Committee. At that time, both Jameson and LaRochelle supported the demands of the associations for some sort of machinery—either in the form of a national council or appeal board—to adjudicate the complaints and grievances of civil servants.[19] Roche, on the other hand, adamantly opposed the creation of a body to hear appeals. Civil servants, he reasoned, did not require such a body because the very extent and nature of the CSC's powers made such machinery superfluous: "The Civil Service Commission of Canada, I will admit, has been given more jurisdiction over the service than is usual with the ordinary Civil Service Commissions in other countries, and I do not see the same necessity for a board of appeal from the decisions of the Civil Service Commission in Canada, as in Canada the Commission is practically an appointed body." The CSC, as far as he was concerned, had enough power and authority to allow it to function as an appeal board against its own decisions as it was presently doing. He also pointed out that if, for any reason, civil servants were dissatisfied with a ruling of the CSC, "they have the right to have their marks re-read by the Commission." Asked if it would not be better to have someone outside the CSC, like a judge, review such cases, Roche replied: "Well,

I would suggest that the Civil Service Commissioners, with all due modesty, have studied the Act and administered it for seven years. . . . They would be in a better position to judge than a judge outside the service."[20]

What is most remarkable in Roche's testimony is his opinion that the interests of the civil servants were best served and protected through the CSC's impartial administration of the merit system. This attitude would seem to suggest a strong influence from the philosophy of scientific management and its concomitant concept of staff relations, both of which underlay the classification system. In its early days before World War I, scientific management was an extremely employer-centred philosophy. According to its conception of employer-employee relations, employees had rights only by virtue of the position they occupied, not by virtue of their dignity as human beings. In the eyes of the scientific management practitioners, fair and decent treatment of employees had a positive value. But it had a value not in terms of the rights of an employee, but because such conditions contributed to good morale which allowed the employee to apply himself to his job in a better manner. By the same measure, anything which could not be interpreted as conducive to the smooth functioning of the system was considered irrelevant. Passing over into the Canadian civil service through the agency of the classification system, such ideas came to the surface in the Report of Transmission,[21] and seem to have deeply impressed themselves upon Roche, and probably Foran as well. Actually the Report was quite progressive and enlightened as far as employee relations were concerned,[22] but Roche seems to have concentrated on the more paternalistic aspects inherent in the philosophy. To him, civil servants had no prior rights outside the functioning of the merit system. The CSC's sole concern was with the administration of the merit system, and any benefits that it secured for civil servants, which today might look like fundamental rights of employees, could, in the 1920s and 1930s, be justified only on the basis that they contributed to the strengthening of this system.

This philosophy emerged to some extent in the CSC's advocacy of a superannuation system. Superannuation arrangements for civil servants —or, a "scientific system of retirement"—had been strongly advocated in the Report of Transmission in terms of the scientific management philosophy of the day.[23] Similarly, the CSC from 1918 to 1924 made a strong plea for the establishment of a superannuation system, not as an employee right, but as a vital component of the merit system. A "scientific system of retirement" was a natural complement to the "scientific selection" and the "scientific management" of employees:

It is believed that a superannuation scheme will prove one of the best means of promoting efficiency in the service. No system of classification or improved methods of administration will be operated satisfactorily in the Civil Service until a comprehensive measure of superannuation is in force. The advantages of superannuation in the public interest are apparent inasmuch as it relieves the Government of the embarrassment and extravagance of retaining the services of officers who have outlived their usefulness; creates a proper flow of promotions; renders the service more mobile; deters efficient officers from leaving the public service for private employment where emolument and opportunity may be greater; helps to attract a better class of applicants for positions in the service and in general tends to promote efficiency in every way.[24]

The CSC's sponsorship of such policies convinced the civil servants and the associations of its ultimate benevolence toward their needs. But they failed to realize that such benefits were never sought or granted as ends in themselves, but were simply by-products of the merit system. In Roche's view, the merit system and its needs were supreme above all other considerations.

It is not difficult to discern that what constituted the needs of the merit system in Roche's conception did not always involve the best interests of the civil servants. This is nowhere more clearly demonstrated than in his idea that the civil service did not require an appeal board. In fact, apart from the rather dubious practice of a body hearing appeals against its own decisions, the CSC fell far short of operating as an appeal board. CSC regulations limited all communication on questions of appointments, promotions, classifications, increases in salary, and transfers between departments only to the deputy heads of departments. Any individual who attempted to influence a member or officer of the CSC on his own behalf faced the possibility of immediate dismissal from the service.[25] But without any formal procedure for hearing appeals, what constituted the difference between attempted influence and an appeal? All appeals are in a sense an attempt to influence, and the associations and civil servants complained on various occasions that they hesitated to bring individual grievances to the attention of the CSC for fear of possible consequences if misinterpreted.[26] In some instances, as during the salary issue, the CSC even tried to prevent the lodging of appeals through the deputy head in the approved manner. Roche's reason for consenting to the salary recommendations in 1927, it will be recalled, was on the condition that the Government would stop deputy heads from making further appeals for increases on behalf of individual employees. Although his attitude had unfortunate results for civil servants, it eventually gained the upper hand in the CSC. Jameson and LaRochelle retired in 1926, but Roche remained in his position until 1935. As we shall see, Charles Bland, his successor as chairman, was also basically of the same mind as Roche on the matter.

Fortunately for the CSC, its employer-centred ideas matched the general atmosphere of the time and did not dissuade the associations from offering it their continued support. This was perhaps most dramatically shown during the salary issue. Despite their sense of irritation and outrage with the CSC's low salary proposals, the associations managed to contain their anger so that their criticisms never expanded to the point where they questioned the CSC's overall role or its relationship to civil servants. Those associations with postal employees among their membership did criticize its role in setting salaries, but they were generally quick to add that they supported it in all other matters.[27] The simple fact was that the CSC's failure to support the associations on this issue had not been significant enough to outweigh the benefits they received from its presence.

Moreover, their disaffection with the CSC was short-lived, for, in the events that followed, the CSC's earlier reprehensible conduct was largely forgotten. In 1929 much of the salary issue was removed from the CSC's jurisdiction for the time being and handed to the Beatty Commission. But with the single exception of the Professional Institute whose members stood to benefit by the inquiry, the associations felt that the Government had stooped to unfair discrimination by studying only the salaries of the professional and technical employees. Their objections resulted in the reconvening of the Beatty Commission in the summer of 1930 under the title of the Royal Commission on the Public Service, with terms of reference calling for a survey of the entire service. With the change of government in 1930 and the deepening of the Depression, however, the Royal Commission lapsed into inactivity, and was eventually terminated without a report having been made. The spectre of patronage which the associations discerned standing over some of the Beatty recommendations made them doubly wary. The Beatty Commission had suggested, for example, that deputy ministers acquire more authority in making appointments and promotions in the professional and technical classes. The associations, of course, saw the possibility of departmental and political patronage occurring and rallied to the support of the CSC.[28]

THE ASSOCIATIONS AND THE GOVERNMENT

The sense of partnership with the Civil Service Commission on the part of the staff associations stands in sharp contrast to the relationship among the associations themselves. Their dealings with one another were generally marked with a bitterness and rancour which completely prevented them from finding a common meeting ground and from presenting a common front to the Government. This fact contributed no small part to their repeated failure to gain their objectives. For example, in contrast to Meighen himself, G. D. Robertson, the Minister of Labour in the Meighen Government, had looked with some favour upon the creation of advisory councils along the lines of those established in some industries. But he foresaw a problem in that "it would be impossible for an Industrial Council to function so long as the civil servants are divided into factions themselves and are not represented through any one organized medium."[29] The same conclusion was reached by the 1923 Committee. It recommended the creation of advisory councils on the departmental level, but owing to "the diversity of evidence submitted," refused to make any specific suggestions on a national council to deal with more important concerns.[30]

The inability of the associations to act in a concerted manner in this regard allowed the Government to continually hold out the creation of councils as an election plum. King had expressed his sympathy with the council idea during the election campaign of 1921,[31] but his Government had done nothing on the matter. During the election campaign of 1926, King again renewed his interest and promised councils if elected.[32] Again nothing was done. In 1928, J. L. Woodsworth introduced a bill designed to provide for the establishment of a Whitley Council system, together with a board of appeal against suspension, dismissal, or any unjust treatment. The bill was sent to the Standing Committee on Industrial and International Relations which then received delegations from several civil service organizations and reported back favourably on the measure.[33] After the House adopted the Report of the Standing Committee, the Government again moved slowly until a couple of months prior to the general election of 1930. In May it passed an Order in Council creating a Drafting Committee for a National Civil Service Council to be composed of equal representatives from the ten largest staff associations and the Government.[34] A month later it appointed Peter Heenan, the Labour Minister, as the chairman of the Committee and set a meeting for October 7. When Bennett came to power later in the summer, G. D. Robertson once again became Minister of Labour. As the new chairman of the Drafting Committee, he called one meeting for the fall. Later, in his capacity as labour minister, he called several meetings of civil service organizations in which he made it clear that the Government was of the opinion that departmental councils should be established first and the creation of a national council deferred until the success of the former became apparent.[35] Owing to the Depression, however, the scheme was dropped, and no council of any sort was created.

While the associations met with repeated defeat in their attempts to secure an appeal board or council, they did gain a momentary degree of satisfaction in 1928 with the creation of an Advisory Committee on the Superannuation Act. In an ill-concealed attempt to quell discontent over the fact that the Government was obviously not going to act on the Report of the 1928 Committee, King's Government established the Advisory Committee in December, 1928.[36] The Committee was composed of five representatives from the staff side and five nominees of the Government. The associations represented on the Committee, the CSF, CSAO, Professional Institute, Postal Workers Association, and ACSC, were picked by the Government in a unilateral decision. The Committee was to act in an advisory fashion and to report to Treasury Board on matters of a general nature pertaining to the administration of the Act, to specific questions referred to it by Treasury Board, and to proposed amendments to the Act and regulations. Despite the sense of accomplishment and the back-patting that went on in the associations as a result of the creation of the Advisory Committee, dissatisfaction soon set in. The Committee made numerous suggestions, particularly with respect to legislative changes in the Act, but neither Bennett's nor King's Government was prone to accept these changes because they invariably meant increased or wider coverage necessitating greater government expenditures. The dissatisfaction in the service eventually led to the creation of a parliamentary Committee on the Superannuation Act in 1938 which, in turn, produced increased dissatisfaction when its recommendations went unheeded for many years.

DANCING WITH THE DEVIL

During the 1920s the dominant characteristic of the staff associations had been to align their fortunes with those of the Civil Service Commission. This attitude changed little in the early years of the Depression. On the one hand, the Bennett period was marked by renewed demands for political patronage and attacks upon the merit system so that the associations were once again forced to come to the defence of the CSC. In 1931 the Gagnon Bill, which proposed to emasculate the power of the CSC, was introduced by a Conservative member from Quebec and appeared to meet with support from many members of the House. Fortunately, the threat of the bill was effectively diverted by the Prime Minister himself, who authorized the creation of the Lawson Committee to inquire into the proposed changes. By the time the Committee devised its final report, the radical nature of the Gagnon proposal had been dissipated—which is what Bennett had expected since only moderate members had been appointed.[37] Although it would thus appear that the Bennett Government never had any intention of ousting the CSC or the merit system, many persons saw the ugly head of patronage rising again, and the staff associations, as well as numerous other noncivil service organizations and newspaper editorialists, sprang to the defence of the CSC and the merit system.[38]

Perhaps more important in maintaining the associations' support of the CSC was the growing power of the Treasury Board. With the 10 percent cut in the salaries of the civil servants, the Board increasingly became the object of the associations' wrath.[39] By the 1940s, in fact, the Board seems to have displaced the "patronage mongers" as the chief villain of the associations, so that one civil service publication could easily rail against that "sleepless ogre known as Treasury Board."[40] In this state of affairs the CSC, which continually protested that the Board's parsimonious and restrictive policies were detrimental to the merit system, appeared as a welcome bulwark against a Government which seemed to be thrusting ever deeper into the civil servants' already depleted pockets.

Despite their apprehension with the Board, by the middle of the thirties the associations also began to exhibit a growing ambivalence toward the CSC. The opening shot of criticism came over the issue of the Grade IV clerks. The associations strongly protested against the introduction of university graduates at this level, asserting that the creation of a privileged group destroyed the merit principle and hindered the opportunities of regular employees for advancement.[41]

What prevented this issue from becoming merely an isolated case of irritation was the slowly emerging feeling among the organized service that the new Chairman, Charles Bland, was on many occasions all too ready to compromise with such powerful forces as the Treasury Board, the department heads, and the politicians, and was too hesitant in asserting the CSC's independence. As Bland's method of operation began to manifest itself, little by little it forced the realization upon the associations that the CSC had become, through default, as much to blame as any other body for unfavourable conditions in the civil service. In effect, the CSC, the symbol of all that was good and holy, was dancing with the devil himself. As they saw it, it was their duty to redeem the CSC, to destroy this illicit alliance, and to restore the purity of the merit system.

This new mission centred primarily on two problems. The first of these concerned the existence of many anomalies in salaries and classifications as a result of the Depression. The fact that the CSC never used its investigational powers to correct these situations dismayed the associations and weakened their faith in the CSC as the protector of civil servants. The CSC seemed to be acting as a mere errand boy for the departments, closing its eyes to any matters which the department heads did not want changed.[42] The associations also felt that the CSC allowed departmental officials too much leeway in settling promotional ratings, thus opening the back door to "office politics." They believed that both these problems could be solved if the CSC were to resume its rightful place of authority. If it was unable to do so on its own initiative, then Parliament should amend the 1918 Act to give the organization new statutory powers.[43]

The interesting point to note in these criticisms is the extent to which the associations persisted in identifying their fortunes and interests with the preservation of the CSC as the guardian of the merit system. The frustrations and irritations they suffered had once again not proved great enough to induce them to question either their relationship to the CSC or the CSC's relationship to the merit system. Instead, they fell back on the traditional answer that the whole problem could be solved by simply strengthening the CSC. But the old verities were becoming more contradictory and difficult to defend all the time, a fact which was dramatically demonstrated before the Pouliot Committee of 1938.

The requests for a national civil service council and an appeal board had diminished in the early years of the Depression, but were resurrected once again for the benefit of the Pouliot Committee. The President of the Professional Institute, for example, advocated the formation of an advisory service council under which an appeal board would operate. When the Pouliot Committee expressed concern over the fact that such a council might conflict with the powers of the CSC, he explained that it would not deal with specific matters of administration, but rather with "general principles."[44] On all detailed matters the associations would continue to make representations to the CSC. The Institute had unfortunately put little thought into its proposals, and a little probing by the Committee quickly discredited the entire scheme, as well as casting some doubts on the credibility of the Institute's spokesmen.[45] The Civil Service Federation, perhaps learning from the experience of the Institute before the Committee, did not mention the issue of councils, but did stress the need for an appeal board for promotions and other matters. But to the Committee, the CSF was contradicting itself: if, as the associations had testified, the departments played such a large part in promotions, then the CSC could act as an appeal board; if, on the other hand, the CSC was strengthened as the associations demanded, why would they require a separate appeal board?[46] At the same time that they were arguing that the future of the merit system depended on a revitalized, more aggressive CSC, the associations were also demanding for themselves some of the prerogatives which up until then had belonged, at least nominally, to the CSC. When confronted with this evident contradiction, they were unable to put their arguments on a

178

more logically sound basis, and were treated with hostility and derision by the Pouliot Committee.[47]

Regardless of their unfortunate experiences before the Pouliot Committee, the associations did gain one consolation: Chairman Bland agreed that the CSC should establish a promotional appeal board. During the 1920s and 1930s an informal system of meetings between the CSC and the associations had grown up in which the latter were given an opportunity of airing grievances of a general nature. But individual cases were rarely raised, and the CSC retained full discretionary authority in all matters. Although the parliamentary committees of 1923 and 1932 had recognized the justice of the associations' demands for more formal procedures to hear individual grievances, Chairman Roche's belief in the infallibility of the merit system had stood in the way of such machinery. Bland now *appeared* to accept the position of the associations, and thus moved to recapture some of the CSC's fading support from that quarter. In reality, however, it was more in the way of a public relations manoeuvre on behalf of the CSC and the merit system. As Bland explained to the Pouliot Committee:

> The employees, the sixty thousand people in the service, are vitally interested in their chances for promotion in the service. If they do not understand clearly how promotions are made and especially if they feel that they have not been fairly made, it is not going to conduce to the efficiency and morale of that service, and my feeling is that all cases of promotion, particularly in appeal cases, the employees themselves should be given a chance to see how the system works and to make representations if they feel it is not working fairly.[48]

In other words, appeal boards would strengthen the existing system through publicity concerning its operations.

That Bland's acceptance of appeal boards did not mean a real change in outlook in the CSC becomes even more apparent when his cautious behaviour in establishing such boards is examined. The Pouliot Committee had recommended a three-man body, consisting of a nominee of the association chosen by the complainant, a nominee of the CSC, and a nominee of the department concerned. The Committee had also intended that the board would deal with appeals on a number of matters. Bland began instead by testing the concept on an unofficial level on promotional appeals only, with the CSC retaining the authority to decide whether appeals were justified before a board was called. In 1938 only one appeal was heard and was apparently decided in favour of the CSC.[49] Only in the following year did the CSC pass regulations establishing formal procedures. Yet

what Bland gave with one hand he took away with the other: only promotional appeals were to be heard, CSC officials were to decide first if
appeals were justified, and the CSC could reject a decision of the board.[50]
The associations were exceedingly disappointed, and there was even some
consideration given in the CSAO, at least, to refusing participation in such
an emasculated scheme. Finally, however, they agreed to make the best
of a bad situation, and cooperate.[51]

The first twenty years after the passage of the 1918 Act, then, had not
been a period of significant achievement for the civil service staff associations. Although civil servants' actual working conditions—security of
tenure, holiday and leave benefits, pension and insurance benefits—may
have been among the best in the country, the associations had gained no
power to participate in any meaningful way in the decisions taken on these
matters, or on matters regarding their salaries, classification, and other
related issues. At least part of this failure can be attributed to their understandable reluctance throughout the twenties and thirties to separate their
interests from those of the CSC. But it was becoming increasingly evident
that if they were to gain any measure of success, they would soon have
to separate their rights from the interests of the CSC and to enunciate their
demands in terms of their own needs. The associations, nevertheless, continued to steer clear of this course. By 1940 they had become less hesitant
about criticizing the CSC, but they still viewed its preservation with its
current statutory powers as the cornerstone in the establishment of a more
adequate employer-employee relationship. This policy was pursued even
after the disappointment they had received over the matter of appeal
boards, and dominated their demands in the next decade. Only in the
1950s, when it became perfectly clear to them that the CSC was incapable
of effectively resisting the growing power of the Treasury Board, were new
alternatives to their dilemma sought.

NOTES

1. *Civil Service News*, April, 1927, p. 11.
2. Ibid., February 24, 1921, p. 3. After 1927 the *News* became the organ
of the CSAO alone when the CSF established its own monthly, *Civil Service
Review*.

3. The name of this organization was changed to the Associated Federal Employees of Canada sometime between 1921 and 1923. For the sake of clarity, all references to it will use its original title.

4. The attitude of the AFEO toward the CSC is taken from testimony before parliamentary committees and from memoranda sent to the Government. See H.C., Special Committee on Bill No. 122, An Act to Amend the Civil Service Act, 1918 [1921], *Proceedings and Evidence,* testimony of F. W. Patterson, pp. 312–16; H.C., Special Committee Appointed to Inquire into the Operation of Chapter 12, 8–9 George V, An Act Respecting the Civil Service of Canada, 1923, *Proceedings and Evidence,* memorandum and testimony of H. C. House, pp. 288–94, 367–403; AFEO to Meighen, undated (received March 9, 1921), March 22, 1921, and September 16, 1921, Meighen Papers, vol. 18, 10480–86, 10536–43, and vol. 19, 10746–48 respectively.

5. AFEO to Meighen, March 22, 1921, Meighen Papers, vol. 18, 10543.

6. 1923 Committee, p. 379.

7. Ibid., memoranda of H. C. House (read by F. W. Patterson), p. 293. For the full AFEO plans with regard to councils, see the memoranda and testimony of House and the testimony of Patterson before the Committee, pp. 288–403. See also the three memoranda from the AFEO to Meighen cited earlier.

8. See the letter from House to the members of the Committee, along with his testimony, 1923 Committee, pp. 54–55, 285–88.

9. AFEO to Meighen, March 2, 1921, Meighen Papers, vol. 18, 10475–79.

10. Private secretary of Meighen (unnamed) to Patterson, February 23, 1921, vol. 18, 10466.

11. *Civil Service News,* February 24, 1921, p. 2.

12. Ibid., Roche, LaRochelle, and Foran all wrote letters of appreciation to the CSF for its support.

13. The letters to the Government from the staff associations are too numerous to enumerate here, but they can be found in the Public Archives collections of the papers of Sir Robert Borden, Arthur Meighen, and Mackenzie King. The Spinney Committee of 1921 and the Malcolm Committee of 1923 are also full of arguments from the associations for the establishment of a Whitley Council system. Their journals, too, are replete with suggestions and proposals of this kind.

14. The 1920 Annual Report of the CSF made this fact quite evident: "The Executive is convinced that in the extension of this idea [that the Board should hear personal appeals on the departmental level] and the enlargement of duties of the Board to cover other problems lie the solution of many of our difficulties. Your Executive recommends that the plan under which the Board of Hearing functions should be enlarged in scope to take up other Civil Service matters, and that the Board's functions be extended to embrace the smallest units in the Service, all of which is to be in cooperation with the Civil Service Commission." (*Civil Service News,* March 14, 1921, p. 7) See also the testimony of George A. Mountain (President of the Professional Institute), 1923 Committee, p. 264.

15. 1923 Committee, testimony of J. A. Elrick, p. 405.

16. *Civil Service Review* 1 (September, 1928), p. 124. The only association to differ from this approach was the Professional Institute of the Civil Service which did not see the need for a council in the first place. See p. 123.

17. Ibid., p. 118.

18. 1923 Committee, p. 287.

19. Ibid., pp. 878–79, 929.

20. Ibid., p. 844.

21. Explaining the role of working conditions and welfare of employees in the scientific management of employees, the Report stated: "That phase of the employment problem that relates to the improvement of physical and mental conditions affecting the personal efficiency of employees is . . . broad and complex. . . . It involves consideration of all those things that affect directly or indirectly the welfare of employees; *particularly those conditions that have a bearing on their ability to give continuous and contented attention to the tasks that they are employed to perform*." (Arthur Young and Company, *Report of Transmission to Accompany the Classification of the Civil Service of Canada*, p. 59. Emphasis added)

22. Ibid., pp. 60–62.

23. Ibid., pp. 55–57.

24. CSC, *Annual Report*, 1922, p. xiv.

25. This regulation had been embodied in an Order in Council, P.C. 1761 (September 7, 1922).

26. See the letter from the ACSC to James Malcolm (Chairman of the 1923 Committee), undated, *The Organizer* (organ of the ACSC), July, 1923, pp. 1–2. See also H.C., Select Special Committee on Civil Service and Civil Service Act, 1932, *Proceedings and Evidence*, p. 832.

27. *The Organizer*, July, 1924, p. 1 and December, 1925, p. 1. *The Organizer* maintained that the CSC was "not a success" as far as setting salaries was concerned, but otherwise strongly supported it.

28. See, for example, *Civil Service News*, April, 1930, pp. 6–10; *The Organizer*, April, 1930, pp. 5–6.

29. Robertson to Meighen, April 1, 1921, Meighen Papers, vol. 18, 10545.

30. 1923 Committee, *Report*, pp. x–xi.

31. *Civil Service Review* 1 (September, 1928), p. 122.

32. Ibid.

33. Second Report of the Committee on Industrial and International Relations, *Debates*, March 27, 1928, pp. 1725–26.

34. P.C. 970 (May 7, 1930).

35. *Civil Service Review* 4 (June, 1931), p. 72.

36. P.C. 2232 (December 22, 1928).

37. Neither Mr. Gagnon nor an Ontario member, Mr. McGibbon, who had a somewhat similar proposal before Parliament, was named to the Committee.

38. Organizations such as the Canadian Legion and Boards of Trade flooded the Prime Minister's Office with protests.

39. In 1935 the *Civil Service News* told its readers that "a certain uneasiness . . . is inevitable at the prospect that the question of promotions and classifications, with which the Civil Service Commission is charged by statute, is to be removed to the jurisdiction of treasury board. Our members may rest assured that a close watch on the situation will be kept, and the Association will lose no time in taking such steps as may be necessary to protect the interests of those affected." (Vol. 13 [July, 1935], pp. 303–4)

40. *Civil Servants Digest*, May, 1946, p. 2.

41. See chapter 17.

42. H.C., Special Committee on the Operation of the Civil Service Act, 1938, *Proceedings and Evidence*, testimony of Phelan and J. C. Beauchamp, pp. 1353–55; 1368–74; 1410–20. See also "Submission of the Professional Institute to the 1938 Committee," ibid., pp. 1395–1403.

43. 1938 Committee, testimony of Beauchamp and Phelan, pp. 1353–55; 1368–78; 1387–88; 1399.

44. This caused an outburst from Chairman Pouliot, who detected a plea for a "brain-trust," and informed the Committee that "they are all crazy . . . in all countries of the world there are brain-trusts, and the brain-trusts are awful in the United States; and I do not see why we should have them here." (Ibid., p. 1314)

45. One member of the Committee told the President of the Professional Institute: "If you have followed [the Committee's hearings] you would have found out that the commission is required by law to follow out these principles but they do not always do it, they do not always follow out the principles laid down in the Act. There are very few amendments in the Act, it is nearly perfect, only we find that it is not applied. And then witnesses like yourself come before us and complain about the Act and you do not know either the Act or the regulations. How can you expect them to apply them when you yourselves do not know what you are asking for?" (1938 Committee, p. 1311)

46. Ibid., pp. 1388–92.

47. Pouliot later remarked that the President of the Professional Institute had impressed him as a man with "the pride of Il Duce and the ambition of Der Fuehrer. On the other hand, he has the pull of a mountain type locomotive and the brains of a humming-bird." (H.C., Special Committee on the Operation of the Civil Service Act, 1939, *Proceedings and Evidence*, p. 195)

48. 1938 Committee, p. 179.

49. CSC, *Annual Report*, 1938, p. 7.

50. *Civil Service News* 17 (October, 1939), pp. 297–98.

51. The *Civil Service Review* said the CSC explained that the present system should be tried out thoroughly before any changes were to be considered. Resigning itself to the CSC's decision, the CSF, according to the *Review*, "feels that in the circumstances the Commission's suggestion will have to be followed." (Vol. 12 [December, 1939], p. 179)

Chapter Nine
The War Years, 1939–1945

*Underlying developments in the philosophy
of government and the increase in responsibilities of the State produced a challenge
for the Civil Service which, in its magnitude and complexity, was undoubtedly
greater than that faced by any other large
administrative organization in our society.
It is useful to examine how this challenge
was met. Here it is important to recall that
in the first instance it came rather suddenly
at the outbreak of the war. It became
necessary over a very short period to mobilize the entire resources of the country
under the direction of a highly centralized
administrative machine. On the basis of
this overriding national necessity it was
possible to make short cuts, to experiment,
to adopt expedients, to undertake on a
large scale programmes that had never
been tried before, and to enlist the best
administrative talent which would not
otherwise have been available. Under conditions of forced draft, administrative
techniques were tried, perfected, and
proven in a remarkably short time.*

J. J. Deutsch, "Some Thoughts on the Public Service"

WHEN WORLD WAR II began in September, 1939, Canada, not unlike most other countries, was slowly recovering from a decade of economic depression. Underemployed resources remained the fundamental problem

185

facing all levels of government in the country. Unemployment formed approximately 20 percent of the industrial working force or around six hundred thousand persons.[1] Nearly one million people were on direct relief, and unemployed employables on direct urban relief numbered close to two hundred thousand. In short, Canada began a war with a high proportion of her human resources idle or underemployed.

Within eight months this situation changed drastically. The German conquest of the Netherlands, the capitulation of France, and the evacuation of British troops at Dunkirk created heavy demands on Canadian resources for war material to combat the German juggernaut. The spring of 1940 was therefore a period of hectic improvisation. The Federal Government, more than ever before in Canadian history, actively intervened in areas which heretofore were considered the province of the private sector of the economy. Departments, notably National Defence, the Post Office, and Munitions and Supply, expanded at unprecedented speed. The latter Department was perhaps the most classic case in point. Created in September, 1939, a staff of 1,024 persons was assembled within the year. By 1941 this staff had more than doubled, and by 1942 quadrupled (see Appendix, table 1).[2] Ottawa became, in the words of R. MacGregor Dawson, "one great big blooming buzzing confusion."[3] Whereas in the past decade of austerity, one of the main concerns in government personnel administration was how to keep people *out* of the bureaucracy, it now became urgent to keep people *in* their jobs and to search out much needed talent for national emergency service.[4] This fact is dramatically illustrated by the figures presented in table 2 (see Appendix). For the six-year period from 1938 to 1943, total appointments under the Civil Service Act rose from 6,406 to 56,342—close to a tenfold increase!

The heavy influx of personnel to cope with the multitudinous tasks which the Canadian Government had assumed since the outbreak of hostilities created a revolution in customary administrative and personnel practices in Ottawa. The War Measures Act, proclaimed on September 1, 1939,[5] preempted the Civil Service Act of 1918, and administrative innovation of a kind previously prohibited within the civil service became accepted practice.[6] The outstanding example of this kind of innovation was the Department of Munitions and Supply. Dawson noted that this Department, only "a few weeks old with nothing more than a skeleton staff," was handed an "assignment so varied, so novel, so complex" as to dismay "a government department of long standing." Taking note of the heavy influx of staff from private industry, and the creation of a plethora of quasi-independent corporations, Dawson concluded that nothing short of a "Canadian industrial revolution had begun."[7]

This sudden changing of the accepted rules of administrative behaviour was almost certain to create confusion and, ultimately, chaos. Within months after the outbreak of hostilities, the Treasury Board noted the attendant problems of coordination in personnel administration fostered by this period of growth and innovation. The mushrooming agencies, boards, and crown corporations, taking full advantage of the emergency powers granted to them under the War Measures Act and the War Appropriations Act, created a situation where at least fifty different and independent organizations in the public service began hiring personnel and devised their own pay scales at will.[8] Within months after the outbreak of war the Treasury Board moved to fill the vacuum: an Order in Council dated April 19, 1940, directed the Civil Service Commission to investigate and report on all requests for staff. New staff would be selected through the CSC, except where the Board directed otherwise. The Board would review all increases in temporary staff.[9] In a sense, this Order enlarged the CSC's role even beyond its statutory powers, since it was now expected to report on exempt positions as well as those covered by the Civil Service Act. The net effect of the Order in Council, however, was to allow the Board to assume its full statutory powers of control in setting policy on staff and salary increases, utilizing the CSC as an investigating agency to ensure that policy directives were being expedited throughout the public service.[10] Thus, the administrative arrangements for which the Board's senior staff had argued during the thirties became a *de jure* reality during this period of crisis.[11]

In May, 1940, an Order in Council reintroduced the staff control quotas that had been suspended in August, 1939. The Order in Council indicated that the Treasury Board was most concerned that wartime pressures for staff increases should not lead to unwarranted and exaggerated salary increases. The CSC was charged with investigating and reporting to the Board on increases to temporary staff working in units engaged exclusively on war work.[12] A series of Orders in Council after May, 1940, prohibited unrestricted competition for personnel between the departments.[13] Provisions were made for the payment of war duties supplements to temporary employees who were not subject to promotion or reclassification, even though they had, in many cases, assumed increasing responsibility. As one writer has suggested, "The history of salary policy during the remaining years of the war consisted of a series of amendments to this rigid anti-inflationary position."[14]

THE COON COMMITTEE AND THE NATIONAL JOINT COUNCIL

By the summer of 1940 it had become patently clear to the civil service community that the Treasury Board was in the driver's seat in determining virtually all policy in federal personnel administration. As a consequence, the Board was continuously swamped with work. Yet the Assistant Secretary of the Board firmly insisted that only a small staff was required.[15] During the war years, the Board maintained a staff of around thirty persons: eighteen to twenty stenographers, about ten young men who were university graduates in commerce or economics, and the Assistant Secretary.[16] From this small group, approximately seven members concerned themselves with the weighty personnel matters coming under the Board's jurisdiction.[17]

During World War II, Treasury Board's officials deliberately developed an Olympian posture in all their dealings with the civil service. Reasons for policy decisions were never given, and no one on the Board's staff was ever accessible to explain to bewildered civil servants why the Board had refused a particular financial request.[18] In part, this attitude was due to the voluminous amount of work placed before the Treasury Board for deliberation: it became a sheer impossibility to give reasoned decisions for every refusal. The notion that the Board was to be occupied solely with broad policy matters became more apparent than real: of the 92,350 items of business issued by the Governor in Council between August, 1939, and September, 1945, 45 percent were approval of contracts, 50 to 51 percent were other administrative acts such as appointments, refunds, and establishments, and 4 to 5 percent were acts of a legislative or policy character. From this immense stream of formal executive proceedings, 36,148, or approximately 40 percent, were a direct result of Treasury Board's proceedings.[19]

Some Board officials argued that this type of operation was possible because Treasury Board was concerned only with policy issues in personnel administration and not with the minutiae of day-to-day administrative details.[20] Indeed, by 1947 one Board official, C. J. Mackenzie, publicly claimed that by utilizing the Civil Service Commission for the administrative details an increase, and not a diminution, of the central personnel agency's responsibilities had occurred:

> While it may be thought by some that the practice of the Treasury Board in personnel matters departs in some degree from the objectives of the Civil Service Act, it cannot be assumed that the duties and responsibilities of the Civil Service Commission have decreased. The reverse is, in fact, the case. If, as has been noted, certain general policies have been laid down by the Treasury Board in line with government policy, and certain final decisions on staff matters are reserved to the government through the Treasury Board, the necessary investigational functions and the responsibility of recommendation and selection of staff rest primarily with the Civil Service Commission. Not only do

these duties and responsibilities obtain with respect to positions falling within the provisions of the Civil Service Act, but, as a result of action on the part of the Treasury Board, with respect to many exempt positions.[21]

But the situation outlined by Mackenzie was all too obviously one whose logic derived more from the ad hoc compromises made necessary by a long bureaucratic struggle than from any rational overview of a functional distribution of authority.[22] A glimpse of how this modus vivendi actually worked can be obtained from the manner in which the two central agencies handled the payments of war supplements. The Order in Council authorizing supplemental payments to public servants gave the Board the sole authority to expedite the payments, and "if any doubt arises as to the interpretation of any provisions hereof, the decision of the Treasury Board on any such questions shall be final and conclusive."[23] Yet, five years later the Assistant Secretary of the Board, W. C. Ronson, admitted to the Gordon Commission: "For a considerable time we concealed the fact that [the war duties supplements] were all referred to the Civil Service Commission. But I think it is well known now that that is what happens to them. Treasury Board nearly always takes the view of the Civil Service Commission as to the amount of the supplement."[24] This statement emphatically reveals the attitude the Board's officials took toward the CSC: Treasury Board desperately needed the CSC's resources in order to operate effectively. But at the same time the Board wanted it clearly understood that, it, and it alone, was in charge of broad policy, while the CSC was an instrumental agency under the Board's control. The Board's view can be discerned in the following exchange between W. C. Ronson and members of the Gordon Commission:

Sir Thomas Gardiner: But the effect of all this is that the Treasury Board have the final say in regard to the emoluments of civil servants. . . .

Mr. Ronson: That is correct, yes . . . Treasury Board, acting in nearly all cases on advice from the Civil Service Commission.

The Chairman: You have to use their machinery for investigation, and so on?

Mr. Ronson: Yes.

The Chairman: You have not any machinery of your own for that sort of thing?

Mr. Ronson: No, we have none at all. That applies, of course, to the areas which are under the Civil Service Act, and not to [the] exempted areas. . . .

Sir Thomas Gardiner: I suppose that from time to time differences of opinion develop between the department primarily concerned and the Civil Service Commission on the one hand, and Treasury Board on the other?

Mr. Ronson: Yes, that happens frequently.

Sir Thomas Gardiner: It is inevitable, human nature being what it is.

Mr. Ronson: Yes.

Sir Thomas Gardiner: What happens then?

Mr. Ronson: Treasury Board has the final say.

The Chairman: Let us suppose the Department says they need so many people, of such-and-such a class, that they are backed up by the Civil Service Commission, and so on. How can you do anything about it?

Mr. Ronson: It is a very exceptional circumstance that the Treasury Board would reverse decisions of that kind. However, I have a very keen recollection a few years ago of a department recommending and insisting that they needed 40 additional clerks, before the war. The Civil Service Commission concurred in it, and Treasury Board flatly refused to pass it. That was that.

Sir Thomas Gardiner: But then if the head of the department says, "if you will not give me 40 clerks, I cannot do the work," what do you do then?

Mr. Ronson: That is the reason for that arrangement. Treasury Board can still say, "You can get along." But the Civil Service Commission cannot say that, because they are civil servants themselves.

Sir Thomas Gardiner: When you say, "You can get along" do you mean, "You must get along"?

Mr. Ronson: Yes.[25]

This tight-fisted Treasury control of monetary and fiscal matters ran counter to the then "radical" Keynesian economics which offered a completely new line of thinking with respect to the causes of economic fluctuations and of unemployment, the determinants of the level of economic activity, and policy prescriptions to correct some of the inherent defects of economic systems.[26] Although Lord Keynes was a frequent visitor to

Ottawa during the war on official business, only a handful of senior public servants were aware of the new Keynesian economics, which was to revolutionize the Government's own conception of its economic role by the end of the war. There was no deep appreciation on the Treasury Board staff of how government expenditure could be utilized as an instrument of government policy in maintaining full employment. Instead the Board stuck closely to the old philosophy of holding down spending regardless of the employment situation.[27]

To place the sole responsibility of this rigid pre-Keynesian economics on the shoulders of the Board's staff would, however, be rather inaccurate. Both the Bennett and the pre-1945 King Governments fostered this negative and restrictive role of government, and many ministers of finance, including Dunning, Ralston, and Ilsley, actively used the Board to control other ministers.[28] Moreover, opposition forces in the House of Commons, hardly numbering more than a corporal's guard for most of the period of the war, suffered from a lack of knowledge of the inner workings of the Board, and were not very conversant with new trends in economic thought and their relevance to Canadian public finance.[29]

Two important events in personnel administration during the war served to highlight the dominating position of the Board and the reasons why it incurred the wrath of the public service population. The staff control regulations mentioned earlier in this chapter effectively stopped all but the most urgent promotions and reclassifications in the public service. Treasury Board, moreover, maintained a rigid control on salaries. In August, 1939, with the cost-of-living index at 101.8, the average public service annual salary was $1,536. By December, 1947, the average annual earnings of public servants was $1,741, and the cost-of-living index stood at 146.0![30] Furthermore, the war duties supplements, which provided a salary bonus to some public servants and not to others, created an additional reason for discontent within civil service circles.[31] The Government was, therefore, well aware of the multitude of grievances in the service as a result of the constant stream of memoranda and representations from the associations.

In March, 1942, the Assistant Secretary of the Treasury Board urged the Government to appoint a special committee to classify the greatly enlarged public service, and "to study and report on existing problems, mainly due to the war, and also on problems related to rehabilitation in outside employment of large war staffs at the end of the war."[32] A further suggestion was made that the Government should take the opportunity to centralize all personnel functions, with the exception of recruitment, in some body under the authority of Treasury Board.[33] The Government proceeded much more cautiously, however, and in January of the following year appointed H. J. Coon, an executive assistant in the main office of the Bank of Nova Scotia, to head a committee to study various problems concerning the conditions of employment.[34]

The Coon Committee was established as a purely advisory body, reporting directly to the Treasury Board.[35] Besides Coon, the Committee was composed of W. C. Ronson and B. J. Roberts, a member of the National Harbours Board. CSC Commissioners Bland and Thivierge also agreed to sit on the Committee, but only after being assured that it was not created to preempt the *de jure* jurisdiction of the CSC.[36] The Coon Committee heard representations from the staff associations, the departments, and the CSC on a wide variety of civil service personnel problems: there were submissions on staff control and overtime regulations, the war duties supplements, superannuation, and statutory increases.[37] Fully confident in the justice of their cause, the staff associations eagerly awaited the publication of the findings of the Committee, but when an interim Report was presented to Treasury Board on March 17, 1943, the Government decided to keep the document secret.

At first glance this appears as a somewhat puzzling decision: a perusal of the secret Report indicates that the Coon Committee had gone a long way in meeting the complaints of the civil servants, and that the Treasury Board was by no means antagonistic to the Committee's recommendations. Indeed, on June 1, 1943, the Board issued a statement of changes in personnel policy which accepted outright many, if not most, of the recommendations of the secret Report.[38] However, in one vital area of concern to civil servants, statutory increases, Treasury Board refused to accept any changes. Since the beginning of the war, statutory increases had been limited to a maximum compensation ceiling of $3,000. The Coon Committee had strongly recommended that this ceiling be removed. The Board, however, accepted an accompanying recommendation which deplored the fact that statutory increases had largely become automatic, thus no longer serving as an incentive for greater efficiency in public administration. Civil servants were told quite bluntly that in future this practice would be terminated. The Board also refused to accept the Coon Committee's recommendation on overtime compensation, which advocated some adjustments in the rate paid to clerical, stenographic, and office employees, recommending instead that the policy of compensatory leave be extended to all departments.

The associations had placed a great deal of emphasis on the removal of the ceiling on statutory increases and the demands for adequate overtime compensation. The Board was not prepared to meet these demands, and thus may have felt that it would have served no useful purpose to release the Report.[39] Whatever the reasons for keeping the Report secret, the decision incensed the staff associations to a degree which no other single issue had, except the classification and reorganization of 1919–21. They suspected, wrongly in part, that the Coon Committee had recognized the justice of all their demands, and had perhaps made many recommendations benefitting all public employees. Beyond this they expressed a sense of outrage that the Government was treating them in its usual high-handed manner, for it had refused the associations' supplications to be allowed to sit on the Coon Committee, and had now further added insult to injury by refusing to release the Report.[40]

The recalcitrance of the Board was laid at the doorstep of none other than "that *bête noir* of civil servants' existence," W. C. Ronson.[41] The feelings of the associations on this matter were fully revealed three years later in the proceedings of the Gordon Commission where Ronson was accused of dictatorial and high-handed methods in dealing with their salary demands. In one revealing passage of evidence Ronson was even portrayed as an omnipotent one-man Treasury Board callously manipulating cabinet ministers as in a Punch and Judy show:

> *The Chairman:* Do you suggest that that individual who, at the present time, is nameless, makes the decisions?
>
> *Dr. Wright:* Yes, he does make them. He said he made them. One of the officers of the professional institute went to him and said, "Do you make the decisions?" And he said, "Yes, I make all the decisions." He said he did, and the Board is so weak that after Treasury Board meets he tells them about it. The man said, "If any of these things are stopped, then you are to blame for stopping them?" And he said "Yes." Then he said, "The only thing to do is to get rid of you?" And he said "Yes," —and there it stands. Whether we get rid of him or not is another point; perhaps you can help.[42]

Faced with the vitriolic criticisms of the staff associations, the Government began to give serious consideration to the creation of an employer-employee council.[43] It is not clear whether the Government and Treasury Board staff anticipated the reaction of civil servants to the secrecy surrounding the Coon Committee Report, but on March 17, the same day the Report was dated, the Government asked CSC Chairman Bland for information regarding the composition of advisory councils in Britain. Bland's reply suggested that there was no need for a council on which the associations were actually represented.[44] But even if the erstwhile champion of the associations was not concerned with securing their direct representation, the Government had already made up its mind. Eleven months later, on February 24, 1944, Finance Minister Ilsley announced in the

House of Commons that Treasury Board had decided to provide for the creation of a National Joint Council of the Public Service. Supposedly based on the Whitley Council model, "with the necessary adaptations to suit Canadian conditions," the NJC was created to act in an advisory capacity to Treasury Board, while "in certain fields their recommendations may appropriately be made directly to the Civil Service Commission."[45]

A careful examination of the NJC's terms of reference and a comparison of its machinery with that of the National Whitley Council in the United Kingdom suggest that the Canadian Government did not expect this "consultative body" to be anything other than a discussion forum. The stated purposes of the NJC were taken practically verbatim from the constitution of the National Whitley Council, but with one very significant exception. The constitution of the latter provided that "the decisions of the Council shall be arrived at by agreement between the two sides, shall be signed by the Chairman and Vice-Chairman, shall be reported to the Cabinet, and *thereupon shall become operative.*"[46] In other words, an agreement between the official and staff sides must be binding if the machinery was to be worthwhile.[47] In Canada the situation was altogether different. In his announcement to Parliament concerning the Government's intentions to create this Council, Ilsley was careful to emphasize the "spirit of camaraderie" which could result if this machinery were utilized effectively during a period of national crisis. The body was to be advisory only, and could not, in the words of the Minister, "impair the responsibility of the Cabinet or Treasury Board or Civil Service Commission, or possibly infringe on the authority of Parliament."[48] The Council was given a mandate to deal with a variety of problems, such as recommendations for proposed civil service legislation and the improvement of office procedures and organization; but in the area of most vital concern to civil servants, namely, conditions of employment, the Council was limited to a discussion of "general principles." Although the NJC was precisely the type of deliberative body which the associations had been demanding for twenty years, it soon became abundantly clear that the constraints on its jurisdiction would prove unsatisfactory to organized civil servants.[49]

From its beginnings the Council amounted to little more than an attempt to put a damper on the flaming tempers of the time. The Order in Council of May, 1944, which put the official seal of approval on the NJC, stressed that the organization was created *"for explaining to members of the public service of Canada the policies of the Government which affect them as employees."*[50] The problems of the government as employer, and not those of the employees, were to be the central focus of concern.[51] Two factors no doubt contributed to this position held by the Government. The spectre of wartime inflation was a serious threat which the Government

194

was determined to check. Under the War Measures Act it had taken drastic measures in the private sector to ensure that wage and price controls were effective.[52] An example, therefore, had to be set in the public sector as well. Second, the Government was all too aware of the very weak position of the staff associations. Less than 50 percent of civil servants at the time were organized, and the leaders of the various staff associations were certainly distrustful of one another, untried and untrained in the art of skilful negotiations.[53] On the other hand, an examination of the roster of the official representatives for the Government indicated that the associations confronted, for the most part, a galaxy of some of the most influential men in the civil service at the time. It is, therefore, plausible to suggest that the NJC was to be some sort of "training school" for the staff associations, as well as a forum of communication, as suggested earlier.

Insight into the Government's intentions toward the NJC may be obtained from the manner in which it handled the issue of the need for publicity of the Council's deliberations. The staff associations argued that deliberations must be made public in order to educate civil servants in general about staff relations in the public service. If this publicity is denied, they contended, "it would handicap the Council in that civil servants, being unaware of what was proceeding, would not be in a position to assess the value of the Council's work."[54] The subject was discussed at length at the first two meetings of the Council, with Dr. W. A. Mackintosh, the Chairman, summing up what he called an inconclusive but final debate on the matter:

1. Undoubtedly it was more important to staff members than to official members to be able to give some publicity to the proceedings of the Council.
2. It would be difficult, if not impossible, to foresee all circumstances in advance, and to attempt to set forth on paper precisely what policy should be followed on all occasions, would appear to be very difficult.
3. Generally speaking, staff representatives should be in a position to discuss with their associates and members, matters coming before, or already before, the Council.
4. There might be some instances when for a time matters would have to be regarded confidential, but perhaps these cases would not be numerous.
5. All agreed that individual members of the Council should feel free to voice their opinions without fear of having individual opinions quoted elsewhere.
6. Both official and staff representatives would have to consult frequently with those whom they represent.[55]

Given these two factors of the Government's reluctance at the time to enter into any specific discussions on salaries in a period of economic and political crisis and the inherent weaknesses of the staff associations' positions, the NJC was not, and realistically could not be expected to be, an organization which would somehow fill a gap in employer-employee relations that had existed for close to thirty years.[56] This is not to argue that the NJC failed to provide an extremely useful forum for the discussion and settlement of many issues important in employer-employee relations.[57] One could quite justifiably argue that because the staff associations were at that stage still inexperienced negotiators, the NJC forum was a much needed device to provide them with the opportunity to advance beyond the stage of merely making unheeded submissions to an indifferent Government. Whereas in the past they could make inflated demands knowing full well that the Government would not listen to them anyway, now they were being "educated" to put forward proposals reached through the interplay of two-way "negotiations."

ROLE OF THE CIVIL SERVICE COMMISSION

The experience of the Coon Committee and the National Joint Council during the war years dramatized the growing recognition of the inadequacies of the 1918 Civil Service Act and the attempts at ad hoc arrangements to control federal personnel administration. As described earlier, the responsibility of coordination fell increasingly on the willing shoulders of the Treasury Board and its staff. While it is clear that the basic groundwork for Treasury Board's powers in this area was laid during the depression years, the war years were critically important for the consolidation and aggrandizement of that power. It would appear that the perception of the Board's powers only came into full focus with the war, and most precisely with the passage of the War Measures Act in 1940. But the accruing of most of these powers was viewed as a short-term contingency. After all, the Civil Service Commission, according to the Civil Service Act of 1918–19, was still legally vested with enormous powers in the field of personnel administration. However, despite its legal status, the CSC entertained few illusions as to the dramatic emergency changes which further enhanced the powers of the Treasury Board. The series of Orders in Council in the autumn of 1939 and the spring of 1940, dealing with the personnel function, made it patently clear that the Government had, at least for the duration of the war, effectively revised the intent of the 1918 Civil Service Act, and had brought personnel policy firmly within the orbit of direct executive control. The CSC was being reduced from a control agency to a kind of service agency, *even in the area of selection and ap-*

196

pointment. However, it is important to re-emphasize that it is doubtful this transformation was seen as long term in its duration. First of all, the concepts of control *versus* service had not been developed to the extent that it was to be following the war. Second, the war years were a crisis period, and it was generally felt that many extraordinary arrangements would disappear in a postwar return to "normalcy": the permanent character of many of these changes was thus obscured. Nevertheless, the seeds of the Glassco and post-Glassco changes in the CSC's status were obviously sown in the war years, when the desperate need for effective management control of the public service overrode the old patronage-merit complex which lay at the base of the CSC's power.

Within this context of fiscal austerity and control, certain fundamental internal changes were also occurring in the CSC. Gradually, and almost imperceptibly, the central personnel agency began adopting the economizing ideology of Treasury Board as its own raison d'être. Guarding the public treasury was the Board's basic function: the CSC, on the other hand, had developed a role as the guardian not of the public treasury but of public morals. Yet in a paper prepared for the Wartime Information Board in 1944, the CSC strongly justified its existence by its economizing role—even to the extent of publishing a table of dollars and cents saved.[58] Moreover, the CSC continually maintained that it was an "independent" body which could act as an honest broker between the civil service associations and the government. Clearly its two self-images were contradictory.[59] An organization which sat in the secret conclaves of the wartime Coon Commission, which was identified, along with Treasury Board representatives, as the official side of the NJC, and which by the end of the war even informed a royal commission that its basic function was to enforce economy in government spending[60]—such an organization could not at the same time realistically pose as an independent arbitrator between the government and its employees.

The vicissitudes of the Organization Branch of the CSC point up the paradoxical nature of the central personnel agency's position. Chapters 5 and 7 have already described how the CSC's failure to carry out any real reorganizational work (and doubts as to the efficacy of reorganizational work being entrusted to such a body in the first place) had led to suggestions in the 1930s that the Organization Branch should be transferred to Treasury Board. Toward the end of the war, doubts even seem to have penetrated into the staff of the Branch itself, as evidenced by an internal memorandum of the Branch which suggested that while organizational analysis was the most "satisfying" aspect of work in the CSC, insufficient time and resources were available to do the job properly, and that Treasury Board was the agency best suited to carry out such work.[61] As a member

197

of the CSC staff has recalled, the Organization Branch before 1939 was capable only of "slow and not very efficient analysis"; during World War II, with the proliferation of agencies and general increase in staff throughout the service, classification became the primary concern of the CSC and organization studies receded to a subsidiary level of importance: "Frankly, there was not much time to do this kind of work."[62]

It is scarcely surprising, then, that the efficiency side of the economy-efficiency philosophy was neglected during the two decades which elapsed between the Griffenhagen inquiry of the early 1920s and the end of the war. Economy was well taken care of by the Treasury Board and even, purportedly, by the CSC. But efficiency as a distinct concept—one which could in fact suffer from a single-minded emphasis on economy—was obviously not dealt with in any specific fashion. Indeed, it would seem that reorganization became a rather marginal aspect of the classification process. While reclassifying employees, a CSC representative might suggest that duties of employees within a small section be redistributed. CSC employees who were interviewed emphasized the minor importance of such work and were quick to point out that no reorganization would be attempted without the agreement and cooperation of the deputy minister of the department.[63] In the rare cases in which larger scale organizational work was undertaken by the CSC, it was still only at the initiative and at the specific request of the department heads. In other words, the CSC was acting only in an advisory capacity, in the provision of a service for the departments, a service which was rarely required. As for the Treasury Board assuming responsibility for initiating such work, "Ronson did not want it. His main concern was the estimates."[64] And so the need for constant independent evaluation of the efficiency of administrative procedures fell squarely between the CSC and the Board.

And yet, this account of the paradoxical position of the CSC remains only one side of the ledger in this odyssey of federal personnel administration. During the eight-year period from 1939 to 1946, the CSC, partly due to circumstances not of its own making, underwent dramatic developments both as an *organization* and as an *institution*. As a "rational instrument engineered to do a job," the CSC performed admirably in the area of recruitment and selection of personnel.[65] Approximately three hundred thousand assignments were made in the public service during the period of the war, not to mention the countless other applicants who had to be rejected for one reason or another. The story of the CSC's response to external environmental demands on its resources is fully explored in chapter 15 and need not be reiterated here. Suffice to state that many senior civil servants in retrospect have praised the central personnel agency's performance in expediting its recruitment and selection functions.

The public comments of a former Secretary of the Board serve as an example:

> The enormous elaboration of the administrative system during the war was built round the existing structure of the civil service. Under all this weight the structure did not collapse. Indeed, after the war the new elements were smoothly absorbed and adapted into the regular mould of the career service. The fact that it was possible to do this is evidence of the essential strength and soundness of the system, and it is a tribute to those responsible for this task, particularly the Civil Service Commission.[66]

One significant illustration of the manner in which the CSC rose to the occasion was in the recruitment of returning servicemen to the ranks of the civil service. At the end of the war the CSC mobilized its services in an unprecedented manner to attract applications from veterans and to ensure the success of such applications.[67]

Phillip Selznick has emphasized that the process of transformation of an expendable organization into an institution is marked by a concern for self-maintenance. Thus, "infusion with value" and "self-maintenance" become mutually inclusive: a living association, he notes, "blends technical aims and procedures with personal desires and group interests. As a result, various elements in the association have a stake in its continued existence."[68] Indeed, increasingly during the war years, the organized civil service community realized that it had a vital stake in the maintenance of the CSC. Treasury Board's cold hand of fiscal austerity, combined with its condoning of lower salary levels for the permanent civil service as compared to the salaries paid to temporary employees, created a reservoir of mistrust and aversion for the Board's role in federal personnel administration. However, the CSC, despite its paradoxical position described earlier, had been consistent throughout in advocating the removal of a degree of this financial disparity between temporary and permanent employees in the public service. For example, it stated in its 1941 Annual Report:

> The Commission renewed its recommendations during the year, that provision should be made whereby permanent employees who have been loaned for work in the war departments, should be granted the compensation which properly belongs to the duties which they are performing. While permanent public servants are glad to make every sacrifice in the war effort, the Commission does not believe it to be desirable in the interests of efficiency or morale that there should be too great a discrepancy between the salary of a permanent public servant and the salary of a temporary employee when both are doing the same work.[69]

Consequently, it is hardly surprising that the staff associations were resolute and continuous in their support of the CSC in its verbal battles with the Board. Almost without exception staff associations' witnesses before the Gordon Commission argued that the activities of the CSC, in dealing with professional, scientific, and administrative positions, "should be expanded greatly, both quantitatively and qualitatively."[70] Dr. L. Austin Wright of the Engineering Institute of Canada assured the Commissioners that the CSC was fully competent to handle all facets of personnel administration in the public service and noted: "If someone will take the restrictions off them, I know they can act. They know what is wrong with all this, but their hands are tied. Their hands are tied by the Treasury Board, as a matter of fact. Treasury Board meets them at every turn, and I think this thing should be emphasized and criticized. I do not know whether your report would include that in any way, but Treasury Board has throttled the attempt of various members of the Civil Service Commission and the heads of departments to get adjustments."[71]

The central personnel agency's service image was also buttressed by the large proportion of agencies and crown corporations availing themselves of its growing expertise in personnel administration.[72] However, while the CSC welcomed this new advisory function, there was no conscious attempt on its part to decentralize the personnel function within the departments, or to encourage the growth of imaginative and trained personnel for personnel administration. Consequently, by 1945 the personnel function within the departments operated in an atmosphere of low prestige and lack of appreciation. "The existing machinery and procedures for the administration of personnel matters," the Gordon Commission observed, "are generally rudimentary in form and routine in operation."[73] On balance, the period from 1939 onwards had, according to Taylor Cole, "furnished a leaven but only the merest beginnings of change."[74]

By the end of the war Treasury Board had consolidated its powerful position as the barometer for financial control of all aspects of federal government administration. But the seeds of change had been deeply planted for basic changes to occur in both the Board and the CSC. The central personnel agency's position was more obvious: despite its successes in improving its procedural methods in personnel selection and placement, the organization had its serious problems. The Gordon Commission strongly indicted the CSC when it found that within the service there were inordinate improvisation in personnel administration, co-opting from the outside, heavy burdens placed on senior officials in the departments, and special organizational devices employed to "escape the procedures of the civil service machinery" which were far more cumbersome "than would have been required under a more flexible system."[75]

The Treasury Board's problems were far more subtle, though just as profound. By the war's end, it was becoming increasingly clear that Government was to take on new dimensions and new directions in the management of the economy. The new Keynesian economic theories, combined with the growing electoral threat of the CCF and the concrete example of the government-directed war effort in bringing the economy out of depression and into a state of full employment, had revolutionized the Government's own conception of its economic role. The White Paper of 1945 was the culmination of the shifting government thinking on this area of activity.[76] While it symbolized a vast new body of responsibility to be assumed by the federal bureaucracy, it also signalled the death knell of the old Treasury Board of the depression and war-crisis eras.

Almost all the knowledgeable economists in both the government service and the universities expected that the end of the war would bring about a return to the prewar conditions of unemployment and depression. The White Paper committed the Government to maintain full employment through interventionist fiscal and monetary policies of a countercyclical nature. The old Bennett-Ronson philosophy of austerity as the answer to depressions was not only outmoded, it had in fact been stood on its head. As Joan Robinson has explained, Bernard Mandeville had unsettled the classical economists by pointing out in *The Fable of the Bees* that underlying their theories was the assumption that private vices (greed and luxury) led to public benefits (full employment). Keynes brought forward an even more shocking doctrine: "Worse than private vices being public benefits, it seemed that the new doctrine was the still more disconcerting proposition that private virtues (of thriftiness and careful husbandry) were public vices."[77] Now, following Keynes, the Federal Government seemed prepared to meet a depression by acting in a "profligate" manner, to happily incur large debts, and, worst of all, not even to worry excessively about the level of its spending—so long as purchasing power got into the hands of the people. In reality, the Government had by no means embraced the Keynesian program in all its ramifications and, as events were to show, the business community never really accepted it at all. But the point needs emphasizing: the government strategy for dealing with a depressed economy had been turned on its head in all essentials. What then of Treasury Board, that powerful agency for cutting down spending regardless of circumstances? It was obvious that the agency itself was an extremely useful tool for maintaining executive control of the bureaucracy, and there was no real chance that the war's end would bring with it any significant reversal of the Board's growing power; but it was just as obvious that a change at the top of the Board's permanent staff was imminent.[78]

1. A. F. W. Plumptre, *Mobilizing Canada's Resources for War*, pp. 1–17.

2. Another "instant department" with an impressive growth in personnel was the Wartime Prices and Trade Board. Between 1939 and 1941 the Board was limited in its jurisdiction. Just before its second birthday, however, the Board was drastically reconstituted, its powers strengthened, and its jurisdiction extended. The growth in staff mirrored this change. For a good résumé of the Board's activities, see R. MacGregor Dawson, *Canada in World Affairs*, pp. 42–43.

3. Dawson, *Canada in World Affairs*, pp. 42–43.

4. During the 1920s and the 1930s civil service employment as a percentage of the civilian labour force was consistently about 1.1 percent. This amounted to about 4.4 civil servants per thousand of the population. By the end of World War II civil service employment had risen to 2.5 percent of the civilian labour force, or about 9.8 civil servants per thousand of population. For some further comments on this growth, see J. J. Deutsch, "Some Thoughts on the Public Service," in J. E. Hodgetts and D. C. Corbett, eds., *Canadian Public Administration*, pp. 297–304.

5. On September 1, 1939, the proclamation issued declared that a state of "apprehended war exists and has existed as and from the twenty-fifth day of August." (*Proclamations and Orders in Council passed under the Authority of the War Measures Act* [Ottawa: King's Printer, 1940], vol. 1, pp. 19–20)

6. C. J. Mackenzie, former assistant secretary of the Treasury Board, explains the sweeping changes in these terms: "The War Measures Act and the War Appropriations Act provided complete exemption from the provisions of the Civil Service Act. In addition many specific exemptions from the Civil Service Act were being approved by the Governor in Council. Appointments were being made, salaries approved and important changes in organization affected without consultation with the Civil Service Commission." ("The Treasury Board," a speech delivered to the Junior Administrative Officers' Course, CSC, December 7, 1947 [mimeograph], p. 8)

7. Dawson, *Canada in World Affairs*, p. 34.

8. Royal Commission on Administrative Classifications in the Public Service, 1946, "Proceedings" (typescript) 1, testimony of W. C. Ronson, pp. 68–69. Hereafter cited as Gordon Commission Proceedings.

9. P.C. 1/1569 (April 19, 1940).

10. In the words of the CSC, "the Commission has acted as the investigating body for the Treasury Board in connection with the organization of departments, the need for new appointments and the proper compensation to be paid." (CSC, *Annual Report*, 1940, p. 5)

11. See chapter 7.

12. P.C. 32/1905 (May 10, 1940).

13. See, for example, P.C. 6/4937 (July 9, 1941); P.C. 854½ (November 1, 1941); P.C. 6286 (November 7, 1940).

14. J. H. Young, "Principles and Practice of Remuneration in the Canadian Civil Service, 1926–1949."

15. See chapter 7. As late as 1939 the Board's staff consisted of only around eight persons.

16. Gordon Commission Proceedings, 1, pp. 81–82.

17. Mackenzie, "The Treasury Board," pp. 13–14.

18. Senior civil servants interviewed remembered the terse statement: "The

Board has considered and has not approved," which constituted the only information received when requests were denied.

19. A. D. P. Heeney, "Cabinet Government in Canada: Some Recent Developments in the Machinery of the Central Executive," pp. 286–87. Heeney further notes: "Of the impressive total of over 90,000 proceedings passed by Council during six years of war, not more than 5 percent represented emergency legislation by the executive. The other acts were of an administrative nature only, representing an immense increase in number and extent but of no real significance in relation to the exercise of extraordinary powers." (P. 286)

20. Interview.

21. Mackenzie, "The Treasury Board," p. 11.

22. Arguments put forward by Mackenzie to justify the Board's preeminence were that the Board and the Cabinet were synonymous and also that the concept of the royal prerogative—"the principle that powers not specifically taken away from the Crown by statute remain with the Crown and can be exercised by the Crown on the advice of its ministers"—could be applied in this instance. Ibid., p. 19.

23. P.C. 6702 (August 26, 1941).

24. Gordon Commission Proceedings, 1, pp. 70–71.

25. Ibid., pp. 77–79.

26. John M. Keynes, *The General Theory of Employment, Interest and Money*.

27. Interview.

28. Walter White reports Ronson as stating: "Members of the government (ministers) were opposed to the Board. There was a row every time the big spending ministers came. They could not take the checks set up by Treasury Board. I have a great deal of admiration for Mr. Ilsley, he was an active minister who used the Board effectively to check on expenditures." (White, "The Treasury Board in Canada," p. 121)

29. Ibid., pp. 169–74.

30. Treasury Board Files, File no. 1101-0.

31. Gordon Commission Proceedings, 1. See the evidence of Ronson, pp. 70–72.

32. Ronson to J. L. Ilsley, March 18, 1942, Treasury Board Files, File no. 101-53-3.

33. Ibid. The suggestion to centralize all the personnel functions was contained in an accompanying draft report to council dated January 26, 1942.

34. P.C. 2/584 (January 23, 1943).

35. Indeed both the King and St. Laurent Governments had consistently taken the stand over the years that advisory bodies to the Board would not be permitted to publicly divulge any of their advice given to the Government. See *Debates*, May 19, 1950, pp. 2653–54.

36. W. C. Clark to Ilsley, January 21, 1943, Treasury Board Files, File no. 101-53-3.

37. Summary of the submissions, Treasury Board Files, File no. 101-53-3. This file contains the Treasury Board's official copy of the Coon Committee Report.

38. See the statement of Treasury Board on personnel policy, issued June 1, 1943, cited in *Civil Service Review* 16 (June, 1943), pp. 124–26.

39. Finance Minister Ilsley was asked to table the Coon Committee Report in the House, but he refused to do so on the grounds that it was purely advisory and confidential.

40. *Civil Servants Digest* argued: "If we look for an incentive for more vigorous organization we need only consider the Treasury Board's decisions in connection with the Coon Committee findings. That the Treasury Board decisions have left the service a load of dissatisfaction cannot be denied; that the remedy lies largely in our own hands cannot be too strongly recommended." ("A Year of Commendable Achievement," September, 1943, p. 3)

41. Interview.

42. Gordon Commission Proceedings, 3, p. 474. Dr. Wright was one of the official spokesmen of the Engineering Institute of Canada to appear before the Commission.

43. *Civil Servants Digest*, August, 1943, p. 2.

44. C. H. Bland to J. W. Pickersgill, March 18, 1943, King Papers, Corr., Post 1939 Series, vol. 54, 80123. The Coon Committee was never officially terminated after handing in its first and only Report. One of its terms of reference called for recommendations dealing with future demobilization problems, but the Committee never spent any time considering this area of concern. In December, 1944, Ilsley wrote to Coon to informally terminate the Committee's existence.

45. *Debates*, February 24, 1944, pp. 778–79. Originally the NJC was to consist of six representatives of the staff side and six of the official or employer side. Because of disputes over the joint representative for the three postal associations, the Government acquiesced in allowing all three to name their respective representative to the Council. Comprising nine representatives for the staff side and six for the official side, one could hardly expect this organization to be anything but advisory in nature.

46. "Constitution of the National Whitley Council," printed as an appendix to *Staff Relations in the Civil Service* (London: H. M. Stationery Office, 1955).

47. Binding in the sense that, in a spirit of goodwill, the Government was normally committed to accept the recommendations. The limitation of the authority of the official side of the Whitley Council was always recognized, although it did not prevent the continuation of the Council's deliberations or the resort to compulsory arbitration. A statement approved by both sides of a National Council Committee made this point very clear in 1949: "In our view it is impossible, even if it were desirable, that a Whitley Council in the Civil Service should function as a legislative body. The members of the official side possess no power or authority except what is delegated to them by ministers. The provision that the decisions of the Council shall be reported to the Cabinet and thereupon shall become operative, appears to us to be a misstatement of the position. In fact, the position is, and must remain, that, unless the Cabinet through Ministers authorizes the Official Side to agree, no agreement can be reached on the Council." (H. M. Treasury, *Staff Relations in the Civil Service* [London: H. M. Stationery Office, 1949], p. 12)

48. Quoted in the *National Joint Council of the Public Service of Canada*, 1944–1954 (Ottawa: Queen's Printer, 1954), p. 14.

49. Commenting on the Council's "advisory role on general principles," and noting that "the millennium on the basis of an announcement of Government policy" was far from being a reality, the *Civil Servants Digest* continued: "Act-

ing as an advisory committee to Government is of little value in itself, unless the Government is prepared in a large measure to accept and act upon the advice received. . . . In practice there has been plenty of advice the Government has ignored . . . it should be remembered that a militant, well-organized staff side, united by a common purpose will accomplish far more. ORGANIZE, EDUCATE, AMALGAMATE." (March, 1944, p. 8)

50. P.C. 3676 (May 16, 1944). (Emphasis added.)

51. This impression is further substantiated by other evidence. In December, 1944, Ilsley wrote to Coon thanking him for his services. Noting that at the time of the creation of the Coon Committee, civil service problems were causing the Government a great deal of worry, he added that with the establishing of the NJC the situation had become "much easier than it was at the time your Committee was sitting." On the whole, the NJC "has been functioning not very actively, but I think satisfactorily." (Ilsley to Coon, December 6, 1944, Treasury Board Files, File no. 101-53-3)

52. See Donald Gordon, "Price Control and the Wage Earner," October 19, 1944.

53. The structural weakness of the staff associations as they faced the Government in negotiations is exemplified by the following statement of a civil servant: "There is a tendency first in the jockeying for position for attention to be diverted from some of the fundamental, day-to-day functions such as representation of individual members for the same groups of employees, there will be a natural tendency for each association to 'beat the other to the draw' to demonstrate its alertness and aggressiveness. This brings with it in turn the danger of the 'quick trigger finger' and hasty aim." (M. M. Maclean, "Problems of Jurisdiction and Structure Facing Staff Associations in the Canadian Civil Service," pp. 34–35)

54. *Civil Service Review* 17 (June, 1944), p. 140.

55. Ibid., p. 141. The *Review* was under no illusions after quoting Dr. Mackintosh's summary: "The Chairman's statement as quoted appears to fix the policy in relation to publishing or reporting the proceedings of the meetings."

56. Fixed attitudes were also a problem with which to contend. The staff associations were weak partly because civil servants were not prepared to give them the full support they desired: "The conditions that give rise to unionism are not as intensely felt in Government as in the business setting. The major reason, however, is probably because Government workers largely consist of white-collar and professional workers who have not joined unions in private industry in large numbers either. Primarily, this seems to be because the social identifications and attitudes of this group do not run in the direction of collective action but rather in terms of individual advancement." (W. R. Dymond, "The Role of the Union in the Public Service as Opposed to Its Role in Private Business," p. 59)

57. For the many accomplishments of the Council over a two-decade period, see C. W. Rump, "The National Joint Council of the Public Service of Canada" (mimeograph). Rump could point to well over twenty-two significant achievements in personnel matters. Chief among them were the establishment of the five-day week, the development of safety standards and group surgical medical plans, and the semimonthly payment of civil service salaries.

58. Wartime Information Board, "The Civil Service Commission," Reference Paper no. 32, January 19, 1944 (mimeograph), p. 2.

59. For some perceptive criticisms concerning the CSC's contradictory positions, see Saul J. Frankel, *Staff Relations in the Civil Service: The Canadian Experience.*

60. In his testimony before the Gordon Commission, CSC Chairman Bland spent much of his time justifying the Government's position on salaries and personnel problems, and, in one of the strangest definitions ever put forward of the function of the CSC, suggested that "there must be coordination and control where the spending of public money is concerned. In fact, that was one of the primary reasons why there is such a thing as a Civil Service Commission, or a Treasury Board." (Gordon Commission Proceedings, 1, p. 25)

61. Memorandum from D. M. Watters to George Jackson, chief of the Organization Branch, Files of the CSC, PAC.

62. Interview.

63. Interview.

64. Interview.

65. Phillip Selznick, *Leadership in Administration*, p. 5.

66. Deutsch, "Some Thoughts on the Public Service," p. 299.

67. For a full discussion of this mobilization, see chapter 18.

68. Selznick, *Leadership in Administration*, p. 20.

69. CSC, *Annual Report*, 1941, p. 10. The CSC was, however, not arguing that all civil servants should be paid the same as their private equivalents. When Chairman Bland testified before the Gordon Commission, he strongly justified the fact that civil servants were paid less because of their job security and the special prestige attached to their positions. Gordon Commission Proceedings, 1, p. 13.

70. Gordon Commission Proceedings, 3, p. 428.

71. Ibid., pp. 472, 473.

72. Interview. The commercial corporations such as Polymer paid no attention to public personnel administration. Their whole philosophy was of course based on industrial practices in the private sector. Agencies such as NRD and CMHC did model their personnel function after CSC's practices.

73. Royal Commission on Administrative Classifications in the Public Service, 1946, *Report*, p. 21.

74. Taylor Cole, *The Canadian Bureaucracy*, p. 43.

75. Gordon Commission, *Report*, pp. 11–12.

76. White Paper on Employment and Income, April, 1945.

77. Joan Robinson, *Economic Philosophy* (Harmondsworth, Middlesex: Penguin, 1964), p. 73.

78. For an account of this redirection in the Board's philosophy, and the changes which were finally concretized in the passing of the Financial Administration Act, 1951, see White, "The Treasury Board in Canada," pp. 117–25.

Chapter Ten
The Postwar Decade:
Interagency Impasse and
Organizational Growth

"Cheshire Puss, . . . Would you tell me,
please, which way I ought to walk from
here?"
"That depends a good deal on where you
want to get to," said the Cat.

Lewis Carroll, *Alice in Wonderland*

THE GORDON ROYAL COMMISSION

THE PERSONNEL PROBLEM in the higher levels of the public service became
acute by the end of World War II. The dispersal of the talent attracted
to Ottawa on a wartime basis was one factor. Another was the vastly expanded requirements of the federal government for technical, professional,
and administrative personnel, arising out of its new role in managing the
economy. In late 1945, an interdepartmental committee on technical and
professional personnel in government employment reported to the Cabinet
that salary levels for these categories were inadequate if requirements
were to be fulfilled. It also referred to "delays in procedure employed in
hiring personnel and to the desirability of improved general arrangements
for promotion and for transfer between departments."[1] Although this
committee did not deal with administrative classifications, it did suggest
that this was an area which the Government ought to explore.

W. C. Clark and his officials in the Department of Finance, as well as
Norman Robertson in External Affairs, strongly recommended that the
top levels of administration should be examined as a first step toward
increasing the general efficiency of administrative machinery.[2] As a result,
Walter Gordon was approached to head a royal commission inquiry into
administrative classifications. Although Clark knew what he wanted done,
it was considered advisable that an outside body be charged with making
the recommendations. The Civil Service Commission was ruled out at the
start; as one source of our information recalled, it had become "very weak"
during the war years, and it was therefore not considered politic to ask

the central personnel agency to fulfil part of its statutory mandate to undertake a major revision of the classification system.[3] Yet the Finance Department was no more capable of assuming the task. The Treasury Board, which at this time was still an adjunct of the Finance Department, had the unfavourable Olympian image described in the previous chapter. Hence any study openly spearheaded by this body would have been suspect from the very beginning.

The Royal Commission on Administrative Classifications in the Public Service was composed of three members: Gordon, a former wartime civil servant in the Department of Finance, and at the time of his appointment a member of a leading Toronto firm of business consultants; Sir Thomas Gardiner of the British civil service; and Major-General Edouard de B. Panet, a retired official of the Canadian Pacific Railway Company.[4] Very early in the investigation both Gordon and his two colleagues seemed to have agreed on the inability of the CSC to institute needed changes in federal personnel administration. A former Commissioner of the CSC complained that the Gordon inquiry met only once in a brief interview with senior officials of the central personnel agency ("for about an hour"), and that "our side of the story" was not given the full attention it deserved by the Royal Commission.[5] This same official added that in his opinion the system was working quite well and that nothing needed to be changed. Since the reason for the Gordon Commission was to overhaul the machinery of personnel administration, it is not surprising that Gordon and his colleagues found little to discuss with the CSC. The CSC appeared in the Royal Commission's eyes as a roadblock en route to a better system. The result was that the CSC did not meaningfully participate in the search for improved methods of personnel management.

When the members of the Gordon Commission brought the wider perspective of independent investigators to bear upon the problem, they were appalled:

> With the increasing complexity of society there has been a steady growth in the activities and responsibilities of government which has imposed increasing demands upon the civil service and particularly upon its principal officials. It appears to us that as a result of this rapid expansion four principal defects in the organization of the service have emerged:
>
> 1. There are not enough men of high calibre in the senior and intermediate grades. This means that the Deputy Ministers and other principal officials—we suggest Ministers as well—are unable to delegate to others as much work as they should, with the result that they are themselves seriously overburdened.

2. There is no clear-cut assignment of responsibility for the overall management and direction of the service. As a result there is no effective machinery for adequately training, seeking out, transferring and promoting able men and women in the junior and intermediate ranks of the service.

3. There is no machinery capable of dealing decisively and promptly with the changes in organization which are needed continuously in any institution as large and varied as the Canadian Civil Service or with the problem of redundant, unsuitable or incompetent personnel.

4. There are very considerable delays in making appointments and promotions at all levels of the service.[6]

These basic flaws in the personnel administrative system stemmed from an "overlapping of duties and responsibilities between the Civil Service Commission and Treasury Board."[7] The Gordon Commission thus neatly summed up the irrationality of the existing system: "The Treasury Board has the authority in relation to all matters of establishment and organization but not the immediate responsibility; the Civil Service Commission has the responsibility but not the authority. This division of duties is the outstanding weakness in the central direction and control of the service and must be eliminated." To rectify, in the words of the Commission's Report, this "incomprehensible" and "cumbersome" state of affairs, Gordon and his colleagues proposed that the CSC be divested of most of its statutory powers given to it under the 1918 civil service legislation. The CSC would then be able "to concentrate on the primary and all-important task of recruitment, in which regard there is need for considerable improvement." More specifically, the CSC was to be given responsibility for recruitment "on a merit basis" of personnel for all classes; for review of recommendations by department heads for promotions in grades other than administrative, scientific, technical, and professional; for transfers in these same grades; and for "general guidance" to departments on in-service training programs.[8]

The Gordon Commission also recommended that the proliferating boards, commissions, and agencies of government around Ottawa should all be brought under the provisions of the Civil Service Act. To coordinate government personnel policy a Director-General of Establishments should be appointed to head an Establishments and Personnel Division in the Treasury Board. This officer would be accorded the rank of deputy minister and, with the assistance of an advisory committee, be given broad powers over organization and establishments of the departments, pay scales, promotions, training, selection, and working conditions—all functions which were to be transferred from the CSC to the Treasury

Board under the new order. "It should," the Report suggested, "be a principal responsibility of the Director-General to make recommendations respecting the reorganization or clearing out of obsolete and unnecessary branches and divisions throughout the service, including the transfer of the personnel therein."[9] In short, the Gordon Commission was suggesting that the age-old problem of reorganizational work in the interests of efficiency could be solved by the creation of a kind of permanent Griffenhagen. Also, with the approval of the Director-General, the jurisdiction of the deputy ministers over promotions in the professional, administrative, scientific, and technical classes in the civil service was to be final.[10]

The Government had one specific individual in mind for the job of Director-General: Mr. Dave Sim, the Deputy Minister of Customs and Excise. Both Prime Minister King and Finance Minister Ilsley exerted some pressures on Sim to accept the appointment, but Sim declined for personal reasons. The question of the Government's sincerity is somewhat unclear. It is the recollection of most people associated with the affair that Sim was not only the leading choice for the job but the *only* choice. Indeed, when Sim refused the job, the whole idea collapsed. What was often mentioned by officials interviewed during the course of this study was that the Gordon Commission may have made a major tactical error by suggesting that the Director-General's office be within the Treasury Board. It was widely believed that the new position would not have sufficient authority since "nobody believed that Treasury Board would give up its powers."[11] The Secretary of the Gordon Commission, J. J. Deutsch, later remarked that the Director-General should have been established separately, because the departments were not willing to accept the formal predominance of the Finance Department and Treasury Board.[12] Sim himself recalled that "when the smoke had cleared, it was evident that there was a growing discontent in the Civil Service against the handling of monetary matters by the Treasury Board."[13] Whatever the precise reasons, the Director-General of Establishments was a stillborn infant. And with this setback to its key recommendation, the internal logic of the rest of the Gordon Report became open to serious questioning.

The Gordon Commission articulated, for the first time, a critical analysis of the Government's system of personnel management. Yet the Commission's recommendations had little effect in the civil service environment of 1946. Instead of making waves, the Gordon Report dropped like a small stone into the deep waters of the civil service, with scarcely a sound announcing its disappearance. "Gordon had much less influence on people's minds than Glassco," recalled one former CSC official. "I did not feel the impact of his report at all."[14] The inquiry was hurriedly completed, as Gordon was pressed by his own private business concerns in Toronto. Moreover, as Taylor Cole reported, "Sir Thomas Gardiner was the only member of the Commission to give full time to his work, and it was his well-known views which were most prominent in the completed document."[15] Only superficial studies were done on comparative personnel systems. For example, Sir Thomas Gardiner and Major-General Panet, "unaccompanied by the chairman or secretary made a flying trip of a few days to Washington for an 'over-all view' of the budget and personnel systems."[16]

This superficiality seems to have had at least two damaging effects on the Commission's impact. The Report failed to sketch out in adequate detail the concrete steps which would have to be taken to realize the substantial changes recommended. Also, there was no time taken to actively prepare the civil service or the public for the proposed changes. For example, the Report's criticism of the classification was severe. Twenty-five years later, Mr. Gordon recalled that the CSC's classification system "just had everybody tied up in knots. There were separate categories for everybody, and it was clear to us in 1946 that the classification system had to be thrown out."[17] Yet, except for the age-old appeal for a "simpler" system, the Report offered no concrete alternative. One leading civil servant suggested that the Gordon Report was simply too brief and facile to form the basis of a large-scale change in the organization of the service. Selection, appointment, promotion, classification, and establishment were, in his view, too intertwined to be easily sorted out. In only one area was any success achieved by the Gordon Commission: salary increases were granted to the top administrative categories, although these were in fact achieved through the mechanism of a second, secret, report by Gordon to the Prime Minister.

In retrospect we can now see that the Gordon Report made the error in mistaking the CSC's apparent lack of imagination and initiative for political weakness. The Commission diagnosed the inefficiency of the system, but did not consider the concrete historical factors which had led to the existing situation. The abstract solution which it presented, while no doubt technically superior, did not reflect the actual power relationships within the bureaucracy. Nor did it take into account the survival instinct of the CSC, which, like every entrenched organization with a long historical background, had developed its own raison d'être. The Gordon inquiry looked at the public service merely as an instrument of government, but did not adequately deal with the service as a microcosm of the political system, with an internal logic born both because of realistic power relationships between bureaucratic agencies, as well as the need for technical efficiency in the implementation of policy. The CSC was satisfied with things as they were, and was ready to resist tooth and claw any change. It was in this sense not entirely relevant that, in the broad perspectives of the Gordon inquiry, the position of the CSC seemed unjustifiable; the fact was that it had survived and found a level at which it could rest. Others were implicated in this situation through the immediate pursuit of their own interests. As the Gordon Commission was to find out, it is not easy to destroy the basis of such an accommodation by the stroke of a pen, however skilfully wielded.

The CSC Commissioners, especially Chairman Bland, had been able to build up at least some political credit with the executive. "I suppose," Mr. Gordon himself recalled, "that the reason the recommendations did not see the light of day . . . was due to the fact that Bland with his protestations got to the PM." A leading CSC official of this period observed that Mr. Bland spent much time at the House of Commons and "courted" the M.P.'s. When the Gordon Report was released, according to this same official, Bland, along with Commissioner Stanley Nelson, was able to personally present the CSC case to King. King was apparently swayed by their arguments that the Gordon people had made up their minds before the investigation had begun and that the CSC had not been given adequate opportunity to present its views. Finally, a former Secretary of the Treasury Board recalled that Mr. Bland "could still go directly to the Prime Minister on a matter which he considered of vital importance. This he did after the Gordon Commission Report. He could get around Treasury Board because of his independence."

Nor was Treasury Board itself in favour of the proposed changes. W. C. Ronson, only a short time from retirement, wanted no part of the recommendations, except those concerning salary changes. The Gordon Commission also failed to take into account the utilitarian value of the CSC to the Treasury Board. The situation in which the CSC did the detailed personnel work, with the Board exercising ultimate and Olympian authority, was a situation not at all unpopular with the Board. Even though the departure of Ronson would be marked by an increase in Treasury Board staff and the development of specialized units dealing with personnel matters, it is nevertheless apparent that the leadership of the Board, even after Ronson, did not favour proposals which would have saddled the staff with an enormous amount of numbing detail—especially as the Board was at the same time becoming increasingly involved in the financial minutiae of departmental affairs through the estimates procedures. What the Board was essentially concerned with was ensuring that expenditures were kept within manageable limits; if the CSC staff could be utilized for this purpose, then so much the better. Further, so long as ultimate power rested with the Board, the CSC could serve the necessary legitimizing function, because of its public image as defender of the merit system.

For both administrative and *political* reasons, then, Ronson's successor as Treasury Board's assistant secretary, R. B. Bryce, held the opinion that fundamental changes in machinery were inopportune at that particular time. A former colleague of Mr. Bryce suggested that Bryce liked to see the Board involved in matters of "policy and principle," exercising its capacity for "logical thought" unburdened by the routine work which was charged to the CSC. Thus, even if the Gordon Commission were correct in viewing Ronson's leadership as outdated, the solution offered by the Commission failed to take into account the political dimensions of which Ronson's astute successor was most keenly aware.

As one moves beyond the confines of the CSC and the Board, and into the realm of the departments, the failure of the Gordon inquiry to grasp political realities becomes further clarified. One leading civil servant suggested that Bland's flexibility and Ronson's toughness were in a sense Bland's strength and Ronson's weakness. This same official felt that neither the CSC nor the Board had leadership of sufficient calibre at this time, but that Bland was more useful to active deputy ministers precisely because of his deference to departmental plans. Ronson, on the other hand, was not easy to deal with, and the department heads were deeply afraid of the Board's purely negative powers. J. J. Deutsch, who became secretary of the Treasury Board after Bryce, admitted freely that any increase in the Board's power was widely feared at the time. Many deputy ministers and even cabinet ministers did not want the Ronson Board to have too much control, and many preferred the old, loose system.[18] "The central control mechanism was deemed too powerful, and the staff associations and civil servants in general felt that the CSC was a much easier body to deal with than the Treasury Board." Deutsch added, significantly, that "it was not feasible to change this mechanism by fiat." He also believed that the CSC was still looked upon as the protector of civil servants, serving as a bulwark against the omnipotent powers of Treasury Board.[19]

This observation was indeed a correct one. The Amalgamated Civil Servants of Canada, in a most memorable phrase, dubbed the Treasury Board as the "sleepless ogre," and criticized the Gordon Report, likening it to a "Parson's egg that was good in some spots and bad in others."[20] The fear of political and administrative patronage still remained one of the overriding concerns of the staff associations:

It seems to us most contradictory for a Royal Commission recommend [*sic*] a closed door to patronage on entry into the Service, and an open door to patronage in respect to promotion within it. The recommendation regarding appointment is good, very good; the recommendation in respect to promotion is so bad that we class it as horrid. . . .

We would be the last people in the world to aver that the operations of the Civil Service Commission are perfect, or that some of the criticisms of the Royal Commission are ill-founded, but we very much object, and will continue to object, to any proposals aimed at changing the Civil Service Commission into nothing more than a recruiting station. One of the faults of the Civil Service Commission from the staff viewpoint, has been the fact that some of its recommendations have been made on the basis of "what the Treasury Board would stand for" and not on the basis of what is the right and proper thing to do.

Notwithstanding these faults, this staff association commented:

The remedy for the ills of the Civil Service lies not in going back to the old order of things, either in whole or in part, but by strengthening the power and authority of the institution created for the purpose of eliminating patronage, both in respect to appointment and promotion in the public service of this country.[21]

Other identifiable groups were roused to opposition by the Gordon recommendations. Although the CSC had never been noted as a strong defender of French-speaking civil servants, the Department of Finance was seen as a veritable Anglo-Saxon bastion. The Gordon recommendations thus encountered "politically effective opposition . . . from a number of French Canadians."[22] The Gordon Commission had also criticized the operation of the veterans preference, which roused the powerful opposition of the Canadian Legion and other veterans' groups to the Report as a whole.[23]

Finally, the perspective of the Government itself must be taken into account. "I have always had the feeling," recalled an influential deputy minister of the period, "that the Government was sitting back and consciously playing the CSC against the Treasury Board."[24] With this observation, the picture of the complex of bureaucratic power relationships is complete. The CSC, drawing on its remaining statutory powers, its public image, and its large staff, continued to play a leading role in personnel management. The Treasury Board, believing that the CSC's reputation for independence was in open question, maintained the CSC for routine labour and as a legitimizing agent for its own power. The staff associations, believing that the CSC's reputation for independence was valid and that it was a bulwark against patronage, supported the CSC as their spokesman. The deputy ministers, believing that the CSC had some independence from the Board, but also believing it to be ineffectual, wished to maintain it as a means of fending off the Board, which they feared as being all too powerful. And finally the Government itself was thoughtfully guarding the guardians, by making certain that two control agencies should be in competition, rather than having one in command. It was thus not surprising that the Gordon Commission met an impasse. Kingsley Martin's comments on Montesquieu's theory of checks and balances are appropriate: "Since there is no animating principle, no directing head or organic life, the result would seem to be a motionless equilibrium. Sheridan might even have had it in mind when he constructed the scene in his play, *The Critic,* where each member of the cast desires to stab his neighbour, but is prevented by his neighbour's attempt to stab him, the whole remaining in tableau, each unable to act because the balance of forces is precise."[25]

THE CSC AND TREASURY BOARD, 1946–1956

By the war's end it had become clear that the Federal Government was preparing to take on new directions in the management of the Canadian economy. The new Keynesian economic theories, combined with the growing electoral threat of the CCF and the concrete example of the government-directed war mobilization in bringing the country out of the depression and into a state of full employment, had revolutionized the Government's own conception of its economic role. If Assistant Secretary Ronson had been of a more flexible cast of mind, if he had been as ready to adapt to the new thinking as were some other leading civil servants, he might have survived the changes in the Board's orientation. He seems instead to have been one of those men whose public lives revolve around a single *idée fixe*—in his case, that spending is bad; saving is good.[26] A leading deputy minister of the period recalled that Ronson was inflexible and could not innovate: "He was not the restless type of man W. C. Clark was." One of Ronson's own successors described him as a "purely negative type of person—a real old-style Treasury type who resisted change." Another of Ronson's successors spoke of the "antiquated" ideology which permeated the Board at this time, and the "untenable" situation the old leadership found itself in.[27] Walter White reports that by 1947 both the Minister of Finance and the Deputy Minister of Finance were convinced that Ronson's methods were creating a "bottleneck in administrative procedure." They felt that the Board needed a secretary "with an appreciation of the priorities in expenditure which could effect employment, interest rates and other fiscal policy matters." They discussed how Treasury Board could be used to coordinate expenditures to the fiscal advantage of the Government, and concluded that Ronson was "incapable of appreciating the new approach."[28]

In 1947 Ronson was retired from the Board to become Master of the Mint, a fitting enough appointment for a man who had spent his life guarding the public treasury. His successor was R. B. Bryce, whose arrival at the Board signalled many changes. Staff increased in quality as well as quantity, as the Board took aim at the highest calibre of university graduates, with considerable success. A senior deputy minister interviewed by White suggested that "the job of Secretary to the Board changes with each incumbent. The boundaries of the job are unclear so that the personality and ability of the Secretary is terribly important. . . . Bryce made the Treasury Board staff a dynamic organization." White reported that senior officials were in agreement that Bryce's appointment was an important milestone in the development of the modern Treasury Board. Bryce was above all interested in planning and coordinating, with a view to making the Board into "a positive agency" to solve "long standing problems." It is also clear to White that the Gordon Commission's recommendation that establishments and organizations be under Treasury Board affected Bryce's assessment of the secretary's job.[29] As Treasury Board developed a more specialized and professional staff under Bryce and Deutsch, a separate personnel policy section also developed within the Board—a form of specialization of which Ronson had always disapproved. This section dealt with reports from the CSC or departments on problems of pay and working conditions, developed recommendations on establishments, and was the sole control agency for public employees not under the jurisdiction of the Civil Service Act.[30]

The transition from the Ronson Board to a newer type of organization was not, however, achieved solely by changing the top leadership. Many permanent staff members had received their early training under Ronson's leadership, and his influence did not vanish with his own departure. One senior Board official recalled that some members of the staff, although "brilliant young men in their own right," had been "nurtured and had all their experience" in the 1930s and wartime climate of depression and austerity, and had to be gradually placed in other positions.[31] Nor had Bryce's own leadership been entirely exempt from such criticism. White reported that some of the younger postwar university graduates felt that Bryce was to an extent still rooted in the ethos of the prewar service.[32] While such criticism may well be exaggerated, it does seem that the revolution in the Board's functioning, while planned and initiated under Bryce, achieved its culmination when Deutsch succeeded Bryce as secretary in the early fifties. A former Board official told White that "Deutsch brought a refreshing attitude to the job of Secretary. Bryce felt that there was something mysterious about the Board. He had a standard little saying—no reasons. Deutsch felt it was both foolish and futile to

218

comment on whether the National Research Council needed a new chemist's position. He pushed the idea that you must place the responsibility with the departments."[33] One external factor which made progress much easier for the Board was the economic buoyancy of the postwar decade. With the Government collecting rising revenues, the environment was "ideal . . . for an imaginative and able administrator at the centre of financial policy planning and administration."[34] It was thus not until the late fifties when economic recession set in that real resentment began to manifest itself against the restrictions applied to departmental plans.

In contrast to the ferment in Treasury Board, the Civil Service Commission in this period was in a somewhat different state. While the leadership of the Board was being changed, the Government in 1945 reappointed Charles Bland for a second ten-year term as chairman. At the same time, another civil servant, Stanley G. Nelson, a man who had spent his entire career as a CSC employee, was promoted to the post of second English-speaking Commissioner, thus ensuring that for the next decade, control of the CSC would remain in the hands of men whose lives had been associated with the organization since 1908 and 1922, respectively. The French-speaking Commissioner at that time was Arthur Thivierge, also a career CSC employee. While Bland had done a remarkable job of steering the CSC through the perils of the depression years, he was unable by the late forties and the early fifties to offer imaginative or dynamic institutional leadership. By force of circumstance the CSC was to continue to grow as an organization with statutory duties to be performed. More and more the central personnel agency was being staffed by dedicated professional personnel, but senior civil servants interviewed felt that what was most needed at the time was a change in leadership.[35]

One improvement in the relationship between the CSC and the Treasury Board had taken place: there were at least moves afoot to improve the dialogue between the two central agencies. This improvement was however only marginal. One official with extensive experience in both agencies, who had long maintained that methods of determining salary levels were hopelessly unscientific, recalls that "from 1947 onwards, they did begin talking to each other somewhat, but with no marked accomplishments."[36] The CSC tried relating pay increases to DBS cost-of-living indices, but only in a very rough way. The Board continued to carry out the occasional exercise of arbitrary and somewhat inexplicable authority. Deutsch, who had obtained first-hand knowledge of the CSC–Treasury Board imbroglio while serving as secretary to the Gordon Commission, found the situation to be little improved when he later took over direction of the Board's staff. As secretary to the Board, he immediately recognized the fundamental flaw in governmental machinery which was publicly identified by the Gordon Commission some years previously. There was, he argued, this "double system of negativism and cumbersome duplication." The CSC was rigidly expediting what it conceived to be the merit principle; the Board was still largely preoccupied with "hard-nosed" economizing. Deutsch concluded that "there were no positive approaches, no division of responsibilities in a positive way. Consequently the public service suffered."[37] Some observers during this period also concluded that the process of personnel administration did not seem to improve, despite the many changes. Indeed, as the public service expanded in size, it may even be argued that personnel administration began to deteriorate. As Dowdell states:

> By the mid 1950s, centralized personnel administration began to break down under its own weight. Cumbersome staffing procedures could not respond quickly enough to secure talent in a continually tight employment market. The system of across-the-board salary increases was a sluggish, undifferentiated, and often inaccurate attempt to maintain a competitive position in the labour market, and to retain staff in the face of attractive opportunities in the prosperous private sector. An increasingly professionalized management *cadre* in departments fretted under the restrictions imposed on them.

Nor, Dowdell adds, did Treasury Board offer a solution, for the Board was preoccupied by the financial side of personnel matters and was trapped by a "myriad of trivial administrative matters," with little time for planning.[38]

POSTWAR CHANGES

Despite the fundamental flaws in interagency relationships and the apparent failure of the Government to implement the recommendations of the Gordon Commission, there was a recognition in the Civil Service Commission that changes had to be made in certain areas of personnel management. This recognition of a "crisis" in personnel administration was precipitated by two events. A vacuum in leadership quality in the civil service had occurred owing to the exodus of wartime management returning to their peacetime professions or positions in industry. But at the same time the Canadian Government had committed itself to undertake extensive postwar reconstruction, expansion of welfare services, and rehabilitation and antidepression measures. These new functions required increasing numbers of people with specialized skills; specialists such as these were in short supply. Furthermore, the direction and coordination of these diverse specialists required skilled managers, an improved system of classification and pay to ensure their attraction and retention, and improvements in administrative structures and methods.

By 1945 the CSC still retained the same three primary branches that had been in existence for over two decades: Examination, Organization, and Assignment Branches. When Commissioner Stitt retired in 1945, his place was taken by Stanley G. Nelson, the chief of the Examination Branch and chief executive officer of the CSC. A replacement for Nelson became of paramount importance, faced as the Government was with the need to improve staffing methods in the civil service. In September, 1946, Dr. O. E. Ault joined the staff of the CSC as the new director of the Personnel Selection Branch (as the Examination Branch was retitled). Ault brought with him a breath of change. He had worked for the Ottawa Board of Education prior to 1939 and, as a Lieutenant-Colonel during World War II, had obtained experience in the area of personnel selection. The mandate given to him by Commissioner Bland was to attempt to improve the merit system by devising better selection methods in recruitment. This new activity resulted in the creation of the Testing Division in 1946 which experimented with and finally implemented the newer multiple-choice type of examinations which could be machine scored.[39]

Since 1942 the CSC had sponsored training classes for stenographers and typists through the agency of the Vocational Training Branch of the Department of Labour. This service turned out to be of tremendous value to the departments. In its 1946 Annual Report, the CSC enthusiastically urged the expansion of such programs, and in April, 1947, established a Staff Training Division attached to the Personnel Selection Branch to further promote this end. The courses provided by the Department of Labour served as a basis for the initial program, and the Staff Training Division soon took over this activity altogether. To acquire specialists in this field, the CSC created the separate classification of staff training officer.[40]

Rudimentary changes in the departmental personnel functions also began to take place during this postwar era. The Gordon Commission had criticized the inadequacy of machinery for the administration of departmental personnel matters and recommended "the appointment in every department of an experienced and properly qualified personnel officer with adequate rank and power."[41] The CSC agreed with this recommendation, and in the following year, there began a series of appointments of directors of personnel in many of the large and decentralized departments of government.[42] While personnel management certainly began to grow in importance during this period, these marginal changes in no way meant that the function was fully recognized as having "come of age" in the federal public service. According to Dowdell: "Until the early 1960's there was no consensus in the public service as to what the role of the departmental personnel officer should be or how the personnel unit should be organized, either internally or in relation to other elements of the departmental hierarchy. Many personnel divisions were several levels removed from top management and exerted little influence. Standards of selection for personnel officers were low and training was inadequate."[43]

Be that as it may, one of the roles which seemed to have been recognized was the personnel officer's responsibility for training at the departmental level. Thus, soon after the CSC established its Staff Training Division in the newly organized Personnel Selection Branch, it began to decentralize the training function to make the departmental training units responsible for training in their respective departments. The CSC, however, continued to serve as a source of specialized advice to these departments, as well as coordinating and administering training which applied to government departments on a whole.[44]

Departmental directors of personnel also found themselves drawn into the competition process. Before 1944 appeals were limited to promotional competitions only. With the end of the war and the withdrawal of restrictions on appeals, the number grew sharply: from seventy-four promotional appeals in 1944 to well over three hundred by 1949. In addition, the CSC was also hearing appeals against the refusal of annual increases.[45] Faced with these added duties, the CSC eliminated its preliminary review boards for promotional appeals, and convened all reviews as regular appeal boards. Departmental personnel officers were gradually given responsibilities for intradepartmental competitions. The CSC retained control by performing an audit of procedure on these competitions, and also by using the new appeals machinery as a control device as well.

The CSC's attempts to meet its responsibilities under the Civil Service Act for investigating and reporting upon organizational changes in the departments continued to present difficulties in implementation. In 1946 the CSC hired several specialists in Organization and Methods (O & M) for the express purpose of aiding in "the development of existing services to departments and other agencies in respect to organization and operations problems."[46] The central personnel agency reminded its public that "management consciousness" had spread in the governments of the United Kingdom, the United States, France, and others, and that advisory services on organization and methods had been established in these places as an aid to operating departmental agencies. The CSC itself was further aware that "great benefits, in terms of increased efficiency and economy, can be realized by the intensive study and adjustment of organizational structure and the simplification and modernization of systems and methods."[47] This latter point, in the CSC's estimation, served as an additional reason for the development of this service. Furthermore, there was a need to consolidate and reduce the size of the civil service which had greatly expanded during the war, and it was hoped that the specialists in O & M would prove helpful in this regard.[48]

In 1948 these specialists were formally recognized as the Organization and Methods Division. Additional staff were recruited so that by the end of 1949 there were twenty-two officers in the Division.[49] The duties and responsibilities of the new Division were defined as follows: "To afford practical assistance to departments and agencies of government through the systematic examination of the structure and operations, and the procedures and work methods employed in their various branches, divisions, and sections, and to engage in such other related studies as will contribute to the progressive improvement of public management as a whole."[50] Although this implied that the Division was to act in an advisory capacity, it soon began to initiate studies, often without the consent of the department involved. While conducting unit surveys of classification in departments, officers of the Organization Branch frequently spotted problems that they felt should be remedied by the application of Organization and Methods techniques, and under the direction of George Jackson, the chief of the Branch, the O & M Division was ordered to undertake studies of these situations. This caused a furious debate within the Branch between those who espoused the idea that O & M should be purely advisory in scope and those who advocated that the service should be actively imposed on the departments. Many of the O & M officers themselves complained that Treasury Board was often responsible for many of the studies they were ordered to undertake, and that the results were then used for control purposes, much to the dismay of the department concerned and of the O & M Division.[51] Indeed, one department was so infuriated by this very fact that it refused to allow the O & M Division on its premises for twenty years afterwards.[52]

The debate within the Division continued for several years, and was not really solved until James C. Gardiner became chief of the Division in 1951. Gardiner was a firm adherent to the concept of the advisory nature of O & M's service, and under his direction this aspect was emphasized, and the service was never again imposed. It acted only on the request of departments, and reports were considered departmental property with implementation left solely to their discretion. Moreover, although the Division remained attached to the Organization Branch, Gardiner was operationally responsible directly to the Commissioners, while matters of policy were to be worked out with the chief of the Organization Branch. Any difference of opinion in this regard was to be referred to the Commissioners for a decision.[53] With its new orientation, the O & M Division met with much more success in its studies. The number of implementations of its reports sharply increased from 50 percent in 1951 to 90 percent in 1960.[54]

The postwar period also witnessed an expansion of the activities of the district offices. Similar to the process at the headquarters during these years, the district officers were continually being granted greater authority and responsibility. In 1948 the CSC began to hold more qualifying examinations for permanent appointments on the local level instead of on a dominion-wide basis as was hitherto the practice. The majority of these examinations were conducted through the district offices.[55] The district offices also became more active in promotional competitions, appeal boards, and character investigations.[56] By 1950 they were authorized to compile and complete eligible lists for their own competitions, subject to headquarters' audit.[57] In 1958 this responsibility was again significantly altered when the headquarters' unit terminated the practice of checking the eligible lists from the district offices. CSC officials in the field were now to assume full responsibility for appointments made from their local eligible lists, subject only to direction, control, and audit from headquarters. Moreover, the practice of sending to Ottawa all papers relating to recruitment and competitions conducted in the field was discontinued. District offices were given full responsibility for the accuracy of work relating to selection and appointment of candidates, subject to the same condition as in the case of the eligible lists.[58] In the following year, they were also granted the authority to issue their own certificates of appointment, instead of having this done in Ottawa.[59] Thus, by 1960, administrative delegation which began in the postwar period had reached the point where district offices were completely responsible for virtually all appointments, at intermediate salary levels, in their respective districts.

The expanding authority of the district offices was however limited to delegation of responsibilities coming under the Personnel Selection and Assignment Branches. In the late forties an officer of the Organization Branch was stationed in the Montreal office, but the experiment did not meet with a great deal of success. The officer in question received his instructions from Ottawa, and in the opinion of the director of the Montreal office, "he was just taking up space as far as we were concerned."[60] The district offices expanded further during the postwar years. By 1950, there were ten district offices situated in St. John's, Halifax, St. John, Montreal, Ottawa, Toronto, Winnipeg, Regina, Edmonton, and Vancouver. In addition, there were suboffices located in Moncton, Quebec, Calgary, and Victoria. In 1954, two more suboffices were added in London and Saskatoon, bringing the total number of offices to sixteen.

In 1951, one of the more important statutory authorities bearing on the organization and responsibilities of the Treasury Board was enacted. The

224

Financial Administration Act consolidated in statutory form many of the powers which the Board had gathered under Orders in Council during the depression and war years,[61] and under the authority of the War Measures Act. First of all, the Act provided for the statutory establishment of the Treasury Board, which shall act as "a committee of the Queen's Privy Council for Canada on all matters relating to finance, revenue . . . establishments, the terms and conditions of employment of persons in the Public Service, and general administrative policy in the Public Service referred to the Board by the Governor in Council or on which the Board considers it desirable to report to the Governor in Council, or on which the Board considers it necessary to act under powers conferred by this or any other Act."[62]

Moreover, the Board was authorized "to exercise all or any of the powers, other than powers of appointment, of the Governor in Council under the *Civil Service Act*." The Board was also allowed to make regulations "subject to any other Act, prescribing rates of compensation, hours of work and other conditions of employment," and "subject to any other act, for any purpose necessary for the efficient administration of the public service."[63] The Treasury Board was also given the authority to make regulations:

(d) notwithstanding the Civil Service Act,

(i) authorizing the payment to persons in the Public Service of compensation or other rewards for inventions or practical suggestions for improvements and

(ii) governing payments to persons in the Public Service by way of reimbursement for travelling or other expenses and allowances to meet special expenses arising out of their duties; and

(e) subject to any other Act, for any other purpose necessary for the efficient administration of the Public Service.[64]

Personnel responsibilities were only a small part of the overall duties entrusted to the Board. Mallory comments that the vast increase in governmental activities during and after the war burdened the Cabinet with too much routine detail; the 1951 Act shifted responsibility for this work to Treasury Board.[65] White interprets this Act as a further "upgrading of the Board's role": "The Board now assumed final authority in the management, both in administration and organization, of the public service. It also assumed under the Financial Administration Act the authority of the Governor in Council which strengthened its hand in the day to day relations with departments. This was the first step in releasing the supreme operational executive for matters of high policy and delegating to Treasury Board day to day management responsibilities."[66]

In view of the Board's extension into so many areas since the early thirties, a comment from the then Secretary, R. B. Bryce, at the time of the passage of the 1951 Act, was very much to the point. Asked by a member of the Public Accounts Committee if the general purpose of the legislation was not to increase the powers of the Board, Bryce replied: "Yes, it will increase its powers, or clarify its powers."[67] The latter term, "clarify," perhaps best describes the effects of the 1951 Act.

Superficially, it might appear to an outside observer that "Treasury Board" meant simply the committee of cabinet ministers which bore that name. In fact, a vast amount of work was being delegated to the permanent staff. The Board's status as a committee of ministers seems somehow to have fundamentally obscured its status as a bureaucratic organization, with permanent interests of its own. Just how much influence the Board's staff did in fact exert can be glimpsed in the forthright words of C. J. Mackenzie in a discussion with George Jackson of the CSC and a departmental personnel director in the early fifties:

> The effect of the Financial Administration Act [is] that, in general, Treasury Board Minutes to Council for issue in the form of Orders in Council, are dealt with again in a purely routine manner by Council. I don't think they're ever looked at unless some major item of policy is involved such as a general salary revision, when the Board's staff would see to it that the Ministers in Council were fully briefed on the case. The Minutes go up in a large binder stapled together, and they lie on the table, and the Ministers can open this binder if they want to but they would probably get lost in the series of Superannuation cases which look very dull in the form of a Minute, and they wouldn't be attracted to further investigation.[68]

Moreover, while the Civil Service Act itself specified that the Governor in Council was to retain certain prerogatives, an Order in Council of October, 1953, delegated to the Treasury Board almost all such prerogatives.[69]

A further regularization of relationships between the CSC and the Treasury Board took place in 1953–54 with the inauguration of the Establishment Review Committee system. These new procedures were, in effect, an institutionalization of the Treasury Board–CSC modus vivendi on establishments as it had taken shape during the war. Drawing on the example of the British civil service,[70] a committee system was set up to examine and report upon departmental staff requirements for the ensuing year, within the context of the estimate procedure. One committee was established for each department, to consist of a CSC representative who was to act as chairman, a representative of Treasury Board, and a representative of the department in question, usually the director of personnel.

In June of each year the Secretary of the Treasury Board sent to all the deputy ministers what was known as the "sermon on the amounts," a document which set the general government policy guidelines for expenditure for the following year. The Establishment Review Committees then met, with the CSC representative concerning himself particularly with questions of classification and with examining proposals "in the light of his knowledge about standards of work load."[71] The Treasury representative was more concerned with the total numbers proposed by departments in the light of government policy. The report of the Committee was written by the CSC representative, and then submitted to Treasury Board by the department as part of its estimates material. The final decisions, of course, lay with the Board.

Stead reported in 1955 that "by bringing together the three organizations around the table it is possible for the responsibilities of the department, the Treasury Board and the Civil Service Commission to be discharged in one motion."[72] Other observers were less sanguine. Dowdell argues that the review procedure "tended to deal almost exclusively with proposed additions to the staff complement, rather than with the total use of manpower in relation to program priorities. Often the discussions weltered in minutiae and ended in a compromise between what the department considered essential and the Board's staff considered reasonable, with neither party having much objective evidence to support its position."[73] The Glassco Commission investigated this system at some length in the early sixties, and pronounced itself less than impressed: the system, it concluded, "imposes damaging delays, creates frustrating inflexibility, and is expensive.[74] The delays in obtaining new staff might range from a low of nine months to as long as two and a half years. The inflexibility of the procedure inhibited long-range planning and forced departments to think in immediate, year-by-year terms. Worst of all, the system did little to reduce that fatal division of responsibility pointed out by the Gordon Commission at the end of the war. As the Glassco Report reiterated:

The Civil Service Commission controls some matters, the Treasury Board others; both are involved in such issues as classification and related pay-scales in the sense that the Commission formulates and recommends and the Board accepts or rejects. The two agencies, together with a given department, constitute a complex triangle of authority and responsibility in countless detailed problems and requests sometimes travel lengthy circuitous routes before decisions are made and action taken.[75]

In a sense, then, the Establishment Review Committees were only an institutionalization of an inefficient ad hoc system. Once again, it can be seen that the real problem lay in the overlapping of powers and responsibilities. Until that thorny problem was dealt with, no amount of gimmickry could clear up the source of inefficiency.

That the old problems of conflict between the CSC and the Treasury Board persisted through the fifties is beyond doubt. A 1956 internal CSC report on personnel administration in the government service reviewed the historical record in some detail, and gave major prominence to the rivalry between the two agencies.[76] After noting that in the ten years following the Gordon Report the size of the CSC staff had fallen from 713 to 621, while that of the Treasury Board had risen from 30 to 96 (of which 21 were in the Board's personnel policy section), the study concluded flatly that the CSC had gradually been forced to play a "policing, legalistic role, without too much power behind it."[77] Even in recruitment, the Board had made its power felt. However, the Board itself was not solely responsible:

> The Civil Service Commission, for reasons which need not be exposed, has been extremely weak in defending its legal position, and has often lost ground to Treasury Board because of its own inactivity or inability, or unwillingness to take positive action and to cope with new problems and situations as they presented themselves.[78]

The same study listed a number of specific grievances against the arbitrary exercise of authority by Treasury Board, and noted that since the rise of the Board in the thirties, the Board's staff had not met with the Commissioners "more than a dozen times" to discuss personnel policy:

> This almost unbelievable absence of direct contact between the Commission and the Government on personnel problems has considerably weakened the position of the Commission, and lowered its prestige in the eyes of Departments, of Staff Associations, and of the Government itself. . . . Members of Treasury Board Staff invariably speak on civil service problems as if they were the Personnel Agency of the Government.[79]

These complaints, of course, only underscore the validity of the Gordon Commission's analysis in 1946. They are symptomatic of an unhealthy situation, of the inevitable difficulties into which the CSC was forced by the system of two control agencies competing, unequally, over the same jurisdiction. The developments of the early fifties provided no solutions, but merely put off the day of reckoning.

1. J. R. Baldwin, Secretary, Cabinet Committee on Reconstruction, Confidential Report on Technical and Professional Personnel—Government Employment, November 30, 1945; Interdepartmental Committee on Public Investment, Secret Report on Problems of Civil Service Employment, October 30, 1945, PSC Files.

2. Interview.

3. Interview.

4. P.C. 563 (February 15, 1946).

5. Interview.

6. Royal Commission on Administrative Classifications in the Public Service, 1946, *Report*, pp. 5–6.

7. Ibid., p. 9.

8. Ibid., pp. 17, 11, 23.

9. Ibid., p. 24.

10. Ibid., p. 9.

11. Interview.

12. Interview.

13. Interview.

14. Interview. This statement is not meant to imply that absolutely nothing came of the Report. Indeed, the changes in personnel administration after 1946 (described later in this chapter) seemed to have been spurred by the criticisms voiced during the Gordon Commission inquiry, although one could not attribute them directly to its recommendations.

15. Taylor Cole, *The Canadian Bureaucracy*, p. 55.

16. Ibid.

17. This quotation and much of the following information come from various interviews.

18. Cabinet ministers not included on Treasury Board had special grievances, as they tended to feel that their departments had greater difficulty in obtaining funds than those whose heads were also members of the Board. Interview.

19. Interview.

20. *Civil Servants Digest*, May, 1946, p. 2, and August, 1946, p. 2.

21. Ibid., pp. 2–3. For other criticisms along the same lines, see *Civil Service Review* 19 (June, 1946), p. 108; *Civil Service News* 24 (August, 1946), p. 181.

22. Cole, *The Canadian Bureaucracy*, p. 56.

23. Ibid., pp. 57 and 100.

24. Interview.

25. Kingsley Martin, *The Rise of French Liberal Thought: A Study of Political Ideas from Bayle to Condorcet* (New York: New York University Press, 1954), p. 166.

26. A full discussion of the factors influencing the formation of this philosophy is found in chapter 7.

27. Interviews.

28. Walter L. White, "The Treasury Board in Canada," pp. 121–22.

29. Ibid., pp. 122, 123, and 124–25.

30. G. W. Stead, "The Treasury Board of Canada," p. 85.

31. Interview.

32. White, "The Treasury Board in Canada," pp. 215–16.

33. Ibid., p. 215.

34. Ibid., pp. 124–25.

35. Indeed, in at least three interviews, senior civil servants felt that many of the criticisms of personnel administration aired by the 1960–62 Glassco Royal Commission might have been unnecessary if this change in leadership had been effected sixteen years previously.

36. Interview.

37. Interview.

38. R. H. Dowdell, "Personnel Administration in the Federal Public Service," in A. M. Willms and W. D. K. Kernaghan, eds., *Public Administration in Canada: Selected Readings*, p. 368.

39. Interview.

40. CSC, *Annual Report*, 1947, p. 8.

41. Royal Commission on Administrative Classifications in the Public Service, 1946, *Report*, p. 21.

42. Many of the personnel appointed were former CSC employees, while others were departmental employees who had previously engaged in departmental personnel matters, sometimes marginally. By 1945 National Defence was perhaps the only department with a director of personnel. In 1947, a director of personnel was appointed in the Department of Transport. Others soon followed: National Revenue–Customs and Excise, 1948, Mines and Technical Surveys and the Post Office, 1949, Agriculture, 1950, Northern Affairs and National Resources, 1951, and Veterans Affairs, 1952. D. R. Cameron, "The Origins of the Personnel Administration Staffing Program" (mimeograph), p. 7.

43. Dowdell, "Personnel Administration," p. 376.

44. For example, courses in work methods, administrative theory, and general orientation courses.

45. In its response to the Coon Committee Report, Treasury Board had stated its intention to end the practice whereby annual increases had almost become automatic. In 1944 an Order in Council instructed the CSC to prepare an annual efficiency report to aid the Government in determining whether or not an employee was eligible for an annual increase. The Order also provided for the CSC to hear appeals against the refusal of the annual increment. See the statement of Treasury Board on personnel policy, issued June 1, 1943, cited in *Civil Service Review* 16 (June, 1943), pp. 124–26. See also P.C. 126/9180 (1944).

46. CSC, *Annual Report*, 1947, p. 12.

47. Ibid.

48. Mohammad Afzal, "Management Analysis: An Emerging Staff Function," p. 274.

49. James C. Gardiner, "The Management Analysis Division," prepared for the Civil Service Commission, December 30, 1960 (mimeograph), p. 1.

50. CSC, *Annual Report*, 1948, p. 10.

51. Interview; Gardiner, "The Management Analysis Division," p. 2.

52. Interview.

53. Interview; Gardiner, "The Management Analysis Division," p. 2.

54. Interview; Afzal, "Management Analysis," p. 280.

55. CSC, *Annual Report*, 1948, p. 7.

56. CSC, *Annual Report*, 1949, p. 10.

57. CSC, *Annual Report*, 1950, p. 9.

58. See CSC Minute 58/4 (January 7, 1958), recommendations 12 and 15, and CSC Minute 58/60 (April 3, 1958), recommendations 12 and 15, Secretary's Office, PSC.

59. CSC, *Annual Report*, 1960, p. 23.

60. G. Beaudry, "Civil Service Commission District Offices," speech to an unidentified group, n.d. (mimeograph), p. 1; for a description of the development of district offices in these years see also PSC, Staffing Branch, W. E. Sinclair, "District Offices," internal study, June 1, 1967 (mimeograph), pp. 1–7.

61. 15–16 George VI (1951), c. 12.

62. Ibid., s. 5(1).

63. Ibid., s. 5(2); s. 5(2)(c); s. 5(2)(e).

64. Ibid., s. 5(7).

65. J. R. Mallory, "Delegated Legislation in Canada: Recent Changes in Machinery," p. 468.

66. White, "The Treasury Board in Canada," p. 120.

67. Quoted in "Personnel Administration in the Government Service," internal document prepared for the Commissioners, 1956 (typescript).

68. "The Relationship between the Civil Service Commission, Treasury Board and the Departments," minutes of discussion between G. T. Jackson (CSC), C. J. Mackenzie (Treasury Board staff), and L. J. Rodger (Department of Trade and Commerce), n.d. (mimeograph), pp. 15–16. Internal evidence indicates that the discussion must have taken place during 1951 and 1952. It would appear to have been arranged for an audience of civil servants, probably staff members of the CSC and the Board, and departmental personnel officers.

69. P.C. 1553–68 (October 14, 1953).

70. Interview.

71. H. J. Hodder, "The Functions and the Organization of the Treasury Board," May 26, 1960, p. 8, files of the Royal Commission on Government Organization, vol. 1.

72. Stead, "The Treasury Board of Canada," p. 88.

73. Dowdell, "Personnel Administration," p. 379.

74. Royal Commission on Government Organization, 1960–62, *Report*, 1, p. 356.

75. Ibid., p. 362.

76. It has not been possible to determine the exact authorship of this report.

77. "Personnel Administration in the Government Service," p. 31.

78. Ibid., p. 24.

79. Ibid., p. 23.

Chapter Eleven

The Precursors of Change: The 1954 Secret Committee and the Heeney Report

*I would be less than candid if I did not say
at once that nothing which has yet come
before the present Commissioners leads
me to believe that the part which the Commission should undertake in a reformed
régime is likely to be less onerous or less
authoritative than that which it has under
present law and practice. Indeed, it may
well prove that, because of the Commission's independence, we shall find strong
argument for an extension of its responsibilities in some areas beyond the terrain
it now occupies under the law.*

From a speech made by A. D. P. Heeney
to the annual meeting of the Canadian
Political Science Association, June 6,
1958

THROUGHOUT THE EARLY fifties the Government appeared seemingly un-
concerned with the growing problems in the field of personnel management
in the civil service. Yet, despite its relatively impassive public face, it was
not entirely unaware of the changes which had occurred over the years. The
great deficiencies inherent in a system whereby responsibility was divided
between the Treasury Board and the Civil Service Commission were, in
fact, obvious to Prime Minister St. Laurent, who recognized that fundamental changes had to be carried out, with a wholesale revamping of the
Civil Service Act as a projected goal. Perhaps as early as 1953, and certainly by 1954, Mr. St. Laurent had decided that A. D. P. Heeney, then the
Canadian Ambassador to the United States, should be placed in command
of the CSC at the earliest convenient moment as part of an infusion of new
blood into the organization.[1]

In the meantime, however, the Prime Minister decided to seek top-level advice on new directions for civil service legislation. In mid-1954, the Cabinet agreed to the Prime Minister's proposal that a small group of officials be convened by the Cabinet Secretary, R. B. Bryce, which was to include, among others, the Civil Service Commissioners, the Secretary of the Treasury Board, and, when possible, Heeney. This committee was to review the Civil Service Act and report "whether and in what manner it should be revised." Realizing the political sensitivity of any change in legislation concerning civil servants, the Cabinet emphasized that "the study should be carried out as quietly and confidentially as possible to avoid undesirable publicity and speculation, especially in Ottawa."[2]

Bryce prepared an agenda for discussion which touched on a wide array of problems ranging from the veterans preference and responsibility for promotions to career planning and prevailing rates employees. A key point for discussion was the relationship between the CSC and Treasury Board. In Bryce's words:

The role of the Commission and the Treasury Board and the Governor in Council should be modernized and clarified. It is suggested that, in general terms, the Civil Service Commission should be primarily and perhaps wholly responsible for the classification of positions, subject only to such general influence as the Treasury Board must inevitably exert in determining the salary appropriations. On the other hand, it is suggested that the pay rates for particular classes should be established by the Governor in Council in law and the Treasury Board in practice, after receiving advice from the Civil Service Commission rather than recommendation. In this connection it should be considered whether it is desirable to build up a situation where the Commission can ultimately act as a mediator and arbitrator between the government and its organized employees. If the pressure for collective bargaining grows, it may well be desirable to have some sort of mediator of this kind on a continuing basis. It is suggested that the Treasury Board should be made definitely responsible for determining the number of positions in an establishment as this is a type of decision for which the government must basically accept responsibility. In fact, they will probably rely to a considerable degree on the advice of the classification officers of the Commission in coming to any conclusion in regard to the numbers that should be allowed, as well of course on the information received from the departments concerned and from the officers of the Board.[3]

The first meeting of the committee was dominated by the three Commissioners Bland, Nelson, and Boudreau. The result was an apparent lack of enthusiasm for change. Bryce confided privately to Heeney, who had been absent, that the meeting had served mainly to allow the Commissioners to "overcome the first shock" of contemplating a major revision of the Civil Service Act:

> The whole group was heavily weighted with Civil Service Commissioners and I had to do most of the talking and all of the proposing of any consequence.
>
> It is clear that the Civil Service Commissioners are far from keen to make any amendments to the Act and will come along only reluctantly. On being pressed they recognize that the Act is seriously out of date, but they contend that one way or another they are getting along and adapting it to present circumstances reasonably well. There is some truth in this but of course it depends on how much zest one has for improvement and logic.
>
> I think Bland would like to be left alone to enjoy his last year or two without the prospect of a long Parliamentary battle and himself on the witness stand a good deal. The other Commissioners have no particular zeal for opening up the Veterans Preference on the one hand and the position of French Canadians on the other.[4]

Bryce foresaw a "good deal of cacophony," and a "very lukewarm Chairman of the Commission in putting it across."[5] Believing that if revisions were not brought in at the coming session of Parliament years might elapse before the initiative was recovered, Bryce speculated on "whether we will be able to persuade the Prime Minister that it is worthwhile taking on the troubles he will have in the House of Commons with this measure in order to get an Act more logical and up-to-date." In reply, Heeney commented directly on the CSC:

> The reluctance of our friends on the Commission to grasp some of these thistles is hardly surprising, but I do hope that the rest of us will be able to bring them along, at least in the more important sectors. I suppose that one of the endemic problems in this whole business tends to be the inertia of those in nominal control. Probably the only treatment is periodic shakeup.[6]

A second meeting grappled inconclusively with the problem of whether the CSC or Treasury Board should control classification. It was all too evident that no consensus was going to emerge.[7] Background papers were prepared on various problems, but somehow, by this stage, the initiative seems to have passed out of the committee's hands. In late November of

1954, Heeney expressed fears that "the project for amendment of the Act is . . . going to be allowed to wither and die." He added that "perhaps the real difficulty is in getting time for such a long term planning exercise in the midst of so many varied urgencies."[8] Heeney's fears were confirmed when the Prime Minister indicated that he would not introduce amendments to the Act at the coming session.[9] No changes were proposed to Parliament either in 1955 or 1956.

Heeney was quite correct in suggesting that long-term changes could not be devised by busy officials with only a few spare moments to devote to such a special task. In fact, the Government was more concerned with the appointment of Heeney to the CSC as the best means of reform. With the Suez crisis and other international problems, Heeney could not leave Washington until 1957.[10] Until then, no changes were possible. Thus the situation in government personnel management at the close of the first postwar decade was as inconclusive as it had been at the end of the war. In retrospect, however, this decade appears merely as the calm before the storm.

Staff Associations and the Demand for Collective Bargaining

If the first postwar decade had failed to see the resolution of long-standing conflicts between the Civil Service Commission and Treasury Board, it was also a period of increasing tension on another front: the relationship between the Government and its organized employees. In this conflict, the CSC was also a central figure, and the outcome was to be a critical factor in determining the future role of that organization.

By the early 1950s the staff associations had become restless under the National Joint Council system of employer-employee relations. Such time-honoured terms as "staff participation" and "negotiation" began in some cases to be replaced by more militant formulations such as "arbitration" and "collective bargaining." In 1953 the Civil Service Federation, the largest of the staff associations, began to make forthright demands for collective bargaining (without the right to strike) along the lines laid down in the federal Industrial Relations and Disputes Investigations Act.[11] In 1955 the Civil Service Association of Ottawa called for the adoption of a negotiating procedure and the resort to arbitration where necessary. It also requested that the Government establish a royal commission "to inquire into the problems of employer-employee relations in the Federal Civil Service."[12] This was the first formal resolution in favour of compulsory arbitration by a major staff association.

This evidence of growing militancy among the organized civil servants is related to several factors. There appears, first of all, to have been an infusion of new and younger leadership into the associations. The old leadership, with its experience drawn from the twenties and thirties, was being replaced by younger, more energetic, and well-educated personnel. This factor cannot be emphasized too strongly; it is borne out by the position of many of these younger men in the upper echelons of the federal bureaucracy and private industry today. The concrete result of this new talent in the fifties was the increasing statistical and logical sophistication of the associations' briefs. Prior to the fifties, the CSC felt that most of the statistical material prepared by the associations betrayed a lack of familiarity with simple statistical concepts, particularly the use of index figures.[13] A new respect now had to be accorded to the arguments of the associations.

Another factor lay in the changing attitudes among the leadership of the associations toward trade union activity. Even more than most white-collar employees, civil servants had been traditionally reluctant to be identified with organized labour. But the prolonged postwar inflation, coupled with the Government's adamant refusal to engage in meaningful wage negotiations, forced many civil servants into a more radical attitude concerning their own status. By 1956 a leading staff association official could make the observation: "Up to comparatively recent years most civil servants viewed their various Organizations as 'Associations,' and objected to being regarded as 'Unions' in a labour sense. There has been a significant movement from this position, which has been due in part to a greater awareness of the role of organized labour, and in part due to the rising demands for some form of collective bargaining."[14]

This development soon began to arouse the interest of the large labour federations, the Canadian Labour Congress (CLC) and the Trades and Labour Congress (TLC). The fifties were, on the whole, a rather static period for trade union membership in Canada. Although civil service staff associations represented less than half the total number of civil servants in 1956, their membership and financial position were in fact being strengthened, aided, no doubt, by the check-off of membership dues won through the auspices of the NJC. Since white-collar labour, especially in government employment, was a growing component of the total labour force in Canada, since government employees were receiving wages below the average for private employees, and since a plethora of competing associations were facing an arbitrary employer, the federal civil service must have appeared an attractive area for the expansion of an organized labour movement facing a levelling-off of its membership. Nor were the advantages of an alliance with the labour movement lost on some of the staff association officials: "There is no doubt . . . that some link with the general trade union movement as represented in the labour congresses in Canada is necessary to strengthen the staff associations. We already are receiving many improvements in working conditions in the public service which were first secured in industry through trade union organization. Governments being what they are, are very sensitive to public opinion and will not move toward improvements until such have become the common practice in other employment."[15] There was, in addition, the feeling that affiliation with the large labour federations would make extensive research resources available to the associations which they then lacked.[16]

To many observers, the logic of the situation thus pointed to some type of union affiliation to ensure more equitable treatment of civil servants by their employers. Both the CLC and TLC formally petitioned the Government to grant civil servants as a whole the right to bargain collectively. Yet, while some of the more radical associations did affiliate, the majority of civil servants remained aloof. Suspicion of the CLC's motives was no doubt fostered by that organization's full-scale participation in the creation of the New Democratic Party. The press spoke of a "CLC-CCF merger," and the election of Stanley Knowles, defeated CCF Member of Parliament, as a vice-president of the CLC "heightened the impression that the new party was to be some sort of amalgam of the socialist party and the labour congress itself."[17] Since civil servants were supposed to be politically neutral, it was widely feared that affiliation with the CLC would create more difficulties than it would solve, despite the CLC's assurances to the contrary.[18] But even if the civil service activities of the CSC in the fifties were not substantially rewarded with membership increases, it cannot be denied that the intervention of organized labour hastened the era of collective bargaining in the public service. It enhanced the staff associations' consciousness of their own power and helped focus the attention of the Government on their demands.

But despite the growing clamour for collective bargaining and arbitration, until 1956 the Government seems to have successfully ignored the developments occurring within the associations. The arguments utilized to combat the criticisms of the civil servants generally followed a fairly consistent pattern during these years.[19] The first of these arguments involved the traditional objection that the Government was a "sovereign employer" and could not be party to a binding agreement. Second, the Government apparently believed that a bargaining regime and the merit system would be mutually exclusive; it feared that the granting of bargaining rights would eventually lead to a closed or union shop, thereby damaging the merit principle. The Prime Minister stated this belief quite explicitly in 1953 in reply to a TLC brief: "Collective bargaining and the Civil Service Commission just do not go together. If you had the one you would not have the other."[20] He added that the majority of the public would be "incensed" if the CSC, as a representative body given control of the civil service by Parliament, were to be set aside.

Closely connected with this argument was the objection that the CSC provided a substitute for bargaining. In rejecting the demand from the postal associations for a conciliation board during a salary dispute in 1955, the Prime Minister offered the opinion that

> the Civil Service Commission is an independent body, established by Parliament and not subject to any direction by the government, which has the duty of investigating questions of this kind, hearing the views of the associations, and making recommendations to the government as to the action which it should take. I feel that this special full-time tribunal established by Parliament, and assisted by a large and expert staff, is far better able to give proper consideration to proposals . . . than would some ad hoc conciliation board.[21]

The CSC itself strongly maintained this position for obvious reasons, claiming that it held a "unique position" as an "independent, impartial arbiter" between management and its employees.[22]

All these arguments were, of course, very much open to question at this time,[23] but it is important to note that the third argument in particular was beginning to show signs of strain. The success of this argument depended upon the success of the Government and the CSC in maintaining the "independence" of the CSC. Yet during the 1950s their ability to do so was greatly weakened. On the one hand, it was manifestly evident that while the CSC might be independent in law, the degree of independence was conditioned by the fact that the Cabinet held the power of appointing and reappointing Commissioners.[24] In addition, the staff associations were becoming more acutely aware of the CSC's quasi-managerial position. As one observer in this period pointed out, the associations had to deal with "a number of authorities acting in an employer's capacity, including Department heads, the Civil Service Commission, the Official Side of the National Joint Council, and various Cabinet Ministers. All of these perform certain of the functions of an employer: none is prepared to admit to having full responsibility, and the ball can quite easily get passed back and forth to the frustration of the staff groups."[25] The CSC's position on the NJC scarcely commended itself to the associations, as well, for instead of acting as an impartial chairman, the CSC representative functioned as a management spokesman.[26] Eventually some of the associations began to openly question this aspect of the CSC's independence: "While it cannot be denied that the Commission has the employees' interests at heart, its 'heavy responsibilities' towards the 'executive agencies' preclude it taking the objective view required of a tribunal."[27] All in all, as J. D. Love, President of the CSAO, suggested in 1956, "It is possibly fair to say that the day-to-day relationship between the Commission and the government is such that the degree of its independence is less in practice than it is in law."[28]

Doubts concerning the position of the CSC had, by 1956, even begun to penetrate the organization itself. Speaking before the convention of the Civil Service Federation, Commissioner Boudreau sent up a trial balloon for the consideration of civil servants. After asserting that the CSC was "very definitely" questioning the theory that the NJC was able to take care of all conflicts between the Government and its employees, Boudreau termed the NJC an "official discussion group" or "study group." He then went so far as to suggest that

> the Civil Service Commission is not afraid of arbitration. We are carefully studying the possibility of suggesting to the powers that be a form of arbitration. . . . We believe that there are essential differences between industrial workers and employees of the Queen, but we believe that taking cognizance of those differences it would and should be possible to define a proper and mutually satisfactory negotiating procedure between organized civil servants and their employer, which is the Government.[29]

Although it was not clear precisely what kind of arrangement Boudreau was advocating, nor what the role of the CSC was to be, the Government moved quickly to quell any hopes for a system of arbitration. On the day following Boudreau's address, Walter Harris, the Minister of Finance, told the convention that

> the Commissioners have their own views and of course are free to express them. For that reason up to the present time, we have felt that the ultimate decision on these matters would of course have to be made by the Government itself because Parliament, as you know, is rather jealous of the expenditure of public monies and prefers to do that itself and not have it done by others.[30]

The Government, it seemed, was determined to remain obdurate on the matter of bargaining and arbitration.

THE 1956 SECRET COMMITTEE AND THE APPOINTMENT OF HEENEY TO THE CSC

Despite Harris' forthright opposition to arbitration, however, there are indications that the growing militancy of the associations was forcing the

Government to reconsider its position. In his book on staff relations in the civil service, Professor Frankel detected a new willingness beginning in 1956 on the part of the Prime Minister to consider arbitration as a matter open for discussion.[31] It is interesting to discover exactly what lay below this "softening" in attitude.

The years of 1954 and 1955, for reasons discussed by Frankel, had been marked by a significant toning down of demands on the part of the associations. But in 1956 they once again became more aggressive.[32] In anticipation of renewed pressure, the Prime Minister requested Bryce to establish a committee of senior officials, which was to include the Civil Service Commissioners, to consider the question of collective bargaining and arbitration. At its first meeting on July 18, 1956, the committee showed itself fairly unanimous in its opposition to full collective bargaining for civil servants because of the multitude of problems it would raise. As an alternative, however, Bryce raised the idea of putting some real meaning into the CSC's claim to being an arbiter between management and the employees by enhancing it as the third party in a triangular negotiating process—a concept he had originally introduced during the meetings of the 1954 secret committee:

> I advanced the thesis that . . . it would seem best to plan over the next few years to develop and stress the independence of the Civil Service Commission, and use it eventually as a body that would enjoy the confidence of both the organized employees and the government as an employer, and could mediate between the two when the routine processes did not bring results that were acceptable to both sides. I said that if we were to follow this strategy, we should have it in mind in developing the role of the Commission almost from now on. It has been possible in the past to leave this role somewhat ambiguous, but the more we get into discussions with employees over salary problems, the more difficult it is to leave unanswered the question as to whether the Civil Service Commission is representing the government as an employer, or whether it is an independent tribunal which can be brought in instead of outside mediators or arbitrators.[33]

Interestingly enough, while the Treasury Board Secretary and two Deputy Ministers, Dave Sim and Arthur Brown, expressed general agreement with the idea of the CSC developing into an independent tribunal, opposition came from the Commissioners themselves. Chairman Nelson was "noncommittal," while Boudreau "was inclined to feel that the Commission should be the personnel agency of the government and not an independent tribunal," since he believed that an agency charged with recruitment and classification could not separate itself from management in recommending pay and other conditions of employment.[34]

If Bryce's proposal met with an unenthusiastic reception from the Commissioners, it seems to have held a great deal of appeal for the Government since it offered an apparent way out of its dilemma. From this point the Government seems to have pursued Bryce's plan with deliberate single-mindedness. It is possible to discern a distinct attempt to stress the independence of the CSC. It no longer offered the CSC as an alternative to arbitration, but instead began to suggest that a form of arbitration could take place through an independent CSC. A speech made by the Prime Minister to the Professional Institute in February, 1957, is fairly indicative of the approach adopted.

> I feel that the proper use and development of the Civil Service Commission offers more hope in securing the fair and effective settlement and revision of the terms of service of Civil Servants than would the creation of some ad hoc arbitration body. I would suggest that before advocating special new machinery for arbitration, we should give serious thought to the proper use of the body already created by Parliament with authority in this field. Here we have, in the Commission a specialized, impartial and experienced tribunal, armed with a detailed law that enjoys a great deal of public support, made up of members who may only be dismissed by Parliament; a body that is not subject to any direction by the government and which is provided with a large and expert staff. This organization is able to understand the views of both the Civil Service and the government and its departments. It has the duty and qualifications to advise and inform both the government as an employer and the Civil Servants as employees. It can mediate effectively between them if it is given an opportunity.[35]

The obvious lack of enthusiasm on the part of the CSC for its proposed new role made the Government more than ever determined to appoint Heeney to the chairmanship. Bland had retired in 1955 after completing forty-seven years in the public service and his second ten-year term as chairman. Stanley Nelson, although ailing, had been persuaded to assume the chairmanship on an interim basis, but in 1956 he found the strains of office too great and offered his resignation. In October, Prime Minister St. Laurent wrote Heeney in Washington to once again renew the offer of appointment to the CSC. The Prime Minister described the task he wanted done in these terms:

> We are not satisfied with the way the Commission has developed and operated in recent years and we believe that it needs strong leadership

and substantial re-organization if it is to fulfill its proper functions in our machinery of government. Moreover, much attention needs to be given to the best role for the Commission in the changing problems and conditions of the labour market and of the relations between the government as employer and its employees and their organizations. The Civil Service Act itself, which has been in substantially its present form for more than thirty-five years, is in need of a thorough review and revision, and I would hope you could advise the government on what should be done with it. . . .

I recognize that what I am suggesting for you is a difficult task, but it is one which at this juncture we believe to be quite important for the future development of the public service as a whole.[36]

Coupled with the Prime Minister's statement to the Professional Institute in the following February, this letter makes it clear that in the revision of the Act Heeney was to take into special account the role of the CSC in the employer-employee relationship along the lines earlier proposed by Bryce.

Besides this forthright mandate, the Government also offered Heeney attractive terms to take on the job it wanted done. The Prime Minister pointed out that while Heeney's appointment would be for a ten-year period, he might resign at such time as he felt the main tasks had been accomplished. The figure of three to four years was mentioned with approval. To attract a man of Heeney's stature to the CSC, the highest level of salary payable to a deputy minister was offered. Also, in accepting the Prime Minister's offer, Heeney was not only filling the post of chairman himself, but was also assuming responsibility for choosing the two other Commissioners who would sit with him. The only conditions attached to these choices were the tacit understanding that one must, of course, be French speaking, and the explicit stipulation that the other must be a woman.[37] This latter stipulation, clearly agreed upon by Cabinet, marked an innovation in the "representativeness" of the Commissioners. Assisted by Bryce, Heeney chose Ruth Addison and then added Paul Pelletier as his own choice for the post.[38] Both understood Heeney's assignment, and were apparently willing to allow the Chairman the initiative in directing changes.[39] The three Commissioners officially assumed office in March, 1957.

The new Chairman thus commenced his term of office in a position of unquestioned supremacy within the CSC, and with what he himself described as a "carte blanche" from the Prime Minister. For the first time in over twenty years the CSC was under leadership which was not basically committed to a defence of the status quo, a leadership, moreover, which was drawn entirely from outside the CSC's permanent staff. For the first time since the 1918 Act, the CSC had been given a direct mandate to innovate from the Prime Minister himself. Yet, just at this auspicious moment, fate intervened in the form of the Canadian electorate. On June 10, 1957, twenty-two years of Liberal rule came to an end with the upset victory of John Diefenbaker's Progressive Conservative Party. Once again, Civil Service Commissioners appointed by a previous government faced a new government whose attitude toward them was at best, cool, and at worst, hostile. Certainly the long association of Heeney with the late Mackenzie King could scarcely commend his political neutrality to a Progressive Conservative government which already held "Liberal bureaucrats" in grave suspicion.

One of Heeney's first tasks as chairman was thus to determine whether the new Government wished to continue the mandate granted by St. Laurent. In August he spoke privately to the new Prime Minister, who, he reported to his colleagues, appeared somewhat "cool." The outlook was cloudy, as Mr. Diefenbaker was not yet ready to declare the Government's position on the role of the CSC and the revision of the Act. "He had had it in mind," Heeney reported, "to have an investigation made by an outside agency . . . along the lines of the Hoover Commission in the United States. . . . He would not wish to have any duplication in investigations into the Civil Service."[40] Heeney, for his part, suggested that a Hoover-type inquiry need not involve any duplication of the CSC's own "intramural" examination. Although the Prime Minister agreed that "anomalies and imperfections" were inevitable in any legislation which had been in operation for as long as the Civil Service Act, the meeting ended on a rather inconclusive note, with Heeney being directed to consult further with the Minister of Finance.

The following month, Heeney lunched with Donald Fleming, the Finance Minister, to discuss the CSC's mandate at greater length. In urging Mr. Fleming to help the Government come to some firm decision on this matter, Heeney also asked for further clarification of the Government's attitude toward a role for the CSC as an independent arbiter. In reply, Fleming clearly stated that the Government had no intention of accepting collective bargaining as such, and added that he himself was inclined to favour the development of an independent role for the CSC, although he would not go so far as to believe that the CSC "could become in any real sense an arbitrator in wage matters." In any event, he saw no reason why the CSC should not go ahead with its own review, whatever shape the Hoover-type inquiry of the bureaucracy as a whole might take.[41]

Two weeks later, Fleming reported to Heeney that the Prime Minister would "go along with" Fleming's own views, which were favourable to the review.[42] Finally, the Prime Minister agreed in writing that the CSC should continue its special mandate for "reviewing the Civil Service Act and procedure and examining the role of the Commission in the machinery of government."[43]

The Attempt to Make the CSC into an Independent Arbiter

Although Heeney had received approval to proceed with the study of the Act, the attitude of the Conservative Government toward an independent arbiter role for the Civil Service Commission remained very unclear. To Heeney himself, this matter was obviously the single most important part of his original mandate, and as it turned out, it was the problem which was to occupy most of his time as chairman. Like Bryce he was convinced that the Government could not accede to collective bargaining at this time because of the problems it entailed. Apart from the question of principle, Heeney felt that the practical difficulty of framing and passing legislation on the matter was simply too great. Moreover, he recognized that the differences among the associations as to what exactly they wanted presented an insurmountable barrier at present. The opposition of the Diefenbaker Government to collective bargaining only confirmed his thoughts and convinced him of the efficacy of Bryce's plan. Within several weeks he was presented with an opportunity to advance his ideas on the subject.

In the summer of 1957 the Civil Service Federation began to renew its demands for some form of bargaining within the civil service. This put the Government in a situation not unlike that faced by the Liberal Government in 1956, and in October the Minister of Finance approached a small group of senior officials for advice on how to handle the matter. At its first meeting, the group of officials generally concurred in the plan put forward by Heeney, and over the next few months he presented several memoranda to the ministers appointed to deal with the situation, attempting to interest them in the project.[44] These memoranda are instructive in demonstrating how Heeney seized upon and developed Bryce's idea of using the CSC as an independent arbiter in staff relations. They contained, moreover, essentially the same plan which Heeney later presented and attempted to induce the Government to adopt in the Heeney Report.

Essentially, Heeney's plan, as it evolved in these memoranda, proposed that the Government go part way toward meeting the demands of the associations by accepting the desirability of discussing wages and salaries with them in a "systematic manner" under the auspices of the CSC. In this scheme, Treasury Board and the relevant departments would sit on the Government's side, while the staff associations would devise a common front to represent the employees. With a representative of the CSC acting

245

as chairman, discussions would proceed on the basis of information provided by the CSC's new Pay Research Bureau. The CSC would then deliberate and announce its recommendations simultaneously to the Government and to the staff associations. Although the final decision on wages and salaries would obviously reside with the Government, Heeney's plan was clearly based on the hope that the CSC's recommendations would appear fair and impartial, and so prove basically acceptable to both sides. To ensure this, Heeney realized that it would be necessary to lay a great deal of emphasis upon "the impartial, quasi-judicial role of the Commission in this field and to promote the 'conciliatory' aspect of the Commission's dealings with the Government on the one side and the organized employees on the other." The huge benefit of this plan in Heeney's eyes was that the whole thing could be accomplished within the present statutory enactments; it would be necessary simply to emphasize the independence in salary matters which, according to law, the CSC already possessed. To further enhance its independence from management, the CSC would withdraw from the NJC which would, with improvements in its procedure, handle all other matters relating to working conditions. In addition to the CSC's impartiality, which would serve to commend its recommendations to the associations, Heeney hoped that the public revelation of its proposals would induce the Government to adopt them or be prepared to offer very sound reasons for refusal. At any rate, with the termination of the secrecy surrounding salary proposals, the Government and the Treasury Board would no longer be able to "pass the buck" to the CSC.

Faced with militant staff associations, Heeney's plan naturally carried some appeal for the ministers to whom it was presented. Following his first communication on the subject in October, they asked him to pursue the ideas further and to develop a more detailed plan on how to deal with the current situation. On November 7, 1957, after holding talks with Bryce and George Davidson, Chairman of the NJC, Heeney recommended that Davidson be instructed to explore, in confidence and without commitment on the part of the Government, the views of the staff association representatives as to the proposed role for the CSC. These talks, Heeney noted, "should at least serve to reduce temporarily the pressure from the Associations. At worst, there is time to be gained without commitment on the Government's part; at best the Associations may be persuaded that the course proposed may afford them a substantial substitute for the more drastic courses they have supported publicly."[45]

The Cabinet approved of this recommendation early in the next year, 1958, and Davidson subsequently met secretly with the representatives of four major associations. Surprisingly enough, in marked contrast to their public demands for collective bargaining and arbitration, Davidson found the representatives amenable to the proposition, but for obvious reasons they were insistent that it not be revealed that they had been engaged in such discussions.[46]

Yet despite this encouraging response, the plan to make the CSC into an independent arbiter seems to have reached its apex at this point. Heeney assiduously endeavoured to get the Government to adopt the scheme formally by announcing it in the House and by writing to the staff associations informing them of the new procedure. But, for reasons which are not entirely clear, the Government displayed a distinct lack of enthusiasm for carrying it to this stage. When Heeney wrote to Mr. Diefenbaker asking him for an opportunity to explain the plan, the Prime Minister turned him aside, telling him to get in touch with Mr. Fleming who handled matters relating to the civil service.[47] Unfortunately, Heeney was equally unable to obtain a firm commitment from Fleming and the other ministers with whom he had been dealing. Their hesitation on the matter was likely linked to reservations they were certain to entertain over the question of publicly revealing the CSC's salary recommendations, since this would certainly put a degree of pressure on the Government not found in the present arrangement. Whatever the full reasons for the Government's refusal, Heeney seems to have reconciled himself to putting it forward at a later date in the report on personnel administration, then well under way in the CSC, in the hope that all parties involved would be favourably influenced at that time.

THE HEENEY REPORT

Regardless of the importance of finding a solution to the employer-employee relationship, this matter was only one aspect of the mandate handed to Heeney in 1957. Almost as pressing at this time was the continuing problem of the divided responsibility between the Civil Service Commission and the Treasury Board in personnel matters. These two problems were, of course, linked closely together so that changes in one area could not but have great repercussions on the other. However, given Heeney's conviction that the CSC could play a vital role in the employer-employee relationship under its present responsibilities in pay matters, it was inevitable that the attempt to redistribute responsibilities and functions in the other areas of personnel administration could only be conducted within the limits imposed by the first of these goals. In short, the philosophy upon which Heeney and the CSC staff were to operate in recommending a rationalization of the functions between the CSC and Treasury Board was the overriding concern for making the CSC into an independent arbiter.

This fact becomes quite evident in the events leading up to the Heeney

Report. Once the Conservative Government had given the signal to proceed with the review of the Act in 1957, sections of the CSC were mobilized for the purpose. Inquiries were launched into all phases of the operation of the Act, and a large amount of data was gathered not only on the Canadian civil service, but on the British service as well. As part of this inquiry, deputy ministers and other leading civil servants were asked to give their departments' views on new directions for the Civil Service Act and on the proper role for the CSC. The replies to this inquiry provide an invaluable indication of the image of the CSC and of attitudes toward civil service legislation among the top ranks of the public service in the fifties.[48]

Among the answers it received, the comments of Treasury Board are of particular interest. D. M. Watters, who was at this time secretary of the Board, set down that organization's views at length. Noting that the Board "has encountered nearly as many difficulties and problems as has the Civil Service Commission in endeavouring to play its part in developing an appropriate personnel policy for the government service in the light of rapidly changing conditions while fettered by obsolete legislation," he went on to outline a number of general recommendations. First, he called for a broader act to include most of those employees then excluded, and for more precise regulatory authority to govern those who would continue to be excluded. Such a comprehensive act, Watters asserted, should clearly outline the Government's responsibilities as employer and the CSC's as independent agency:

> Much of the difficulty which has been experienced in recent years in determining consistent employment policies, and much of the unrest and suspicion which has been demonstrated by the organized staff associations, has stemmed from the attempts of the Civil Service Commission to combine the irreconcilable functions of management agency, with almost final authority in such matters as pay, classification and establishment, with that of independent umpire or arbiter, interposed and mediating between the government as employer and its employees. *We consider that organization, establishments, pay, classification, fringe benefits and working conditions are, under our constitutional system, clearly the function of management—the government—and that the final responsibility for determinations in these areas must be entrusted to a management agency,* be it the Governor in Council, the Treasury Board, or as the Royal Commission on Administrative Classifications suggested more than a decade ago, a Director General. On the other hand, recruitment, selection, appointment, some aspects of training, appeals, grievance machinery and mediation can only be entrusted to

an independent agency if the merit system is to be, and appear to be, preserved.

In general, the Board was willing to see the CSC retain its watchdog role over the merit system, but not to the extent that it could impair efficiency, for Watters was quick to add that "the fight against political patronage and moral turpitude has been largely won" and further warned that "over-zealous" attention to merit safeguards might degenerate into the protection of incompetence. Watters also foreshadowed the Glassco recommendations on the delegation of authority in personnel matters when he stated the Board's belief that

> legislation should be so drafted as to clear the channel of communica-
> tion between the Department, as employer, and its employees, so that
> control agencies such as the Treasury Board and the Civil Service Com-
> mission do not interpose themselves in this direct line. It should be
> necessary only for these control agencies to establish clearly and defi-
> nitely the rules and regulations governing employment policy, and then
> to delegate authority and responsibility clearly and precisely to the
> departments to deal with their staffs, providing appeal machinery only
> where the employer-employee relationship has clearly broken down.

Finally, on the old question of reorganizational work—now called Organization and Methods—the Board's response was that the CSC should retain
control "as part of its research machinery." Watters candidly admitted
that such a view "cannot be adequately defended in logic," but suggested
that from the standpoint of "employee and public relations" it should not
appear to be a direct tool of management.[49]

Several months later, in April, 1958, Watters got the opportunity to
present his views on these matters directly to the Government. When the
Minister of Finance asked him to prepare a memorandum on the limitations which the Civil Service Act placed on the executive with regard to
the creation of positions, pay determination, and other related matters,
Watters informed the Minister that many sections of the Act which had no
direct connection with the merit system nevertheless conferred wide powers on the CSC, including areas that infringed on such "management prerogatives" as establishments, pay determination, and working conditions.[50]
Watters, however, did point out to Fleming that "by the exercise of patience and tact the staffs of the Civil Service Commission and Treasury
Board were able to make the present arrangement work."

Watters' arguments contained a great deal of logic, particularly when
one realizes that the Glassco Commission adopted an almost identical

position on the matter several years later. But at this point in time his out-look obviously conflicted with the role which Heeney had planned for the CSC in staff relations. When asked by Watters to comment on the memorandum to Fleming, Heeney strongly challenged the view that "management prerogatives" should be preempted by the executive. For one thing, central to Heeney's scheme was the fact that the CSC would continue to make pay recommendations to the Government. What made the matter all the more grave was that he was at this very moment occupied behind the scenes with attempting to get the Government to adopt his plan. Thus he cautioned Watters that if the CSC were to be deprived of its right to initiate pay recommendations, the Government would face much stronger demands for full collective bargaining. In support of his own program he noted that in private industry, management is limited by collective agreements; the limitations placed on the Government by his plan were "less onerous" and "more appropriate to a Parliamentary regime." Finally, he maintained that classification was so closely connected with pay that the CSC should retain that responsibility as well. He concluded with these rather pointed remarks:

> I do not believe that revisions of the kind implied and expressed in your memorandum, particularly with regard to pay in the Civil Service, would be progressive or in any way desirable. It is not, in my opinion, along such lines that improvements should be sought.
>
> Since the Minister of Finance and members of Treasury Board have had the benefit of your views on these subjects, Mr. Fleming might think it appropriate that they should be made aware of the viewpoint of the Commission as well.[51]

When it was finally completed in December, 1958, the report on personnel administration in the public service,[52] or as it is better known, the Heeney Report, reflected these views and, by implication, rejected those of the Treasury Board. The Report maintained from the outset that "the basic and central issue involved in all questions of public personnel administration" was "how to provide the freedom and flexibility required to enable the administrator to do the job and, at the same time, maintain the measure of central control necessary to ensure a career service based on the merit principle and governed by uniform standards." After reviewing the changing conditions of the civil service from Confederation to the present, the Report recognized that while both political and bureaucratic patronage were still forces which had to be held in check by an independent agency, "a monolithic merit system is not in itself enough." The objectives of new legislation ought then to be the preservation of the basic merit system, tempered by other considerations, such as greater speed and flexibility, progressive administrative methods, greater autonomy in decision-making for the departments, greater participation by employees in the determination of their conditions of employment, clearer definition of the division of authority between the executive and the CSC, a unified set of standards to cover the entire service, and the clarification of the "rights and obligations" of civil servants.[53] The Report, in appendix A, set out detailed proposals for changes in the Act and regulations; appendix B contained the plan and recommendations for utilizing the CSC as an independent arbiter in joint consultations between the Government and the staff associations over pay and salary matters.

In recommending changes to the Act, the Heeney Report attempted to meet the objectives which it set forth. On the one hand, it attempted to establish, more clearly than in the past, the CSC's independent and exclusive role in those functions relating directly to the maintenance of the merit system. With this in mind it recommended that the CSC continue to retain final responsibility for recruitment, selection, appointment, and promotion. Guided, on the other hand, by the desire to unfetter departmental management, it attempted to end the CSC's cumbersome control over matters not directly related to the merit principle. In this regard it recommended that deputy ministers be granted greater power and responsibility for effecting intradepartmental promotions. Similarly it suggested that the ultimate responsibility for determining the organizational structure of departments be taken from the CSC and be placed with the Government or its agent, Treasury Board.

But cutting directly across these goals and objectives was the aim to put forth the concept of the CSC as an independent arbiter as a solution to the employer-employee relationship. So central was this goal to the Heeney Report, in fact, that only when this scheme is understood do many of the other recommendations begin to fall into a comprehensible and logical pattern. For one thing, although the Report recommended the transfer of some of the CSC's traditional powers to the executive on the grounds that these responsibilities had no bearing on the merit system, but were, on the contrary, of concern to management, it did not recommend a diminution of power in the areas of pay, classification, conditions of employment, and appeal procedures. But these functions, as Watters had earlier informed Heeney, were of vital concern to management. The reason for the different approach lay, of course, in the fact that Heeney wanted to retain control over those matters which were of critical importance in staff relations so as to allow the CSC to fulfil the role he had projected for it in this field. It was on this basis that the Heeney Report recommended the CSC's jurisdiction be expanded to include even the Superannuation Branch of the

Department of Finance and the Civil Service Health Division of the Department of National Health and Welfare. While these functions obviously had no connection to the merit system, they did fall into the area of "fringe benefits" and would thus allow the CSC to offer the "package deals" for which the associations were beginning to press. Finally, it will be recalled that Heeney placed great value and importance upon the independence of the CSC if it were to assume its new role, and this helps to explain the tremendous emphasis the Report attached to this factor, particularly with regard to the CSC's independence in making salary recommendations.[54]

In sum it is important to realize that the Heeney Report represented the first major attempt since 1918 to rethink the role and purpose of the CSC. In effect it proposed a partial abandonment of the old merit ideology by which the organization had, since the early twenties, always justified its existence. Instead, Heeney attempted on the one hand to redefine the concept of merit by recognizing that in at least some areas, such as organization structure, questions of managerial efficiency overrode merit considerations and should no longer constitute part of the CSC's duties. At the same time he recognized that the merit principle itself was not an absolute and immutable concept, but needed to be tempered by the other considerations mentioned earlier, such as greater speed and flexibility and greater autonomy in decision-making for departments. Second, and most important, he endeavoured to add a more contemporary role and purpose to the CSC by establishing it as an independent arbiter in staff relations.

The new role posited by Heeney, however, was open to serious question. In his book on staff relations in the civil service written several years after the publication of the Heeney Report, Professor Frankel commented that in attempting to make itself into a "quasi-arbitral tribunal," the CSC overlooked a major difficulty:

> If after receiving a recommendation from the Commission, a recommendation which was also communicated to the staff associations, the Government rejected it, the Commission should suffer a serious loss of confidence and prestige. Its ability to play an effective part in staff relations would be undermined. If, on the other hand, the Government felt bound to accept the recommendation on the grounds that it represented the objective findings of an independent and competent tribunal, it would imply submission to *compulsory* arbitration in its least desirable form—arbitration without prior negotiation.[55]

Frankel, admittedly, had the benefit of hindsight in this observation. But perhaps an even more basic and perceptive criticism was one he made privately to Heeney in 1958. While Heeney's plan revolved around the concept of an independent CSC, Frankel entertained doubts that the organization could ever attain the degree of independence it required, not so much legally as psychologically:

> On the question of the "independent" role of the Commission as between employer and employee, it seems to me that the issue is not whether an agency can conform to the technical definition of independence but whether it is in fact perceived as being independent by the parties concerned. When I talked with you last November I certainly gained the impression that a real movement towards asserting the legal independence of the Commission was under way. However, in thinking about it I felt that the energy for this movement was not inherent in the machinery of the Commission but in its new Chairman. I would say that in the long run the imperatives of financial co-ordination and parliamentary responsibility require that the initiative in personnel policy, with the exception of recruitment and promotion, should come from the government. If disagreement between the government and the organizations of its employees warrants the intervention of a third party, that third party should have terms of reference similar to those given to the conciliation boards or arbitration tribunals that are set up in private industrial disputes.[56]

As it was to turn out, the problems and difficulties mentioned by Frankel were to make themselves quite evident so that Heeney's plan was never implemented.

But these considerations were not so obvious to Heeney and others at the time. Although he had been unable to get a firm commitment from the ministers on the matter of the CSC as an independent arbiter during the previous summer, and although he had been unable to interest the Prime Minister in the plan, Heeney and others in the bureaucracy were quite optimistic that the principal recommendations of the Report, especially those contained in appendix B, would be adopted.[57] So confident was Heeney of this fact that ten days before submitting the Report to the Prime Minister, he and Bryce began planning both a draft of a new Civil Service Act for submission to the Cabinet early in February, 1959, and a proposal for a parliamentary committee to study the new bill shortly thereafter.[58] A week after he had presented the Report to the Prime Minister, Heeney reported: "It was evident that Mr. Diefenbaker took considerable personal interest in the report and that he was contemplating parliamentary action upon it during the next session and probably the reference of consequential legislation to a Parliamentary Committee."[59] At another meeting in January, 1959, Heeney emerged hopeful: "He evinced interest in our recommendations, particularly those dealing with employer-employee relations in the Service."[60]

Whatever Heeney's impressions, however, the Government acted with extreme caution on the matter, and the haste with which Heeney had hoped to move was completely lost. Public release of the Heeney Report was delayed until the Prime Minister and the Cabinet had the opportunity to scrutinize it carefully. Moreover, when the public release did come in the middle of January, it was followed within hours by the announcement that Heeney was to resume immediately his former duties as Canadian Ambassador in Washington. It is possible to read too much significance into this announcement: after all, in the original agreement made between St. Laurent and Heeney, it had been specified that Heeney could leave the CSC as soon as his specific task of reviewing legislation had been completed. The argument that Heeney was needed immediately in Washington, however, has been the subject of some speculation.[61] In any event, the author of the Heeney Report, and the most prestigious and formidable figure ever to head the CSC, would not be there while the Government decided on the disposition of his recommendations.

The issue left most in doubt by this situation was Heeney's central philosophical tenet of the CSC as an independent arbiter in staff relations. On this point, and indeed on the whole Report, the Government remained completely noncommittal. Unfortunately for the CSC, the attempt to jump from one boat to another always entails the risk of missing altogether, and of ending up entirely at sea. Actually, the CSC did not try to jump completely off the merit principle, but tried instead to keep one leg on familiar footing while reaching out with the other for new ground. Unknown to the CSC, the Government was about to yank its new foothold out from under it. The CSC was thus to find itself in an unsightly position, poised over a target which had just been removed.

NOTES

1. Interview.
2. "Committee for Revision of Civil Service Act," confidential memorandum of R. B. Bryce, July 29, 1954. This memorandum is contained in one of several private files of memoranda and correspondence belonging to A. D. P. Heeney

and held in the Chairman's Office of the PSC. (Hereafter cited as Heeney Files.) All the correspondence and memoranda in this chapter, unless cited otherwise, are from these files.

3. Ibid.

4. Bryce to Heeney, July 23, 1954.

5. It is interesting in this regard that Bland clearly recognized that, if the Act was opened up, the CSC would be under a great deal of pressure to give up many of its present statutory powers. In preparation for this he took preliminary steps to mobilize the CSC's traditional sources of support. On July 21, he wrote to the Secretary of State, saying that if changes were to be made in the Act, "I assume that it would also be considered desirable before a final decision is reached that there should be obtained the ideas and reactions of civil servants themselves, as expressed by their various organizations; of the great body of veterans who are affected by the preference and who might logically be expected to speak through the veterans' associations; and of the public at large, who at the time of the last revision of the Act (1938) expressed through the press a very decided interest in the conditions under which its Civil Service was to operate." (Bland to Roch Pinard, July 21, 1954)

6. Heeney to Bryce, July 29, 1954.

7. Bryce to Heeney, August 30, 1954.

8. Heeney to Bryce, November 22, 1954.

9. Bryce to Heeney, November 24, 1954.

10. Interview.

11. Saul J. Frankel, *Staff Relations in the Civil Service: The Canadian Experience*, pp. 117–18. See too M. M. Maclean, "Problems of Jurisdiction and Structure Facing Staff Associations in the Canadian Civil Service," pp. 7–8.

12. *Civil Service News*, January, 1956, p. 9; Frankel, *Staff Relations in the Civil Service*, p. 121.

13. Memorandum from M. M. Maclean to G. T. Jackson, August 9, 1950, contained in the private papers of Maclean, a former Secretary of the CSC.

14. Trevor Gough, "Single Versus Multiple Organization," *Civil Service Review* 29 (June, 1956), p. 138.

15. L. R. Menzies to Victor Johnson, May 7, 1955, in *Civil Service Review* 27 (June, 1955), pp. 173–74.

16. Interview.

17. Gad Horowitz, *Canadian Labour in Politics*, p. 242.

18. See the exchange of views at the 1956 convention of the CSF, "The Federation and the Trades and Labour Congress of Canada," *Civil Service Review* 29 (June, 1956), pp. 156–61. See also the testimony of Claude Jodoin, CLC President, in H.C., Special Committee on the Civil Service Act, 1960–61, *Proceedings and Evidence*, p. 143. There is even evidence indicating that from 1957 onwards, the associations successfully fought to block the CLC from obtaining the right of check-off privileges for prevailing rates employees. David Kwavnick, "Organized Labour and Government: The Canadian Labour Congress as a Political Interest Group During the Diefenbaker and Pearson Administrations," pp. 406–9.

19. For its information regarding the staff associations and collective bargaining, this chapter is heavily indebted to J. D. Love, "Employee Organizations in the Federal Public Service and the Problems of Collective Bargaining," November, 1956.

20. Cited in *Trades and Labour Congress Journal* 32 (December, 1953), p. 14.

21. St. Laurent to H. A. Clarke, November 2, 1955, cited in the *Railway Mail Clerk* 33 (December, 1955), p. 14.

22. CSC, *Annual Report*, 1956, p. 7.

23. See Love, "Employee Organizations," pp. 41–45; Frankel, *Staff Relations in the Civil Service*, pp. 11–15.

24. In a speech to the Canadian Postal Employees' Association in 1956, Walter Turnbull, then Deputy Postmaster-General, was reported as suggesting that the Commissioners might have "a tendency to please the boss" when their ten-year terms were about to expire. (*Ottawa Citizen*, September 20, 1956)

25. John Mainwaring, "Some Reflections on the Problem of Collective Bargaining by Federal Public Servants," February, 1957, p. 10.

26. Frankel, *Staff Relations in the Civil Service*, p. 79.

27. "Negotiation-Arbitration," *Professional Public Service* 36 (October, 1957), p. 7. The quoted phrases are from the CSC's own official pronouncements.

28. Love, "Employee Organizations," p. 45.

29. Address by A. J. Boudreau, July 9, 1956, cited in *Civil Service Review* 29 (September, 1956), pp. 359–60.

30. Address by the Honourable Walter Harris, July 10, 1956, cited in *Civil Service Review* 29, (September, 1956), p. 342.

31. Frankel, *Staff Relations in the Civil Service*, p. 123. Frankel dates the first noticeable sign of this change to April 11, 1956, when the Prime Minister tabled in the House his reply to a letter from the Association of Canadian Postal Employees. It read: "This subject [collective bargaining] is a rather fundamental one and I will not endeavour at this time to outline the position of the government upon it nor to comment on the various statements made in your letter on related subjects. This detailed exposition of yours, however, will be of use to the government in its consideration of this subject." (Cited in *Civil Service Review* 29 [June, 1956], p. 135)

32. Frankel, *Staff Relations in the Civil Service*, pp. 119–21.

33. Confidential memorandum from Bryce to the Prime Minister, July 19, 1956.

34. Ibid.

35. Address by the Prime Minister to the Professional Institute, February 23, 1957, cited in *Civil Service Review* 30 (March, 1957), p. 12.

36. St. Laurent to Heeney, October 9, 1956.

37. Ibid.

38. Interview. See also St. Laurent Papers, PAC, 1956, c-12-3-w.

39. Interview.

40. Heeney to Addison and Pelletier, August 8, 1957.

41. Heeney to Addison and Pelletier, September 6, 1957.

42. Heeney to Addison and Pelletier, September 16, 1957.

43. Diefenbaker to Heeney, September 24, 1957.

44. The ministers concerned were Mr. Starr, the Minister of Labour, Mrs. Fairclough, the Secretary of State, and Mr. Fleming, the Minister of Finance. There are numerous memoranda and letters on the subject in Heeney's private files, both for circulation to the ministers and for file purposes. See in particular "Memorandum for Ministers," prepared by Heeney, October 11,

1957, with the enclosed memorandum "The Civil Service and Collective Bargaining," prepared by Heeney, October 9, 1957; memorandum from Heeney to the Minister of Finance, November 7, 1957; and "Memorandum to Ministers," prepared by Heeney, May 28, 1958.

45. Heeney to the Minister of Finance, November 7, 1957.

46. "Memorandum to Ministers," prepared by Heeney, May 28, 1958.

47. Heeney to Diefenbaker, May 29, 1958, and Diefenbaker to Heeney, June 6, 1958.

48. "Views of the Deputy Heads," compiled by G. A. Blackburn, February 19, 1958, Confidential Background Papers to the Heeney Report, Chairman's Office, PSC.

49. D. M. Watters to Heeney, January 29, 1958, ibid. (Emphasis added.)

50. Memorandum to the Treasury Board members, prepared by Watters, April 28, 1958.

51. Heeney to Watters, June 2, 1958.

52. CSC, *Personnel Administration in the Public Service: A Review of Civil Service Legislation*, December, 1958.

53. Ibid., pp. 3, 8, 9–10.

54. At one point the Report stated for example: "Although it is not, perhaps, widely appreciated, it seems to us that the independent status of the Commission in matters of pay and conditions of work is as important a characteristic of our system as its independence in relation to appointment and promotion. In its recommendations on pay, the Commission is no more subject to Government direction than it is to influence by organized employees. It is as immune to outside pressures as the law can make it. Its sole duty is to read, within the framework of accepted principles, conclusions based on objective examination and analysis through its Pay Research Bureau and such other sources as may be available to it." (Ibid., p. 23) See also ibid., appendix B, p. 132.

55. Frankel, *Staff Relations in the Civil Service*, pp. 155–56.

56. Frankel to Heeney, May 23, 1958. It is interesting that beside Frankel's last two sentences quoted here, Heeney had penned in the comment "[I] cannot (and will not) agree."

57. Heeney's optimism on this point was obviously encouraged in part by a speech made by Mr. Diefenbaker in May, 1958, at which time he said that civil servants "should have a greater voice in the process of determining Civil Service salaries." He argued that this could be achieved within the present framework of institutions and laws, using the Civil Service Commission, but left the details rather vague. Heeney, however, was encouraged at the time, particularly since Diefenbaker had also emphasized the independence of the CSC. (See "An Address on the Civil Service," delivered by the Right Honourable John G. Diefenbaker to the CSAC, p. 3) See also Heeney to Diefenbaker, May 28, 1958.

58. Heeney to Bryce, December 12, 1958.

59. Memorandum for file, prepared by Heeney, December 30, 1958.

60. Memorandum for file, prepared by Heeney, January 8, 1959.

61. Interview.

Chapter Twelve
Implementing the Heeney Report

A funny thing happened on the way to
Parliament . . .

THREE MAJOR FACTORS ultimately doomed the central philosophy of the
Heeney Report. First, the pay disputes of 1958 and 1959 seriously weakened the CSC's credibility as an independent arbiter. Second, the pending
report of the Glassco Royal Commission on Government Organization
gravely challenged the CSC's future as a control agency. Finally, the growing militancy of the staff associations and their rising demands for full
collective bargaining directly with Treasury Board threatened to remove
the Civil Service Commission from the staff relations scene altogether. All
these factors can be seen in retrospect to have had a strong, perhaps decisive, impact on the fate of the Heeney Report.

THE PAY DISPUTES OF 1958–1959

To understand the critical importance of the 1958 and 1959 pay disputes it is first necessary to retrace some ground in the period of the
Heeney chairmanship, and to examine the creation and performance of
the Pay Research Bureau. In its determination of wage and salary levels
to be recommended to Treasury Board, the Civil Service Commission had
been traditionally guided by an established government policy on compensation. Prime Minister Diefenbaker, in a speech in 1958, expressed
the guiding philosophy which had been accepted by both Liberal and Conservative administrations over the years:

> For many years it has been generally accepted that two main principles
> should guide the determination of salaries in the Service. First the sal-
> aries must be enough to do the job, that is to attract enough of the right
> kind of men and women into the Service and keep them in it; second,
> they must be fair as between Civil Servants and people outside the Ser-
> vice, the taxpayers if you will, which means that the salaries we pay for

259

any class of work should be comparable with those paid by private employers for similar classes of work, taking into account the other terms of employment that are necessary to make a fair comparison. I think these principles should continue to guide us.[1]

Until 1957, the CSC implemented this general policy through its Organization and Classification Branch, but this proved to be an unsatisfactory arrangement, for the Branch was not organized on a formal basis for this type of work and was not properly staffed for the detailed studies which were required. The process of arriving at pay recommendations was consequently marked by a rather haphazard and unscientific methodology.[2]

The first postwar decade was characterized economically by full employment and a tight labour market, with the Government consequently facing strong competition from the private sector.[3] Moreover, "the postwar problem of conducting research to support the rate-setting process was greatly intensified by the dynamic upward trend of wages and salaries, and by the emergence of fringe benefits as an important part of the total remuneration of industrial employees."[4] The staff associations were also growing very restless with the existing process. They were no longer content to make pay representations to the CSC based on their own, often inadequate, sources of information. Demands were being made to obtain access to the data available to the CSC, so that the associations could challenge, if necessary, the Commission's recommendations to the Government.[5]

Events in Canada were also influenced by certain developments in the civil service of the United Kingdom. The Priestly Royal Commission of 1953–55 had recommended the establishment of a pay research unit to rationalize the pay determination process:

> We recommend, first, that fact-finding should be assigned to a branch of the Civil Service not directly connected with those divisions of the Treasury responsible for questions of pay and conditions of service. . . .
>
> Secondly, we think it essential that means should be found of enabling the staff associations to participate fully in the work of fact-finding. . . .
>
> We believe that steps of this kind would go a long way towards remedying one of the most serious sources of difficulty at the present time, namely the suspicion in the minds of the associations that the Treasury as pay negotiators are able to secure and interpret facts on outside jobs and rates of pay that are not available to the associations.[6]

This recommendation had a decisive influence in Canada. In February of 1957, Prime Minister St. Laurent told a meeting of the Professional Institute that the Government was considering the establishment of some form of fact-finding machinery on salaries and working conditions, the information from which could be made available to the staff associations as well as to the Government.[7] The associations were highly enthusiastic; in March, three major associations submitted a brief to the Government calling for the establishment of an independent pay research unit, along the lines recommended in Britain.[8]

The idea of a pay research unit had certain intrinsic attractions to all of the parties involved. Dissatisfaction on the part of the associations was threatening to drive them into the arms of organized labour, for it appears that the Canadian Labour Congress would have been more than happy to supply civil servants with its research data. The Treasury Board was also hampered by lack of adequate machinery. An across-the-board wage increase threw the budgetary process into disorder, since revenue had not been raised by the previous year's taxation.[9] General increases, moreover, were on the whole unsatisfactory: in certain parts of the service there were employees who were well paid in comparison with outside practice, while many other groups were consistently underpaid by comparison. It seemed desirable to devise a method of pay determination which would take into consideration the peculiar characteristics of the various classes in the public service. Moreover, as a purely fact-finding agency which would not itself make specific recommendations, but would merely provide data to all parties, the independent unit could gain the trust of all the various interests involved, and could thus create a healthier climate for cooperation. For these various reasons, then, the concept of a pay research unit seemed attractive to both the Government and its employees alike.

Soon after Heeney's appointment to the CSC chairmanship, a committee was set up to study the feasibility of establishing a research unit to investigate rates of pay, conditions of employment, and related personnel practices. This move obviously met with the full approval of the new Diefenbaker Government,[10] and on September 2, 1957, the formation of the Pay Research Bureau (PRB) was formally announced. The new Bureau was

> to provide objective information on compensation and working conditions in Government, business and industry and to assemble and analyse factual evidence of trends in outside employment.[11]

> The Commission is responsible, under the Civil Service Act, for recommending to the Government of Canada salary rates for all classified civil servants. The information upon which the Commission's recommendations are based will now be centralized in the new Bureau, which will form an integral part of the Commission's organization.[12]

As Frankel notes, the decision to make the PRB an integral part of the CSC seems to have inspired remarkably little comment. The CSC did establish an advisory committee—made up of representatives of the staff associations and Treasury Board as well as the CSC—to "advise and assist" the Bureau in its work, but the PRB was itself entirely a CSC creature. Heeney himself placed a very high value on the PRB's importance for the CSC's projected new role. In fact, it was obviously of central importance to his blueprint for the CSC's future. The fate of the PRB— hence of the CSC's power to independently recommend pay scales—was thus a critical indicator of the fate of the ideas embodied in the Heeney Report.

In August of 1958, after the PRB had been in operation for less than a year, a report was submitted by the CSC to the Minister of Finance which recommended that no general salary increase be granted. The associations had not been consulted in the CSC's interpretation of the admittedly limited data assembled by the PRB, and were not consulted by the Government itself.[13] The Government, which was obviously anxious to avoid paying for salary increases, seized eagerly upon the CSC's advice, and attempted to deflect strong criticism from the associations onto the CSC. Frankel comments:

> One has the impression that the Minister was particularly anxious to connect the report of the Commission with the work of the Bureau. He thus intended to justify what was in fact a unilateral policy on the grounds that it was based on the supposedly objective and unequivocal facts collected by the Bureau on whose advisory committee the staff associations were represented. . . .
>
> The Minister stressed the statutory duty of the Commission to make recommendations on pay to the Governor in Council. "Thus in fact, as well as in law, the Commission is the independent source of advice to the Government in all matters of salaries and wages to civil servants and this has been so since the Civil Service Act was enacted by Parliament in 1918."[14]

Fleming also told the associations that they should not try to bring their complaints to the Government but should talk to the CSC, since it was the CSC which held the "statutory responsibility" for pay determination. Although at first glance the behaviour of the Finance Minister might seem to lend some credence to Heeney's "independent" Commission idea, the appearances were misleading. As events the following year were to demonstrate, the Government was only willing to accept the CSC's recommendations in 1958 because it agreed with them, not because it respected the CSC's *right* to set pay rates. The Government was obviously trying to shunt the criticism of the associations onto the CSC's shoulders.

As Heeney himself was well aware, the "statutory responsibility" of the CSC had been for many years a legal fiction. Frankel expressed considerable doubt that the 1918 Act had actually given the CSC the sole responsibility for recommending pay rates.[15] However, Frankel does not seem to be aware of the events in the early 1920s when the CSC did in fact attempt to independently set pay rates—in this case, at lower levels than the Government wanted. As explained in chapter 6, the CSC refused to modify its recommendations and the Government sought a legal ruling from the Justice Department. This ruling stated that the Government could only accept or reject the CSC's recommendations, but could not amend them. The Government, however, rather easily overcame this restriction by simply returning CSC salary recommendations until the Commission presented an acceptable schedule. Thus the CSC had gained sole authority, *in theory*; the practical reality was, on the other hand, quite the contrary. Frankel does suggest that the overwhelming impression given to him by both CSC and Treasury Board officials was that preliminary consultation always took place on pay recommendations, although he was forced to admit that he could find no "documentary evidence" of such a practice.[16] There can be no doubt that Frankel's suspicions were well founded. Interviews conducted for this study confirmed that the legal concept of the CSC recommending, and the Government either accepting or rejecting but not amending, had little basis in reality. The Commission staff was usually aware of just what salary changes were acceptable to the Board, and tended to avoid conflict by recommending only such changes as were likely to be accepted by the Board. When differences did develop the Board did, on occasion, impose its own changes.[17] While its statutory power to carry out amendments to the CSC's recommendations might be in some doubt, the CSC was itself often unwilling to challenge the Board. The reality, then, was that in one way or another, the Board had assumed a preeminent position in pay determination. By the mid-fifties, this position was becoming increasingly recognized.[18]

Heeney, who wished to infuse some backbone into the CSC's stance before Parliament and the public, saw pay determination as a critical area. He believed strongly that the CSC should play an independent role. In the past the CSC would consult with Treasury Board, and then present the staff associations with a fait accompli. Heeney wished to firmly establish the PRB, obtain the objective facts about pay determination, present these facts along with CSC recommendations to the Board, and then allow the Government to either accept or reject the recommendations as it saw fit, while stating in Parliament its reasons.[19] In the 1958 situation, Fleming refused to state publicly why the CSC's recommendations had been accepted by the Government. To Heeney's chagrin, the Government effectively turned the wrath of the associations toward the CSC. Faced with demands that the whole question be reopened by the CSC, Heeney had to issue a public statement: "There is no question of any investigation of the whole basis under which the Commission made its recommendation to the Government. There will be no 'probe' or 'review' of the methods and operations of the Pay Research Bureau. . . . If new evidence, in the judgment of the Commission, invalidates the decision against an increase, then the Commission will send new recommendations to the Government."[20]

It was in this rather unsatisfactory state that the 1958 salaries question was left. Much worse was to follow the next year, however, and from the CSC's point of view, the events of 1959 came at a particularly difficult time. It will be remembered that immediately following the tabling of the Heeney Report in Parliament in January of 1959, it was announced that Heeney was returning to Washington. Mr. Justice Hughes of the Ontario Supreme Court was Diefenbaker's choice as Heeney's successor, but Hughes himself was not entirely enthusiastic about accepting such an appointment.[21] The result was a hiatus between February 1, when Heeney left, and July 1, when Hughes finally took over. For six months the CSC was without a chairman, and was under the direction of Commissioners Addison and Pelletier.

In May of 1959 the PRB made its second Annual Report on salary levels. The facts presented seemed to point to a general increase, and the associations assumed this to be the case. The next month the CSC sent its confidential recommendations to the Government and stated that a majority of classified civil servants should be granted increases. The Government, for its part, sat on the recommendations for almost three months. When questioned in the House, Mr. Fleming acknowledged that he had received the recommendations, but cautioned: "The matter is not final as between the Civil Service Commission and the Government, because further discussions must be held with the Commission on it before I would be prepared to regard it as a final submission on the part of the Commission to the Government."[22] Although Fleming later tried to maintain that he in no way wished to undermine the CSC's independence, the implication was clear. The Government was trying to amend the recommendations privately with the CSC. This was directly counter to Heeney's idea that the Government either accept or reject the recommendations with full public explanations in Parliament. Finally on October 13, the Government announced in a press release that it was rejecting the CSC's recommendations because the Government could not afford such increases as had been suggested, and because the Government had doubts about both the PRB's statistical data and the interpretation provided by the CSC. The press release also contained a pointed reference to the "Civil Service Commission, as constituted in June, 1959." Frankel notes that "this reference was noticed and widely interpreted as an expression of lack of confidence in the two members of the Commission responsible for the salary recommendations."[23] Certainly the Government had publicly questioned the credibility of both the CSC and the PRB. Most importantly, the Heeney Report concept of a new role for the CSC as arbiter between the Government and its organized staff had been badly damaged. As Frankel suggests: "By its unilateral action the Government undercut the fragile structure of staff relations that had been so assiduously built up in the preceding two years. This . . . was based on the notion that the Commission performed a quasi-arbitral role. Indeed the Government's action exposed the fundamental weakness of this structure."[24] Treasury Board, with the Minister of Finance lending his full support, had once again exercised its power successfully. Yet it must also be noted that the mere exercise of power could not, and did not, provide a final "solution" to the problem of pay determination. The 1959 outcome left the entire structure of pay in the civil service in an unsatisfactory state, including some very serious lags with pay scales in the private sector. The following year some large pay increases proved to be necessary, putting the 1959 decision of the Treasury Board in a bad light, and thus adding greatly to the growing pressures for collective bargaining.

In the long run, the introduction of the PRB into the pay determination system can be seen to have had many positive aspects. The visits of the PRB staff to the "outside world" provided the Government with much needed insights into contemporary concepts and techniques of personnel management in the more progressive private corporations; in this way, they helped to create in the CSC, and to a lesser extent in the Treasury Board, an urge to reform that was consistent with the mood Heeney had tried to create. Moreover, the efforts of the PRB to design a survey format that would serve the pay determination requirements of the civil service revealed in a variety of concrete ways the very considerable shortcomings of the existing classification system, and thus gave rise to the first tentative efforts to achieve some rational form of occupational grouping of classes. In a sense, then, the PRB served to fertilize the ground on which the criticisms of the Glassco Commission were to fall, and on which the structure of collective bargaining was later to be built.

For the moment, however, neither the PRB nor the Heeney Report concept of the CSC itself appeared to be very successful, in the face of overt governmental hostility. In attempting to jump off the old merit platform onto Heeney's new staff relations platform, the CSC had missed and found itself yet again in an embarrassing position.

THE HUGHES CHAIRMANSHIP

The advent of Mr. Justice Hughes as chairman of the Civil Service Commission seemed a good omen in a generally discouraging situation for the CSC. If the Government was possibly mistrustful of the two remaining appointments of the former government, Hughes was the definite personal choice of the Prime Minister—who was in fact extremely anxious to secure his services—as well as a prestigious outsider unidentified with the CSC's past. Indeed, the appointment of a Justice of the Ontario Supreme Court to the chairmanship could be viewed as further confirmation of the new prestige which Heeney's appointment had conferred on the CSC. It was unclear, however, just what type of mandate Hughes was being given. The Prime Minister did not want him to simply undo the work of the Heeney Report, but it seemed that major changes would be introduced. Mr. Diefenbaker had pledged his Government to maintain the CSC's "independence" and the staff associations could be expected to watch the Government's behaviour closely on this matter; on the other hand, just what such "independence" was to mean in *specific* terms was rather problematic. The one point which was clear was that the Report would not be implemented directly. The Prime Minister had expressed a desire to have the Heeney Report scrutinized by fresh eyes. While the Heeney recommendations were generally accepted by the Government as constituting a kind of model system, not all specific points were viewed as *politically* feasible. A trained legal mind such as Hughes possessed could be expected to transform the general intent of the Heeney recommendations into specific legal form, and while some of the more contentious political issues, such as modifying the veterans preference, might be de-emphasized, the prospects for enactment of the basic Heeney philosophy might have seemed good. Two factors, however, loomed ominously over the Hughes chairmanship. One was the memory of the pay disputes of 1958 and 1959 and the hard fact that after Fleming's actions the Heeney concept of the CSC as arbiter in staff relations had diminished in credibility. It was clear that the Treasury staff had Fleming's ear and that the Government was leaning strongly toward complete Treasury authority in pay determination. The other ominious factor lay in the future, with the coming report of the Glassco Commission on Government Organization. It will be remembered that both Diefenbaker and Fleming had mentioned the possibility of a Hoover-type inquiry early in 1957 when Heeney had sought reassurance on the status of his mandate. In 1960 the Glassco Commission was set up and began its investigations; it fell like a shadow across the CSC's plans for the future.

To Hughes there was never the slightest question about where the Glassco inquiry stood on the issue of the CSC's status. The inquiry's working documents indicate a uniform hostility to the CSC and all its works. And not only was the inquiry hostile to what it saw as the CSC's use of the merit principle as a rationalization of inefficiency, but as a management-oriented inquiry it also had no sympathy for Heeney's projected new role in staff relations. The blend of private enterprise ideology with the Treasury control philosophy represented by Watson Sellar, a Glassco Commissioner who had been for many years an ally of W. C. Ronson, left no doubt in Hughes' mind that the Glassco Report would turn out to be a high-powered replay of the 1946 Gordon Report, this time more thorough, more formidable, and more devastating.

It was against this darkening horizon that Hughes set about drafting a new Civil Service Act. The Glassco Commissioners were in fact displeased that the CSC was proceeding with a new Act, which was bound to be in conflict with their own concepts. For his part, Hughes was quite unsympathetic to the Glassco approach, which he felt wrongly equated government with private enterprise, and which demonstrated an inadequate grasp of the moral and rational necessity for a definite *control* function not only to guard against both political and departmental patronage, but also to establish uniform standards throughout the public service. In short, Hughes was unwilling to allow the CSC to be turned into a mere rubber stamp. This perspective he shared with Heeney. But working under the threat of the coming Glassco report, the new Chairman in effect transmuted much of the central thrust of the Heeney Report into another projected role for the CSC, this time as a judicial body to hear appeals by civil servants. It is not perhaps surprising that a man of Hughes' legal background should have moved along such lines, but in any event, it served to emphasize an independent CSC role which had not been emphasized by Heeney. Hughes had recognized that the appeals systems then in force was antiquated, lacking in any statutory basis, and rather erratically ad hoc in operation. He set out to rectify this situation.

Hughes was, in fact, rather skeptical of Heeney's concept of the CSC as arbiter in setting pay rates independently of the Government. This, he felt, would put Parliament in the absurd position of acting as an instrument of its own creature. But if the CSC could not fully play the particular role Heeney had planned for it, it could adopt a new role as independent judicial body to preside over a rationalized appeal system. This emphasis on the judicial function may be seen as the central innovation introduced into the CSC's operations by Hughes, and it was in effect to be the cornerstone of the CSC's independent strength in the Hughes scheme. The new concept was not dissimilar, in many ways, to the Heeney concept, and both were predicated upon the existence of a strong and independent CSC. But as we have described the events of 1958 and 1959, the Heeney concept had already been made rather irrelevant, and as we shall see, the changing attitudes of the staff associations were making it even more irrelevant. The Hughes revision of the Heeney Report thus projected yet another platform for the CSC to stand on.

Curiously, then, the Diefenbaker Government was on the one hand encouraging the CSC to prepare a new Civil Service Act which would reinforce its control functions, and attempt to carve out new areas of independence, and on the other hand had set up a royal commission inquiry which was to recommend the virtual abolition of the CSC as a control agency with power over personnel management. A collision course had obviously been set. A leading CSC official explained simply that "Mr. Diefenbaker never really thought the thing through thoroughly."[25]

STAFF RELATIONS AND THE CIVIL SERVICE ACT OF 1961

If the Heeney concept of the Civil Service Commission as third-party arbiter had been seriously damaged by the pay disputes of 1958 and 1959 and was threatened by the coming report of the Glassco Commission, it was also under fire from yet another quarter: the staff associations. There is a rather fine irony in the fact that during their decades of dependency on the CSC, the associations would have accepted the Heeney Report as a Utopia on earth; yet when the offer was finally made, the associations saw it as a rather quaint anachronism, the usefulness of which had long since passed. The concept developed by Bryce and Heeney failed to take into account the rapidly developing militancy and sophistication of the organized employees. The latter part of the 1950s and the early 1960s were periods of flux and turmoil in staff relations, as the old staff associations transformed themselves into contemporary style mass-based industrial trade unions. Of course these developments did not come out of the blue; they had been building beneath the surface for many years. Bryce and Heeney had seen that new pressures were ready to burst forth and had tried to anticipate events. But they had not quite gauged the depth of the changes taking place, and hence the solution they proffered was, quite simply, overtaken by events.

As early as October of 1958—two months before the Prime Minister was to receive the Heeney Report, and three months before its public release—the Civil Service Association of Canada wrote to Mr. Diefenbaker to complain about the CSC's role in the 1958 pay dispute.[26] In so doing a point of conflict with the Government was revealed which went well beyond the specific situation of 1959, and in fact established a basic philosophical rejection of the Heeney Report in advance. The dispute, argued the CSAC, was no longer one of salary, but one of principle, "of how much longer decisions are to remain unilateral ones." The CSAC, moreover, explicitly dissociated itself from the traditional cap-in-hand approach:

> We do not desire to ask for favour, but only such fairness of condition as is current in industry and we must, therefore, reject the confusion and uneven treatment of the paternal approach.
>
> No employer, not even the Government, should have the final judging of a dispute with its employees, or the final decision as to whether it will or will not act in every matter concerning its employees. This task should be given to some arbitration body that is independent in all respects, with all parties abiding by the decision rendered.
>
> We are not unmindful of the fact that some form of negotiation procedure and arbitration would not in itself be an unmixed blessing. It could be a two edged sword, but at least it would have some promise that it would not always be our necks that were under the blade.
>
> Civil Servants have reached some maturity in organization, and their responsibility should now be recognized by an Employer-Employee relationship that is in keeping with the times.
>
> We would ask that speedy consideration be given to our recent recommendations for a form of collective bargaining for the service, that is meaningful within the concept of the terms, together with provision for independent arbitration authority.

The Prime Minister, in reply, maintained that the CSC was in fact independent, and that "no additional independent arbitration authority" apart from the CSC, was to be considered by the Government.[27] Yet this answer scarcely grappled with the very real questions the CSAC had raised, and as can be seen in retrospect, failed to square with the Government's own conduct in the pay dispute.

Following the more serious and overt pay dispute of 1959, the staff associations went even further in shedding their old illusions. At a conference on civil service staff relations sponsored by the Canadian Labour Congress in 1960, the President of the CSAC was bluntly straightforward on the question of the independence of the CSC:

> Whether the Civil Service Commission may or may not want to accept the fact, it is primarily the Government's recruiting agency. Regardless

of statements to the contrary, by-and-large, it is much more sensitive to Government policies and statements than it is to those of employee associations. This does much to raise doubts about the theory of an independent commission on pay and monetary matters. The present relationship on such matters is triangular. The Commission, the Minister of Finance (Treasury Board) and the staff associations. What is needed is not a triangular relationship but a dual one. Eliminate the Commission entirely from the bargaining aspects of pay and working conditions and substitute the vastly more practical and satisfactory system of Treasury Board–Association negotiations.[28]

The position which the associations had arrived at by the beginning of the 1960s was a clear-cut demand for collective bargaining, with provision for compulsory arbitration. Except for the militant postal unions, there was no sentiment at this time for the right to strike. Moreover, not all the associations were equally ready to move to full collective bargaining, nor were they wholly united within their own executives: there seems to have been some conflict between the new, postwar leadership and the more traditional elements still remaining. The general drift of staff association thinking was, however, irrevocably in the direction of collective bargaining in some form. And this spelled failure for the Heeney Report recommendations on staff relations and pay determination.

Hughes himself quickly accepted the fact that the associations were opposed to the implementation of the Heeney concept, and were aiming for collective bargaining. However, Hughes did not form a particularly high opinion of the leadership of the associations, citing what he felt to be their "very immature" behaviour over the 1959 pay dispute. He consequently downplayed the extent of their demands, and asserted that the phrase "collective bargaining" indicated rather less than met the eye. In the early fall of 1959, he suggested: "The staff associations desire what they term 'collective bargaining,' and although this phrase does not suggest what they really want, it appears to me that the essence of their aims is the right to discuss directly with the government, represented by the Treasury, their pay demands and to obtain, if not all that they are asking for, at least some compromise which they could then take back to their membership as a token of victorious achievement."[29] Believing that it would be "advantageous to make a gesture in the direction of the staff associations," Hughes put forward an alternative concept to the Heeney Report in which the associations would consult with the CSC, the CSC would make its recommendations to the government, and then the associations would "sit down with the representatives of the government and discuss the Commission's recommendations, which would be made available, confidentially, to them." This procedure would, in Hughes' view, achieve the "atmosphere of 'collective bargaining,' " as well as freeing the government of the necessity to grant "as much or as little of the Commission's recommendations as it felt desirable." This would in turn give public recognition to what "is undoubtedly the fact now, that the government does not have to accept the Commission's proposals in an uncritical way." Finally, the "curse of secrecy," which made the CSC's recommendations subject to suspicion, could be lifted "particularly when it is clearly understood that the government is not bound to accept [them] and [they are] still subject to discussion between the government and the associations."[30]

In effect, Hughes was suggesting nothing less than the dismantlement not only of the Heeney recommendations, but also of the pretence under which the CSC, Treasury Board, and the staff associations had always operated in matters of pay determination. The Hughes alternative was, however, very much in the nature of a compromise between the old system and a more realistic new system, a compromise which quite obviously fell far short of immediate collective bargaining in any meaningful sense of that term. Hughes himself saw it not only as a compromise but as an opened door through which the staff associations could proceed, step by step, to a more comprehensive stage of collective bargaining when conditions were favourable. Hughes' proposal was in fact received much more cordially by the Government than Heeney's had been, and ultimately formed the basis of staff relations in the new Civil Service Act.

In late 1959, a cabinet committee was set up to consider the drafting of the new Act. By early January, 1960, the committee had reported to the full Cabinet that the revision of civil service legislation should in general follow the lines of the Heeney Report, except for a number of points where the present Government differed. Many of these differences were matters of detail; some, such as the refusal to tamper with the operations of the veterans preference, were of rather wider significance. But as to the key point in the Heeney Report, the differences were fundamental. First, it was recommended that the determination of pay become the responsibility of the Governor in Council, who in turn would delegate it to the Treasury Board. The CSC was to report its recommendations to the Governor in Council, but the Government was no longer to be bound by the practice of either accepting or rejecting, but not amending, these recommendations. In a statutory sense, it could do as it pleased, whatever the CSC's recommendations.[31] Under this arrangement, the CSC could scarcely play the role of independent arbiter which Heeney had envisaged.

What was still left in doubt by this fomulation was the precise form that staff relations were to take under the new legislation. Hughes clearly considered this to be an open-ended question, subject only to the limitation

271

that the Conservative Government did not favour full collective bargaining in the industrial sense, certainly not with the right to strike nor with compulsory third-party arbitration, and also subject perhaps to the further limitation that, in Hughes' view, the staff associations were not yet mature enough to assume the responsibility that full collective bargaining would require. The Minister of Finance, after some tentative probing by Hughes, instructed C. J. Mackenzie of the Treasury Board staff to prepare a paper on "collective bargaining or consultation with the recognized staff associations on pay questions."[32] Mackenzie advised Fleming that the CSC "cannot be in the line of administration and arbitrator at one and the same time," that the associations wanted bilateral discussions, and that the Treasury Board staff should "undertake negotiations on pay matters with a joint negotiating Committee of the recognized staff organizations," after the CSC's recommendations had been received *in confidence*. Contrary to the CSC's views, Mackenzie believed that any open conflict within "managerial ranks" would worsen the negotiating atmosphere. Thus the only major disagreement remaining between the CSC and the Treasury Board was on the matter of publicity. Mackenzie also believed that "some experience with negotiations should be developed before the question of arbitration, compulsory or otherwise, is envisaged,"[33] but this was just as clearly Hughes' view as well.

At a meeting of the cabinet committee in March, the Minister of Finance took a rather harder line than the Government had hitherto revealed. There was simply no question, Mr. Fleming asserted, of granting either collective bargaining or arbitration: it was therefore "a question of what it was expedient to say about consultation." It was finally agreed that some form of "qualified obligation" should be laid on both the CSC and the Minister of Finance to consult with the organized employees. Significantly, "it was recognized that a clause of this kind was to have chiefly a propaganda value rather than to lay down a procedure of or requirement for consultation on all pay changes."[34] It would thus appear that the open-ended attitude of Hughes and the more negative attitude of the Government, or at least of the Department of Finance, could come together in the new Act—although with rather different motives involved.

In the following week members of the cabinet committee met with representatives of the Joint Action Committee from the associations to discuss the situation with regard to the new Act. The representatives of the associations reiterated their desire for "collective bargaining," and used the threat of certain extremists who were agitating for the right to strike as a lever for more moderate concessions. While they were in agreement among themselves that direct negotiations with Treasury Board were the only satisfactory procedure, there appears to have been some disagreement beyond this stage. One representative suggested that "a form of discussion leading to agreement but not the signing of a formal collective agreement" would be involved, while another suggested that a formal Arbitration Board report would be presented to Parliament. The Minister of Finance did not reject the concept of collective bargaining out of hand, but instead warned the associations that statutory provisions for arbitration and conciliation might introduce legislative "rigidity" which would harm the associations themselves. Considering the views that Fleming had expressed privately the week before, this argument was not entirely ingenuous, and for their part, the associations were adamant that the Government give an explicit statement of principle, if not in the new Act, then in Parliament. On this inconclusive note the consultation with the staff associations on the new civil service legislation came to an end.[35]

In a draft bill prepared by the Justice Department in April, a provision was included for consultations at the request of the CSC or the Minister of Finance, which was inserted "merely to raise the point and to ensure that it will not be overlooked."[36] The CSAC continued to argue for the right of the associations to initiate such consultations.[37] And Hughes himself, believing that the associations "are committed to indefinite agitation on the subject, and refusal even to discuss the pros and cons would be needlessly provocative," suggested a committee representative of both the management and staff sides to investigate the possibility of a system of collective bargaining with provision for the submission of disputes to compulsory arbitration, thus transferring the "odium of making unpopular decisions on pay, which now attaches to the Government . . . to an arbitrator." Such an arbitrator, Hughes was quick to add, should *not* be the CSC, but could come from the judicial branch of government. However, Hughes freely admitted to Fleming that the two other Commissioners did not share his views in this matter and that the introduction of any form of negotiation would necessarily entail "serious administrative problems."[38]

The new legislation was introduced too late in the 1960 session to get past the stage of first reading, and thus a new session in 1960–61 gave all the participants the opportunity to explore the staff relations issue further. Fleming took up the objections raised by the staff associations, as well as by Hughes, to the provision for consultations only at the request of the CSC or the Minister of Finance and suggested to the cabinet committee that some more magnanimous gesture might be made to the associations.[39] The Cabinet then decided to introduce a provision for consultations to be held "at the request of" the associations, as well as at the initiative of the CSC or the Minister of Finance,[40] and it was in this form that the legislation received first reading and proceeded to the committee stage. Although the associations went before the special parliamentary committee reviewing the bill to demand that the consultation provision be expanded to include provision for bargaining and arbitration,[41] these concepts were not introduced into the legislation. The clause in question was altered in the committee stage at the instigation of the Minister of Finance, but only in such a way as to make the predominant role of Treasury Board in pay determination even more explicit. Section 7 of the new Civil Service Act in its final form read as follows:

(1) The Minister of Finance or such members of the public service as he may designate shall from time to time consult with representatives of appropriate organizations and associations of employees with respect to remuneration, at the request of such representatives or whenever in the opinion of the Minister of Finance such consultation is necessary or desirable.

(2) The Commission and such members of the public service as the Minister of Finance may designate shall from time to time consult with representatives of appropriate organizations and associations of employees with respect to the terms and conditions of employment referred to in sub-section (1) of section 68, at the request of such representatives or whenever in the opinion of the Commission and the Minister of Finance such consultation is necessary or desirable.

(3) The Commission shall from time to time consult with representatives of appropriate organizations and associations of employees with respect to such terms and conditions of employment as come within the exclusive jurisdiction of the Commission under this Act and the regulations, at the request of such representatives or whenever in the opinion of the Commission such consultation is necessary or desirable.[42]

While the CSC was still to make recommendations on pay, and was to consult with the associations in formulating its recommendations, the new Act also specified:

(11) The Governor in Council, after the Commission has had an opportunity of considering the matter and after considering any recommendations made by the Commission, shall
    (a) establish rates of pay for each grade; and
    (b) establish the allowances that may be paid in addition to pay.

The central core of Heeney's vision of the CSC as an independent arbiter was thus officially dead, although the fatal blows had been struck long before the legislation achieved final form. The final decisions on pay now lay squarely between Treasury Board and the organized public servants.

The Government clearly believed that section 7 had gone a long way toward meeting the demands of the staff associations. Not only had they been given official recognition for the first time, but they had also been granted the right to initiate consultations with the Government. Hughes had on a number of occasions stated publicly his belief that the new Civil Service Act provided the framework within which collective bargaining could develop. Both Hughes on the one hand, and the Minister of Finance, Treasury Board, and the two other Commissioners on the other, were more or less in agreement that no legislative blueprint for collective bargaining and arbitration procedures should be written into legislation. But whereas Hughes would appear to have genuinely believed that an evolution toward collective bargaining would be positively beneficial, the Minister of Finance as well as the two Commissioners appear to have seen far more difficulties than benefits in such a scheme. Yet despite the somewhat differing motives of the various parties involved, there was a consensus that fundamental transformations in staff relations ought not to be established by legislative fiat. The Progressive Conservative Government, as well as Hughes, who was of an old Conservative family, was suspicious of rationalistic blueprints, and preferred to develop solutions through "precedent." Hughes himself spoke of a system which "based upon precedent, will stand the test of time."[43] And in Parliament, Richard Bell, a Conservative member from the civil-servant-dominated constituency of Carleton, defended the new Act by suggesting that "techniques, like freedom, ought to broaden down from precedent to precedent."[44] This philosophic conservatism was in rather sharp contrast to the Liberal attitude a few years later, when a precise legislative blueprint for collective bargaining was set up.

The conservative argument that human relationships cannot be legislated but must develop in an evolutionary fashion drew much strength from the example of the British civil service, where the Whitley Council system of joint consultation had developed without any precise legislative foundation. Unfortunately for the Government, however, the essential *trust* upon which such an evolution could take place had, on both sides, deteriorated to a marked degree. The leadership of the associations was suspicious of the Government's motives, and, as we have already seen, with some reason. Moreover, the new consultation system was quickly to prove a cumbersome and frustrating procedure to the associations. First they would consult with the CSC, then they would have to begin all over again with the Treasury Board. It was all too obviously an irrational system, and as it turned out, in the first year of operation, Treasury Board was to cut back severely on the CSC recommendations, thus calling into question the value of consulting with the CSC at all.[45] The conservative argument simply did not sit well with the employees. The associations were now at a point where a distinct break with the past was positively desired. An appeal to history had little attraction to those who saw tradition as a chain to be broken.

THE HEENEY REPORT AND THE 1961 ACT

An article by Hughes in the *Public Personnel Review* of 1962 maintained that the new Act followed the recommendations of the Heeney Report with only two major exceptions—the decision not to alter the veterans preference, and the refusal to apply the Act to previously excluded sections of the service.[46] While these changes were indeed direct revisions of the Heeney recommendations, to limit the number of revisions to these two is to seriously misunderstand the extent to which the basic Heeney philosophy had been altered by the time the proposals had reached legislative form. Far more important from Heeney's point of view than either of the changes cited by Hughes was the clear removal from the Civil Service Commission of the power to act as an independent arbiter in staff relations and pay determination. The fact that Treasury Board could now amend at will the CSC's recommendations effectively put an end to that concept. There were, of course, sound reasons for this, but it is nevertheless curious that so many observers, in missing the main point of the Heeney Report, also missed the main point of its revision.

The major innovation in the new Act was, as we have already indicated, in the area of appeals. Basically, civil servants were given the *right* of appeal against a number of administrative actions. The ad hoc type of appeal procedures which had hitherto existed in sketchy form in the regulations, or merely in custom and usage, were extended and rationalized within the Act itself.[47] The CSC was to hear all appeals and its decision was to be final on all matters except dismissals, where its judgement was to be in the form of a recommendation to the Governor in Council. Beyond the CSC, however, civil servants could have recourse to the civil courts—although this right would presumably be exercised only rarely. Before the passage of the new Act, the CSC only heard appeals against promotion or denial of a statutory increase. Under the Act, transfers, demotions, suspensions, and dismissals could be appealed to the CSC. Provision was also made for establishing grievance machinery to deal with grievances arising from the administration of the Act and its regulations. The provisions governing appeals were referred to at the time as the "Magna Carta of the Clerk 2."

In view of the importance which Hughes placed on the appeals function, it is interesting to note that the rest of the CSC was not unanimous in its support of the new concept. During the House of Commons hearings on the 1961 Act, Hughes hinted that an additional number of Commissioners might be useful to handle the large volume of appeals expected. Commissioner Addison quickly interjected: "I can see Mr. Hughes' point about appeals, but this is a separate field. . . . One has to stop and think: Why was this commission set up? It was for a definite purpose, namely, to preserve the merit system, and to carry out the terms of the Civil Service Act." Commissioner Pelletier followed by advising the committee that "it must not be forgotten . . . that there is not only the question of appeals in the civil service, but also that of appointments, demotions, transfers and so on, for which the commission is responsible."[48]

As Heeney himself had recommended, responsibility for organizational changes was transferred to the Treasury Board, with the CSC giving up all control functions in this regard and retaining only an advisory role. Thus the old ghost of Griffenhagen was at last laid to rest. On the two major points of pay determination and organization, Treasury Board had finally been awarded fairly clear responsibility. In other areas, however, the verdict was different. Heeney had argued that classification should remain with the CSC, and remain it did, despite a strong challenge from Treasury Board, supported by the Minister of Finance. On April 21, 1960, Fleming had written to the Associate Deputy Minister of Justice, who was drafting the new bill, and stated explicitly: "It is the intention of the Cabinet Committee that ultimate authority in the field of classification, as in the case of pay, should be in the hands of the Governor in Council with the Civil Service Commission serving as expert advisors."[49] Hughes strongly resisted this and disputed C. J. Mackenzie's interpretation of the cabinet committee's views, upon which Fleming was acting.[50] When the Justice Department produced the first draft, having attempted, as they put it, to "give effect to the views of the Chairman of the Civil Service Commission as well as to the views of [Fleming's] officials," the change requested by Fleming was not included, apparently because it had been received rather late in the process.[51] The CSC argued that the same proposal had been put before it by Treasury Board during the preparation of the Heeney Report and that it had been "violently opposed whenever it came up during the meetings of Deputy Heads."[52] As it turned out, the Cabinet decided that the Fleming-Mackenzie interpretation had not been the correct one, and the responsibility for classification remained with the CSC.[53]

In other areas as well, the *control* aspect of appointments, promotions, and conditions of employment, remained very much in evidence in the new legislation. Hughes strongly believed in the necessity of a central control function, and was very adverse to revolutionary transformations of an organization which was rooted firmly in the soil of the Canadian political system. He recalled: "I had some strong views on the need for a strong central Commission, in the spirit of the previous Act—an organization which had a part to play in government and which had a long life history in the events of yesteryear."[54] As was suggested in the previous chapter on the Heeney Report, Heeney had generally tried to divest the CSC of its management functions not related to the maintenance of the merit system, but that in the pursuit of his central vision of the CSC as an independent arbiter in staff relations, he had wished to retain certain management control functions which he saw as essential to the performance of its projected new role. This was the crux of the argument which developed between Heeney and Watters of the Treasury Board in 1958.[55] But Heeney's argument for the continued division of management responsibility made sense only so long as the CSC was to act as an independent arbiter. When this role was removed, as it was by 1961, Watters' arguments take on far more cogency. In fact Watters anticipated by four years the essential recommendations of the Glassco Commission. The Civil Service Act of 1961 was thus in the nature of a compromise between two quite divergent views of the role of the CSC, at a time when the possibility of meaningful compromise was drawing rapidly to a close.

The preparation of the 1961 legislation reveals very clearly the continuation of the decades-old rivalry between the CSC and the Treasury Board. It was no secret that the Board was unhappy with the new Act as not going far enough in divesting the CSC of its non-merit responsibilities. The radically divergent views revealed in the earlier Heeney-Watters exchange continued, despite the victory which Treasury Board had won over the CSC on pay determination. The new Act was, after all, a CSC project. Mr. C. J. Mackenzie, Assistant Secretary of the Board, appeared as a witness before the special parliamentary committee considering the bill at the same time as the three Commissioners, and a number of conflicts were revealed, all of them turning on matters which the Board considered to be management prerogatives. Interestingly enough, on at least one occasion, Hughes took the side of the Treasury Board against the other Commissioners on the point of making clear the exclusion of prevailing rates employees from the Act.[56]

The somewhat confused face which the CSC presented to Parliament was only a reflection of the confusion into which it had fallen after its long years of rather comfortable quiet. Heeney had tried to start the CSC off in a new direction, but that had proved abortive. Hughes tried to point them in another direction with his emphasis on the appeals function, but could not line up the CSC solidly behind him. Meanwhile, Glassco was formulating its own views. An internal paper of the manpower project of the

Glassco inquiry dated December 1, 1961, rejected the 1961 Act as being grievously inadequate. It suggested that

> the focal point of our study is the nature and extent of delegation of authority and responsibility to departments and agencies. The basic problem in this focus is the tripartite nature of decision-making in the areas of manpower management. The concept is traditional: the roles of the Civil Service Commission, Governor in Council (through the Minister of Finance or Treasury Board) and departments were cast in the Civil Service Act of 1918. As the scenes changed, the makeup and characterization modified. But the "eternal triangle" as played out in government service remained. The Civil Service Act of 1961 did not represent a dramatic change in any sense of the word.[57]

The 1961 Act had taken some four years to produce. Events moved so quickly that its life span scarcely outlasted its period of gestation. With the CSC heading off in various directions at once, and with the Glassco Report in the making, the whole question of the management of personnel in the public service, and of the CSC's role in this process, was in a greater state of flux than at any time since the passage of the 1918 Act. In retrospect it can be seen that the decade between the appointment of Heeney in 1957 and the passage of the 1967 public service legislation was by far the most turbulent period in the Commission's history since the 1918–21 period of classification and reorganization. The influence which was eventually to prove the strongest in shaping the CSC's future came not from within, despite the efforts of men like Heeney and Hughes, but from without, from the Glassco inquiry and from the Preparatory Committee on Collective Bargaining.

NOTES

1. "An Address on the Civil Service," delivered by the Right Honourable John G. Diefenbaker to the Civil Service Association of Canada, p. 4.
2. Interview.
3. J. D. Love, speech to the International Conference of the Public Personnel Association, Vancouver and Victoria, October, 1967 (mimeograph).

4. Georges E. Gauthier, "The Canadian Pay Research Bureau," p. 269.

5. T. J. Wilkins, "The Pay Research Bureau," *Civil Service Review* 40 (September, 1967), p. 4.

6. Great Britain, *Report of the Royal Commission on the Civil Service*, 1953–55, Cmd. 9613, p. 37.

7. Quoted in "Memorandum to Ministers," prepared by Heeney, May 28, 1958, Heeney Files.

8. Gauthier, "Canadian Pay Research Bureau," p. 269.

9. Interview.

10. Diefenbaker, "Address on the Civil Service," p. 4.

11. Quoted in Preparatory Committee on Collective Bargaining in the Public Service, "Pay Determination in the Canadian Civil Service," Staff Reference Paper no. 14, January, 1964, pp. 3–4.

12. CSC, Press Release, September 4, 1957, cited in Saul J. Frankel, *Staff Relations in the Civil Service: The Canadian Experience*, p. 136. See also Gauthier, "Canadian Pay Research Bureau," p. 270.

13. Frankel, *Staff Relations in the Civil Service*, p. 142.

14. Ibid., pp. 141–42.

15. Ibid., pp. 174–75.

16. Ibid., p. 174.

17. Although direct documentary evidence on this point was almost impossible to obtain, former civil servants confirmed in confidential interviews that it did occur.

18. As an internal CSC report noted, "When the recent increase in civil service salaries was authorized, a meeting of representatives of all Staff Associations to explain the increase was called and chaired by a Treasury Board official." ("Personnel Administration in the Government Service," internal document prepared for the Commissioners, 1956 [typescript], p. 23)

19. Interview.

20. *Ottawa Journal*, September 18, 1958, cited in Frankel, *Staff Relations in the Civil Service*, p. 143.

21. Interview.

22. *Debates*, July 9, 1959, p. 5704.

23. Frankel, *Staff Relations in the Civil Service*, p. 157.

24. Ibid., pp. 147–48.

25. Interview.

26. Trevor Gough to Diefenbaker, October 23, 1958, Heeney Files.

27. Diefenbaker to Gough, October 24, 1958, ibid.

28. J. C. Best, "The Heeney Report," p. 5.

29. "Memorandum on Joint Discussions on Pay in the Civil Service," prepared by Hughes, n.d., PSC File 041-91, PSC Central Registry. The memorandum would appear to have been written in September or October of 1959.

30. Ibid.

31. Record of Cabinet Decision (Meeting of January 4, 1960), PSC File 041-91, PSC Central Registry.

32. Fleming to Bryce, February 9, 1960, ibid. It is perhaps not without significance that Hughes himself wrote "collective bargaining" within quotation marks. (Hughes to Fleming, February 12, 1960, ibid.)

33. Memorandum from C. J. Mackenzie to the Cabinet Committee on the Civil Service Act, February 19, 1960, ibid.

34. Memorandum on meeting of the Cabinet Committee on the Revision of the Civil Service Act, held March 7, 1960, prepared by Bryce, March 16, 1960, ibid.

35. Memorandum of meeting with the Joint Action Committee of the staff associations, March 15, 1960, prepared by C. J. Mackenzie, ibid.

36. F. A. Driedger to Fleming, April 26, 1960, ibid.

37. J. C. Best to Hughes, October 13, 1960, ibid.

38. Hughes to Fleming, December 8, 1960, ibid.

39. Memorandum on meeting of the Cabinet Committee on the Revision of the Civil Service Act, held January 4, 1961, prepared by Bryce, January 11, 1961, and draft memorandum for Cabinet, prepared by Bryce, January 11, 1961, ibid.

40. Record of Cabinet Decision (Meeting of January 19, 1961), ibid.

41. CSF, "Submission Pertaining to Bill C-71," April 13, 1961; and CSAC, "Views and Recommendations on Bill C-71, An Act Respecting the Civil Service of Canada," April, 1961, PSC File 041-92.

42. 9–10 Elizabeth II (1961), c. 71, s. 7.

43. Hughes to Fleming, June 22, 1961, PSC File 041-92.

44. *Debates*, March 10, 1961, p. 2868.

45. See chapter 13 for details.

46. S. H. S. Hughes, "The New Civil Service Act: A Comparison of the Old and New Civil Service Acts," p. 19.

47. Interview.

48. H.C., Special Committee on the Civil Service Act (Bill C-71), 1960–61, *Proceedings and Evidence*, pp. 349–50.

49. Fleming to Driedger, April 21, 1960, PSC File 041-91.

50. Hughes to Fleming, April 25, 1960, and memorandum from K. R. Scobie to Hughes, May 12, 1960, ibid.

51. Driedger to Fleming, April 26, 1960, ibid.

52. G. A. Blackburn to Hughes, May 4, 1960, ibid.

53. "Memorandum on Suggested Changes in the Civil Service Bill," prepared by Hughes, December 28, 1960, ibid. The Cabinet Committee did not, however, take up Hughes' suggestion that the classification function was "of such importance as to warrant its inclusion in a statement of general powers and duties." (Memorandum on meeting of the Cabinet Committee on the Revision of the Civil Service Act, held January 4, 1961, prepared by Bryce, January 11, 1961, ibid.)

54. Interview.

55. See chapter 11.

56. 1961 Committee, p. 330. Prevailing rates employees were outside the provisions of the Civil Service Act and were paid the prevailing rate of pay of the district or locality in which they were employed.

57. "The Civil Service Act," Manpower Project Discussion Paper no. 20, December 1, 1961, files of the Royal Commission on Government Organization, vol. 62.

Chapter Thirteen
The Search for a New Role,
1962–1964

I have always been sorry that it has not
been possible for the Civil Service Com-
mission to detach itself from the role of
management more than it has. I think the
Civil Service Commission ... has been
willing to take over as the "chief personnel
agency" of government much too readily,
that it has been associated in the minds of
employees with management much more
than it should have been. ... But I am not
satisfied ... that [the Glassco Commission]
has fully taken on board, not only the
historic, but the actual importance of this
institution of the Civil Service Commis-
sion and the role that it is capable of play-
ing, under more flexible and efficient
conditions for management than have
existed hitherto. I am not appearing in the
guise of a defender of the status quo ante
or the Civil Service Commission or indeed
any of our existing arrangements. But
here is something under our system which
I do not think has been fully appreciated
by these able men.

A. D. P. Heeney at the 1962 annual conference
of the Institute of Public Administration of Canada

NINETEEN SIXTY-TWO was not a good year for the Civil Service Commission. In that one year it encountered more difficulty and criticism than it
had been subjected to for any time since the Pouliot inquiry more than

twenty years earlier. The CSC's troubles primarily derived from two sources: the inauguration of the system of consultation over pay determination provided in the 1961 Act, and the release of the Report of the Royal Commission on Government Organization (the Glassco Commission). These events demonstrated, on the one hand, great deficiencies in the state of employer-employee relations in the civil service and, on the other, the sorry state of personnel management. In both areas the CSC was made to bear a major portion of the guilt. By the end of the year it became increasingly evident that the traditional role of the CSC would be severely circumscribed from its former limits. The problem facing the CSC in the years following 1962 involved no small task: it had to discover the boundaries of its powers and to redefine and reassert its priorities within its new limits.

PROBLEMS OF CONSULTATION

THE PAY DETERMINATION PROCESS

On April 1, 1962, the three-tiered system of consultation with staff associations for the determination of salary schedules came into operation. From the beginning it failed to satisfy all parties involved and far from settled the problem of employer-employee relations. The major difficulty with the system from the point of view of the Civil Service Commission resided in the fact that the Treasury Board had come to adopt what the CSC referred to as "a rather extreme 'management position.'"[1] Prior to the 1961 Act, as we saw, the machinery for pay determination was relatively simple. To recapitulate briefly, the Pay Research Bureau conducted studies and made a report containing comparative analyses of industrial and civil service rates of pay. Working with these reports, the CSC subsequently made recommendations to the Treasury Board which then had the choice of accepting or rejecting the recommendations, but could not amend them. During this period differences of opinion began to develop between the officials of the Treasury Board and the CSC over the use and interpretation of the information produced by the PRB. Problems that could not be solved at this time eventually resolved themselves into four fundamental questions of policy which came to a head roughly at the same time as the commencement of the consultation system in 1962.

The first of these problems revolved around the PRB's choice of the area of outside comparison. Historically, the Government had usually maintained that the terms and conditions of employment offered civil servants should ideally be guided by a rough comparison to the policies and practices of firms in the private sector that could be considered "good employers." To develop its studies, it was necessary for the PRB to define

284

what was meant by a good employer, and it eventually developed five criteria on which to judge this. The Treasury Board officials, however, began to object that the criteria used were too restrictive, producing a "rich" sample. With time the arguments became more developed and centred upon the minimum standards of comparison used by the PRB to obtain its sample. Although the CSC in general agreed with the PRB's position, it supported attempts to modify the minimum standards, but these efforts were blocked by the staff associations sitting on the Advisory Committee on Pay Research. Little progress was made, consequently, with both the staff associations and the Treasury Board maintaining their basic positions.

Second, differences of opinion occurred over the method of comparing outside rates with those in the service. Over the years the PRB had come to develop two methods of comparison. The first of these involved comparing the maximum rates for classes in the service with the third quartile of their outside sample. (The outside sample was divided into four quartiles so that the third quartile represented rates immediately below the top level.) The second method involved a comparison of the mean rates both outside and in the service. The CSC maintained that both measures were significant and should be used in the determination of pay, but the Treasury Board disagreed, and instead used only the data on the comparison of mean rates which usually produced a lower rate of comparison.

The third area of difficulty centred on the differences in industrial rates of pay for blue-collar occupations in various parts of the country, and here three different views emerged. The CSC felt that the geographic factor in pay should at times temper the market rates suggested by the results of a national survey, but saw no value in any formula which attempted to accomplish this in an automatic fashion. Like its stand on the question of comparative rate measures, the CSC argued that the two factors were significant, and depending on the case in question, one should dominate over the other. The officials of the Board, on the other hand, argued strongly that the geographic factor was of crucial importance and attempted to arrive at a mechanical formula which would take it into consideration in all cases. In direct opposition to this position stood the representatives of the staff associations who asserted that the rates in the economy at large should be allowed to dominate.

The fourth area of difficulty concerned the matter of fringe benefits. In 1961, the PRB conducted a comparative study of expenditures on employee benefits. This project was the most ambitious of its kind ever undertaken in Canada to that time, and because of the problems the PRB had encountered, the CSC regarded the findings as somewhat experimental in nature. Once again it felt the study useful and worthy of consideration among other factors, but, as before, the Treasury Board tended to adopt a hard-line approach. During the 1961 pay determination process the officers of the Board announced their intention of making provision over a period of years for adjustments equal to the full amount of the difference between the civil service and industrial rates of expenditure on employee benefits. Because the PRB's study had indicated that fringe benefits in the civil service were more generous than those in the industrial sector, bitter debate followed the announcement, with a strong negative response from the staff associations.

While these issues had caused problems and complications in the pay determination process prior to 1962, they all but made a mockery of the consultation process after that date. The fact that the 1961 Act made it no longer incumbent upon the Government merely to accept or reject the CSC recommendations meant that, when they reached the Board, these recommendations regularly underwent modification. The first of these occurred, in fact, in 1962, shortly after the Act came into operation when the Treasury Board took it upon itself to reduce the salary levels recommended by the CSC. A rather acrimonious debate ensued between the CSC, the Board, and the staff associations. This produced an extremely frustrating situation for both the CSC and the associations. The representatives of the associations found that after their "negotiations" with the CSC, they had to begin "negotiations" all over again with the Treasury Board.[2] The officials of the CSC, on the other hand, were deeply disturbed because of the damaging effect of this situation upon the Commission's prestige.

By July of the following year the whole consultation and pay determination situation had deteriorated to such an extent that the Commissioners sent a memorandum to Walter Gordon, the Minister of Finance of the recently elected Liberal Government, elaborating on the difficulties caused by the Board's "extreme management position" and asking him to consider modifications in the pay determination process along lines which bore a remarkable similarity to the process earlier envisaged by Heeney. They suggested that consultations between the Treasury Board and the associations should take place under CSC auspices *before* the CSC made its recommendations to the Treasury Board: "In the event of agreement between the two sides, the Commission would recommend the rates agreed upon. In the event of failure to agree, the Commission would take into consideration the arguments presented by both sides and recommend whatever rates it considered appropriate. The recommendations of the Commission would be made public and it would be understood that, in normal circumstances, they would be accepted by the Government."[3] If the Government, "for reasons of overriding national concern," found itself

286

unable to accept the recommendations of the CSC in either event, the Commissioners suggested that it should make its refusal and the reasons behind the refusal public. In the opinion of the Commissioners, "there is good reason to believe that, in such circumstances, a public explanation would result in widespread civil service support for the decision of the Government." Despite the efforts of the CSC, however, the Government seems to have had reservations about modifying a procedure that was little more than a year old, so that nothing substantial was done on the matter.

REPORT OF THE GLASSCO COMMISSION

In September of 1962, in the midst of the troubles which the Civil Service Commission was beginning to encounter with the pay determination process, the Glassco Commission published its Report. Not unexpectedly, the Report, among other things, sharply criticized the state of personnel management in the civil service. To begin with, instead of any centralized or overall planning, it discovered only a plethora of detailed controls split among the CSC, the Treasury Board, and the departments. The resultant situation was, in its estimation, disastrous for the civil service:

> The charges laid at the doorstep of the personnel management system, and largely confirmed by our investigation, can be bluntly stated: there is a waste of human resources, because of the failure to give orderly consideration to the best methods of providing and utilizing people and the consequent frustration of many individual careers; the procedures are costly and time-consuming; personnel management in departments is generally misdirected, mainly because accountability for the effective use of personnel is fragmented or virtually non-existent.[4]

The main villain emerging from the pages of the Glassco Report was the CSC, the body historically concerned with most facets of personnel management, and because of its desire to ensure uniformity of treatment for civil servants, the organization largely responsible for the growth of controls. The Glassco Commission found these controls permeating all activities which were the responsibility of the CSC. In commenting on this, the Report made an important distinction:

> It was the intention of the Civil Service Act of 1918 to establish the "merit principle" as the guide to recruitment, selection and promotion in the public service. The merit principle has been endorsed in all subsequent appraisals, and has the full support of your Commissioners. A distinction however, must be made between the merit principle and the

287

"merit system," i.e., that collection of rules, regulations, policies and procedures peculiar to the Canadian civil service which have been designed to implement the principle. The merit system, in many of its current practices, frustrates the attainment of the principle; in its name many absurd procedures are tolerated; the system has become an end in itself, overriding the need to "get the job done"; and all too frequently it has engendered such delays in the attempt to get the "best" man that his loss to a more nimble employer was ensured. It is paradoxical, to say the least, that a system designed to improve the public service by eliminating improper influences on appointments should exact, in the process, such high costs.[5]

In the area of promotions and transfers the Glassco Commission found machinery equally heavy-handed, designed in this instance to protect the service from internal patronage. Again, there was evidence that the procedures and machinery in operation for this purpose were perhaps more costly "in terms of delay, unfilled positions, poor selection of personnel, and general frustration of responsible supervisors" than they were worth in terms of control.[6]

Other areas, too, fared no better. The Royal Commissioners, for example, were "forced to conclude that, in general, training and development have received inadequate attention in the public service for many years." The classification system was "too elaborate and complicated," and the combination of the classification, recruitment, and placement functions of the CSC in one branch was a move of "debatable wisdom" when compared with the experience of the industrial sector. They found the remuneration system "essentially negative" owing to its lack of provision for "positive recognition of superior performance." The whole area of pay determination was "marked by duplication of machinery and effort and a failure to achieve reasonable co-ordination and common guiding principles." There was also a serious lack of suitable departmental grievance procedure and a too-formalized and complicated general appeal machinery.[7]

In dealing with these problems the Glassco Commission endeavoured to identify the various functions of personnel management in the civil service. It suggested that those concerned with the central direction of the bureaucracy as a whole, that is, those functions generally concerned with the development and coordination of personnel policy for the entire bureaucracy, should be centralized in a personnel policy branch of a reconstituted Treasury Board.[8] On the other hand, it recommended that the more operational end of personnel administration should be performed by the departments, which would be held correspondingly accountable. This outlook had grave implications for the future of the CSC. In the area of recruitment and selection, the Glassco Commission greatly deplored the fact that managers had historically been granted little choice in the appointment of subordinate officers. Accordingly, because "recruitment and selection are obviously of such critical importance to management," the Glassco Commission recommended that these functions become the prime responsibilities of the departments. In a similar vein, promotions and transfers were an inherent duty of management because of their connection with career development, and the Glassco Commission recommended that the CSC be absolved from all responsibility in this area.

Within this context the Glassco Commission foresaw that the CSC would be left with only two staffing activities. It would simply function as a certifying agent in initial appointments, ensuring that the selection was free from political considerations, and "that the method used has been reasonably calculated to obtain personnel qualified for the position to be filled."[9] Second, the Royal Commissioners felt that the CSC could provide a common recruiting service for a great many of the lower salary classes, while departments would perform their own recruitment and selection of the more senior executives, administrative, and technical personnel. The dividing line suggested was a starting salary level of $5,200. Initial appointments to positions below this level, estimated to constitute about 95 percent of the total by the Report, would be made by the CSC while the remainder were to be the sole responsibility of the departments. Even where it was directly involved, the CSC was to lose all control functions to become completely service oriented, simply meeting departmental requirements and needs.[10]

In accordance with its enunciated policy, the Glassco Commission also suggested that all the other management functions presently performed by the CSC be removed from its jurisdiction and handed to the departments and Treasury Board. Once this was accomplished the departments would be responsible for their own manpower inventories and for the identification of their own future requirements. In addition, they would bear responsibility for the appraisal and career development of employees, including the conduct of intradepartmental training programs, for the classification of departmental positions, as well as for the establishment of the pay ranges for these positions, and for internal staff relations including grievance procedures. All these functions would be conducted within the broad policy and general guidelines established by the Treasury Board.

These recommendations, thus, contained a complete reassessment of the CSC's position within the bureaucracy. The CSC would become a much smaller organization with responsibility only for several relatively simple and unimpressive tasks; in the opinion of A. D. P. Heeney, the former Chairman, the CSC was to be "emasculated."[11] Besides certifying initial appointments and providing a common recruiting service, the CSC would, as the Glassco Commission envisaged it, function as a final court of appeal on grievances relating to disciplinary matters, would operate common training programs and facilities under the guidelines established by the Treasury Board, and would assist the departments and agencies in the conduct of interdepartmental competitions. The Treasury Board was to assume sole responsibility for wage and salary adjustments, as well as for changes in employee benefit plans. In this regard the PRB would remain with the CSC, but would make its data available to the Treasury Board and staff associations.

Following the publication of the Glassco Report, then, most observers could easily predict that extensive alterations would be made in the traditional role of the CSC. This anticipation was given added force by the creation of the Committee of Senior Officials in the fall of 1962, under the chairmanship of R. B. Bryce, which had the task of considering the Glassco Report and of making recommendations on its implementation to a cabinet committee established for this purpose. The task was larger than first anticipated, however, so that in January of 1963 the Bureau of Government Organization (BOGO) was formed in the Privy Council Office under the direction of George Davidson, who also assumed the chairmanship of the Senior Officials Committee. The Committee continued its consideration of those recommendations which had an impact on the relationships between departments and the various central agencies, while the BOGO, conversely, dealt with those recommendations affecting the relationships among departments and with those affecting only one or two departments.[12]

These developments clearly necessitated some public response from the CSC. In retrospect it is evident that three possible paths of action lay open to it at this time. It could mount a strong defence of itself and its traditional role, attempting to divert the tides of change (as it had done after the Report of the Gordon Commission in 1946); it could publicly accept much of the Glassco Commission's criticism as valid and submit to its recommendations; or it could acknowledge the criticisms and endeavour to carve a new role for itself. Unfortunately, in the same month that the Glassco Report was published, the very moment that the CSC required strong, dynamic leadership in order to ride out the storm of criticism in one or another of these ways, Chairman Hughes left the organization to return to the Ontario Supreme Court.

When the two remaining Commissioners, Pelletier and Addison, turned to the senior officials of the CSC for their reaction to the Glassco Report, the majority of answers they received did not simplify their own predicament. Virtually all the senior CSC officials at this time had been connected with the organization for well over a decade, in some cases for almost twenty years. Quite understandably, the Glassco criticisms represented something of a personal affront to them. While these officers demonstrated an admirable ability to acknowledge the justice of many of the criticisms and the need for change, they were unable to suggest what the CSC's overall response should be: rather they tended to dwell at length on the detailed recommendations contained in the Report, querying their validity or seeking to identify errors in the Commission's findings.[13]

There was one response, however, which took a decidedly different turn. In his remarkably perceptive comments on the Report, J. D. Love, the Assistant Director of the PRB, was the only official to argue that the CSC should attempt to carve out a new role for itself based at least partially upon the Glassco proposals. His comments merit full consideration because of the eventual impact they had in helping to determine the course followed by the CSC over the next two years. While he expressed reservations concerning many of the recommendations, the general tone of Love's assessment was that the present situation, whereby authority and responsibility for personnel management was splintered and divided between the CSC and the Treasury Board, did nothing to enhance the CSC's prestige. On the contrary, in fact, he suggested that it might prove to the CSC's great benefit to reconsider its role in light of the Glassco proposals.

Essentially Love's plan revolved around the Glassco Commission's attempt to rationalize the bureaucracy by investing the Treasury Board with the general management of the civil service. Love looked upon this suggestion with considerable favour for two reasons. On the one hand, he felt that if the CSC was relieved of its management functions, it could perhaps continue to play an important role in recruitment and selection. He felt that the Glassco Commission had seriously misjudged the extent of the patronage problem and suggested that if it acted quickly, the CSC could "endeavour to head off the Royal Commission proposals on this subject by developing . . . a coherent plan for the exercise on a significant scale of its relatively new powers of delegation" which had been granted it by the 1961 Act.[14] He also suggested that the CSC take the opportunity to define with greater clarity its role in the selection process by becoming more service oriented as the Glassco Commission had recommended. Second, Love recognized that the rationalization of the bureaucracy would in the long run tend to solve what is today generally regarded as the major deficiency of the Glassco Report—its failure to deal with the problem of employer-employee relations:

In one sense . . . the shortcoming may carry with it the seeds of self-correction. Implementation of the recommendations of the Royal Commission would substantially alter the institutional environment in which the present employer-employee relationship has developed and, in doing so, would inevitably work changes in the relationship itself. The establishment of a reconstituted Treasury Board as the clearly defined focal point of managerial authority; the disappearance of the Civil Service Commission from the process of classification and pay determination; a substantial increase in departmental authority in the personnel field: these changes would be bound to have their effect on association aims and attitudes. There is good chance that they would rather quickly produce situations and release pressures leading to some form of a bargaining relationship between the associations and the government.[15]

With this in view, he did not oppose the transfer of the responsibility for classification and pay determination to the Treasury Board if it meant that "in performing their function, the staff of the Treasury Board would be regulated by a requirement to engage in meaningful negotiations with the associations." Such a transfer could, far from weakening the CSC, perhaps lead to an expanded role for it. By clarifying a confused situation and by removing functions from the CSC which in the past tended to identify it as an "arm of management," the way would be free to consider "the eventual use of the Commission as a third party in disputes arising out of the failure of Treasury Board and the associations to reach agreement."[16]

Love thus suggested that the Glassco Report offered the CSC a unique opportunity to fashion a new role for itself, a role which essentially consisted of two parts:

In conclusion, I would like to say that, in my view, the Civil Service Commission could gain substantially from implementation of many of the recommendations of the Royal Commission. It would lose certain functions and its sphere of influence would be curtailed but it might be thereby placed in a stronger position to do a really effective job in the field of recruitment and selection, and in the long run its clearly defined status as an independent agency might attract to it important new functions in the field of labour-management relations. I am satisfied that there is little reason to defend the status quo.[17]

The force and logic of Love's arguments were impossible to ignore in the face of the confusing situation in which the CSC found itself after the publication of the Glassco Report. Moreover, with the creation of the Senior Officials Committee, the Civil Service Commissioners realized the necessity of quick action if the CSC was to have a hand in determining its own role. Consequently, in December they established a special secretariat under Love's direction which was to aid the Commissioners in the consideration and implementation of the Glassco recommendations pertaining to the CSC.

Love's secretariat began its work by approaching the branch directors to once again test their reaction to the Glassco Report and gain their suggestions as to the proposed role of the CSC. The secretariat also established a special committee composed of several senior departmental officials which it used to secure the reaction of departments to the Glassco Report and as a sounding board to test its own ideas. The result of these meetings and subsequent discussions seems to have convinced Love not only of the validity of his original proposals, but also that the CSC could continue to play an important role in promotions and transfers which he had earlier doubted. Accordingly he began to pursue two separate lines of action. On the one hand, he endeavoured to get the Commissioners to commit themselves to a redefinition of the basic role of the CSC. As he observed, "It will be difficult for the Commission to fashion a convincing response to the Glassco proposals unless it can come to a conclusion about the basic objective it wants to pursue." He recommended that the best alternative was that of "the independent agency, impartial in matters giving rise to disputes between the Government and staff associations, with responsibility for recruitment, selection, promotions, transfers and the appeals procedure, arbitration of grievances, pay research and the arbitration of disputes over pay and conditions of employment."[18] Love suggested that not only would this role stand the best chance of allowing the CSC to respond to the Glassco Report "in a convincing fashion," but that, in addition, it "would be supported to a substantial degree within the Commission and in other parts of the Service."

Second, it was realized that even if the CSC were to retain its present appointment function, it would be necessary to become much more service oriented by granting the departments a greater role in recruitment and selection and by delegating many of its other responsibilities. The branch directors were generally amenable to this approach, and planning was initiated for the modification and delegation of recruitment and selection procedures and for the preparation of extensive delegation of promotion competitions.[19]

But at this point, the CSC's attempt to redefine its role and objectives ran into conflict with the Senior Officials Committee. On January 25, 1963, the Commissioners met with the Committee to discuss the Glassco recommendations on initial appointment, recruitment and selection, promotion and transfer. At this meeting Addison and Pelletier took the approach fashioned by Love and insisted that the CSC should retain legal authority

293

and ultimate responsibility for these functions, but should delegate and share its responsibility to an extensive degree.[20]

The Committee, however, had different ideas. Because of its nature and purpose, the Senior Officials Committee operated primarily from the standpoint of the administrative efficiency of the civil service. It had no authority to consider the possible future course of the employer-employee relationship upon which the CSC, under Love's guidance, had partially based its case. Consequently, while the Committee took issue with specific points of the Glassco Commission's recommendations, on the whole it agreed with its criticism of the current arrangement and wished to see a significant restructuring of the control agencies, and a greater degree of responsibility for personnel management granted to the departments.[21] In this atmosphere, and operating on these premises, the Committee tended to look upon the CSC's arguments simply as a feeble and conservative attempt to stand in the path of change. At this first meeting with the Commissioners, in fact, the CSC came under heavy criticism and condemnation.

The Commissioners seem to have been somewhat surprised at the extent of the opposition they encountered and made haste to explain the reasons for their stand in greater detail. Six days later, on January 31, they submitted a memorandum to Davidson in which they described the CSC's concern for the nonpolitical character of the service as the justification for retaining final responsibility for recruitment, selection, appointment, promotion, and transfer. They also reiterated their desire to witness extensive delegation and procedural changes in these areas. The memorandum, in addition, made it explicitly clear that the CSC's position on these matters was directly related to the possibility that a bargaining arrangement would be introduced into the civil service in the future. If this occurred, the Commissioners indicated they would be willing to transfer responsibility for classification and pay to the Treasury Board and suggested that consideration should then be given to locating the arbitration machinery in the CSC. In the view of the Commissioners, an independent CSC with responsibility in all these areas "seems to offer the best means of creating a workable system based on the general objectives of the Royal Commission."[22]

With time the major point of difference between the Senior Officials Committee and the CSC narrowed itself down to the role of the CSC in promotions and transfers. On this issue no agreement could be reached, so that when the Committee submitted its review of the Glassco Commission's Report on personnel management in May, it was still the outstanding point of contention, with a semblance of consensus reached on the other points. Like the Glassco Commission, the Committee recommended that departments be granted a more active role in recruitment and selection and be given greater freedom to act on their own initiative, particularly with regard to the more senior appointments, as well as those calling for professional or other special qualifications. However, the Committee differed from the Royal Commission in that it felt that legal authority and ultimate responsibility for initial appointments should continue to reside with the CSC. This meant that while the CSC might delegate its recruitment function quite widely, it should take an active part with the departments on the selection boards and prescribe the rules for their operation. On the other hand, in the case of promotions and transfers, the Committee envisaged a role for the CSC somewhat similar to that proposed for it by the Glassco Commission in initial appointments—that of a mere certifying agency. It recommended that because promotion and transfer are essentially management functions, they should reside with the deputy heads, who would act in accordance with the general policies established by the Treasury Board. In the majority of cases the role of the CSC would simply be to certify that promotions and transfers conformed to the rules of procedure which it would establish to guard against internal patronage. However, in promotions to the more senior positions, the Committee agreed with the Glassco Commission that "certification by the Civil Service Commission is inconsistent with the general responsibility of departments and the government for the efficiency of administration in the public service." Accordingly, it suggested that selected officers be certified in advance by the CSC as being eligible for promotion and transfer to a general list of senior positions specified by the Treasury Board or the Governor in Council.[23]

The Commissioners remained dissatisfied with the Senior Officials Committee's recommendations on promotions and transfers, and on May 22 submitted a minority report on the subject to the cabinet committee dealing with the implementation of the Glassco Report. They expressed the fear that, if adopted, the recommendations "would result in a confusing and inefficient division of authority and responsibility similar to that which has produced operating difficulties and public criticism in the field of classification and pay. Furthermore, it would cast the Commission in an uncertain but essentially negative role that could not be performed without interference in departmental affairs of a type that might prove to be both ineffectual and objectionable."[24] They also reiterated their argument that the objectives of the Glassco Commission could best be met if the CSC retained responsibility in these areas and mentioned that planning was currently being conducted to delegate these functions to an even greater extent.

Fortunately for the CSC, the Government did not at this time ratify all the Committee's recommendations, most likely because it had recently committed itself to collective bargaining, and as a result, these questions would again be open for discussion. By June, it had approved in principle only four of the recommendations in the area of personnel management, and of these only two related directly to the role of the CSC. However, neither of these contained a critical reappraisal of the CSC's place within the bureaucracy. The first recommendation made provision for the compilation of personnel statistics in accordance with a standard guide developed by the CSC and approved by Treasury Board. This actually represented something of a victory for the CSC since the Glassco Report had not seen fit to include it at all in its recommendation on this point. Second, the Government gave a modified approval to the Glassco Commission recommendation that departments be given authority to manage their own personnel and be held accountable for efficient performance.[25]

On this basis the CSC continued to proceed with its plans for delegation. In October it made the first significant move in this direction by delegating full responsibility to deputy heads to conduct intradepartmental closed promotion and transfer competitions up to the senior salary level of $13,100 without reference to the CSC. After obtaining approval from the CSC, departments could also conduct similar competitions for positions above this level or interdepartmental competitions for certain specified classes. In addition prior CSC approval was required for all cases in which the general public was to be included in the area of competition.[26]

The Preparatory Committee and the CSC

To this point, then, the Civil Service Commission had escaped relatively unscathed from the criticism of the Glassco Commission. But it was not to be left alone to define its own role, for by August of 1963 there was a new actor upon the scene with an acute interest in defining the limits of the CSC's powers. The Preparatory Committee on Collective Bargaining (PCCB), in fact, more than any other single body, ultimately became responsible for determining its sphere of action.

The creation of the PCCB resulted from the combination of several factors. By 1961 most staff associations had already committed themselves to some form of collective bargaining, and over the next two years their arguments gained added force. The inauguration of the consultation system in 1962 had, as we saw, far from satisfied the aspirations of civil servants. The dispute over the data supplied by the Pay Research Bureau served to underline the fact that the real nature of the problem did not revolve solely around the need for sound and objective statistical information, but essentially involved the components of pay policy and the interpretation of the data presented—and this could only be solved by collective agreements between the Government and its employees. The proposed rationalization of the management functions in the bureaucracy by the Glassco Commission only increased the pressure for collective bargaining, as Love had earlier foreseen. Prior to the general election in April, 1963, Claude Edwards, the President of the Civil Service Federation, seized the opportunity to write to the four major political parties asking them to publicly declare their respective party's position on the issue of collective bargaining for federal public servants. Within four weeks all four parties had endorsed the principle of collective bargaining, although some of them had expressed certain reservations about strike action. However, as an electoral promise, collective bargaining was by no means assured after the federal elections had come and gone. For one thing, the parties had committed themselves without really understanding all the issues and problems involved. In addition, the Treasury Board had serious reservations about a system which it understood as reducing its area of discretion in dealing with personnel policy and, more specifically, in establishing rates of pay. Collective bargaining, it was felt, would place unacceptable limits on the Government's economic policies.

It will be recalled that Love's plan for the CSC's response to the Glassco Commission had consisted basically of two parts. On the one hand, the CSC had attempted to head off criticism by greater delegation of many of its responsibilities, while, on the other, it attempted to use the opportunity to fashion a new role for itself. This role was itself to consist of two parts: a reassertion of CSC responsibility in the area of recruitment, selection, promotion, and transfer, and the possible location in the CSC of the arbitration machinery in what was anticipated would soon become a new system of employer-employee relations in the civil service. In a sense, Love's whole argument for the CSC's new role, and therefore its success in offsetting the Glassco recommendations, was predicated on the future development of a bargaining system. This, certainly, was of great interest to Love himself. He had been a president of the Civil Service Association of Ottawa, had been a representative of that association on the National Joint Council, and was a long-time advocate of collective bargaining. Thus, at the same time that he was attempting to preserve CSC responsibility in promotions and transfers from his vantage point in the special secretariat, he remained intensely interested in seeing changes in the employer-employee relationship as part of the overall rationalization of the bureaucracy. Fortunately, with the general election of 1963 and the Government's commitment to collective bargaining, a situation developed which presented Love with a chance to exert some initiative in this area.

Shortly following the Liberal victory at the polls, R. G. MacNeill, the recently appointed chairman of the CSC,[27] on Love's urging, wrote several letters to the Secretary of State reminding him of the Government's commitment. The first of these, written on April 24, only briefly broached the subject but did result in a meeting between the Secretary, J. W. Pickersgill, and MacNeill.[28] The second letter attempted to make the Government more aware of the magnitude of the problem by drawing an explicit picture of the issues involved. In it MacNeill pointed to the unsatisfactory consultation arrangement of employer-employee relations currently in operation and observed that, before the Government could hope to honour its pre-election commitment, several interrelated matters would have to be considered. The most important of these was the divided responsibility between the CSC and the Treasury Board for pay determination. He also observed, however, that if the Government accepted the Glassco Commission's recommendations on the rationalization of the bureaucratic machinery, the CSC would no longer have any responsibility for recommending rates of pay, and in view of the Government's promise on collective bargaining, urged acceptance of this proposal. Among other matters meriting consideration, MacNeill noted, were the mode of employee representation, the areas of employment to which the system of bargaining and arbitration would apply, the subject matter of bargaining and arbitration, and the membership, method of operation, and terms of reference of the arbitration body. In addition, he indicated that the classification system needed a basic overhaul, and it would be necessary that "the Government should at least have a detailed blue-print of the changes it would like to introduce in this area." Otherwise, "without this, the system of bargaining and arbitration could prove to be an obstacle to highly developed reforms in an important area of personnel administration." Finally he advised:

> Because of the complexity of some of the problems involved and the importance of devising solutions that will establish a firm foundation for the new relationship between staff associations and the government, some considerable time will be needed for study and consultation. Additional time will be required for the preparation and passage through Parliament of required changes in legislation. Ideally, the system of bargaining and arbitration would not be introduced until July 1, 1965, at the beginning of the third cycle of salary reviews. We believe that the associations would be willing to accept a delay of this duration if the Government were prepared at an early date to make in Parliament a formal statement of policy accepting the principles involved, indicating the manner in which the staff associations will be consulted in the development of procedures, and setting forth a schedule of target dates for their introduction.[29]

The letter obviously did everything but actually propose the establishment of a special body to study the whole question.

This letter in particular seems to have produced a significant effect. The Government became convinced that a great deal of study was required, and extensive discussions followed between MacNeill, the Deputy Minister of Finance, the Secretary of the Treasury Board, and several government ministers, notably Walter Gordon, the new Minister of Finance. The discussions dealt primarily with the status and terms of reference of whatever body would be charged with the responsibility of recommending to the Government concrete proposals for a collective bargaining regime.[30]

The resolution of this issue was achieved only after a heated debate between the CSC and the Treasury Board. Both Love and MacNeill recognized that to gain the confidence of the staff associations a body studying the matter would have to be free from any taint of contamination from the present control agencies. Accordingly, in these discussions MacNeill advocated the creation of a high-powered, broadly based working group whose members were to be drawn from a variety of agencies and departments.[31] The Treasury Board, on the other hand, remained somewhat suspicious of collective bargaining and wished to keep the project under its own wing. Its representatives thus argued that policy recommendations in this regard could best be dealt with by a group of Treasury Board staffers. Sometime during May, the CSC's argument triumphed, however, and the decision was taken to create a committee of senior public servants to develop proposals for a collective bargaining regime under the aegis of a committee of ministers. In August, 1963, an Order in Council established the Preparatory Committee on Collective Bargaining with terms of reference "to make preparations for the introduction into the Public Service of an appropriate form of collective bargaining and arbitration and to examine the need for reforms in the system of classification and pay applying to civil servants and prevailing rate employees."[32] The creation of the PCCB, in the final analysis, serves to illustrate the kind of influence a handful of key civil servants can achieve in inducing the Government to adopt a certain course of action.

As an administrative technique, the PCCB proved highly successful in expediting the task before it. Certainly much of this success is due in large measure to its composition and structure. One of its strongest assets was that A. D. P. Heeney, the former Chairman of the CSC and a highly respected civil servant, served as its chairman. Because of the delicate nature of the subject matter there was a great need to reconcile opposing views, to allay fears, and to gain a consensus within the bureaucracy for the decisions of the PCCB. Heeney was just the person required for the job. His years in the Privy Council Office, the Cabinet Secretariat, and as the

Canadian Ambassador to Washington had made him a master in diplomacy, the very talent which was needed. Also, his two years as chairman of the CSC gave him a grasp of the important issues.

In addition to the chairman, the other members of the PCCB were chosen to reflect segments of the public service with an interest in collective bargaining, or because of special qualifications. Among them were MacNeill, Davidson, and G. G. E. Steele, the Secretary of the Treasury Board.[33] The staff of the PCCB were similarly carefully chosen. The first appointment was that of Love who was named secretary, and in this capacity played an important role in the selection of the other members of the permanent staff. He realized that with its terms of reference the PCCB would need experts in a number of subjects. Accordingly, eleven other officers were selected on the basis of their special knowledge of one or more of the subject areas thought to require study. Of these, six were seconded from government departments, four from managerial positions in industry, and one from a trade union. They were generally brought in on a rotational basis, most serving from three to six months.[34]

Among the various problems facing the PCCB were several which contained serious implications for the future of the CSC. The first and most basic of these concerned the need to identify the management functions and to decide in what body these would be vested so that it could represent the Government as employer. Here the groundwork had obviously been laid by the Glassco Commission. Thus, basing its decision on the Government's commitment to bargaining and arbitration and the conclusions reached by the Senior Officials Committee, the PCCB very early in its existence proceeded on the assumption that responsibility for classification and pay administration and for the determination of the more important conditions of employment would be vested solely in the Treasury Board, which would, accordingly, represent the employer on the general management level in the bargaining relationship.[35]

In addition, it became quickly evident to the PCCB, just as MacNeill had earlier indicated to Pickersgill, that the classification and pay system was in drastic need of a transformation.[36] In the opinion of the PCCB the present system was "a patchwork of concepts and techniques, difficult to explain and defend, difficult to comprehend."[37] In its second progress report to the Government, made on March 31, 1964, the PCCB explained that the system consisted of 680 classes, 1,725 grades, and 320 salary ranges. In its view, "reforms designed to simplify and rationalize the system" were no longer merely desirable, but were "a precondition to an orderly approach to collective bargaining." It outlined at that time a proposed fundamental framework for a completely new system based upon a horizontal division of the civil service into six occupational groups and an initial fifty subgroups (more were later added). In such a system, the PCCB argued, it would be possible to vary the approach to salary administration and personnel policy from one basic group to another.[38]

The PCCB continued to think along these lines and to give the matters raised further consideration. Two months later, at the end of May, it submitted for cabinet approval its first proposals which included all those points contained in its earlier progress report. Among other things, it also proposed to establish a departmental grievance procedure.[39]

These proposals caused considerable apprehension within the CSC when they became known in 1964. Despite the efforts of Love to define a new role, morale within the CSC had begun to deteriorate rapidly. The recommendations of the Senior Officials Committee only served to aggravate the morale problem further for, although it proposed that the CSC would retain final responsibility for recruitment, selection, and appointment, it was clear that the CSC's role was not to be very elaborate or prestigious. The fact that the Government had not immediately approved all the recommendations had done little to remedy the uncertain future of the organization; it merely appeared that the day of reckoning had been postponed. The PCCB's assumption that the administration of the classification and pay system would be transferred to the Treasury Board now appeared to many in the CSC as the first substantial step in the implementation of the Glassco recommendations. Although MacNeill, Addison, and Pelletier had all earlier advocated this transfer if a system of bargaining was introduced, they had made the proposal on the grounds that the CSC would retain final responsibility for its present staffing responsibilities. But this matter was still far from settled in early 1964, so that any proposal calling for a substantial erosion of the central personnel agency's authority could by this time expect to encounter a reasonable degree of opposition from some elements in the CSC.

The feeling of apprehension within the CSC gained an ear and an advocate after Jean Boucher was appointed as Commissioner in October, 1963, to replace Pelletier.[40] Boucher was a strong-willed Commissioner with a deep conviction concerning the need for the continued role of the CSC in the civil service. He felt that the Glassco Commission had adopted a wholly negative attitude toward the CSC, and once appointed Commissioner seems to have made it his purpose to defend the organization from what he considered unfair criticism and unacceptable recommendations. His initial departure with the Glassco Report centred on the fundamental issue of the endeavour to rationalize the bureaucracy.[41] Boucher's argument was that the present state of personnel management was a product of historical evolution and that any attempt to rationalize the structure could only be moderately successful. Although this evolution had produced a very complicated situation and had given the CSC "a rather complex purpose," so that all its activities, including appointments, in some degree pertained to management, the division of responsibility between it and the Treasury Board provided a balance wheel of sorts. With some degree of foresight, Boucher felt that the attempt to assign all management functions in the vaguely defined field of personnel management to the Treasury Board, even with the balancing factor of collective bargaining, would lay the groundwork for the growth of a super control agency which could stifle all initiative and programs in the CSC, and presumably in the departments also, which were not specifically enshrined in the act. Moreover, he displayed reservations over "the advisability of charging an agency, whose paramount statutory and professional concern lies in the cost of programmes, with the exclusive responsibility also not only for controlling but for programming the development of human resources."[42] Boucher, in short, did not oppose the introduction of collective bargaining, but held the opinion that extreme caution should be employed in restructuring the two control agencies. He had no argument with the transfer of pay determination to the Treasury Board, but felt more consideration should be given before transferring responsibility for classification and conditions of employment. It was apparently with these considerations in mind that he informed MacNeill he had "all sorts of reservations" concerning the PCCB's proposals.[43]

Regardless of the rationale behind Boucher's opposition, it is evident that the situation was aggravated by the state of relationship between the PCCB and the CSC. Although MacNeill sat on the PCCB, it was never specifically clarified, either there or in the CSC, in what capacity he was acting; that is, whether he sat simply as an individual or as a delegate of sorts from the CSC. Under normal circumstances this would have been an irrelevant consideration, the two elements merging together. But in this case difficulties arose over the fact that there was a sharp difference of opinion in the CSC over the future role and powers of the organization. While Boucher and certain segments of the staff were urging caution on the one hand, MacNeill found himself in general agreement with the need to rationalize the bureaucracy in order to prepare the way for the advent of collective bargaining. This difference of outlook, it is true, only widened a rift which had already appeared prior to Boucher's appointment between the Chairman and his two colleagues as a result of several other factors. But the two approaches soon led to a rapid and serious breakdown of communication among the leadership.[44] This in turn gravely affected Boucher's lines of communication with the PCCB. For one thing, neither he nor Addison seems to have been made aware of the specific lines being followed by the PCCB until they received its second progress report to the Government at the beginning of April, 1964. Second, because MacNeill generally agreed with the PCCB and as a member had endorsed its proposals and recommendations, it appeared to Boucher that the PCCB was acting in a unilateral fashion, arriving at decisions affecting the future of the CSC without taking adequate consideration of contrary views held in the CSC.[45]

Boucher's opposition to the recommendations of the PCCB proved so formidable that for a time it stalled action in the cabinet committee on legislation on those provisions designed in part to provide for the transfer of the administration of classification, pay, and conditions of employment.[46] However, from a contemporary perspective it is evident that Boucher was waging a losing battle. The points he raised, while certainly valid to some extent, could be argued just as strongly the other way, and with the urgent need for a system of bargaining, they were not allowed to stand for long in the path of progress toward this goal. The matter was finally resolved at a meeting held on August 5, attended by the three Commissioners, the Secretary of the Treasury Board, and the Chairman of the PCCB at which time Boucher capitulated and agreed to the transfer of the functions in dispute to the Treasury Board.[47]

While the planning for this transfer got under way once again, plans were also being made for the creation of a special task force to further develop the PCCB's proposed classification and pay system and to merge the old system into the new. Cabinet approval had come on July 9 for this reclassification, which was to be conducted under the authority of the CSC since it still held statutory responsibility for classification matters. The revision, however, was to be undertaken "in close collaboration with staffs of the Preparatory Committee and the Treasury Board."[48] Following this decision, there was some controversy over the exact terms of reference for the task force, centring mostly on its relationship with the CSC. At first the CSC advocated terms which would have linked its task of designing the new system closely to its ongoing function of developing pay revisions and of classifying positions for present classes. Because of the magnitude of the reclassification program, it was feared that the task would never be accomplished if the study group was to be diverted by the day-to-day crises involved in the ongoing classification work. After considerable discussion, terms of reference were agreed upon which excluded functions associated with the administration of the old classification system. A classification policy group was also established, consisting of the three Commissioners, the Secretary of the Treasury Board, and the Chairman of the PCCB, with the Chairman of the CSC acting as chairman of the body. On October 1,

1964, the Bureau of Classification Revision (BCR) of the CSC became officially established, and in a short time its structure and method of operation had been approved and its staffing completed.[49]

THE ARGUMENT FOR THIRD-PARTY FUNCTIONS

At the same time that Boucher was endeavouring to protect the traditional role of the Civil Service Commission, it was recognized elsewhere in the CSC that the best hope for the future perhaps lay in redefining the goals of the organization within the boundaries circumscribed for it by the PCCB. The first major effort to discover these limits and to establish priorities within them was begun by G. A. Blackburn, the Executive Secretary and a long-term senior official of the CSC. In the early summer of 1964, Blackburn had represented the CSC on a committee consisting of, besides himself, representatives of the PCCB, Treasury Board, and the Department of Justice to explore the legislative changes that would be required if the PCCB's recommendations were approved. MacNeill had also asked him and his assistant, S. H. Mansbridge, to give consideration to all the implications of the PCCB's recommendations for the future role and activities of the CSC. On June 26, Blackburn prepared a paper in which he made specific proposals for goals he felt that the CSC should pursue.

Unlike Boucher, Blackburn was of the opinion that the CSC had little argument to offer against the transfer of pay, classification, and conditions of employment to the Treasury Board.[50] He acknowledged that this transfer would severely circumscribe the CSC's area of operation, but felt that there remained for it several important functions. The first of these was appointments. If the Government chose to adopt the PCCB's proposal to enlarge the civil service by the inclusion of many hitherto exempt agencies, the CSC might argue that it should be given greater scope for exercising its judgement and discretion in developing regulations relating to appointments appropriate to the various elements of the public service. A case in point was the recruitment and selection program for physical and social scientists. He felt that if the CSC was to be able to recruit the best-qualified people in these fields, it should be given greater authority and responsibility to make decisions unencumbered by such factors as locality preference and the veterans preference. If this was done, "the responsibility of the Commission would be much enlarged and, if it had the degree of flexibility required for the purpose, it could become a tremendously influential body in developing recruitment, selection, and appointment processes for the general good of the Public Service, and this in an independent atmosphere."[51]

Blackburn felt that if the CSC was to lose its management functions and become truly independent, it could continue to operate the PRB and to hear appeals on appointments. The question of training, however, was another matter. He observed that in the final resort it was essentially a function of management and, accordingly, ultimate responsibility should be with the Personnel Policy Branch of Treasury Board. Although this did not rule out the arrangement recommended by the Glassco Commission whereby the actual conduct of centralized training programs was left in the hands of the CSC while the Treasury Board established the policy, Blackburn nevertheless warned that "if the Commission wants to be completely independent it should probably give up the whole training function to the Treasury Board or some other agency." The same basic logic, he argued, also applied to management services which again were essentially "a management function."[52]

The main thrust of Blackburn's argument, however, was reserved for a proposal originally suggested by Love in 1962. The one function which the CSC as a completely independent body might perform, and which would serve to "re-establish the Commission as a significant and influential body in matters relating to public personnel administration," was that of the "third party" in the collective bargaining regime. In its proposals to the Government, the PCCB had recommended the creation of a Public Service Staff Relations Board (PSSRB) to assume the third-party functions. Blackburn, however, perceived "a good deal of uneasiness on the part of a number of members of the Preparatory Committee in connection with the Committee's recommendation." The proposal, he observed, "adds a fourth institution, more or less autonomous to the machinery of Government. We now have the deputy heads, Treasury Board and the Commission entangled in most aspects of public personnel administration; to add a fourth, or even contemplate a fourth institution would, in my view, be enough to cause some anxiety."[53] Accordingly, he argued that since the certification and arbitration machinery could only be situated in an independent agency, the CSC could make a strong case for locating the third-party functions within its jurisdiction, if it were to relinquish its management functions.

The PCCB had first investigated very early in its existence the problem of where to locate the third-party functions. At that time, both the CSC and the Canada Labour Relations Board had come under consideration but were set aside in favour of a new body, the PSSRB. Rejection of the CSC was based perhaps as much upon psychological considerations as upon any other. The need was for a body which was completely neutral and independent from management not only in theory but also in practice. The fact that, with the possible exception of staffing, the CSC would lose its management functions did nothing to alter the decision of the PCCB for by 1963 the staff associations were somewhat distrustful and resentful of the CSC, primarily as a result of the breakdown of the consultation process. The old pay determination system simply held too many unpleasant memories for the staff associations, and the PCCB reasoned that this fact might serve to compromise the CSC's ability to command their trust and confidence as the home of the third-party functions.[54] Because of this, the PCCB had no intention of altering its resolve to argue for the creation of the PSSRB, despite the fact that Blackburn may have perceived some apprehension among the staff.

The unfortunate fact that this resolve went unrecognized by Blackburn and other CSC officers cannot be attributed to anything more than the poor state of communications between the Commissioners and Chairman MacNeill, and, consequently, between the staff of the CSC and the PCCB. Blackburn's proposal, therefore, held considerable appeal for an organization desperately seeking to find some significant reason for its existence, and the idea was further pursued and developed in two papers by S. H. Mansbridge.[55] On October 8, Boucher took up the issue with the PCCB when he wrote Heeney, informing him that since "the Commission has not formally conveyed its opinion on the location of the third party functions which will be created by the introduction of collective bargaining . . . we now believe it desirable to express our opinion in writing, before the stage of final decision is reached."[56] Although he laid the CSC's case before Heeney, it is evident that the final decision had, in fact, already been reached and the issue seems to have died there.

Thus far the central personnel agency had met with defeat both in its attempt to defend its traditional role and in its endeavour to forge a new one. However, even while the argument was being made to locate the third-party functions in the CSC, a more successful attempt to redefine the role and goals of the agency in an even narrower area was under way in the organization.

NOTES

1. This opinion was expressed in a memorandum from the CSC to the Minister of Finance on the pay determination process in 1963. "Problems of Pay Determination," memorandum from MacNeill, Addison, and Pelletier to the Minister of Finance, July 3, 1963, p. 6, PSC File 625. The discussion on the problems of pay determination following this quotation is also largely taken from this source.

2. Interviews.

3. "Problems of Pay Determination," p. 7.

4. Royal Commission on Government Organization, 1960–62, *Report*, 1, p. 255.

5. Ibid., pp. 261–62.

6. Ibid., p. 268.

7. Ibid., pp. 271, 292, 415, 421, 442, 388–90.

8. The Glassco Commission listed these functions at one point. See ibid., p. 52.

9. Ibid., pp. 262–63.

10. Ibid., pp. 263–65.

11. Heeney made this remark during a panel discussion on the Glassco Report at the annual meeting of the Canadian Institute of Public Administration in September, 1962. See "The Glassco Commission Report: A Panel Discussion," *Canadian Public Administration* 5 (December, 1962), p. 392.

12. Davidson explained this relationship to the CSC at some length. See Davidson to J. M. Hamel (Secretary of the CSC), January 22, 1963, PSC File 044-23.

13. PSC File 044-24.

14. Memorandum from Love to G. E. Gauthier (Director of the PRB), October 1, 1962, PSC File 044-22L7.

15. Ibid. A. D. P. Heeney also recognized the great deficiency of the Glassco Report. His remarks were made during the panel discussion cited earlier. See "The Glassco Commission Report: A Panel Discussion," pp. 393–94.

16. Ibid.

17. Ibid.

18. Memorandum from Love to the Commissioners, January 8, 1963, PSC File 044-22L4.

19. There are various memoranda dealing with these plans in PSC File 044-22L3.

20. See memorandum from Addison (Acting Chairman) to Davidson, January 25, 1963, PSC File 044-22L3.

21. In its report to the Government on the personnel management recommendations in the Glassco Report, the Senior Officials Committee stated: "Deputy Heads are at present hindered in fulfilling their responsibility for personnel management by an accumulation of detailed external controls and the inherent disadvantages of the present system are compounded by the ambiguous division of authority between the Treasury Board and the Civil Service Commission. . . . Your Committee agree [with the Glassco Commission] that, subject to the restrictions proposed in their report, departments should be given greater authority to manage their own personnel, so as to enable deputy heads to fulfil their responsibility for personnel administration. However, wider delegation of authority for personnel management must be related to the recommended establishment of a Personnel Division in the Treasury Board to formulate policies and assess departmental performance." (Review by Senior Officials Committee of the Glassco Commission Report no. 3, "Personnel Management," Privy Council Office, May 14, 1963, p. 2, PSC File 044-22L11)

22. Memorandum from Addison and Pelletier to Davidson, January 31, 1963, PSC File 044-22L3.

23. Review by Senior Officials Committee of the Glassco Commission Report no. 3, pp. 6–7, 10–12.

24. Memorandum from MacNeill, Addison, and Pelletier to the Cabinet Committee, May 22, 1963, PSC File 044-22L11.

25. "Glassco Recommendations Proposed for Acceptance in Principle," n.d., p. 3, PSC File 044-22L11. This was a list of recommendations approved in principle by the Government. See also Love to MacNeill, June 11, 1963, ibid.

26. CSC, *Annual Report*, 1963, p. 16. See also memorandum from A. E. Russell to C. R. Patterson, March 12, 1964, PSC File 044-22.

27. Mr. MacNeill, a former Assistant Secretary of the Treasury Board and Assistant Deputy Minister of National Defence, was appointed chairman in February, 1963.

28. A draft copy (undated) of this letter is contained in PSC File 044-22L7.

29. MacNeill to Pickersgill, May 2, 1963, PSC File 625.

30. Unless cited otherwise, much of the information on the PCCB comes from Jean Carrière, "The Preparatory Committee on Collective Bargaining" (prepared for the PSC, October, 1967), Chairman's Office Files, PSC.

31. Interview; Carrière, "Preparatory Committee on Collective Bargaining," pp. 22–23.

32. Preparatory Committee on Collective Bargaining in the Public Service, *Report*, p. 1.

33. The other members of the PCCB were G. L. Lalonde, Deputy Minister of Public Works; R. C. Labarge, Deputy Minister (Customs and Excise), Department of National Revenue; Guy Roberge, Chairman, National Film Board; W. R. Dymond, Assistant Deputy Minister, Department of Labour; and F. T. Rosser, Vice-President (Administration), National Research Council.

34. See Carrière, "Preparatory Committee on Collective Bargaining," pp. 23–29; also, for a discussion of the PCCB staff composition and its success as a device in policy-making, see G. Bruce Doern, "The Role of Interdepartmental Committees in the Policy Process" (M.A. thesis, Carleton University, 1966).

35. Preparatory Committee on Collective Bargaining in the Public Service, "Basic Problems: Bargaining and Arbitration in the Public Service," Staff Reference Paper no. 4, October, 1963, pp. 8–10. The staff reference papers were the internal working documents of the PCCB, a set of which is deposited in the PSC Library.

36. The first staff reference paper, in fact, dealt with this problem. PCCB, "System of Classification and Pay," Staff Reference Paper no. 1, October, 1963.

37. "Second Progress Report; Review of Tentative Conclusions," memorandum from Heeney to the Cabinet, March 31, 1964, p. 1, PSC File 625-1, vol. 1. See also PCCB, "Classification and Pay: The Development of a Tentative Framework of Occupational Groupings," Staff Reference Paper no. 9, November, 1963.

38. "Second Progress Report," pp. 1–2. The six categories proposed by the PCCB, which were to form the basic framework that was later adopted in creating the new classification system, were the management category (later

called the executive category), the professional category (later called the scientific and professional category), the general administration category (later called the administrative category), the general clerical category, the technical category, and the service and maintenance category (later called collectively the operational category).

39. "Proposals for a System of Collective Bargaining and Arbitration," memorandum from Heeney to the Cabinet, May 27, 1964, PSC File 625-1, vol. 1. See in particular paragraphs 4, 5, 6, 19, and 26.

40. Pelletier left the CSC to become the deputy minister of Veterans Affairs. Boucher came from the Department of Citizenship and Immigration where he had been since 1950, holding the posts of assistant to the deputy minister, director of administrative services, and director of citizenship.

41. Most of the information on Boucher's views at this time comes from the memorandum from Boucher to the Commission, July 5, 1964, PSC File 044-22L4.

42. Ibid., pp. 2–3.

43. Boucher's comment was pencilled in on a letter from Sylvain Cloutier (Assistant Secretary of the PCCB) to MacNeill, April 1, 1964, enclosing the PCCB's "Second Progress Report" to the Cabinet, PSC File 625-1, vol. 1.

44. One aspect of this breakdown appeared in the fact that the Commissioners' formal meetings became less important, dealing less and less with policy matters and more with minor administrative matters. They also became more infrequent than the weekly meetings established during Heeney's chairmanship, sometimes being held only once a month or less. For further aspects of this problem see chapter 16.

45. Boucher's attitude made itself evident when he received a copy of the PCCB's first recommendations to the Government on May 27. He wrote MacNeill that "surely Cabinet cannot approve these recommendations . . . without having the views of the Commission on (those paragraphs concerning the transfer of classification, pay, and conditions of employment) on which we may have strong reservations." Boucher's notation was made on a covering letter from Heeney to MacNeill, June 9, 1964, PSC File 625-1, vol. 1.

46. Carrière, "Preparatory Committee on Collective Bargaining," p. 48.

47. Ibid.

48. Cited in ibid., p. 46.

49. Much of the background to the Bureau of Classification Revision comes from Carrière, "Preparatory Committee on Collective Bargaining," pp. 44–49.

50. Memorandum from Blackburn to the Commissioners, June 26, 1964, p. 2, PSC File 044-22L4. Blackburn provided several formidable arguments for his reasoning in this regard. He pointed out that the Heeney Report had argued that an equitable classification plan controlled by a central body was an essential ingredient of a sound merit system, and that because this function was separate from pay determination, it should be the responsibility of an independent body. However, when they reorganized the CSC in 1960 after Heeney's departure, the Commissioners reversed this position. They acknowledged the connection between pay policy and classification policy by uniting the functions in the Pay and Standards Branch. At the same time they acknowledged that the responsibility for the actual classification of positions was an operational matter and could be separated from the standard setting function. Accordingly, the Operations Branch was given the task of classifying

positions. Blackburn thus noted that the position of the CSC and PCCB was identical on these points. The PCCB had concluded that the development of pay policy and class standards should be the joint responsibility of one centre of authority (the Treasury Board) while the actual classification of positions could be accomplished as a separate operation (by the departments).

51. Memorandum from Blackburn to the Commissioners, ibid., p. 4.

52. Ibid., pp. 4 and 5.

53. Ibid., pp. 5 and 6.

54. Interview.

55. See "Preliminary Paper on the Definition of the Future Role and Tasks of the Civil Service Commission," internal document prepared by S. H. Mansbridge, August 21, 1964, and "Paper on the Definition of the Role and Tasks of Civil Service Commission," revised edition, September 3, 1964, PSC File 044-22L4.

56. Boucher to Heeney, October 8, 1964, PSC File 625-1, vol. 1. This letter also shows the confusion over MacNeill's role on the PCCB. Boucher mentioned that the CSC had not formally conveyed its opinion on the matter to the PCCB. But MacNeill had in fact already endorsed the recommendation to the Government that the PSSRB be created.

Chapter Fourteen

Defining a New Role:
The Central Staffing Agency,
1964–1968

*There is nothing more difficult to take in
hand, more perilous to conduct, or more
uncertain in its success, than to take the
lead in the introduction of a new order
of things.*

Machiavelli, *The Prince*

ALTHOUGH THE CIVIL SERVICE Commission's endeavour to argue for the
third-party functions had proved unsuccessful, Blackburn's paper on the
implications of the PCCB's recommendations, which had originally proposed this role, had also pointed in another possible direction. Blackburn
had observed that the CSC could rely upon a substantial degree of support
from the deputy heads for retaining its responsibility for initial appointments. He had also argued that the CSC should strive to develop new
methods and techniques of recruitment and selection, especially if its jurisdiction was to be widened by the inclusion of some hitherto exempt agencies. S. H. Mansbridge, Chief of Special Projects in the Commission, now
seized upon this problem. He successfully urged the Commissioners to
establish a small task force within the CSC to study the matter. The ideas
pursued and developed by this group were then refined by Mansbridge
into several working papers.[1]

In his first effort, completed in August, 1964, Mansbridge pointed to
the fact that it was probable the CSC would lose its responsibility for pay
determination, classification, and conditions of employment. In addition,
he mentioned that there had been some discussion about transferring the
responsibility for management services to the Treasury Board. Nevertheless, he observed:

If all these changes occurred, the Commission would retain by far the
greater proportion of its present staff for its dominant and vital role of
meeting the staff requirements of the Civil Service. The concentration
of effort in the Civil Service Commission on staffing the service, and the

313

continuing relationship of this activity with the peripheral functions which may be located elsewhere, demand a careful redefinition of the role and tasks of the Commission, a reconsideration of organizational needs, and a study of the machinery for essential co-ordination.[2]

It was these objectives which he now attempted to explore.

The ideas and concepts evolved by Mansbridge on this subject over a period of two months represent a significant achievement, for they eventually had much to do with restoring, or at least retaining, the CSC as a fundamental and central force in the bureaucracy. In its final form, Mansbridge's paper essentially rested upon two basic concepts. Although the thoughts behind these concepts did not entail a wholly new approach, they were the first attempt to bring together and clearly articulate trends that had been occurring in the bureaucracy. The first of these involved an attempt to demonstrate the interrelationship of the numerous processes concerned with filling vacancies in the bureaucracy and to argue that the CSC had a legitimate interest and responsibility in all these activities. Until this time it had been the general attitude to think of recruitment, selection, appointment, promotion, and transfer as essentially rather simple activities having little in common with one another, except, perhaps, a past relationship to the merit system. This explained the tendency of the Glassco Commission to separate them and to suggest that they should basically be the responsibility of the various departments. Mansbridge, however, expressed the idea that they were all part of a complex process. As he put it: "From the outset, the specific act of selecting a candidate to fill a particular vacancy has never been more than the mid-point of a series of activities on a continuum which, in its total length, may be termed the 'staffing function.' It is this broad function which, over the years and even more recently, has undergone a gradual evolution towards greater significance and complexity and which this paper will attempt to describe in its most immediate implications."[3] The second theme running throughout the paper was that delegation to departments by no means ended CSC interest and concern with staffing. Rather, by delegating its routine tasks and operational responsibility, the CSC could assume a position somewhat analogous to the role which the Glassco Commission had foreseen for the Treasury Board in personnel management: it was freeing itself for the broad role of establishing overall policy and of supplying centralized service.

The great significance of these concepts was that they offered the CSC an attractive and sophisticated alternative to the rubber stamp role proposed for it by the Glassco Commission and by other sectors of the bureaucracy. They supplied, in fact, a logical framework and a philosophical basis for retaining CSC responsibility for recruitment, selection, appointment, promotions, and transfers. As Mansbridge saw it, the very complexity and interrelatedness of the various staffing activities was a case for a central staffing agency. But the CSC was also to be more than the mere service-oriented agency proposed by the Senior Officials Committee. In its role of establishing overall policy, it was necessary to shed its former passive approach to staffing, whereby it simply filled departmental requests, in favour of exercising initiative and creative leadership. It was insufficient for the CSC "merely to respond to needs as they arise; on the contrary, it is apparent that the Commission must foresee trends and needs, and initiate action accordingly."[4]

As a justification for this new dynamic approach to staffing, Mansbridge endeavoured to identify the various elements of the staffing process, to explain their complexity, and to assert the CSC's concern in each area. To begin with, he pointed out that an efficient recruitment program necessitated extensive and intimate knowledge of both demand for and supply of manpower. The implication here was that this knowledge could best be gathered and analysed by the CSC as a central staffing agency. On the one hand, the CSC would need to determine and analyse the requirements of client departments in order to relate this effectively to the sources of supply. In this regard it had an abiding need for the preparation of forecasts related to manpower inventories, which would supply it with data on the changing structure and nature of the service according to such things as occupation, age, and other carefully defined items. Additionally, it would require knowledge of such things as departmental programs and organization plans so as to effectively relate these to the manpower situation. Second, an efficient recruitment program implied a comprehensive and current familiarity with the sources of supply of manpower. This meant not only improving and specializing the contacts already maintained with the universities in order to compete for the best talent available, but, as well, that the CSC would have to extend its relationship with technological institutes and secondary schools and would need to establish contacts with appropriate professional and trade associations.

A third feature of an effective recruitment program was the need to develop and improve recruitment standards, methods, and techniques. In the past the CSC's ability to do this was always hampered by the fact that these subjects were simply one of a number of factors for consideration in the development of classification standards, which had to be designed also to serve organizational needs, the needs of pay plans, or for the purpose of career development. But with the proposed transfer of classification and pay to the Treasury Board, Mansbridge suggested that the CSC could now concentrate on the greater perfection of its recruitment and selection standards and methods. It could begin to employ more modern techniques such as executive search. It would also be necessary, if the CSC was to staff the service effectively, to develop a consultation process with the Treasury Board so that staffing requirements would continue to exercise some degree of influence upon classification standards.

This approach to recruitment implied throughout that its complexity required the continued presence of the CSC to coordinate and develop the different features of the function. It stood in sharp contrast to the thoughts expressed on the subject by the Glassco Commission and the Senior Officials Committee, both of which had felt that the recruitment function could be decentralized to a large extent. But apart from recruitment, Mansbridge also attempted to assert the CSC's interest and responsibility for all aspects of selection and placement, even when the operational processes had been delegated to the departments:

> The filling of a vacant position raises important problems of choice. A candidate can be sought from outside the public service (the importation of "new blood"), or from within the public service or selected segments of it. Alternatively, the position could be filled by the transfer process as part of a career development programme, or the maintenance of high morale might demand a strictly localized promotion competition. Along with others, the Commission has inescapable responsibilities in this matter which demand initiative and action, and no less in those activities, such as promotion competitions, where authority is delegated.[5]

The responsibility of the CSC was "to bring independent judgements to bear, to ensure that the appropriate skills are used in the process, and, by advice and example, to provide leadership of a high order in this aspect of personnel management."[6]

Another area in which Mansbridge felt the CSC had a legitimate interest to oversee was that of the effective use of the probationary period. Although the major responsibility for this did lie with the employing department, the CSC was involved because probation represents the completion of the selection process and is a limited measure of the success of the original competition.

All the foregoing elements in the staffing process could be applied to the case of initial appointments only. However, Mansbridge was prepared to argue that the CSC should retain overall responsibility for promotions and interdepartmental transfers from the point of view that they were a logical extension of the staffing process since they were concerned with the filling of vacancies. Moreover, he asserted that while performance appraisal and review were primarily departmental responsibilities, the CSC had an interest in them. On the one hand, it could offer guidance and help to those departments with slender personnel resources, and, on the other, coordinate an across-the-service operation of appraisal and development for certain classes. Mansbridge also argued that the CSC should continue to retain primary responsibility for the administration of senior appointments and for the Advisory Panel on Senior Appointments which it had created to help with the task in 1957.

Finally, despite the fact he recognized that staff training and development was primarily a departmental responsibility, Mansbridge saw its close connections with the staffing function[7] and attempted to argue that central responsibility should thus reside with the CSC, rather than with the Treasury Board as recommended in the Glassco Report. As a central planning and coordinating body, he thought that the CSC could not only set the overall policy and assist departments with departmental programs when requested, but could also plan and conduct central programs.

Apart from the logic and relative novelty of Mansbridge's arguments, his paper is interesting in that it marked the culmination of a process that had initially begun during the Heeney years. It will be recalled that the Heeney Report recognized in part that the reasons for the existence of the CSC needed a reassessment and redefinition after forty years. Most important, it had argued that the CSC could not longer stand upon the merit principle as its sole and primary raison d'être; the merit principle, while still of great importance, had to be tied to the dramatic changes and developments which had occurred in the field of personnel management after the war. Mansbridge drew this argument to its obvious conclusion by defining the organization's existence solely in terms of the personnel management system. It was the logic of the system itself, due to the complexity of the staffing process, which warranted the continued presence of the CSC as a vital part of the bureaucracy; although alluded to at the outset of his paper, the merit principle was clearly a marginal concept in Mansbridge's proposed scheme.[8]

But this fact seems to have completely escaped notice at the time in the midst of the result which Mansbridge's paper produced. Not surprisingly, the proposals and arguments contained in his paper had an immediate and significant effect upon the organization. The paper healed to some extent the division among the Commissioners, for it presented a proposed role to which they could at last all give their full and enthusiastic support. In addition, the paper began to reverse the declining morale among the senior and intermediate officers which had begun to reach serious proportions. It was circulated among the branch directors and the special task force of senior CSC officers at each stage of its development where it generated a great deal of discussion and enthusiasm.

This internal support was further sustained and enhanced by the creation of a small internal working group in October, the successor to the earlier task force, to study the implications of the proposed role for the CSC's method of operation and organizational needs. This committee produced a report in short order which, besides refining and expanding upon the concepts enunciated by Mansbridge, contained proposals which were to have a great bearing on the future of the CSC. Entitled "Staffing the Civil Service Through a Class Programme System," the report made specific recommendations for the creation of a staffing branch embodying a whole new approach to the staffing problem. Essentially the new system rested on the broad interpretation given the staffing function in Mansbridge's paper:

> If staffing activities are carried out independently of each other they are rendered inefficient and unproductive resulting in improper utilization and development of present staff and in inadequate provision of new staff. Thus, for example, where promotion activities are carried on without being integrated with staff appraisal and staff training programmes no effective staff development is done. Where recruitment-selection is carried on without being sufficiently integrated with staff appraisal, promotion, training, transfer and rotation activities the most obvious consequence is that it is done on an unpredictable demand response rather than on a planned basis.[9]

Within this broad framework, the report implied that it was no longer valid to think of staffing merely in terms of ensuring that the best-qualified staff were available to fill vacancies as they occurred. Rather, because of the "interrelatedness and interdependence of all staffing activities," it was necessary also to conceive of it as the attempt to ensure that the staff resources within the government were properly and fully utilized. To meet these two objectives, the committee designed a system which represented a sharp break with the traditional approach adopted to recruitment and selection. Instead of orienting its operation toward fulfilling the recruitment needs of specific departments, as it did at present, the report suggested that the CSC restructure its operation completely along functional lines based upon staffing programs for an occupational class or a group of classes. A staffing program could then attempt to treat the various staffing processes as part of an interrelated whole, so that such activities as recruitment and selection were conducted in conjunction with, and as an integral part of, the activities of promoting, transferring, training, and appraising persons in the class in question.

What was most significant for the CSC in this approach was that it obviously further re-emphasized and strengthened the concept of a dynamic central staffing agency. This point cannot be stressed too greatly. For two years the CSC had been facing a future which seemed to hold little promise for any really challenging or interesting role within the bureaucracy. But with the proposed creation of the new staffing system, the dark cloud over its future began to disperse Although the committee's report emphasized the fact that the system envisaged extensive delegation and departmental participation, it constantly reiterated the need for a strong CSC as a central focus of the whole plan.[10] The CSC's role, however, was to differ substantially from its former status as a "control agency." Rather, the new staffing system demanded a considerable amount of centrally located expertise and reserve of talent on such matters as training methods, written examinations, selection methods, recruiting methods, research, and public relations, all of which the CSC would provide as a service to departments. To operate the staffing programs successfully would require "a high degree of professional competence on the part of Programme Officers" and the CSC itself would have to adopt a "research-developmental" orientation instead of the "administration-procedural" approach then in force. In addition, there was a need for centralized planning and scheduling so that the recruitment-selection methods of the individual programs would anticipate and meet departmental needs and the conditions of the employee market.[11] The CSC's proposed role, in short, would serve to restore it to a place of prestige within the bureaucracy, and, as well, would help to revive the waning level of morale in the organization:

The Committee has recognized the need at the present time for a formulation of the future role of the Commission. The Committee realizes that its approach is not a new one and that it has been accepted and partially used with success in a number of areas. It feels, however, that its adoption as a system generally to be followed will serve to give a new look and direction to the Commission's role. The need for a new look at this time seemed apparent to the Committee since the morale of the Commission staff is now at a low ebb. A number of factors have contributed to this, including frustration over the lack of time and of facilities to carry out the more professional aspects of the staffing function, insecurity in respect of the Commission's future and the loss of prestige which Commission Officers have suffered as a result of criticisms levelled from a number of quarters such as the Glassco Commission. It was the Committee's opinion that staff morale could be dramatically raised by the Commission's public adoption of a new approach to the staffing function and by its assurance to the staff that steps would be taken to provide the resources they would need to carry out these functions in a responsible and creditable manner. The establishment of a climate within the Commission which will foster pride of profession should result in a higher standard of performance of its employees, the retention of its highly trained staff and the attraction to its ranks of superior and well qualified recruits.[12]

REACTION FROM THE BUREAUCRACY

Apart from the strong internal appeal of the attempt to define the Civil Service Commission as the central staffing agency, it is obvious that other segments of the bureaucracy could not be expected to have reacted with similar enthusiasm. The proposed role for the CSC, for example, impinged upon several areas which the Glassco Commission and the Senior Officials Committee had earlier suggested were the rightful prerogatives of the Treasury Board and the departments. The Board in particular might be expected to have had reservations on this subject. It had always looked with considerable favour upon many of the Glassco recommendations since they had the effect of increasing its power at the expense of that of the CSC. Moreover, in recent years it had acquired several senior officers who had been involved in one way or another with the Glassco Report or its implementation. For instance, George Davidson, the Director of the Bureau of Government Organization and Chairman of the Senior Officials Committee, became secretary of the Board in the spring of 1964, while John Carson, the former project director on personnel management for the Glassco Commission, also joined the Board later that year as a special consultant. Naturally, then, there was still some concern in the Treasury Board in ensuring that many of the original Glassco recommendations were not lost by the wayside during the drive for collective bargaining.[13]

This concern exhibited itself in the Treasury Board's reaction to the role the CSC had proposed for itself. On October 21, 1964, MacNeill forwarded a copy of Mansbridge's paper to Davidson for his information, and three weeks later received a strongly worded reply which left no doubts as to the Board's feelings on the matter. Davidson's quarrel with the paper rested on two factors. On the one hand, he indicated his displeasure with the fact that the CSC "has initiated this internal review of its own function and role,—as it conceives it" in an "unilateral" manner without consulting with the Treasury Board and the departments, although both would obviously be deeply affected and concerned by decisions in the personnel management field. He stated that in his opinion all parties concerned should be given an opportunity to present their points of view and suggested that the proper place for this to occur would be in the Senior Officials Committee. Second, and more significant, besides criticizing the method the CSC used to define its new role, Davidson took strong issue with the paper's attempt to install the CSC as the central staffing agency:

> As I read your paper, it is based on the thesis that the Commission should not merely discharge the duties which are assigned to it under the Civil Service Act, but that it should be, in fact, the central staffing agency of the Civil Service.
>
> Such a concept of the role of the Commission is, of course, in sharp contrast with the views of the Glassco Commission as reflected in the Personnel Management report and recommendations. More than this, you will agree I am sure that it runs counter to the clear consensus of the Senior Officers Committee appointed by the government to review the Glassco Report.
>
> Most of the issues raised by the Commission in its draft paper were also raised in the Glassco Report. On most of these questions the Senior Officers Committee has already recorded its point of view for the government's consideration. In some instances, it disagreed with the Glassco Commission: in others it took a position which the Civil Service Commissioners could not accept and in respect of which they saw fit to present a minority report. On most questions, however, as you will recall,—and you and your colleagues took part in the deliberations of the Committee,—there was a general consensus to the views which should be presented to the government concerning the roles of the Commission, the departments and the Treasury Board in the field of Personnel Management. I do not think that the views of such a committee,—composed as it was of a specially selected group of senior deputy ministers and other agency heads,—can be left out of account in assessing the Commission's present proposals as to the role which it should assume. Yet the Commission's paper seems to me,—and I say this with every respect for the position of the Commission,—to leave both the views of the Glassco Commission and the view of the Senior Officers Committee largely out of account.[14]

Davidson concluded by again suggesting that the matter be discussed at the Senior Officials Committee.

Davidson's letter caused some concern and debate within the CSC, but did little to change the direction of the course it had begun to take. Mac-Neill met with Davidson and subsequently sent him a letter in an effort to better acquaint him with the CSC's position. Mansbridge's paper, he informed Davidson, was strictly for the internal purpose of the CSC and had not attempted to argue for powers which it did not already possess. Nor did it try to reassert the old control functions of the CSC. Indeed, "we took care to distinguish among responsibilities which were clearly ours, responsibilities which we shared with Treasury Board, and responsibilities we shared in a participative manner with the various departments of the Government Service." MacNeill observed that the CSC was motivated in its endeavour by the fact that, among other things, "there had been a progressive deterioration in the morale of the Commission officers arising from the irresolution of certain of the Glassco Commission proposals, and the time had come to combat the malaise of indecisiveness surrounding the Commission's role and to organize its resources to give improved service to departments." In addition, the CSC "had no reason to expect any other significant or fundamental changes being made in our statutory responsibilities, at least in the foreseeable future."[15]

This last point is particularly significant for it reveals that by this time the CSC expected that it could be fairly well assured of support for its stand from the Preparatory Committee on Collective Bargaining. During the course of its studies, the PCCB had begun to arrive by a separate route at conclusions concerning the limits of CSC responsibilities which essentially complemented those proposed by Mansbridge. As they proceeded with their consideration of the subject matter of bargaining, the staff of the PCCB generally came to feel that, although appointments and promotions were management functions, special considerations and safeguards were still necessary, as they were in the past. In their opinion, a real need existed to ensure that the bureaucracy was broadly representative of the entire community, and, at the same time, to guard against both political patronage and bureaucratic nepotism. Although it may not have been defined in such clear terms in 1964, Heeney later told the special parliamentary committee that the only way these considerations could be guarded was to remove appointments and promotions from the collective bargaining process altogether: "On the basis of our analysis of the patterns of collective bargaining elsewhere, we were not persuaded that the parties in bargaining could always be depended upon to preserve the public interest in these two vital areas." Accordingly, "we therefore recommended that a Civil Service Commission responsible to Parliament and independent of both the government of the day and of employee organizations, should continue to regulate the entry of Canadian citizens to the public service and to establish and control the standards by which public servants would be promoted, demoted or released."[16]

The inclusion of promotion within the boundaries of the merit system was something of a contentious issue, however, and was not as easily settled as that of initial appointments. Although there are strong arguments for retaining promotions in the merit system, a strong case could be made, and was made during the 1966–67 parliamentary committee hearings,[17] that they should be subject to the bargaining process, as they were in the private sector. Moreover, both the Glassco Commission and the Senior Officials Committee had stressed management's need to control promotions as a device in career development. The PCCB's decision to define promotions as falling within the merit system, therefore, while basically sound and logical, still constituted something of an arbitrary action of sorts. One senior civil servant connected with the PCCB has suggested that the element which tipped the scales was the PCCB's need to establish a broad consensus within the bureaucracy for its "radical" proposals. It recognized that the Commissioners and staff of the CSC would strongly resist any further erosion of CSC authority and the PCCB did not wish to imperil its report by making recommendations which the CSC would be sure to oppose publicly.[18]

Whatever the full reasons for the PCCB's decision, the CSC, at the very least, could reasonably expect no opposition to Mansbridge's paper from this corner, and it went ahead with its studies on the staffing function without interruption. Treasury Board's resistance to the proposed role, in fact, seems to have amounted in the end to nothing greater than a tempest in a teapot, and represents the only occasion when the broad role of the central staffing agency encountered serious opposition from another governmental body.[19]

But besides offering the CSC tacit support for the limits of its proposed powers, it is important to note that by predicating the CSC's existence in terms of preserving the merit system, the PCCB supplied a crucial factor in the rationale for a powerful CSC which had been largely ignored or assumed by Mansbridge. This clearly gave the role proposed within the CSC a legitimacy in many eyes which it might have otherwise lacked. New techniques of staffing, combined with the traditional source of the CSC's power, produced a very compelling reason for preserving the organization as a vital force within the bureaucracy.

That this was the case was made obvious by the fact that with time the concept of the central staffing agency gained many new adherents, including many of those who had earlier entertained substantially different thoughts on the matter. By far the most significant of these individuals was John Carson, who was appointed to replace MacNeill as chairman of the CSC in September, 1965.[20] Although he had been known as one of the chief critics of the CSC in the past as a result of his connection with the Glassco Commission, Carson had come to re-evaluate many of his opinions in the year he spent as special adviser to the Treasury Board. In particular, he came to feel that the Glassco Commission had dismissed the problem of political patronage and departmental nepotism too easily, and this made him see a need for a continued role for the CSC in areas other than that of strictly initial appointments.[21] But, in addition, Carson had become convinced that the CSC could also play a vital and dynamic role in the staffiing process; in his own words, issued shortly after his appointment, he wanted it "to become the most efficient facilitator and coordinator of public service staffing in the democratic world."[22] Carson consequently proceeded with the planning for the CSC's new role, and within the first few weeks of his appointment announced the creation of the Staffing Branch.

By means of the establishment of this Branch, Carson and his colleagues, Ruth Addison and Sylvian Cloutier, attempted to implement the system outlined earlier.[23] In order to provide the "systematic forward planning" elaborated by Mansbridge and the internal working committee, the Commissioners created an initial eight staffing programs, using the occupational classes and groups designed by the Bureau of Classification Revision.[24] A Research and Planning Service was also created to provide assistance to the program directors. As well, they created a new Training and Development Service to provide "a reservoir of experts to guide staffing officers and departmental personnel advisors."[25]

Within this system, the Commissioners anticipated "massive delegation" of the CSC's operational responsibilities. This delegation was essentially to consist of two parts. First, it involved decentralization within the CSC itself. In keeping with the Glassco Commission dictum to let the managers manage, the Commissioners delegated extensive staffing authority to Blackburn, the Director-General of the Staffing Branch, except in relation to the most senior appointments in the service.[26] Blackburn similarly delegated authority to staffing officers at the headquarters and in the regional offices. Second, Blackburn's staff began planning for extensive delegation to the departments. This stage, however, proceeded at a much slower pace because of the need to develop departmental personnel facilities and a monitoring system within the CSC. Once again the fact should be re-emphasized: this was to be a delegation of operational responsibility only; the CSC was to still have a very important planning, coordinating, and centralized service role.

The Public Service Employment Act

In 1966 negotiations were conducted within the bureaucracy over three new acts required to provide for collective bargaining and to rationalize and restructure the public service. Fortunately these discussions were considerably facilitated by the fact that Davidson and the Treasury Board had largely come to share Carson's views as to the proposed role for the Civil Service Commission—the first time in nearly forty years that the

Treasury Board and the CSC had been able to reach agreement on the respective roles of the two agencies. Thus, when the acts were passed in 1967, both organizations received them with a degree of satisfaction and accomplishment. Essentially, the Public Service Staff Relations Act created a collective bargaining regime in the civil service, while the amendments to the Financial Administration Act installed the Treasury Board as the general manager of the public service, with the authority to enter collective agreements on behalf of the government.[27] In this regard the responsibility for classification, pay determination, and most conditions of employment was transferred from the CSC to the Board. The Public Service Employment Act,[28] on the other hand, basically put the stamp of approval on the proposed new role for the CSC. As this was really the first totally new piece of legislation regarding the CSC since 1918—the 1961 Act notwithstanding—it might be worthwhile to discuss briefly the provisions relating to the staffing function.

The intent of the Public Service Employment Act was to give to one central body the ultimate responsibility for all the elements of the staffing process, and to provide it with the resources and discretionary powers necessary to enter into manpower planning and the development of an efficient staffing service. Perhaps most significant, the Act acknowledged the continuing need for a quasi-independent commission to execute the task of staffing the service. Section 3 began by renaming the CSC the Public Service Commission (PSC) to reflect more accurately the PSC's wider jurisdiction. As in the 1918 legislation, each Commissioner was to hold office contingent upon good behaviour for a period of ten years, and was to be removable only by the Governor in Council upon address of the Senate and the House of Commons. The Commissioners were to have the rank and standing of deputy head, and their salaries were to be paid out of the Consolidated Revenue Fund.

After establishing the independence of the PSC, the Act went on, in section 8, to provide it with the "exclusive right and authority to make appointments to or from within the Public Service of persons for whose appointment there is no authority in or under any other Act of Parliament." Not only did this supply the broad basis for the staffing function, but, as well, extended the PSC's jurisdiction over certain groups, such as prevailing rate employees and revenue postmasters, which had historically stood outside the provisions of the Civil Service Act. Within the broad limits established by section 8, section 10 provided that:

Appointments to or from within the Public Service shall be based on selection according to merit, as determined by the Commission, and shall be made by the Commission, at the request of the deputy head concerned, by competition or by such other process of personnel selection designed to establish the merit of candidates as the Commission considers is in the best interests of the Public Service.

Additionally, section 12 stated:

> The Commission may, in determining pursuant to section 10 the basis of assessment of merit in relation to any position or class of positions, prescribe selection standards as to education, knowledge, experience, language, age, residence or any other matters that, in the opinion of the Commission, are necessary or desirable having regard to the nature of the duties to be performed, but any such selection standards shall not be inconsistent with any classification standard prescribed pursuant to the Financial Administration Act for that position or any position in that class.

These two sections are particularly significant since they supplied the PSC with the discretionary powers it required to function as the central staffing agency. On the one hand, they provided that appointments were to continue to be made on the basis of merit, but at the same time recognized the changing conception of "merit" by allowing the PSC to determine the exact meaning of the term for any position or class of positions within the limits established by section 12. Second, these specific sections of the Act allowed the PSC to use means other than the competition process to make appointments, when it considered the alternative to be in the best interests of the service. This flexibility was designed to enable the PSC to enter upon such modern selection practices as continuous staffing programs and executive search. In addition, these two sections allowed the PSC to develop more meaningful personnel development and career planning programs. Finally, section 12 gave the organization wide discretion to frame selection standards in its role of establishing staffing policy for the bureaucracy.

Other sections of the Act likewise supplied the PSC with similar discretionary powers. Section 17, for example, changed the former provision regarding eligible lists in order to allow it to create successive eligible lists in continuing competitions. Continuing competitions had been found to be the best recruitment device in some occupational areas, such as science, where demand outstripped supply. (This was not a new method but had been employed during the war under the authority of an Order in Council for stenographic and other related classes.) Section 17 also empowered the PSC to limit the length of eligible lists to the number of persons who could reasonably be expected to be offered positions during the life of the lists and to determine the length of time an eligible list would remain in force. Section 18 provided the PSC with discretionary power to pick candidates other than the one standing highest on the eligible list, as was the current requirement, when special qualifications were required for a position.

Finally, section 6 empowered the PSC to delegate to deputy heads any or all of its powers of recruitment, selection, and appointment. It also allowed the PSC to rescind or reinstate delegated authority as it saw fit. Section 7 provided the central staffing agency with access to departmental staffing documents in order to monitor and review the delegated functions. Concomitant to this, section 21 established the PSC's appeals function on most staffing matters, which essentially gave it another monitoring device to safeguard the merit principle.

Following the passage of the Act, delegation procedures moved ahead with considerable speed. In 1967 the PSC made only one delegation of staffing authority as a test case of sorts, but by the end of 1968 it had delegated staffing authority to several departments for 96 percent of the total number of positions in the operational category, and for approximately 60 percent of the positions in the administrative support category.[29] From the earliest the CSC, and later the PSC, had recognized that if patronage and nepotism were going to occur, they would more likely take place in the higher salary brackets, and consequently it had decided to proceed with delegation in an opposite fashion to that suggested by the Glassco Commission, beginning with the lower salaried classes first. It was planned that delegation of staffing authority would encompass recruitment, selection, appointment, and certification. Where only some of these functions were handled by the department, the arrangement was referred to as "work sharing" instead of delegation.[30] Coincidentally to these developments, the PSC developed its monitoring system. Departmental selection and appointment procedures were also periodically reviewed to ensure that the principle of merit, the Act, and regulations had been adhered to.[31]

BILINGUALISM AND THE MERIT PRINCIPLE

Before passing on to the other functions which the Public Service Commission assumed or retained under the Public Service Employment Act, it should be noted that one additional factor helped to support the idea of a central staffing agency. Although it is impossible to judge just how much of an effect it had on defining the CSC's role, the growing need to develop a bilingual and bicultural public service was certainly an argument in favour of allowing the CSC to retain control over all aspects of what became known as the staffing function.

The historical background to the development of the recognition of the need for a bilingual public service will be dealt with at greater length in chapter 18, but at this point it is important to realize that the major impetus in the bilingual movement came from the Glassco Commission, and, in particular, from the minority report of Commissioner Therrien. The Commission's Report had approved of attempts to provide service to the public in the mother tongue of the two official linguistic groups in the country, and, as well, supported the endeavour to create a working environment in which French Canadians could operate in their mother tongue. It indicated that the solution to these problems lay in two directions—in language training for public servants in an effort to make certain selected officers bilingual, and in a more active recruitment program in French Canada aimed at attracting talented and capable French Canadians to the public service.[32] In his minority report on the subject, Commissioner Therrien drew a stark picture of a host of factors that stood in the way of developing a truly bilingual public service, and suggested that no expense should be spared to overcome these obstacles.[33]

From this point onwards, measures accelerated in order to meet these criticisms and recommendations. When in December, 1962, Prime Minister Diefenbaker announced the creation of what became the Bureau of Government Organization, he mentioned that the staff was to work "on measures to implement the recommendations of the Royal Commission on government organization, with particular reference to the views expressed in those recommendations by Mr. Therrien, one of the Commissioners."[34] In May of the following year, the Senior Officials Committee recommended the creation of a special body of senior civil servants "to give sustained attention" to the issues raised by Therrien and to recommend steps to overcome these difficulties.[35] On August 2, the Cabinet concurred and established the Interdepartmental Committee on Bilingualism to oversee the implementation of measures designed to cope with the problem. The 1961 Act had given the CSC the authority to determine whether the number of employees serving in a department or a local office was sufficient to enable the department "to perform its functions adequately and to give effective service to the public."[36] On this basis the Cabinet directed the CSC at this time "to prepare proposals for consideration by the interdepartmental committee on recruitment, training, promotion, and assignment policies and practices in order more fully to meet the bilingual needs of the Federal Public Service."[37]

Under Boucher's general initiative and direction, the CSC proceeded to draw up plans and in March, 1964, forwarded a paper on the topic to the Interdepartmental Committee. Essentially the CSC's paper rested upon the proposition implied in the cabinet directive that the bureaucracy should be generally representative of the two official language groups of the country. The CSC informed the Committee that the central feature of its program to promote this representativeness was the realization that "in Canada, *language requirements are an essential element of the merit principle and of a policy of effective public administration.*"[38] Accordingly it proposed several measures in which these facts could be made operational. On the one hand, the Commission would attempt to guarantee "for every member of the public the benefit of written communication in the official language he uses, and, wherever this member belongs to an official mother-tongue group representing at least ten percent of the particular public involved, the benefit of oral communication and direct service with minimum referral, and without interpretation or translation." Concomitantly, the CSC was also determined, among other things, "to ensure the overall bilingual effectiveness and bicultural representativeness of administrative units as well as the dispatch of particular tasks in these units." It noted that it had already recommended that bilingual skills be financially remunerated in the case of stenographers and typists.

In order to provide both a bilingual service and working environment, the CSC proposed that in competitions bilingual skills, or the willingness to acquire such skills, would be counted as an asset and be rated accordingly. It also informed the Committee that its recruitment program was being considerably expanded in order to attract more French Canadians to the public service. Additionally, it would place more emphasis on the use of general intelligence tests rather than culturally conditioned knowledge tests (which had been one of Therrien's most pointed criticisms), and would ensure that examination boards were composed of persons capable of fully assessing each candidate's education and experience, and able to interview the candidate in his or her mother tongue. The CSC indicated that it would endeavour to break with past practice in order to provide reception, orientation, and briefing programs in French for the new French-Canadian recruits. Moreover, it would attempt "to place bilingual and French Canadian recruits in situations where departmental management is committed to make use of bilingual skills or at least to foster bilingualism effectively."

Regardless of the CSC's intentions, it was not able to exercise the initiative and leadership which it would have liked at this time, owing to the uncertainty of its role. Bilingualism was still somewhat of a contentious issue in 1964—the Government had not yet enunciated any specific policy on the matter—and the leadership of the CSC, quite understandably, was not willing to commit itself publicly to any specific measures or program without having a firm or certain base upon which to stand. In particular, because of the vague nature of the limits of the CSC's power regarding

language in the 1961 Act, the extent to which the CSC could enforce bilingual requirements in the working environment of the departments was
not at all clear. Consequently, a week after sending the document, Mac-
Neill wrote Davidson a further explanatory note:

> In many respects, the position taken by the Commission is open to
> further exposition, adjustment, and possible rectification. Indeed, the
> only provision which can be implemented with any degree of complete-
> ness and immediacy are those related to the establishment of machinery
> within the Commission to initiate action towards the objectives listed
> in the document. . . . Therefore, the Commission can only apply itself,
> over the coming months, to make a start on all of them and hopefully
> to incorporate the 1964 contingent of university graduates in the new
> induction and language training programmes.[39]

He indicated that for the time being the CSC would not pursue the measures outlined to their fullest extent, unless it received specific instructions
on the matter from the Government or Parliament. "With such guidance,"
he added, "the Commission would be better able and only too willing to
press the matter further."

Unfortunately, because of the general state of flux in the public service
at this time, the CSC seems to have received no firm guidelines, with the
result that little headway was made on implementing its proposed measures in 1964. But as its role as the central staffing agency began to acquire
a more definite shape, it became willing to take the initiative in the question of bilingualism, even without the guidelines. This was especially true
after Sylvain Cloutier arrived in the CSC. One senior public servant has
suggested that while Boucher had perhaps been a "philosopher" on the
bilingualism issue, pinpointing problems and suggesting the general direction in which reforms could be made, Cloutier was "program oriented"
and prepared to meet the problem in a more immediate way. Shortly after
Cloutier's appointment the Commissioners decided to adopt the central feature of the CSC's earlier proposals by recognizing proficiency
in the two official languages as an element of merit in selection for appointments and promotions in the Ottawa-Hull area, and in other centres where
the public being served sufficiently reflected the two cultures.[40] In these
cases proficiency in the two languages was considered an asset and accorded 10 percent of the total selection rating score.

But Cloutier realized that this measure was far from adequate, and
after Carson's appointment, he proceeded to develop further plans and
policies with the enthusiastic support and approval of his two colleagues.
In the two years previous to his appointment, the CSC had intensified its

recruitment program at the French-language universities, but the results had not been commensurate with the efforts. Cloutier felt that what was lacking was a publicly enunciated policy on bilingualism that would serve to assure French Canadians that neither their language nor their culture would be imperilled by accepting a job with the federal government. In the absence of any publicly announced policy he convinced his colleagues that the CSC should take the initiative and partially fill the gap by enunciating some policy as far as its own responsibilities went. Accordingly, in a speech to the Federal Institute of Management on February 1, 1966, Carson formally announced the CSC's decision regarding the fact that bilingualism would be an element of merit in the national capital area. Additionally he stated the intention of the CSC to make "bilingual proficiency, or the willingness to take the necessary steps to acquire it within a prescribed period of time through appropriate training at public expense an element of merit in the selection of all university graduates recruited for administrative trainee positions." He indicated that the CSC was determined to apply the same basic policy in appointments and promotions to executive and administrative positions, so that bilingualism, or a willingness to acquire it, "will be a criterion of selection in locations where a need for bilingualism exists and will be considered an element of merit, or an additional asset, in the case of positions located in other centres."[41]

On the basis of Cloutier's plan, as elaborated by Carson, the Staffing Branch drew up explicit instructions in March in which it indicated the degree of language proficiency required in different situations.[42] The CSC's initiative on this question basically received official approval in the following month when Prime Minister Pearson announced the Government's policy on bilingualism. The Prime Minister in effect reiterated the policy enunciated by Carson, and, as well, accepted the fundamental arguments of the CSC's 1964 paper on bilingualism. He stated that Canadians should be able to communicate with the federal bureaucracy in either English or French, and that within the bureaucracy itself, public servants should be able to express themselves in either language in the course of their work. He also announced the plan, suggested by the CSC in 1964, of incentive pay to stenographic and typist positions in which there was a requirement for a knowledge of both languages.[43]

One of the most noticeable results of the Prime Minister's statement was that it greatly facilitated the CSC's recruitment program in French Canada. Whereas it had been able to attract only eighteen French-speaking graduates into the administrative trainee program in the 1965–66 season, it secured the services of forty-two graduates for this program in the following season.[44]

What all this made clear was that the spread of bilingualism could be far better promoted by a central agency with authority over all aspects of staffing, as well as having responsibility for the merit principle, than it could had that authority been diffused and the boundaries of the merit principle sharply circumscribed as suggested by both the Glassco Report and the Senior Officials Committee. The CSC's willingness to take the initiative in this area and to create uniform standards, provided, as it were, another argument in favour of a central staffing agency.

The increasing importance of bilingualism and the CSC's role in promoting it were subsequently recognized by the Public Service Employment Act. Sections 12 and 20 of the Act considerably broadened the discretionary powers of the PSC in this field by giving it the responsibility to determine the language proficiency required of candidates in order to qualify for appointment to any position under its jurisdiction.[45] Under this authority the PSC proceeded to draw up regulations which essentially gave the instructions issued in March, 1966, the full force of law. The most significant addition to these instructions at this time was the provision that "any headquarters establishment in the National Capital Region should be considered as serving all Canadians and should, accordingly, be staffed with employees competent in French and English in proportion to the English and French-speaking population distribution in Canada (i.e., about 30 percent of the employees should be competent in the use of French)." In addition, skills in both languages were to be regarded as "desirable" qualifications for future appointment to a position in a headquarters establishment in the national capital region.[46]

APPEALS, TRAINING, AND MANAGEMENT SERVICES

In the years following the publication of the Glassco Report, the main focus of attention in the Civil Service Commission had been on the activities which composed a part of what became known, after 1964, as the staffing function. But responsibility for several other activities peripheral to staffing, in which the CSC had been engaged for years, had now to be determined. Responsibility in these areas could not really be decided, however, until the central role and purpose of the CSC had been clarified. Thus, as its role as the central staffing agency began to emerge, this helped to determine the disposition of the other functions.

The first of these matters to be settled was the appeal function. It will be recalled that the CSC had been hearing appeals against promotions since 1939 and against the denial of the annual increase since 1944, but that prior to the 1961 Act, it had had no statutory basis for this function.[47] Besides making statutory provision, the 1961 Act widened the basis of appeals to include transfers, demotion and suspension, and dismissal.[48]

Chairman Hughes, as we saw, had been primarily responsible for gaining statutory recognition for the right of appeal, but had accomplished this against apprehension expressed within the CSC that the whole process would be "too legalistic" and unwieldy.

After the inauguration of the new system in 1962, the fears of Hughes' colleagues and of the CSC officers seemed to prove true. Appeals could now be lodged on these matters for any reason whatever, and because the right was enshrined in the Act, the CSC had no authority to dispose of frivolous or invalid appeals at the outset. Rather, it had to conduct a hearing for all appeals before an appeal board. Not only did the CSC find this situation basically unsatisfactory,[49] but the Glassco Commission also criticized the formality of the procedure. It recommended that adequate departmental grievance procedure be established and that the CSC serve as a final court of appeal on disciplinary matters only. This would have removed promotions and transfers from the appealable items.[50]

The problem of appeals was further complicated by the Government's intention to institute collective bargaining into the civil service. As it progressed with its studies, the Preparatory Committee on Collective Bargaining recognized the need to establish both departmental grievance machinery and a grievance arbitration procedure for matters which generally fell outside the bargaining arena. It worked on the assumption that several of the matters currently appealable to the CSC, specifically, suspension, demotion, and discharge, would be subject to the grievance arbitration procedure because they concerned departmental disciplinary matters. Similarly, transfers and the denial of the annual increase, because they were a management prerogative, would be subject to departmental grievance procedure.[51] This meant that the CSC's appeal system would be seriously circumscribed, being left to deal only with appeals against promotion.

But as the CSC began to define its role in staffing, this solution became clearly unacceptable from its point of view. For its own part, the CSC began to discern between appeals lodged as the result of staffing actions, and those which concerned managerial decisions or disciplinary matters. On this basis, it agreed that appeals against transfers and the refusal of the annual increase should indeed be removed from the Civil Service Act since they both concerned management decisions and did not fall within the interests of the staffing system. On the other hand, it was felt that since promotions were in reality appointments clearly connected with the merit system, appeals in this area should continue to be the responsibility of the CSC. Furthermore, a distinction was made between suspensions and demotions made for incompetence, and those made for misconduct. The argument was put forward that incompetence was directly related to the merit principle (an absence of merit), so that suspensions and demotions made on this basis should be subject to appeal to the CSC. As such, appeals lodged on the basis of incompetence should continue to be the concern of the CSC. Conversely, it was recognized that misconduct and its penalties could be matters covered by collective bargaining agreements, and therefore appeals against suspension or demotion for reasons of misconduct were more properly matters subject to grievance adjudication. Finally, the staff of the CSC felt that if dismissals were, in the final resort, to continue to be the responsibility of the Governor in Council, the CSC might also continue to hear appeals on this matter.[52]

These distinctions were basically supported by the PCCB the further it progressed with its studies. As it arrived at the decision to leave staffing matters, with the exception of transfers, outside the bargaining system, it also came to adopt the same basic stance on appeals as that of the CSC. Consequently, in its public report of July, 1965, the PCCB recommended that those matters relating to disciplinary action, then subject to direct appeal to the CSC, should be made subject instead to the grievance procedure it proposed to establish. At the same time, "because the 'merit principle' is directly involved, appeals against promotions and against release for reasons of incompetence or incapacity should continue to be governed by the provisions of the Civil Service Act."[53] This solution was found generally acceptable and was the arrangement ratified by the Public Service Employment Act.[54]

Unlike the situation with appeals, much less difficulty was encountered in affixing responsibility for training and development programs. The Glassco Commission had observed that these matters were essentially a management concern because of their connection with career development, and it had recommended that, while the CSC might continue to operate central training programs, ultimate responsibility for establishing policy should reside with the Treasury Board. Although Mansbridge had earlier attempted to dispute this and argued that training was an inherent part of the staffing process, when it came to framing legislation, most participants acknowledged the connection of training with the management function. The solution finally adopted in the legislation introduced in 1967 was the one suggested by the Glassco Commission. By the terms of the Financial Administration Act amendment, the Treasury Board was to "determine the requirements for training and development of personnel in the public service and fix the terms on which such training and development may be carried out."[55] The CSC, meanwhile, by the terms of the Public Service Employment Act, was to conduct centralized programs, within Treasury Board's guidelines, and to assist departmental managers with the conduct of intramural programs.[56] Although the efficacy of splitting the policy-framing function from the operational responsibility for centralized programs was questioned in the CSC when the Glassco Report was originally published,[57] there seems to have been little comment on this in 1966 and 1967.

The third area which required settlement was that of management services. In this case the primary difficulty centred more on the need for centralized service than on the problem of affixing responsibility for the service itself. Since the late forties, as we saw in chapter 10, the CSC had been providing some elements of a management consulting service through its Management Analysis and Organizational Analysis Divisions. After the publication of the Glassco Report, the Treasury Board proceeded to establish a Management Improvement Branch which was designed to establish overall policy in this area and to initiate and direct specific studies and projects. The Comptroller of the Treasury had also become involved in the central consulting service area with the creation of an Accounting Advisory Services Division and a Central Data Processing Bureau. In addition, many departments had established their own management advisory services, while private consultants were being used by various departments with increasing frequency.

This diffusion of effort had caused some concern and had been the subject of at least one study since the publication of the Glassco Report. The general consensus seems to have been that the overriding need was for a grouping and centralized location for all management services.[58] In February of 1966 Mansbridge prepared a memorandum for the Commissioners in which he strongly argued that actual location for the service was of secondary importance. Ever since the CSC had become involved in the area, it had been a moot question whether it would be better to situate the service in the CSC or the Treasury Board. Mansbridge indicated that strong cases could be made for locating the service in either body. However, "the most important thing in this whole area is to eliminate the wastefulness of parallel development, of duplication, of purposeless rivalry, and of confusion."[59]

This, generally, was the approach taken by the Commissioners in the negotiations over the framing of the new legislation in 1966. As the CSC's role as the central staffing agency was of prime concern, it was realized that management services constituted something of an additional duty of the CSC and was not by any means an inherent part of this role. As Carson expressed it to Davidson in November, 1966, the major concern of the CSC was to ensure the development of an effective service:

You will recall that the question whether the Commission's advisory services should continue under the Commission's jurisdiction or be transferred to the Treasury Board has been discussed between the two of us on numerous occasions. In each of these discussions I have made it clear that the Commission is not possessive: indeed I think I have indicated that the transfer of these functions to the Treasury Board (the emerging "general manager" of the Service) seemed to make organizational sense. However, I also added that, should it be the wish of the Government, the Commission would be quite prepared to continue to provide these advisory services, and in such a case we would want to develop these resources into a really first class service. Our position has not changed. But we do believe that the reaching of a decision, on the basis of the merits of the matter, should not be postponed or delayed any longer. Because of the potential overlapping responsibility between the Board and the Commission in this field we are having some difficulty in building and maintaining high staff morale.[60]

Carson observed that in the past there had been no statutory provision for the CSC's performance of this activity. However, since the proposed Public Service Employment Act provided a clear mandate for the CSC's staffing and training activities, he wished for a clear mandate from the Governor in Council if the CSC were to retain responsibility.

The settlement finally agreed upon was to leave management services with the CSC, as an assigned function, most likely as a result of the desire to leave the Treasury Board unburdened with any direct operational responsibility. Nothing was done at this time about the dispersal of the various management services throughout the civil service, although negotiations and talks continued on the efficacy of uniting them under one roof after the passage of the new legislation. However, in the spring of 1967, at Carson's invitation, Mansbridge formed the Bureau of Management Consulting Services and became its first Director-General. This began a process of consolidation and development of these services which was continued until the fall of 1968 when a major government reorganization provided for the transfer of the Bureau to the newly formed Department of Supply and Services.

Language Training

The fourth and final matter requiring settlement in the new legislation was that of language training, the area over which there was the least dispute as far as responsibility for the function was concerned. Actually, in the dark days following the release of the Glassco Report, when all the CSC's other functions were being questioned and examined, language training was the one area where its responsibility continued to grow and expand, so that during the negotiations over the new legislation few questions were raised as to the efficacy of transferring responsibility elsewhere. The CSC has become involved in language training only recently, and it might prove helpful to digress briefly to explain how this had occurred and how the language-training program had developed.

Over the years the slow and gradual recognition of the need to develop a bilingual civil service had led several departments to provide French-language courses for their employees, with varying degrees of success. But on the whole, little had actually been accomplished. The need for a more concerted effort was fast becoming apparent and was given strong voice in the Glassco Report. Since the growing interest in bilingualism occurred at the same time that the CSC's traditional role within the bureaucracy was cast into doubt, it was natural that hopes were raised within the CSC that it might assume a central and important role in providing language-training courses. In anticipation of this possibility, the CSC began to inquire into the different methods of language training and to develop concrete proposals, so that when the time came, it was able to assert some degree of initiative and leadership.

The time to exercise this leadership was not far off. In May, 1963, the Senior Officials Committee recommended that the Government provide "language training facilities for senior and intermediate officers under arrangements co-ordinated by the Civil Service Commission."[61] On June 25 Commissioner Pelletier sent a memorandum to Maurice Lamontagne, the President of the Privy Council, urging the establishment of such language-training classes under the aegis of the CSC and outlining several proposals the CSC had developed for the language courses.[62] Pelletier's request met with a fair degree of success, for on August 2, when the Government established the Interdepartmental Committee on Bilingualism, it also directed the CSC to proceed with the preparation of a comprehensive proposal to provide language-training facilities for the public service at Ottawa.

The Commissioners submitted their proposals on language training three weeks later, on August 26.[63] The most notable feature about the submission is what today appears as naive optimism regarding the results they hoped to achieve. This is clearly due to the fact that language training on the scale proposed was such a relatively novel development in Canada. The Commissioners noted that there were in Ottawa some fifty thousand public servants, and they suggested that a reasonable objective would be to train about twenty-four thousand of these to a minimal level of competence in a second language represented by approximately two thousand words. They felt that apart from those public servants who would require a higher degree of competence, this objective would "develop a working vocabulary appropriate to the needs of the Public Service and do this at a pace which, in four years, will ensure that headquarters and other selected officials and staff will be able to attend the business of government in the English or French language more or less interchangeably, and this in both inter office business and business with the public."[64] They suggested that the objective could be accomplished over the four-year period from 1963 to 1967 at a cost of about $200 per student. It was estimated that when in full operation the program would cost about $900,000 annually, but that after the original four-year period, a "substantially reduced" program would suffice to train new entrants to the public service at the headquarters.

To accomplish these objectives the Commissioners envisaged the creation of twelve training units under the direction of a coordinator of language training within the CSC. Each unit would contain, besides the necessary equipment, five instructors and a small secretarial and clerical staff. The Commissioners proposed that the CSC actually operate only two central classes for its own needs and those of smaller departments, while the other ten would be operated by departments but in conjunction with the CSC. However, because of the CSC's relative inexperience with language training, and because of the urgent need to train instructors in the Saint-Cloud system, the teaching method they proposed to adopt, the Commissioners suggested the establishment of a pilot project of one unit to provide both English- and French-language training facilities and to train more instructors. After an initial one-year period of experience, they hoped to bring the full twelve units into operation by the end of 1964.

Cabinet approval for the pilot project was quickly forthcoming, and the CSC made haste to set up its program. Early in the new year it established a Language Training Centre; four courses were inaugurated, three for English-speaking public servants to be taught French (one full-time, one part-time, and one slow-paced), and another for French-speaking public servants to be taught English.[65]

From the beginning the CSC began to encounter difficulties which indicated that the problem of language training, and of French-language training in particular, was much more complex, complicated, and costly than it had first anticipated. For one thing it met with serious problems in attempting to find competent instructors for the French program. The St-Cloud system, or more specifically the "Voix et Images de France" method, had been developed by the Centre de Recherche et Etude pour la Diffusion de Français under the aegis of the French National Ministry of Education. To be fully effective the method had to be applied by instructors thoroughly trained in the method, and, in fact, one of the copy-

338

right requirements was that the instructor had to be officially licensed in the use of the method. At that time this training could be acquired only in a small number of centres, mostly in France. Because the method itself was relatively new, there was a serious shortage of instructors available, and this effectively limited the expansion program proposed earlier. Through an arrangement with the French National Ministry of Education, the CSC was able to obtain one credited instructor for the first French classes. This instructor also undertook to train a number of assistants. But it was realized that if language training was to be successful, the CSC would have to secure a greater number of competent instructors and an expert in methodology to provide professional supervision of subordinate instructors.[66]

Within this first year a host of other factors also became apparent. Experience indicated that the number of students which could be trained in one year by a given number of instructors was much smaller than initially thought. In its memorandum of August, 1963, the Commissioners had predicted that five teachers could train 450 students in one year. By August of 1964 the figure had been revised to about 100 students trained for every five instructors.[67] Similarly it became evident that the costs of training equipment and material, and of instructors' salaries, were going to be substantially higher than originally forecast. It was also discovered that students would require a much higher degree of competency in French than the two thousand words first suggested if bilingualism was to be at all meaningful. The first degree of the "Voix et Images" method proved effective in developing elementary training in the French language, but was not sufficient to develop a useful working knowledge. Accordingly, the CSC proceeded with plans to introduce the second degree of this method for officers who had completed the first degree and for more advanced students.[68] Finally, the CSC discovered that to be successful each class would have to consist of about eight to ten full-time students with roughly the same level of knowledge, learning capacity, and aptitude. This finding indicated that only a large-scale approach to language training would be effective so as to obtain the small, homogeneous groupings desired.[69]

As the complexity of the situation began to unfold, the CSC started to re-evaluate its proposed role in language training. In the original plan it was anticipated that the CSC would merely act as a coordinator—a term that had been left rather vague—and would provide central courses for the smaller departments. During the period of experimentation with its own pilot project, the CSC had endeavoured to follow this plan and had concurred in the establishment of several departmental language-training programs. However, as more departments contemplated the establishment of programs, the CSC began to express apprehension over the lack of central direction with respect to the content and the equipment used in the courses. As well, there was another problem in that departmental programs tended to cause competition for the small number of teachers available. At first the attitude within the CSC was that it should assume a strong supervisory role to ensure some degree of essential uniformity of content and standardization of material.[70] But as the results of its pilot project became clearer, the CSC's Coordinator of Language Training, J. J. Gerin, began to have doubts as to the efficacy of departmental programs altogether. As he explained to Blackburn in September, 1964:

> It should be noted that many departments have been allowed to engage in language training and as such have been authorized establishments and funds. The CSC Language Training Centre, where teachers have been selected with great care, has serious reservations concerning programmes which are at times run by unqualified staff, using various methods still unproven in the field of second language teaching. It is considered that in order to effect economies and to ensure the success of the Government language training programme, such a programme should be centralized under one agency which would have the responsibility to train teachers in a well recognized audio-visual method, organize a scientific testing programme and supervise the calibre of instruction.[71]

This argument quickly gained the upper hand in the CSC. Later that month, Commissioner Boucher presented a memorandum to the Interdepartmental Committee in which the CSC set forth, among other things, its objections to departmental programs and argued that "the only efficient and effective way to provide non-specialized language training is on a highly centralized basis, with as far as possible, all students undergoing instruction on a half-time or full-time basis. Any alternative arrangement is bound to be more costly and produce an undesirable variation in the degree of language training throughout the Public Service."[72] The Committee concurred with the CSC's analysis of the situation,[73] and afterwards G. G. E. Steele, the Chairman of the Committee, sent a letter to all deputy ministers and heads of agencies in which he indicated that "the role of departments and agencies in language training should be the determination of their own peculiar requirements and, possibly, the provision of supplementary courses of a specialized nature." He accordingly asked that departments and agencies "co-operate in using the central facilities to the maximum extent, rather than seeking to establish or expand their own programs."[74]

From this point CSC responsibility for language training was fairly well assured. To complement these developments, the Treasury Board soon began to frown upon supplying funds to departmental programs that duplicated those already in existence at the CSC Language Centre.[75] The CSC subsequently began negotiations with the Department of Northern Affairs and National Resources, which had conducted perhaps the most successful departmental program, eventually leading to the assumption of the administration of the program by the CSC. Expansion and course development also continued at a rapid pace so that during the consultations in 1966 over the framing of the Public Service Employment Act, there was really no contention concerning responsibility for language-training programs. Although responsibility was not in doubt, the legislation was framed so that it consisted partly of a statutory and partly of an assigned duty of the CSC. Under section 5(b) of the Act the CSC was to operate training programs, which by implication also meant language-training programs, for employees coming under the jurisdiction of the Act. Section 5(f), in addition, directed the CSC to perform such functions as assigned to it by the Governor in Council, and under the provision the CSC undertook to provide language training for a wide variety of officials not subject to the Public Service Employment Act. Consequently, Members of Parliament, deputy heads, members of boards and commissions, and employees of crown corporations were also included in the language-training programs.[76] In November, 1968, this category of students amounted to approximately 16 percent of the total number of public servants enrolled in second language training.[77]

Following the passage of the Act, the PSC created the Language Bureau with G. A. Blackburn, the former head of the Staffing Branch, as Director-General. By 1966–67 enrolment at the Language Centre was 3,200 students with a waiting list of 10,000 public servants.[78] Since that time the language-training program has continued to grow both in cost and in importance to the country. By 1970 the budget had reached $9 million with an annual enrolment of 6,918 students.

The passage of the Public Service Employment Act marked the culmination of a process that had started more than a decade earlier, with the 1954 secret committee on the Civil Service Act. Although questions concerning the proper role for the Civil Service Commission in the bureaucracy had been raised ever since 1918, it was not until 1954 that the Government actively began to consider changes in its duties. The re-evaluation of the CSC's position continued during the Heeney years, but took place only within the boundaries of Heeney's larger purpose of having the CSC play a vital role in the employer-employee relationship. Whereas Heeney had perhaps erred on the one side, by attempting to carve out a role for the CSC which it was incapable of performing, the Glassco Commission subsequently erred on the other, by completely overlooking the important role which it could perform, and by relegating it to a position of relative insignificance. But the Glassco Report left a dramatic impression on the bureaucracy, and in the years immediately following its publication, the continued existence of the CSC as a vital institution of government was more in doubt than at any time since 1918. In the final resort, it was an ad hoc task force, the Preparatory Committee, and not the Glassco Commission, which had the major part to play in defining the limits of the CSC's responsibilities. And yet, it had been left to the CSC to define what role it would assume within these limits. The elaboration of the concept of the central staffing agency and its development into specific plans and programs of action, while perhaps long overdue in many respects, essentially stand as a credit to the organization's ability to reassess itself critically and to renew its goals and purposes.

NOTES

1. It was in the first two of these papers that he also examined the implications of locating the third-party functions in the CSC.

2. "Preliminary Paper on the Definition of the Future Role and Tasks of the Civil Service Commission," internal document prepared by S. H. Mansbridge, August 21, 1964, p. 1, PSC File 044-22L4.

3. "A Definition of the Role and Tasks of the Civil Service Commission in Staffing the Civil Service," prepared by S. H. Mansbridge, October, 1964, p. 1, ibid.

4. Ibid., p. 11.

5. Ibid., p. 6.

6. Ibid.

7. Although Mansbridge did not explain this connection in detail in the final draft, the earlier copies did so. Basically his argument for linking training and development to staffing consisted of two parts. "First, when specific skills are needed in the service and they cannot be obtained in the market, then, as part of the staffing function, suitable persons must be obtained and trained within the service. This is properly a part of the recruitment and staffing task and, for reasons of economy alone, should be the responsibility of the Commission as the central staffing agency." Second, training also had the purpose of developing employees to allow them to better fit their present tasks for the future needs of the service. (See "Preliminary Paper," p. 6)

8. Mansbridge wrote: "While, throughout the history of the Commission,

the preservation of the merit principle has remained the underlying preoccupation which has conditioned all its activities, a changing milieu with the growing awareness of the need for professional services in the management of human resources has gradually led the Commission to develop its more creative functions so as to meet the needs and best interests of the service." ("Role and Tasks," p. 1)

9. "The Staffing Function: A Proposal for a Staffing System for the Civil Service Commission," in "Staffing the Civil Service Through a Class Programme System," internal document prepared for the CSC, November 16, 1964 (mimeograph), p. 1.

10. The committee wrote, for example: "This staffing system focuses attention on the role of the Civil Service Commission in the staffing function because of the fact that great numbers of employees distributed on both departmental and geographical bases call for a central personnel agency, not only to co-ordinate complex recruitment-selection activities, but also to provide a strong element of leadership in all aspects of personnel administration. Furthermore, at the present time the Personnel Administration group and personnel services in the government are at a stage of development when strong leadership is required: a system centered in the Civil Service [Commission] can provide this. In brief, the system is based upon the conviction that initiative in developing a staffing system for the Service lies with the Civil Service Commission." (Ibid.)

11. Ibid., pp. 2–3.

12. "Memorandum to the Commission re: the Commission's Staffing Role," in "Staffing the Civil Service," pp. 2–3.

13. This attitude made itself evident to some extent in an article by Carson published in April, 1965. In attempting to explain the wide range of changes introduced into the Federal Government as a result of the Glassco Commission, Carson also pointed to several areas which he felt still merited further consideration. The first of these was the "redefinition of the Civil Service Commission's role in the staffing function, *with an emphasis placed on initial appointment.*" J. J. Carson, "What's Happened to Glassco?" p. 72. (Emphasis added.)

14. Davidson to MacNeill, November 12, 1964, PSC File 044-22L4.

15. MacNeill to Davidson, November 24, 1964, ibid.

16. Special Joint Committee of Senate and House of Commons on Employer-Employee Relations in the Public Service of Canada, 1966–67, *Proceedings and Evidence*, p. 352.

17. See the criticisms of David Lewis, ibid., p. 653.

18. Interview. This is not meant to cast doubt on the sincerity of Heeney's statement before the parliamentary committee, cited earlier. Heeney personally believed strongly in the need for a merit system and felt that promotions had an inherent part in this scheme. This is made obvious from the Heeney Report. But, nevertheless, for some of the other members and for some of the staff of the PCCB, who did not hold quite as strong views on the subject as did Heeney, it is clear that the deciding factor was the PCCB's need to establish this consensus.

19. Although the Senior Officials Committee originally recommended that the Treasury Board be responsible for establishing the guidelines within which the departments would have the authority to promote and transfer, the Gov-

ernment did not accept the proposal in this form. On February 9, 1965, it gave approval in principle to a modified recommendation which made the CSC, instead of the Treasury Board, responsible for establishing the guidelines. An undated, untitled copy of the list of recommendations approved at this time is found in PSC File 044-22.

20. MacNeill resigned at this time to accept the position of Canadian Consul-General at New Orleans.

21. Interview.

22. J. J. Carson, "The New Role of the Civil Service Commission," p. 3.

23. Boucher resigned in April, 1965, to accept the position of director of the Canada Council. He was replaced by Cloutier who had been Associate Secretary of the PCCB, and prior to that, Director of Administration and Personnel in the office of the Comptroller of the Treasury for three years.

24. These programs consisted of the Senior Officer or Executive Program, which was assisted by the Advisory Panel on Senior Appointments, and the General Administration, Personnel Administration, Financial Administration, Socio-Economic, Bio-physical Sciences, Applied Sciences, and the Administrative Support and Occupational Programs.

25. CSC, *Annual Report*, 1965, p. 7.

26. See "Position Definition—Director General, Staffing," September 22, 1965, PSC File 023-12; also, CSC Document 66/5 (January 13, 1966), and CSC Minute 66/10 (January 19, 1966), Secretary's Office, PSC.

27. See 14–15–16 Elizabeth II (1967), c. 72 and 14–15–16 Elizabeth II (1967), c. 74, respectively.

28. See 14–15–16 Elizabeth II (1967), c. 71.

29. PSC, *Annual Report*, 1968, pp. 4, 16; appendix B, p. 54; and appendix J, p. 70.

30. PSC, *Annual Report*, 1967, p. 8.

31. PSC, *Annual Report*, 1968, p. 16.

32. Royal Commission on Government Organization, 1960–62, *Report*, 1, p. 267. Hereafter cited as Glassco Report.

33. Ibid., pp. 67–77.

34. *Debates*, December 20, 1962, p. 2849.

35. Review by Senior Officials Committee of the Glassco Commission Report no. 3, May 14, 1963, PSC File 044-22L11, p. 7.

36. 9–10 Elizabeth II (1961), c. 57, s. 47.

37. Quoted in CSC Document 64/10, "Measures Taken by the Civil Service Commission to meet the Bilingual Needs of the Civil Service of Canada," March, 1964.

38. Ibid. (Emphasis added.) This document was forwarded to Davidson in March. See MacNeill to Davidson, March 12, 1964, PSC File 533-6, vol. 1. The following quotations are also from this document.

39. MacNeill to Davidson, March 18, 1964, PSC File 533-6, vol. 1.

40. See CSC Minute 65/11 (May 19, 1965). Although it was not specifically stated that language was to become an element of merit, the Commissioners decided that language requirements for certain positions were to be specified on recruiting posters.

41. Carson, "The New Role of the Civil Service Commission," pp. 15 and 13.

42. As Blackburn explained it, the CSC directed, among other things, that

344

"(a) the language composition of the clientele of a department or portion of a department (e.g., a field office) should determine the range of linguistic skills required; (b) where 10 percent or more of the clientele was a minority using the English or French language, skill in the second language should always be regarded as an asset in the assessment of qualifications; (c) where 10 to 40 percent of the clientele was a minority speaking English or French, the number of employees competent in the use of both English and French should be ultimately at least in the same proportion to the whole staff as the minority was to the total number of persons served; (d) where 40 percent or more of the clientele was a minority speaking English or French, all employees ought to be or become competent in the use of both languages; (e) when in any unit there were both unilingual French-speaking and English-speaking employees, the supervisor of that unit must be competent in the use of both languages." ("A Bilingual and Bicultural Public Service," pp. 36–37)

43. *Debates*, April 6, 1966, pp. 3915–17.

44. PSC, *Annual Report*, 1967, table 1, p. 10. During the same period the number of English-speaking administrative trainees increased from 120 to 160.

45. 14–15–16 Elizabeth II (1967), c. 17, ss. 12 and 20.

46. Blackburn, "Bilingual and Bicultural Public Service," p. 37. See also PSC, *Annual Report*, 1968, appendix A, pp. 44–50. The PSC made a distinction in its 1967 Report between "essential" and "desirable" language qualifications: "Where language proficiency is an essential qualification, only those with the required degree of proficiency in both languages can qualify for appointment. . . . Where language proficiency is a desirable as distinct from an essential qualification, the candidates for the position who have attained a pass mark on the qualifications (for the job, i.e., the non-language qualifications) are rated on their proficiency in the second language." (PSC, *Annual Report*, 1967, p. 22)

47. See chapter 10.

48. 9–10 Elizabeth II (1961), c. 57, ss. 27, 56(3), 60(2).

49. See the unsigned memorandum, "Appeals Against Promotions and Transfers," March 18, 1963, PSC File 044-22L2.

50. Glassco Report, 1, pp. 283, 372, 388–90.

51. "Commentary on Selected Aspects of the Legislative Drafting Instructions for a Bill Providing for Collective Bargaining and Arbitration in the Public Service," internal document of the PCCB, November 12, 1964, pp. 6–9, PSC File 625-1, vol. 1.

52. See the internal memorandum prepared by Mansbridge, December 2, 1964, ibid.

53. Preparatory Committee on Collective Bargaining in the Public Service, *Report*, p. 38.

54. 14–15–16 Elizabeth II (1967), c. 71, ss. 21, 31(3), 32(6).

55. 14–15–16 Elizabeth II (1967), c. 74, s. 3.

56. 14–15–16 Elizabeth II (1967), c. 71, s. 5(b).

57. See "Training," unsigned, undated memorandum, PSC File 044-22L10. Although undated, the memorandum is contained with other material concerning the CSC's initial reaction to the Glassco Report.

58. The study mentioned here had suggested that the Department of the Secretary of State serve as this location. Steele to Davidson, January 17, 1966, PSC File 080-1.

59. Memorandum from Mansbridge to the Commissioners, February 14, 1966, ibid. Mansbridge's concern for the centralization of this service was at least partly motivated by the realization that "a division of responsibility between the Civil Service Commission and the Treasury Board could result in the Commission carrying out the routine survey and studies, while the Board concentrated on the more interesting and challenging tasks, and the formulation of relative policy regulations. With such a division of interest, the Commission would find it difficult to attract and hold competent people in the Advisory Services Branch." (CSC Minute 66/28 [March 30, 1966])

60. Carson to Davidson, November 21, 1966, PSC File 061-11.

61. Review by Senior Officials Committee of the Glassco Commission Report no. 3, May 14, 1963, PSC File 044-22L11, p. 8.

62. Memorandum from Pelletier to Lamontagne, June 25, 1963, PSC File 533-6, vol. 1. Pelletier realized that bilingualism was only one side of the issue: "Efficiency in the use of the two official languages will, however, only enable one civil servant to understand what another civil servant or a member of the public is saying but not necessarily what he is thinking." Accordingly he also urged the creation of an Institute of Canadian Affairs attended on a compulsory basis by senior officials in the hope that it would "enable senior civil servants of one cultural background to understand their masters, colleagues and clients who happen to belong to the other ethnic group."

63. Memorandum from the CSC to the Interdepartmental Committee on Bilingualism, August 26, 1963, PSC File 533-6, vol. 1. Also see the memorandum from Lamontagne to the Cabinet, September 3, 1963, ibid.

64. Memorandum from the CSC to the Interdepartmental Committee on Bilingualism, August 26, 1963, PSC File 533-6, vol. 1, pp. 2–3.

65. The pilot project consisted of forty-two students: ten French-speaking and thirty-two English-speaking.

66. Much of this information comes from various memoranda and letters in PSC Files 533-6, vol. 1; 533-6, vol. 2; and 533-6, vol. 3.

67. Memorandum from J. J. Gerin (Coordinator of Language Training) to Blackburn, August 19, 1964, PSC File 533-6, vol. 2.

68. Memorandum from the CSC to Interdepartmental Committee on Bilingualism, n.d., pp. 4, 6–7, ibid. (This memorandum was presented to the Committee on September 18, 1964.) In keeping with the recognition that further training would be necessary to bring public servants to an acceptable level of competence in a second language, the time required to accomplish this was revised from 300 hours to 600 hours.

69. Ibid., p. 5. For a discussion of some of the methodological problems encountered in the language-training program, see Blackburn, "Bilingual and Bicultural Public Service."

70. Memorandum from J. M. Hamel to the Commissioners, April 16, 1964, PSC File 533-6, vol. 2. (Hamel preceded Gerin as Coordinator of Language Training.) The CSC convinced Treasury Board of the need for better coordination, and in September the Board circularized the departments asking that they consult with the CSC before establishing their own language-training courses. See D. Watters to deputy ministers and heads of agencies, September 14, 1964, PSC File 533-6, vol. 1.

71. Memorandum from Gerin to Blackburn, September 4, 1964, PSC File 533-6, vol. 3.

72. Memorandum from the CSC to the Interdepartmental Committee on Bilingualism, n.d., PSC File 533-6, vol. 2, p. 6.

73. Minutes of the nineteenth meeting of the Interdepartmental Committee on Bilingualism, September 18, 1964, PSC File 533-6, vol. 2.

74. Steele to MacNeill, September 23, 1964, ibid.

75. Memorandum from Gerin to Blackburn, October 15, 1964, ibid.

76. PSC, *Annual Report*, 1968, p. 26.

77. Ibid.

78. Blackburn, "Bilingual and Bicultural Public Service," p. 38.

Part Two

Chapter Fifteen

Internal Administration of the
Civil Service Commission,
1918–1968

HON. MR. CALDER: *That is the whole point, all this red tape is gone through merely to satisfy an idea that the Civil Service [Commission] is protective.*

MR. GRIESBACH: *That idea is as old as civilization. You tell a boy that it is in the Bible that if he tells a lie he will go to hell. That is why he tells the truth. The evidence of all the deputy ministers goes to prove that while they do not think a deuce of a lot of the Civil Service Commission, still they think that it protects them from patronage. . . . It is a phenomenon that exists and we cannot get away from it.*

From testimony before the 1921 Committee

TO THIS POINT, this study has been primarily engaged in viewing the Civil Service Commission in relation to its external environment. It has been concerned with the goals the organization enunciated in response to its original environment and in demonstrating how the leadership either modified or failed to modify these over the years in order to reflect the changing external conditions. It might be worthwhile to look briefly at the organization from another point of view—from the standpoint of the internal development of the CSC. For, as the external environment changed, the internal needs of the CSC similarly changed; this in turn became reflected in the organization's structure, administration, and style of leadership.

THE MERIT SYSTEM MACHINE

Until 1918 the Civil Service Commission was a relatively small organization devoted to the examination of candidates for appointment to the

Inside Service. The figures given for the number of its employees at this time vary slightly according to source, but the number appears to be somewhere between twelve and twenty-five.[1] With the new duties handed to it by the 1918 Act, however, the organization soon swelled to a high point of 272 employees in the early twenties.[2] To assist in organizing the employees for the task confronting them, and particularly for establishing the procedure to be followed within the CSC, the Commissioners secured the services of the Arthur Young Company in the summer of 1918. Its Report, completed in November, 1918, divided the CSC into three branches under the general direction of the Secretary, William Foran.[3] The first of these, the Administration Branch, later called the Assignment Branch, was the CSC's administrative arm performing the general office management of its business. The other two branches, the Examination Branch and the Organization Branch, consisted of its operational arms. The Examination Branch set and conducted all examinations for appointments and promotions, rated the candidates, and established a list of comparative merit for each examination—the eligible list. The Organization Branch was concerned with all matters of classification, the establishment of salary rates, investigations, and reports on the organization of the departments and the operation of the Civil Service Act, and in conducting special investigations. As outlined in the Report, the clerks, examiners, and investigators in each of the three branches were to work under the general direction of a chief who reported to the Commissioners through the secretary. In fact the organization did differ from the ideal set up in the Report in that duties of the chief of the Examination Branch were shared between two men, C. H. Bland and J. R. A. Baril, who supervised the English and French examination procedures respectively. After a few years this situation was brought into line with the suggested organization when Bland became the sole chief of the Branch.

Directly above the chiefs of the respective branches stood the secretary and his staff. As secretary, Foran's position lay at the organizational crossroads of the CSC. He was to "attend the meetings of the Commission, present matters for its consideration, assist in its deliberations and execute its decisions."[4] He also acted as the CSC's representative in dealing with the public, the departments, and the civil servants. In addition, the branch chiefs reported to the Commissioners through him and he also acted as the chief executive officer. Although this latter duty primarily involved the execution of the Commissioners' decisions relating to internal administrative matters, Foran, as we shall see, exercised considerable influence on these decisions.

Overseeing the entire organization were the three Commissioners. The Report envisaged their duties to be primarily those of policy-making: "The

Commissioners, meeting daily except Sundays and holidays, shall determine general policies with regard to the interpretation and administration of the Civil Service Act and the relation of the Civil Service Commission to departments." To aid in this policy-making, the Report suggested that each Commissioner familiarize himself with one or more specific phases of civil service administration, such as salary matters or examination problems, so that "when any broad policy is under consideration, the Commission may have the expert counsel and advice from one of its own members."[5] This proposal was never implemented; the Commissioners, as we shall see, became so deeply immersed in the daily routine of the organization from the beginning that they failed to attain the detachment necessary for such policy-making.

Chapter 5 has tried to show that by the early twenties the CSC had shifted its raison d'être away from an emphasis upon economy and efficiency toward the establishment of a merit system of appointment and promotion as an alternative to the patronage system. One of the dominating features of this campaign was the tendency to picture the patronage temptation as an almost overwhelming urge which sooner or later took possession of most people in any position to dispense it. The only recourse was simply to place patronage out of reach, and it was precisely this which the CSC claimed to be doing. When it came to the actual implementation of a system to meet this requirement, it involved the CSC in a complicated procedural network of checks and balances designed to detect the insidious influence of patronage before it could do any harm. The responsibility for making all appointments and promotions within the CSC was thus split among the three branches and involved both Foran and the Commissioners. Within the branches the procedure involved virtually no delegation of decision-making authority; rather, it consisted of a series of checks at different levels with the final decision in all matters, even the most simple and routine, reserved for the Commissioners.

In order to illustrate how this system functioned in actual practice, it might be useful to trace the path which a departmental requisition for an appointment took when it entered the CSC. On its arrival, the requisition went first to the Assignment Branch to be registered. From there it proceeded to the Organization Branch which provided the authority to fill the position by ensuring that it was properly classified. If the appointment involved a new position, the Organization Branch sent out an investigator to classify the position and establish the salary schedule. Following this, it went to the chief of the Organization Branch who initialled it, sent it back for revision, or put his comments and suggestions upon it. Next it went to the Commissioners, who, if they approved of the new classification, recommended its creation to the Privy Council. Once the position was established, the Assignment Branch again received the requisition. If no eligible list existed for the class in question, the requisition proceeded to the Examination Branch where an examiner prepared a report for the Commissioners for authority to hold examination. In his report the examiner set out the proposed procedure for the entire competition, including the duties of the position, the qualifications required for it, and the recommended scheme of examination (written or oral, and the marking scheme). The report also suggested to whom the competition would be open; that is, whether it would be intradepartmental (a promotional competition), interdepartmental, restricted to the general public within a certain locality, or open to all the residents of Canada. After the report passed through the hands of Bland, the Chief Examiner, and of Foran, both of whom initialled it and offered comments, it proceeded to the Commissioners for their approval. Once approval was received, posters were drawn up and distributed, applications received, an examination held, and a list made of the successful candidates arranged in their relative order of merit—the eligible list. As before, this list then passed through the hands of Bland and Foran for approval from the Commissioners. Once it was approved, the Assignment Branch made the appointment from the first name on the list and submitted the selection to the Commissioners for final approval.

It should be noted that in many cases, the requisition for appointment concerned a position which already existed and a classification for which an eligible list was already available. In these instances the requisition's route of travel was still rather tortuous. It first went from the Assignment Branch to the Organization Branch to ensure the correctness of the classification. From there it went to the Examination Branch where an examiner checked with the Assignment Branch to discover if an eligible list already existed. If there was, he returned the requisition to the Assignment Branch, which appointed the first name on the list. The appointment then went to the Commissioners for their approval.

Since all this took some time, business was not always expedited quickly. In addition, in some cases the Assignment Branch took a considerable amount of time to make the appointment. The eligible lists were prepared for future, and not necessarily for present, vacancies in the service. By the time a vacancy arose for a certain position, the person standing first on the list might choose to refuse the offer of appointment. The CSC then had to contact the person ranking second and so on down the list. Most eligible lists had a life span of two years so that some applicants had to wait a considerable length of time for appointment. The problem of tracing people after this time lapse can well be imagined. To delay appointments even more, the Assignment Branch had no authority to routinely fill positions to which departments requested the appointment of persons with special skills, such as bilingualism. Instead, it submitted the full eligible list, along with the qualifications of all persons on it, to the Commissioners who then chose the highest standing eligible with the proper qualifications.[6]

This complicated procedure of checks and double checks applied to more than simply appointments and promotions. It was felt necessary to protect all CSC business from undue influence so that all classifications and reclassifications, the establishment of salary rates, and changes in departmental organization and establishments went through a series of checks with the Commissioners rendering the ultimate decision in the end.

What is quite evident from this description is the extent to which the Commissioners themselves formed an integral and vital link in the daily routine and procedure of the CSC. By retaining all authority and responsibility for decisions within their hands, the Commissioners possessed an intimate knowledge of all work processed within the organization and were ideally in a position to guard against political influence on subordinate officers. As a further complicating factor, the Commissioners operated among themselves in a similarly involved fashion. The Act had stipulated that one of the Commissioners was to act as chairman, but beyond this had failed to assign him any preferential duties in relation to his colleagues. The Arthur Young Company's report on the internal administration of the CSC had interpreted this as meaning that the Commissioners must function only as a corporate body.[7] Whether or not the interpretation was correct, and no other seems possible in view of the terms of the Act, it was one which the Commissioners were disposed to accept because it suited the mechanistic procedure by better allowing them to guard against political influence through checking one another's work.

Each Commissioner was given charge over a specific number of government departments, and when a file came forward to be presented to the Commissioners, it went first to the desk of the Commissioner having charge over the department concerned. From this point it rotated in turn among the other two Commissioners. All three Commissioners usually perused every file, but matters required only the initials of two to be considered valid. One of the approval initials on a file, however, had to be that of the Commissioner having specific charge over the department involved. Most matters were processed in a routine fashion, but when a special problem arose, such as an appointment necessitating special qualifications, or one which was politically volatile, it was set aside to be brought forward again when the Commissioners met in a formal body on Tuesdays and Thursdays. On these occasions policy questions and matters demanding special attention were discussed. The chairman conducted all these sessions, and when questions under discussion could not be resolved unanimously, a vote was taken. The chairman did not have an overriding vote in these instances so that a simple majority decided matters.

This method of processing work was obviously open to grave procedural difficulties. For one thing, the prominence of the Commissioners in the overall procedure of the organization frequently resulted in bottlenecks and delays. If one Commissioner was absent from his office, all appointments, promotions, classifications, and all other CSC responsibilities in the departments under his purview were unduly delayed, so that even routine matters took months to process in some cases.[8] More fundamentally yet, delay was built into the system by the very fact that the Commissioners were so deeply involved in the daily routine that they often dealt with hundreds of files daily, and that any one file might have to pass over the desk of each Commissioner several times before final action was taken. In addition to the problems on this level, difficulties were encountered by the fact that responsibility for much of the work was split among three different branches and that all documents had to proceed through a series of checks before reaching the Commissioners. All work on any specific matter was stopped until approval was forthcoming from the proper CSC officers and the Commissioners at the various stages of its process through the organization. Any matter deviating at all from the norm simply caused further difficulties.

These delays greatly irritated the CSC's relations with departmental officials. Throughout the twenties and thirties deputy heads often indulged in bitter criticism of the slow wheels of CSC procedure at every opportunity—even those who supported the idea of the CSC as an independent appointing authority. It was generally alleged and acknowledged that most appointments and promotions took several months to make, while in some instances they ran to over a year. In one case in the early twenties the CSC appointed to a position a man who had been dead for six months.[9] Other CSC business was processed no more quickly, so that it often took up to a year simply to approve of reorganization work which departments had conducted on their own.[10]

The combination of the mechanistic method of processing work in the CSC and the corporate method of operation among the Commissioners was thus completed at the expense of the very efficiency of the CSC as a whole. Yet, despite the problems it created, the CSC's complicated procedure came to play a vital role in the defence of its existence. As an organization endeavouring to establish a base of support, the CSC laboured under the compulsion to explain the reason for its special role in making appointments, promotions, and in conducting classification work.

This was particularly true during the 1920s when the call arose for a return to the patronage system. The charge frequently levelled at this time was that the system which the CSC administered was not really any more efficient than the patronage system it had replaced. Members of Parliament argued that in appointments to local positions throughout the country, all the Civil Service Act had done was to take away the powers of patronage from the elected representatives, giving the appointing authority to three Commissioners who had neither knowledge of local conditions nor accountability to the local population for their actions.[11] Some deputy ministers, as well, insisted that they could make better appointments to their headquarters' staff in Ottawa than could the CSC.[12] To counteract these accusations, the CSC had to prove that the merit system was more efficient and could produce better appointments to the service than could either the M.P.'s or deputy heads. In this effort it was aided immeasurably by the union of the mechanistic conception of the CSC's operations with the whole body of scientific management thought which was so prevalent in the service at this time as a result of the efforts to introduce a "scientific" classification system. Not only could the CSC argue that the classification system operated according to scientific principles, but it could also imply that the "scientific selection of employees"[13] removed the appointment process from the dictates of mere human judgement and raised it to the realm of science. By giving its procedure, in practice and in theory, the attributes of a machine which scientifically and remorselessly chose the one best candidate for any given job, the CSC could justify its special competence to perform these tasks.

It was essentially on this basis that the CSC lodged its defence. In a booklet published in 1920 as a guide to the intricacies of its procedure, the CSC stated that "the Selection of employees nowadays has become an approved and established science with definite rules and laws." It explained that the booklet was intended for the use of departmental officials, "so that they may understand why at times the examination machinery of the Commission would seem to be moving slowly when, in reality, it is carefully weeding out undesirables in order to obtain eligibles. If departments can appreciate the large quantity of work involved in this connection, there is no doubt but that they will endeavour to anticipate their needs in the interest of efficiency and give the Commission time to examine applicants with all the care and precision that normal scientific selection demands."[14] It is interesting, in fact, to find the extent to which the CSC employed machine imagery to describe its procedure,[15] imagery which could at times reach rather ludicrous proportions:

Dr. MacTavish: Would it be in order, Mr. Chairman . . . to make a

357

verbal statement? . . . I mean, probably, a descriptive statement of my visualization, one might put it, of the Civil Service . . . Act, and of the Commission by which it is administered. I would like to put it this way, if you will permit me, that the Civil Service Act if you can conceive it— picture it—is a huge machine which has ramifications all over the Dominion. I have heard it, and have seen it, described in newspapers once, as having tentacles reaching out all over. It has ramifications all over the country. It is a huge machine if I might put it that way, this Act of Parliament, working under the Civil Service Commission. I merely use this manner of describing it, because I think you gentlemen might visualize it more clearly if I gave just a few minutes to it.

Now, we have that machine in operation like any other great machine and it goes along just turning out men and women for positions; it has the process all the time of elimination—if you get the idea of elimination. . . .

The Chairman (Mr. Lawson): Elimination of aspirants in order to get down to the irreducible minimum?

Dr. MacTavish: A good many people I know are all the time wondering how appointments are made.

Mr. Ernst: It is survival of the fittest?

Dr. MacTavish: Survival of the fittest. It is a long process in that survival of the fittest because the fittest have to be fitted throughout the country into the various ramifications of this machine.

Now the Civil Service Commission itself has a staff of 140 . . . and that group of individuals is keeping this machine going.[16]

Within this impersonal, mechanistic system the Commissioners seemingly occupied only a small place. Although they entered into the actual procedure in a large way, set in perspective against the overall background they merged completely into the machine: they were simply the final check in the system. CSC officers, in fact, were quick to note that the Commissioners were very rarely called upon to exercise their personal discretion and question work which had already been processed on the lower levels.[17] The Commissioners were, in other words, simply another cog in the wheel of the merit system machine.

This mystification of CSC procedure had far-reaching results. For one thing, it led the CSC to view its appointment procedure as being almost infallible. This becomes evident from the dispute over the rejection of its appointees which the CSC conducted with the departments in the late

1920s and early 1930s. In its Annual Report for 1925 the CSC noted that less than 1.5 percent of appointments to permanent positions were rejected by the departments during the probationary period. The CSC proudly boasted that this state of affairs was "an indication of the suitability for their posts of those selected and assigned by the Civil Service Commission."[18] Nevertheless, despite these glowing statistics, the CSC was not satisfied and protested that a portion of the 1.5 percent rejected were not given sufficient trial on the job. The Annual Reports repeated this argument year after year,[19] and Commissioner Roche lodged the same protest before the 1932 Committee.[20] At that time he explained that out of fifty-four rejections made in 1931 during the probationary period, at least fifteen were rejected for no reason other than that they were described as being "unsuitable." In his judgement this was insufficient cause. Roche also informed the Committee that the CSC had referred the question to the Justice Department but that its decision had upheld the departments' side of the case. The Committee thought that the CSC was making a mountain out of a molehill, and got MacTavish to admit that the whole issue really revolved around the CSC's refusal to admit the departments' right to reject appointees and its own desire to be made the supreme arbiter in matters of this kind.[21] The CSC eventually triumphed in this regard as the 1932 amendment made it incumbent upon a department to assign sufficient reason for rejecting CSC appointees.[22] The dispute illustrates to some extent the great emphasis which the CSC placed upon the irrevocably meritorious nature of its appointment procedure.

The firm belief in the essential righteousness of its procedure also led to a problem of another order. The scientific approach to the administration of the merit system encountered a dilemma in the need to denigrate the part which the personal judgement of the Commissioners or CSC officials played in making appointments and promotions. To establish the eligible list and to make promotions, a numerical rating system, based on 100 percent for perfection, was used. The rating took into account such factors as the candidate's experience, ability, education, and suitability to the job in question. The Organization Branch established the basis upon which the rating was performed, and it was intended that individual examiners use these "objective" standards so that personal value judgements would have no part in rating a candidate.

Despite its mechanical and scientific procedure, CSC employees were not machines, and it was simply impossible to deny that the individual judgement of officers was often instrumental in picking one candidate over another. CSC objections to the contrary, to the 1932 Committee it was obvious that in promotional competitions examiners sometimes gave preference to persons temporarily occupying positions at the time of the competition. Such preference, the Committee felt, did not square with the CSC's own description of a truly competitive merit system.[23] The responses of the Commissioners and CSC officers to the question put to them were rather muddled and contradictory—and were obviously attempts to avoid admitting to the Committee (as well as to themselves) that the personal discretion of examiners did in fact play some part in producing an eligible list.[24]

The CSC subsequently managed to deal with such aberrations from the perfection of its system. Bland, ever the diplomat, explained in 1938 that while the examination system was in itself not perfect, its imperfections were guarded by the probationary period for all new appointments.[25] Since by the 1932 amendment the CSC controlled the terms under which the departments could dismiss appointees, Bland was, in reality, suggesting that the CSC's overall procedure was still relatively free from error.

RESISTANCE TO CHANGE

Despite these effects, it was from the point of view of its own organization and methods of work that the Civil Service Commission's procedure probably had the most drastic result. Here it delayed for almost twenty-five years any substantial simplification in either area. Because its procedure played such a large part in the defence of its existence, all pressures for change were met with active resistance. This is nowhere more evident than in the furor over the Kemmis-Simmins affair in 1927. Since it demonstrates the attitudes described above, as well as exhibiting some of the problems relating to the leadership of the CSC, it may be enlightening to describe the affair briefly.

Less than a year after taking office, MacTavish and Tremblay initiated a study of the organization and procedure within the CSC. The immediate reason for the project, MacTavish later said, was that both he and Tremblay had received numerous complaints concerning the tardiness of its procedure.[26] The two Commissioners proceeded by appointing Major R. G. Simmins, a junior investigator in the Organization Branch, and A. C. Kemmis, a junior examiner, to conduct the study. Both appointments were made without the immediate knowledge of Roche and over the heads of Bland, the chief of the Examination Branch, and C. V. Putman, the chief of the Organization Branch. These latter officials were not involved because, as MacTavish explained, they would have undoubtedly produced a report favourable to the procedure because they were so closely connected with it. Similarly, Roche was not made aware of the study at first because "he would be put in the embarrassing position of having to dissent." Roche was only informed of the project by Bland and

Putman two days after Kemmis and Simmins were appointed. He immediately protested that the matter should be conducted in the usual manner through the heads of the branches, and predicted that "the suggested departure from this procedure will in my opinion prove subversive of good discipline, and will unnecessarily engender ill feeling of the staff."

The situation was further exacerbated when the Report was finished. In an attempt to placate the officials of the CSC, MacTavish and Tremblay had agreed to submit the Kemmis-Simmins Report to them for their comments. This, unfortunately, produced the opposite effect. The Report suggested a centralization of the CSC in which one Commissioner was to have direct supervision of the Examination Branch and the other Commissioner to have direct charge over the Organization Branch. The chairman was left in a nebulous position coordinating these two sections. Moreover, in streamlining the procedure the Report had the examiners and investigators reporting directly to the Commissioner in charge, bypassing the chiefs of the branches and the secretary.

The officials who submitted their comments on the Report to the Commissioner with one exception offered nothing but their implacable enmity to the scheme.[27] Aspersions were cast upon the character and ability of both Kemmis and Simmins by their superiors. MacTavish and Tremblay were exceedingly upset by this state of affairs and considered taking action against what they now considered as the "unauthorized preparation" of these counter-documents by the CSC officials. Fortunately, nothing was done in this regard, but the affair did spill over the boundaries of the CSC. Roche caught the ear of E. J. Garland, an M.P., who complained of the matter to King.[28] Apparently MacTavish and Tremblay then approached members of King's Cabinet to tell their side of the story.[29] King, however, refused to become involved, maintaining, quite rightly, that the CSC had been granted the power to establish its own procedure.[30]

In the end the opposition of the CSC officials made it impossible to implement the Report and it became a dead letter, but not until Roche's earlier predictions on the matter had come to pass. The affair produced incredible bad feelings within the organization. At one point some employees induced Major Simmins to join them for a drink after work in Hull. There they filled him with beer, and afterwards went out back and roughed him up so badly that he was unable to report to work for several days.[31] Five years later the bad taste had still not left the mouth of Bland, and he reported that "every time I think of it I get so mad I can't talk."[32]

The Report, admittedly, was initiated under the wrong conditions and conducted in an improper manner. The high-handed method by which MacTavish and Tremblay had begun the project produced only ill will and left the impression that they may have been acting under instruction from outside the CSC. The organizational changes also met with understandable resistance. Not only were senior officers insulted that their positions had been overlooked in the new scheme, but the grouping of the two main branches under MacTavish and Tremblay made it appear to the members of the 1932 Committee as an attempt to divest Roche of all power. Apart from this, CSC officials charged that the new organization would add appreciably to the work which the Commissioners already had.[33]

The actual procedural suggestions contained in the Report, however, are more difficult to dismiss than the reaction of the CSC officers would tend to indicate. Despite the defects of its recommendations on organization—and there is, incidentally, no concrete proof that it had been the intent of the two authors to organizationally isolate Roche—the Kemmis-Simmins Report contained some valuable and useful suggestions with regard to the procedure. Much of the "cumbersome routine" which the Lawson Committee of 1932 later found to exist in the CSC would have been eradicated by the procedure recommended in the Report.[34] The conclusion of Kemmis and Simmins, in fact, was that the present procedure was unnecessarily complicated and inefficient:

> At the present time it would appear that there are too many steps interposed between those officers entrusted with making original recommendations and those whose function it is to decide on those recommendations (the Commissioners). In other ways there is much unnecessary handling and passing of files to various branches or officials in carrying out routine. Every time that a file is passed for a purpose that is not absolutely necessary, delay is incurred, and the time of employees to some extent wasted.
>
> It would therefore be an improvement if the routine of both special and routine matters could be simplified so as to release senior officers from needless work and to economize the time of juniors. Senior officers should, as far as possible, be allowed to give all their attention to the special matters which have been confided to them.[35]

Basically, the Report suggested an elimination of the elaborate system of checks by simplifying or consolidating many of the steps of the various office procedures and by bypassing the branch chiefs.

The attitude of the CSC officers to these suggestions was somewhat contradictory. While they acknowledged the individual merit of many of the suggestions, they offered their implacable opposition to the sum total of the changes recommended. The great problem with the Report, aside from the conditions under which it was made, was that it struck at the very base upon which the defence of the CSC was situated: the suggested simplified procedure and organization conflicted with the need for a complicated and mechanistic procedure of checks and double checks. Thus the CSC officers saw the recommendations of the Kemmis-Simmins Report as a direct threat to the CSC. As J. R. A. Baril, the senior French examiner, explained:

> There would be very little economy in time or staff and when one thinks of all the trouble we would get into if we did away with the present checking, it is evident that a change of procedure would be unwise. The present checking system has not been created at one stroke: it has been built up gradually to prevent the repetition of errors and misunderstandings into which we have fallen in the past. It is surprising the different kinds of mistakes that can be made in dealing with the thousands of positions in the Service. And when a mistake is made we are bound to hear from it.[36]

Both Putman and Bland took special argument with the suggested functional division of the Commissioners' duties. They maintained that the responsibilities of the Commissioners could not be divided because their duties were of a judicial nature and they could thus function only as a corporate body.[37] Finally, Bland dismissed the whole Report complaining that the recommendations it contained endangered the merit system itself: "If . . . the present suggestions of Messrs. Kemmis and Simmins, ill informed and pervasive as I consider them, are accepted as a whole, they can have one effect and one effect only, namely, the weakening of the administration of the Civil Service Act, with the ultimate result, if persisted in, of the loss of the public confidence in the Civil Service Commission and the destruction of the merit system."[38] This perhaps explains the fact that, although they recognized the validity of many of the individual suggestions in the Report, the officials of the CSC never adopted any of them.

At this point, it is important to realize that the mechanical method of operation within the CSC served as a defence of the organization on more than one level. Whereas, on the one hand, this method united with the ideas of scientific management to justify its complicated procedure, it united, on the other, with a judicial conception of the Commissioners' duties to provide it with an explanation of the Commissioners' role within the bureaucracy. In protecting the civil service from patronage the Commissioners essentially saw themselves as judges of sorts whose duty it was to weigh all the factors bearing on appointments, promotions, and all other matters under their jurisdiction and to render decisions on these.[39] This line of reasoning was particularly attractive to the CSC after the brief but unfortunate experience with the classification venture in 1918–20. The Commissioners did not see it as their place to act as innovators within the bureaucracy; on the contrary, they performed a semi-judicial function, mechanically administering the law within the narrow confines of the Act. As Roche told the Spinney Committee in 1921:

> We are trying to enforce the Act which you members have put in the Statute Book, but the difficulty is that you members have placed a certain Act, and a drastic Act it is, a very advanced Act—but it is there by legislation, and the members of parliament while most of them are very, very reasonable, some of them blame the Commission for enforcing their own Act; that is unfair, insofar as the commission is concerned. We are living up to the provisions of the Act, and if you desire to change the Act, do so, and we will then dutifully carry out whatever provisions the Act may provide.[40]

The concept of the Commissioners as a judicial body in a sense was simply an extension of the description of CSC procedure as an impersonal scientific machine. That the Commissioners in the final resort made virtually every decision in the organization corporately could be justified by the need for a rigorous system of checks, as well as on the grounds that CSC business was essentially of a judicial nature and decisions, therefore, could not be delegated to subordinates. Both arguments had in fact been used to argue against the functional division of Commissioners' duties as proposed in the Kemmis-Simmins Report.

This attitude of resistance to organizational and procedural change continued to make itself quite evident in events subsequent to the Kemmis-Simmins affair. In 1930 the CSC conducted another internal study, this time by the Organization Branch. While minor alterations were made, basically little was found wanting. The 1932 Committee investigation, on the other hand, acknowledged the departmental criticisms of the CSC, and sharply reprimanded it for the "unnecessary delays" in appointments and promotions due to the "cumbersome routine" of its procedure.[41]

As a result of these and other criticisms, the CSC proceeded with an internal reorganization. Although the progress made in this regard pleased the Committee of 1934,[42] the change does not seem to have been too extensive. The division of work between the French and English examiners and clerks in the Examination Branch became part of the organizational framework with the creation of individual French and English sections. The Assignment Branch also divided along functional lines so that the CSC was now composed of four branches. The section of the Assignment

Branch which had dealt with the internal services of the Commission, such as the central registry, the typing pool, and personnel services, split off to become the Administrative and Personnel Services Branch and was attached to the Secretary's Office. It was under the direction of Miss Elsie Saunders, a CSC employee of long standing, who had the rank of assistant secretary. The remaining part of the Assignment Branch was under the direction of Arthur Thivierge, a future Commissioner. His position was further enhanced when a group of twenty M.P.'s met with Bland in 1936 to complain about the fact that the CSC had no French-speaking employee to answer French correspondence. As a result of this meeting the CSC split the duties of the assistant secretary between Thivierge and Miss Saunders.[43]

During the 1930s the majority of changes made within the Civil Service Commission had primarily involved the organizational framework, with little done by way of procedural simplification. Moreover, with the exception that by 1939 the Examination Branch bypassed the secretary and reported directly to the Commissioners, until his retirement in February, 1939, none of the reorganizations touched upon Foran's power. As earlier chapters have shown, Foran was an instrumental figure within the CSC. Not only was he active in the movement for civil service reform and in engendering support for the CSC's cause, but he occupied a crucial position in the organizational and procedural framework. He also showed an amazing ability to retain his power and position in the face of a great deal of parliamentary criticism directed his way. The 1932 Committee, for example, was strongly critical of the centralization of power in his hands and linked many of the difficulties in the CSC to this situation:

> Your Committee is of the opinion that there is a great deal of overlapping in the performance of duties by the heads of different branches of the Civil Service Commission, owing to matters receiving the attention of the secretary of the Commission which are in no way related to secretarial duties.
>
> Your Committee, therefore, recommends that the secretary of the Civil Service Commission be called to perform only those duties which are peculiarly those of a secretary and that the Civil Service Commission consider ways and means of eliminating duplication of correspondence and departmental memoranda which now pass through the secretary to the commissioners.[44]

Nothing was done by the Commissioners in this regard, and six years later the 1938 Committee reiterated the earlier criticisms.[45] This Committee also called for an end or alteration of all the forms and documents in use which required the approval or disapproval of the secretary before they were passed to the Commissioners.

These changes had to await the retirement of Foran in the following year. When this occurred the Commissioners divided the duties performed by Foran among three different persons so that no single officer had the position of power that he had held. The executive work was entrusted to S. G. Nelson, the Chief Examiner, while the secretarial duties were divided between Miss Saunders and Thivierge. In addition, the four branches of the CSC no longer reported through the secretary, but instead reported directly to the Commissioners so, as Bland explained, "to prevent the secretary's office in any way delaying matters, or in any way being a bottleneck for matters coming from the staff to the Commission for action."[46] CSC forms were also altered to meet the criticism of the 1938 Committee. The change eliminated the space formerly provided on documents for the recommendations of the secretary before they proceeded to the Commissioners' offices.

While these changes enhanced the power of the Commissioners within the organization, they did little to remedy the complicated procedure in the various branches of the CSC. In an internal memorandum to Bland, submitted a month after Foran's retirement, Putman noted the procedural difficulties still remaining. He pointed out that since 1918 the CSC staff had grown from 15 or 20 to nearly 300 and to handle this growth, and the increasing complexity of business, procedures had been installed and allowed to remain in existence, although they did not always integrate well with procedures as a whole. Yet nothing had been done to change this state of affairs. He also indicated that if the CSC was not to be subject to increasing criticism for causing delays, something would soon have to be done about the matter.[47]

Putman's observations are interesting for they reveal that the CSC was at last beginning to move away from its old protective mentality. This is also suggested by the fact that by the late thirties the Commissioners tended to rely upon their senior officers to a greater degree by perfunctorily signing many documents that had already received the approval of the branch chiefs. Unfortunately, this changing attitude was not reflected to any marked extent elsewhere in the organization, nor did Putman's comments spark any movement toward further simplification. The Commissioners still retained all signing authority and took final responsibility for all decisions. The rudimentary delegation of authority to the branch chiefs was, moreover, quite haphazard since no coherent policy had been enunciated on it. The Commissioners might read in full any file which happened to catch their eye, even though it had received the approval of one of the branch chiefs. Even as late as 1939 the Commissioners' desks were apparently piled with files several feet in height requiring their signatures.[48] The CSC failed to escape, to any meaningful extent, from the system that had encumbered it for twenty years.

THE CSC'S RESPONSE TO THE WAR

Although internal frustration had not proved great enough to initiate substantial changes in the Civil Service Commission's organization and procedure, the rapid external developments during the war made internal change inevitable. As described in chapter 9, the most striking and dramatic of the changes in the CSC's environment after 1939 was the tremendous increase in the number of appointments required in the bureaucracy and the problem of planning and organizing staff to meet the wartime exigencies. In the year prior to the outbreak of hostilities, the CSC had made a total of 6,406 appointments to the civil service,[49] but by contrast was making over 56,000 appointments in 1943[50]—almost a ninefold increase. While this added tremendously to the work load of the Examination Branch, the Organization Branch was far removed from the relative idleness which had characterized it during the 1930s. In some cases it had to formulate plans for new services, salary schedules, and staff organizations on a dominion-wide basis within a matter of a few days or weeks. Rapid changes in wartime organizations and the reallocation of duties also frequently necessitated the reclassification of a great many temporary employees after a complete survey of various units. Clearly, the highly centralized and mechanical operation in the CSC had to be altered because of the sheer physical impossibility of continuing in the old fashion.

In response to the situation the CSC first attempted to contract its procedure and to simplify and shorten its tests and methods of selection. In some areas, particularly those involving the examination of candidates, this succeeded quite well. A wartime Order in Council of 1940 had given the CSC the authority to make appointments "after such tests of qualifications as the Commission considers practicable and in the public interest."[51] Under this provision, the CSC hastened to dispense with many time-consuming procedures and requirements that had grown up around the examination function. The rising demand for office employees, coupled with the facts that the number of refusals of employment had greatly multiplied as a result of the offer of better employment conditions from outside the civil service, and that many eligibles had enlisted in the armed forces, meant that the eligible lists became rapidly depleted. To cope with the problem, more examinations were held on a dominion-wide basis, waiving the locality preference. Requirements as to maximum age were also relaxed, and the examinations themselves modified. In many classes, such as the stenographic, in which demand always outstripped supply, the practice of holding competitive examinations on a fixed date was terminated. Instead, continuous eligible lists were established, and as new applicants were found, they wrote the examination, and if qualified, their names were entered in order of merit on the list. In many cases these qualifying, rather than competitive, examinations were the only test given prior to appointment, while in other classes the only formality was an oral interview.

The endeavour to expedite CSC business at this level was matched by a similar attempt to remedy what had always been the biggest bottleneck in CSC procedure: the preeminent role played by the Commissioners themselves in the day-to-day operation of the CSC. At the beginning of the war all files had required the individual attention of all three Commissioners at the various stages of their progress through the CSC. But as the work grew, it became no longer possible to operate in such a manner. As a result, files dealing with most routine matters of business were retained in the Personnel Services Branch of the Secretary's Office where a list of the cases and recommended action in each instance was drawn up. These List Minutes, as they were called, were then submitted to the Commissioners for their approval. If a question was raised with respect to any case, the corresponding file would be produced for their consideration. Once the Commissioners had signed the List Minutes, the files were stamped and released from the Branch.

This worked well at first, but when the volume of work continued to grow unabated it became necessary to have virtually all files handled in this fashion. The only cases not appearing on the List Minutes were those concerning policy or procedure, exceptional cases, all appointments of postmasters, or cases which involved positions carrying salaries of $4,000 or over. Files relating to these matters still necessitated the individual attention of the Commissioners.[52]

In conjunction with the reformation of the procedure on this level, it was also found necessary to grant greater *operational* responsibility to the branch heads. Toward the middle of the war when the CSC's work was at its heaviest, their meagre responsibility was expanded when they were given signing authority in some of the more routine matters, particularly in the area of temporary positions. The tremendous expansion of departments, branches, and sections connected to the war effort had necessitated the creation of literally thousands of temporary positions which were to remain only as long as the war continued. The establishment of these positions was a pretty routine affair, running into very little opposition from Treasury Board, which generally acquiesced in the CSC's recommendations. Similarly, the filling of these positions was not particularly complicated or involved. To prevent the List Minutes from becoming filled with the record of action taken in each of these cases, the Commissioners granted the three branch heads the power to establish and fill temporary positions up to a certain level on their own authority. The head of the Organization Branch, George Jackson,[53] also had additional authority to act in matters concerning war duties supplements without further reference. (In practice the war duties supplements were used as a means of circumventing Treasury Board's restrictions on reclassifications.) It is not too clear whether any of this authority was delegated in a formal manner and recorded in the CSC minutes, or whether it was simply an informal arrangement, but, in any event, it constituted the first real occasion of any significant delegation of the Commissioners' operational role.[54]

Apart from these changes, the greatly increased work load and the expansion of staff during the war years also forced the CSC to arrive at a more structured arrangement for conducting the work in its two main branches. Prior to the war a very informal situation for delegating tasks had reigned in both the Examination and Organization Branches. While personal inclination or qualifications often dictated that one examiner would be more proficient at conducting examinations for certain classes rather than for others with which he had less familiarity, the relatively small staff meant that there was no clear-cut specialization. In the Organization Branch a similar situation prevailed with respect to classification and organizational matters. But this method of operation, like that of the Commissioners', was no longer completely possible during the war years, for in this period the staff of the CSC more than doubled from 235 employees in 1939 to 591 in 1944.[55] The new employees were composed primarily of office and clerical staff and were largely absorbed by the Organization and Examination Branches. But the professional staff also increased greatly in these years. Although precise figures are difficult to obtain, by the end of the war the Examination Branch contained about thirty-eight examiners compared to about eleven in the immediate prewar years. The Organization and Classification Branch, as the Organization Branch was officially titled after 1942, similarly expanded from about eight investigators in 1938 to about thirty-three by 1946.[56] To further complicate the matter, by 1945 the CSC found itself physically separated and divided among six different buildings around Ottawa. Under these circumstances the informal method of delegating work in the branches was simply too unsophisticated to cope with the demands now placed upon it.

In order to create a more structured arrangement, the CSC made a formal division of duties first among the examiners and then among the investigators in the Organization Branch. In each case the majority of the officers were divided into groups specializing in meeting the needs and requirements of a specific number of departments, which were grouped largely on the basis of a similarity of occupational content in each of them. In addition, one experimental group in the Examination Branch was aligned on a functional, rather than departmental, basis. It concentrated on meeting the overwhelming demand from all departments for stenographic and clerical assistance.

Although the departmental division of duties improved the situation, and allowed the CSC to better handle the increased work load, it did not eradicate the problem by any means; the CSC continued to be responsible for lengthy delays in meeting the requirements of the departments. Essentially, the crux of the difficulty lay in the old mechanistic procedure of checks and balances which the CSC had inherited from the 1920s and 1930s. In practice this system had resulted in a flow of files among the branches of the CSC, and between the branches and the offices of the Commissioners. This had always been somewhat of a problem causing bottlenecks and delays, but during the war the problem was greatly amplified owing to the increased work load. The creation of the List Minutes had been the first step toward finding a remedy for the problem by partially decreasing the file flow to the Commissioners. But the routing of the files among the three branches of the CSC was more of a problem than ever. Files not only had to travel between floors in the same building, but in many cases even between different buildings. In these conditions the old mechanistic system showed severe strains. Delays, in fact, simply multiplied with the amount of work and at times brought the entire organization to a standstill.[57]

This system, along with its breakdowns, was pretty well left to limp along untouched for most of the war, except for the improvements where the Commissioners were concerned. Toward the close of the war, however, a physical reorganization improved the problem considerably by bringing the Examination and Organization Branches closer together. To ease the flow of files, examiners and investigators dealing with roughly the same departments were grouped, along with clerical staff, together into close physical proximity to one another. As a further aid, the central registry was largely decentralized and a portion of it attached to each of these units. Although the units maintained the rigid branch separation with each group of examiners and investigators working under its own supervisor, the file flow was greatly reduced by having a number of operations performed in one place. The units processed all the paper work for appointments up to the final certification of the candidate which remained the prerogative of the Assignment Branch. At first, considerable discussion was given to the efficacy of also attaching this latter Branch to these units, but the scheme was dropped when it met the hostile resistance of the chief of the Branch. Apparently he recognized that because the Assignment Branch was largely a mechanical operation involved primarily with certifying successful candidates, it would become a mere appendage to the unit with a resultant loss of his authority.[58]

Left as it was, however, the unit system did not in any manner take precedence over the branches or impinge upon the powers of the branch heads. It was a purely physical arrangement designed for procedural purposes, mostly relating to making appointments. The other normal work of each branch went on in the units under the direction of the supervisor of each group. In addition, there were some specialists in each branch who remained outside the unit system. A growing specialization in the area of test development in the Examination Branch and with pay matters and organizational and classification problems in the Organization Branch meant that some officers never became deeply involved in any one unit.

As well as the procedural changes introduced to deal with the wartime conditions, there were also several organizational changes in these years. By far the most important of these was the creation of the district offices. A great many of the appointments which the CSC was called to make during the war were to positions in localities far from Ottawa. Until this time examiners were required to travel to these localities to administer their tests, but it was now simply impossible to do the amount of travelling required. To aid it in making the local appointments, the CSC established in 1942 the first district offices. Early that year four of these offices were opened in Montreal, Toronto, Winnipeg, and Vancouver. They were followed with five others later in the year at Halifax, St. John, Quebec, Regina, and Edmonton. By the end of the war the CSC had added an additional four suboffices which were served at least one day a week. These offices in 1945 were staffed by a total of seventy-four employees with an additional eleven persons at the headquarters' unit in Ottawa.[59]

In their first few years of operation, the district offices were simply a physical extension of the Examination and Assignment Branches of the CSC at Ottawa, and were primarily concerned with the local recruitment of temporary war staff. While physical separation from headquarters necessitated the making of some decisions without consultation, basically the district officers were given no more authority than the Ottawa examiners. As the CSC itself admitted, the district office scheme was decentralization but "under strong central control and direction."[60] The procedure for making appointments amply demonstrated this fact. All actions undertaken by the district officers, like those of the examiners in Ottawa, still had to have the approval of the Commissioners. In the great majority of cases, the district officers held an examination only after authority came from Ottawa and then sent the results back to headquarters where the eligible list was drawn up. In a few cases the district officers did have the authority to maintain their own eligible lists without reference to Ottawa, but all appointments made from these lists had to be entered in the List Minutes.

Although it was tightly controlled from Ottawa during this period, the district office system did prove to be a great aid to the CSC, relieving the headquarters of a great deal of travelling and routine work and providing better service to departments in the field. While these offices were originally designed to deal with wholly wartime positions, by the close of the war they were handling virtually all examinations and assignment work for both wartime and peacetime positions in their respective districts.

THE POSTWAR ERA, 1945–1957

The war years had drastically altered the face of the civil service and, with it, the CSC. While this period had created a totally different set of conditions to which the CSC had to adjust, there was no indication immediately following the war that the situation would return to prewar normality. Events, in fact, suggested just the opposite, for 1946 in many respects presented a heavier work load for the CSC than had any of the war years. With the termination of the War Measures Act, the normal method of appointing candidates through regular competitive examinations replaced the ad hoc selection methods in force. Qualified veterans also had to be placed in the civil service, and it was necessary to convert classification and organization from a wartime to a normal basis. During the war the majority of examinations for permanent appointment had been discontinued in an attempt to mete out fair treatment to the personnel on active service. Now that these persons were returning to their old positions the CSC had to mount an extensive program of competitions for permanency. Promotional competitions had also been greatly reduced by Treasury Board restrictions during the war, but with the loosening of these restrictions in 1945 a backlog of examinations was required. The continued growth, reorganization, and development programs of many departments meant that there was no diminution in the demand for staff in the immediate postwar years. The civil service also faced a very great staff turnover rate at the war's end which further augmented the demand for staff.[61]

Under these circumstances a return to the prewar method of operation in the CSC was completely out of the question. On the contrary, as the external environment continued to alter and change after the war, it was evident that further changes would have to be made to the internal structure of the CSC. This proved to be something of a problem. At the beginning of the war the CSC had inherited an organization and procedure which had developed in response to the particular environment of the twenties and thirties. During the war years attempts had been made to adapt what was a cumbersome and now-antiquated system to the demands of a new environment. Yet, all the changes which had been made consisted mostly of adaptations to the original system and did not constitute a reassessment of the organizational and procedural framework. It was a quantitative rather than qualitative change.

The system, as a result, continued to provide plentiful delays, as it had in the prewar years. If one single operation was not performed properly or was delayed while authority was obtained, the next officer in line could not proceed with any work on the file until the problem was remedied. Consequently, even routine work sometimes took up to a year to process. At one examination a prospective candidate had submitted his application so long before that he had to be reminded what position it was he was being examined for.[62] Matters of special difficulty which might require follow-up action on the part of an officer often became sidetracked from the regular flow of work—the "conveyor belt" as it was sometimes called—and were left unattended for long periods among the countless files of the CSC. Under these circumstances, searching for one particular file buried somewhere among the various units, sections, and branches could easily consume the better part of a day and still produce no results.

The delays and difficulties which the CSC continued to face after the war was a cause of concern to both the Commissioners and the officers of the organization. The copies of minutes of meetings of the Commissioners and the memoranda to the branch heads which still survive from this period exhibit that a great deal of attention was being given to this problem and record several studies into the matter.[63] The staff meetings from this period also show deep concern over the problem. In these latter meetings the problem became identified as falling into two basic areas. First, the tremendous growth of staff had caused severe problems of coordination within the branches. Officers had become specialized in the work of their own area and were too cut off from the work of other officers within the same branch. Intraorganizational rivalry between branches also resulted in a frequent lack of cooperation between individual investigators and examiners.

Second, and more important, there was a growing awareness among both the Commissioners and the officers that the mechanistic method of checks and balances had begun to outlive its usefulness. In the past the CSC's mechanistic procedure, although slow and complicated, had served as a justification for its distinctive competence to make appointments and promotions. But by 1946 the CSC had entered a new era where different responses were demanded from it. The need after the war was not only for a system to protect the service from patronage, but also for a positive instrument of personnel policy. In this environment the inefficiency of the system became a distinct liability. Under this stimulus, and aided by the great influx of younger officers during the war who were unconnected with the trials of the past, the organization slowly began to shed its protective and defensive character. There was a growing awareness that the merit principle no longer required all the protections that had been built up around it in the past, and that it was now time to concentrate on effecting improvements in the system.[64] This attitude pervaded the whole organization; as Bland himself told one staff meeting in early 1946:

> Delay is our chief enemy now. Executive impatience sometimes exercised in the Commission comes mainly from the fact that our competitive system can be attacked only through its weaknesses. We are not vulnerable now to attack on the score of favouritism, weak appointments, inaccuracy, and so forth, but the common criticism made by high Government officials of the CSC is that we are too slow.
>
> In the past, in guarding against any possible criticism on other scores, we have had an elaborate system of check and balance, so that it was always possible to prove, by documents, why the CSC had taken any specific action. But if we don't get some types of appointments made more quickly we are going to lose them, and that would be definitely bad, since our appointments are better than those of any alternative system.[65]

The attempts to deal with this situation provided the basis for the first really significant change in the system and the first real rethinking of the place of the Commissioners within the organization.

In the summer of 1946 the Commissioners took the first step toward changing the old procedural system by formally delegating a wide expanse of operational authority to CSC officers. In July they granted to about nineteen CSC officers the authority to act on their behalf in many designated cases. This included most promotions, promotional appeals, leaves of absence, transfers from one department to another, authority to advertise competitions, eligible lists, wartime duties and supplements, and appointments, assignments, and reclassifications to temporary positions up to a maximum salary level of $4,000. Matters that required submissions to Council—briefly, exemptions, permanent reclassifications, reorganizations, the establishment of new positions and abolition of old ones, and recommended retirements under the Superannuation Act—were to be investigated and reported upon without prior approval or without reference to the Commissioners except for their final signature before submission. In conjunction with this, the List Minutes were discontinued, and it was the intention that the regular minutes of the CSC would become primarily a record of standing instructions of the Commissioners and of changes and interpretations of these.[66]

This new arrangement significantly altered the role of the Commissioners within the organization by taking them out of the daily routine to a large extent and leading to a specialization of the matters which came to their attention. Basically the Commissioners now concerned themselves with policy questions, exceptional cases, all permanent appointments, and all matters relating to senior positions with a maximum salary over $4,000. While these latter two matters ensured that the Commissioners were not removed altogether from the daily operations, they constituted only a small portion of the total business. Most matters dealt with by the CSC concerned positions below $4,000, and permanent appointments accounted for only about one-seventh of all the appointments made in the immediate postwar years.

Although it produced a significant effect on the procedural role of the Commissioners, this delegation did not eradicate all the vestiges of the old system at one stroke. The CSC moved only cautiously and for many years remained pretty much of a hierarchical structure. In addition to the chiefs of the Examination and Organization Branches, the Commissioners had designated six other officers in each of these branches, who could act on their behalf. Yet the work of these supervisory officers had to be reviewed by the chief of their respective branches or his assistants. In the Examination Branch, for example, all work by subordinate officers was generally completed under the supervision of those officers with signing authority. This work, although initialled by these supervisory officers, was then submitted for a further review to two senior examiners, C. Garrett and L. W. Moffit, who handled the files on a departmental basis.[67] An exception to this appeared in all files relating to positions in Quebec or where bilingual qualifications were concerned. After initialling these files on behalf of the Commissioners, the supervising officers then passed them along for a final check to O. A. Lefebvre, a senior examiner. Once any of these three persons had stamped and initialled a file, official action could be taken by the Examination Branch. A similar situation prevailed in the Organization Branch where the chief, G. Jackson, and his assistant, D. Watters, countersigned or reviewed all the files.[68]

But despite its initial defects, the delegation of authority did represent the first major step away from the cumbersome system of checks and balances. While it by no means eliminated all causes of delay, CSC business was expedited by the removal of many of the encumbrances at the Commissioners' level. Moreover, as the CSC began to creep away from its old protective mechanism, CSC officers were increasingly granted authority to deal with additional matters at levels higher than $4,000. In the future, authority was also delegated, slowly but consistently, to more and more officers at lower levels. Although there was some difficulty in convincing one branch head to delegate his authority to junior officers, CSC officers slowly gained the responsibility and authority to use their own discretion to a greater degree.

This was matched on another level by the endeavour to relieve the officers of some of the more mechanical aspects of their jobs. One of the holdovers from the days of a smaller CSC was the great amount of routine clerical work performed by the officers. Such work consumed valuable time that might be better spent in other ways. During the late forties the CSC officers were successful in getting additional clerical assistance to aid them in the more mechanical features of their work, partially solving the problem. In addition to this Dr. O. E. Ault, since 1946 the chief of the Personnel Selection Branch (as the Examination Branch was now called), consistently tried to get his officers to break away from the rigid application of rules and regulations and to use their own personal discretion to a greater extent. One of the most absurd features of the old system had been the insistence that the personal judgement of an examiner rarely went into the creation of an eligible list. The need to picture the CSC as a strictly objective and impartial machine had produced a tendency among the officers to rigidly apply rules and regulations and to use as little of their own judgement on matters as possible. By the time Ault entered the CSC, this need had largely disappeared, however, and he quickly recognized the drawbacks of the system. Over the years he successfully urged the examiners to apply common sense and their own reasoned discretion in dealing with positions and qualifications.[69] He also obtained the relaxation of many of the rules and regulations to better enable them to perform in this manner.[70]

These facts had profound effects on the methods of operation within the CSC. Largely as a result of the continued delegation of authority, combined with the efforts of people like Ault on another level, by the time of Bland's retirement in 1955 the CSC had to a great extent escaped from the elaborate system of checks which had characterized the old system. CSC officers, in fact, probably had as much, if not more, operational responsibility and authority as did officers in most government departments.

Although the system of checks was rapidly disappearing from sight in the postwar years, CSC operations nevertheless continued to encounter problems. This was in part due to the fact that not all the procedural developments of these years conduced toward expediting business. During the late 1940s and in the 1950s there was a steady movement toward a greater specialization of duties in the recruitment function. While this specialization did increase the output of individual persons within certain limits, it also increased the number of hands through which a recruitment request passed. In the long run the added handling very often resulted in difficulties in coordination and an increase in processing time.[71] The processing time for the professional classes such as engineers was further hampered in the postwar years by the drastic shortage of candidates who were more readily attracted to the private sector.

By far the greatest difficulty, however, lay in the fact that all the procedural developments of the postwar years had taken place within the context of the old organizational structure. Responsibility for recruitment, selection, and promotion remained divided among the different branches of the CSC. Even when junior officers had sufficient authority to process their own work without reference to a supervisor, requisitions still had to pass from one branch to another exactly in the same pattern as in the prewar years, before all processes were completed. In routine cases the flow of work basically constituted a clerical operation and ran smoothly and swiftly, primarily as a result of the procedural improvements of these years. But cases which might require a change in classification or which presented some other problem really hampered the flow of work and increased the processing time. An internal study of recruitment and selection procedures commissioned in 1958 noted that when requisitions entered the CSC they could start on any one of a variety of procedural patterns. Some of these requests, particularly those concerned with cases not strictly ordinary or routine, might entail as many as *fifty* changes of supervisory responsibility involving *seven* major organizational units before the request would be met. Delays resulting from this state of affairs meant that the *average* time for processing a requisition in 1958 which required a Canada-wide competition was 194 days from the time of entry into the CSC until the final assignment.[72] This time span had actually increased from several years earlier.[73]

Interestingly enough, the CSC did not always let the division of responsibility hinder it when the occasion called for a special effort. In 1948 it was given the rush job of setting the establishment and work procedures in the Income Tax Department which had, until this time, been exempt from the Civil Service Act. The CSC was also to gain jurisdiction over all positions with an annual salary level up to $3,000. Positions had to be classified, procedures developed, competitions held for those positions blanketed under the Act, and certificates of appointment issued. To handle the situation the CSC set up a special group under K. R. Scobie, a senior investigator, which combined the functions of the Organization, Examination, and Assignment Branches. The experiment worked well and the task was completed within the time limit. Such approaches were used on different occasions whenever the situation warranted it, but at the completion of these projects the group always disbanded into the old organizational framework without ever provoking a total reassessment of the current set-up.

The major obstacle in the path of such an organizational reassessment seems to have been sheer inertia. Former CSC officers feel that Bland himself did not oppose such changes, but that other CSC officers, comfortable in their old positions, did not wish to be shaken. But by the late 1950s it was becoming increasingly difficult for inertia and entrenched interests to prevent obvious conclusions from reaching the surface. Throughout the postwar period the CSC had expanded its activities into many different areas. Although this had resulted in the creation of several new branches and divisions within the CSC,[74] it had been accomplished with virtually no increase in the number of officers. The pressures this created upon the old organizational and procedural framework, and the pressures for staff expansion, clearly necessitated a reorganization of the CSC. In 1958 the study of the recruitment and selection procedures quickly drew the conclusion that any procedural changes would not amount to much without sufficient organizational changes as a background within which to place these improvements.[75] It identified the major source of difficulty as the division of responsibility for recruitment and selection between the Personnel Selection and the Organization and Classification officers.[76] (The Assignment Branch had already been united with the Personnel Selection Branch earlier in 1958.) The central recommendation of the report was the termination of this state of affairs with the Personnel Selection Branch alone having the duty of receiving and processing requests from the departments to fill positions.[77] The report in effect signalled the final defeat of the old mechanistic system of checks and balances which had been in existence in one way or another for forty years.

THE 1960 REORGANIZATION

The growing arguments in favour of a full-scale reorganization were given an added dimension in the late fifties by the internal study of the Civil Service Act and federal personnel administration which resulted in the Heeney Report. It was quickly realized that the present structure would not support the changes which the Report proposed. As Heeney wrote to Bryce in 1958: "If and when a bill is passed . . . we will have a pretty major reorganization job to do in the Commission before we will be ready to establish and operate a new regime."[78] Heeney also informed the Prime Minister of the need for a reorganization, adding that, "in this connection it should be noted that in recent years the Commission's establishment has remained virtually static pending its anticipated reorganization. A comprehensive study of this important question of administrative reorganization is now under way."[79] The study continued after Heeney's departure early in the next year and was completed after Hughes became chairman. This endeavour constituted the first total reassessment of the organization and ended the existence of the Personnel Selection (Examination) Branch and the Organization Branch, both of which had lingered around for over forty years.

The chief feature of the reorganization was the attempt "to achieve homogeneous groupings of functions and responsibilities, and to bring together closely related activities under single directing authorities."[80] Among other things, one of the guiding principles of the reorganization was to avoid "fragmentation of responsibility" whereby autonomous units had responsibility for different facets of any one CSC task.[81] This pitfall, as we saw, was one of the most cumbersome features of the old system, with responsibility for the same tasks split between the Organization and Examination Branches. An attempt was also made, in Hughes' words, "to disentangle the more reflective pursuits of the advisory services from the operational routine."[82]

To accomplish these objectives the various duties of the CSC, which until this time had been split between the various branches, were identified, separated from the old branches, and combined into new functional units. By far the most significant feature of the reorganization was the virtual union of the old Personnel Selection and Organization Branches into a new Operations Branch. This one Branch now became responsible for the recruitment, selection, appointment, promotion, probation, transfer, and lay-off functions of the Personnel Selection Branch, as well as for the consideration of classification and compensation for individual positions, and the reclassification duties of the Organization Branch. The Operations Branch in effect assumed responsibility for nearly all the day-to-day operational services to departments.

Most of what remained of the Organization Branch was removed to the new Pay and Standards Branch. The latter dealt with CSC responsibilities in the area of pay and conditions of employment, as well as in the related area of the development of standards applicable throughout the service. The Pay Division of the Branch was responsible for the development of the CSC's recommendations on rates of pay based on information gathered by the Pay Research Bureau. In addition, it was concerned with the standards of discipline and employment conditions such as the various types of leave, hours of work, and overtime. The Standards Division was concerned with what might be termed the more theoretical aspects of classification. Briefly, the Operations Branch conducted the classification of individual positions using the classification specifications (duties and qualifications of positions) developed by the Standards Division. This unit was also responsible for recommending changes in existing classes and the creation of new ones.

Apart from the Operations and the Pay and Standards Branches, several other units were created at this time. The decision to broaden the base of appeals in the civil service bill currently before Parliament in 1960 was reflected within the organization by a similar expansion in the size of the Appeals Branch, which now became the Appeals and Service Relations Branch. As well as dealing with appeals, this Branch was to handle the CSC's consultation with the staff associations, as outlined in the proposed legislation. The endeavour to separate the advisory services of the CSC from its operational responsibilities resulted in the creation of an Advisory Services Branch with the responsibilities of organizational analysis, management analysis, and staff development and training. Finally, the Pay Research Bureau remained unchanged in the reorganization, while the Administrative and Personnel Branch took over the internal services of the organization from the Administration Branch. The Secretary's Office remained virtually unchanged in the new scheme, basically serving as an appendage to the Commissioners' offices.

The reorganization of the CSC proceeded quite smoothly and was largely completed by the end of October, 1960. Although consideration was given to bringing in men from outside the organization to fill the top positions in the new structure, this suggestion was passed over in favour of appointment from within the present ranks. All the officers within the CSC were assessed by appraisal boards which included personnel officers loaned by departments to ensure objectivity, and officers were subsequently assigned to their new positions by a memorandum issued in late 1960.

DEVELOPMENT OF THE CENTRAL STAFFING AGENCY

Following the 1960 reorganization, the Civil Service Commission entered upon the most turbulent period of its history, ending with a complete reassessment of its role within the bureaucracy. As a result, the procedural and organizational framework established in 1960 did not remain static very long. On the one hand, the unsettled condition of its role produced several changes in the structure of the organization, none of which need detain us here.[83] Second, and more important, the eventual development of the central staffing agency concept demanded a fresh new approach to the problem of staffing which the present structure was incapable of fulfilling. By 1965 it was recognized that if the CSC were to assume its new role, it would have to undergo another reorganization even more fundamental than that of 1960.

The most dominant feature of the central staffing agency idea from the point of view of the CSC's operations was that it represented the culmination of an evolutionary process that had been occurring since the war. During the twenties and thirties the CSC's operations had been characterized by what might be termed a passive approach to staffing: it simply filled departmental requisitions and requests when demanded. In the loose labour market of these years with its ready supply of talent, the CSC rarely had to adopt the initiative or go to any extraordinary lengths to secure the services of those it appointed. Even during the forties with the tighter labour markets, this orientation predominated within the organization so that its day-to-day service was arranged primarily on a departmental basis; that is, officers were grouped on the basis of the departments they served. However, for some areas in which particular difficulty was encountered in finding suitable candidates, an increasing amount of functionalism was introduced, so that some officers became grouped on the basis of the classes they handled. Much of this had been terminated with the end of the war, but some classes difficult to fill, like those in the physical sciences group, continued to be handled functionally. The 1960 reorganization had represented something of a compromise between the two approaches. In the Operations Branch departmental requests were met by two divisions, one of which was organized on a departmental basis, while the other was organized on the basis of the classes it handled. The former division was divided into six departmental units and the latter contained three functional units designed to handle clerical and related classes, technical and scientific classes, and general professional classes such as finance officers and statisticians.

This compromise system lasted only until 1965 when the elaboration of the central staffing agency rendered it obsolete. Essentially the new system proposed to replace the former passive approach to staffing by a new dynamic approach characterized by "the provision for formal and systematic forward planning, based on a careful assessment of the manpower needs of departments and the manpower resources available both within and outside the civil service."[84] The CSC was thus no longer to await notification of departmental needs but was to actively anticipate the needs and requirements of the service as a whole. Within the organization this approach effectively completed the revolution from a departmental to a completely functional system. As one internal document explained in 1965:

> Internally . . . the new system will demand a new orientation designed to respond to the needs of the service as a whole in respect of each occupational group or cluster of closely related occupational groups. By adopting this basic system, the Commission will be able to develop service-wide assessments and programs for specific occupations. It will mean the abandonment of an internal organization based on individual departments so that the responsibility for assessing and co-ordinating the personnel needs of a specific department or agency will be exercised by officials of the department concerned, where it correctly and logically belongs.[85]

In September of 1965 the Commissioners attempted to implement the new functional system when they disbanded the Operations Branch and in its place created the Staffing Branch. The latter consisted of an initial eight staffing programs based on the occupational classes and groups of classes designed by the Bureau of Classification Revision. The first of these programs was the Advisory Panel on Senior Appointments which retained responsibility for the management of the senior officer program. The ten occupational groups of the administrative category were arranged into three staffing programs: general, financial, and personnel. The professional and scientific category was divided into three programs: the socio-economic, the bio-physical sciences, and the applied sciences. The final staffing program contained the administrative support (clerical), the operational (service and maintenance), and the remaining technical and occupational groups. A new Research and Planning Service was created at this time to provide assistance to the program directors, primarily in the areas of making the most effective use of manpower resources, of improving the capacity of the service to attract and retain qualified and competent people, and of creating an understanding of the technological and sociological changes occurring in the public service. As well, the CSC created a new Training and Development Service to provide "a reservoir of experts to guide the staffing program officers and departmental personnel advisors."[86] With the appearance of this Branch the CSC gained the capability to conduct the staffing action for any position within the framework of the staffing plans formulated for the class or group of classes to which that position belonged.

Closely related to the new orientation adopted at this time was the greater use made of the continuous recruitment and selection process. In a sense this process typified the new dynamic approach to staffing. In the past the CSC had conducted competitions for many positions on an annual basis only or when a vacancy arose for which there was no qualified eligible. This worked well for classes in which occasional vacancies arose, but in areas where demand outstripped supply, it was still necessary to make all potential candidates wait until the date set for the next examination so that an eligible list could be established. Since the war continuing competitions had been used to an increasingly greater extent, and they considerably eased this situation by having candidates examined as they were found and appointed as they passed. In this way the eligible list for the class in question was continually being depleted and replenished at the same time. In order to improve the CSC's ability to provide quick service to departments, it was decided to make even greater use of this process. As the CSC explained:

> The most important single technique or method in the new system will be the process of continuous recruitment and selection, which will correspond with the unbroken continuity of the requirements of departments. Continuous processes will be developed for these occupational groups for which there is a continuing need for immediate reaction to demands from departments for the filling of positions and will be supported by "banks and inventories" of qualified persons, and underpinned by up-to-date reports and progress analysis.[87]

By 1966 the continuing competition had proved a great aid by helping the CSC to meet nearly all the requirements for legal officers. It also enabled the CSC to increase its intake of economists and statisticians by 40 percent over the intake of the previous year. In the area of financial administration it allowed a reduction in the time between receipt of a requisition for appointment and the filling of the position from eighteen weeks to only four. The regional offices, which now had responsibility for staffing the administrative support and operational categories, also used the continuing competition with great success.[88]

When the Public Service Employment Act was passed in 1967, approving the new role for the Public Service Commission (PSC), it became necessary to make some organizational changes beyond what had been done in 1965. For one thing, the PSC lost several duties which it had been performing since 1918. With the transfer of overall responsibility for pay, classification, and conditions of service to the Treasury Board, the Pay and Standards Branch (which by 1967 had been renamed the Pay and Conditions of Service Branch) was disbanded. Similarly the Pay Research

Bureau, part of the CSC's organization since 1957, was moved to the Public Service Staff Relations Board. At the same time, the increasing importance of many of the functions which the PSC retained forced it to make further organizational accommodations. In this regard language training was separated from the other duties of the PSC, and a Language Bureau was created to meet the organization's responsibilities in this area. Within the Staffing Branch two new divisions were established, one to create selection standards to accompany the revised class system, and the other to provide for the process of delegating the PSC's staffing authority, and for the development of a monitoring and auditing system. As well, the Data Processing and Inventory Service, formed several years earlier, was reorganized into a Manpower Inventory Service into which all manpower inventories of the Staffing Branch were integrated. It provided an information base for staffing programs through its accumulation and dissemination of information on manpower needs and resources of the service and on labour market conditions. Finally, the advisory services of the PSC were reorganized into the Bureau of Management Consulting Services. This body, however, remained with the PSC only until the following year, at which time, following a governmental reorganization, it was removed to the Department of Supply and Services. The year 1968 saw the creation of the Bureau of Staff Training and Development whose expanded training functions replaced the Training and Development Service of the Staffing Branch. The Bureau had the overall responsibility for assisting departments and agencies to conduct their own training and development programs, for conducting centrally operated programs where such programs were warranted, for advising the Treasury Board on development and training needs, and for ensuring effective use of all training resources employed within the public service.

In this history of the internal developments within the CSC, 1965 stands as a very significant date. For not only did the creation of the staffing programs in that year allow the CSC to fulfil the new role planned for it, but the shift to a completely functional system erased the final heritage of the old framework established when its original role had been defined nearly fifty years earlier. In protecting the civil service from patronage, the CSC had proceeded on the assumption that, like the case with liquor, it was necessary to protect a person from the baser drives and urges of one's own nature. Patronage was thus to be placed out of reach by the CSC's complicated and involved procedural system. But as the external environment changed and altered with time, the internal needs of the organization changed too. With the great expansion and development in the field of personnel administration during and after the war, no longer was the need simply for a system aimed at protecting the service from patronage. However, institutions are always slow to change, and although the CSC expanded the scope of its activities to a considerable degree to meet the situation, the internal structure continued to reflect the original intentions of its creators long after the need for such a system had largely disappeared. While the 1960 reorganization attempted to level the old structure and to install an entirely new one in its place, it is significant that not until the CSC had defined and implemented a new role for itself were the last remaining vestiges of the system so closely connected with its old role finally swept away.

NOTES

1. H.C., Special Committee Appointed to Inquire into the Operation of Chapter 12, 8–9 George V, An Act Respecting the Civil Service of Canada, 1923, *Proceedings and Evidence*, testimony of Jameson, pp. 893–95. Foran agreed with Jameson that it was somewhere around twelve. Ibid., p. 3. The Spinney Committee of 1921, however, lists the staff in 1917–18 as twenty-four, including temporaries. H.C., Special Committee on Bill No. 122, An Act to Amend the Civil Service Act, 1918 [1921], *Proceedings and Evidence*, appendix no. 2, p. 415. A study completed by the Organization Branch in 1932 lists the staff at seventeen in 1918. CSC, Organization Branch, "Reorganization Work Effected through the Agency of the Civil Service Commission under the Civil Service Act," April 28, 1932 (mimeograph), p. 1. A memorandum to the 1938 Committee from the CSC puts the staff at twenty-five in 1917–18. Files of the CSC, PAC, vol. 376.

2. 1921 Committee, appendix no. 2, p. 415. It is listed here as 235 employees, but in 1923 Foran told the Malcolm Committee that the high point in employment with the Commission was 272. 1923 Committee, p. 3. The Organization Branch study of 1932 lists it at 246. "Reorganization Work by the CSC," p. 1.

3. Arthur Young and Company, "Civil Service Commission of Canada: Report on Office Organization and Procedure containing Proposed Manual of Rules," November 30, 1918 (typescript).

4. Ibid., p. 17.

5. Ibid., p. 15.

6. The information on the procedure within the CSC comes primarily from the testimony of the Commissioners and various CSC officials before the parliamentary committees on the civil service of 1921, 1923, and 1932.

7. Young, "Report on Office Organization and Procedure," pp. 15, 48.

8. H.C., Select Special Committee on Civil Service and Civil Service Act, 1932, *Proceedings and Evidence*, pp. 699–700, 882. MacTavish, for example, was absent for more than 700 days—nearly two years—during his six-year tenure, which greatly delayed business.

9. 1921 Committee, p. 64. Roche blamed the department concerned for not informing the Commission of the man's death.

10. See, for example, the testimony of Mr. Desbarats and Mr. Beauchesne, 1932 Committee, pp. 362–67, 466.

11. *Debates*, April 12, 1918, pp. 707ff; May 10, 1918, pp. 1725ff.

12. See, for example, Report of the Committee of Deputy Ministers on Civil Service Matters, December, 1922, King Papers, *Memoranda and Notes*, vol. 61, C48184–92.

13. This term was used originally by the Arthur Young Company in the *Report of Transmission to Accompany the Classification of the Civil Service of Canada*, p. 40.

14. CSC, *Civil Service Appointments: Guide to Procedure* (Ottawa: Government Printing Bureau, 1920), p. 14.

15. CSC, *Annual Report*, 1918–19, p. 9; CSC, *Annual Report*, 1920, pp. 10–11, 13; 1921 Committee, testimony of Foran, p. 52; H.C., Special Committee on the Operation of the Civil Service Act, 1938, *Proceedings and Evidence*, pp. 179, 219, 713; W. Foran, "The Status of the Federal Civil Service and the Accomplishments of the Civil Service Commission since its Inception," address made during the Canadian Civil Service Research Conference, *Proceedings of the Third Annual Convention*, 1926, p. 63.

16. 1932 Committee, p. 34.

17. 1923 Committee, pp. 72–73, 98, 128–29.

18. CSC, *Annual Report*, 1925, p. x.

19. CSC, *Annual Report*, 1925, p. viii; 1927, p. ix; 1928, pp. viii–ix; 1929, p. x; 1931, p. xix.

20. 1932 Committee, pp. 7–9. See also the testimony of MacTavish on this point, pp. 35–40.

21. Ibid., pp. 37–39.

22. 22–23 George V (1932), c. 40, s. 5.

23. 1932 Committee, pp. 75–81, 83–88, 148–52, 496–567.

24. Ibid.

25. 1938 Committee, pp. 57–58.

26. The information regarding the Kemmis-Simmins affair comes from the testimony of the Commissioners and various officials before the 1932 Committee and from a collection of documents relating to the whole affair in the PSC Library. Unless cited otherwise, all the following material is from these two sources.

27. The exception was Arthur Thivierge, the future Commissioner. The Report placed him in charge of a new Certification Branch and over his then superior Miss Elsie Saunders.

28. E. J. Garland to King, April 28 and June 6, 1927, King Papers, Corr., Prim. Ser., vol. 143, 121773–74, 121775.

29. Garland mentioned this fact in his letter of April 28, 1927.

30. King to Garland, June 14, 1927, King Papers, Corr., Prim. Ser., vol. 143, 121779–82.

31. Interview.

32. 1932 Committee, p. 651.

33. Memoranda of Gilchrist, Putman, and Bland in *Papers Relating to the Kemmis-Simmins Affair.*

34. 1932 Committee, *Report*, p. viii.

35. Report of Kemmis and Simmins, *Papers Relating to the Kemmis-Simmins Affair.*

36. Memorandum of Baril.

37. Memoranda of Putman and Bland.

38. Memorandum of Bland.

39. In a letter to Bennett in 1931 LaRochelle maintained that he had taken "the attitude of a magistrate" in appointments and promotions. LaRochelle to Bennett, July 9, 1931, Bennett Papers, no. 137, 91852.

40. 1921 Committee, pp. 103–4.

41. 1932 Committee, *Report*, pp. viii-ix.

42. H.C., Select Special Committee on Civil Service Act, 1934, *Report*, p. 386.

43. 1938 Committee, testimony of Bland, pp. 1518–19.

44. 1932 Committee, *Report*, p. viii.

45. 1938 Committee, *Report*, p. 1552.

46. H.C., Special Committee on the Operation of the Civil Service Act, 1939, *Proceedings and Evidence*, p. 3.

47. Memorandum from C. V. Putman to Bland, March 3, 1939, "Special Reports 1937–39" (mimeograph). This document is contained in the PSC Library.

48. Interview.

49. CSC, *Annual Report*, 1938, p. 30. Of these 6,406 appointments, 5,563 were to temporary positions and 843 were to permanent positions.

50. CSC, *Annual Report*, 1943, p. 30. This figure included 55,239 temporary appointments and 681 permanent.

51. P.C. 1/1569 (April 19, 1940) as cited in CSC, *Annual Report*, 1940, pp. 12–14.

52. This and much of the following material on the war and postwar years was taken from the information provided by the records of the Examination Branch staff meetings. Beginning in 1945, and continuing throughout the forties and into the fifties, frequent meetings of the staff of the Examination Branch were held at which papers were delivered or panel discussions took place. The papers and discussions largely centred on the problems of the Branch, but at times also dealt with topics related to the CSC's organization, procedure, and responsibilities. A fairly complete set of these meetings is held in the Staffing Branch Files of the PSC. All further references to staff meetings are to these.

53. In late 1939 or early 1940 Putman stepped down from head of the Organization Branch to take a position elsewhere in the CSC. He was succeeded by George H. Gilchrist, and when Gilchrist died in 1942, Jackson became chief of the Branch.

54. This information comes primarily from interviews. The authority granted to Jackson to deal with war duties supplements and with changes in the classification of temporary positions was not formally delegated until June, 1946, at which time the decision was recorded in the minutes of the CSC. Copy of CSC Minutes, June 19, 1946, Staffing Branch Files.

55. Wartime Information Board, "The Civil Service Commission," Reference Paper no. 32, January 19, 1944 (mimeograph), p. 17.

56. The figures for the branch staff in 1938 are based on the organization chart, dated February of that year, in the files of the CSC, PAC, vol. 377, File 26-10. The figures for 1946 are based on an organization chart prepared for the Gordon Commission, dated February 26, 1946, and contained in the private files of J. A. Murray, a former director of the CSC's Organization Branch.

57. Staff Meeting no. 50, October 21, 1946, p. 1.

58. Interview. See also Staff Meeting no. 50, pp. 5–6.

59. Staff Meeting no. 18, October 22, 1945, p. 2.

60. CSC, *Annual Report*, 1941, p. 6.

61. In 1946 turnover accounted for more than half of the total 52,638 appointments made. Approximately 80 percent of these appointments were of persons not previously employed in the public service. The remainder were largely cases of reassignments from departments or branches where personnel had become surplus. CSC, *Annual Report*, 1946, p. 5.

62. Staff Meeting no. 52, November 4, 1946, p. 2.

63. Copies of certain selected minutes are to be found in the information unit of the Staffing Branch of the PSC. These give evidence that the Commissioners several times initiated studies into the procedure of the CSC with a view to cutting delays.

64. This point was stated specifically in these terms by D. L. Gow at Staff Meeting no. 80, April 12, 1945, p. 1.

65. Staff Meeting no. 28, January 28, 1946, p. 4.

66. See the Memorandum to Examiners, no. 1946–63 (July 19, 1946).

67. Memorandum to Examiners, no. 1946–40 (April 17, 1946).

68. Memorandum to Examiners, no. 1946–16 (February 18, 1946) and Memorandum to Examiners, no. 1946–63.

69. See, for example, Staff Meeting no. 80, p. 2.

70. As a result of Ault's endeavours, the Organization Branch gave examining boards greater discretion in deciding the matter of qualifications for jobs instead of insisting on such things as the strict requirement that the appointee have a specific number of years experience. The examining boards were allowed more leeway in deciding if other factors compensated for a deficiency in one area. Staff Meeting no. 69, October 6, 1947, p. 2.

71. CSC, Organization and Methods Service, "Report on the Personnel Recruitment and Selection Procedure in the Civil Service Commission," Project no. 416, November, 1958 (mimeograph), pp. 4, 8.

72. Ibid., p. 8 and appendix C, p. 4. For interdepartmental promotional competitions the average time taken was 146 days, while competitions for local positions took somewhat less time at 137 days.

73. In 1953 an internal study found that the average time taken for all processes involved in Canada-wide competitions was 95.5 days. This time period, however, did not include the time taken for possible appeals which the 1958 study had considered. J. F. Dawe, "A Study of Canada-Wide Open Competitions," November 13, 1953, PSC File 543-R-14.

74. See chapter 10. Between 1945 and 1957 a Testing Division and a Staff Training Division were formed within the Personnel Selection Branch, an Organization and Methods Division created within the Organization Branch, and an Appeals Branch and a Planning and Development Branch established

in their own right. As well, the district offices were expanded and granted greater responsibility.

75. The terms of reference of the study called for a consideration of "the work processes of the Civil Service Commission in order to determine the feasibility of establishing procedural controls designed to expedite recruitment and selection." In its first few pages the report pointed out the futility of looking at procedure alone in this regard: "In brief it was found that it would be difficult, if not impossible to design and administer procedural controls without considering changes in organization." ("Recruitment and Selection Procedure," p. 3)

76. Ibid., pp. 10–15.

77. Ibid., pp. 41–45.

78. Heeney to Bryce, December 12, 1958, Heeney Files.

79. Heeney to Diefenbaker, December 22, 1959, ibid.

80. "Reorganization of the Civil Service Commission," internal document prepared for the Commissioners by S. H. Mansbridge, January, 1961 (typescript), p. 3.

81. Ibid.

82. Cited in W. J. Trudeau, "The New Structure of the Civil Service Commission," *Professional Public Service* 39 (December, 1960), p. 10.

83. Chapter 16 deals with the creation of the position of executive secretary, the most significant organizational development of these years.

84. "A Description of the New Approach to be Adopted by the Civil Service Commission to Fulfill its Role and Purpose in Staffing the Civil Service," internal document prepared November, 1965 (mimeograph), p. 2.

85. Ibid.

86. CSC, *Annual Report*, 1965, p. 7.

87. "A Description of the New Approach to be Adopted by the CSC," p. 3.

88. CSC, *Annual Report*, 1966, pp. 6–8.

Chapter Sixteen
Role of Leadership in the Civil Service Commission, 1918–1968

The whole idea of having three men to do
such an executive job was wrong from the
first. A commission is an admirable body
to investigate and report; in an executive,
unity of command is necessary. If the
C.P.R. ever wishes to go into bankruptcy,
it could hardly find a better way than to
put its general managership into commis-
sion and to give any two commissioners
power to overrule the third. Any old-timer
who remembers Sir William Van Horne
will think with joy of the language that
artist in profanity would have used to
describe such a suggestion.

Ask any of our great corporations or banks
what they would think of putting such a
three-headed Cerberus in their chief
executive position. To replace the present
three commissioners by one strong man is
the first essential.

W. L. Grant in the *Montreal Gazette,*
1931

ALL FORMS OF MANAGEMENT contain inherent problems particular to
them, and in this respect the three-member Civil Service Commission is
certainly no exception. Although these problems made themselves more
evident in the first fifteen or twenty years after 1918, the difficulty of functioning as a corporate body and of resolving disagreements and conflicts
among a body of three supposedly co-equal members has plagued the CSC
from time to time throughout its history.

When the new appointees, W. J. Roche and C. Jameson, joined Commissioner LaRochelle in the CSC in 1917, they were faced with a rather peculiar situation. The 1912 Civil Service Act amendment had stipulated that a chairman was to be designated from among the Commissioners, but had failed to assign him any superior role in relation to his colleagues.[1] This situation was perpetuated by the 1918 Act.[2] From a modern management standpoint the failure to provide a special role for the chairman might appear as a great oversight; but at the time there was probably a very good reason for its absence. The prevailing view was that the Commissioners were judges of sorts who essentially performed a semi-judicial function in making appointments and promotions to the civil service.[3]

Because their positions within the bureaucracy were seen in judicial terms, and because of the need for a mechanistic procedure on an operational level, it was felt that the Commissioners could operate only as a corporate body. As we saw in the previous chapter, this was at least the attitude adopted by the Commissioners themselves. Moreover, the corporate method of operation extended to all matters coming to the Commissioners' attention. All files and documents reaching their offices required the approval of at least two of the Commissioners before further action could be taken. Furthermore, no distinction was made between matters relating to general policy, routine business, or the internal administration of the CSC. Decisions were reached on the basis of the rotation of files between the three offices, while problem cases were dealt with at formal meetings, held twice a week. The chairman had no overriding vote on these occasions, so that a simple majority decided issues.

This method of management, while difficult enough to operate under normal circumstances, had serious consequences in view of some of the weak personalities the Government appointed to the CSC. During the chairmanship of Roche, Jameson and LaRochelle were able to outvote him and give a salary increase to the official in the Customs Department from whom they had received cases of liquor. Similarly, when MacTavish and Tremblay occupied the CSC, Roche's position was insufficient to offset the more deleterious effects of his less diligent colleagues.[4] These problems revealed one of the basic weaknesses of the three-man body. In comparison to his colleagues, Roche, also a political appointee, was a dedicated Commissioner whose integrity went unchallenged. It is possible that alone he might have spared the organization a great deal of the disrepute brought to it by his colleagues. By 1931 the justification for a three-man Commission had begun to wear rather thin for some people, leading to such attacks as that of W. L. Grant, quoted in the epigraph of this chapter.

The provision for a three-man body had come in 1912 after Adam Shortt complained of difficulties in reaching unanimous decisions with La-

Rochelle. Shortt, it seems, would have preferred a one-man CSC,[5] but the Government preferred the three-man arrangement and this provision became embodied in the legislation. Not surprisingly, there was little or no discussion of the possibility of a single Commissioner in 1918. At this time the three-man body was perhaps needed for symbolic value which it embodied. The elimination of patronage was an intensely emotional issue, and it might be argued that in this atmosphere the creation of a three-man CSC would have a greater psychological impact in representing the defeat of patronage in a way that a single Commissioner could not have done. Three men could also guard against the influence of patronage on one of their members. There was, however, an additional reason for the continuance of the triumvirate body. The 1918 Act had delegated a wide range of duties to the CSC, and there was some doubt expressed as to whether even three men alone could handle the "Herculean task." A. K. Maclean actually suggested the possibility that Parliament might have to appoint additional Commissioners in the following year.[6]

The first few years of administering the Act bore out the predictions for a heavy work load. Following the classification of the service, reclassification work began so that, while additional Commissioners were never added, the incumbents were far from idle. By the 1930s, however, the situation had changed greatly. Although CSC officials continued to complain publicly about their heavy tasks,[7] there is some doubt as to the veracity of their statements. With the Depression and the freeze upon all positions, the Examination Branch did not have a great deal to do. The Organization Branch, on the other hand, was in a complete state of doldrums. Reclassification work halted, as did reorganization work, which, indeed, never did consume a great deal of attention of the Branch in the first place. Of the six investigators in the Organization Branch in the early 1930s, only one, George Jackson, who was in charge of paring away excess employees in various departments, seems to have had anything substantial to do.[8] Although the Commissioners, like their employees, complained of their arduous duties, in such a situation they had little to do.

At the same time that the Depression greatly decreased the volume of work, the scandals in which Newton MacTavish and J. E. Tremblay became implicated demonstrated the bankruptcy of the supposed need for three Commissioners. The lesson was not lost to the percipient Secretary, William Foran. In an obvious effort to save the CSC from further embarrassment, Foran wrote to the Hon. Mr. Manion, the Minister of Railways and Lands, in 1932 suggesting that, "When the question comes up, as it must very soon, of appointing new Civil Service Commissioners, I should like you to take the attitude that there is no possible justification for the naming of three Commissioners." The immediate pretext for the recommendation lay in the small amount of work the Commissioners then had:

> I give you my word, as one who has been in the job since the Commission was established in 1908, that there is not at the present time sufficient work to keep one man busy let alone three. The Government has very wisely decreed that all positions through the Service which are not absolutely necessary should be abolished, and if in the face of such a decision three civil service commissioners were appointed, I am afraid that the action of the Government would, to say the least, seem inconsistent. . . . I feel very strongly that it would not be a bad move on the part of the Prime Minister, or some member of the cabinet named by him for the purpose, to talk over the situation here with Mr. Bland and myself.[9]

Manion relayed Foran's recommendation to Prime Minister Bennett, and a few days later the Government made an encouraging response but raised the problem of French-Canadian representation on a one-man body.[10] In his reply, Foran pointed to various studies in the United States that recommended one-man civil service commissions, and suggested that the interests of French Canadians were protected by conducting examinations in both languages. His plan, moreover, contained an additional protection to their interests:

> My suggestion would be as follows: Retire the present commissioners as ordered by Parliament; appoint one man for the present to carry on the work here; bring down legislation during the next session of Parliament, preferably after the Christmas adjournment, amending the Civil Service Act by providing for a commission composed of one commissioner and an assistant commissioner who shall also act as secretary; when this legislation becomes law, retire the present secretary and appoint in his stead a French Canadian as assistant commissioner and secretary. I am quite sure that this arrangement would be perfectly satisfactory to the French Canadian element.

As a measure of his own goodwill and selflessness, Foran added: "Personally, I did not intend to retire for another three years; but so convinced am I that the proposal I make is in the interests of the Government, the public, and the Commission itself, that I am prepared to take my superannuation now rather than see the old arrangement continue."[11]

Foran's efforts to spare the organization from further scandals by changing to a one-man body proved to be in vain. There is no record of the Government's response to this final request, but nothing was ever done in this regard, probably because of the political difficulty of ensuring French-Canadian representation.

BLAND'S LEADERSHIP, 1935–1955

Although Foran failed to remedy the difficulty of managing with three Commissioners, C. H. Bland managed to handle the problem in his own manner after he became chairman in 1935. His first significant move in this direction was to increase his influence among the Commissioners by procedural means. Sometime after becoming chairman, Bland terminated the departmental division of initial responsibility among the Commissioners so that all major matters came to his desk first before rotating to his two colleagues. This arrangement clearly put him in a controlling position. For one thing, it meant that he had carefully noted his decision on each major case before it came to the attention of his colleagues. Their view on these issues was thus easily coloured by his interpretation and decision. During the thirties and early forties there was also a degree of moral suasion accompanying his decision by virtue of the fact that he had been with the Civil Service Commission since 1909 and was acutely familiar with civil service matters, while Commissioners A. Potvin and J. H. Stitt were relative newcomers. Indications are that, unlike the situation in former years, the Commissioners rarely disagreed with the chairman's assessment; they simply initialled the file in question.[12]

This particular procedural arrangement applied only to major issues. Routine matters which involved little interpretation went first to the most junior Commissioner and lastly to Bland. In these cases Bland usually agreed with the assessment of his colleagues, or in the eventuality of a division of opinion, with the Commissioner whose judgement he trusted the most. Virtually all procedural and minor policy questions were handled in this manner. Thus, not only was Bland able to make his will predominate on all major policy decisions, but he never allowed the occasion to arise in any routine matter where he could be outvoted.

Bland's next move was to consolidate his power within the organization which meant, specifically, dealing with the power of the secretary. Foran, as we saw, was a crucial figure in the organizational and procedural framework of the CSC. All files passed through his hands before proceeding to the Commissioners, and he could, on his own volition, return the files for revision or forward them on with his remarks and comments upon them. He also attended the meetings of the Commissioners, could present matters for consideration, participated in the discussions, and executed their decisions. The suggestion remains that with his acute awareness of civil service matters, coupled with his forceful personality and vital position, he could not but exert a great influence upon the decisions of the Commissioners.

Even if he had wanted to, Bland was far too wise to tackle the secretary's power while Foran occupied the position. Two parliamentary committees had attempted to curb Foran's influence but to no avail. The reason for his ability to retain a hold on the position despite vociferous parliamentary criticism seems to have rested on the presence of a base of support independent of the organization, and in the face of which both the Commissioners and politicians were helpless to act. On the one hand, Foran was widely known to the general public, particularly to those concerned with the preservation of the merit system. To have removed him or to have reduced his influence would have brought forth cries of protest.[13] On the other hand, Foran seems to have exercised some degree of personal influence with various Prime Ministers. He often communicated his views on various civil service matters directly to the Prime Minister or his ministers—and not always in his official capacity as secretary of the CSC. He sometimes requested personal interviews with the Prime Minister and at other times his views were solicited by both King and Bennett, as well as by Borden earlier.[14] At the very least this leads one to suspect that his opinions held some weight in these official circles. This is perhaps indicated by the fact that following the hearings of the 1938 Committee, Pouliot wrote several letters to King urging him to fire Foran (the secretary had been appointed by Order in Council), but the Prime Minister does not seem to have looked with favour upon the suggestion and left Foran alone to retire on his own the following year, several years after the normal retirement age of sixty-five.[15]

Once Foran retired, however, Bland immediately seized upon the opportunity to divide up the secretary's duties among several different officers, so that the position could never again become a locus of power to rival that of the Commissioners. This put Bland in the commanding position in the organization. Not only was he preeminent among the Commissioners, but now, without Foran present, the heads of the branches reported directly to the chairman so that the staff was in effect solely responsible to him.

The procedural developments within the CSC during the war and postwar years only served to further consolidate Bland's position. The creation of the List Minutes and the subsequent delegation of authority to CSC officers reduced the procedural preeminence of the Commissioners within the organization. At the same time that the number of matters coming to their attention was greatly reduced, the lack of any formally delegated duties among them meant that Bland's two colleagues had nothing else of substantial importance with which to occupy their free time. Although this situation might normally have increased their propensity to direct their energies to other activities, none of Bland's wartime colleagues seems to have been particularly motivated to do so. Nor, since virtually all their contact with the organization existed through Bland, did they enjoy a sufficient base of support within the organization to allow them to do so. Consequently, the Commissioners had to satisfy themselves with what responsibility Bland gave them. This appears to have been very little indeed. Stitt had legal training and apparently interested himself in the occasional legal problem which came before the CSC. But beyond this, he acquiesced in the new arrangement and sometimes found himself at loose ends, even in the midst of the frenzied work in the other parts of the organization during the war. Different officers formerly serving with the CSC tell of being invited into Stitt's office on several occasions to chat because, as he said, he was "lonely" sitting by himself with nothing to do. Potvin seems to have found himself in a similar predicament, except that his training as a translator did not even prepare him for a role similar to that accorded Stitt, meagre though it was.

The declining influence of Stitt and Potvin is reflected by the fact that sometime after 1939, probably at approximately the same time as the List Minutes were created, the Commissioners suspended their twice weekly formal meetings. Regular meetings, in fact, were suspended altogether, and the Commissioners now met as a formal body only occasionally and sporadically to consider special issues. This development was probably due less to the pressure of war work than to the unassertive personalities of Bland's colleagues at this time. Neither Stitt nor Potvin was prone to question Bland's judgement on major issues, while on routine matters Bland's opinion decided any deadlocks.

This situation changed little with the appointment of Arthur Thivierge to replace Potvin in 1942. Thivierge had been an employee of longstanding on the CSC and was eager to avoid the problems the CSC had encountered in the past. He thought the same as Bland in most instances, and because, as the former head of the Assignment Branch, the least significant of the CSC's activities, he had not had an opportunity to acquire a wide range of experience, he was prone to defer to Bland's opinion on any major issue. The CSC, as a result, simply did not encounter the deep conflicts among the Commissioners that had characterized Roche's tenure. Since Bland's will predominated, it obviated the need for regular formal meetings as an opportunity to discuss problem cases. Formal meetings were now called on the rare occasions when a contentious matter arose. The Commissioners continued to function as a corporate body in the sense that all decisions necessitated the approval of at least two of their number, but virtually all decisions, even policy questions, were now reached simply by means of rotating files.

By the end of the war, then, Bland had succeeded in making the chairman's position preeminent in the organization. He had accomplished this by interposing himself between the other Commissioners and the staff and by ensuring through the force of his personality, combined with procedural arrangements, that his opinions on all major matters went unchallenged.

After the appointment of Stanley G. Nelson as Commissioner in 1945 to fill the vacant position left by Stitt's retirement, the relationship among the Commissioners changed to some extent. Bland and Nelson had been long-time colleagues on the CSC, both serving on it through the troubles of the twenties and thirties. Nelson had entered the CSC in 1921 and had followed in Bland's footsteps, becoming Chief Examiner in 1935. Over the years of working together in the Examination Branch, these two men had built up a considerable amount of trust and confidence in one another. Their close relationship naturally persisted after Nelson's appointment and exercised a dominant influence in the Commissioners' method of operation.

Basically Bland and Nelson, as one former CSC official has remarked, "operated in one another's pockets." Although Bland continued to be the dominant partner, he informally distributed some of the Commissioners' tasks between the two of them. Without enunciating policy on the matter and without altering the corporate conception of their duties, problems arising in the sphere of examinations were generally referred first to Nelson, while all other important matters continued to come first to the attention of Bland. Their close working relationship also made formal meetings even fewer. Meetings, in fact, often occurred when Bland or Nelson entered the office of the other with some problem or difficulty to discuss. Branch directors or other officials might be called in for consultation if their opinion was desired, but they took part in the deliberations in a very minimal and peripheral way. If and when a decision was reached on the matter under discussion, a secretary from the Secretary's Office was summoned to record the final result. Although the third Commissioner was frequently absent from these "board meetings," a memorandum noting the decision taken was circulated among the three Commissioners for their signature. Once approved, the memorandum was entered into the minutes along with the other decisions arrived at through the circulation of files.

It is significant that although the corporate method of operation among the Commissioners was perhaps more apparent than real after Nelson's appointment, the Commissioners never took steps to formally distribute duties between themselves. In the twenties and thirties the corporate method of management had been inextricably bound up with the mechanical method of processing work throughout the whole CSC; it was simply part of the process of protecting all levels of the organization from the malign influence of politics and nepotism. But during and after the war the CSC began to acquire a more complex purpose than that of merely safeguarding the merit principle; there was also the need for it to develop as a positive instrument of personnel policy. Although it was slow in actually developing this feature—it was forced into it by events rather than by design—the shift of emphasis was reflected within the CSC by the Commissioners' willingness to move away from the more mechanistic features of the merit system by delegating a good deal of operational responsibility to CSC officers. It is somewhat ironic, then, that this reassessment of its operations on the lower levels was not matched by changes on the Commissioners' level, where the corporate method of operation continued, with modifications, to hold sway on all matters coming to their attention. Admittedly the Commissioners still worked under the provisions of the 1918 Act. But Bland was a master at adapting such things to the changing needs of the organization, and it cannot be argued that the Act presented an impediment to change in this area. After Bland's retirement, in fact, the Commissioners proceeded with a functional division of duties without a change in the Act.

Yet there was a rationale on Bland's part for preserving this antiquated method of operation, for, combined with the lack of operational structure among the Commissioners, it allowed him to remain at the central and controlling point in the organization. By preventing a formal division of functions among the Commissioners, the corporate method of operation made him the sole channel between the Commissioners and the employees. All branches of the CSC and all officials were responsible directly to him so that no Commissioner was presented with the opportunity to build an independent base of power within the organization. Conversely, by delegating duties in an informal manner and by holding board meetings in the fluid way in which he did, Bland could effectively withhold a degree of responsibility from the third Commissioner and could share it with Nelson in whom he had implicit trust.

While this situation ensured that no single Commissioner was in a position to pose a threat to his power, it also ensured that no branch director could acquire an inordinate amount of power. The lack of a functional division of duties among the Commissioners prevented any single branch director or employee from building up his position by playing off the Commissioners against each other. Similarly, this situation acted as a balancing factor to the delegation of responsibility within the CSC during the postwar years. Although CSC officials received considerable operational

399

responsibility, all new, experimental, or policy matters were carefully scrutinized by the Commissioners, particularly Bland. Also officials were granted little discretion in deciding matters deviating at all from the norm, and the Commissioners insisted that all exceptional cases and even minor problem cases be referred to them.[16] While branch directors might be consulted on any of these matters, the relative secrecy of the board meetings, and the fact that they did not really assist in the final deliberations, meant that they had little ability to influence important or major decisions, and were frequently left with little knowledge concerning the basis on which such decisions were made. Bland, in short, made his will effectively predominate over the entire organization. As one former employee of the CSC aptly put it, "Bland was the king and he knew how to play the role."

Bland's ability to centralize all effective power within the organization saved the CSC from the strong disagreements over policy matters that had characterized Roche's term of office and which had led to intraorganizational conflict and subsequent public scandals. At the same time, it also provided a unity of direction in internal staff matters that had been woefully lacking during the Roche years. The 1918 Act, it will be recalled, had not granted the chairman any special precedence regarding matters of internal administration. Historically this meant that the Commissioners were corporately responsible for the internal administration of the CSC and that they handled these matters in exactly the same fashion as all other issues coming before them. The shortcomings of the method of operation had become painfully obvious in the Kemmis-Simmins affair in which there was a sharp conflict among the Commissioners over a matter of internal procedure. Unfortunately, the existence of the separate position of chief executive officer, occupied prior to the war by Foran, did nothing to remedy the problem. Although it was originally intended that the chief executive officer be primarily concerned with executing the internal administrative decisions of the Commissioners, Foran's powerful personality meant that often four, instead of three, minds were brought to bear on these matters. On his departure from the CSC the Commissioners separated the chief executive officer's position from that of the secretary's, and conferred upon Nelson the former appointment in addition to his duties as chief examiner. The position now lost a great deal of the significance it had formerly enjoyed and became more strictly limited to the simple execution of the Commissioners' decisions. Bland's accumulation of power in the forties in effect dispelled the need for an officer interposed between the Commissioners and the staff, and the position subsequently disappeared after Nelson's appointment as Commissioner in 1945.

Although the Commissioners continued to function as a corporate body in internal matters, Bland, by virtue of his preeminent role among them, was in effect the *de facto* chief executive officer. This became quite evident in the meetings of the 1954 secret committee studying the Civil Service Act. R. B. Bryce was concerned by the fact that the Act had failed to give the chairman a preferred role in relation to his colleagues and suggested that, as in the recent establishment of the St. Lawrence Seaway Authority, it should be made clear that the chairman was the chief executive officer, having control over the staff of the CSC. He also felt that the Act should specifically stipulate what duties were to be exercised collectively by the Commissioners and what duties should be exercised by the chairman alone as the chief executive officer. That Bland had coped with the situation to his satisfaction was made patently obvious at the first meeting of the committee. When the suggested changes were put forward, Bryce recorded, "Mr. Bland said he doubted whether such a change was necessary."[17]

Despite Bland's success in remedying one of the worst features of Roche's term of office by providing the staff with a unity of direction, one serious staff problem smouldered during his tenure. Although his method of operation had prevented any staff members from acquiring an inordinate amount of power by virtue of their organizational positions, some officers were able to exert a degree of influence within the organization out of proportion to the peer group to which they belonged. This was due to the fact that prior to the war the CSC was essentially a small, closely knit organization and that many of the officers from these years continued to have warm, friendly relationships with Bland, Nelson, and Thivierge with whom they were on a first-name basis. This group of employees basically constituted the "old guard" within the CSC and shared the Commissioners' misgivings about radical, innovative change. With the influx of younger officers during and after the war who were unconnected with the trials of the past, a situation developed in which the staff often divided over issues and plans according to the length of time they had been with the CSC. Because of the intimacy they enjoyed with the Commissioners, some of these older officers were able to get their own way in many of these matters.[18] These officers at times could go over the heads of their supervising officers and lay their case directly on the doorstep of the Commissioners to receive a sympathetic hearing. This situation was certainly not conducive to good morale within the organization and constitutes one of the major criticisms to be made of Bland's regime.

One interesting additional effect of Bland's method of decision-making was the change it produced in the role of the Secretary's Office. When Foran had occupied the position of secretary, he was to "attend the meetings of the Commission, present matters for its consideration, assist in its deliberations, and execute its decisions." With the informality which began to characterize the operations of the Commissioners following Foran's retirement, however, the secretary's role changed drastically. He no longer personally attended the meetings of the Commissioners: their decisions were recorded by a minor official from his Office. The Secretary's Office, in fact, gradually assumed the central housekeeping functions of the CSC. It handled all the internal services of the organization, as well as keeping the minutes and official records.

It is extremely difficult to attempt any overall assessment of Bland's leadership of the CSC. He had become chairman at a time when the organization had been drastically weakened by the trials of its existence in the twenties and early thirties. He took the CSC's poor position within the bureaucracy as a given fact, and starting from this point, managed to conserve and consolidate what power had remained with it. By working within the existing system of power relationships and by adapting the CSC to the changing external situation, he succeeded in deterring until after his retirement any radical reassessment of the Civil Service Act and the CSC's position in the bureaucracy. Whatever the merits of this fact, it was a considerable task.

At the same time, however, the fact cannot be overlooked that the Act and the CSC were long overdue for drastic alterations, and it is tempting to consider what another type of leadership might have accomplished in the same situation. Although everyone is attracted to the innovative and dynamic leader, it is dubious what results such leadership would have brought unless the organization possessed the support and authority of the Government in this task. That the CSC never enjoyed this support until 1957 was perhaps partly due to its own shortcomings, but it dictated to Bland the impossibility of acting in any innovative manner. Perhaps the best and the worst that can be said of Bland's style of leadership is that it suited conditions of the times.

The same conclusion might equally apply to Bland's style of leadership within the CSC, the question that really concerns us here. Former employees of the CSC in these years tend to be of two minds concerning Bland. They are in general agreement that he granted CSC officials a great deal of operational responsibility in the postwar years in order to meet the external demands placed upon the organization. But several officials also criticized the extreme caution with which he approached any innovative thinking. Suggestions for changes, or for new developments, always came from below and were decided rather authoritatively by the Commissioners. Moreover, his occasional tendency to compromise the merit system—or, in his own words, to "sacrifice the little things in order to protect the bigger things"—often frustrated officers who were of the strong opinion that the CSC should at times make a stand upon principle. Generally they were prone to feel that while they did possess a good deal of responsibility for the daily operations of the CSC, they had little influence on, or participation in, the critical decisions determining the course of the organization. They were often not even aware when questions of this sort were under consideration.

Yet, if such leadership is not entirely excusable, it is understandable. Bland had become chairman of an organization in 1935 which had suffered because his predecessor had not been in a strong enough position to avert the more unfortunate tendencies of his less diligent colleagues. By consolidating power in his hands, Bland successfully ensured that his judgement on all important matters reigned supreme, thereby saving the organization from many of the problems of its earlier years. At the same time it allowed him to adapt the CSC within given limits to meet the changing external environment. Bland, in the final analysis, offered exactly the same style of leadership within the organization that had characterized his guidance and direction of the CSC within the bureaucracy: he was no innovator; instead he simply manipulated the situation as he found it to arrive at a satisfactory working relationship designed to protect the organization. It is doubtful whether, under the circumstances, anything more could be expected.

ROLE OF THE FRENCH-SPEAKING COMMISSIONER, 1918–1957

Although Bland had successfully made his position preeminent among the Commissioners, preventing either of his colleagues from building a position of power within the organization, the French-speaking Commissioner always enjoyed a potential base of support independent of the organization. This support rested on the fact that, on the one hand, his appointment necessitated the approval of the Quebec wing of the Cabinet,[19] while, on the other, his role was generally taken by the public and the politicians "to represent the interests of the French Canadians before the Civil Service Commission."[20] The French Commissioner, in fact, was often seen from both within and without the bureaucracy as an ombudsman of sorts for French Canadians. Members of Parliament from Quebec were often in the habit of phoning or writing him to recommend a candidate or to air a complaint. Prospective candidates frequently contacted him on their own behalf and French-speaking civil servants informed him of cases of suspected discrimination. In addition, departments often consulted him on their own initiative concerning appointments and promotions in Quebec.

During the twenties and thirties, and even in the early forties, the conception of the French Commissioner as representing the interests of

French Canadians had little basis in actual fact. For one thing, in view of the supposed impartiality of the merit system, this representation had no means by which it could make itself felt. The idea inherent in the merit system was that there was one best man for any given job and that this was independent of the mother tongue of the candidate, whether French or English. In 1938 Bland set down on record the policy that the Civil Service Commission was in no way to actively promote bilingualism. He judged the only duty of the CSC to be that of filling positions according to the requirements stipulated by the department. If a department required a bilingual person then the CSC would make such an appointment from the highest ranking bilingual person on the eligible list. But in the absence of such a requirement it was not, under any circumstances, the duty of the CSC to stipulate that a certain position should be filled by a bilingual person.[21] Within the context of the impartial "machinery" of the CSC, the French Commissioner could have no special interests to represent.

Actually, we can probably better define the role of the French Commissioner in terms of *protecting* rather than *representing* the interests of French Canadians. The presence of the French Commissioner would tend to ensure that French Canadians were treated as objectively and impartially as all other candidates. In an operational context this simply meant that the French Commissioner merely represented an extension of the CSC procedure which attempted to produce this result. During the early 1930s the examiners and clerical assistants in the Examination Branch had been divided into two sections, one of which was to concern itself with examinations administered in French. All appointments within Quebec also had to secure the approval of the head French examiner before the chief of the Examination Branch approved them. It is not known whether LaRochelle then took any special authority over Quebec appointments from this point, but during Tremblay's term all such matters came first to his attention regardless of whether or not they concerned departments over which he had the initial division of responsibility.[22] Although this allowed Tremblay to delay appointments at times under the guise of "suiting the department" whenever the deputy minister requested his indulgence, the majority of cases probably passed through his hands in the usual fashion. The practice of routing files in this manner continued after Tremblay's retirement, but his successors seem to have been less prone to act solely on the departments' wishes. They all worked under the same pressures that Tremblay did, but investigated only those cases they considered valid in terms of the merit system and resisted the more questionable requests for their influence.

Apart from this rather meagre acknowledgement of their special status within the bureaucracy, the French Commissioners did not perform any other duties out of the ordinary within the CSC. Bland's accumulation of power during the war effectively prevented any organizational base for a distinctive role. With the advent of the delegation of operational responsibility to CSC officers, the French Commissioner actually occupied a position of less responsibility within the organization than in the prewar years. Although this might normally have increased the propensity of the French Commissioner to fall back upon his special base of power outside the organization, neither of Bland's French-Canadian colleagues during the war was personally inclined to exploit these possibilities. Potvin's ability to do so was seriously curtailed after 1935 because he was a known Conservative serving during a Liberal term of office. Consequently he seems to have satisfied himself with his existing position.

Arthur Thivierge, Potvin's successor in 1942, was similarly not inclined to take advantage of the situation, if for different reasons. Prior to his appointment, Thivierge had occupied the position of chief of the Assignment Branch of the CSC, not a particularly prestigious position within the bureaucracy, or the CSC, for that matter. He was, simply, in many respects a relatively junior employee. Once appointed Commissioner, this factor gravely limited his ability to use his independent source of power. He has been described as a man who felt inferior to his colleagues on the CSC and to the deputy ministers with whom he was often forced to deal. Consequently, Thivierge, like Potvin, usually deferred to Bland on all matters.[23]

Thivierge's successor, however, was, as one former officer put it, "another kettle of fish, altogether." Alexander J. Boudreau, appointed in 1948 after Thivierge's death, was remarkably well educated for the position—actually, he was the first Commissioner since Shortt who could boast such academic attainments. Boudreau had graduated from Levis College and had attended the Agricultural College at Ste. Anne de la Pocatière where he received a Bachelor of Agricultural Science with a specialty in rural economics. After teaching at this college for some time, he was granted a Littauer Fellowship by the Graduate School of Public Administration at Harvard University in 1942, and in the following year received the degree of Master of Public Administration. Boudreau then proceeded to Laval University where he became a professor of organization and administration.

Boudreau was not the type of man to satisfy himself with the relatively inactive role of his predecessors on the CSC, and from the beginning set about to carve out his own distinct role, separate from and independent of the internal needs of the organization. He had originally been sought out and approached by the Jean Committee, or "the Committee of Five," the semi-official group of five Quebec M.P.'s formed in the late forties which attempted to attract well-qualified French Canadians to the federal services. After his appointment, Boudreau seems to have taken it upon himself to promote the same end as the Jean Committee from a position within the bureaucracy. In his capacity as Commissioner he made a great many speeches in Quebec, particularly at the universities, aimed at arousing interest in the opportunities of employment with the federal government. He also took the part of French Canadians in the civil service. He fought with departments and deputy ministers to end discrimination against French-Canadian employees and to induce them to appoint French Canadians to more responsible positions. Some senior civil servants recall Boudreau as "a real fighter" and one of the persons primarily responsible for "waking them up" (the Ottawa civil service establishment) to the plight of French Canadians.

Boudreau's activities in this regard were made all the more difficult by the frequent departmental resentment which his concern caused. In addition, the more he espoused his cause, the greater the tendency of French Canadians to contact him. This placed a great burden and responsibility upon his shoulders. Various officials have in fact described the job of the French Commissioner in this period as "the toughest job in the civil service." One former CSC employee who officiated for Boudreau while the Commissioner spent some time in Cambodia with the United Nations claimed that his mail ran two to three times that received by Bland or Nelson, and that he was continually beseiged by calls from Quebec M.P.'s and from French Canadians. In view of what he did manage to accomplish, it is regrettable that Boudreau's effectiveness was muted to some extent by his unfortunate propensity to come to public attention under what were not always the best of circumstances.

Within the CSC, Boudreau seems to have been left pretty much on his own to carve out a separate role as he saw fit. Bland continued to dominate the Commissioners on all matters other than those specifically concerned with CSC business in Quebec, in which case Boudreau probably exercised the decisive influence. Boudreau did take a degree of interest in all matters before the CSC and at times ran into conflict with his two colleagues. As a rule, though, his primary concern was with cases dealing with French Canadians, and he was generally willing to follow Bland's lead in other areas. Boudreau, in essence, occupied what one senior French-speaking civil servant formerly with the CSC has called "a French ghetto" within the organization. When Paul Pelletier, Boudreau's successor on the CSC, visited the Commissioner before his own appointment, he came away with the distinct impression that Boudreau was "not in the mainstream of the Commission." He existed, on the contrary, somewhere on the periphery of CSC activities, pursuing his primary interest on his own.

This arrangement worked fairly well during Bland's term of office, but caused problems for his successor. Bland was a skilful leader well practised in effecting a consensus among disparate elements. While Boudreau's degree of independence may have at times created problems, the CSC usually presented a united front in public. But when Bland retired in 1955, things changed perceptibly. Although Nelson was appointed chairman, he did not immediately assume a position which had the same trappings of power and authority as that of his predecessor. It had taken Bland several years to create his position of power, a position which was based very much upon the force of his personality. Now, with his absence, the situation reverted almost to what it had been prior to 1935. To make matters worse, no third Commissioner was appointed so that the CSC faced the same problem of agreement between two Commissioners which had caused problems for Shortt and LaRochelle. Boudreau's independent bent of mind, along with conduct which provided a continual source of embarrassment for the CSC, meant that the consensus which Bland had been able to effect for twenty years fell apart to a large extent and rifts began to appear on the CSC's hitherto united front. Fortunately for the CSC, this situation was not of long duration owing to the Government's determination to appoint Heeney to the chairmanship at his earliest convenience.

THE HEENEY YEARS

In 1957 Nelson expressed to Prime Minister St. Laurent his desire to retire from the Civil Service Commission on account of ill health. The Government willingly accepted, for A. D. P. Heeney was at last free to accept the appointment to the chairmanship. Boudreau also tendered his resignation at this time to accept the position of Consul-General for Canada at Boston, leaving the way clear for the appointment of a full new Commission. Heeney was given a free hand to choose his two colleagues and to accompany him he chose Ruth Addison and Paul Pelletier.

The appointment of Heeney had a tremendous impact upon the organization. Never before had a man of his stature occupied the chairmanship. He had been the person primarily responsible for organizing the cabinet Secretariat during the war and had been a former Under Secretary of State for External Affairs and Ambassador to the United States. Combined with the mandate handed him to study the administration of the Civil Service Act and the employer-employee relationship, his appointment signalled a hopeful new future for the CSC. His colleagues, too, added considerable stature to the CSC. Miss Addison, the first woman Commissioner, as well as the first woman to attain such high rank in the federal civil service, had entered the service in 1941 after several years with the Manitoba government. She had served with three different departments before becoming executive assistant to the deputy minister of the newly created Department of Defence Production in 1951, from where she was appointed to the CSC. Paul Pelletier had gained a considerable knowledge of civil service matters from the vantage point of the Privy Council Office where he was assistant secretary at the time of his appointment. He had also served as assistant secretary to the Gordon Commission in 1946 and secretary to the Federal-Provincial Conferences of 1950 and 1955–56, as well as secretary to the Royal Commission on Broadcasting in 1956.

It is not at all surprising that with their impressive experience the three Commissioners found the administrative arrangement within the CSC somewhat constraining. The corporate method of operation had resulted in the practice that all matters referred to the Commissioners for a decision required the approval of at least two of their number before being considered valid. Consequently the Commissioners were often required to approve many documents about which they might have little knowledge, or which involved trivial matters, and might otherwise have been conveniently dealt with by one Commissioner. Pelletier recalled that the number of relatively insignificant matters requiring his attention, "hit me right in the face when I first came into the Commission." Heeney, in particular, might be expected to have found this system a hindrance. He was an intensely organized person and Mackenzie King had made good use of his abilities to develop the cabinet Secretariat. Files remaining with the Public Service Commission reveal him also as a man who carried this penchant for organizing into his daily approach to work. He kept meticulous notes of important conversations and letters of all important transactions and collected these into topical files for future reference. The haphazard method of operation among the Commissioners which he inherited was simply not suited to his style of leadership.

The CSC quickly benefitted from Heeney's abilities. Shortly after assuming their new positions, the Commissioners, on Heeney's suggestion, agreed to a functional, as well as a departmental, division of duties among themselves. Addison took general supervision over all pay and classification matters, as well as those in the area of conditions of employment, civil service staff organizations, and the National Joint Council. Pelletier took charge of selection, recruitment, appointment, and promotion matters and also dealt with issues in the areas of appeals, transfers, reassignments, layoffs, exemptions, regulations, rejections, dismissals, and answers to parliamentary questions. As well as providing general direction to the review of the Civil Service Act and regulations, Heeney handled planning and research, training, public relations, annual establishment reviews, and shared with Addison some duties in the area of salary research. Heeney also handled all problems relating to CSC personnel and administration. All files, memoranda, and formal submissions coming to the attention of the Commissioners for information, decisions, or formal approval were to be referred on the basis of the areas of initial responsibility. Matters which did not submit to this functional division or departmental matters of a general nature were referred to either Addison or Pelletier on the basis of a departmental division of duties between them.[24]

The division of responsibility significantly altered the reporting relationships of the branches. Branch heads no longer reported directly to the chairman but to the Commissioner having charge over their area of jurisdiction. The Organization and Classification Branch thus reported to Addison, while the Personnel Selection and Appeals Branches reported to Pelletier. The Planning and Development Branch and the Secretary's Office continued to be the responsibility of the chairman. This allowed the Commissioners to handle singly, and without reference to one another, many matters relating to any one branch, including policy questions, which had formerly required the approval of all three. Many documents, particularly submissions to Council, continued to require their joint signature, but on the whole the number of matters needing this sort of approval was considerably reduced. All recommendations requiring the formal approval of the Treasury Board, for example, were forwarded under the signature of the Commissioner having relevant jurisdiction over the matter in question.

To complement the developments in this area, the Commissioners instituted formal weekly meetings. These had the practical advantage of co-ordinating the activities of the Commissioners by keeping them informed and aware of the overall operation of the CSC. The meetings provided an opportunity to discuss outstanding matters of importance, to identify special problem areas, and to consider policy questions relating to the whole organization or to one or more branches. Branch directors and other CSC officials attended these meetings when matters pertaining to their respective jurisdiction were under discussion. Unlike the situation in former years, they were not merely consulted but actively participated in the deliberations. Heeney chaired these meetings which were conducted in a relatively formal manner, closely following an agenda circulated beforehand.

What made this method of operation work successfully when a similar structural arrangement had created such problems during Roche's term of office was the status of the chairman. Bland had succeeded, where Roche had failed, by building up his personal power as the unchallenged leader within the organization, but had accomplished this with neither official nor unofficial government recognition of the fact. The Government simply took no notice of the situation, according Bland no more prominence than that set out in the Act and holding all three Commissioners equally accountable for the deeds of the CSC. Although the Act remained unchanged at the time of Heeney's appointment, there was a significant change in the factors surrounding the stature of the chairman. Heeney was one of the most senior men in the civil service in 1957, and one of the best known and most respected. He had been chosen by the Government to perform a specific task on the CSC because of the abilities he possessed, and had even been given the responsibility of choosing the two colleagues to aid him in this task—the first time a government had handed such responsibility to the chairman. In short, personal stature and prestige combined with government recognition to make him the acknowledged leader among the Commissioners in a way none of his predecessors had been. As Heeney himself has said: "It was a *carte blanche* appointment. I was not *primus inter pares*, I was *primus* among the Commissioners. . . . They knew they were junior to me; they knew my assignment, and there was no question as to who was the commanding officer. . . . I really did not care what the Act said [respecting the fact that it did not give the chairman a preeminent position]: this was the situation, the others knew it and they abided by it."

This allowed Heeney to do what neither Roche, Bland, nor Nelson had been capable of doing. Because he was the person primarily responsible for the *operation* of the CSC, he occupied a position somewhat analogous to that of a deputy head of an operating department. In other words, Heeney was in a much more obvious way than Bland the acknowledged chief executive officer of the CSC. Accordingly, he was always careful to distinguish between matters related to the internal administration and work of the CSC, for which he considered himself solely responsible, and matters of general policy or interpretations of the Act and regulations, for which he felt the Commissioners were corporately responsible.[25] In his capacity of chief executive officer, Heeney could thus easily distribute operational responsibility to his two colleagues for certain of the CSC's functions.

While this arrangement in theory meant that he could be outvoted on a policy issue, in practice this situation never arose. Because of his personal stature and force of personality, it was natural that his opinion would carry a great deal of weight in deliberations and could not help but influence the outcome of the decision. At the same time, Heeney never used his preeminent position to coerce his colleagues into accepting decisions which were not really their own—besides it is unlikely that either

410

Pelletier or Addison would have found this acceptable. Rather, Heeney was masterly at arriving at a consensus which reflected all points of view. In debate he would listen to all sides and would sum up what impressed him as the main points put forward and the conclusion to be reached. It was rare for a dissenting voice to be raised against his summation.

It is interesting that despite Heeney's preeminent position within the organization, his chairmanship paradoxically constituted what was in effect a democratization of the CSC. Although he provided the organization with strong direction, Heeney's two colleagues, as well as the officers of the CSC, were granted a great deal more power and responsibility than any of their immediate predecessors had enjoyed. Bland's colleagues had had responsibility without power, while CSC officers had enjoyed a measure of power without responsibility. The delegation of duties among the Commissioners in 1957 now provided all Commissioners with a vital role in the CSC's operations and greatly extended their influence within the organization. Within this decentralization of power the Commissioners worked closely together, attempting to harmonize their actions; as Pelletier has said, "We operated as a team." Heeney was careful to respect the authority granted to the other two Commissioners and never used his position to interfere unduly in matters under their purview. At the same time, he was diligent in keeping Pelletier and Addison informed of affairs under his area of jurisdiction. The files of the PSC show that during the negotiations with the Government over the Heeney Report, he carefully recorded what had transpired at each meeting and circulated the report to his colleagues.

The officers of the CSC reaped similar benefits during his tenure by acquiring a broader role in helping to determine the major decisions and the direction of the CSC. At the weekly meetings of the Commissioners their views were actively sought, and they aided in the deliberations of the Commissioners. Unlike the situation in former years, they had first-hand knowledge of matters under consideration and had a vital opportunity to influence decisions.

The changing operational role of the Commissioners and CSC officials during this period serves to underline the evolution of the policy-making role of the Commissioners within the bureaucracy and within the organization itself. It will be recalled from the previous chapter that during the twenties and thirties the Commissioners conceived of their role within the bureaucracy in judicial terms. From their viewpoint, their role was not to innovate but to administer faithfully Parliament's wishes; they were judicial administrators, not policy-makers. Within the organization this mentality became reflected in the deep involvement of the Commissioners in the daily routine, so that there was little differentiation between policy matters and other matters of daily business. But after 1945 the CSC responded to the changing nature of the civil service by developing and expanding its services in many areas. It is significant, however, that while the CSC's role changed on an operational level, it was not accompanied by any re-evaluation of its role within the bureaucracy. The Commissioners still saw their job essentially in judicial terms and did not actively speculate on or plan the direction in which the CSC moved in these years. On the contrary, new ideas, plans, and policies inevitably arose at the lower levels of the organization as the situation demanded and were forwarded to the Commissioners for a decision. The CSC, as a result, rarely evolved consistent policy in any one direction, but simply reacted to situations as they arose. When, on one occasion, it did attempt to assess the situation in which it found itself, the effort was doomed to failure. In 1956 it attempted to define its position in a study entitled "Personnel Administration in the Government Service." Unfortunately, instead of using the opportunity to fashion a proposed future role, the Report concerned itself almost wholly with detailing how the Treasury Board over the years had usurped the CSC's powers. The Report argued not for a new role, but instead looked back to what it saw as the CSC's golden age—the period before the rise of the Treasury Board. It argued, quite ineffectively, that the CSC should be recognized and strengthened as the central personnel agency of the Government.[26]

During the Heeney years, however, a new element was added to the role of the Commissioners. Within the bureaucracy, the Commissioners, and Heeney in particular, became innovators of sorts due to the study undertaken on the Act and the creation of the Pay Research Bureau. Within the organization the same general situation came to prevail. The Commissioners became involved in the planning and policy-making in a more direct and active manner. This is perhaps most dramatically illustrated by the fact that the central thesis of the Heeney Report concerning the CSC's proposed role as an independent arbiter in staff relations originated with Heeney himself. The Commissioners, in short, became more than mere administrators within the organization; they were equally as much policy-makers who were responsible for defining the role of the organization in different areas.

But neither was this merely a passing phenomenon connected only with the study of the Act; the Commissioners saw this innovative and policy-framing role as an inherent part of their duties and made some attempt to institutionalize their new activity. On the one hand, the Heeney Report endeavoured to establish their new role within the bureaucracy. It essentially proposed a relatively basic, rather bare, Civil Service Act which would leave the Commissioners free to administer it within wide limits.

Within these wide limits they could, using their own discretion in the matter, enunciate personnel policy and develop programs on the basis of what one former senior CSC officer had described as "humanitarian principles." It can be readily seen that this conception of their role stands in sharp contrast to the picture presented from the Roche and Bland years of Commissioners functioning within strictly defined limits.

Similarly, within the organization the Commissioners attempted to firmly establish their policy-making role by freeing themselves from some of the relatively trivial detail which occupied their time. Exceptional matters, policy questions, and problem cases had always been referred to the Commissioners during Bland's and Nelson's rule. But after 1957, while all policy questions still came to the attention of the Commissioners, the CSC officers received wider authority to act on their behalf in many of these other cases.[27]

Paradoxically, while the general bureaucratic role of the Commissioners became less judicial and more innovative, the role of the French-speaking Commissioner became less innovative and more administrative. This was the direct result of the fact that, in contrast to Boudreau, Pelletier assumed a more influential role within the organization which took away any personal need for a role independent and separate from it. Pelletier had visited Boudreau before assuming his new duties and came away determined not to accept his peripheral position within the organization. It was, in fact, only on the understanding that he would be a vital part of the CSC that he agreed to his appointment.

Once in his new position, Pelletier, with the approval and support of Heeney and Addison, attempted to alter fundamentally the role of the French Commissioner as Boudreau had left it. It was no easy task. He tried to circulate the news that he had no exclusive concern with French-Canadian matters, but it was some time before this information went abroad in the bureaucracy and among the politicians. Despite his endeavours, he estimated that 80 to 85 percent of his time was originally spent on matters of this nature. Quebec M.P.'s and prospective candidates continued to contact him to elicit his aid, and he was still seen as something of a French-Canadian ombudsman. Pelletier stood firm, however, and with time he was able to devote more attention to other matters. By the time of his retirement from the CSC in 1963 he had met with considerable success in his purpose. His successor, Jean Boucher, stated that he was rarely, if ever, bothered by the sort of calls which had earlier plagued Pelletier.

The changing roles of the Commissioners within the organization at this time also had fundamental implications for the role of the secretary of the CSC. The latter now attended every meeting of the Commissioners, recorded their decisions, and informed CSC officers of decisions relevant to them. In keeping with the more active role of the secretary, the Secretary's Office was divided, with the internal personnel function and financial services becoming the Administration and Personnel Branch. The functions more strictly pertaining to secretarial duties, such as the maintenance of the minutes, the official documents, and the regulations of the CSC, were retained in the Secretary's Office, which became more clearly an appendage to the Commissioners' offices.

It is virtually impossible to overestimate the effect which Heeney's appointment and leadership had upon the organization. During his tenure the CSC regained a unifying sense of purpose and direction reminiscent of the 1917–19 period. Most of this enthusiasm centred around the study of the Civil Service Act and the creation of the Pay Research Bureau, but it spilled over to inspire the entire organization. It was also accentuated by Heeney's ability to attract talented and intelligent persons to the CSC to work on the study of the Act and in the PRB. Officers formerly with the CSC during these few years fondly recall it as being at the zenith of its powers and influence at this time, and they are fairly well unanimous in the opinion that Heeney was the best chairman the CSC has ever had. In his two short years as chief executive officer, Heeney thus left an indelible imprint upon the organization. Perhaps the only unfortunate aspect of his tenure is that he built up hopes and aspirations for the future within the organization which were dashed with the publication of the Glassco Report.

THE HUGHES YEARS

When Heeney left the Civil Service Commission in early 1959 to return to Washington as Canadian Ambassador, the Government had some difficulty in finding an immediate successor to replace him. As a result the CSC was once again left with only two Commissioners. Although this situation did not produce the deadlock which similar situations had presented earlier, it did create problems. Addison and Pelletier worked well together and were able to avoid conflict, but neither was willing to assume the leadership of the CSC in the absence of a chairman. This had the unfortunate tendency to rupture the high level of enthusiasm which had characterized the organization for the past two years. Heeney had given the CSC direction and purpose, but with the completion of the Heeney Report, his departure, and the Government's noncommittal reaction, much of this was lost. The CSC needed strong, immediate leadership to commit and channel the energies of the organization. The two Commissioners continued with the planning on the proposed reorganization of the CSC, but there was no one to supply initiative in other areas.

Unfortunately for Hughes, when he became chairman in July, 1959, it

414

was not at the most propitious moment in the CSC's history. He succeeded a man who rallied and inspired the CSC to an unprecedented degree; Heeney's shoes were difficult to fill. To complicate matters, Hughes had some serious reservations about portions of the Heeney Report, the very document that had served as the major rallying point in the CSC. Moreover, while the Government had not shown itself particularly disposed to officially adopt the Heeney Report, it had failed to indicate what the future role of the CSC was to be. Hughes' mandate, in other words, was not overly clear. All these factors made his job particularly difficult and contributed to problems during his tenure. For one thing, Pelletier and Addison had been deeply committed to the Heeney Report, and the appearance of a chairman who was not in full agreement with many of its recommendations sometimes resulted in conflict among them. There was, in fact, often a deep division of opinion between Addison and Pelletier on the one hand and Hughes on the other.

Among the officers of the CSC the situation was somewhat similar. Because of the noncommittal stand of the Government, Hughes was unable to disperse the uncertainty surrounding the CSC's future role. Consequently, the enthusiasm and momentum built up under Heeney continued to deteriorate during Hughes' term of office. This problem was aggravated by Hughes' personal style of leadership, which was distinctly different from what the organization had been accustomed to for the past two years. He basically retained the same functional division of duties left by Heeney, as well as the same reporting relationships, but his approach was altogether different. He apparently had little patience with some of the more mundane aspects of administration with which he had to deal and tended to concentrate on those which did interest him. Moreover, civil servants connected with the CSC at this time invariably describe Hughes as excessively "legal-minded." These two factors combined to produce an overriding concern with the CSC's appeal function.

Before 1961 there was no statutory basis for appeals; the CSC heard appeals against promotions and the refusal of statutory increase on the authority of regulations passed by it. As a former judge of the Ontario Supreme Court, Hughes felt this situation to be deplorable. He was particularly distressed that appeals were not granted as a matter of right to civil servants but were simply at the pleasure of the CSC. One of his favourite phrases was that "one must not only be fair, but one must appear to be fair," and this maxim guided his desire for a statutory basis for appeals. He took particular interest in ensuring that the proposed legislative changes of 1961 contained clauses which would remedy the situation.

This caused some dissension within the organization. Many CSC officers felt that to recognize appeals in law would take away much of the flexibility of the system. They agreed that the basis on which appeals could be lodged should be widened, as the Heeney Report had suggested, but strongly urged that the system not become too legalistic. They were of the opinion that there were other functions of the CSC, such as Organization and Methods work, which were just as important as appeals, and should be recognized in law, as the Heeney Report had recommended. Hughes, however, persisted in his original aim.[28]

It is evident that the division of opinion in the CSC at this time went much deeper than a mere conflict over particulars in the Heeney Report and over the CSC's appeal function. Whether it was recognized at the time or not, the real problem was centred around the issue of the role of the CSC within the bureaucracy. In contrast to Heeney, and to Pelletier and Addison, Hughes, probably as a result of his legal experience, wanted a fairly detailed Civil Service Act which would have the CSC operating within clearly delineated limits and on clearly defined principles. It was, in a sense, to be a return to the original conception of the CSC for he saw the role of the Commissioners as almost exclusively judicial in form. Issues would be brought before them and the Commissioners, weighing the pros and cons, would render a decision in each case. There would be very little room to exercise discretion on humanitarian grounds as Heeney had wanted; the Commissioners would simply make judgements based on the principles set down in the Act.

With such a variant conception of the CSC and the role of the Commissioners within the bureaucracy, it is not at all surprising that Hughes was unable to unite the organization or to provide it with strong direction. Persons serving the CSC during these years recall Hughes as a warmer and more approachable man than Heeney but feel that he was not the leader Heeney was. Yet it is helpful to remember that the leadership problem was just one of a number of problems facing the CSC at this time and assumes relative insignificance beside some of the others. For, by the end of 1960, although the Government had decided on the basic outline of the new Act, the Glassco Commission study had begun, thereby throwing the future role of the CSC again into doubt. Consequently, the organization tended to drift along in these years not entirely certain of where it was going. As one former senior officer put it, the Hughes years were "not a happy period" for the CSC. If this was the case, it was perhaps less the fault of the Chairman than of the uncertain situation in which the CSC found itself.

PROBLEMS OF INTERNAL MANAGEMENT, 1959–1962

Apart from the troubles relating to Civil Service Commission policy in these years, there were also increasing difficulties in the area of the internal management of the organization. The lack of any statutory provision for a special role for the chairman in internal administrative matters had, as we saw, caused considerable trouble during Roche's tenure. Both Bland and Heeney coped with the problem, each in his own distinctive way. But since each of them had accomplished this in an ad hoc and unofficial manner, the roots of the difficulty still remained to provide a stumbling block. This was particularly true of Heeney's solution, for while Bland had at least maintained the outward appearance of corporate leadership in this respect, it was an open question whether or not Heeney's arrangement deviated from a strict interpretation of the Act.

These problems once again came to light when Hughes became chairman. Although he stepped into the arrangement left by Heeney, he had more difficulty making it work. The functional division of operational responsibility among the Commissioners could at times make it extremely difficult to differentiate between what constituted administrative direction of the staff by the *de facto* chief executive officer and what constituted interference into the responsibilities of fellow Commissioners. This had not presented too great a problem to Heeney since his two colleagues were usually in agreement with him on most matters. Hughes, on the other hand, faced a somewhat different situation. The differences of outlook on the part of the Commissioners on occasion served to obscure their ability to make this distinction.

The proposed reorganization of the CSC along functional lines only promised to make this problem all the more acute. To remedy what could easily develop into conflicting and overlapping staff direction, consideration was given during the planning for the 1960 reorganization as to the efficacy of interposing an executive director between the Commissioners and the staff. The plan was eventually rejected, however, when it encountered the opposition of the Commissioners:

> There was some discussion of the role of the Commissioners, both individually and collectively. It appeared that the Commissioners would find unacceptable a restrictive role of policy making only, leaving the management of the Commission's total operations to an Executive Director. On the other hand, if the Commissioners were to perform the normal management role of a Deputy Minister or General Manager, then it was obviously desirable to determine a logical division of interest and responsibility.[29]

At the same time that vain attempts were being made at this level to correct the problem, Hughes was searching for a solution through other channels. In the fall of 1959 the Government approached him to gain his personal views on the Heeney Report. In the last pages of his lengthy memorandum submitted on this subject, Hughes turned to the management problem within the CSC:

> It seems to me that provision must be made for the possibility of the Chairman of the Commission being over-ruled by his colleagues. This may not be of importance on questions of policy because these are quite properly the subject of discussion and the Commissioners should, if possible, present a united front thereon. But as the Commission is at present organized, individual Commissioners have operational responsibilities which may never reach the stage of discussion and on which it is physically impossible to achieve a united front by joint decision. Only recently I was able, with the concurrence of the other Commissioners, to reinstate the practice of having all submissions to Treasury Board signed by all three Commissioners, at least when they were all in Ottawa. It is important in my view for the Act to state clearly, as in the Parole Act, that the Chairman shall be the chief executive officer of the Commission and responsible for its operations. Other jurisdictions have recognized this need particularly in the case of the United States Civil Service Commission and the New York State Civil Service Commission. As things stand at present the Chairman in Canada can only use his influence as *primus inter pares.*

Hughes also suggested that consideration should be given to increasing the number of Commissioners, "particularly if the importance of the appellate functions of the Commission is recognized." In addition he pointed out that the present tenure arrangements were insufficient to guard the independence of the Commissioners: "It is at least questionable that real independence can be achieved by Commissioners who are appointed for ten years only. As the period of appointment draws to an end and a Commissioner looks for a further term he must necessarily become more sensitive to pressure by the political officers who hold the next ten years in their gift." Interestingly enough, he suggested, as had Borden in 1908, that they should be put in the same position as judges subject to retirement at the usual civil service age of sixty-five.[30]

With the exception of the last two of these recommendations, the Government appears to have looked with favour upon Hughes' suggestions. In February of 1960 it issued a cabinet decision on the changes which it would contemplate in the Civil Service Act. This decision primarily concerned itself with what features of the Heeney Report were to be adopted in the proposed act, but in passing also dealt with the composition of the CSC and the powers of the chairman: "The Commission should consist of

418

a Chairman and not more than four other members appointed by the Governor in Council. . . . The Chairman shall be the chief executive officer of the Commission and as such shall have power to give directions to the staff of the Commission and carry out its operations but not to exercise the corporate powers of the Commission."[31] Clauses embodying these decisions were then framed and included in Bill C-77, which after second reading was referred to a parliamentary committee.

These provisions caused considerable controversy within the CSC. For although Hughes and some staff associations felt the need for more than three Commissioners,[32] both Pelletier and Addison disapproved, as did much of the CSC staff. They felt that this measure would make the organization too top heavy and unwieldy.[33] Eventually these arguments won the day for although the original bill introduced in 1960 contained provision for five Commissioners, when it was reintroduced in 1961 as Bill C-71, it provided for only three.

Second, both the bills of 1960 and of 1961 had made use of Hughes' suggestions by stipulating that the chairman was to be the chief executive officer and was to have "supervision over the direction of the work and staff of the Commission." Both Pelletier and Addison saw the threat of considerable danger and difficulty if this position was implemented. As Addison explained to Hughes:

> This goes without saying [that the Chairman is chief executive officer] but by putting it in the Act would seem to imply a special status which could affect the principle of having more than one opinion brought to bear on matters affecting the merit system and give undue weight to the authority of the Chairman. The concept of the Commission has always been that of three persons exercising their best judgment as equals to uphold the merit principle.[34]

Addison had struck upon an interesting and important point. By making the chairman preeminent in internal staff matters, as well as giving him supervision over and direction of the work of the CSC, the Act ran the risk of giving him an added prestige which easily might increase his influence upon the corporate decisions of the Commissioners. It was not simply a question of giving the chairman control of the staff, but involved a deeper principle: the very composition of the CSC. The problem of three co-equal Commissioners had caused problems for the CSC since 1917, however, and it might be fairly argued that the general preeminence of the chairman was not an undesirable feature. Moreover it cannot be denied that although they maintained the practice of corporate responsibility in matters respecting the merit system, Bland, Heeney, and to a lesser extent

419

Hughes, by virtue of the stature they already possessed, exercised a degree of influence in these decisions somewhat greater than those of their colleagues.

Nevertheless it was the intention of neither the Government nor Hughes to give the impression that the chairman was to have the deciding voice in all major decisions of the CSC. After some private negotiations with the special committee studying Bill C-71, the solution finally agreed upon, and subsequently passed by the House, was to designate the chairman simply as the chief executive officer and in a second clause stipulate that, "for the purposes of this Act, the Commission and the staff of the Commission constitute a department and the Chairman is the deputy head in relation thereto."[35] It was apparently felt that this would make the chairman more clearly responsible only for internal administrative and staff matters, and the Commissioners as a whole corporately responsible for all other matters.

While these clauses essentially gave legal recognition to what had been an actual fact for several years and removed any pressure on the chairman to cope with internal administrative matters in an ad hoc manner, they by no means remedied all the problems relating to the internal management of the CSC. They did not really remove the danger of which Addison had warned nor did the simple designation of the chairman as the chief executive officer help to clarify the problem of conflicting jurisdictions. The difficult, if not impossible, task of differentiating policy matters from administrative matters continued at times to cause problems in distinguishing between the responsibilities of the chairman as chief executive officer, the functional responsibilities of the individual Commissioners, and the corporate responsibility of the Commissioners as a whole. This fact became evident to a member of the Glassco Commission studying the CSC in 1961:

> While the Chairman is the chief executive officer of the Commission, his signature, in theory, holds sway only in situations affecting the supervision and direction over the work and staff of the Commission. The approval of at least two Commissioners is required before any matter affecting the Federal Service which lies within the jurisdiction of the Commission, becomes legal. . . .
>
> The problems inherent in such a form of management will not be dealt with in this paper. Senior personnel in the Civil Service Commission, however, did comment during interviews that the distinction between the exercise of authority by the Commission itself, and any of the Commissioners individually is often confusing. The Chairman is required and has authority to approve some matters in the capacity of the Commission Chairman—that is as a Deputy Head of a Department

420

but in others, the approval of the whole Commission is required and he must obtain the approval of at least one other Commissioner. Except that this troika may sometimes produce delays, there was no evidence during interviews with Commission staff that it interfered with the decision-making process.[36]

It is necessary to recognize that there are particular problems inherent with any three-man body of co-equal members, as indeed there is with any form of management. It is doubtful, on the other hand, that it is possible to prevent one of their number from sooner or later exercising a decisive influence in their corporate decisions. And, as the Glassco study recognized, there is always the problem of conflicting jurisdiction as soon as the members take on functional responsibilities.

LEADERSHIP OF THE CSC, 1963–1965

Although the Glassco researcher cited above may have found little hindrance in the decision-making process within the Civil Service Commission in 1961, problems began to appear shortly thereafter. In the latter part of Hughes' term and during the period between his retirement and MacNeill's appointment, the Commissioners' meetings began to deteriorate to the point where they served less and less as a forum for discussion of policy matters and became progressively more concerned with minor administrative matters.[37] This was an extremely unfortunate situation since it was at precisely this moment that the CSC needed strong dynamic leadership to guide it through the storm of criticism produced by the Glassco Report.

The appointment of R. G. MacNeill early in 1963 did little to remedy the problem. Because of the differences of opinion and the general lack of communication which soon developed between MacNeill and his two colleagues, the CSC was without the united leadership among the Commissioners it so badly needed. In fact, as we saw in chapter 13, due to these circumstances certain Commissioners and staff officers were attempting to formulate plans for a defence of the CSC and for a proposed new role, all without having adequate knowledge of the decisions which were being made on these subjects elsewhere in the bureaucracy. MacNeill, in addition, does not seem to have been as appreciative as were Heeney and Hughes for the need to distinguish between the corporate powers of the Commissioners and the individual responsibilities of the chairman. Consequently the Commissioners sometimes found themselves committed to positions which did not accurately reflect their own views.

The problem of securing a consensus among the Commissioners during

MacNeill's term of office further contributed to the deterioration of the Commissioners' meetings. These meetings assumed such relative unimportance that they became much more infrequent than the weekly meetings conducted under Heeney and Hughes, sometimes occurring only once a month or less. This in turn produced two major results. On the one hand, policy formulation and decision-making of any importance tended to be taken from this locality and was conducted instead among several senior officials of the CSC in informal consultation with the various Commissioners. Second, the lack of any effective policy coordination created difficulties for the functional division of operational responsibilities among the Commissioners. To a large extent the division of responsibility fell apart in these years leaving a vacuum in the direction and supervision of the staff. Much of the history of the problems of management in the CSC during this period is essentially a record of attempts to cope with these two problems.

The policy formulation vacuum, which was to some degree a holdover from the Hughes years, was partially filled in early 1963 when J. D. Love was appointed special assistant to the chairman. Although the appointment was only official acknowledgement of what he had been doing for several months, Love essentially took charge of deciding the CSC's response to the Glassco Report. When he left the CSC in the late summer of 1963 for the Preparatory Committee, however, the vacuum once again reappeared. On this occasion it was partially filled with the creation of the position of executive secretary in October. One of the chief purposes of this position, occupied from the beginning by G. A. Blackburn, a long-term senior CSC officer, was to attempt to coordinate and provide an orderly basis for the development of general and procedural policy. In this regard, all proposals of branch directors for policy changes passed through Blackburn's hands. He was to review all such proposals and was expected to perform much of the basic background work on policy proposals before consideration by the Commissioners. He ensured that other directors who would be affected, directly or indirectly, by any specific proposal were made aware of such proposals and were given the opportunity to comment. While he had no power to change any proposal coming from the directors, he was to view all proposals from the overall responsibilities of the CSC and could, on the strength of this, return proposals to the originating director and suggest revisions. In addition, Blackburn undertook any projects of special character which involved major policy changes or major new programs. Under this responsibility he became deeply involved in helping to develop the CSC's language-training facilities.

Although Blackburn's position was to be primarily one of coordination as far as policy was concerned, it was inevitable that because of the existing vacuum, he and his assistant, S. H. Mansbridge, came to play a crucial role in formulating policy in many areas. To some extent both men picked up where Love had left off, but with the creation of the Preparatory Committee on Collective Bargaining the scene had changed somewhat, and they both became deeply involved in attempting to plan a new role for the CSC. The major outcome of this effort was Mansbridge's paper on the staffing function which served as a basis for the later creation of the Staffing Branch.

Despite their vital role in the organization, both Blackburn and Mansbridge realized that their degree of influence was at best a temporary solution to an old problem, and they made continual attempts to re-establish the primacy of the Commissioners in the management of the CSC. In December of 1963, Blackburn forwarded a memorandum on the management problem prepared earlier that year by Love. Love had made the point that with the breakdown of Commissioners' meetings there was a very real lack of any formalized procedure for policy formulation and coordination. He made suggestions along several lines which represented in effect a significant departure from procedures in the past.[38] Only Commissioner Pelletier seems to have seen the original memorandum, and there is no indication of his reaction. Although the Commissioners rejected Love's specific proposals when Blackburn resubmitted the document in December, they did use it as a basis for discussing their method of operation. Blackburn was able to secure a measure of consensus among them on what constituted the role of the Commissioners as a corporate body, the role of the individual Commissioners, and the role of the chairman as chief executive officer. Basically, these respective roles bore a rough resemblance to those of the Heeney period except that the chairman was not accorded the same degree of power.[39]

The next step, however, created more of a problem. On the strength of this consensus, Blackburn drew up a list of CSC activities grouped on a functional basis which he hoped would serve as a basis for a division of areas of prime interest among the Commissioners. Although a similar arrangement had worked well during the Heeney period, both Addison and Boucher were now apprehensive about accepting such a division of responsibility. The fact that the CSC's role was in itself far from being settled and that they already felt cut off from developments elsewhere in the bureaucracy made them understandably cautious about losing personal contact with some areas of the organization's duties and responsibilities. While they eventually agreed to a functional division of operational responsibility, it was not clearly defined and did not go to the extent that it did in the Heeney and Hughes years.

While troubles continued to plague the CSC on the level of policy formation and coordination, internal management problems once again arose to cause some difficulty. Because of the slow and sporadic nature of the evolution of delegation of functions, responsibilities, and authority within the CSC, there was no clear idea as to the exact extent of the powers of the branch heads in relation to those of the Commissioners. This created problems in two areas. On the one hand, the Commissioners expressed some concern that the branch directors might be deciding matters upon which they felt it was more correctly their prerogative to make judgements. Although a study of this subject was commissioned,[40] the matter seems to have never been settled to any satisfaction during MacNeill's term of office. Second, this ill-defined relationship meant that the Commissioners tended to become involved in a wide range of daily, routine business. By using their positions to direct special attention to specific questions in the work of the different branches, they also tended to distort work priorities. Moreover, they created morale problems on some occasions by going over the heads of several management levels to deal directly with subordinate officers.[41]

In a paper on the CSC's organization, prepared in early 1965 at the request of the Chairman, Mansbridge suggested that the best solution for these various problems would be for the Commissioners to extricate themselves from routine matters and become more clearly involved only with policy. He also urged that they should once again try to arrive at primary areas of interest among themselves, and "once this has been done, to respect the divisions in a meaningful manner." He added that this would not mean the exclusion of any one Commissioner from a particular policy area, but would simply be a procedural means of bringing all relevant policy matters before the Commissioners. Policy matters would be referred to the Commissioner having the primary concern in each policy area. Each Commissioner would be responsible for the basic examination of policy questions arising in his area and would arrange to bring a considered appraisal and proposals before his colleagues.[42] Unfortunately, like the problem relating to the extent of the responsibility and authority of the branch directors, this second difficulty was never satisfactorily settled during Mac-Neill's tenure.

LEADERSHIP OF THE CSC, 1965–1967

Fortunately for the Civil Service Commission, MacNeill's successor, John Carson, met with greater success in coping with the organization's internal management and administrative problems. From the time of his entry into the Civil Service Commission, in September, 1965, Carson drew a clear distinction between the corporate powers of the Commissioners and the individual responsibilities of the chairman as chief executive officer. Like Heeney and Hughes, Carson conceived of himself as being solely responsible for the administration and operation of the CSC. His solution, however, was somewhat different from that of his predecessors. He terminated all functional responsibilities among the Commissioners so that the branch directors were in the first instance responsible to him alone. This accumulation of power was balanced by Carson's desire to follow the precept of the Glassco Commission to "let the managers manage." The creation of the Staffing Branch shortly following his appointment allowed the Commissioners to put this precept into practice, and Blackburn, now the director-general of the new Branch, was granted a degree of operational responsibility much more extensive than had hitherto been the practice in the CSC.

The improvements in this area were matched by the endeavour to restore the Commissioners as the central policy-framing body in the organization. This was largely accomplished by removing them from the routine administrative matters with which they had been to a great extent occupying their time. The Commissioners' meetings were also restored to a weekly basis so that they once again served a policy coordinating purpose. In addition to the consideration of policy matters, the Commissioners turned their attention to special problems or activities of which they agreed, after mutual discussion, to take charge.

This latter arrangement worked well at the time owing to the great number of special matters requiring the Commissioners' attention. But there was some apprehension that after the passage of the new Act, and with delegation of staffing authority to departments, the organization might become too top heavy. For a time consideration was given to having the Commissioners double as branch heads, but this idea was passed by when it was realized that the problems it was likely to generate would far outweigh any benefits it would bestow. In 1966 the Commissioners tried to arrive at a different solution when they recommended in the first draft of the proposed act that the CSC should consist only of a full-time chairman and two part-time Commissioners. The Cabinet, however, seems to have felt that this was not politically feasible and rejected the proposal. The Commissioners later attempted yet another solution when they once again assumed a partial functional responsibility for CSC activities. In this case one Commissioner was given supervision over the appeals function and the other over issues and activities related to the official languages. This supervision pertained to policy matters only, and the chairman retained full administrative responsibility in the sense that he had full and final control over the money and staff involved.

Carson's solution to the method of operation among the Commissioners basically constituted the first successful attempt since Heeney's chairman-ship to cope with the problem. Although the two solutions differ in some respects, the reason for their success seems to hinge to a great extent upon the stature and power of the chairman. While he perhaps lacked Heeney's prestige due to his relative newness to the bureaucracy, Carson clearly emerged as the central point of focus among the Commissioners. On the one hand, he managed to provide a unity of direction in internal staff mat-ters lacking since Hughes, and, at the same time, without impinging upon the corporate powers of the Commissioners, supplied the organization with strong direction and guidance within the bureaucracy as did Heeney. In this regard it is interesting to find that under Carson the Commissioners' conception of their role within the bureaucracy closely resembled that of Heeney's; Carson, in fact, brought to fruition Heeney's plans for an inno-vative CSC. The Commissioners basically saw the merit principle as something that changes with time to reflect the different values of society at various stages of its development. They felt that it was the duty of the organization to be cognizant and sensitive to these changes and within certain limits to make the bureaucracy similarly aware of them by acting as their sponsor. In the area of language policy and training, for example, the Commissioners, as we saw, played an innovative role in securing the Government's commitment to the program enunciated by Prime Minister Pearson in April, 1966. The PSC appeared similarly intent on making the bureaucracy aware of the problems which women face in the public service through its sponsorship of such studies as Dr. Archibald's *Sex and the Public Service.*

In conclusion it might be well to observe that the problems with the three-member Civil Service Commission, as with any three-man body, has made it a very awkward instrument of management and decision-making. Although the specific problems have changed and shifted over the years, the difficulty of finding a suitable working arrangement for the three Com-missioners has been a source of trouble for the organization since 1918. Having said this, however, it is equally as evident that the three-man Com-mission has also proved to be a workable proposition—Bland, Heeney, and Carson all handled the problem successfully, each in his own distinc-tive manner. But it is important to reiterate that these periods of relative stability have been marked by the presence of a strong-willed chairman who has clearly attained a preeminent position among his colleagues. In the final resort perhaps the only question that remains to be answered is whether the reoccurring problems with this form of management continue to outweigh those of any other.

426

1. 2 George V (1912), c. 10.
2. 8–9 George V (1918), c. 12, s. 3.
3. In 1907 Robert Borden, then leader of the Opposition, likened the proposed positions of the Civil Service Commissioners to those of judgeships. *Debates,* June 25, 1908, pp. 11339–41.
4. See chapters 5 and 7.
5. See chapter 2.
6. *Debates,* May 11, 1918, p. 1801.
7. H.C., Select Special Committee on Civil Service and Civil Service Act, 1932, *Proceedings and Evidence,* p. 175.
8. Interview.
9. These comments of Foran were contained in a letter from Manion to Bennett, September 17, 1932, Bennett Papers, no. 136, 91517.
10. The fact of the Government's response became evident in a letter from Foran to Manion who forwarded a copy to Bennett, September 22, 1932, ibid., 91523–25.
11. Ibid.
12. Unless cited otherwise the quotations and information in this chapter come from interviews.
13. In his articles in the *Gazette* in 1931 in which he attacked the three Commissioners and suggested that they be replaced with a single Commissioner, W. L. Grant highly praised Foran and felt that he should continue in his present position. See the *Montreal Gazette,* 1931.
14. The private papers of Borden, King, and Bennett in the Public Archives are all rife with letters to and from Foran on a great many subjects.
15. J. F. Pouliot to King, November 14, 1938, and November 22, 1938, King Papers, Corr., Prim. Ser., vol. 257, 218900–904 and 218905–8 respectively.
16. The memorandum that had announced the original delegation of responsibility in 1946 had also contained the directive that "in any case where there was no standing instructions of the Commission applicable to the case, or an officer does not fully understand the instructions or the relevant provisions of the Act or Regulation, he shall refer the matter to the Commission for a decision." (Memorandum to Examiners, no. 1946–63 [July 19, 1946]) Apparently some officers began to use too much of their own discretion for at a staff meeting in 1947, Dr. Ault advised the examiners that "the Commissioners had expressed the wish to see more of the cases which deviated from the ordinary procedure." (Staff Meeting no. 67, September 8, 1947, p. 1) In 1950 a revised list of officers who had the authority to sign on behalf of the Commissioners contained the warning that "such delegated authority can be exercised only on matters in which the policy and practice of the Commission have been well established." (Memorandum to Heads of Branches, February 26, 1950, Staffing Branch Files)
17. R. B. Bryce, "Summary Minutes of a Preliminary Meeting to Consider a Revision of the Civil Service Act," July 23, 1954, Heeney Files.
18. The conservative attitude of some of the older CSC officers becomes quite evident in reading over the accounts of the staff meetings in the Examination Branch. At two meetings in 1946 one examiner, Mr. Lochnan, suggested that in some cases the departments were in a better position than the CSC to find and select suitable appointees and that the possibility should be explored

of turning the recruiting job over to them in some instances: "Mr. Lochnan thought that the departments were genuinely anxious to obtain the best qualified personnel and that administrative necessity would cause them to proceed in accordance with our principles." A senior examiner, Dr. L. Moffit, although not a particularly long-term CSC employee, shared some of the attitudes of the older employees. He expressed shock at the suggestion, calling it "a bombshell." Dr. Moffit suggested that "none of us is so naive as to believe that the departments alone would adhere to the necessary regulations and procedure for a competitive merit system." (Staff Meeting no. 53, November 18, 1946, p. 4, and Staff Meeting no. 54, November 25, 1946, p. 1)

At another meeting earlier in 1946 a different aspect of this conservative, protective mentality was revealed when Charlie Garrett, an employee of the CSC since the early 1920s, spoke on "The Ethics and Conduct of a Civil Service Examiner." Garrett warned that examiners should beware of all discussions of politics, even with intimate friends. Although they are subject to abuse and insults, examiners should bear their burden stoically: "They must control their impulse to retaliate with physical violence. Self-control is an essential for a Civil Service Examiner or he could soon disgrace his profession and the Commission that employs him." Moreover, "our conduct both in and out of office hours undoubtedly reflects on the Civil Service Commission, favourably or unfavourably. Our private time is our own, but the moment our actions take a turn where they are likely to cause complications for the Commission, or bring injury to its prestige, we are no longer acting ethically. . . . If over-familiarity with spirits lets down one's control of the temper or the tongue so that unseemly brawling or gossiping on official matters occurs, ask yourself— is that ethical conduct on the part of a Civil Service Examiner?" In fact, an examiner should avoid talking about official matters and office gossip at all times, even to his wife, and in particular to the press which was "a certain road to trouble." (Staff Meeting no. 31, February 18, 1946, pp. 4, 7, 8)

19. While little is actually known of the circumstances surrounding the appointments of LaRochelle and Tremblay, more information exists on the appointment of Potvin. It is clear from Bennett's private papers that after Tremblay's retirement the Prime Minister turned over the power of nomination of the French Commissioner to the ministers from Quebec. This actually caused some difficulty as they could not immediately agree on one candidate. See chapter 7. Similarly when Potvin retired in 1942, it is evident that King's Quebec colleagues had a great deal of influence in appointing Thivierge. See J. A. Blanchette to King, July 30, 1942, King Papers, Corr., Post 1939 Ser., vol. 39, 64174; Norman McLarty to King, July 20, 1942, ibid., vol. 46, 71433.

20. This was the sentiment expressed to King by one Quebec M.P. at the time of Thivierge's appointment. A. Goulet to King, July 19, 1942, ibid., vol. 42, 67481.

21. Files of the CSC, PAC, vol. 376.

22. 1932 Committee, pp. 721, 752.

23. Interviews.

24. "Division of Duties between Commissioners," Internal Procedure no. 1 (July, 1957, and amendments of August and September, 1957), Maclean Files.

25. Heeney's realization that at times he acted in two different capacities is perhaps best illustrated by an amusing example. At one point a branch head

in the CSC devised an elaborate scheme similar to those put forward by departments to justify more staff. He approached Heeney with the plan and the Chairman agreed to place it on the agenda of the next meeting of the Commissioners. At the meeting a few days later, Heeney introduced the item saying that as deputy head of an operating agency, he had an interesting proposal to consider regarding a requested increase in the establishment of one of the branches. In the next sentence he announced, however, that as chairman of the CSC, he found the proposal outrageous and completely lacking in merit. Interview.

26. "Personnel Administration in the Government Service," internal document prepared for the Commissioners, 1956 (typescript).

27. See, for example, "Delegation to Branch Heads," Internal Procedure no. 2 (July, 1957), Maclean Files.

28. In this regard, the remarks and impressions of an officer who interviewed Hughes for the Glassco Commission are interesting and informative:

Mr. Hughes' interests are strongly centred on a new and elaborate appeal procedure in the Bill presently before the House. His approach to this is almost wholly legalistic. The appeal procedure has the atmosphere of a court. There will be opportunities for applicants to be represented by counsel, all of which is very much to Mr. Hughes' liking. He feels strongly that appeals should be as much the right of the Civil Servant as is his right to draw pay. . . .

Mr. Hughes seems completely unimpressed and uninterested with any suggestion that ordinary grievance procedures might be far more effective and helpful than the cumbersome appeal procedure contemplated by the Act. . . .

It would be, I take it, within the powers of the Commission to make regulations outlining the steps to be taken before a formal appeal is lodged with the Commission and these steps would be, presumably, the usual grievance procedure. There is no interest in, or intention of doing, any such thing and, in my opinion, a great gap exists in the personnel organization as a result.

The present plan must mean that there will be a considerable increase in appeals when the new Act comes into force and that many of these appeals will be either frivolous or based on misinformation and misunderstanding, which normal grievance procedure and counselling could easily eliminate. It was impossible for Mr. Hughes to see this. . . .

Mr. Hughes feels the new Bill will provide more flexibility and a greater exercise of judgement on the part of the Commission staff and on the part of the responsibilities delegated to Deputy Ministers. (Interview with Mr. Hughes, June 22, 1961, files of the Royal Commission on Government Organization, vol. 52)

29. "Reorganization of the Civil Service Commission," internal document prepared for the Commissioners by S. H. Mansbridge, January, 1961 (typescript), p. 17.

30. "Observations on the Heeney Report," memorandum enclosed in a letter from Hughes to Fleming, November 16, 1959, PSC File 041-91.

31. Record of Cabinet Decision (Meeting of January 7, 1960), ibid.

32. H.C., Special Committee on the Civil Service Act (Bill C-71), 1960–61, *Proceedings and Evidence*, pp. 34, 75, 194, 349.

33. Pelletier to Hughes, May 12, 1960, and Addison to Hughes, May 30, 1960, PSC File 041-91. See also 1961 Committee, pp. 349–51.

34. Addison to Hughes, May 30, 1960, PSC File 041-91.

35. 9–10 Elizabeth II (1961), c. 57, s. 5(1) and (2). The wording in the second clause was essentially that proposed by Pelletier in a memorandum to the special committee in May of 1961. In the recommendations he made at this time, however, Pelletier did not include provision for naming the chairman as the chief executive officer. It seems that he would have wished only for the one clause. "Memorandum for the Special Committee on the Civil Service Act," contained in a letter from Pelletier to R. S. MacLellan, May 17, 1961, PSC File 041-92.

36. Manpower Project, "The Civil Service Commission," Interim Report no. 54, November 28, 1961, files of the Royal Commission on Government Organization, vol. 89.

37. This fact becomes quite evident from looking at the minutes of the Commissioners' meetings in these years. The fact, too, was apparent to at least one member of the staff. In a memorandum "Policy Formation, Policy Co-ordination and Management in the Civil Service Commission," J. D. Love attempted to suggest ways of improving the situation. He began by contrasting the past procedure with that of the present: "At the present time there are two closely related instruments of policy co-ordination in use, the Commissioners' meeting and the Secretary's Office, both of which have a long history. In the pre-war days . . . the Commissioners' meeting was an important institution. Control over the documentation put before the meeting and (control) over the minutes recording the decisions reached was firmly in the hands of the Secretary, who functioned much in the same manner as would an Executive Director. Without tracing all the stages of evolution, it can be said that there has been a tendency to retain the form but not the substance of the Commissioners' meetings. In recent times at least, discussion at these meetings has been concerned for the most part with relatively minor matters, major questions of policy being aired and disposed of in other ways. There has been a parallel decline in the role of the Secretary's Office, which has found it increasingly difficult to maintain touch with the process of policy formulation." (Memorandum from Love to the Commissioners, March 3, 1963, PSC File 044-22L8)

38. Love felt that the chairman should be more clearly recognized as the focal point of administrative control for all the branches. In his scheme all branch directors would report to the chairman who would deal with all matters on the basis of policy established jointly by the Commissioners. Cases posing problems of policy determination or concerning matters on which there was no clearly enunciated policy would be referred to the other Commissioners for consideration. He also felt that the traditional Commissioners' meetings had outlived their usefulness. In their place he suggested that a series of standing committees be established, each concerned with one of the basic functions of the CSC such as recruitment and selection, promotions, transfers and appeals, and classification and pay. The membership of these committees would be made up from the directors and senior officers of the CSC. The committees would not only concern themselves with new problems of policy, but would also review the existing body of policy affecting the function in question. They would be served by the Secretary's Office which would also be concerned with

430

policy from the aspect of coordination and in following up decisions. The other two Commissioners would be relieved of their responsibility for day-to-day administration and would devote the bulk of their time to the committees on which they would be ex-officio members. They would be expected to bring to fruition inquiries into major problems of policy identified in the discussions of the standing committees. They would also maintain contact with other institutions, organizations, societies, and associations whose activities were related to the functions of the CSC. Ibid.

39. See the memorandum from Blackburn to the chairman, January 9, 1964, PSC File 044-22L8. The consensus was that the Commissioners would be corporately responsible for general and procedural policy, for setting operational objectives, goals, and priorities for the branch heads, for the assignment of senior people in the CSC, and for examining the operational effectiveness of the branches. Individually, the Commissioners would accept prime areas of interest in CSC activities (in effect they would individually provide supervision of various CSC functions), would supervise, and perhaps conduct, special studies in the areas of interest under their purview, and would communicate and consult with departments. The role of the chairman within this arrangement seems to have been left somewhat vague.

40. See unsigned memorandum to the chairman, January 24, 1964, PSC File 044-22L8. An attached notation indicates that the memorandum was prepared by Blackburn.

41. See the memorandum from Mansbridge to the Commissioners, February 2, 1965, ibid.

42. Ibid.

Chapter Seventeen

Management Development in the Canadian Federal Bureaucracy, 1935–1967

*What is called executive development is
really a harvesting of one important
product—administrative ability—out of
a total training program designed to promote the development of persons in many
ways and in all ranks. In other words, it
should be the function of the executive
development program to develop administrative ability which is over and above
professional, vocational or technical proficiency—the capacity to understand and
direct the work of others, to accept responsibility, to exercise good judgment in
making difficult decisions, and to give
confidence to others in trying circumstances.*

The Hoover Commission

WITHIN THE LAST two decades, two of the most important elements in the
staffing process of the Canadian federal civil service, namely, the recruitment and development of managerial talent,[1] have assumed increasing importance in governmental circles. The reasons for this have been varied,
but these trends have been justified because of the continued expansion of
the civil service in response to new governmental activities, and the growing demand for governmental agencies to provide administrative leadership of an increasingly sophisticated character.[2]

For many years within the public service of Canada, the concept of
management development came under the all-encompassing label of training and development, with no clear conception of the goals and purposes
of this element of staffing.[3] Indeed most of the literature dealing with training and development has been imprecise in distinguishing between the two

433

elements. Moreover, the distinction continues to lack clarity up to the present day. The Glassco Report, among other government documents, attempted to clarify the confusion in meaning between the two terms: "Training is the process of teaching skills to an individual so that he may improve his performance on a particular job. Development is the process whereby an individual acquires new knowledge, habits, attitudes, self-awareness, and values or maturity. *Training courses and development programmes, therefore entail different methods.*" (Emphasis added.) Unfortunately, the Report failed to elaborate on the distinction. It would have been instructive, for example, to have been given some understanding of why the Report felt it was important to separate the acquisition of technical knowledge from the knowledge acquired by habits, attitudes, and self-awareness.

Technical training, or the acquisition of a technique to ensure proficiency in a particular job situation, has been conducted for many years in some government departments in Ottawa. For example, in the early part of this century, technical departments were engaged in training personnel to meet departmental requirements for specific jobs.[4] After assuming full responsibility for staffing in 1918, the Civil Service Commission continued to view training as primarily the responsibility of the individual civil servant supplemented, wherever the need arose, by well-defined departmental programs confined to the immediate duties of the position and based on the principle of "learn to do by doing."[5]

As chapter 10 has already shown, by the early 1940s this orientation began to change when the CSC increasingly provided leadership, on a service-wide basis, in training personnel such as stenographers, tradesmen, and stationary engineers. However, the idea that development is a learning process distinct from training, and existing apart from programs devised to foster proficiency in techniques, received relatively little attention, until quite recently, in the staffing process of the public service.

It has been difficult to isolate the specific reasons for the growth of this attitude, but in part it seems attributable to an educational system and a work environment which visualize all development in terms of the acquisition of technical proficiency. The idea that genuine knowledge can be imparted to recruits participating, for instance, in orientation programs not geared to technical training, and where, as Michael Oakeshott puts it, they have an opportunity of "learning the nuances which compose the tradition and standard of behaviour which belong to a great profession,"[6] seemed remote and esoteric. This is particularly well mirrored in the approach taken in job classification toward the work environment: the individual was fitted to the duties and responsibilities enumerated for the position, with no conscious attempt being made to define the position in terms of the unique qualities the personality must contribute to ensure success on the job. Scientific management, in its early attempts to eradicate imprecise criteria based on personality characteristics and the like, specified very carefully the job and its attendant duties. The recruit was therefore required to bring to the work environment those "scientific" qualities, *and only those qualities*, needed to fulfil the job's requirements. Consequently both training and development courses were considered low priorities in personnel administration because a good classification system precluded the need for such. Thus as in Canada, Mosher, Kingsley, and Stahl report that in the United States the prevalent attitude has been "that employees hired under a merit system are already qualified, are already 'trained,' therefore, for their jobs. To superimpose in-service training on top of this is either wasteful 'boondoggling' or an evidence that the initial selection of personnel was inadequate."[7]

This criterion of precise job requirements for selection dovetailed rather neatly with the concerns of civil service reformers bent on eliminating all "irrelevant" considerations in the recruitment of personnel. By scientifically specifying the job requirement, the work environment would be kept free of all personnel attempting to use influence as a means of recruitment or promotion. Furthermore, advocates denied the criticism that by the application of such a rigid mechanistic system of scientific job specifications, personnel from the lower levels of the bureaucracy were effectively blocked from the senior echelons.[8] Indeed, the scheme fortified the Horatio Alger myth by encouraging the most enterprising employees to be ever on the alert for vacant job positions which could be filled by open competition, and which would provide the necessary training for the individual on his way up the hierarchical ladder.[9] One provincial civil service commissioner informed the late Professor Keith Callard of McGill of the prevailing view that "good administrators are born, not made, and that if proper steps are taken to identify younger men who reveal an aptitude for administrative work, they will, through gradual promotion and experience, make good administrators without anything in the way of formal training."[10] The Horatio Alger myth was therefore still a viable concept: incorporated into the classification scheme, it made better Horatio Algers out of personnel who were naturally endowed with enterprise and foresight.

History, however, turned out to be on the side of the critics. Dawson's criticisms were indeed prophetic in pinpointing one of the basic flaws of the classification scheme, namely, its inability to produce personnel suited for managerial positions:

The . . . objectionable feature of the present classification is the scheme of gradation and promotion which it contains. The experts of 1919 had apparently been unable to shake off the influence of their early environment, and the works of Horatio Alger, Jr., still made a strong appeal to their imaginations. "Bound to Rise, or From Office Boy to President" may be said to have inspired the present classification, for the entire scheme is avowedly built about the idea of a continual flow of promotions from the bottom to the top.

The Civil Service Commission in attempting to apply the classification is thus frequently faced with three alternatives in filling a vacancy: first, to promote an employee and waive many of the educational qualifications which are required, in other words, appoint an inferior man; second, to fill the position from outside the service, and so depart from the cherished ideal of the whole plan; or, third, to grant leave of absence to certain employees so that they may, by continuing their education outside the service, obtain the necessary qualifications for advancement. When any of these alternatives must be employed, to that extent the classification has usually proved inadequate and has failed to meet the legitimate needs of the service. Unfortunately it appears that the first and second alternatives are being constantly resorted to, and men without the stated qualifications are promoted or others are being brought in from the outside. The Civil Service Commission as a result is being forced to regard the classification as little more than a general guide to determining the eligibility of candidates for promotion and as a useful gauge and means of control in maintaining a range of salaries: they have made the classification workable by quietly ignoring many of its inconvenient provisions. . . . The lines of promotion have had to be abandoned so frequently that they represent in many cases nothing more troublesome than a pious aspiration and a gesture to the shades of Horatio Alger, Jr.[11]

For close to two decades the CSC appeared oblivious to some of these basic defects in the scheme. The central personnel agency of the federal government allowed itself to be trapped by an approach to selection and promotion which emphasized staffing processes based essentially on the technical or quasi-technical knowledge of all applicants. In addition, the job was erroneously conceptualized as a static phenomenon, divorced wholly from its encumbent and treated as a short-cycle set of functions performed within any given day. Underlying this clinical treatment of the work environment was the tacit assumption that a senior officer's position could be dissected in the same manner as a stenographer's or a messenger's. Thus, as Dawson complained, the CSC was apparently content to abide by the idea that "no officer class as such should be separately introduced and trained, nor should any express provision be made for revivifying the service by the addition of highly educated material from the ranks of university graduates."[12]

By 1932 some senior officials from the CSC were publicly indicating that they were having second thoughts on the matter. Appearing before the Lawson Committee, Assistant Secretary Bland expressed some misgivings about the workings of the scheme:

> This point has to do with the principle of promotions, Mr. Chairman, and I am heartily in favour with the principle of promotion, but I do believe that in certain cases it may be overdone and abused. By that I mean this: If the entire service—outside of technical positions to which I am not referring for the moment—is to be recruited only from the lowest grades and the higher positions are to be continuously and completely filled by promotion, I think you are going to have a weakening in your structure, perhaps not for a few years, but in ten or fifteen years you will have a decided weakening.
>
> *Q.* Unless you increase the qualifications required?
>
> *A.* Even that, Mr. Chairman, would be an improvement. I mentioned a little while ago about the British system where there are, so to speak, two stories: an upper story for which the highest academic qualifications are required, and a lower story which is about similar to our present entrance grade. From 1908 to 1915 we had in Canada a somewhat similar system whereby appointment to the service was really by means of two grades,—a lower grade such as we have at present, and a higher grade known as the second division. It had some benefits and some difficulties, and I am not suggesting that we should adopt completely the British system.[13]

The 1933 Annual Report of the CSC mirrored essentially the same concerns expressed by the Assistant Secretary a year previously.[14] However, Bland's position before the 1932 Committee, even though reinforced by the Annual Report, was not endorsed unanimously within the central personnel agency. Secretary Foran, who some fourteen years previously was instrumental in condemning the pre-1918 divisions as "unscientific" and "founded on no definite principle, a happy-go-lucky hit or miss affair," visualized this method of recruitment as a threat to the rationale of the classification system, and refused to give his assent to a new scheme of university recruitment.[15] One civil service staff association interpreted the CSC's announcement as a confession that the classification scheme had failed to produce experienced senior administrators befitting the enthusiastic expectations of 1919, and that "not a sufficient number of persons who qualify for promotions to higher positions are secured through the present entrance system."[16]

By 1935, then, the system had proved inadequate in supplying talent for the senior positions in the administrative system. In August, 1934, the CSC argued before the Treasury Board that most departments suffered from an acute shortage of experienced, capable officers, and that it was necessary to infuse new life into the whole system by "a considered plan for recruitment and careful anticipation of the needs of each department."[17] This lack of suitable senior personnel in the departments was attributable to the influx of junior clerks with little or no higher education, and a classification system which, when applied to the civil service, obviated the use of jobs for developmental purposes.[18] The Commissioners, finding support in the identical experience of the American Civil Service Commission, concluded that university graduates had the best potential for the more senior administrative positions in the service.[19] The CSC, however, did not favour the creation of a separate and isolated "administrative class," for it felt that this would be unacceptable both to the Canadian public and to the style and needs of the Canadian federal bureaucracy. The administrative clerkship was therefore not made an exclusive preserve of university graduates, and capable nongraduate clerks, Grade IV, or chief clerks were considered in the general pool, making it "reasonably certain that qualified employees . . . [would] be available to compete for responsible positions when vacancies occur."[20] The plan, however, possessed a novel feature in departing from the traditional method of recruitment aimed at specific positions, and, as the CSC argued, "its purpose is to provide the various departments with young men and women who have the capacity to develop into senior officers"[21] and not "to perform the duties of the class to which they seek to be appointed."[22]

Thus, the changes suggested in 1933, and which finally came to fruition in 1935, were the first faint realization that managers had to be consciously developed for the public service of the country.

MANAGEMENT DEVELOPMENT, 1935–1946

In announcing the new program of recruitment to the public, the Civil Service Commission stressed that it would begin the venture "by severely restricting the eligible list to the small number who can be absorbed into the departments, to obtain only the best material which the universities have to offer; and to make the best use of the material thus secured by assigning from this list to positions where intensive training and watchful supervision are guaranteed."[23] This "intensive training" was limited to male recruits only, the CSC announcing that "it would be unfair to invite applications from female candidates when no positions were at present available to them." The Canadian Seminar of Public Administration was engaged to conduct the lecture and seminar courses for new recruits to the Grade IV clerkships.[24] The results of this enterprise seemed to have been satisfactory to the CSC. By 1945 C. H. Bland, now the Chairman of the CSC, could proudly announce to the Canadian Political Science Association annual meeting that an important stage in the recruitment for administrative positions had taken place: "[in] . . . the last ten years, or more properly, the five years preceding the war, when the British system was more closely followed . . . an endeavour was made to secure the best minds among university graduates, the emphasis being placed on quality, adaptability, and promise of development rather than upon specific knowledge in any particular field."[25]

Three appropriate observations follow from this and previous statements made by the CSC officials. Although Bland did not expressly state it, his remarks implied that the Treasury Board's cold hand of fiscal austerity forced a curtailment of the program during the war years in particular. The Board's retrenchment on salary levels, its solid freeze on "normal levels" of appointments, and its veto on promotions had left the CSC somewhat restricted in developing a program for attracting high-quality university graduates to the civil service.

Second, it was not entirely accurate to assert that the clerkship scheme was akin to the British model of the administrative class: the concept of postentry training given to both university graduates and nongraduates in a specific category was definitely American in conception.[26] Contrary to popular opinion the British civil service fared no better at this time than the Canadian service in training and career management programs, a theme to which we will return later in the chapter. Furthermore, no Canadian federal departments were allowed special positions on their establishments for these new recruits, the CSC making this point very clear in its submission to the Treasury Board: "The attention of the Treasury Board is especially directed to the point that it is not proposed to create new positions for the appointment of these Administrative Clerks, but merely to utilize such positions as Clerks, Grade IV, or higher as may fall vacant in departments where the need of better trained administrative officers is apparent."[27] The proposals by the CSC did, however, allow departments, with special orientations, to develop career programs for their specific needs: the Departments of Trade and Commerce and of External Affairs, when resuming their normal recruitment of foreign service officers after the war, found the scheme adaptable to their own personnel requirements.

Third, no pattern of career development had ever been suggested for normal progression from a Grade IV clerk to the higher echelons of the civil service. The young entrant tended to remain in the same department to which he was originally assigned, thus being deprived of the opportunity to gain a more varied experience to fit him for administrative positions elsewhere in the federal bureaucracy. As one former Civil Service Commissioner expressed it: "We had no concept of career development as they do today. In those days the departments held on to their bright young men once they were recruited to the departmental ranks."[28]

The barriers to career development were reinforced, as noted previously, by the view that training and career management were antithetical to the merit ideology which the CSC had successfully initiated and nurtured in the reforms of 1918–19. Moreover, although initial reaction by civil servants to the classification system was strongly adverse,[29] ten years after it was adopted many accepted the Horatio Alger orientation implied in the scheme: an office boy, diligently applying himself to his work, had the capacity in time to become a senior departmental official. Additionally it placed an *undue* emphasis on seniority as an "objective" qualification for promotion. At first glance the Horatio Alger and the promotion by seniority concepts appear to be somewhat antithetical. The Horatio Alger concept meant than an individual could fight his way to the top on the basis of his personal merits, whereas the seniority concept implied that only longevity—and not merit—was recognized. The fact remains, however, that the Horatio Alger myth was primarily applied to entrants to the public service. It was supposed to serve the egalitarian purpose of being a "leveller" for all recruits regardless of educational qualifications. Once in the public service the employee then found that his personality together with his seniority accounted for much more in his promotional successes than his training. By 1927, for example, the *Civil Service News* could triumphantly declare: "It is within the power of *each* and *every* civil servant of Canada to so perform the duties assigned them (even though they may at present be lowly) with such zeal and regard for efficiency that their very efficiency will produce the result most desired by them—a promotion to higher duties which they can perform with equal energy."[30] Consequently to the staff associations, developmental courses for a chosen few implied both favouritism in promotion, and the nurturing of "crown princes" for senior positions in the hierarchy.[31] When the Grade IV clerkship program was reviewed in 1938, the enmity of the civil service rank and file to these "crown princes" was so considerable that the CSC seriously entertained a proposal to have the young recruits removed from established positions and attached as understudies to senior officers, in the hope of relieving the objections of staff who resented the prospect of having to contend with the newcomers for available vacancies.[32] Even as recently as the 1950s the

440

underlying assumptions of this attitude were still present in the civil service: so strong was the fear that training would undermine the merit system that in the summary of the Senior Personnel Officers' Conference on executive and professional development in May, 1957, one conclusion reached was that "it is necessary to counter the belief that the program (that is, staff development) is designed primarily to develop people for promotion. It must be quite clear that the program is designed to improve performance on the job, to improve morale, and thirdly in order of importance to prepare people for promotion."[33]

Underlying these attitudes were some rather basic assumptions which are widespread in North American society. For many the notion of seeking out excellence for special development had elitist connotations which contradicted the ideal of equality by which liberal democratic societies are judged. According to this line of reasoning excellence should therefore be left to rise on its own: the natural laws of evolution would ensure the survival of the fittest.

Assigned for years to specific duties in one or, at best, two departments, and lacking exposure to some planned variety of administrative experiences so vital for executive development, personnel reaching the top echelons of government departments were generally deemed to be unprepared for their new positions.[34] The Royal Commission on Administrative Classifications in the Public Service was highly critical of this lack of administrative expertise at the senior levels of the federal government:

It is significant that a substantial proportion of the Deputy Ministers and other principal officials have been appointed to their present positions from outside the service. The truth is that the Canadian Civil Service as presently organized and managed does not provide its own leadership. No doubt, it is desirable, from time to time, to bring in from the outside, to fill important senior positions, persons who are exceptionally qualified, but the extent to which this has been done leaves little question that there is something seriously wrong with the management of what is intended to be a career service.

This condition is, in our view, the result of a combination of circumstances. The methods of recruitment, the almost total lack of training programs, the systems and procedures for classification, remuneration, transfer and promotion, as well as the absence of a clearly assigned central responsibility for personnel planning, have all contributed to it. However that may be, it is clear that there are not enough men of high quality and training in senior and administrative positions.[35]

As the Gordon Commission discovered, the classification system remained one of the obstacles to career management in the civil service. For implicit in the theory and method of position classification which most North American public bureaucracies utilized were certain static assumptions about work which divorced the man from the job and which conceived training for administration strictly in utilitarian terms.[36] Critics like the late Professor K. Callard of McGill continued to point to the consequences of this orientation:

> Nearly all Canadian public servants are recruited as specialists unless they enter in the clerical grades. If they have no technical or professional training before they enter, their assignment to one branch of the service is likely to lead them to acquire an area of specialization by experience. The more able are then expected to advance up the ladder within that branch. Having reached the top of a branch they may then hope for promotion to a wider sphere. Promotion used to be normally a matter of selecting the highest qualified candidate within the branch or department with some allowance being made for seniority. The theory was that, by ability and hard work, a man might advance from office boy to Deputy Minister. This is, in some ways, a noble ideal, and in the province of Alberta I am told there is a Deputy Minister who has worked continuously for the provincial government since the age of twelve. This is the negative "merit system," designed to keep the wrong people out of jobs rather than to put the right ones in. There is not . . . anything approaching a service-wide pool of administrators, capable of being allocated according to need.[37]

However, certain other factors must be remembered. Criticisms about the lack of adequate staffing practices were essentially correct, but in all fairness it should be observed that the strictures on the Canadian situation expressed were being reiterated in other jurisdictions as well.[38] The "ideal" British civil service, to which admiring Canadian commentators looked for inspiration, possessed some serious deficiencies of its own. Almost nothing was done in the United Kingdom about training and development for civil servants until the Assheton Report of 1944.[39] As in the Canadian civil service, training and development were considered "frill" activities and usually suffered during economy drives.[40] Moreover, the job rotation concept, which admiring commentators hoped the Canadian federal civil service would adopt, possessed some serious defects. As the Fulton Committee reported:

> We found that much of the movement of staff from job to job arranged

by Establishment offices masqueraded as career planning. This was because in the Civil Service all movement is thought of as good and contributing to the development of a career; promotion boards like and demand broad experience and, . . . consider expertise to be "narrowing." Indeed, we frequently met cases where valuable expertise was dissipated by the enforced transfer of officers in the alleged interest of their careers.[41]

These arguments should not be taken as a defence for the slow developments in training and career management exhibited in the Canadian experience. However when compared with similar practices in other western civil services at that particular period of time, they do serve to place our experience in perspective.

EVENTS AFTER THE GORDON COMMISSION, 1946–1958

Although the Gordon Commission's recommendations failed to be implemented, the Civil Service Commission had the political clairvoyance to realize that there were strong principalities and powers within the civil service urging basic reforms in personnel administration, and that Prime Minister Mackenzie King's refusal to act on the Royal Commission's major recommendations could only be, at best, a staying action. Within two months after the release of the Royal Commission's Report, the CSC employed Dr. O. E. Ault, a former Canadian army psychologist, to devise new methods for the selection of prospective civil servants and for the training and development of young administrative entrants. The groundwork for new training programs and the development of the junior administrative category began immediately.[42] A committee, organized to look into the feasibility of setting up the junior category, reported rather favourably that it was incumbent on the Civil Service Commission to "strengthen and improve the calibre of Canadian public administration at the directing and policy development levels, by injecting into the traditional and functional career streams of the service, a group of specially selected and specially trained officers, whose primary interest and responsibility is administration in the broadest sense of the term."[43]

In 1947 the CSC instituted the junior administrative assistant's developmental program to orient the new recruits. Plans for the new category called for recruiting approximately twenty university graduates each year, and the competitive selection of an equal number of recruits already within the ranks of the civil service. In 1950, for example, the competition was open to Ottawa employees with three years' service who had not yet reached a position higher than principal clerk. The CSC's Annual Report indicated that "about eight hundred civil servants applied and over five hundred sat for the examination . . . the top sixty on the written test were then selected for oral examination . . . eighteen were chosen for the course in administration."[44]

The program followed was designed in the form of weekly lectures and forum discussions on the nature of governmental administration. For one year the recruits were rotated in selected government departments in Ottawa, and following the completion of this period of training, were assigned to regular posts "in accordance with the needs of the employing department and the aptitude of the individual in each case."[45] After two years of trial, the program was modified to place "greater emphasis . . . on student participation, and consequently there has been an increase in the number of panel discussions, open forums and conference groups."[46] Between 1947 and 1961 two hundred and ninety-three administrative officers successfully completed the program and were placed in twenty-six departments in the federal government.[47]

The advent of the junior administrative assistant category did nothing, however, to change the basic structure of the classification scheme as such. No department of government had junior executive *positions* on its establishment. Like the university graduates entering the service in the mid-thirties, the junior officers were used to fill vacancies at a variety of levels and classifications already determined from the old schema. There was no pattern for a normal progression from the junior executive category to one of the occupational groupings, for progression was determined by the accidental result of the choice of departments or area of specialization. Thus, if the young recruit entered the Finance Department, he became known as a finance officer for the most part of his career progression in the federal bureaucracy.

This almost static orientation toward all levels of work was also evident in the intermediate and senior categories of the civil service: the functional specialist orientation precluded the development of broad categories suited for general administrative duties.[48] The Federal Government, observed Professor Callard, continued to

recruit men and women for specific and immediate tasks. A member of the United Kingdom Civil Service Commission has given this criterion as a basis for the selection of administrative recruits: "Is this a man (or woman) who in ten years, or fifteen, will develop into an experienced and competent administrator who will be an asset to the service?" By contrast, the legislation governing most Canadian personnel agencies would require the following criterion: "Is this the man best suited to be an Economist, Grade I, starting on the first of the month?"[49]

Partly in response to some of these criticisms, the CSC created a Planning and Development Branch in 1953. Among its first duties was a study of the related problems of filling senior positions and the development of senior officers. In 1954, developmental courses were established for groups of intermediate and senior administrative officers in the Ottawa area. The intermediate course took the form of a two-week in-service program conducted in Arnprior, Ontario, while the senior program for the directorate and assistant deputy minister's levels consisted of four weeks' instruction at the Agricultural College at Kemptville, Ontario.[50] These developments, although viewed by many senior public servants as definite progress, were still considered inadequate in dealing with the problem of developing senior personnel. Many held the opinion that only a revised civil service act, with specific provisions for the effective management of the senior ranks of the service through transfers and career planning, could ameliorate the problem. However, the CSC's leadership, as it was then constituted, was not prepared to entertain the idea of revamping the 1918 legislation.[51]

Early 1957 saw the advent of new leadership at the CSC which sought, and immediately obtained, Treasury Board's permission to establish three new grades in the senior officer's category to replace a proliferation of specific categories:

> A senior officer classification series, with three grades, and embracing senior positions up to and including the level of Assistant Deputy Minister, was established by the Commission in mid-year. The new series was intended to eliminate fine distinctions between departmental positions. The new grades replace, for classification, establishment, and salary purposes, approximately 100 previous classes, most of them "one-man" classes.[52]

In that same year the Advisory Panel on Senior Appointments was formed to assist the CSC in the selection of potential appointees. The panel, comprising the three Civil Service Commissioners, nine deputy ministers representing the departments, and the Secretary of Treasury Board, provided a means whereby the CSC could discuss the administration of the senior classes with selected officials, and obtain their views on specific appointments, promotions, or transfers under consideration.[53]

The Heeney Report of 1958 advocated the consolidation of these changes by recommending the greater involvement of deputy ministers in the transfer of personnel both within and between departments. Planned transfers for select personnel were vital "not only as a means of ensuring that the best use is made of the talent available, but also as a means of providing promising civil servants with more productive and more attractive careers. The Commission heartily endorses this view."[54]

"Career Planning" and Promotion by 1962

The Glassco Royal Commission in 1962 conceded that the Civil Service Commission had shown some "imagination and capacity" in its efforts in the area of management development. Glassco, however, made explicit what senior officers in the public service had stressed for many years: that the classification system was chaotic, and remained an impediment to further development of the service into broad occupational categories.[55] In attempting to slay the dragon of classification rigidity the Royal Commission declared:

> Some informal management development activity exists. One device is "classification creeping"—a process for avoiding promotion competitions. Another, is the placing of employees in positions with the justification "that no one else in the department is as well qualified." *Of over 200 civil servants attending the Senior Officers' Course from 1954 to 1960, most had received their promotions by such routes rather than through the established system of promotion competitions.*
>
> A few departments, in which management development receives more attention, have attempted to carry out systematic planned rotation of individuals, carefully selected for management development. Such programmes have the support of the central control agencies in principle, but despite this, the establishment review and the estimates procedures tend to frustrate staff rotation for management development purposes.[56]

Outside observers have been extremely critical of the Canadian civil service's inability to develop a service with clearly defined promotional avenues to the senior levels, or as sociologist John Porter calls it, "a fully developed bureaucratic career."[57] Winning one's way to the senior categories by being "next to policy," or "sitting on interdepartmental committees where one gets known," or "winning promotion by alertness in noticing another opening," or "winning in a competition without reference to the performance in one's work"—in short, any promotion achieved in a manner other than through devoted work together with commitment and capability—has been seen by the critics as a valuable reward for enterprise but certainly not suited for the development of a career civil service.[58]

As a whole, the Canadian federal service does not conform to the "model" of a career civil service as outlined by Professor John Porter.[59] Although small segments of the federal bureaucracy have developed fairly defined career patterns over the years,[60] it nevertheless remained true that within the general clerical sections certain factors militated against any clearly defined courses of action which would have shaped the federal bureaucracy in the likeness and image of the British civil service.[61]

In the early fifties the CSC seemed to be faced with a dilemma on this issue. Having embraced a philosophy and a system for well over three to four decades, and then allowing both to become almost inviolate and immutable, the central personnel agency experienced considerable difficulties in attempting to innovate in personnel administration. The whole area of reclassification for promotional or developmental purposes was a case in point.

As discussed in chapter 4, scientific management theory, as applied to job classification, postulated a rigid relationship between the rank (or the classification) and the job. This rigidity meant that a change of positions required a change in classification, and conversely a change in classification conflicted with the preservation of the previous position. Promotion and open-ended developmental schemes, such as the junior executive positions, tended to throw the whole establishment into confusion—hence the "creeping classification" and the departmental intrigues on which the Glassco Royal Commission commented.

Our argument is best illustrated by diverging somewhat to assess the way in which the junior administrative officers concept worked over the years it was in operation. Each year when asking the departments to state the number of administrative officers required for their establishment, the CSC would declare: "The purpose of the Junior Administrative Officer is to provide potential administrators for training and for long-term administrative requirements. Therefore, we suggest that you do not ask for the services of persons to do immediate specific jobs."[62] The departments, however, faced with a congeries of classes, with each class having its own particular functions to perform, reacted predictably each year. Traditionally the organization has always been conceived in terms of positions, and any attempt to tinker piecemeal with the whole complex business of classification only created confusion and misunderstanding. The departments always replied by requesting personnel with particular skills or personnel who would be required to fill a particular slot and a particular job. Thus the recruitment of the nonspecialist class landed back again on the proximity of the familiar quest for specialists. The criticisms of Dawson and other academics returned once more to haunt the CSC.

The CSC's attempts to rectify the problem by admonishing the departments that this was a wrong application of its scheme for career planning evidently met with little success. The departments assigned to the junior administrative officers duties of a conventional character, keeping the young recruits from the rotation which had been planned for developmental purposes. At times a "get tough" policy was resorted to by the CSC in refusing to appoint officers to departments which were the chief offenders.[63] By 1955 a modus vivendi was arrived at in an attempt to reconcile the particularistic practices and expectations of the departments with the generalist central planning of the personnel agency, a modus vivendi, incidentally, which was identical to that adopted by the United States federal government some twenty years earlier.[64]

"We propose now," wrote the Chairman of the CSC to the departments, "to meet both needs by setting up two lists from our present competition." These were: "(1) Junior Administrative Officer (A) from which assignments will be made to the Administrative type of position only and (2) Junior Administrative Officer (B) on which will be successful candidates with special interests and education for such Departmental jobs as Citizenship Officer, Treasury Officer, etc."[65] This scheme was followed until 1967 when the revamping of the whole classification scheme and the adoption of the administrative trainee category eliminated these tinkering adjustments in classification.

Traditionally within the public service of Canada there have been three avenues of promotion. Reclassification or, as the Glassco Commission derisively dubbed it, "creeping classification," remained the least favoured of the three. The most common has been the winning of an open competition for a position further up the hierarchical scale.[66] The winner of that competition must contend with all other candidates who have applied, civil servants and members of the public at large, and he enjoys no special privileges because of his civil service status.[67]

Another avenue of promotion has been the promotion competition aimed at civil servants employed within a limited sector of the public service. This route is the most hazardous to depend on, for success is achieved by a continual alertness throughout one's career for momentary opportunities. If a potential applicant does not apply, regardless of long, capable, and devoted service, he remains at the level at which he was hired. In reality, all three avenues of promotion do not possess any semblance of career planning for capable individuals, and the policies and programs presently being devised by the Government, and which will be described shortly, are attempts at rectifying, in part, this inadequacy.

In order to gain some insight into the incidence of competition in promotions, as practised in the general civil service, a research study of the individual files of a sector of the service was conducted in 1957 by Dr. M. Z. Prives of McGill University.[68] The sector analysed included all the officers receiving salaries of $7,500 or more per annum. The sample number was 863 and represented a wide cross section of the civil service population, scientists, professionals, and administrative officers included. Dr. Prives found that 385 officers did not participate successfully in any promotion competition, 139 succeeded in one, 85 in two, 84 in three, 73 in four, 48 in five, 22 in six, 14 in seven, 9 in eight, 3 in nine, and 1 officer succeeded in ten competitions. Among those who did not participate successfully in the promotion competitions of the federal service, Dr. Prives found 140 medical and scientific officers whose usual promotion avenue led through reclassification. Dr. Prives' general conclusions were that the career paths of these officers were dictated by patternless chance, and that in the civil service of Canada only a small percentage remain as civil servants for any long period of time. Within the occupational groupings which could be called the administrative category he concluded:

> Only the first two steps of promotion are planned and controlled, while from the level of Administrative Officer I up the employee advances on his own initiative and in the usual haphazard manner, through a variety of classes and titles. This haphazard manner of promotion is chiefly responsible for making the course of the official life of an employee a private enterprise of his own, responsive to chance impulses rather than to plan and guidance. Without any value judgments as to the desirability or otherwise of this phenomenon, it must be recognized that a career service is an institution built in accordance to plan and responsive to planning and guidance, an institution characterized by stability and permanence.[69]

Senior civil servants who were interviewed admitted that there is this aspect of "patternless chance" in the career avenues within the federal public service, but they contend that the nature of Canadian society proscribes any full development of a clearly delineated career path for the chosen elect who were identified as potential senior officer material. One senior civil servant involved in the 1965 reclassification of the civil service indicated the difficulties involved as he perceived them: "The Preparatory Committee on Collective Bargaining did set up a category for potentials or, as the British call them, 'flyers.' As we discussed this among ourselves on the Committee, and with senior officials throughout the public service, we gradually realized that the creation of such a group would be a serious mistake. . . . Elitism was suspected. There had to be a studious avoidance of establishing any apparent grouping of 'crown princes.' "[70]

Notwithstanding this "aversion to elitism," there was only a rudimentary development of comprehensive, sustained development programs which would facilitate early identification and selection of people with some promise and potential for growth and development. The basic criticism of the effects of the classification system remained essentially valid: recruitment of personnel was heavily weighted in favour of persons with special technical qualifications, and any administrative skills were acquired in the performance of the job. Men who reached the top in the civil service were mostly those who had risen through their own respective departments. "As a result some of our most senior departmental officers had no administrative experience of any consequence outside their narrow specialization. They failed to have a broad perspective, a view of the public service as a total entity."[71]

EXECUTIVE DEVELOPMENT SINCE THE GLASSCO COMMISSION

By 1960 it was generally agreed by senior public servants that one of the essential problems in the public service of Canada was how to transform the present and potential crop of "departmental executives" into a broader occupational group, and how to train these people to develop an orientation devoid of departmental parochialism. The Glassco Report enunciated this management philosophy:

A good plan of organization and an appropriate concept of management—essential as they are—provide no automatic guarantee of good administration. The essential ingredient is good people, especially at the top. The goals pursued by departments are matters of public policy but the effectiveness of their activity will depend primarily on the quality of administrative leadership. There must be, throughout the public service, senior administrators of outstanding ability with a strong sense of purpose and a clear grasp of their responsibilities.[72]

The Glassco Commission repeated essentially the criticisms of the Gordon Commission of 1946 by asserting that management development in the public service continued to suffer as a result of a lack of a coordinated program supervised by a single, central managerial group with responsibility for policy-making in this area. Furthermore, management development had suffered from "those quirks in the merit system, as applied, which make it difficult if not impossible to plan promotions and transfers."[73]

Glassco did not envision a significant role for the Civil Service Commission in this undertaking and argued that this whole area of management development was, and should be, the responsibility of the Treasury Board.[74] As events turned out, the CSC, under new leadership, continues to play an important role in executive development for the public service. The 1965 Preparatory Committee on Collective Bargaining, in revamping the classification scheme, also took the initiative in establishing broader occupational groupings to accommodate "career planning" and pay determination. The Committee recommended the distinct recognition of senior positions in the public service: "The Committee has concluded that all senior positions in which the incumbents are essential to the effective management of the Public Service should be clearly identified. The identification of managerial positions is desirable initially for purposes of classification and pay administration, and ultimately to permit distinctive and appropriate treatment of managerial personnel in all aspects of personnel administration."[75]

Between 1965 and 1967 the CSC, in cooperation with the Treasury Board Secretariat and the Clerk of the Privy Council, studied ways and means of implementing the recommendations of the Preparatory Committee. In 1966, a management consultant team, Hickling-Johnston Limited of Toronto, was engaged by the Government to conduct a study on the executive category. The consultants opted for an elite corps of senior officers possessing special privileges and carefully screened for high I.Q.'s and other attributes. Some of these recommendations were found to be unacceptable to the Government. The Hickling-Johnston study was, however, instrumental in emphasizing one of the fundamental weaknesses of personnel administration in the Canadian federal bureaucracy: "We found that almost no central planning and very little departmental planning had been done, or was being done, to ensure that well qualified individuals were being prepared for more senior responsibilities and that these same individuals were meeting their own growth needs."[76]

Hickling-Johnston also identified a sizeable group of Horatio Algers in the public service, men who have had to consciously plan their careers by themselves in order to ascend the hierarchical ladder in government service:

A second group of comparable size was made up of individuals who had quite consciously planned their careers in the Service. In the Public Service of Canada, it is much easier to do this than in most private organizations because of the competition system whereby a number of intermediate vacancies are open for service-wide competition and thus give the individual who is managing his own career the opportunity to apply for selected positions. Most individuals who planned their careers often took lateral moves into areas that they felt would be required to give them either additional professional experience or necessary political or organizational exposure. Through acquiring such experiences and such exposure, they continued to develop rapidly and had little competition when being considered for more senior posts.[77]

Hickling-Johnston, however, concluded that this mode of career planning was simply inadequate for a large organization such as the federal government to rely on, and that a "substantial group" of civil servants, who, "given more fortuitous circumstances," would have developed equally well, have been left behind. Some semblance of a career planning scheme was urgently required in the federal government.

As a response to this need, the Bureau of Staff Training and Development was organized in April, 1968, to replace the Staff Training and Development Service of the Public Service Commission:

> As agent of the Commission, the bureau has the overall responsibility for assisting departments and agencies to carry out their development and training programmes; for conducting centrally operated programmes where these can more effectively or economically serve the Public Service; for advising the Treasury Board on developmental and training needs indicated by research and evaluation; and for the effective use of training resources employed in training programmes within the Public Service.[78]

The Bureau has worked in conjunction with Treasury Board, and with the departments in the identification, selection, and special assignment of intermediate officers who are considered to have potential for executive development. To meet this need the Bureau has the responsibility for conducting the career assignment program.

Senior officials admit that the measures taken since 1965 are by no means exhaustive and final. However, for the first time, senior management in the Canadian public service has been identified as a group, and steps are being taken to cultivate and train the members of this group to assume administrative responsibilities anywhere they are required to do so in Canada. Opportunities are now being provided to rotate hundreds of individual officers in positions throughout the service.[79] Thus, concern with staff development and training coupled with the massive language-training program assigned to the PSC constituted the two major areas on which the Public Service Commission was to concentrate its attention in the late 1960s and thereafter.

Events in this area of staffing continue to evolve rapidly, and consequently this narrative cannot attempt to be definitive in its assessment of the situation; however, a few concluding general observations are warranted.

First, the classification system, with its myriad of catacomb-like categories, was a definite impediment to the growth of flexible, horizontal divisions of occupational categories which would have easily facilitated the development of an administrative cadre in the Canadian bureaucracy. According to the position classification system which prevailed for so many years in the service, specific qualifications were required of candidates for each position to be filled, and only those persons who could successfully meet this requirement by virtue of specific educational requirements, training, and experience were chosen for higher civil service positions. Since the selection standards were primarily based on the candidate's achievements, productivity, special abilities, and skills in relation to the immediate requirements of the specific position in question, the long-range potential of the employee tended to receive relatively less emphasis in the overall selection process. The result has been the tremendous amount of co-optation of personnel from outside the ranks of the public service to fill positions within because of a deplorable lack of wide administrative expertise.

Second, it now appears rather clear that certain personalities played a significant role in the forties to delay a much needed overhaul of this outdated conception of occupational classification. Steeped in an ideology which was well suited for 1919 perhaps, but getting outdated by 1949, the hierarchy of the Civil Service Commission for many years played the role of King Canute: inevitably the tides of change did inundate their "sand castles" of defence, forcing a revamping of the classification and a consequent growth in importance of development programs for potential executives. These critical comments must however be kept in perspective. Despite the Gordon Commission's strong criticisms, the fact remains that few, if any, private corporations and public services had progressive programs in training and career management. It was only in the 1950s that the need for serious manpower management was widely recognized in North America and Europe.[80]

Having criticized the Civil Service Commission and its past leadership, we must bear in mind the CSC cannot be blamed for a failure, on Canada's part, to develop a career public service where positions were filled solely by career public servants and promotions were based on an "orderly, predictable and reasonably certain system." To be sure the development of some semblance of career planning would have mitigated the "creeping classification" which Glassco commented on, or the "entrepreneurship" which the Hickling-Johnston study uncovered, but these factors were by no means totally responsible for the lack of the model bureaucratic career pattern espoused by some. We were struck by the wide belief held by a disparate collection of senior officials that any attempts to create clearly demarcated categories by which "crown princes" or "flyers" could emerge would have been antithetical to "Canadian values of egalitarianism," and would have been doomed to failure from the outset.

The classification system, the aversion to elitism, the resistance to the idea of planned careers—all these factors relate to a fundamental ethos of North American society, namely, the egalitarian and utilitarian ideas existing in both Canada and the United States. It seems doubtful therefore that any innovations in career development which sought to drastically change these values overnight could ever have hoped to be of marked success in the Canadian federal bureaucracy.

NOTES

1. In this chapter the concepts development and career management are used interchangeably.

2. R. H. Dowdell, "The Elements of Personnel Management in the Civil Service of Canada," p. 49.

3. Various official reports in the past have indicated a gap in government personnel management, beginning with the Arthur Young Company's *Report of Transmission* in 1919. The 1958 Heeney Report felt that "both the Commission and the Departments should . . . do more than has been possible in the past in the development and training of staff and in employment counselling." In 1962, the Glassco Report reiterated essentially the same remarks by asserting: "In proportion to the needs of such a large and complex organization, very little training and development have, in fact, been done." See CSC, *Personnel Administration in the Public Service: A Review of Civil Service Legislation*, December, 1958, p. 16 (hereafter cited as the Heeney Report); and Royal Commission on Government Organization, 1960–62, *Report*, 1, p. 373 (hereafter cited as the Glassco Report).

4. The Arthur Young Company in 1918, while otherwise deploring the lack of training programs throughout the federal civil service, commented rather favourably on the programs devised by the Departments of Insurance, Mines, Customs and Inland Revenue, and the Auditor-General's Department. See *Report of Transmission to Accompany the Classification of the Civil Service of Canada*, pp. 45–46.

5. Ibid., p. 46.

6. Michael Oakeshott, *Rationalism in Politics and Other Essays*, p. 34.

7. William E. Mosher, J. Donald Kingsley, and O. Glenn Stahl, *Public Personnel Administration*, pp. 388–89. The same attitude has been observed in Canada. Senior civil servants in the Canadian federal bureaucracy traditionally viewed training and developmental programs as trimmings to be curtailed in periods of civil service austerity. As one senior civil servant noted: "The old concept was that the recruit should know enough before entering the public service. Old deputy ministers would argue that the idea of staff development programmes was a waste of departments' time and energies. A typical response would be: 'Don't tell me that I have to waste money and time "developing" this new recruit. If I have to do that I do not want him in the first place.' " (Interview)

8. R. MacGregor Dawson, "The Canadian Civil Service," pp. 293–94.

9. Eli Ginzberg, *Human Resources: The Wealth of a Nation*, pp. 105–6.

10. Keith B. Callard, *Advanced Administrative Training in the Public Service*, p. 9.

11. Dawson, "Canadian Civil Service," pp. 294 and 296. Dawson was essentially correct about the quality of personnel being promoted into the senior ranks of the civil service. During the hearings of the Lawson Committee in 1932, the then Assistant Secretary and Chief Examiner of the CSC admitted that many of the CSC's own staff had been promoted in spite of the fact that they did not meet the educational requirements specified for the senior positions. When asked whether he did not find this a "most anomalous situation, of people holding positions who are not now qualified under your own regulations," Mr. Bland replied that this condition was "fairly general in the service." (H.C., Select Special Committee on Civil Service and Civil Service Act, 1932, *Proceedings and Evidence*, p. 158)

12. Dawson, "Canadian Civil Service," p. 296. Principal W. L. Grant of Upper Canada College was equally critical of the recruitment and promotion processes of the federal government. Pointing to a lack of "a fertilizing stream of good brains" needed for the senior positions of government, he added: "An egg-inspector of the second grade may become an egg-inspector of the first grade. But if an egg-inspector of the second grade gives promise of having high administrative qualities of a more general type, it is extremely difficult to transfer him to a position where he may employ them in the service of his country. . . . We have occasionally a way in Canada of adopting an American practice just when the Americans themselves are outgrowing it, and never did we do so more flagrantly than in this case." (W. L. Grant, "The Civil Service of Canada," pp. 436–37)

13. 1932 Committee, p. 865.

14. CSC, *Annual Report*, 1933, p. 10. Calling for persons with "higher educational qualifications and broader general capacity than those obtained by the normal examinations . . . of the service," the Report added that "during the years 1908–1917 similar results were secured in Canada by means of what were then known as Second Division Examinations."

15. On March 2, 1934, in the course of planning the recruitment of non-specialist university graduates as clerks, Grade IV, an internal memorandum of the CSC indicated that "the present system is noted principally for the lack of a comprehensive plan for providing officers adequately equipped to replace the senior officers of the service as their positions fall vacant." Foran strongly dissented from this report when it was considered by the Commissioners. See

M. Z. Prives, "Career in Civil Service: Canada, Great Britain and the United States," p. 92.

16. *Civil Service News* 13 (May, 1935), p. 204.

17. Prives, "Career in Civil Service," p. 41.

18. Dawson highlighted this criticism of the classification scheme by arguing: "It envisages a scheme of promotion which, while attractive enough on paper, proves to be far removed from reality and breaks down badly when tested by practical administrative needs. It provides a system of examinations, undoubtedly successful in filling some positions, but very inadequate indeed for producing the right type of recruits for others. It has failed to appreciate the profound difference in the qualities which must be sought in selecting candidates for specialized and technical offices as contrasted with those where specialization is not needed at entrance but must come later as a result of years of experience and practical work." (Dawson, "Canadian Civil Service," pp. 295–96)

19. Letter from L. D. White, U.S. Civil Service Commissioner, to C. H. Bland, April 19, 1935, cited in Prives, "Career in Civil Service," p. 41.

20. Ibid., p. 42.

21. Bland, "Opportunities in Government Service," broadcast in a series entitled "Canada at Work," August 14, 1955, cited in Prives, "Career in Civil Service," p. 42.

22. *Revised Statutes of Canada*, 1952, c. 48, s. 25(2).

23. CSC, *Annual Report*, 1934, p. 11.

24. In 1934 a group of some thirty men, mostly civil servants and academics, formed the Canadian Seminar of Public Administration with an aim to pursue planned systematic studies on government. The Extension Division of the University of Toronto gave active support to the group by supplying distinguished academics, such as H. A. Innis, Alexander Brady, and Hubert Kemp, to lecture on various aspects of the economic and social history of Canada. Academics from other Canadian universities also took part, as well as visiting senior civil servants from other western democracies, notably the United Kingdom. It is interesting that the first public meeting held by the seminar, some two months after its inaugural meeting, was addressed by Sir Francis Floud, the British High Commissioner in Canada, on the subject "The Relations between Specialist and Administrative Officers in the Public Service." In its first year of operation, the president of the Seminar was N. R. Boutin of the CSC Organization Branch.

25. Bland, "Training for Administrative Posts in the Public Service of Canada," p. 518.

26. For the very important role that the Civil Service Assembly of the United States and Canada played in the development of postentry training in the public service, see Civil Service Assembly of the United States and Canada, *Proceedings of the Twenty-Seventh Annual Meeting* (Milwaukee, Wis., September 26–28, 1935), pp. 80–110. At that time Bland was one of five members of the Assembly's Executive Council, and C. V. Putman, chief of the CSC's Organization Branch, was one of three vice-presidents of the Assembly.

27. Prives, "Career in Civil Service," p. 42.

28. Interview.

29. See chapter 4.

30. *Civil Service News*, April, 1927, p. 11.

31. Commenting in 1949 on the state of personnel administration in the Canadian public service, the Chairman of the CSC, C. H. Bland, is reported to have remarked that "up to ten or fifteen years ago the use of the title personnel officer or training officer would have been sufficient to have one tried for witchcraft." (See Sylvain Cloutier, "The Personnel Revolution: An Interim Report," speech given at the Royal Military College, Kingston, June 19, 1965 [mimeograph], p. 2)

32. Prives, "Career in Civil Service," p. 92.

33. Senior Personnel Officers' Conference, "Summary of Executive and Professional Development Conference," May 20–21, 1957 (mimeograph), p. 4.

34. Canadian critics of the consequences of the classification scheme of the federal government were essentially in agreement with Professor George A. Graham's observations on the subject: "The theory underlying a classification plan is that selection is for a specific post or narrow line of development and that the organization should pay not the man but the job. But when higher positions in the supervisory scale are considered, it is difficult to separate the man from the position. His qualities make the position. He has broad responsibilities which are quite definite. But the way he works, or the steps he takes in meeting the responsibilities, are a matter properly determined by his own personality and habits. Great leeway is justifiable." (George A. Graham, "Personnel Practices in Business and Governmental Organizations" [Monograph 11 of the Commission of Inquiry on Public Service Personnel], in *Problems of the American Public Service* [New York, 1935], pp. 385–86)

35. Royal Commission on Administrative Classifications in the Public Service, 1946, *Report*, p. 15.

36. See J. J. Deutsch, "Some Thoughts on the Public Service," pp. 83–89. W. A. Mackintosh, "Should We Have Specialized Degrees in Public Administration Given by Universities?" pp. 27–33.

37. Callard, *Advanced Administrative Training*, p. 4.

38. In 1948, for example, Dwight Waldo noted: "The argument for and consideration of training for public administration has been largely carried on in ignorance of or indifference to the record of twenty-five centuries of thought about matters educational. . . . There has been consequent confusion and blurring of important distinctions; as one writer has observed, it is impossible to discover from the literature exactly what public administration is, who should teach it, who should learn it, and why!" (*The Administrative State: A Study of the Political Theory of American Public Administration*, pp. 30–31)

39. *Report of the Committee on the Training of Civil Servants*, Cmd. 6526 (1944).

40. See the *Fulton Committee on the Civil Service; Labour Party Evidence* (London: C.W.S. Printing Works, 1967), p. 29.

41. *Report of the Committee on the Civil Service*, 1966–1968, Cmd. 3638 (1968), vol. 2, para. 240.

42. On April 1, 1947, the Staff Training Division of the CSC came into being under Dr. Ault's leadership. See CSC, *Annual Report*, 1947, pp. 8–10.

43. *Report on the Junior Administrative Officers Category*, 1947, internal memorandum of the CSC, p. 3.

44. CSC, *Annual Report*, 1950, p. 11.

45. CSC, *Annual Report*, 1946, p. 7.

46. CSC, *Annual Report*, 1949, p. 10. By 1959 the course had developed into a full-scale program of special seminars and group projects. The formal portion of the course consisted of four parts: I, development of the Canadian democratic system (the Canadian constitution, nature of federalism, etc.); II, the administrative process (functions of a manager, the political context of governmental decision-making, etc.); III, human values in administration (employee motivation, employee appraisal and staff development, employee counselling, etc.); and IV, projects dealing with specific administrative problems for the students to solve. Both Carleton University and the University of Ottawa participated in the program, as well as the professional staff of Parliament (the parliamentary law clerk and the parliamentary counsel of the Senate) and various senior departmental officers. See CSC, *Annual Report*, 1953, p. 11.

47. Data supplied by the Staffing Branch, Public Service Commission. The category's name was changed over the years, but there was no accompanying change in orientation. (It was first known as the junior administrative assistant category, then junior administrative officer, and then junior executive officer.) In 1967 a new category, called the administrative trainee group, with basic changes in orientation, came into existence to replace the junior executive category.

48. By 1946 there was an increasing tendency by the CSC to recognize general administrative abilities as important criteria in the recruitment process. The classification scheme was not revised to accommodate this recognition, and technical positions were simply given the appellation administrative officer, Grade I, II, etc. See G. Y. Lougheed, "Some Aspects of Departmental Administration," speech given to the Junior Administrative Officers' Course, January 14, 1948 (mimeograph), p. 3.

49. Callard, *Advanced Administrative Training*, p. 4.

50. G. S. Follis, "The Senior Course in Public Administration," pp. 37–38; O. E. Ault, "Executive Development in Canadian Government," pp. 37–38.

51. The CSC did in part respond to these pressures by inaugurating, in 1954, a committee of deputy ministers to advise it with regard to the salary, classification, and service conditions of senior officials at levels immediately below the rank of deputy minister.

52. CSC, *Annual Report*, 1957, p. 9. For Treasury Board's approval to revise the compensation schedule to fit this new classification, see TB minutes 522565 (September 19, 1957) and 522734 (September 26, 1957).

53. Interview.

54. Heeney Report, p. 15.

55. Interview.

56. Glassco Report, 1, p. 376. (Emphasis added.)

57. John Porter, *The Vertical Mosaic: An Analysis of Social Class and Power in Canada*, p. 436.

58. The language used in CSC posters and information booklets certainly substantiated this image. Consider the following example: "Announcements of vacant positions, setting forth the duties and qualifications required for the job, will be circulated from time to time. It is to your advantage to read each of them, study the duties and qualifications, and decide whether or not you can fill the bill. If you think you can, by all means apply for the position. You may enter as many competitions as you like—if you fail to qualify it is not

held against you . . . IN A FEW WORDS—PROMOTION IS UP TO YOU."
(CSC, *For Your Information as a Civil Servant* (Ottawa: King's Printer,
1951), pp. 16–17 [Capitals in the original])

59. See Porter, *Vertical Mosaic*.

60. These are the foreign service officers groupings in the Department of
External Affairs and in the Department of Trade and Commerce. See Prives,
"Career in Civil Service," pp. 148–71.

61. Porter, for example, argues that the British civil service "might be taken
as more typical of bureaucracy in the pure sense." (*Vertical Mosaic*, p. 436)

62. From the yearly circular letter sent by the Chairman of the CSC to
heads of departments, asking for departmental requirements in personnel. This
particular note came from a letter dated March 11, 1955, cited in Prives,
"Career in Civil Service," p. 48.

63. Ibid., p. 44.

64. Ibid., pp. 41 and 44.

65. Ibid., pp. 44–45.

66. The Horatio Alger complex is most evident in this avenue of promotion: "To summarize, the civil servant in Canada can rise to senior levels by a
system of competitive promotions even to the office of Assistant Deputy Minister." (Ault, "Executive Development in Canadian Government," pp. 24–29)

67. Commissioner Addison made this point rather clearly in a speech given
to members of the Professional Institute of Canada. "The search for executive
talent could be extended to the Public Service or, to the public at large, . . .
(taking) whatever form may be necessary for effective recruiting including
the technique of executive search based on continuing study of the outside
market." ("The Appraisal and Career Development Programme for Senior
Personnel," p. 9)

68. Prives, "Career in Civil Service," pp. 99–106.

69. M. Z. Prives, "Career and Promotion in the Federal Civil Service of
Canada," p. 190.

70. Interview.

71. Interview.

72. Glassco Report, 1, p. 59.

73. Ibid., pp. 375–76.

74. Ibid., p. 59.

75. Preparatory Committee on Collective Bargaining, "Initial Study of the
Applicability of Criteria Developed for the Management Category," internal
document of the PCCB, n.d. (mimeograph), p. 1.

76. Hickling-Johnston Ltd., *The Executive Category, Public Service of
Canada*, a report to the CSC, November, 1966, pp. 57–58.

77. Ibid., p. 58. (Emphasis added.)

78. CSC, *Annual Report*, 1968.

79. Interview.

80. R. H. Dowdell, "Personnel Administration in the Federal Public Service," in A. M. Willms and W. D. K. Kernaghan, eds., *Public Administration
in Canada: Selected Readings*, pp. 378–79.

Chapter Eighteen
Special Problems in the Administration of the Merit System

All animals are equal.
But some animals are more equal than
others.

George Orwell, *Animal Farm*

IN EARLIER CHAPTERS we discussed the genesis of the merit system in the 1918 Civil Service Act, the Civil Service Commission's own understanding of the merit principle, and the evolving attitudes to the principle on the part of the civil service and successive governments over the years following the original legislation. If we recall that Dowdell has defined the merit principle as including two major propositions, that Canadian citizens should have a reasonable opportunity to be considered for appointment and that selection should be based exclusively on the candidate's fitness for the job,[1] we may now go on to examine in depth some of the persistent problems associated with the administration of the merit system over the past half-century.

The most serious problems associated with the merit system have centred around the definition of what a "reasonable opportunity" to be considered for appointment means, and how "fitness for the job" is determined. One group of Canadians has, on two occasions, been granted very special treatment for appointment to the civil service. The veterans preference constitutes what would appear on the surface to be a direct contradiction of the merit principle. Yet few voices have ever been raised against the practice, and legislative modifications have invariably been in the direction of greater liberality toward the veterans. On the other hand, various identifiable groups within the country have charged that they have been discriminated against in the public service, especially French Canadians and women. The phenomenon of discrimination in employment on the basis of race, language, sex, etc. is hardly unique to Canada, and certainly not to the federal public service, but it is nevertheless a matter of the greatest importance to any understanding of how the merit system has operated in reality.

THE VETERANS PREFERENCE

It is a historical fact of the utmost importance that the abolition of the old patronage system and the establishment of the merit system were brought about in the throes of World War I. Not only did the experience of mobilizaton for war bring home to the Canadian Government and people the high cost of inefficiency in administration, but the return of tens of thousands of soldiers from overseas deeply affected the whole question of "merit."

The terrible experiences of war fostered among the returned soldiers a good deal of democratic discontent, much of which spilled over into radical political opinions about economic privilege and exploitation at home in Canada. James Eayrs has detailed the demands of many of the returning soldiers for a better deal.[2] If the world had been made safe for democracy, then at least some of those who fought for this goal wanted Canada to be democratic as well. Whatever the actual radicalism of the lower ranks— and one doubts either its depth or persistence—the fears of the established order were obvious. With the Russian Revolution of 1917 fresh in mind, many, including cabinet ministers, saw the discontented returned soldier as the bearer of Bolshevism. The Winnipeg General Strike, in which veterans played a leading role, aroused these fears yet further. A memorandum from the Canadian General Staff in 1919 asserted that "the principal peril confronting us at the present moment is the danger of the overthrow of Law and Order in our own Country."[3] In the same year the Acting Prime Minister cabled to Borden in Paris that the Cabinet believed that revolution was imminent in British Columbia: "Bolshevism has made great progress among workers and soldiers there. We cannot get troops absolutely dependable in emergency. . . . Situation is undoubtedly serious and getting out of hand by reason of propaganda from . . . workers and soldiers."[4] The point of our historical interest is not the objective validity of such fears, which were grotesquely overdrawn, but their very existence. The returned soldier was in many ways an object of fear. This element of fear needs some emphasis because its absence from the post-World War II experience has caused it to fade from the historical consciousness. Yet it is probably a major part of the explanation of why the Government went as far as it did to offer special privileges to returned soldiers. They fought off the discontented workers at the same time as they bought off the discontented soldiers.

Fear was, of course, only one element. Undoubtedly more important was a genuine sense of gratitude. Certainly the sentiment of the whole community was behind them. The organized veterans were, and still are, a unique pressure group—one with no organized opposition or counter-pressure group. It is also quite possible that guilt feelings over the slaughter in Europe was assuaged by granting privileges to the survivors.

Whatever the mixture of motives, it is quite apparent that the opposition to political patronage in the civil service was throughout the war very closely identified with the concept of special treatment for veterans. Indeed, when one reads the parliamentary debates during the war years, one cannot fail to be struck by the equation of "merit" with "returned soldier." When it is recalled that charges of war profiteering and corruption were rife, one can begin to glimpse the emergence among many Members of Parliament of the idea that the young men who had proved their worth on the front lines in Europe must not be betrayed by the corrupt practitioners of "political" influence, whether in profiteering or patronage. In the years leading up to the 1918 Act, members often brought forward examples of government jobs being given to party supporters which should have gone to returning soldiers. Patronage was thus identified with those who grew rich at home while others suffered and died in France.

Another possible explanation was offered later by the Veterans Assistance Commission which suggested that at the time of the 1918 Act, the legislators did not feel that they were creating special privileges for returned soldiers but that their intention was "merely to overcome the disadvantage under which those who had been overseas were labouring when they returned to find themselves in competition with those who had been schooling themselves in particular jobs for one, two, three, four or even five years. The disadvantage under which the veteran rested was apparent and onerous. The Veterans Preference sought to overcome this."[5] In this sense the legislation could be seen as simply giving all candidates an equal opportunity.

The legislative provisions for returned soldiers entering the federal service were reworked in 1920 and 1921 to provide a more comprehensive and detailed foundation for the smooth operation of the preference. A former civil servant who had resigned his position to fight overseas was to be placed on the list of the eligible persons for the position from which he had resigned, or for "any other position for which he may have qualified, in the order, as respects other persons, provided by the regulations of the Commission" and his salary on appointment was to be his salary at the time of his resignation, or the minimum salary of the class in which the position was classified, whichever was higher.[6] Among returned men who had not formerly been civil servants, there was to be a list prepared by the CSC of veterans in receipt of pensions by reasons of service who:

(a) have from causes attributable to such service lost capacity for physical exertion to an extent which makes them unfit efficiently to

pursue the avocations which they were pursuing before the war;
(b) have not been successfully re-established in some other avocation; and
(c) desire to be placed on such list.[7]

The CSC was to obtain "as full particulars of each person on such special list, including particulars of his age, education, physical and mental condition, resources and responsibilities, as it is possible to obtain from all available records."[8] In entrance examinations, all persons named on this list "who are found to possess the necessary qualifications" were to be placed above all other successful candidates. Veterans not on this list or their widows were to be placed below this group, but above all other non-veteran candidates.[9] Thus, a three-tiered preference was established with disabled veterans first, able-bodied veterans and war widows second, and non-veterans third.

While legislative provisions were the business of Parliament, the Civil Service Commission took its own initiative as well. A representative of the Canadian Legion, or, infrequently, a representative of another veterans' group, was invited to sit in on examining boards. They were allowed to ask questions, and to satisfy themselves that the interests of the returned men were being accommodated. On occasion they even marked examination papers. It is of interest at this point that special nonstatutory privileges for the organized veterans were not limited to the CSC. Testimony by Legion officials in 1928 indicates that vacancies in post office positions exempted from the Civil Service Act, never advertised owing to their patronage nature, were made known to the Legion which informed veterans in the particular locality where a vacancy existed.

Not all the provisions of the Civil Service Act worked in harmony. Some were in conflict with the veterans preference and these were quickly detected by the alert eyes of veterans' spokesmen. For example, the "locality preference" was attacked by the Canadian Legion, which also pointed out that in 1922, 55 percent of appointments made under the Civil Service Act went to returned soldiers while only 15 percent of exempted positions went to veterans.[10] Veterans also felt themselves to be in competition with other identifiable groups such as French Canadians and women. When a mandatory language requirement was finally added to the list of qualifications for local positions, the veterans quickly pointed it out as a restriction on veterans. As Josie has explained: "Bearing in mind the low enlistment rate for Quebec, the restrictive effect of this clause on the appointment of veterans is indicated by the fact that in 1938 approximately 38 per cent of all appointments outside headquarters at Ottawa were to positions in the province of Quebec where the French language or both languages would usually be specified."[11] Moreover, veterans' groups were always quick to add their voice to attempts to exclude or downgrade female candidates, especially during the depression years.

In terms of actual practice, the impact of the veterans on the public service following World War I was strong initially but quickly subsided. Josie points out that the fairly steady decline in the proportion of veterans appointed cannot be attributed to a decline in the number of applicants, which remained fairly stable. Of course the period of greatest flux in the labour market was at the immediate end of the war, when large numbers of temporary wartime employees were either leaving the service or being removed. Moreover, many of the returning soldiers were of prime age for entry into lifetime career patterns at the war's end. Even though age qualifications as such were specifically waived for veterans, it is probable that the twenty years of the interwar period may have had some effect of attrition on the general quality and suitability of aging veterans. More to the point, however, is the screening influence of the competitive examination system which no doubt filtered the better candidates through in the early years, leaving a residue of less capable candidates as applicants. Another factor to be considered here is that after the initial period of flux following the war, the CSC settled into the practice, encouraged by the Civil Service Act, of filling positions from the ranks wherever possible. Josie quotes Chairman Roche in 1930 to the effect that "only positions which cannot be filled by promotion are thrown open to general competition" so that "there is not a steady demand for higher grade employees before the public."[12]

Yet while the latter point might explain in some degree the decline in the number of successful veteran applicants, its relevance is limited by an analysis of the type of positions actually held by veterans. Even in the period from September, 1918, to the end of 1919, the vast majority of returned soldier appointments were to the bottom grades in the Post Office and in the Department of National Revenue—98 percent of the 558 Post Office appointments were for annual salaries of less than $600. By 1937–38, about one-half of all veterans appointed went to the Post Office and Public Works. Josie suggests that most of these were probably in the categories of letter carrier, postal clerk, caretaker, cleaner and helper, and elevator operator:

> Although accurate information is not readily available it appears safe to generalize to the extent that in the departments where a large proportion of lower grade positions are found the percentage of veteran appointees is relatively high. . . . It appears therefore that the practice of appointing veterans to low grade positions is a procedure of long stand-

ing, and not related to lapse of time. It is these lower grade positions of the caretaker type . . . that are "dead end" jobs from the standpoint of promotion within the service.[13]

The Veterans Assistance Commission made the flat statement that "Canada has deliberately run the risk of weakening the efficiency of her Civil Service in order to pay the debt she owed those who volunteered for service in her hour of peril."[14] In theoretical terms there can be no doubt that a system which gives any veteran who can pass the examination preference over non-veterans is an invitation to weakening the calibre of appointments. Yet the misgivings of the Veterans Assistance Commission— and it must be noted that it was not until the 1930s that even such mild criticism could be given voice—were perhaps less alarming in reality than in theory. If most veterans were, as it appears, placed in such dead-end jobs as caretaker and elevator operator, it is doubtful that the overall efficiency of the service was grossly impaired.

One part of the veterans preference did give rise to justifiable misgivings. The so-called "preference within the preference" granted to disabled veterans raised legitimate fears for efficiency. It also raised the anger of able-bodied veterans. In 1938 Bland was probed by M.P.'s on this point, with illuminating results:

Q. Mr. Chairman, possibly we can get a picture of it in this way: if the total number of marks that could be obtained for a certain position were 100, and the pass marks were 80—

A. Make it 70, it is 70.

Q. Seventy, and the non-veteran might receive a hundred?

A. Yes.

Q. The ordinary veteran might receive 90?

A. Yes.

Q. And the disabled veteran might receive 70?

A. That is a possibility.

Q. The disabled veteran would get the position?

A. Yes.

The Chairman: What would Griffenhagen say about that?

A. You will have to call him, Mr. Chairman.[15]

Five thousand veterans of World War I were appointed under what some

M.P.'s called the "super-preference." If the operation of the veterans preference gave real cause for alarm between the two wars, that alarm was mostly on this question of the preference within the preference. Whether the federal civil service ought to act as a welfare and rehabilitation agency was clearly a relevant question.

The general legislative provisions for the care of veterans returning from World War II were much more extensive than those in force following the first war. By 1945 the Federal Government felt that it had the fiscal resources to accomplish far more than would have been deemed possible in 1918. A spate of laws was passed through Parliament in the last year of the war and in the years that followed. In 1944 veterans were given an entire new department, to be directed by a full-fledged cabinet minister, the sole purpose of which was to look after the interests of veterans. Other relevant legislation included the Veterans Insurance Act, the War Services Grants Act, the Veterans Land Act, the War Veterans Allowance Act, and the Civilian War Pensions and Allowances Act—all passed in the period from 1944 to 1946. For our purposes the single most important piece of legislation was the Veterans Rehabilitation Act.[16] This provided for allowances to be paid any veteran attending vocational training courses, universities, or taking correspondence courses "likely to fit him for employment or re-employment or to enable him to obtain better or more suitable employment." Fees would be paid, allowances were provided for dependents, and tax exemptions were provided. An amendment the following year provided loans and the payment of travel and other expenses,[17] and allowed special rights to disabled veterans. All this provided a golden opportunity for returned servicemen to acquire an education which they might otherwise never have received. It also had profound implications for the operations of the veterans preference in the civil service.

As we have already noted, the bulk of returned soldiers appointed to the civil service after 1918 went to bottom-level dead-end jobs. This pattern does not appear to have recurred after the second war. The CSC itself maintained that veterans were appointed to all levels, including the top salary levels; unfortunately, it never provided any statistical information. In 1948 the CSC did note that the ratio of veterans to total male appointments would appear even higher "if junior grades having little appeal for veterans were disregarded."[18] Although precise information as to the type of positions to which veterans were appointed is not available, it is possible to compute the distribution of initial appointments by departments. The results indicate that the educational advantages available to veterans had an equalizing effect on their opportunities vis-à-vis non-veteran males. Detailed statistical tables upon which the following pages are based may be found in the Appendix, pp. 501–506.

Table 3 shows the number of veterans and non-veteran males appointed to permanent positions in the civil service from 1945 to 1954 by departments for an overall picture for the ten-year postwar period. A total of 24,309 veterans were appointed.[19] Of these about 30 percent went to the Post Office or received postmasterships. About 17 percent went to the new Department of Veterans Affairs, 11 percent to National Revenue, and 9 percent to the Unemployment Insurance Commission. Among non-veteran male appointments, 22 percent went to the Post Office, 15 percent to Revenue, 13 percent to Transport, and 10 percent to UIC. Comparing the distribution of the two groups by department, we find that only two departments show a significant surplus of veterans: 8 percent more veterans than non-veterans went to the Post Office, and almost 16 percent more went to Veterans Affairs. It is the latter which offers the most startling contrast, with less than 1 percent of non-veterans against almost 17 percent of veterans. Thus, it would appear likely that, with the exception of transfers from other departments, positions at *all* levels must have gone to veterans. The only departments to show a preference for non-veteran males were Transport, where 9 percent more non-veteran than veterans were appointed, and Agriculture, Revenue, and the Resources group, with smaller differences. It is of some interest that no significant preference was shown for veterans by Public Works, a haven for veterans of the first war.

We can also examine temporary appointments for the same ten-year period in table 4. Once again Veterans Affairs was a channel for veterans, 24 percent of veterans being appointed to this department as opposed to only 6 percent of non-veterans—a net difference of 18 percent. The comparative distribution among other departments showed no equivalent divergences, although Transport, Resources, and Agriculture (together with Defence) once again showed a comparatively greater number of non-veterans.

From 1955 to 1962 the Annual Reports of the Civil Service Commission indicated the distribution by department of all appointments, both permanent and temporary. Computing the overall distributions for this eight-year period in table 5, we find that the Department of National Defence suddenly emerged as the largest employer of veterans. Almost 28 percent of veterans appointed went initially to Defence, while only 13 percent now went to Veterans Affairs. Meanwhile, almost 19 percent of non-veteran male appointments went initially to Defence, and 5 percent to Veterans Affairs. Thus Defence took 9 percent more veterans than non-veterans, whereas Veterans Affairs took 8 percent more veterans than non-veterans. The sudden shifting of veterans into Defence during the second postwar decade may be explained by two factors: the transfer of armed forces personnel into the civilian side of the Department and the delayed action effects of the subsidized education of veterans. National Defence emerged during the cold war in the 1950s as one of the largest and most prestigious of government departments. The combination of a military department and the advantages of the veterans preference apparently proved a successful one with many ex-servicemen. While the comparative distribution in the Post Office continued to level off, it is of interest that Public Works did begin to show a slight tendency to hire comparatively more veterans—although in contrast to the post-World War I situation, most of these were apparently for technical and professional positions, following the graduation of many veterans from engineering faculties. The Resources group of departments again showed a comparative disinclination to hire veterans, as did Revenue and Agriculture on a smaller scale. However, the relative number of veterans hired by Transport more than doubled.

We may also look at all appointments, permanent and temporary, over an eighteen-year period following the war in table 6. With the exception of Veterans Affairs, it cannot be said that any significant concentrations of ex-servicemen can be detected. Unlike the experience following World War I, veterans preference appointments were distributed in a fashion not significantly different from the distribution of non-veteran male appointments. All the indications are, moreover, that veteran appointments were to a far wider range of positions and salary levels; there is no evidence that the bulk went to dead-end jobs, as had previously occurred.

When we turn to the overall impact of the veterans on civil service recruitment, we also find a change from the earlier experience. Far more veterans took advantage of the veterans preference to enter the service than following the previous war. Unfortunately, information does not seem to be available concerning the number of veteran *applicants* for government jobs; therefore we cannot determine if World War II veterans applied in proportionately greater numbers or if they were relatively more successful than their predecessors in achieving passing grades on examinations. Perhaps a combination of these two factors may have come into play. It is possible that the government service may have seemed a more attractive career possibility in the 1940s and 1950s than it had in the 1920s. More to the point, perhaps, is the impact of subsidized education on the success of veterans in meeting the qualifications for entry into the service.

When we examine in table 7 all appointments of veterans by year as a percentage of all male appointments, and of all appointments, male and female, we find that from 1945 to 1962, 525,555 persons, both male and female, were appointed to permanent or temporary positions within the civil service. Of this number, 143,833 or 27 percent, were veterans. In the same period, appointments of male veterans constituted 45 percent of all male appointments. Table 8 shows that from 1945 to 1954, 44,602 persons, male and female, were given permanent appointments. Of these positions, 24,409, or 55 percent, were to veterans. Taking the number of male veterans appointed as a percentage of permanent male appointments only, we reach a figure of 66 percent. In other words, two out of every three males given permanent positions in the civil service in the decade following World War II came in under the veterans preference, and one out of every two appointments, male or female, went to a veteran. Moreover, as the CSC itself noted, as early as 1948: "Another 14,000 veterans have been re-assigned from department to department in the same period [1945 to 1948]. This latter figure reflects the steps taken to protect their interests when wartime departments drastically reduce their personnel or disappear altogether. [This] becomes a source of added satisfaction when it is remembered that over-all civil service strength was reduced appreciably in the same period."[20]

The peak impact of the veterans on the civil service was in 1946. (We are speaking here in a *quantitative* sense. In the *qualitative* sense, the years 1951 and 1952 were significant to the service, as the mass of veterans who had entered university courses under the Veterans Preference Act graduated and entered the labour force.) Since 1946, and especially since the close of the 1940s, the input of veterans into the service has been a declining factor as can be seen in Appendix, figures 1 and 2. Although the CSC no longer publishes records of the frequency with which the veterans preference is used, it is safe to suggest that its use is by now infrequent and insignificant to the overall picture, with the possible exception of military officers with war service moving into the civilian side of National Defence or allied departments, a process perhaps accelerated in recent years by the unification of the armed services with its attendant strains.

No major changes were made to the Civil Service Act to accommodate the returning veterans in 1945. The legislative provision of absolute preference in force since the first war was more than sufficient. The CSC did, however, mobilize its services in an unprecedented manner to attract applications from veterans and to ensure the success of such applications. The CSC's own attitude toward the veterans appears also to have shifted from laissez-faire in the first instance to a positively interventionist approach in the second. While war was still raging in Europe, the CSC set up a London office for the benefit of servicemen. Competitions were advertised among the fighting forces by means of daily routine orders, service publications, service personnel officers, and educational officers. Examining boards operated in France, Belgium, Holland, Italy, and England. Other government departments, especially National Defence and External Affairs, cooperated in these endeavours. Special veterans' information offices

470

were established in Ottawa and in district offices throughout Canada. The CSC and its various agencies worked closely with the Department of Veterans Affairs, Defence discharge depots, and veterans' organizations. A Government Services Selection and Release Committee was set up in 1945 under the chairmanship of the CSC to recommend the release from the armed forces of persons whose services were demanded by government departments.[21] The CSC also continued the practice begun after World War I of including a representative of the Canadian Legion or of other veterans' associations on selection boards to ensure that the interests of veteran applicants were being properly safeguarded. This practice was not a statutory requirement but was undertaken at the initiative of the CSC itself, and was in effect the responsibility of the CSC alone.

In 1946 the Veterans' Information Office interviewed more than eighteen thousand servicemen. Interestingly enough, the CSC noted with some pride that the VIO "as a result of special tests, effected the placement of thirty-four hundred veterans additional to those who had entered the service through regular competitive examination." The examinations themselves were revamped to measure more "clearly" the potentialities of veterans, with their different "background of experience." A special placement service for disabled veterans was set up, and special attention was given to "those veterans of both wars for whom the problem of finding suitable employment is made particularly difficult by age, family responsibilities and other factors."[22] In this same period, the CSC, which had always shown a reluctance to institute in-service training for civil servants, began providing training to veterans.[23] By the end of 1947 the special functions of the VIO were absorbed into the mainstream of the CSC, after the Office had interviewed some thirty-five thousand veterans between 1944 and 1947 and had placed more than five thousand in the public service, in additon to the veterans appointed through the regular competitive examination.[24] While the VIO went out of existence as such, however, it quickly rose phoenix-like as the Public Relations Office. Nor was this metamorphosis entirely accidental, for as Commissioner Nelson told a group of American colleagues at the 1948 Civil Service Assembly, the CSC did not always have to engage directly in public relations since "we get a good deal of publicity through veterans' periodicals."[25] The CSC had, in effect, fostered a new constituency for itself, and a new pillar of public support.

The "preference within the prefrence," the extra preference given disabled veterans over able-bodied veterans, continued in force following World War II. The CSC stated in 1949 that five thousand disabled veterans had been given positions under this special preference,[26] a total over four years which matched the total accumulated over twenty-five years following World War I. Curiously enough, this particular aspect of the

471

veterans preference seems to have attracted much less criticism following the second war, even though it appears to have been taken advantage of more extensively, and would appear to be less justifiable, given the more generous context of social welfare measures, both specifically for veterans and generally for all citizens. The lack of criticism on the part of able-bodied veterans may indeed offer further proof for the proposition that veterans from the second war were more evenly distributed throughout the many levels of the service: it may well have been that disabled veterans were not competing with other veterans, but were instead being assigned to the bottom-level dead-end jobs such as elevator operator and caretaker into which the bulk of veterans had been channelled following the first war.

The first attempt to draw attention to the implications of the veterans preference for the efficiency of the service came as early as 1946 in the Report of the Gordon Royal Commission. Expressing misgivings over the rigidity and "not wholly satisfactory" nature of absolute preference, Gordon pointed with approval to United States and British practices, and then simply suggested a new system "that is designed to be both in the best long-term interests of the whole body of veterans as citizens and in the best interests of the present and future efficiency of the public service" without providing any concrete details of such a system.[27] Taylor Cole points out that the sole impact of this vague recommendation was to add the voice of the Canadian Legion to the chorus of opposition to the Gordon Report.[28]

The second attempt to examine the implications of the veterans preference for the service came a dozen years later. The Heeney Report of 1958 noted that the absolute preference system was "to the best of our knowledge more generous than that in any other country." The "absolute and overriding" character of the preference was cause for "general concern":

Under the present law this can operate to exclude entirely other Canadian citizens with outstanding qualifications. Recognizing that Parliament's purpose in granting such preferential treatment was to give the veteran an advantage in competition for appointment not only to compensate for time lost from his regular employment but also as a recognition by the State that the ex-serviceman has risked life and limb in the defence of his country, we have considered other means of achieving this end which would not entail the unsatisfactory administrative factors and inequities of the present law.[29]

After considering various alternatives, the Heeney Report recommended that the present preference for disabled veterans be continued without advancing any reasons why this aspect, the most questionable from an efficiency viewpoint, should be left unchallenged. At the same time, Heeney recommended that other veterans be accorded a 5 percent point bonus preference, to be limited to one occasion at the veteran's option—a recommendation later echoed, with as much effect, by the Glassco Commission.[30] The Diefenbaker Government was clearly hostile to any limitation of the preference, and Heeney's successor as CSC chairman, S. H. Hughes, had no intention of implementing this section of the Report.[31] As Hughes explained publicly, "The government took the view that this long standing preference was in the nature of a compact with those who had served the nation so nobly in times of great peril and consequently did not feel disposed to alter in any particular the absolute preference."[32] The Civil Service Act of 1961 thus kept the preference system intact, while spelling out in great detail who was not eligible for the preference. Finally, the 1967 Public Service Employment Act once again maintained the preference system intact.

FRENCH-SPEAKING CIVIL SERVANTS

The Royal Commission on Bilingualism and Biculturalism has carried out an exhaustive study of the place of French-speaking civil servants in the federal bureaucracy.[33] There would be little point in attempting to reproduce this research effort. We will therefore draw largely on the highlights of the work of the Royal Commission.

Although it is somewhat difficult to gather firm statistical evidence, it would appear that there has been a steady decline in the proportion of French-speaking civil servants throughout the last hundred years. Hodgetts has estimated that in 1863, 36 percent of the Government's employees were French-speaking—although these same employees accounted for less than 20 percent of the payroll.[34] In 1918, French-speaking employees numbered 22 percent of the total. In 1946, the proportion had dropped to 13 percent. In examining these figures it should not be forgotten that the proportion of French-speaking Canadians in the population as a whole was also declining over this same period, as new provinces were added and immigration increased. Nevertheless, it is obvious that other factors were at work. Among these factors the most important was probably the advent of the merit system and competitive examinations.

The patronage system undoubtedly allowed for a degree of representativeness in the selection of administrative staff. The constitutional provisions for the representation of Quebec in the House of Commons, as well as *de facto* arrangements for representation in the Cabinet, would tend to ensure that under a patronage regime, *mutatis mutandis*, government posts could be distributed in a roughly similar proportion. Even in the absence of any official policy encouraging bilingualism in service to the public, some degree of bilingualism must have existed because of the presence of relatively large numbers of French-speaking employees.

It is revealing that when the merit principle was being advanced as a great moral benefit to the body politic, there seems to have been no discussion of its potentially differential impact on the two linguistic and cultural groups in Canada. It was quite simply assumed that the competitive examination was a neutral device capable of detecting the universal "merits" of any and all candidates, regardless of cultural, linguistic, or educational background. The question of whether the civil service ought to be bilingual and bicultural was not raised. The Civil Service Commission thus cannot, in retrospect, be fixed with individual blame for the decline of French representation which accompanied its own establishment and growth: bilingualism and biculturalism in the contemporary sense were simply not part of the universe of political discourse.

Even the Quebec M.P.'s did not appear to differ significantly from their English-Canadian colleagues in their attitudes toward the 1918–19 legislation. There were defenders of patronage and proponents of the merit system in both groups. Indeed, the most vocal defender of patronage was Sir Sam Hughes, scarcely a figure around whom Quebecers would rally. Many Quebec M.P.'s expressed the same relief at ridding themselves of the "incubus" and the same hopes for the merit system as their English colleagues. Three factors, however, soon combined to severely strain Quebec support for the merit system.

The veterans preference was not only at odds with the usual formulation of the merit principle, but was in its actual impact a roadblock thrown directly and immediately into the path of French-speaking representation. The very basis of the conscription crisis of 1917 had of course been the failure of Quebecers to volunteer for service in anything like the numbers in which English-speaking Canadians had come forward. Now the mainly English-speaking returned men were entering into the civil service under an absolute preference system. Worse, they were competing for the lower rank positions in which French-speaking employees were concentrated. Worse yet, the 1918–19 legislation contained no provision concerning the language capabilities of employees serving areas which were predominantly French speaking.

This last point leads to the second factor which weakened the value of the merit system in Quebec's eyes. Despite the professed concern for the efficiency of the public service, neither the new legislation nor the CSC recognized that the existence of over two million French-speaking citizens required special efforts to ensure French-language service to the public.

Curiously, the sheer *inefficiency* of unilingual service in a bilingual country does not seem to have impressed itself upon English Canadians at the time.

The third factor which hindered French-speaking civil servants was the examination system. Although examinations could be written in French at the candidate's option, language was in itself only a minor problem. More important by far was the differing educational backgrounds of the two groups: English technical and commercial skills versus the French classical education. The CSC never took this into account. As the Royal Commission on Bilingualism noted, "Its examinations, even when translated into French, reflected the patterns of thought and cultural style of English-speaking Canada."[35] Nor were the language skills of French-speaking candidates given any credit in determining their qualifications, despite the fact that virtually the only bilingual candidates were French speaking.

Many of these same factors operated to lower the levels of French-speaking *participation* within the bureaucratic process, as well as the levels of those entering the service. It was a clear fact of life that it was much more difficult for French-speaking civil servants to reach middle or senior levels. The resulting imbalance in the distribution of the two groups was first made apparent to the top ranks of the bureaucracy in 1932, when a delegation was chosen to represent Canada at the Imperial Economic Conference. Not a single French-speaking official was numbered among the civil servants in the delegation. A controversy was sparked by Quebec M.P.'s. The Under Secretary of State for External Affairs, O. D. Skelton, was shaken to find that not a single French-speaking official of sufficient rank was to be found in the civil service. Skelton immediately began a program of encouraging French-speaking university graduates to enter the bureaucracy.

French Canadians inside or outside the bureaucracy who were aware of the inequity of the system found that protest was usually untenable, as it was associated with attacks on the merit principle. Any pleas on behalf of the French as a group were generally categorized as attempts at gaining "special privileges" to which the individual members of the group were not entitled, or as veiled moves toward the old patronage system. The attitude of most Quebec cabinet ministers and M.P.'s did little to indicate that political patronage was not at the root of all French discontent. These spokesmen, according to the Royal Commission Report, "showed little interest in the Civil Service Commission's new staffing policies; they were content to perpetuate the old practices rather than to try to work out ways in which the Public Service might modify its interpretation of efficiency and rationalization to fit the talents and needs of their constituents."[36] The witch-hunting atmosphere of the Pouliot Committee in 1938 probably reinforced this image, with its French-speaking chairman and its strong hostility to the CSC.

After 1935, however, an increasing level of protest and demands could be detected from French Canadians across Canada. This discontent centred around the lack of French-language service to the public. In 1938 Wilfred Lacroix, Liberal member for Quebec-Montmorency, succeeded in adding an amendment to the Civil Service Act which specified that a candidate must be qualified in the knowledge and usage of the language of the majority of people with whom he would have to deal.[37] The Lacroix amendment was the first explicit recognition in the Civil Service Act of the value of the French language to bureaucratic efficiency. It does not, however, appear to have been taken very seriously. In 1942 a civil service regulation gave the deputy heads the right to determine the language qualifications for any particular position.[38] It would seem that they largely ignored the provision. Early in 1944 Lacroix himself wrote to Prime Minister King to point out that a unilingual English-speaking official had been appointed clerk appraiser, postal parcels and express, in Montreal. When pressed by Lacroix, CSC Chairman Bland denied that knowledge of the French language was necessary for this post. The Minister of National Revenue concurred in this judgement and ignored Lacroix's protest.[39]

Research of the Royal Commission on Bilingualism has brought out the key role played by Ernest Lapointe in fighting behind the scenes for a greater French role in the civil service. As King's chief Quebec lieutenant, Lapointe was in no position to wage an open confrontation with the English establishment, but he tirelessly used his influence in personal appeals, not in any attempt to re-establish patronage (of which he had always been a critic) but to effect a recogniton of the efficiency of a bilingual civil service in a bilingual country. Despite the sincerity of his convictions, his efforts met with virtually no response: "Lapointe was fighting a strong historical tradition: the worlds of politics and administration were permeated by the conviction that the use of the two languages would weaken efficiency. There was no new legislation in language use in the Public Service between the amendment of 1898 (which had awarded a $50 bonus to bilingual civil servants) and the Lacroix amendment of 1938, and the latter was allowed to become a dead letter due to the exigencies of the war."[40]

Lapointe had hoped that the Lacroix amendment would have led to an increase in French-speaking civil servants, but legislation by itself is impotent without the will to enforce and utilize it. This latter intention was clearly lacking. The advent of World War II administered the coup de grâce to the Lacroix amendment. The enormous expansion of the service during the war, and the virtual suspension of normal staffing procedures, meant that the English character of the bureaucracy became even more pronounced: "In the haste to recruit staff in an atmosphere of emergency, informal networks of personal and professional acquaintances became more than ever before the chief means of finding new recruits. The Francophones were even more left out in the cold, and the purposes of the amendment were forgotten."[41]

Some of the resistance which Lapointe met was extreme. For example, at one time he received a flood of complaints from Quebec M.P.'s that telephone calls to the CSC were answered by unilingual secretaries. Lapointe attempted to arrange for special telephones for each Commissioner so that French calls could go directly to the French Commissioner. The Comptroller of the Treasury issued a flat rejection of this request. "It took Lapointe weeks of importuning before the Minister of Finance reversed this ruling."[42]

The role of the CSC in the issue of French in the civil service was somewhat ambiguous. As the defender of the merit system and the guardian of the veterans preference, the CSC could well be seen as an enemy of the French. It is no doubt the case that at least part of J. F. Pouliot's hostility to the CSC arose from his feeling that it was an anti-French, anti-Quebec device. Yet from its very beginnings, the CSC had maintained a certain place for the French minority within its own organization. One Commissioner was always French speaking, and there is evidence that the Quebec caucus of the party in power had considerable influence in the selection of this Commissioner. A separate French Examination Branch operated alongside the larger English Branch, and there were separate English and French clerical sections. Yet these token recognitions of the French masked a general indifference. The CSC was traditionally opposed to any positive action to promote the French language. A former Commissioner disclosed in an interview that it had always been his policy that bilingualism was entirely a departmental affair and no concern of the CSC as such.

It is a mark of the desperate neglect into which French-speaking civil servants had fallen that even the CSC's neutrality and indifference could on occasion inspire gratitude and loyalty. This state of affairs was revealed in 1946 when the Gordon Royal Commission recommended that the CSC be stripped of almost all its powers, which were to be transferred to Treasury Board. As Chairman Bland whipped up opposition to the Gordon Report, French-speaking civil servants, Members of Parliament, and independent organizations rallied enthusiastically to Bland's side, on the grounds that the Department of Finance and Treasury Board were bastions of Anglo-Saxon, anti-French prejudice.[43] In an environment so unsympathetic, even indifference could be taken as reason for gratitude.

If World War II caused further deterioration of the position of French-speaking civil servants, the war's aftermath was even more shattering. Although many French Canadians had fought overseas, the armed forces had nevertheless been overwhelmingly English speaking. The removal of large numbers of employees to make way for returning veterans with an absolute preference would clearly be at the expense of the French as a group. As previously noted, the proportion of French-speaking employees dropped to 13 percent in 1946, the peak year for the entry of veterans into the service.

The onslaught of the veterans, together with the disregard for French evidenced in the Gordon Report, sparked an outburst of protest among French nationalists in the postwar period. In Parliament, a group of five Quebec M.P.'s began meeting on an informal basis to discuss the situation and possible solutions. Prime Minister King recognized the group officially in 1947; they were constituted as a committee under Solicitor-General Joseph Jean to investigate French participation in all federal departments and agencies. They recommended the appointment of three French-speaking deputy ministers and of dual French and English deputies for the Departments of Agriculture, Mines and Resources, Justice, and Trade and Commerce. Comment was hostile. The report was never tabled or published. Jean himself was appointed to the Bench, and his committee was dissolved.

In 1950 Commissioner Boudreau circulated a memorandum stating his personal opposition to the exclusive determination of language requirements by departments. He argued that "since the measurement of linguistic ability was difficult at best, the Civil Service Commission, unlike individual departments, was at least in a position to ensure uniform and adequate standards throughout the Service."[44] The other Commissioners, however, did not agree.

The decade of the 1950s was generally a period of increased restiveness in Quebec. Some of the more prescient government officials could see the growing discontent and understood at least some of its implications for the public service. The committee of leading civil servants which met in the early 1950s under Robert Bryce to consider changes in the Civil Service Act realized that greater consideration must be given to the place of the French language and to the position of French-speaking civil servants. No action, however, followed.

Beyond a general statement that the civil service ought to be *representative* of the population it served, the Heeney Report of 1958 gave little prominence to the question of language, but did find the Lacroix amendment and the corresponding regulation 32 "not wholly satisfactory." Heeney went on to recommend that where both English and French-speaking citizens were served by a government office, it would be preferable to have bilingual officials serving the public rather than those with "knowledge and use of the language of the majority" (section 19). Heeney also suggested that the CSC should determine the language qualifications to be attached to any given position, rather than allowing the departments to set qualifications.[45] The Civil Service Act of 1961 incorporated the following change: "The number of employees appointed to serve in any department or in any local office of a department who are qualified in the knowledge and use of the English or French language or both shall, in the opinion of the Commission, be sufficient to enable the department or local office to perform its functions adequately and to give effective service to the public."[46]

The Glassco Royal Commission focussed attention on bilingualism in the central machinery of government rather than on local offices. Glassco made the point very clearly that a representative French-speaking presence in the bureaucracy was the essential goal, and that the creation of an administrative environment attractive to those of French culture and education was necessary. The CSC was moreover charged with the responsibility for intensifying recruitment efforts in French Canada. Glassco was, however, short on details. The French-speaking member of the Royal Commission, F. Eugène Therrien, submitted a separate statement, "Bilingualism in the Federal Administration," in which he called for a far more extensive program than had been outlined in the main Report.[47]

By the time the Report of the Glassco Commission was published, Jean Lesage and the Liberals had deposed the Union Nationale in Quebec, the so-called Quiet Revolution was well under way, separatism was becoming a serious alternative, and the Federal Government began to realize that a bilingual and bicultural civil service might be more than a generous gift to the French minority and that it might instead be a political necessity to keep the nation together. The return of the Liberals to power in Ottawa with strong Quebec backing, the establishment of the Royal Commission on Bilingualism and Biculturalism, the granting of bonuses to bilingual employees, and the encouragement of top Quebec university graduates, academics, and public officials to come to Ottawa to make careers in the federal civil service, all indicated a vastly altered attitude toward French in the public service. The CSC, with its new role in language training, found itself near the centre of one of the largest transformations ever attempted in the bureaucracy. The election victory of Pierre Elliott Trudeau in 1968 and the subsequent passage of the Official Languages Bill consolidated this trend: a mandate was given to effect a *bilingual* civil service. But the civil service legislation of 1967 had already laid the groundwork for the CSC's own role in this process.

The Public Service Employment Act of 1967 includes three sections bearing on language.[48] According to section 10:

Appointments to or from within the Public Service shall be based on selection according to merit, as determined by the Commission, and shall be made by the Commission, at the request of the deputy head concerned, by competition or by other such process of personnel selection designed to establish the merit of candidates as the Commission considers is in the best interests of the Public Service.

12(1) The Commission may, in determining pursuant to section 10 the basis of assessment of merit in relation to any position or class of positions, prescribe selection standards as to education, knowledge, experience, language, age, residence or any other matters that, in the opinion of the Commission, are necessary or desirable having regard to the nature of the duties to be performed. . . .

Section 16(2) gives the CSC power to determine the language qualifications of candidates by conducting examinations in the language to be tested, as well as in the language chosen at the candidate's own option. Section 20 states that:

Employees appointed to serve in any department or other portion of the Public Service, or part thereof, shall be qualified in the knowledge and use of the English or French language, or both, to the extent that the Commission deems necessary in order that the functions of such department, portion or part, can be performed adequately and effective service can be provided to the public.

The decade of the 1960s has thus witnessed a startling change in direction on this issue. However, it is well to place the transformations of this decade within the perspective of the entire half-century of the merit system. In this connection it is worth quoting the Royal Commission on Bilingualism at some length.

The history of language use and participation in the federal Public Service . . . has been strongly influenced by a particular interpretation of the concept of efficiency.

Both Francophone and Anglophone federal politicians and public servants accepted the prevailing orthodoxies linking unilingualism with rationality and efficiency. For Anglophones, the concept of efficiency was an article of faith. . . . But the idea that language ability in French alone—or even in both French and English—might be a component of merit and efficiency rarely made an impression. . . .

French speaking Canada's complaints could always be interpreted as a "political" appeal to return to the bad old days of patronage and, therefore, to inefficiency if not corruption, and the French language partisans were put in the position of appearing to be opposed to efficiency as an administrative aim. Most Francophone politicians and officials probably accepted the dominant Anglophone definition of the situation.

Anglophones enjoyed the benefits of a unilingual public service, but generally did so unconsciously, for consciousness implies some element of choice, and no alternatives were seriously debated. What we can consider today as effective discrimination against the French language and Francophones, earlier generations took to be the natural order of things. The Anglophones did not see that such one-sidedness corroded Anglo-French harmony and the continued existence of Canada; the Francophones were lulled into quiescence by patronage and honorific positions. All in all, the history of the Public Service from the two standpoints of language use and Francophone participation represents a tragic failure of Canadian political imagination.[49]

As this lengthy quotation points out most admirably, both the English and the French were prisoners not only of the particular historical circumstances in which they found themselves, but also of that ubiquitous and all-encompassing concept of "efficiency" which seemed to lie at the end of every road. Yet the disregard shown even for the concept of providing service to the public in both official languages indicates a deeper level yet of Anglo-Saxon indifference. Since even serving the French-speaking public in the language they could best understand was not considered a matter of efficiency, *it is scarcely surprising that the far more complex question of the place of French-Canadian civil servants within the bureaucracy was left untouched.*

The small proportion and low ranking of French officials did not rest on positively discriminatory rules but rather on a failure to recognize the social and cultural content of the supposedly neutral structure of the merit system. By setting up impartial machinery which was in fact derived from an English-Canadian cultural and educational framework, the CSC was in effect helping to perpetuate and indeed to consolidate an already existing social inequality. Yet it would clearly be a historical injustice to lay any special blame on the CSC for this state of affairs. In the context of the times, it was simply fulfilling the role that others expected it to fulfil. There can be little doubt that majority opinion in the country at large, in Parliament, and in the bureaucracy itself, would have rejected out of hand any concept of special treatment for the French minority. But it is also important to note that the case of the veterans preference stands as a thorough refutation of all the theses advanced in the name of the merit principle against special treatment for the French, and a refutation, more-over, backed by the powerful approval of the majority.

In terms of the CSC's own role, the contrast between the case of the French Canadians and the veterans is instructive. Where the Government decided to act as a model employer, the CSC could and did play an inno-vative role, taking initiatives and experimenting with its own machinery in an attempt to smooth the way for the veterans. Where no such decision was taken, the CSC played no positive role whatever. By way of contrast with its historical record in this regard, it is interesting to note the active and innovative role adopted by the CSC now that the *political* decision has been made that the Federal Government should be a model employer of French-speaking Canadians. In the larger sense, this is, of course, as it should be; yet in another sense it is one more bit of historical evidence undermining the CSC's own image of its independence of action.

WOMEN IN THE PUBLIC SERVICE

As with the case of the Royal Commission on Bilingualism Report on French-speaking participation in the civil service, we are fortunate in pos-sessing a major piece of research on female participation in the bureauc-racy: Kathleen Archibald's *Sex and the Public Service*.[50] Much of what follows is drawn from Archibald, along with additional historical data gathered in the course of this study.

It is a universal observation that women have been entering the labour market in ever-increasing numbers throughout the twentieth century. This much is obvious. What is less obvious is the type of work into which women have been channelled. Despite popular opinion, a close study of statistical information on the female labour force in Canada does *not* indi-cate that the twentieth century has witnessed a steady upward movement of women in the work world.[51] The proportion of female professionals, for instance, was lower in 1961 than at any time in this century since 1901. In fact, the major occupational increase in female participation is in the "clerical" category; in 1901, only 22 percent in this category were female, but by 1961 this proportion had risen to 62 percent.[52] In effect, as the economy shifted away from a reliance on heavy industry and primary pro-duction to the present postindustrial situation in which white-collar occu-pations are the most common, women have been brought into the lowest rungs of this burgeoning sector of the economy. When the data show that women are consistently underpaid compared to men,[53] and when it is fur-ther considered that the relative earning power of the clerical category has fallen drastically from 1941 to 1961, that the relative earning power of professional categories has maintained stability, and at the same time that relative earning power of the increasingly male-dominated "service" category has *risen*,[54] it becomes clear that the flooding of the lower white-collar ranks with women has been essentially a utilization of a cheap labour reserve—a process not dissimilar to the drawing of surplus agricultural labour into the factories during the early Industrial Revolution. Moreover, while this long-term trend is the most pronounced throughout the century, two fluctuations within this trend confirm this categorization of women as a cheap labour reserve. In two world wars, and particularly in the second, large numbers of women were brought into factories and heavy industries to take over "male" jobs from soldiers. At war's end, almost all were removed, with no long-term change in occupational patterns resulting. For example, in 1944, seventy-one thousand women were employed in the manufacture of iron products in Canada; in 1946 almost fifty thousand of these were gone.[55] By 1951 the proportion of women in blue-collar manufacturing categories was at its lowest point in the century.[56] In other words, the female labour reserve could be shifted briefly from one sector to another to ease the strains of external events on the labour market as a whole.

A statistical device which can measure the degree of concentration of groups within particular occupational categories is the index of segregation, devised by Duncan and Duncan. This is expressed as a percentage, indicating the number of, in this case, women who would have to change occupations to produce a percentage distribution of females equal to that of males. This index has been computed in the United States for the seven decennial censuses throughout the twentieth century. In 1900 the index was 66.9. It changed only slightly over 60 years, and by 1960 was 68.4—a small *increase*. By way of contrast, the same index for racial segregation in 1960 was only 46.8.[57] All this is of some considerable importance as a perspective on the history of female participation in the public service. Before making sense out of this history, it is necessary to discard the common notion that slowly but surely women have been attaining a better and better position in the work world. It is simply not so.

Until very recently, the Government in general, and the Civil Service Commission in particular, never considered women as employees to be treated on an equal basis with men. Unlike the more subtle forms of covert discrimination against French-speaking civil servants, there was never any particular attempt made to hide the discrimination against women which was, and is, built into the very fabric of civil service legislation and personnel practice. This approach, however straightforward, always presented an incongruous contrast with the merit principle. The clash of these two divergent principles presents a constant theme through the last sixty years.

There were two aspects to the merit system which promised greater equality for women. The patronage system coincided historically with the period when women could not vote. Clearly a system of selection based on electoral support for the party in power would be generally indifferent to those who lacked the franchise. By contrast, the merit system, by denying political influence, appeared to open up avenues for the politically power-less. For example, in 1908 the CSC estimated that seven hundred out of three thousand government employees (23 percent) in the Inside Service were women, although the female proportion in the Outside Service was negligible. Archibald suggests that only part of this difference can be at-tributed to the higher concentration of office support staff in Ottawa; a part must also be attributed to the divergent hiring practices in the two sec-tions,[58] with political considerations less important in the Inside Service.

The second reason why the merit principle would seem to have prompted egalitarian hiring practices lay in the rhetoric with which it was advanced. Under competitive examinations, it was asserted, *individual* merits would be tested. On the face of it, a system which claimed to select those best qualified for any position should have been a system which cut across existing prejudices. Yet despite the otherwise unbounded faith of the CSC in the infallibility of the examination system, it was never willing to apply the system to women on the same basis as men. The reason for this reluctance is twofold. As Archibald suggests: "When opportunities were made available, as in the Ottawa civil service, women flooded in. This suggests the generally low labour force participation rates of women in the early part of this century were more a result of restricted opportunities than of female lack of interest in working."[59] Second, women showed an embarrassing ability to qualify for entry into the service under the competi-tive examination system. The result was, in the words of the Royal Com-mission of 1907–8:

> The Commissioners have to draw attention to another set of circum-stances which has cropped up during the last few years, and that is the great *redundance* of women appointed to the junior branches in the in-side service. . . . In Ottawa in 1906, out of the 206 candidates who passed the qualifying examination, 121 were women. The lower grades of the Post Office, where there are 366 employees altogether, and the lower grades of the Department of the Interior, where there are some 500 employees, are practically filled up with women. While the Com-missioners readily acknowledge that many women are thoroughly en-titled to succeed in the public service, yet the influx of such a large num-ber must, if continued, in the course of time utterly swallow up the lower grades of the service, and by limiting the field of promotion to the higher classes prove detrimental to the higher and more responsible

branches of the service; for it can hardly be admitted yet that the work devolving on the departments can be carried on with a staff composed entirely of women.[60]

There is an Alice-in-Wonderland touch to this line of logic, not dissimilar from arguments used to describe the "problem" of coloured immigrants. But in the early twentieth century, the "problem" of women was taken as real—and even dangerous. As the CSC stated bluntly: "The character and quality of the men entering the service declined. The lower-grade offices were filled with women, which limited the field from which promotions might be made to the higher divisions, and interfered with the development of competent male clerks."[61] The question of whether competence was in fact a sex-linked quality indeed occurred to the CSC, but it perceived the possibility of women displaying equal aptitudes, not as a potential for the enhanced efficiency of the service, but rather as a threat. Astonishingly, the CSC in 1908 stated: "It is freely admitted that there are women who have quite as good executive ability as men, and who might, on the *mere* ground of personal qualifications, fill the higher positions in the service."[62]

Starting from this premise, the defenders of the merit principle went on to introduce restrictions on women which would ensure that they could not achieve advancement on the "mere ground of personal qualifications." Deputy heads were told to segregate occupational categories into male and female groups. Women were then limited to the lowest levels of appointment, such as "stenographers and typewriters." Although the Canadian civil service had never recognized the concept that differential rates of pay be accorded to male and female employees engaged in the same work, the equal pay for equal work doctrine was rendered a mockery by limiting women to the lowest levels without much real hope of advancement, while their male counterparts could advance to new classes and higher levels of salary.

The explanation for the CSC's behaviour is quite apparent. As Archibald explains, "The Commission perceived its problem not as one of keeping women down—that was taken for granted—but as one of keeping down the *number* of women in the civil service."[63] Clearly this goal transcended the merit principle. If on the basis of mere personal qualifications women could be selected and advanced by the merit system, which after all was concerned solely with mere personal qualifications, then the merit system would have to be protected against itself. There was a very curious ambivalence involved here, not unlike an ambivalence usually present when discriminatory rules are being defended. The basis of the rules was the alleged inability of women to fill executive positions; yet the very use of such rules implied a deep fear that women *could* fill such positions; otherwise formal segregation would not have been necessary. Restrictive rules on the other hand ensured that the prejudice would remain untested. That the CSC got itself into such a tangle is an indication of both the power of anti-female prejudice in the society at large and the strength of the merit principle as a standard for selection. The merit principle was a potent social myth which could be partially subverted to accommodate the exigencies of the time, but which left a vague sense of uneasiness among those so manipulating it.

Despite some of the genuinely revolutionary features of the 1918 Civil Service Act, its treatment of female employees could not be numbered among its more audacious aspects. As we noted earlier in our examination of the legislation, the only mention of sex was as a quality which, along with "age, . . . health, habits, residence, moral character," was considered a *limiting* factor on individual qualifications. When the Arthur Young classification experts recommended salaries which were geared to prewar price levels, the resulting hardship was offset by the award of bonuses. However, such bonuses were granted only to "heads of households," thus effectively cutting off women employees from the equal pay for equal work doctrine. The Associated Federal Employees of Ottawa protested to Meighen: "Whether an employee is married or unmarried, male or female, has nothing whatever to do with the question. He or she, as an individual, is paid a certain sum for doing certain work. The problem is to bring as near to normal as may be the purchasing power of the wages as paid."[64] The protest went unheeded.

In 1921 formal restrictions were placed against the employment of married women. Only if they could prove that they were self-supporting and only if a sufficient number of qualified male candidates was lacking, were married women to be appointed, and then largely to temporary positions. Women already holding permanent positions who married had to resign. If there was a need for their services they could be rehired as temporaries and paid only the minimum rate in the class. These restrictions continued for thirty-four years. This did not, however, mean that no married women were working for the Government. For as the CSC later noted, "For a number of years, the Commission had found it necessary to recruit and retain married women as stenographers, typists, office equipment operators, and clerks."[65] What such restrictions did in fact offer was an effective means of control over a cheap labour supply. Even in the depression years, when popular pressures against married women holding jobs became intense, an investigation instigated by the Pouliot Committee revealed that many married women were employed by the civil service in 1938. That not all married women were willing to undergo such discriminatory treatment is indicated by a further Pouliot-inspired investigation which revealed that at least 189 married women were working under their maiden names.[66]

The Depression was a particularly unhappy and insecure period for women in the public service. When jobs became scarce, women, especially married women, were treated as a marginal group with less right to employment than men. The proportion of overall female appointments dropped slightly from the 1920s, but the number of permanent female appointments dropped more sharply than did the proportion of male permanent appointments.

World War II turned previous values on their heads. Suddenly it was the patriotic duty of women to enter the public service and to perform male jobs. In 1938 only 16.5 percent of all appointments to the service were female; by 1943, 65.4 percent of appointments were to women. Throughout the war years the majority of appointments were female. The war's end, however, brought a dramatic reversal. In 1946 the proportion of female appointments was slashed to half the proportion in the last year of the war. Restrictions on the employment of married women were renewed; Archibald remarks that this was "completely unnecessary" since married women were "so eager to return home that the exodus of women from the labour force preceded the return of veterans."[67] Yet despite the undoubted fact that many married women never had any intention of working after the war's end, there was also a considerable degree of coercion employed to open up positions for veterans. It is perhaps worth examining this episode for the light it throws on the whole question of women's place in the civil service of the time.

Earlier in the chapter we have recounted the steps taken to "demobilize" wartime staff, and of the tremendous turnover which permitted the mass entry of veterans. We have also noted in the section on French-speaking civil servants that the veterans preference was a device which clearly worsened the situation of French Canadians. The case is even more sharply drawn with regard to women, only a tiny handful of whom had served overseas. In 1944 the decision was made to release the five thousand to seven thousand married women then in the service, except for those in typing, stenographic, or office appliance operating positions. The latter stipulation is very revealing for it shows that the sex-typing of jobs —the very "evidence" used to show why women could not be capable of filling higher, executive positions—was in large part a function of officially enforced policy. Since the directive was public knowledge, it becomes a doubtful question how many married women left voluntarily, how many left because they recognized the inevitable, and how many were simply released, whatever their own decision. There is, however, much evidence in the CSC records to indicate that a number resisted the official policy and stayed on, with the approval of their own departments. The CSC kept lists and prodded departments to clear their staffs of married women. Efficiency was not a prime consideration. For example, the Deputy Minister of Transport complained that certain married female employees were the only ones qualified for certain jobs. The CSC advised that veterans be trained. The same Deputy Minister maintained that another woman, working part-time, accomplished more than many full-time employees. The CSC was unmoved. There is also evidence that this period of flux was taken advantage of by some officials to exercise generally anti-female policies. An internal CSC memorandum from the period remarks: "Many single female clerks are being released by various departments after several years' service and if there is [sic] not enough OAS [veteran] clerks I would think these people should receive consideration before the non-self-supporting married women."[68]

As it turned out, the actual circumstances of the postwar situation tended to cancel out the intended effects of the official policies. Instead of the economic recession expected by everyone, including the leading government economists, the postwar decade was a period of unprecedented boom. Government had to compete for staff in a labour market marked by short supply and rising wages. The sweeping of married women out of the government ranks never took place on the scale envisaged. In fact secretarial and clerical positions were continuously before the public.

In any event the main lesson to be drawn from the events of 1945 to 1947 is not their actual historical outcome but the intent which lay behind the official directives issued by the Government and by the CSC. Clearly, women were considered the most marginal group in the service, and the most expendable. When fluctuations in the labour market had to be accommodated, such as the return of the veterans, it was the female work force which would have to make way. In this the Government was only following the example of the private sphere. It could not be said to be less humane than private employers, although neither was it any more humane.

In the 1950s the situation became somewhat liberalized. More and more women were entering the service. Moreover, in the private sphere the proportion of married women had been steadily rising, until by 1955 one-third of all working women in Canada were married. The same year the CSC bowed to the inevitable and removed all restrictions on the appointment of married women, although the CSC did not expect "that the new policy will result in any great increase in the number of married

488

women in the Service."[69] Since the CSC did not keep statistics on the marital status of government employees, it is unfortunately impossible to verify or to disprove its belief. The following year, however, the female proportion of all appointees rose by 5 percent. The 1950s also saw the appointment of the first female Civil Service Commissioner, Ruth Addison.

The Heeney Report did not concern itself with the question of female employees. The 1961 Civil Service Act did, however, drop the explicit mention of "sex" as a qualification for positions. The CSC could now "prescribe qualifications as to age, residence or any other matters that in the opinion of the Commission are necessary or desirable having regard to the nature of the duties to be performed."[70] "Any other matters" of course might include the sex of the applicant. That this was possible was made clear by section 33 which forbade discrimination on the basis of "race, national origin, colour or religion"— but not on the basis of sex.

The Glassco Royal Commission gave very brief attention to the problem. After noting that the Canadian Government allowed fewer women to reach senior positions than the American or British governments, Glassco went on to mildly make a suggestion which in fact had revolutionary implications—that the Government ought not simply to follow private practice but should act as a model employer. It was precisely this that the Government had always refused to do.

In 1967 the Public Service Employment Act added "sex" to "race, national origin, colour or creed" as matters upon which individuals could not be discriminated against.[71] This was added to maintain the conditions of an International Labour Organization Convention forbidding employment discrimination on the basis of sex, which was ratified by Canada in 1964. The 1918–19 legislation had now been reversed. As Archibald suggests: "While equal pay for equal work had been official policy for nearly a century, the equal opportunity that would make equal pay meaningful was not endorsed in legislation until 1967."[72]

While the legal framework has changed significantly in the past decade, the actual situation of women in the Government has not changed in any dramatic fashion. While a law can be changed by the stroke of a pen, an actual social situation is under the accumulated weight of a history which cannot be changed and can only be shifted with great difficulty. Archibald and Judek have both demonstrated the serious underutilization of human resources represented by continuing discrimination against female employees.[73] The index of segregation for women in the public service for 1967 is 73.1 percent. While figures are not available for the Canadian private sector as a means of comparison, it is higher than the American index, mentioned earlier, of 68.4 percent for the overall labour force in 1960. In any event, it represents a high degree of occupational segregation. And as Archibald points out:

> Occupational segregation limits freedom of choice and tends to lead to inequality of opportunity. The historical record not only confirms this but reveals that occupational segregation was not inadvertent. It was instituted expressly to limit competition and to discourage females. Competitive examinations for higher level clerical positions and for positions with advancement opportunities were limited to men, not because women were uninterested, or incapable of passing the examinations, but precisely because they were interested and capable.

Even the one area where women have had some small success in reaching higher ranks is determined by history. Again in Archibald's words:

> The greater success of women in professional than in executive classes, noticeable today, has its roots in the early years of the civil service. Advancement to managerial positions was officially restricted for women, whereas discrimination in professional classes, while common, was the product of more informal practices on the part of line managers.[74]

Only in recent years has persistent pressure been brought to bear on the Government to grant greater equality. In the past the public pressures were, if anything, in the other direction. In the past, moreover, the Government always looked to the private sector for its leads. As we indicated in the earlier part of this section, the position of women in the work world has not been in fact improving over the years. Given this context it is not possible to attach special blame to the Government, and even less to the CSC for the state of affairs which has developed. The Government and the CSC were, as usual, simply following the path of least resistance. The almost total absence of public pressures against sex discrimination meant that the path of least resistance was to ignore the radical implications of the merit principle, and to enact restrictive controls, and thus to go with the grain of existing prejudices in the society at large.

A New Role for Government

There is an unsolved dilemma at the root of the merit principle. In defining "merit," the question arises of where the focus should rest, whether on the employer or on the employee. Does merit reside in the services which an employee can potentially render to the government, or is merit to be considered a quality residing in certain citizens which it is the government's duty to reward? While this distinction may appear somewhat abstract, the practical consequences of focussing on either the employee or the employer are great. For instance, the incorporation of the veterans preference within the merit system clearly indicates the choice of an employee-focussed assumption: certain citizens possess a quality (military service) which entitles them to a reward (government job). On the other hand, the classification system rests on an employer-focussed assumption: the qualities of candidates are measured by their potential for fulfilling certain specified duties. Even though these two assumptions are rather divergent in their implications, we find both resting uneasily side by side within the same system of personnel selection. In a sense, both are complementary: fulfilling the functional needs of the organization is necessary for the efficiency of operations; on the other hand, the government pursues certain social goals, such as reintegrating a large number of veterans following the war, or establishing a bilingual federal government, which may require a modification of its own hiring practice. Inevitably, however, strong tensions have been generated by the existence of these two divergent interpretations of merit.

Because of the circumstances of history, the veterans preference was established in a relatively painless manner. Yet this situation obscured the normal face of the merit system, which has historically been more concerned with administrative efficiency in a narrow sense. The special treatment of the veterans was an exception; the fate of French-speaking and female employees is more typical. Opting for a policy of hiring those candidates who will best fulfil its specific functional requirements, the government has turned for justification to the principle that all candidates are treated equally, without regard to race, colour, creed, sex, political affiliation, etc. But if we grant that serious social and economic inequalities already exist within the labour force upon which the government draws, and if we further grant that successive governments have committed themselves to the goal of eradicating these inequalities, then a new dimension in the definition of "efficiency" must be added, one which takes into account not only the immediate goal of administrative output, but also the achievement of important social goals.

The position of French-speaking civil servants, considered historically, has rested for the most part not on positively discriminatory rules, but on an attitude of indifference toward the value of the French language and the participation of French-speaking citizens in the administration of government. Attempts to change this situation were met by the argument that special treatment for a discriminated group is just as immoral as the original discrimination itself. The present language policies of the federal

491

government are a direct refutation of this argument: "special treatment" has now been granted to French-speaking civil servants. In effect, the government has decided that treating unequal persons on a basis of equality is itself a form of inequality. Judging from the historical record of the operation of the merit system in this regard, it is difficult to see how any government committed to bilingualism as a social goal could have decided otherwise. For the government to adopt a policy of "equal treatment" in selection and promotion is, in a sense, to withdraw from direct confrontation with the existing social inequalities. In short, *equal* treatment is not necessarily *equitable* treatment. Present moves toward bilingualism in the public service indicate a definite recognition of the limitations of the traditional merit system, which had previously been ignored. The extension of this recognition to other groups has not yet come about, but it does imply a new role for government, that of the model employer.

The case of the female civil servants is somewhat different, since women have been treated in a positively discriminatory fashion. The basis of this discrimination has been a simple acceptance on the part of government of the prevailing inequalities of the society at large. While the government cannot be blamed for this general condition, it has chosen to go along with the grain of existing prejudices, motivated, presumably, by a desire to "get the job done," to take immediate administrative efficiency as the sole criterion of personnel policy. Yet this view also implies an acceptance of the propostion that because a certain *group* of persons is believed to be less efficient in the work world, each *individual* will be judged by the alleged standards of the group—a proposition in direct contradiction to the merit principle. It has often been argued as well, particularly by International Labour Organization resolutions which Canada supports, that such a policy creates a serious underutilization of human resources, scarcely a situation conducive to efficiency.

The contemporary focussing of popular discontent on the government as the most responsive instrument for effecting change means that the era in which government could simply follow private practice may be now drawing to a close. The concept of government as a model employer who must innovate as an example to the private sector appears to be taking a firmer hold, particularly in the light of the current attempts to make the public service into a bilingual organization. The extension of the model employer concept into other spheres may follow. The Public Service Commission thus faces a new role of trying to anticipate popular pressures and to act in advance. There are indications that it is currently attempting to do this in regard to the employment of women. In 1969 the PSC issued a statement to deputy heads on the subject of sex qualifications which read, in part:

Equal opportunity for all persons employed by or applying for employment with the Canadian Public Service means that decisions on both appointment and career development must be based on the qualifications or suitability of a particular individual and not on the basis of characteristics assumed, accurately or inaccurately, to be associated with a particular category of people. . . .

To make an assumption about the capability or lack of capability of a particular individual solely on the basis of group tendencies is prejudice; to act on that assumption is discrimination. . . . Personal suitability is to be judged on a case-by-case basis, not on the basis of characteristics assumed to be associated with one sex. . . . The traditional sex-typing of a job as male or female is *not* sufficient reason to limit a position to members of one sex only.[75]

What is most interesting about this statement is that fifty years after the establishment of the merit system, it is still the merit principle which serves as a basis for discussion of the rightness or wrongness of employment practices. In many respects, the merit principle may be seen as an important myth—not in the sense of an untruth, but rather of an idea with a kernel of truth, which exerts a profound influence on human behaviour in a basically affective or emotional manner. Like most viable social myths, it has demonstrated a tenacity over time which has outlasted many of the things done in its name. The case of women is particularly interesting in this regard, for a half century of discriminatory practice coexisted with a theory which was itself a critique of such practice. Yet it would appear that the power of the merit myth has continued undiminished while the practice of discrimination has begun to show signs of deterioration.

NOTES

1. R. H. Dowdell, "Personnel Administration in the Federal Public Service," in A. M. Willms and W. D. K. Kernaghan, eds., *Public Administration in Canada: Selected Readings*, p. 367.

2. James Eayrs, *In Defence of Canada: From the Great War to the Great Depression*.

3. Ibid., p. 62.

4. Ibid., p. 48.

5. Veterans Assistance Commission, quoted in H.C., Special Committee on the Operation of the Civil Service Act, 1938, *Proceedings and Evidence*, p. 90.

6. *Revised Statutes*, 1927, c. 22, s. 28.

7. Ibid., s. 29(2).

8. Ibid., s. 29(3).

9. Ibid., s. 29(4).

10. Gordon Josie, "Administration of the Veterans Preference in the Canadian Civil Service," p. 604.

11. Ibid.

12. Ibid., p. 607, quoting an address by Roche to the Canadian Civil Service Research Conference, Toronto, November 6 and 7, 1930.

13. Ibid., p. 608.

14. 1938 Committee, p. 90.

15. Ibid., p. 72.

16. 9–10 George VI (1946), c. 35.

17. 10 George VI (1946), c. 71.

18. CSC, *Annual Report*, 1948, p. 7. Veterans were only appointed to clerk II positions, never to clerk I levels.

19. This figure includes female as well as male veterans. The number of women who were appointed under the veterans preference made up only 2 percent of all veteran appointments.

20. CSC, *Annual Report*, 1948, p. 7.

21. P.C. 4644 (June 28, 1945).

22. CSC, *Annual Report*, 1946, p. 6.

23. P.C. 12/5570 (December 1, 1948).

24. CSC, *Annual Report*, 1947.

25. "The Role of the Commissioner in Public Relations," Civil Service Assembly of the United States and Canada, *Proceedings of the Forty-Eighth Annual Conference* (Ottawa, October 4–7, 1948), p. 18.

26. CSC, *Annual Report*, 1949.

27. Royal Commission on Administrative Classifications in the Public Service, 1946, *Report*, p. 25.

28. Taylor Cole, *The Canadian Bureaucracy*, p. 100.

29. CSC, *Personnel Administration in the Public Service: A Review of Civil Service Legislation*, December, 1958, pp. 19–20. Hereafter cited as the Heeney Report.

30. Royal Commission on Government Organization, 1960–62, *Report*, 1, pp. 267–68. Hereafter cited as the Glassco Report.

31. Interview.

32. S. H. S. Hughes, "The New Civil Service Act," p. 19.

33. Royal Commission on Bilingualism and Biculturalism, *Report*, 5 vols. (Ottawa: Queen's Printer, 1967–70), 3, *The World of Work* (1969). Hereafter cited as RCBB, 3.

34. J. E. Hodgetts, *Pioneer Public Service: An Administrative History of the United Canadas, 1841–1867*, p. 57.

35. RCBB, 3, p. 101.

36. Ibid., p. 103.

494

37. 2 George VI (1938), c. 7, s. 1.

38. Civil service regulation 32, 1942.

39. Lacroix to King, January 19, 1944, King Papers, Corr., Post 1939 Series, vol. 79.

40. RCBB, 3, p. 107. A more detailed study may be found in J. Heward, "History of Bilingualism and Biculturalism in the Canadian Public Service," internal research project of the Royal Commission on Bilingualism and Biculturalism (July, 1966).

41. RCBB, 3, p. 105.

42. Ibid., p. 106.

43. Cole, *Canadian Bureaucracy*, pp. 56–57.

44. RCBB, 3, p. 110.

45. Heeney Report, p. 21.

46. 9–10 Elizabeth II (1961), c. 57, s. 47.

47. Glassco Report, 1, pp. 67–77.

48. 14–15–16 Elizabeth II (1967), c. 71.

49. RCBB, 3, pp. 111–12.

50. Kathleen Archibald, *Sex and the Public Service.*

51. For general statistical data on women in the Canadian labour force, see Sylvia Ostry, *The Female Worker in Canada*; Frank T. Denton and Sylvia Ostry, *Historical Estimates of the Canadian Labour Force*; Noah Meltz, *Changes in the Occupational Composition of the Canadian Labour Force, 1931–1961*; Department of Labour, Women's Bureau, *Changing Patterns in Women's Employment* (Ottawa: Department of Labour, 1966); and Sylvia Ostry, *The Occupational Composition of the Canadian Labour Force.*

52. Ostry, *Occupational Composition of the Labour Force.*

53. Ostry calculated an adjusted ratio of average annual wages of all female wage earners to average annual wages of all male wage earners in 1961 as 59.3; see *Female Worker in Canada*, p. 45.

54. Meltz, *Changes in the Occupational Composition of the Labour Force,* p. 68.

55. DBS, *Canada Yearbooks*, 1947 and 1950.

56. Ostry, *Occupational Composition of the Labour Force.*

57. Archibald, *Sex and the Public Service*, p. 22 and p. 32, fn. 48.

58. Ibid., p. 16.

59. Ibid.

60. CSC, *Report of the Commissioners*, 1908, p. 14. (Emphasis added.)

61. CSC, *Annual Report*, 1918, pp. 13–14.

62. CSC, *Annual Report*, 1908–9, p. 17. (Emphasis added.)

63. Archibald, *Sex and the Public Service*, p. 14.

64. Patterson to Meighen, February 23, 1921, Meighen Papers, vol. 18, 10459.

65. CSC, *Annual Report*, 1955, p. 9.

66. Files of the CSC, PAC, vol. 379, File 26-10-2.

67. Archibald, *Sex and the Public Service*, p. 16.

68. Files of the CSC, PAC.

69. CSC, *Annual Report*, 1955, p. 9.

70. 9–10 Elizabeth II (1961), c. 57, s. 33.

71. 14–15–16 Elizabeth II (1967), c. 71.

72. Archibald, *Sex and the Public Service*, p. 18.
73. Stanislaw Judek, *Women in the Public Service: Their Utilization and Employment.*
74. Archibald, *Sex and the Public Service*, pp. 18–19.
75. Quoted in ibid., appendix D, pp. 213–14.

Appendix

TABLE 1

Temporary Appointments in the Federal Civil Service, 1938–1948

DEPARTMENT	1938	1939	1940	1941	1942	1943	1944	1945	1946	1947	1948
Agriculture	894	1118	859	710	863	759	765	844	1293	1241	1374
Auditor-General's Office	15	25	104	136	215	120	51	100	36	37	23
Cdn. Pension Comm.	6	7	20	38	57	44	188	169	178	*	*
CSC	50	73	252	297	572	525	429	490	420	286	176
External Affairs	14	35	324	220	163	172	85	197	294	368	339
Finance	166	721	1880	3484	4959	5482	4528	5292	4305	1449	1416
Fisheries	50	63	55	67	53	47	42	44	52	201	169
Govt. Contracts	–	*	*	*	*	*	*	*	*	*	*
Govt. Gen. Sec. Office	2	2	2	3	–	–	–	1	–	2	–
House of Commons	–	–	–	–	–	–	–	–	–	–	–
Insurance	6	–	10	6	9	10	11	15	20	23	14
Justice	24	20	20	25	28	38	15	41	43	69	62
Labour	15	36	47	66	1128	2823	1990	1001	396	170	227
Library of Parliament	–	2	–	–	–	–	–	4	–	2	–
Mines and Resources	536	500	497	616	506	437	510	867	1492	1445	1901
National Defence	224	1362	6004	4617	5314	8194	4374	4348	7145	3255	2074
National Revenue	377	375	435	605	508	360	378	605	1056	1109	2423
Pensions & National Health	178	309	591	878	1182	1626	1985	*	*	*	*
Post Office	1660	1789	2231	3523	4689	4579	3948	3717	5009	3140	3985
Postmasters	28	20	25	17	26	48	85	95	91	75	105
Privy Council	–	3	5	5	10	24	23	15	16	5	14
Public Archives	2	12	6	5	4	3	5	5	9	3	8
Pub. Printing & Stat.	66	99	93	163	164	174	113	96	150	115	141
Public Works	395	425	574	566	614	689	628	629	965	847	755

Department											
RCMP	1	41	100	164	321	310	282	151	141	142	150
Secretary of State	29	93	118	120	156	104	92	112	121	204	139
Senate	1	–	–	–	–	–	–	–	–	–	–
Soldier Settlement of Can.	18	24	33	25	17	104	184	688	1571	600	397
Trade & Commerce	283	256	1214	2051	744	464	561	645	1423	1037	780
Transport	498	595	1223	1222	1680	1454	1275	1128	1901	1493	1397
Transport Commissioners Board	5	12	14	9	12	10	6	7	14	58	31
Munitions & Supply	*	*	1024	2428	4503	4022	2355	1507	*	*	*
National Defence for Air	*	*	*	6124	7452	7269	2947	1542	1858	476	746
National War Services	*	*	*	571	1346	1523	784	303	7	*	*
Unemployment Insur. Comm.	*	*	*	1315	2697	4651	3256	4335	5040	1360	1653
Natl. Defence for Naval Ser.	*	*	*	*	3677	4302	2915	2556	1409	986	1217
Wartime Prices & Trade Board	*	**	**	**	4272	4872	2195	1644	3	*	*
Air Transport Board	*	*	*	*	*	*	3	21	24	17	12
Cdn. Mutual Aid Board	*	*	*	*	*	*	16	26	2	*	*
Reconstruction	*	*	*	*	*	*	7	350	507	107	183
Veterans Affairs	*	*	*	*	*	*	516	6156	14759	8127	3515
Natl. Health & Welfare	*	*	*	*	*	*	22	680	838	701	687
Cdn. Information Service	*	*	*	*	*	*	*	2	50	9	1
Cdn. Maritime Comm.	*	*	*	*	*	*	*	*	*	3	30
National Film Board	*	*	*	*	*	*	*	*	*	3	–
P.M.'s Office	*	*	*	*	*	*	*	*	*	1	3
National Revenue (Tax.)	*	*	*	*	*	*	*	*	*	*	2287

SOURCE: CSC, *Annual Reports*, 1938–48.

*Department not in existence.

**Total appointment figures unknown.

TABLE 2

All Appointments, Permanent and Temporary, in the Federal Civil Service, 1938–1948

YEAR	PERMANENT STATUS (including Seasonal)	TEMPORARY STATUS	TOTAL APPOINTMENTS
1938	843	5,563	6,406
1939	1,166	8,017	9,183
1940	1,540	17,760	19,300
1941	985	30,076	31,061
1942	681	47,941	48,622
1943	1,103	55,239	56,342
1944	1,383	37,569	38,952
1945	651	40,434[1]	41,085
1946	536	52,638[2]	53,174
1947	4,202	29,164[3]	33,366
1948	5,715	28,434[4]	34,149

SOURCE: CSC, *Annual Reports*, 1938–48.

[1] 28,427 of these temporary assignments were new; 12,007 were reassignments.
[2] 41,745 of these temporary assignments were new; 10,893 were reassignments.
[3] 18,659 of these temporary assignments were new; 10,505 were reassignments.
[4] 18,691 of these temporary assignments were new; 9,743 were reassignments.

TABLE 3

PERMANENT APPOINTMENTS IN THE FEDERAL CIVIL SERVICE, 1945–1954

DEPARTMENT	VETERANS		MALE CIVILIANS		VARIATION
	NO.	%	NO.	%	
Veterans Affairs[1]	4,059	16.6	103	0.9	+15.7
Post Office[2]	7,275	29.8	2,652	21.9	+7.9
Defence[3]	1,331	5.5	551	4.6	+0.9
Revenue	2,604	10.7	1,801	14.9	−4.2
UIC	2,168	8.9	1,231	10.2	−1.3
Finance	1,178	4.8	490	4.1	+0.4
Transport[4]	906	3.7	1,578	13.1	−9.4
Public Works	801	3.3	297	2.5	+0.8
Resources[5]	669	2.7	737	6.1	−3.4
Agriculture	663	2.7	1,018	8.4	−5.7
Trade & Commerce	523	2.1	358	3.0	−0.9
Health & Welfare	522	2.1	289	2.4	−0.3
Citizenship & Imm.	499	2.0	153	1.3	+0.7
Fisheries	188	0.8	176	1.5	−.07
External Affairs	263	1.1	105	0.9	+0.2
CSC	99	0.4	60	0.5	−0.1
Labour	97	0.4	85	0.7	−0.3
Secretary of State	43	0.4	108	0.9	−0.5
Justice	53	0.4	30	0.2	+ 0.2
Other	368	1.5	268	2.2	−0.7
Total	24,309	100	12,090	100	

SOURCE: CSC, *Annual Reports*, 1945–54.

[1]Includes Soldiers' Settlement Board.

[2]Includes Postmasters.

[3]Includes Defence Production.

[4]Includes Board of Transport Commissioners.

[5]Mines and Resources, Northern Affairs and National Resources, Mines and Technical Surveys.

TABLE 4

TEMPORARY APPOINTMENTS IN THE FEDERAL CIVIL SERVICE, 1945–1954

DEPARTMENT	VETERANS		MALE CIVILIANS		VARIATION
	NO.	%	NO.	%	
Veterans Affairs	24,007	24.1	4,844	5.9	+18.2
Post Office	17,667	17.8	15,111	18.3	−0.5
Defence	20,616	20.7	19,775	23.9	−3.2
Revenue	6,178	6.2	5,543	6.7	−0.5
UIC	5,743	5.8	3,883	4.7	+1.1
Finance	4,996	5.0	2,600	3.1	−1.9
Transport	3,805	3.8	6,281	7.6	−3.8
Public Works	3,548	3.6	2,845	3.8	−0.2
Resources	3,711	3.7	7,058	8.5	−4.8
Agriculture	2,892	2.9	5,305	6.6	−3.7
Trade & Commerce	2,090	2.1	2,384	2.7	−0.6
Health & Welfare	1,522	1.5	1,757	2.1	−0.6
Citizenship & Imm.	497	0.5	630	0.7	−0.2
Fisheries	512	0.5	479	0.5	−
External Affairs	483	0.5	653	0.7	−0.7
CSC	348	0.3	389	0.4	−0.1
Labour	345	0.3	499	0.6	−0.3
Secretary of State	111	0.1	391	0.4	−0.3
Justice	97	0.1	123	0.1	−0.3
Other[1]	315	0.3	2,246	2.7	−2.4
Total	99,483	100	82,796	100	

SOURCE: CSC, *Annual Reports*, 1945–54.

[1]Includes 308 veterans appointed to the Department of Reconstruction. In the male civilian category 321 were appointed to Reconstruction, 398 to Munitions and Supply, 429 to the Wartime Prices and Trade Board, 53 to National War Services, and 7 to the Mutual Aid Board; 1,208 in all appointed to temporary war departments. Also includes 735 male civilians appointed to Public Printing and Stationery.

TABLE 5

All Appointments,
Permanent and Temporary, in the Federal Civil Service, 1955–1962

DEPARTMENT	VETERANS		MALE CIVILIANS		VARIATION
	NO.	%	NO.	%	
Veterans Affairs	2,599	13.2	4,209	5.0	+8.2
Post Office	4,023	20.4	17,696	21.2	−0.8
Defence	5,502	27.9	15,610	18.7	+9.2
Revenue	761	3.8	6,358	7.6	−3.8
UIC	632	3.2	3,316	3.9	−0.7
Finance	145	0.7	1,570	1.8	−1.1
Transport	1,584	8.0	8,053	9.6	−1.6
Public Works	1,875	9.5	3,911	4.6	+4.9
Resources	455	2.3	7,738	9.2	−6.9
Agriculture	674	3.4	4,931	5.9	−2.5
Trade & Commerce	321	1.6	2,532	3.0	−1.4
Health & Welfare	243	1.2	1,558	1.8	−0.6
Citizenship & Imm.	456	2.3	1,598	1.9	+0.4
Fisheries	183	0.9	625	0.7	+0.2
External Affairs	82	0.4	601	0.7	−0.3
CSC	26	0.1	172	0.2	−0.1
Labour	30	0.2	242	0.2	−
Secretary of State	31	0.2	365	0.4	−0.2
Justice	24	0.1	179	0.2	−0.1
Other	7	0.1	1,986[1]	2.3	−2.2
Total	19,653	100	83,250	100	

SOURCE: CSC, *Annual Reports*, 1955–62.

[1]Includes 654 non-veteran males appointed to Public Printing and Stationery.

TABLE 6

ALL APPOINTMENTS,
PERMANENT AND TEMPORARY, IN THE FEDERAL CIVIL SERVICE, 1945–1962

DEPARTMENT	VETERANS		MALE CIVILIANS		VARIATION
	NO.	%	NO.	%	
Veterans Affairs	30,665	21.3	9,156	5.1	+16.2
Post Office	28,965	20.1	35,459	19.1	+0.2
Defence	27,449	19.1	35,936	20.1	−1.0
Revenue	9,543	6.6	13,702	7.6	−1.0
UIC	8,543	6.0	8,430	4.7	+1.3
Finance	6,319	4.4	4,660	2.6	+1.8
Transport	6,295	4.4	15,912	8.9	−4.5
Public Works	6,224	4.3	7,053	4.0	+0.3
Resources	4,835	3.4	15,533	8.7	−5.3
Agriculture	4,229	2.9	11,254	6.3	−3.4
Trade & Commerce	2,934	2.1	5,274	3.0	−0.9
Health & Welfare	2,287	1.6	3,598	2.0	−0.4
Citizenship & Imm.	1,452	1.0	2,381	1.3	−0.3
Fisheries	883	1.0	1,280	0.7	−0.1
External Affairs	828	0.6	1,359	0.8	−0.2
CSC	473	0.3	621	0.3	−
Labour	472	0.3	826	0.5	−0.2
Secretary of State	185	0.1	864	0.5	−0.4
Justice	174	0.1	332	0.2	−0.1
Other	690	0.5	4,500	2.5	−2.0
Total	143,445	100	178,130	100	

SOURCE: CSC, *Annual Reports*, 1945–62.

TABLE 7

ALL APPOINTMENTS,
PERMANENT AND TEMPORARY, IN THE FEDERAL CIVIL SERVICE, 1945–1962

YEAR	MALE APPOINTMENTS				FEMALE APPOINTMENTS			
	Vet-erans	Civil-ians	Total	Male Veterans as % of All Male Appoint-ments	Vet-erans	Civil-ians	Total	VETERANS AS % OF ALL APPOINT-MENTS
1945	10,835	8,147	18,982	59.2	101	22,002	22,103	24.2
1946	30,100	7,642	37,742	79.8	998	14,434	15,432	58.5
1947	17,372	5,947	23,319	74.5	880	9,167	10,047	54.7
1948	14,421	8,443	22,864	63.1	350	10,935	11,285	43.2
1949	12,752	8,954	21,706	58.7	273	10,273	10,546	40.4
1950	8,279	8,442	16,721	49.5	130	7,362	7,492	34.7
1951	7,563	10,362	17,925	42.2	221	11,617	11,838	26.2
1952	8,060	11,691	19,751	40.8	198	12,313	12,511	25.6
1953	6,605	13,372	19,977	33.1	77	12,605	12,682	20.4
1954	4,928	12,044	16,972	29.0	37	11,630	11,667	17.3
1955	3,332	9,649	12,981	25.7	23	10,853	10,876	14.0
1956	3,050	10,766	13,816	22.0	9	12,267	12,276	11.1
1957	2,640	11,986	14,626	18.0	40	12,411	12,451	9.9
1958	2,446	9,419	11,865	27.9	25	9,454	9,479	11.1
1959	2,218	9,571	11,789	18.8	20	9,561	9,581	10.5
1960	2,056	9,709	11,765	21.3	13	8,278	8,291	10.3
1961	1,735	12,689	14,424	12.3	–	10,435	10,435	7.4
1962	2,046	9,461	11,507	17.8	–	7,831	7,831	10.6
Total	140,438	178,294	318,732	45.3	3,395	203,428	206,823	27.4

SOURCE: CSC, *Annual Reports*, 1945–62.

TABLE 8

PERMANENT APPOINTMENTS IN THE FEDERAL CIVIL SERVICE, 1945–1954

| YEAR | MALE APPOINTMENTS | | | | FEMALE APPOINTMENTS | | | |
	Vet- erans	Civil- ians	Total	Male Veterans as % of All Male Appoint- ments	Vet- erans	Civil- ians	Total	VETERANS AS % OF ALL APPOINT- MENTS
1945	439	106	545	80.6	1	27	28	73.3
1946	420	58	478	87.9	3	28	31	83.1
1947	3,429	629	4,058	84.5	2	114	116	82.2
1948	3,633	1,329	4,962	73.2	46	482	528	67.0
1949	3,378	1,318	4,596	73.5	68	727	795	63.9
1950	3,290	2,327	5,617	58.6	62	1,976	2,038	43.8
1951	3,139	1,687	4,826	65.1	144	1,639	1,783	49.7
1952	3,506	1,904	5,410	64.8	161	1,420	1,581	52.5
1953	1,912	1,601	3,513	54.4	42	771	813	45.2
1954	728	1,231	1,959	37.1	6	919	925	25.5
Total	23,874	12,090	35,964	66.4	535	8,103	8,638	54.7

SOURCE: CSC, *Annual Reports*, 1945–54.

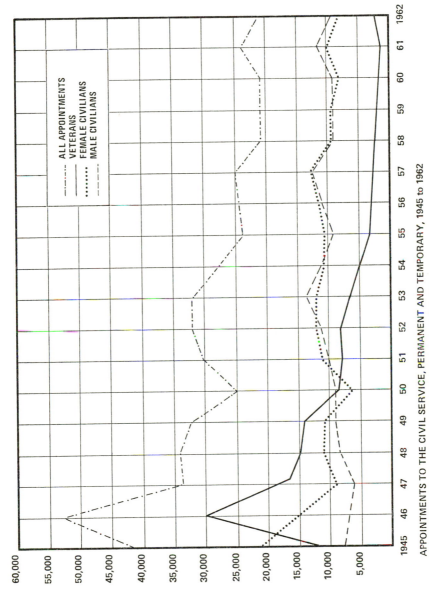

APPOINTMENTS TO THE CIVIL SERVICE, PERMANENT AND TEMPORARY, 1945 to 1962

FIGURE 1

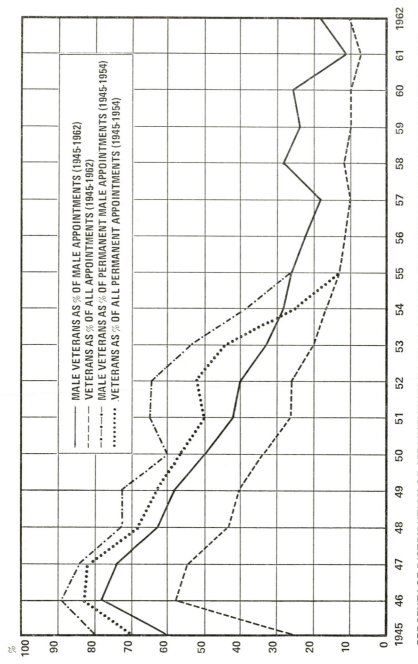

MALE VETERANS AS % OF MALE APPOINTMENTS (1945-1962)

VETERANS AS % OF ALL APPOINTMENTS (1945-1962)

MALE VETERANS AS % OF PERMANENT MALE APPOINTMENTS (1945-1954)

VETERANS AS % OF ALL PERMANENT APPOINTMENTS (1945-1954)

PERCENTAGE DISTRIBUTION OF APPOINTMENTS TO CIVIL SERVICE, PERMANENT AND TEMPORARY, 1945 to 1962

FIGURE 2

Select Bibliography

PRIMARY SOURCES

In 1965 most of the files of the Civil Service Commission covering the period from its inception to 1957 were unfortunately destroyed. As a result, the authors had to turn to other sources for their information on the CSC's history. The following public and private collections of papers, files, and documents represent the major sources consulted. Copies of much of the material consulted were deposited with the library of the Public Service Commission at the completion of the study.

PUBLIC COLLECTIONS

Much of the information on the career and activities of Adam Shortt derives from two sources. The Shortt Papers in the Douglas Library, Queen's University, contain a great deal of his private correspondence and many speeches, both prior to 1908 and during his tenure as Commissioner. The Borden Papers in the Public Archives of Canada also contain some letters and memoranda from Shortt to Borden, as well as other documents relating to the 1908–18 period. Memoranda prepared by Borden a decade or more after his retirement and found in these papers provide a glimpse of events from his point of view. Some documents relating to the activities of Griffenhagen and his associates are also contained here. To a lesser degree the J. S. Willison Papers and the Grey Papers, both in the Public Archives, supplied background material for the period prior to the 1918 reform. The Rowell Papers in the Public Archives helped to fill in the background for the events surrounding the passage of the Civil Service Act of 1918.

The prime source of material from private papers concerning the classification of the civil service by the Arthur Young Company and the reorganization work conducted by Griffenhagen's company comes from the Meighen Papers, with some related documents and information in the Foster Papers, both of which are located in the Public Archives. The Meighen Papers also proved to be a source of information regarding the activities and views of the staff associations in these years.

As a result of Mackenzie King's happy penchant for saving virtually every piece of paper crossing his desk, the King Papers in the Public Archives were invaluable for helping to sketch in the period of the twenties and late thirties during the time he served as prime minister. The files of the Royal Commission on Professional and Technical Services (the Beatty Commission) in the Public Archives contained the correspondence of both the Commissioner and the staff, the minutes of evidence, and submissions from various interested parties, all of which proved helpful in filling in the events surrounding the establishment of the Royal Commission and in supplying information on its activities.

The authors were fortunate that at the time of their research the R. B. Bennett Papers, which are deposited at the University of New Brunswick, were at the Public Archives being microfilmed. They provided a valuable source of information regarding the civil service in the early depression years. The Public Archives also contains some early files and documents from both the Civil Service Commission and the Treasury Board. Only a minimal amount of this material, however, proved to be relevant to the study.

PRIVATE COLLECTIONS

Besides the public collections listed, the authors also had the good fortune of gaining access to several private collections of files, correspondence, and documents. Files and journals in the archives of the Professional Institute of the Public Service of Canada were made available to us through the kind offices of Mr. L. C. W. S. Barnes, the Executive Director of the Institute. Mr. J. F. Telford, former Executive Officer of the Civil Service Association of Canada, also made available to us his complete set of association journals. This access was valuable in giving us some background of civil service associations' activities, particularly in the early part of this century. The post-1940 series of the Mackenzie King Papers and the St. Laurent Papers, both at the Public Archives, provided useful background material for the period of the forties and early fifties. This access was facilitated through the kind offices of the Honourable J. W. Pickersgill. Most of the information concerning the creation and report of the Coon Committee and much of that surrounding the establishment of the National Joint Council are taken from the internal files of the Treasury Board. Several files of correspondence and memoranda belonging to A. D. P. Heeney and held in the Chairman's Office of the Public Service Commission proved immensely helpful in sketching in the events leading up to Heeney's appointment as chairman of the CSC, and in providing a view of his activities while in that position. Also, despite his failing health, the late A. D. P. Heeney was magnanimous in according us two lengthy interviews during which he corroborated much of our interpretation of his chairmanship. The documents of the Royal Commission on Government Organization in the Public Archives yielded information allowing for a fuller picture of the views of the staff studying the state of personnel management in the public service. The internal files of the CSC and PSC in the PSC's central registry were the major source of information on the internal developments within the organization for the whole of the 1957–68 period. Finally, the personal files of J. A. Murray, the former Director of the Organization and Classification Branch of the CSC, and of M. M. Maclean, a former Secretary of the CSC, which were kindly lent to the authors for the duration of the study, supplied valuable background information for the entire period from 1945 to 1965.

PUBLIC DOCUMENTS

Royal Commissions and Commissions of Inquiry

Over the years various commissions have conducted studies into the civil service. Unfortunately many of the earlier commissions possessed no specific title and, as a result, their reports were often issued with a name which bore little relation to the terms of reference under which they were officially constituted. Many of these earlier commissions as well did not refer to themselves as royal commissions. Moreover, some commissions published the minutes of evidence taken before them with their report, while others did not. The following list has endeavoured to keep to the original as closely as possible. The names of the commissions are taken from the terms of reference under which they were constituted, and the names of the reports from the title with which they were published. Notation has also been made where the commission report included minutes of evidence.

Canada.   Commission to Enquire into the Present State and Probable Requirements of the Civil Service, 1868–70. *First Report of the Civil Service Commission*. Ottawa: Hunter, Rose, 1869.

Canada.   Commission to Enquire into the Present State and Probable Requirements of the Civil Service, 1868–70. *Second Report of the Civil Service Commission*. Ottawa: Hunter, Rose, 1869.

Canada.   Commission to Enquire into the Present State and Probable Requirements of the Civil Service, 1868–70. *Final Report of the Civil Service Commissioners*. Ottawa: I. B. Taylor, 1870.

Canada.   Commission to Consider the Needs and Condition of the Civil Service of the Dominion, 1880–81. *First Report of the Civil Service Commission*. Ottawa: MacLean, Roger, 1881. (Includes the *Minutes of Evidence*.)

Canada.   Royal Commission to Enquire into the Present Condition of the Civil Service in Ottawa, 1891–92. *Report of the Royal Commissioners Appointed to Enquire into Certain Matters Relating to the Civil Service of Canada*. Ottawa: Queen's Printer, 1892. (Includes the *Minutes of Evidence*.)

Canada.   Commission to Enquire into and Report upon the Operation of the Civil Service Act and Kindred Legislation, 1907–8. Civil Service Commission. *Report of the Commissioners*. Ottawa: King's Printer, 1908.

Canada. Commission to Enquire into and Report upon the Operation of the Civil Service Act and Kindred Legislation, 1907–8. Civil Service Commission. *Minutes of Evidence.* 2 vols. Ottawa: King's Printer, 1908.

Canada. Commission to Enquire into All Matters Connected with or Affecting the Administration of the Various Departments of the Government and the Conduct of the Public Business Therein, 1911–12. Public Service Commission. Vol. 1, *Report of the Commissioners.* Vols. 2 and 3, *Evidence.* Ottawa: King's Printer, 1913.

Canada. Commission to Inquire into Certain Matters Affecting the Operation of the Civil Service Acts, the Organization of the Public Service and the Methods of Administration under which the Public Business of Canada is Carried On, 1912. *Report on the Organization of the Public Service of Canada.* By Sir George Murray. Ottawa: King's Printer, 1912.

Canada. Royal Commission on Technical and Professional Services, 1929–30. *Report.* Ottawa: King's Printer, 1930.

Canada. Royal Commission on Administrative Classifications in the Public Service, 1946. *Report.* Ottawa: King's Printer, 1946.

Canada. Royal Commission on Administrative Classifications in the Public Service, 1946. "Proceedings." 5 vols. Typescript.

Canada. Royal Commission on Government Organization, 1960–62. *Report.* Vol. 1, *Management of the Public Service.* Ottawa: Queen's Printer, 1962.

Parliamentary Committees

In the following list, where the minutes of proceedings and evidence were printed, they always included the report(s) of the committee.

Canada. Parliament. House of Commons. Select Committee Appointed to Inquire into the Present Condition of the Civil Service, 1877. *Report.* Ottawa: MacLean, Roger, 1877. (Includes the *Minutes of Evidence.*)

Canada. Parliament. House of Commons. Special Committee Appointed to Inquire into the Working of the Staffs of the Inside Civil Service, 1919. *Proceedings and Evidence.* Ottawa: King's Printer, 1919.

Canada. Parliament. House of Commons. Special Committee on Bill No. 122, An Act to Amend the Civil Service Act, 1918 [1921]. *Proceedings and Evidence.* Ottawa: King's Printer, 1921.

Canada. Parliament. House of Commons. Special Committee Appointed to Inquire into the Operation of Chapter 12, 8–9 George V, An Act Respecting the Civil Service of Canada, 1923. *Proceedings and Evidence.* Ottawa: King's Printer, 1923.

Canada. Parliament. Senate. Special Committee on the Civil Service, 1924. *Report.* Ottawa: King's Printer, 1924.

Canada. Parliament. House of Commons. Special Committee Investigating the Administration of the Department of Customs and Excise, 1926. *Proceedings and Evidence.* Ottawa: King's Printer, 1926.

Canada.   Parliament. House of Commons. Select Special Committee on Civil
Service and Civil Service Act, 1932. *Proceedings and Evidence.* Ottawa: King's Printer, 1932.

Canada.   Parliament. House of Commons. Select Special Committee on Civil
Service Act, 1934. *Proceedings and Evidence.* Ottawa: King's Printer,
1934.

Canada.   Parliament. House of Commons. Special Committee on the Operation of the Civil Service Act, 1938. *Proceedings and Evidence.* Ottawa:
King's Printer, 1938.

Canada.   Parliament. House of Commons. Special Committee on the Operation of the Civil Service Act, 1939. *Proceedings and Evidence.* Ottawa: King's Printer, 1939.

Canada.   Parliament. House of Commons. Standing Committee on Estimates,
1959. *Proceedings and Evidence.* Ottawa: Queen's Printer, 1959.

Canada.   Parliament. House of Commons. Special Committee on the Civil
Service Act (Bill C-71), 1960–61. *Proceedings and Evidence.* Ottawa: Queen's Printer, 1961.

Canada.   Parliament. Special Joint Committee of Senate and House of Commons on Employer-Employee Relations in the Public Service of Canada, 1966–67. *Proceedings and Evidence.* Ottawa: Queen's Printer,
1966–67.

Government Publications

Canada.   Parliament. House of Commons. *Debates,* 1870–1970.

Canada.   Civil Service Commission. *Annual Reports,* 1908–66. Ottawa:
King's Printer, 1908–51; Queen's Printer, 1952–67.

Canada.   Civil Service Commission. *Report of Transmission to Accompany
the Classification of the Civil Service of Canada.* By Arthur Young
and Company. Ottawa: King's Printer, 1919.

Canada.   Civil Service Commission. *The Classification of the Civil Service of
Canada.* By Arthur Young and Company, June, 1919. Ottawa: King's
Printer, 1919.

Canada.   Civil Service Commission. *Revised Classification of the Civil Service
of Canada.* By Arthur Young and Company, September, 1919. Ot-
tawa: King's Printer, 1919.

Canada.   Civil Service Commission. *Personnel Administration in the Public
Service: A Review of Civil Service Legislation.* Ottawa: Queen's
Printer, 1959.

Canada.   Preparatory Committee on Collective Bargaining in the Public Service. *Report.* Ottawa: Queen's Printer, 1965.

Canada.   Public Service Commission. *Annual Reports,* 1967–69. Ottawa:
Queen's Printer, 1968–70.

OTHER PUBLICATIONS

Apart from the above sources, several other publications also proved helpful
in providing useful information. All but one of these publications fall into the

513

category of civil service staff association journals. Besides providing the views of their respective associations, these journals often carried news items not found elsewhere, and reported most speeches relating to civil service matters made by any major figure.

Civil Service News, 1920–1958. This journal was the official publication of the Civil Service Association of Ottawa, and from 1920 to 1928 also served as the official organ of the Civil Service Federation of which the CSAO was a member organization. In its early years it was a weekly publication, but it soon changed to a monthly one.

The Organizer, 1920–1939. This journal served as the official organ of the Amalgamated Civil Servants of Canada.

Civil Servants Digest, 1940–1947. After 1939 *The Organizer* was published under this title.

Canadian Civil Servant, 1947–1958. After 1946 the *Civil Servants Digest* was published under this title.

CSAC Journal, 1958–1966. Following the merger of the CSAO and ACSC in 1958 to form the Civil Service Association of Canada, the *Civil Service News* merged with the *Canadian Civil Servant* to become the *CSAC Journal*.

Argus-Journal, 1966–1970. With the creation of the Public Service Alliance in 1966 the *CSAC Journal* was changed to this title.

Civil Service Review, 1928–1970. This quarterly journal served as the official publication of the Civil Service Federation from 1928 until 1966. After 1966 it was published under the same title by the Public Service Alliance.

Institute Bulletin, 1921–1931. It was the official publication of the Professional Institute of the Public Service of Canada.

Institute Journal, 1932–1951. After 1931 the *Institute Bulletin* was changed to this title.

Professional Public Service, 1951–1971. In April, 1951, this became the new title of the *Institute Journal*.

Civil Service Research Conference. *Proceedings of the Annual Conventions*, 1924–31. Toronto: The Citizens' Research Institute of Canada, 1924–31.

INTERVIEWS

The positions of persons in the following list are given at the time they were interviewed. In cases where a person formerly occupied a position of particular interest to this study, a notation has been made.

R. E. ADDISON, Public Service Commissioner.

A. R. K. ANDERSON, Director-General of Staffing, Public Service Commission.

M. ANDRASSY, Chief of the Career Assignment Program, Public Service Commission.

O. E. AULT, retired. Former Director of the Personnel Selection Branch, Civil Service Commission.

LESLIE W. C. S. BARNES, Executive Director, Professional Institute of the Public Service of Canada.

C. W. BARRASS, Chief of the Compensation and Planning Group, Treasury Board. Formerly with the Civil Service Commission.

G. L. BENNETT, Assistant Deputy Minister, Department of National Revenue.

L. T. BLACK, Assistant to the Senior Staff Officer, Public Service Commission.

G. A. BLACKBURN, Director-General of the Language Bureau, Public Service Commission.

JEAN BOUCHER, Deputy Minister, Department of Supply and Services. Former Civil Service Commissioner.

R. B. BRYCE, Deputy Minister, Department of Finance. Former Secretary of the Treasury Board and Clerk of the Privy Council.

R. M. BURNS, Director, Institute of Intergovernmental Relations, Queen's University. Former Director of Dominion-Provincial Relations Branch, Department of Finance.

J. J. CARSON, Chairman, Public Service Commission. Former Project Director on Personnel Management, Royal Commission on Government Organization.

SYLVAIN CLOUTIER, Deputy Minister, Department of National Revenue. Former Civil Service Commissioner and Assistant Secretary of the Preparatory Committee on Collective Bargaining.

R. B. CODE, Director of Personnel, Department of Energy, Mines, and Resources.

GEORGE DAVIDSON, President, Canadian Broadcasting Corporation. Former Secretary of the Treasury Board.

J. J. DEUTSCH, Principal, Queen's University. Former Secretary of the Treasury Board.

R. H. DOWDELL, Director of Personnel, Canadian Air Transport Administration, Department of Transport. Formerly with the Civil Sevice Commission.

G. G. DUCLOS, Director-General, Bureau of Staff Training and Development, Public Service Commission.

N. GAGNON, Director of Personnel, Canadian Radio-Television Commission. Formerly with the Treasury Board.

G. E. GAUTHIER, Vice-Chairman, Public Service Staff Relations Board. Former Director of the Pay Research Bureau, Civil Service Commission.

WALTER GORDON, Clarkson and Gordon Company Ltd., Toronto. Former Minister of Finance in the Pearson Government and Chairman of the Royal Commission on Administrative Classifications in the Public Service.

DONALD GOW, Executive Assistant to the Principal, Queen's University. Formerly with the staffs of the Treasury Board and Civil Service Commission.

J. Y. HARCOURT, Educational Liaison Officer, Public Service Commission.

A. D. P. HEENEY, Chairman, Canadian Section, International Joint Commission. Former Chairman of the Civil Service Commission and Chairman of the Preparatory Committee on Collective Bargaining.

JUSTICE S. H. HUGHES, Supreme Court of Ontario. Former Chairman of the Civil Service Commission.

G. T. JACKSON, retired. Former Director of the Organization and Classification Branch of the Civil Service Commission and also ADM of Public Works.

J. D. LOVE, Deputy Minister, Department of Labour. Former Assistant Director of the Pay Research Bureau and Secretary of the Preparatory Committee on Collective Bargaining.

C. J. MACKENZIE, Secretary-General, National Museums of Canada. Former Assistant Secretary of the Treasury Board.

M. M. MACLEAN, Assistant to the Secretary, Public Service Staff Relations Board. Former Secretary of the Civil Service Commission.

S. H. MANSBRIDGE, Director-General, Bureau of Management Consulting, Department of Supply and Services. Formerly with the Civil Service Commission.

D. MORLEY, Director, Executive Development Program, Public Service Commission.

J. C. MORRISON, Assistant Deputy Minister, Department of Manpower and Immigration.

MARGARET MUNRO, retired. Formerly with the Civil Service Commission.

J. A. MURRAY, Special Assistant to the Chairman, Public Service Staff Relations Board. Former Director of the Organization and Classification Branch, Civil Service Commission.

S. H. NELSON, retired. Former Chairman, Civil Service Commission.

J. R. NEVILLE, Senior Staff Officer, Public Service Commission.

C. R. PATTERSON, National Co-ordinator, Civil Emergency Measures, Department of National Defence. Former Director, Operations Branch, Civil Service Commission.

PAUL PELLETIER, Special Adviser, National Capital Commission. Former Civil Service Commissioner.

G. SABOURIN, Assistant General Administrator, Secretariat, Public Service Commission.

K. R. SCOBIE, Assistant Director, Pay Research Bureau, Public Service Staff Relations Board. Former Director, Pay and Standards Branch, Civil Service Commission.

DAVID SIM, retired. Former Deputy Minister, Department of National Revenue (Customs and Excise).

W. D. SPEER, Director, Ottawa Regional Office, Public Service Commission.

GORDON TAGGART, retired. Former Deputy Minister, Department of Agriculture.

WALTER TURNBULL, retired. Former Deputy Postmaster-General and Principal Secretary to Mackenzie King.

J. VINOKUR, Director, Appeals Branch, Public Service Commission.

DAVE WATTERS, retired. Former Secretary of the Treasury Board.

J. WILEY, Vice-President, Public Service Alliance of Canada.

516

SECONDARY SOURCES

BOOKS AND THESES

AFZAL, MOHAMMAD. "Management Analysis: An Emerging Staff Function." Ph.D. thesis, Cornell University, 1962.

ARCHIBALD, KATHLEEN. *Sex and the Public Service*. Ottawa: Queen's Printer, 1970.

ASHLEY, C. A. and SMAILS, R. G. H. *Canadian Crown Corporations*. Toronto: Macmillan Co., 1965.

BECKER, HOWARD S. *Outsiders: Studies in the Sociology of Deviance*. New York: The Free Press of Glencoe, 1963.

BORDEN, ROBERT LAIRD. *Memoirs of Sir Robert Borden*. Vol. 2. London: Macmillan and Co., 1968.

BRECHER, IRVING. *Monetary and Fiscal Thought and Policy in Canada, 1919–1939*. Toronto: University of Toronto Press, 1956.

CAIDEN, GERALD E. "The Federal Civil Service of Canada." Unpublished manuscript, London, England, 1960.

CALLARD, KEITH B. *Advanced Administrative Training in the Public Service*. Toronto: Institute of Public Administration of Canada, 1956.

COLE, TAYLOR. *The Canadian Bureaucracy*. Durham, N.C.: Duke University Press, 1949.

DAWSON, R. MACGREGOR. *Canada in World Affairs*. Toronto: Oxford University Press, 1943.

————. *The Civil Service of Canada*. London: Oxford University Press, 1929.

DENTON, FRANK T. and OSTRY, SYLVIA. *Historical Estimates of the Canadian Labour Force*. Ottawa: Dominion Bureau of Statistics, 1967.

DOWDELL, R. H. "The Elements of Personnel Management in the Civil Service of Canada." Ottawa, 1965. Typescript.

DOWNS, ANTHONY. *Inside Bureaucracy*. Boston: Little, Brown and Co., 1967.

EAYRS, JAMES. *In Defence of Canada: From the Great War to the Great Depression*. Toronto: University of Toronto Press, 1964.

ETZIONI, AMITAI. *Modern Organizations*. Englewood Cliffs, N.J.: Prentice-Hall, 1964.

FRANKEL, SAUL J. *Staff Relations in the Civil Service: The Canadian Experience*. Montreal: McGill University Press, 1962.

GINZBERG, ELI. *Human Resources: The Wealth of a Nation*. New York: Simon and Schuster, 1958.

GLADDEN, E. N. *Civil Service or Bureaucracy?* London: Staples Press, 1956.

HABER, SAMUEL. *Efficiency and Uplift: Scientific Management in the Progressive Era*. Chicago: University of Chicago Press, 1964.

HEADY, FERREL and STOKES, S. L., eds. *Papers in Comparative Public Administration*. Michigan: Institute of Public Administration, University of Michigan, 1962.

HODGETTS, J. E. *Pioneer Public Service: An Administrative History of the United Canadas, 1841–1867*. Toronto: University of Toronto Press, 1955.

———— and CORBETT, D. C., eds. *Canadian Public Administration*. Toronto: Macmillan Co., 1960.

HOROWITZ, GAD. *Canadian Labour in Politics*. Toronto: University of Toronto Press, 1968.

JUDEK, STANISLAW. *Women in the Public Service: Their Utilization and Employment*. Ottawa: Queen's Printer, 1968.

KEYNES, JOHN M. *The General Theory of Employment, Interest and Money*. New York: Harcourt, Brace and World, 1936.

KWAVNICK, DAVID. "Organized Labour and Government: The Canadian Labour Congress as a Political Interest Group During the Diefenbaker and Pearson Administrations." Ph.D. thesis, Carleton University, 1969.

LANHAM, E. *Job Evaluation*. New York: McGraw-Hill Book Co., 1955.

LING, CYRIL C. *The Management of Personnel Relations: History and Origins*. Homewood, Ill.: Richard D. Irwin, 1965.

LIPSET, SEYMOUR MARTIN. *The First New Nation*. New York: Doubleday and Co., 1963.

LYTLE, CHARLES W. *Job Evaluation Methods*. New York: Ronald Press Co., 1946.

MACLEAN, M. M. "Problems of Jurisdiction and Structure Facing Staff Associations in the Canadian Civil Service." M.A. thesis, Syracuse University, 1958.

MACPHERSON, C. B. *Democracy in Alberta: Social Credit and the Party System*. Toronto: University of Toronto Press, 1962.

MELTZ, NOAH. *Changes in the Occupational Composition of the Canadian Labour Force, 1931–1961*. Ottawa: Department of Labour, 1965.

MERTON, R. K. *Social Theory and Social Structure*. New York: The Free Press, 1957.

MOSHER, WILLIAM E. and KINGSLEY, J. DONALD. *Public Personnel Administration*. New York: Harper and Bros., 1936.

———— and STAHL, O. GLENN. *Public Personnel Administration*. New York: Harper and Bros., 1950.

OAKESHOTT, MICHAEL. *Rationalism in Politics and Other Essays*. London: Metheun, 1962.

OSTRY, SYLVIA. *The Female Worker in Canada*. Ottawa: Dominion Bureau of Statistics, 1968.

————. *The Occupational Composition of the Canadian Labour Force*. Ottawa: Dominion Bureau of Statistics, 1967.

PLUMPTRE, A. F. W. *Mobilizing Canada's Resources for War*. Toronto: University of Toronto Press, 1941.

PORTER, JOHN. *The Vertical Mosaic: An Analysis of Social Class and Power in Canada*. Toronto: University of Toronto Press, 1965.

PRIVES, M. Z. "Career in Civil Service: Canada, Great Britain and the United States." Ph.D. thesis, McGill University, April, 1958.

SAFARIAN, A. E. *The Canadian Economy in the Great Depression*. Toronto: University of Toronto Press, 1959.

SELZNICK, PHILLIP. *Leadership in Administration.* New York: Harper and Row, 1957.

———. *TVA and the Grass Roots.* New York: Harper and Row, 1966.

THORBURN, HUGH, ed. *Party Politics in Canada.* Toronto: Prentice-Hall, 1967.

UNDERHILL, FRANK H. *In Search of Canadian Liberalism.* Toronto: Macmillan Co., 1961.

VAN RIPER, PAUL. *History of the United States Civil Service.* Evanston, Ill.: Row, Peterson, 1958.

WALDO, DWIGHT. *The Administrative State: A Study of the Political Theory of American Public Administration.* New York: Ronald Press Co., 1948.

WARD, NORMAN. *The Public Purse: A Study in Canadian Democracy.* Toronto: University of Toronto Press, 1962.

WHITE, L. D. *The Federalists.* New York: Macmillan Co., 1948.

———. *The Jeffersonians.* New York: Macmillan Co., 1951.

WHITE, WALTER L. "The Treasury Board in Canada." Ph.D. thesis, University of Michigan, 1965.

——— and STRICK, J. C. *Policy, Politics and the Treasury Board in Canadian Government.* Don Mills: Science Research Associates, 1970.

WILBUR, J. R. H., ed. *The Bennett New Deal: Fraud or Portent?* Toronto: Copp Clark Pub. Co., 1968.

WILLMS, A. M. and KERNAGHAN, W. D. K., eds. *Public Administration in Canada: Selected Readings.* Toronto: Methuen Publications, 1968.

ARTICLES AND SPEECHES

ADDISON, RUTH E. "The Appraisal and Career Development Programme for Senior Personnel." *Professional Public Service* 44 (January, 1965).

AULT, O. E. "Executive Development in Canadian Government." *Personnel Administration* 16 (November, 1954).

BENDIX, REINHARD. "Bureaucracy and the Problem of Power." *Public Administration Review* 5 (Summer, 1945).

BEST, J. C. "The Heeney Report." Remarks made to the Canadian Labour Congress Government Employee Conference, Fredericton, New Brunswick, May 5–6, 1960. Mimeograph.

BLACKBURN, G. A. "A Bilingual and Bicultural Public Service." *Canadian Public Administration* 12 (Spring, 1969).

BLAND, C. H. "Training for Administrative Posts in the Public Service of Canada." *Canadian Journal of Economics and Political Science* 11 (November, 1945).

CARSON, J. J. "The New Role of the Civil Service Commission." Speech delivered to the Federal Institute of Management, February 1, 1966. Mimeograph.

———. "What's Happened to Glassco?" *Public Personnel Review* 26 (April, 1965).

CLARK, PETER B. and WILSON, JAMES Q. "Incentive Systems: A Theory of Organizations." *Administrative Science Quarterly* 6 (September, 1961).

DAWSON, HELEN J. "The Consumers' Association of Canada." *Canadian Public Administration* 6 (March, 1963).

DAWSON, R. MACGREGOR. "The Canadian Civil Service." *Canadian Journal of Economics and Political Science* 2 (August, 1936).

———. "The Select Committee on the Civil Service, 1938." *Canadian Journal of Economics and Political Science* 2 (May, 1939).

DEUTSCH, J. J. "Some Thoughts on the Public Service." *Canadian Journal of Economics and Political Science* 23 (February, 1957).

DIEFENBAKER, JOHN G. "An Address on the Civil Service." Delivered to the Civil Service Association of Canada, Ottawa, May 1, 1958. Mimeograph.

DONOVAN, J. J. "Officers of the Civil Service Assembly of the United States and Canada, 1906–1956." *Public Personnel Review* 17 (October, 1956).

DYMOND, W. R. "The Role of the Union in the Public Service as Opposed to Its Role in Private Business." Institute of Public Administration of Canada, *Proceedings of the Fifth Annual Conference*, Saskatoon, September 9–12, 1953.

ERIKSSON, ERIK. "The Federal Civil Service under President Jackson." *Mississippi Valley Historical Review* 13 (1926–27).

FINER, S. E. "Patronage and the Public Service." *Public Administration* 30 (1952).

FOLLIS, G. S. "The Senior Course in Public Administration." *Canadian Public Administration* 3 (March, 1965).

GAUTHIER, GEORGES E. "The Canadian Pay Research Bureau." *Public Personnel Review* 19 (October, 1958).

GORDON, DONALD. "Price Control and the Wage Earner." Address given to the Canadian Congress of Labour, Quebec, October 19, 1944. Mimeograph.

GRANT, W. L. "The Civil Service of Canada." *University of Toronto Quarterly* 3 (July, 1934).

HAYDON, ANDREW. "Adam Shortt." *Queen's Quarterly* 38 (Autumn, 1931).

HEENEY, A. D. P. "Cabinet Government in Canada: Some Recent Developments in the Machinery of the Central Executive." *Canadian Journal of Economics and Political Science* 12 (August, 1946).

HUGHES, S. H. S. "The New Civil Service Act: A Comparison of the Old and New Civil Service Acts." *Public Personnel Review* 23 (January, 1962).

JOSIE, GORDON. "Administration of the Veterans Preference in the Canadian Civil Service." *Canadian Journal of Economics and Political Science* 11 (November, 1945).

LOVE, J. D. "Employee Organizations in the Federal Public Service and the Problems of Collective Bargaining." Paper delivered to the Ottawa chapter of the Canadian Political Science Association, November, 1956. Mimeograph.

MACKINTOSH, W. A.   "Adam Shortt, 1859–1931." *Canadian Journal of Economics and Political Science* 4 (May, 1938).

——. "Should We Have Specialized Degrees in Public Administration Given by Universities?" Institute of Public Administration of Canada, *Proceedings of the First Annual Conference*, Quebec, October 3–4, 1949.

MACLEAN, R. D.   "An Examination of the Role of the Comptroller of the Treasury." *Canadian Public Administration* 7 (March, 1964).

MAINWARING, JOHN.   "Some Reflections on the Problem of Collective Bargaining by Federal Public Servants." Paper delivered to the Ottawa chapter of the Canadian Political Science Association, Industrial Relations Study Group, February, 1957. Mimeograph.

MALLORY, J. R.   "Delegated Legislation in Canada: Recent Changes in Machinery." *Canadian Journal of Economics and Political Science* 19 (November, 1953).

PAYNE, J. L.   "The Civil Servant." *University Magazine* 6 (December, 1907).

PRIVES, M. Z.   "Career and Promotion in the Federal Civil Service of Canada." *Canadian Public Administration* 3 (June, 1960).

SKELTON, O. D.   "Our Foes at Home." *Queen's Quarterly* 23 (July, 1915).

STEAD, G. W.   "The Treasury Board of Canada." Institute of Public Administration of Canada, *Proceedings of the Seventh Annual Conference*, Halifax, Nova Scotia, September 7–10, 1955.

SUBRAMANIAM, V.   "The Relative Status of Specialists and Generalists: An Attempt at a Comparative Historical Explanation." *Public Administration* (Journal of the Royal Institute of Public Administration, London) 46 (Autumn, 1968).

YOUNG, J. H.   "Principles and Practice of Remuneration in the Canadian Civil Service, 1926–1949." Treasury Board Staff Paper, August 15, 1949. Mimeograph.

Index